CAMPAIGN IN WESTERN ASIA

Dharm Pal, ph.d.

OFFICIAL HISTORY OF THE INDIAN ARMED FORCES
IN THE SECOND WORLD WAR
1939-45

CAMPAIGN IN WESTERN ASIA

General Editor
BISHESHWAR PRASAD, D.LITT.

COMBINED INTER-SERVICES HISTORICAL SECTION
(INDIA & PAKISTAN)
1957

The Naval & Military Press Ltd

Published by

The Naval & Military Press Ltd
Unit 5 Riverside, Brambleside
Bellbrook Industrial Estate
Uckfield, East Sussex
TN22 1QQ England

Tel: +44 (0)1825 749494

www.naval-military-press.com
www.nmarchive.com

In reprinting in facsimile from the original, any imperfections are inevitably reproduced and the quality may fall short of modern type and cartographic standards.

TO ALL WHO SERVED

ADVISORY COMMITTEE

Chairman
SECRETARY, MINISTRY OF DEFENCE, INDIA

Members

DR TARA CHAND
DR S. N. SEN
PROF K. A. NILAKANTA SASTRI
PROF MOHAMMAD HABIB
DR R. C. MAJUMDAR
GENERAL K. S. THIMAYYA
LIEUT.-GENERAL SIR DUDLEY RUSSELL
LIEUT.-GENERAL S. P. P. THORAT
MILITARY ADVISER TO THE HIGH COMMISSIONER
    FOR PAKISTAN IN INDIA

Secretary
DR BISHESHWAR PRASAD

CAMPAIGNS IN THE WESTERN THEATRE

- North African Campaign
- East African Campaign
- Campaign in Western Asia
- Campaigns in Italy
- Operations in Greece

PREFACE

The Official History of the Indian Armed Forces in the Second World War was planned by the Combined Inter-Services Historical Section, a joint venture of India and Pakistan, to appear in about twenty volumes, besides those relating to the medical aspect, and is divided into three series, viz., the campaigns in the western theatre, the campaigns in the eastern theatre, and general war administration and organisation. The volumes in the first series relate to the campaigns in Africa and Western Asia. The first volume published in this series narrated the fighting in North Africa. The present volume is the second of the series and carries the narrative further to the lands of Western Asia—Iraq, Syria and Iran, where Indian troops were called upon to block the further progress of Nazi arms and maintain strategic defence of the north-west frontiers of their own country. At a time when Iraq and Iran were definitely drifting under German and Italian influence and there was fear of Axis bases being established in the two states, the Government of India stepped in to prevent the aggressive flow of German forces through Turkey and Syria into the 'Fertile Crescent,' the land of the Euphrates and the Tigris, or across the Zagros and Mount Ararat into the plateau of Iran. The campaigns, though short and swift, against the weak forces of Iraq and Iran or in Syria, had a far-reaching effect on the course of the global war. And the Indian forces were commissioned to garrison these lands, even when the danger of Axis advance had been finally removed, to supervise the transport of supplies of war material to Soviet Russia from her Western Allies.

This volume is divided into four parts, Iraq, Syria, Iran and Paiforce. The first three deal with the operations in each of the three areas, Iraq, Syria and Iran, while the fourth narrates the build-up and the activities of the Persia and Iraq Force which took up later the task of garrisoning these countries. One of the primary functions of this Force was to provide the security of oilfields and oil installations in Iraq and Iran and develop the ports and means of communication of these lands for its own maintenance and speeding up the supplies to Russia. The administrative and strategic planning to achieve these objects had a particular value at the time and may still be of more than mere historical significance. It is these administrative aspects which make the story of these campaigns one of consequence.

As in earlier volumes, every endeavour has been made to present an accurate and objective narrative of events in the background of the factors and forces which conditioned them. Our object has been to reconstruct the situations in which the Indian armed forces were called upon to function, emphasising the strategic and tactical plans which directed their action. In such a study there is naturally greater stress on policies than on personalities.

This volume has been mainly written by Dr. Dharm Pal, Narrator in the Historical Section. I am indebted to him for his unflinching devotion and ungrudging industry. I must also mention the assistance which I received from Mr. P. N. Khera, Narrator in the Historical Section, in editing the volume. He not only prepared the script for the press but also saw it through at every stage of printing. To him my thanks are due. I acknowledge the assistance of Dr. Hari Ram Gupta, who was a Narrator for some time in the Section, in collecting and collating material for the narratives on Iran and Paiforce. The maps, as in the previous volumes, have been prepared by Mr. T. D. Sharma, Cartographer, to whom my thanks are due.

The narratives contained in this volume have been shown to some of the commanders who were responsible for these campaigns in West Asia. I am particularly indebted to General Sir Edward Quinan, Major-General W. A. K. Fraser, Major-General C. O. Harvey and Brigadier C. J. Weld, C.I.E., M.C., for their comments which have greatly helped in clearing obscure points and presenting a correct story. The volume has also been seen by Prof. K. A. Nilakanta Sastri, Dr. Tara Chand, and Prof. Mohammad Habib, members of the Advisory Committee. I am greatly indebted to the Cabinet Historical Section for making valuable suggestions for its improvement.

In conclusion I must acknowledge the encouragement and cooperation which I have received from the Ministries of Defence of India and Pakistan.

New Delhi
May 1957

BISHESHWAR PRASAD

CONTENTS

	Page
INTRODUCTION	xix

IRAQ

CHAPTER		
I.	HISTORICAL BACKGROUND	3
II.	PHYSICAL FEATURES	9
III.	COMMUNICATIONS AND ECONOMIC RESOURCES	15
IV.	PRE-WAR DEFENCE PLANS	25
V.	DEFENCE PLANS (1939—JUNE 1940)	32
VI.	DEFENCE PLANS (JULY 1940—APRIL 1941)	46
VII.	THE DEVELOPMENTS IN IRAQ—1941	57
VIII.	PLANS FOR AN OPPOSED LANDING	66
IX.	BATTLE OF HABBANIYA	77
X.	DEFENCE OF THE BASRA-SHUAIBA AREA	81
XI.	ADVANCE OF KINGCOL TO FALLUJA	86
XII.	AXIS INTERVENTION	97
XIII.	ADVANCE ON BAGHDAD	106
XIV.	IRAQ AS AN OPERATIONAL BASE	113
XV.	INITIAL PLANS TO MEET AXIS THREAT	125
XVI.	PLANNING IN INDIA, IRAQ AND THE MIDDLE EAST	131
XVII.	PROBLEMS CONNECTED WITH THE THREAT TO CAUCASIA	139
XVIII.	MOSUL AND BAGHDAD DEFENCES	148
XIX.	PLAN "WONDERFUL"	156
XX.	FORMATION OF A NEW COMMAND	166

SYRIA

XXI.	PHYSICAL FEATURES AND HISTORICAL SURVEY	171
XXII.	THE PLAN FOR THE INVASION	179
XXIII.	CAPTURE OF SHEIKH MESKINE	191
XXIV.	CAPTURE OF KISSOUE	198
XXV.	VICHY COUNTER-ATTACKS	205
XXVI.	CAPTURE OF MEZZE	210
XXVII.	CAPTURE OF PALMYRA	220
XXVIII.	PLAN FOR THE ATTACK ON DEIR EZ ZOR	227
XXIX.	CAPTURE OF DEIR EZ ZOR	237
XXX.	VICHY COUNTER-ATTACK ON RAQQA	248
XXXI.	ADVANCE TO TELL AALO	256
XXXII.	CAPTURE OF HASSETCHE	262

IRAN

Chapter		Page
XXXIII.	Geographical Survey	271
XXXIV.	Historical Background	278
XXXV.	Military Resources and Organisation	289
XXXVI.	Events Leading to the Action	299
XXXVII.	The Allied Plans	311
XXXVIII.	Abadan	317
XXXIX.	Qasr Shaikh	330
XL.	West Iran Operations	340

PAIFORCE

XLI.	Paiforce and Its Plans	359
XLII.	Plan 'Gherkin'	369
XLIII.	British Projects	380
XLIV.	American Projects	393
XLV.	Development of Ports	405
XLVI.	Development of Roads and Railways	416
XLVII.	Inland Water Transport	430
XLVIII.	Bases and Lines of Communication	447
XLIX.	Supply	455
Appendices		463
Index		563

APPENDICES

1. Proposed Composition of Sabine Force (Exclusive of Sybil Force) —January 1941.
2. Proposed Composition of Sybil Force—January 1941.
3. Letter from the Grand Mufti of Palestine to Herr Hitler.
4. Summary of Order of Battle of Iraq Army—15 April 1941.
5. Royal Iraqi Air Force—15 November 1940.
6. Forces in and around Basra.
7. Main Dispositions of the Iraq Force—20 June 1941.
8. Tenth Army Order of Battle—1 February 1942.
9. Tenth Army Operation Instruction No. 21—25 May 1942.
10. Reorganisation of Commands in Iraq and Persia.
11. 5th Indian Infantry Brigade Operation Order No. 1—5 June 1941.
12. Iraq Force Operation Instruction No. 6—21 June 1941.
13. 21st Indian Infantry Brigade Operation Order No. 9—29 June 1941.
14. Lessons from the Operations of 10th Indian Division in Syria.
15. Agreement for the Cessation of Hostilities in Syria and the Lebanon.
16. Order of Battle, 8th Indian Division—25 August 1941.
17. 8th Indian Division Administration Instructions for the Advance—25 August 1941.
18. Order of Battle 10th Indian Division—25 August 1941.
19. Pamphlet Dropping Operations, from 25 to 28 August 1941.
20. Tenth Army—Order of Battle and Location Statement as on 15 September 1942.
21. Movements Tenth Army, Working Instruction No. 6.
22. "Aid to Russia" Cargo, January 1943—March 1944.
23. Reorganisation of Supply Personnel.
24. Engineering Activities at Ashar—May 1944.

MAPS

	Page
Port of Basra	16
Projected Landings of Force "Trout"	42
Shuaiba Defences—May 1941	99
Basra Area	101
Attack on Habibshawi—24 May 1941	103
Mosul and Surrounding Area	149
Operations of 5 Indian Infantry Brigade in Syria, 8-9 June 1941	188
Kuneitra Defences	206
Damascus Area	211
Palmyra Area	221
21 Indian Infantry Brigade Group's Advance to Tell Abiad, 30 June —9 July 1941	234
Sketch, Deir ez Zor, attack by 4/13 F.F. Rifles, 3 July 1941	243
Raqqa—French counter-attack, 9-10 July 1941	250
Operations in North-East Syria, 2-11 July 1941	259
Iran—areas under the influence of Russia and Great Britain	283
Plan of Operations in South-West Iran—25 to 28 August 1941	312
Sketch map of Abadan	318
Advance into West Iran	341
Division of Military areas in Iraq and Iran	361
Iraq and Iran Transport in Aid to Russia	418

	facing page
Iraq	3
Disposition of Iraqi troops at Habbaniya—1 May 1941	75
Occupation of Maqil—2 May 1941	81
Attack on Falluja—18-23 May 1941	95
Mosul aerodrome area Defences—29 June 1941	121
The Persian Gulf showing Defensive Layout	123
Defence of Iraq—1 September 1941—Plan	135
Plan 'Wonderful'—Proposed demolition zones and devastation areas in Iraq and Iran	165
Iraq and Iran, readjustment of Commands—23 July 1942	167
Syria	171
Deir'ez Zor—attack by 2/10 Gurkha Rifles 3 July 1941	241
Map of Iran	271
Khurramshahr	327
Attack on Qasr Shaikh	331
Plan Garment	359
Caucasia	371
Western Asia	At the end

ILLUSTRATIONS

		Facing page
1.	General Sir Edward Quinan	72
2.	Major-General W. A. K. Fraser	72
3.	Gateway to Iraq	73
4.	Indian Troops arrive at Basra Dock	73
5.	General Sir Claude Auchinleck	192
6.	Indian Troops take a view of picturesque Damascus	192
7.	Brigadier W. L. Lloyd	193
8.	Brigadier C. J. Weld	193
9.	General Sir Archibald Wavell	344
10.	Major-General W. J. Slim	344
11.	Detachment 1/5 Gurkha Rifles, Iran	345
12.	Indian Armoured cars on patrol in Iran	345
13.	Lt.-General Sir Henry Maitland Wilson	378
14.	Indian soldiers going through a pass in Iran on the 'Aid to Russia' route	379
15.	Men of the Kashmir Rifles in Iran on the 'Aid to Russia' route	422
16.	The Bandar Shahpur—Teheran Express carrying war materials to Russia	423
17.	Indian Troops in Iranian mountain passes	423

Abbreviations

AA	Anti-Aircraft.
AFVs	Armoured Fighting Vehicles.
AIOC	Anglo-Iranian Oil Company.
AOC	Army Ordnance Corps.
AQMG	Assistant Quartermaster General.
Arty	Artillery.
A/Tk	Anti-Tank.
BIM	Battalion l'Infanterie de Marine.
BMA	British Military Adviser.
BOD	Base Ordnance Depot.
Br	British.
BT Flight	Bomber Transport Flight.
Bty	Battery.
CE	Chief Engineer.
CGS	Chief of the General Staff.
CIGS	Chief of the Imperial General Staff.
CKD	Complete Knock Down.
Comb	Combined.
Conval	Convalescent.
COS	Chief of Staff.
Coy	Company.
DD	Deputy Director.
DDOS	Deputy Director Ordnance Services.
Det	Detachment.
DMO and I	Directorate of Military Operations and Intelligence.
E & M	Electrical and Mechanical.
Engr	Engineer.
E and Tn	Engineering and Transportation.
FSD	Field Supply Depot.
Fd	Field.
GG	Governor-General.
GHQ	General Headquarters.
GOC-in-C	General Officer Commanding-in-Chief.
GP Tpt	General Purpose Transport.
GR	Gurkha Rifles.
HMAS	His Majesty's Armoured Ship (Sloop).
HMG	His Majesty's Government.
HMIS	His Majesty's Indian Ship (Sloop).
HMS	His Majesty's Ship (Sloop).
Hows	Howitzers.
HQ	Headquarters.
IE	Indian Engineers.
Int	Intelligence.
ISF	Indian States Forces.
IWT	Inland Water Transport.
KEO	King Edward's Own.
KGO	King George's Own.
KLM	Royal Dutch Airlines.

LA	Light Artillery.
L of C	Line of Communication.
LRS	Light Repair Section.
MDI	Military Department, India.
MEF	Middle East Force.
MG	Machine-Gun.
MEFS	Middle East Field Service.
MGRE	Major-General, Royal Engineers.
Mob	Mobile.
Mtn	Mountain.
OI	Operation Instruction.
OO	Operation Order.
Ord	Ordnance.
Paic	Persia and Iraq Command.
Paiforce	Persia and Iraq Force.
Pibas	Persia and Iraq Base.
POL	Petrol Oil and Lubricants.
PWO	Prince of Wales's own.
QMG	Quartermaster General.
QVO	Queen Victoria's Own.
RA	Royal Artillery.
RAF	Royal Air Force.
RASC	Royal Army Service Corps.
RE	Royal Engineers.
RIAF	Royal Indian Air Force.
RIASC	Royal Indian Army Service Corps.
SFTS	Service Flying Training School.
SS	Secretary of State.
S and T	Supply and Transport.
Svy	Survey.
UKCC	United Kingdom Commercial Corporation.
VC	Victoria Cross.
W/D	War Diary.

INTRODUCTION

Western Asia, in the nineteenth century, provided a suitable ground for the inter-play of rival ambitions of the European powers. Great Britain and France were the first in the field as both of them sought control over the regions of Iran and the waters of the Persian Gulf. Soon Russia also exhibited designs dominating diplomatically over the Government at Teheran, and her scarcely veiled territorical expansion in the Caspian region created feelings of nervousness and Russophobia in the British mind. The plans for railway construction sponsored by the British in Iran and the valley of the rivers, Euphrates and Tigris, found their echo in the Russian projects of railway development to the east of the Caspian Sea. All these schemes had one object, that of connecting India with Europe and providing a land line of communications. But rival imperialistic ambitions of European powers prevented their implementation because of their strategic associations; and it was impossible for these powers to co-operate or co-ordinate their efforts for the economic development of the area of the Middle East.

Not till the close of the last century did Germany reveal any commercial, financial or strategic interests in Western Asia. Prince Bismarck, however, despite his aversion to territorial expansion and indifference to the Near Eastern problems, had initiated a programme of peaceful penetration at Constantinople. It did not take Germany long to ingratiate herself with the Porte; and William II could boast of being the protector of millions of Muslims of Asia. Under him was launched the project of the Baghdad Railway, directed towards connecting Baghdad and Basra with Berlin in Europe. The contract provided not merely for the construction of the railway line but also the exploitation of mineral wealth and establishment of plantations in the valleys of the two rivers, Euphrates and Tigris. Thus Baghdad Railway revived the earlier schemes of railway communication in Western Asia and opened the prospect of German control over the Persian Gulf. The British, French and Russian governments were naturally concerned about this fresh interposition in a region of vast potentialities, and, till the opening of the first Great War in 1914, this railway scheme in the Middle East kept the European chancelleries agitated, and diplomatic crises were the order of the day. In the Great War, Mesopotamia became a major field of operations, of intimate concern to the Government of India because of the dangers arising out of the contiguity of the German forces to the Indian borders.

The British had been sensitive, from the very beginning of the last century, about the existence of any influence other than their own in the states of Western Asia. In the past they had established their patronage over the Ottoman Sultans, and the Shahs of Iran, and sought to maintain it. But whenever there was danger to their position of vantage in this region, the British actively resisted any interloper, and did not hesitate to align with themselves elements in the Asian states who might be hostile to the local government. Their championing the cause of the Arabs against the Turkish Sultans, their support to Syrians and the raising of Jewish state in Palestine, clearly reveal this attitude, which is not surprising. For did not the British have vital interests in the region of Western Asia which controlled their imperial communications? The Suez Canal, the Red Sea, the Persian Gulf and the land block extending from the western borders of India to the Mediterranean Sea and overlooking the sea passages, were the life-lines of the British Empire, on the security of which depended the integrity of their far-flung empire in the east and their hold over India. Moreover, the oil resources of Iraq and Iran were necessary to keep the Royal Navy on the seas. Commercial advantages were of no less concern. The protection of all these interests became the paramount principle of British policy, and the Government of India, a subordinate agency of the Whitehall, was fully vigilant in maintaining a watch over these.

The Great War saw the end of the Turkish Empire and out of its possessions three Arab states were created besides the states of Syria, Lebanon and Palestine. Iraq was carved out of the three *vilayets* of Mesopotamia with a king at its head. These states in their infancy were placed under the tutelage of Great Britain or France and were styled Mandated Territories, for the administration of which the great powers were accountable to the League of Nations. Iraq, however, did not long remain in such statu populi, for the British Government relinquished the mandate in 1932, and subject to a treaty of defence, the kingdom was made independent. In the period intervening between independence and the Second World War, Iraq, as perhaps the entire Arab region, became a field for Nazi and Fascist propaganda. German influence was active among the officer ranks of the Iraqi army, and though the Regent of Iraq was friendly to the British, elements in support of the Nazis were not lacking in the country.

German interest in Western Asia had a pre-eminently strategic character, and was primarily directed against the disruption of the vital British imperial communications which passed through Iraq. Control over the Persian Gulf, exploitation of the oil wealth of this region and a strategic position close to the Indian and Russian frontiers were other objects which the Nazis then cherished. In the thirties, thus, there was a revival of the early Drang Nach Osten which had led to the Great War. And in this new move, the Germans were considerably helped by the Arab hostility to Zionism which was presumed to have British support.

The progress of the Second World War greatly accelerated the pace of Nazi propaganda and German activity to acquire a hold over Iraq. Initially German strategy had embraced Western Europe, but with the success in the west as a result of the collapse of France, and the entry of Italy into the arena of war, the Middle East acquired a new significance. The British will to fight had to be broken and a blow aimed at their empire. In 1940 war had entered Africa where the Italian armies, contrary to the expectations of Mussolini, were melting away before the superior fighting power of the meagre British and Indian forces. War had also been introduced in the Balkans, and the omens of Russian participation in it could clearly be discerned. The American benevolence for the British war effort was also mounting up every day. This conjunction of forces might sweep away the structure of German hegemony unless checked in time. Hence came an orientation in German strategy which became global in character, and the Middle East was now brought into it. Axis victory in North Africa predicated the employment of a pincer, one leg of which was to be based on Syria. Russia could be counter-acted and discomfited by a thrust in her under-belly from the south. And the life-line of the British in the Indian Ocean, which brought supplies from the United States or her empire in the east, could be dominated by control over Iraq, which would also threaten the defences of India. The advantages were immense, hence German policy manoeuvred a change of government in Iraq which came about early in 1941.

These German ambitions and machinations did not fail to have their reaction on British policy, particularly in India where the government could not remain absolutely passive to the developments so close to the frontiers. Before the war, India had been assigned the obligation for the defence of British interests in Egypt and the oil-bearing areas of Iraq and Iran. Plans for the despatch of troops had been prepared. The Chatfield Committee had emphasised the vitalness of the Persian Gulf and Suez area for the defence of India. Hence the Government of India felt alarmed at the new developments in Iraq, and demanded immediate action to nip the apprehended trouble in its bud.

For active interference in Iraq, Germany required a base in Syria, but for access there, control over Crete and Greece was the necessary link in the chain. Mussolini had begun his aggressive march into Greece, but he did not meet with success, and German arms had to take up the fight there in April 1941 against the combined resistance of the Greek patriots and their British supporters.

This invasion was a step preliminary to the domination of Iraq, where German policy desired a change of administration as a prelude to active Axis interference. A precise synchronisation was required for the success of this manoeuvre. But unfortunately for Nazi strategy, Rashid Ali's *coup de'etat* at Baghdad came before Hitler was ready to rush into the arena for his assistance. On the first day of April 1941, the Regent fled to the British post at Habbaniya and was flown away to the safety of a British naval ship. The new government was installed in power, but without an immediate prospect of German military support. Meanwhile, the British ambassador had been temporising with the new administration, as the British hold over Iraq was precarious, their force was extremely meagre, and with their arms locked in deadly grip in Ethiopia, Egypt, Greece and Crete, and with the crisis in the Far East impending, there was little hope of reinforcements arriving quickly.

Diplomacy was wavering between active military interposition and appeasement. The War Office in England could not decide, and the Foreign Office was of two minds. It was then that the Government of India took the initiative and forced a decisive step by offering to divert troops intended for Malaya to Basra. The die was cast, and secret preparations were made to land a brigade immediately at Basra and fly a battalion into Habbaniya. This decision was fortunate and the timing of the arrival of these forces opportune, for before the Germans could send effective help to Iraq, its capital, Baghdad, and port Basra had both been occupied by the Indian forces and the rebel government crushed. The fighting for these prizes was nominal as Iraqi resistance had neither sting nor determination. And with the collapse of resistance at the capital, the whole of Iraq lay exposed for the movement of British Indian forces.

The next stage was to organise this area of the Middle East for counteracting any further moves by the Germans in this region. For more than a year, the danger of German invasion through Turkey, Caucasus or Syria was seriously apprehended. The Vichy forces in Syria might afford entry to Germans, hence they had to be eliminated. This involved action in Syria, which was a concomitant of the Iraqian campaign, and a necessary postulate for the protection of Western Asia and India. At the same time Iran was also to be purged of all hostile influences, and the oil-bearing wells made safe for British exploitation. If Russia crumbled and the Germans entered through the Caucasus, their entrance was to be blocked. Thus the importance of Iraq, after its occupation, lay in organising defence against German infiltration from the north, west or east. And though the campaign itself has little interest from the point of military strategy or tactics, the development of the system of defended localities which was adopted there, had a lesson for India when its own defences were to be organised in 1941 and 1942. These self-sufficient defended localities, on the model of medieval forts, were a positive answer to Blitzkrieg, and combined dynamism with static defence. It was a great advance on the Maginot line, and a reorientation of medieval fortification to suit the demands of a highly mobile warfare.

Iraq and Iran were made the responsibility of India, and later when Paiforce was formed for the occupation of these countries, the force was maintained from India. The Government of India realised full well the significance of these West Asian countries for the defence of India and strove hard to keep the western gates and avenues leading to them fully closed. The strength of the forces employed in that region rose to as much as three divisions, the bulk of which came from the Indian army. The Middle East Force was also called upon to bear a part of the load, and for some time the command of these troops lay with the Middle East Command; but it soon reverted to the Commander-in-Chief of India who remained in control of the operations in Iraq and Iran till the creation of a separate command directly under the War Office.

BISHESHWAR PRASAD

IRAQ

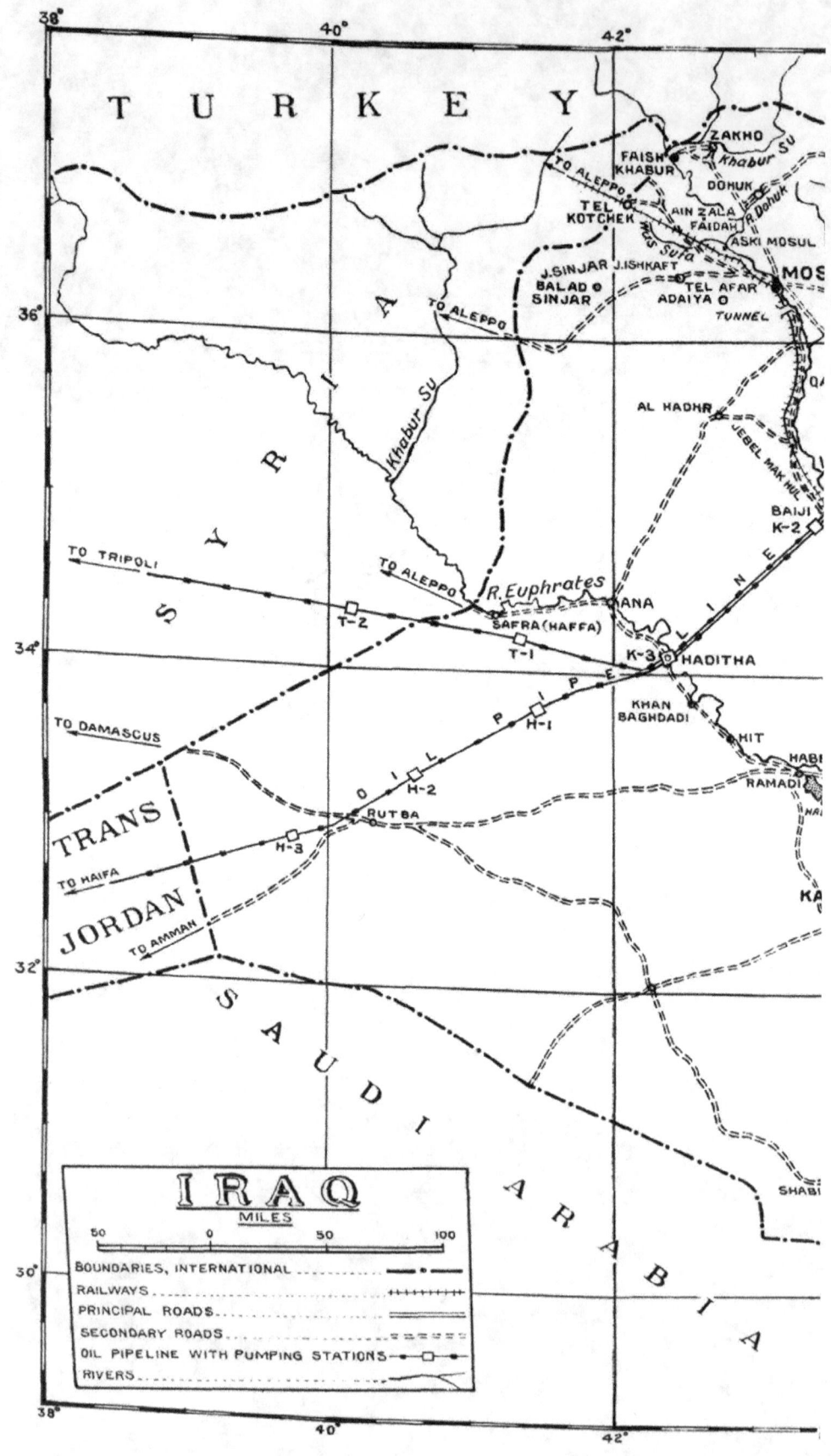

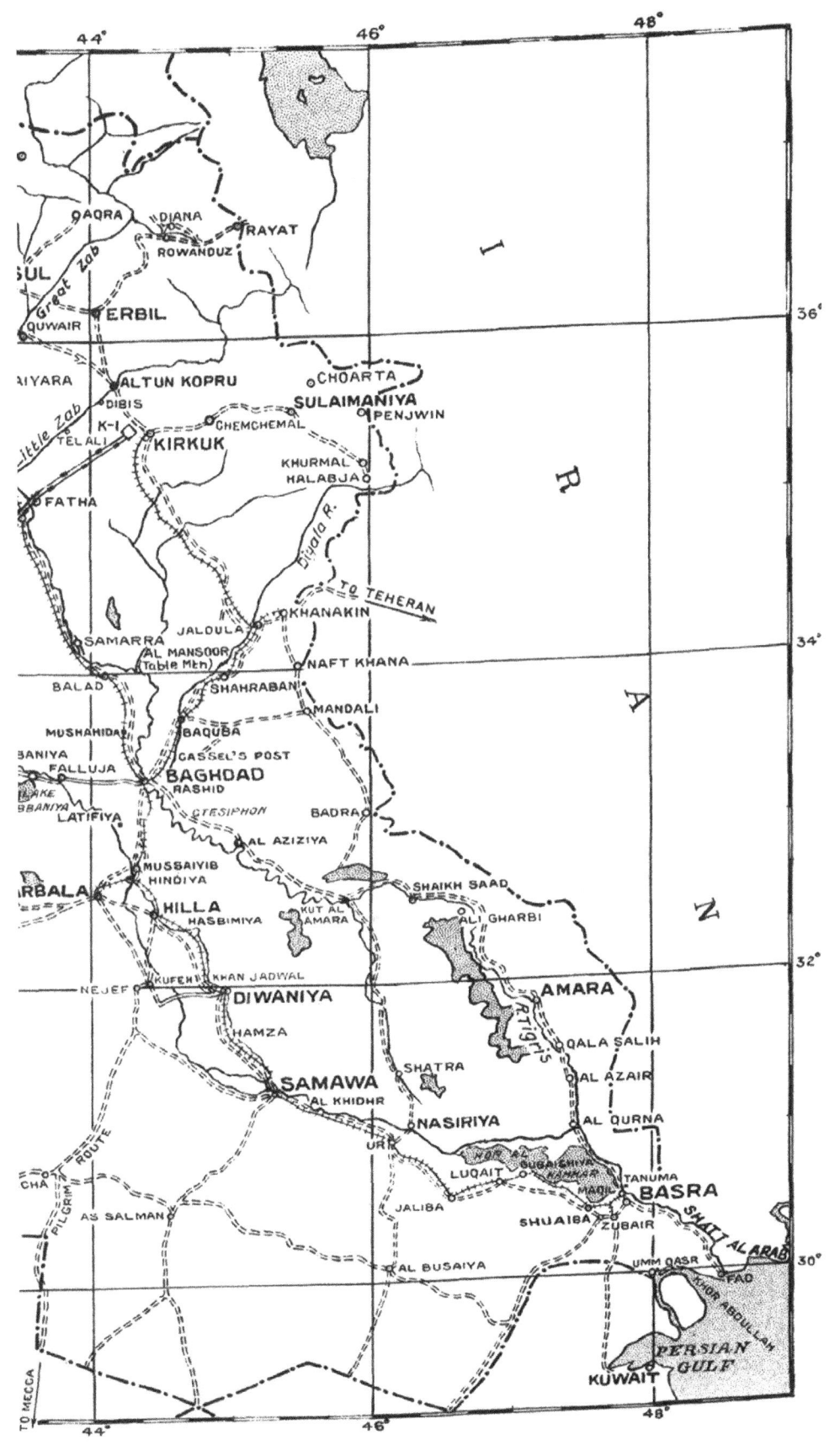

CHAPTER I

Historical Background

Early Hitsory

Modern Iraq has its roots deep in the past. It has played an important part in the evolution of human culture. Within its borders lie buried the seats of many imperial powers of the ancient Orient. The different phases of the history of this remarkable country, between 3,000 B.C. and the 9th century A.D., are marked by the rise to power of the Sumerian, Akkadian, early Babylonian, Assyrian, Chaldean, Persian, Alexandrian, Parthian, Sassanian and Abbasid dynasties. The excavations carried out at Ur, Kish, Babylon, Ninevah, Ctesiphon and Baghdad have thrown a flood of light on the ancient past of this land, the home of one of the earliest, if not the first, of the human civilizations.

The Sumerians considerably enriched the civilization of southern Iraq. On the banks of the rivers Tigris and Euphrates was developed a fairly advanced social organisation; there were built splendid temples, such as Nergal at Kutha or Enlil at Nippur.[1] The Sumerians were followed by the Akkadians, who rose into importance under their able and energetic ruler Sargon. Then Babylon shone in splendour under its remarkable leader Hammurabi. This was followed by the establishment of the Assyrian Empire, which attained the zenith of its glory in the time of Sennacherib who made Ninevah the centre of a rich civilization. After the Assyrians came the Medes from north Iran, to be followed by the Achaemenian Persians, the climax of whose prosperity came in the time of Darius I.

During the later period of history, Iraq successively formed part of the empires of Alexander, the Seleucid Greeks, the Parthians and the Sassanian Persians. It was during this period that the Greeks first gave to this part of the world the name—Mesopotamia, meaning "between the two rivers." Subsequently, as a result of the extensive Muslim conquests, in the 7th century A.D., Iraq became subject to the Omayyad Caliphs. Leadership passed later to the Abbasids who ruled as Caliphs from 750 A.D. to 1258 A.D. The greatest of the Abbasids was Mansur, who built the legend-famed city of Baghdad and made it the centre of a rich civilization. Baghdad was destroyed in 1258 A.D. by Hulagu Khan, grandson of Chinghiz Khan, the famous Mongol leader, who dealt a death

[1] Seton Lloyd: *Twin Rivers* (1943), p. 25.

blow to the prosperity of Iraq. "The Capital was sacked, and the scientific, literary, and artistic records of centuries were wiped out; the system of irrigation, upon which the country depended for its existence, was destroyed; and, after a period of civilization which had lasted for eighty centuries, Mesopotamia once more lay waste —an arid desert, save for the two great rivers which wound their way, past a few scattered vestiges of humanity, towards the Persian Gulf."[2] In 1534 A.D., Baghdad was occupied by the famous Turkish Sultan, Sulaiman the Magnificent, and Iraq thus came to form part of the Ottoman Empire, which broke up during the first World War.

Early British connection with the Persian Gulf

While the Ottoman Turks ruled over the land of the Euphrates and the Tigris, feudal Europe was undergoing a transformation, and European maritime countries were laying the foundations of their colonial empires of the future. First came the discovery of the new lands and new routes across the seas, and then the race for wealth, trade and possessions of the new domains. In this race, England soon acquired a lead over the other European countries. Early in the sixteenth century, she had emerged as a maritime power of some importance and her seagoing vessels were exploring the coasts of the distant seas. Before the end of the century, she had destroyed the Spanish Armada and had established her naval supremacy. Her overseas trade was expanding rapidly. She had chartered more than one trading company, including the East India Company in 1600. In 1622, the latter took from the Portuguese the port of Ormuz, and thus established itself in the Persian Gulf. To protect its trade and shipping, the Company was authorised to maintain two men-of-war in the Gulf. This was the beginning of Great Britain's commercial and political interests in that area.

During the following century, England continued trading with the East, France being her close rival and competitor. Wars between England and France in Europe were generally followed by wars between their colonial possessions. This rivalry reached its height during the Napoleonic wars. Therefore, when Napoleon took Egypt in 1798, the East India Company promptly established a permanent resident at Baghdad to counteract the French influence in the Middle East. Henceforth Great Britain took a steadily growing interest in the Middle East countries, which considerably increased when, later, Iran and Iraq were found to be rich oil-bearing regions, capable of supplying oil for the ships of her navy and the mercantile marine. Besides, due to the development of

[2] R. Evans: *A Brief outline of the Campaign in Mesopotamia* (1926), p. 1.

means of transport and communications and expansion of England's overseas empire, Middle East, and particularly Iraq, had acquired a strategic importance for Great Britain. It was most marked in the later part of the nineteenth century.

During that century, the British had gradually built up for themselves a special position in the region of the Persian Gulf and Lower Iraq. Great Britain undertook to suppress slave trade and piracy as well as to preserve peace and develop trade in the Persian Gulf. She launched a programme of opening the Tigris and the Euphrates to navigation. At the end of the century, Britain was in friendly relations with Turkey and occupied an important position at Baghdad. She practically held a monopoly of the navigation of the Tigris, and in 1910, eighty-seven per cent of the trade of the Persian Gulf was in British hands.

Meanwhile Europe was passing through a phase of industrial development which called for a search for fresh fields for the supply of raw materials and new markets for an ever-increasing output of manufactured goods. This led to a frantic effort for dominating the undeveloped territories and carving out spheres of interest or imperial possessions there. The Near and Middle East were also the victims of this policy. An important corollary of that was the desire to develop the means of communication in their territories. An early endeavour was the opening of the Suez Canal which was made possible by the initiative and effort of France. Schemes for connecting India with the Mediterranean coast by a rail line were mooted by English financiers, but these did not materialise. However, the German Emperor, Kaiser William II, employed a psychological moment to obtain concession for German financiers and engineers to build a railway from Istanbul to Baghdad to connect it with Berlin. The projected railway was to connect the Anatolian railway system with Baghdad by a line running along the north coast of the Mediterranean and on to Aleppo and Mosul. It represented an important feature of the *"drang nach osten"*, or the Austro-German drive to the East. The Berlin-Baghdad railway did not initially materialise owing to objections of Great Britain, Russia and France to the proposed routes. But eventually it was taken up and in the first decade of the twentieth century almost caused a diplomatic crisis. At the same time the construction of the Trans Caucasian and Trans-Caspian railways was progressively bringing Russia nearer the Middle East.

With the discovery of oil near the Karun river, one hundred miles north of the Persian Gulf, and the formation of a company to exploit the oil resources of this region, the Middle East acquired a new importance. Iran and Iraq were already coming to be recognised as rich oil-bearing regions. Just before the outbreak of World

War I, the Persian Gulf region was supplying Great Britain with 75% of the oil needed by her navy.[3] At this time the powers most vitally interested in Iraq were Great Britain, France, Russia and Germany.

World War I

During World War I, Turkey threw her weight on the side of the Central Powers and consequently Great Britain was faced with the initial task of protecting her oil wells and pipelines near the river Karun, from the easy attacks by Turkish troops from Basra. The British Government had oil holdings worth over two and a half million sterling in this area and without this oil British naval supremacy was in danger. It was therefore necessary to act both with energy and caution. Accordingly, as a first step, a naval sloop and a few marines were despatched to attack and capture the fort of Fao, at the mouth of the Shatt al Arab, which they did on 6 November 1914. This was the modest beginning of the Mesopotamian Expeditionary Force. Fao was to be used as a stepping stone to Basra. Basra was captured by the 6th Indian Division on 22 November 1914. Then a force was sent to the Karun river to protect the oil wells and pipelines. This force accomplished its task without encountering any opposition. Indian troops were also sent to occupy Qurna on 9 December 1914, which the Turks relinquished, retreating northwards. Early in 1915, however, the Turks received fresh reinforcements and the situation changed. As a counter-measure, a second division and a cavalry brigade were sent from India and more pressure was brought against the Turks, who gave up Shuaiba and retreated up the Euphrates to Nasiriya, which was captured on 24 July 1915.

Meanwhile, the remainder of the Expeditionary Force under General Townshend was moving up the Tigris with Baghdad as its objective. Amara was captured on 3 June 1915 and Kut occupied on 30 September 1915. Then General Nixon took a step which proved disastrous. Under an apprehension that the Russians, operating in the north-east, might forestall the British in occupying Baghdad, he ordered General Townshend to hasten his advance on Baghdad. The latter carried out the order and moved on with haste, but was met by the Turks at Ctesiphon, and was defeated and obliged to retreat. He retreated precipitately to Kut and was besieged there by the Turks. The siege lasted five months, during which the British Army sustained nearly 23,000 casualties in ineffective attempts to relieve a beleagured garrison of 13,000 troops. Ultimately, General Townshend surrendered with his army of 13,000 on 29 April 1916 and the Mesopotamian campaign became an

[3] *Field Notes Mesopotamia*, General Staff India, 1917.

expensive and prolonged affair. The situation was however retrieved by General Maude, who was appointed to the Supreme Command in Mesopotamia. On 22 February 1917, his troops crossed the Tigris in the rear of Kut and compelled the Turks to retreat.[4] Baghdad was taken on 11 March 1917, and the advance was continued to Mosul. When the Armistice of Mudros was announced on 1 November 1917, British troops were within twelve miles of Mosul. Mosul was however occupied, for according to the British interpretation of the armistice provisions, the invader had the right to occupy the points which were strategically necessary for holding the area already conquered.[5]

The Mesopotamia Commission Report

The surrender of more than a division of the finest troops at Kut on 29 April 1916 was followed by a searching inquiry into the causes of this disaster. The Commission, presided over by Lord George Francis Hamilton, issued its report on 17 May 1917. The Commission held that General Nixon's confident optimism was largely responsible for this disaster. The advance to Baghdad was based upon political and military miscalculations and was attempted with insufficient forces and inadequate preparation. The root cause of the trouble was, however, the division of responsibility between the India Office and the Indian Government. The arrangement, by which the Secretary of State for India controlled the policy and the Indian Government managed the expedition, proved unworkable.[6]

Iraq under British Mandate

The political consequences to Iraq of the Allied victory were great and far-reaching. Iraq was freed from the Turks and recognised as an independent state to be placed under a Mandatory Power. The Mandate was allotted to Great Britain. A provisional Arab government was set up by the British High Commissioner in November 1920; and on 23 August 1921, Emir Feisal was proclaimed King of Iraq. Relations between Iraq and the United Kingdom were defined by a treaty concluded in October 1922. This treaty imposed certain limitations on the sovereignty of Iraq. The government was to be guided by the advice of the British High Commissioner, especially "on all important matters affecting the international and financial obligations and interests" of Great Britain, as well as "the finances of the Iraq Government". No territory in Iraq (with a few exceptions), was to be ceded or leased

---

[4] A. H. Burne: *Mesopotamia—the Last Phase* (1936), p. 3.
[5] Henry A. Foster: *The Making of Modern Iraq* (1935), pp. 41-2.
[6] *The Mesopotamia Commission Report*, 1917.

to any foreign power. The interests of the foreigners were to be safeguarded, but they were not to be appointed as gazetted officials, without the consent of the British High Commissioner.[7]

In 1925 Great Britain succeeded in persuading the League of Nations to award Mosul (which belonged to Turkey) to Iraq. Since Mosul had oil deposits this was as much in the interest of Iraq as of Great Britain. In 1930 the British Government came to have the view that it had fulfilled the trust imposed on it in the Mandate of the League of Nations. Therefore it decided to surrender the Mandate, leaving Iraq completely independent, and to sponsor Iraq's application for admission to the League of Nations, which it did in 1932. Great Britain's original treaty of 1922 with Iraq, in the meanwhile, had been replaced by a new Treaty of Alliance, providing for a diplomatic and defensive alliance to last twenty-five years.[8] By this treaty Britain was to have, in time of peace, air bases at or near Basra and at a point west of Baghdad, which for her were important stations on the air route to India and the Far East. Under other terms of the treaty, Great Britain was given the right to maintain local levies for the ground defence of these bases and a right of transit across Iraq for her military forces and supplies at all times. The ships of H.M's Navy had the use of the Shatt al Arab, on giving notice of their intention to visit the Iraqi ports.

Some squadrons of the Royal Air Force, whose headquarters were at Habbaniya, were retained, but all British land forces were withdrawn from Iraq. The treaty came into force when the Mandate was terminated and Iraq became an independent member of the League of Nations in October 1932. Thereafter Iraq's relations with Great Britain continued to be friendly until April 1941, when Iraq turned hostile to Britain and was invaded by British and Indian troops, leading to military operations which are described in this part of the narrative.

---

[7] Foster: *The Making of Modern Iraq*, pp. 182-6.
[8] D. H. Cole: *Imperial Military Geography* (1937), pp. 335-6.

CHAPTER II

Physical Features

Military operations are affected considerably by the physical features of a country, such as rivers, nature of the terrain, climatic conditions, etc. A short account of the physical features of Iraq would therefore provide a fitting background to a proper appreciation of the operations in that country.

Area

When the Second World War started in September 1939, Iraq had an area of 116,600 square miles. The boundaries of Iraq on the north touch Turkey, on the east Iran, on the south the Persian Gulf, Kuwait and Saudi-Arabia and on the west Transjordan and Syria.

Physical Features

Physically, Iraq falls into four divisions, Lower Iraq, Upper Iraq, the mountains of the north-east (Kurdistan) and the desert fringe.[1] Lower Iraq is a vast plain. Commencing a little above Baghdad, and sloping gradually to the Persian Gulf, it is one flat area of alluvial clay, unrelieved by hills or by a single eminence of any importance. Nowhere is the country more than a hundred feet above sea-level, and the whole zone may be regarded as a northern extension of the Persian Gulf, which at one time probably reached almost to the Mediterranean. In fact, the whole of Lower Iraq is one large river delta, built up by the flood-mud of centuries. After the Arab conquest in the seventh century A.D., a part of this mud-silted area came to be called "Iraq ul Arab, the Arab's mudbank", from which arose the name Iraq. All this area is watered by two rivers—the Tigris and the Euphrates.

Upper Iraq offers a strong contrast to Lower Iraq. It is mostly an undulating plain, with occasional ranges of low hills. Commencing near Baghdad, this region extends in the north to the fold ranges of Asia Minor. It includes the area bounded on two sides by the rivers Euphrates and the Tigris and on the north by the hills of Asia Minor, which region is known as the Jezireh, from an Arabic word meaning 'island'. "For the most part, the Jezireh consists of an undulating plain or low plateau, lying at an altitude of 500 to 1,000 feet above sea-level, with a number of small closed

[1] L. Dudley Stamp: *Asia* (1948), p. 142.

basins, from which there is no drainage outlet. The largest of these basins is a long, narrow trench cut deeply into the plateau and known as the Wadi Tharthar. Streams enter the Wadi from the north but terminate towards the southern end in a salt marsh."[2] To the north-west of the Wadi Tharthar lies the Jebel Sinjar, a prolongation of the Syrian range of hills. The region to the east of Jezireh is known as Assyria. Here the land rises in a succession of sandstone ridges. The first of these ridges, with a maximum height of 1600 feet, faces the Tigris along a part of its course.

The mountains of the north-east chiefly consist of the highland region of Kurdistan on the borders of Turkey and Iran, which can be marked off from the uplands of Upper Iraq by an imaginary line drawn roughly from Faish Khabur through Dohuk, Aqra, Chemchemal and Khanakin. The Zagros mountains which lie between Iraq and Iran, and whose peaks on the Iranian border rise to over 10,000 feet, are remarkable for their scenery. "Rocky defiles and steep-sided canyons intersect the range, torrents of water pour down from a height on to the valleys below, rivers run through the valleys, and the headwaters of the Tigris are to be found among the higher reaches."[3]

The Desert Fringe comprises a portion of the Syrian and Arabian deserts included within the frontiers of Iraq. The sandy plains are uncultivable and almost waterless.

The Rivers

It is necessary here to describe in detail the two rivers—Tigris and the Euphrates—as they are the life-blood of the country. The Euphrates, about 1600 miles long, is the largest river in Western Asia. Its two streams—Murad Su and Firat or Kara Su, forming the headwaters, rise in the area between Lake Van and Erzurum and unite at Samsat. Then the river winds along in great sweeps to Hit, where it enters its alluvial bed, in which it flows towards the Persian Gulf. The river Tigris is about 1,150 miles long. Its two streams, forming the headwaters, rise on the southern edge of the Armenian plateau, cut through the barrier of the Taurus Mountains and unite about twenty miles north of Diyarbekir. The Tigris leaves the mountains one hundred and seventy miles below Diyarbekir, and then flows in a trough through the upper Iraqi plains, passing by Mosul to Samarra. About fifteen miles below the latter place, it enters its alluvial bed and makes its way to the Persian Gulf. The Tigris and the Euphrates approach fairly close to each other at Baghdad, and then turn apart to unite finally at Quramat Ali, below Al Qurna. Between Baghdad and Al Qurna the two

---
[2] W. B. Fisher: *The Middle East* (1950), p. 348.
[3] Mrs. Steuart Erskine: *King Faisal of Iraq* (1933), pp. 217-18.

rivers are connected by several channels and intermittent water courses, of which the chief are the Saqlawiya canal and the Shatt al Hai. From Al Qurna downwards the stream is known as the Shatt al Arab. The Shatt al Arab traverses a flat and fertile plain, dotted with villages and covered with artificially irrigated meadows and date groves. Forty miles above its mouth and twenty miles below Basra, the Shatt al Arab is joined by the Karun river, and here properly begins the delta.

Though the width of the Tigris is less than that of the Euphrates, the volume of water carried is far greater. This is due to the fact that it receives more affluents than the Euphrates. While crossing the north Syrian steppe, the Euphrates receives two large affluents. After that no other tributary joins the Euphrates. On the other hand, as it flows through the hot plains of Iraq, there is considerable evaporation, resulting in greater diminution in its volume of water. The Tigris, on the other hand, receives along the whole length of its course a large number of affluents, the most important of which are the Great Zab, the Little Zab and the Diyala. The Great Zab joins the Tigris, thirty-five miles below Mosul, and the Little Zab enters it sixty-five miles lower down. The Diyala unites with the Tigris a few miles south of Baghdad.

The Tigris is subject to devastating floods on account of the speed of the current and great volume of water. Both the Tigris and the Euphrates are at their lowest in September and October but begin to rise from December onwards. The maximum flood of the Tigris takes place during April and that of the Euphrates in May. As Lower Iraq is an extremely flat plain, floods regularly inundate large areas of the country. Thus in spring, virtually the whole region, enclosed by the triangle Basra—Amara—Nasiriya, is turned into a huge marshland. The floods are controlled to a certain extent by large earthen "bunds" along both banks of the Tigris; none-the-less, the Tigris becomes a raging torrent, with a 5-knot current flowing well above the level of the surrounding country. Hence any breach in these "bunds" leads to the flooding of a very large area of the country, often suddenly.[4]

Population

The population of Iraq according to the census of 1935 was 3,560,456 and consisted mostly of Sunni and Shiah Muslims of Arab nationality. Iranians, Kurds, Turcomans and others inhabited the

---

[4] *Field Notes Mesopotamia*—General Staff India, Feb. 1917; Fisher: *The Middle East*, pp. 340-8; *A Manual of Eurasian Routes* by Naval Staff Intelligence Department, March 1920, C.B. 909, pp. 95-7; Erskine: *King Faisal of Iraq*, pp. 190-2.

border areas, and there were large settlements of Jews and Indians also.[5]

In Iraq about 90 per cent of the inhabitants are grouped along the rivers and canals. The line of the Euphrates is far more densely populated than that of the Tigris, and has been so for thousands of years, because the slope of the ground-levels is more favourable for purposes of irrigation.[6]

Climate

The climate of Iraq is sub-tropical in character. It is dry, though an appreciable amount of rain falls in the winter months. The heat in summer is intense, going up to 130°F. in shade in the daytime. North of Amara the dry heat is easier to bear, but in the marshy areas further south, the moist heat is very trying indeed.[7] In Lower Iraq, i.e. between Baghdad and Al Qurna, the mean monthly maximum for August is 119°F. and the mean monthly minimum in January is 27.5°. In the hilly parts of Upper Iraq the coldest month is January, with an average day temperature of 40°F; the hottest are July and August, with an average of 90°F.[8]

The annual rainfall in Upper Iraq in the hills is 22 inches, the heaviest fall being in December. July, August and September are rainless. In Lower Iraq the average rainfall ranges from 4 to 7 inches. June to September are rainless.[9]

The prevailing winds in Iraq are from the north and north-west. The "Shamal" which comes from the latter direction, normally begins about the middle of June and blows more or less continuously for about forty days, with occasional lulls of 24 to 48 hours' duration. Its velocity frequently reaches 40 miles an hour. It makes the atmosphere dry and affords some relief from the intolerable summer heat. Other winds in Iraq are the "Sharqi" or the East Wind, which increases the temperature, and the South Wind, which is invariably oppressive and accompanied by dust.[10] Sometimes, frightful dust storms, deep amber in colour, rage for hours, resulting in complete blackout and creating serious dislocation.

Health and Sanitation

From the point of health and sanitation, Iraq has little to recommend it. Plague, smallpox, malaria, sandfly fever, dysentery and Baghdad boils are not uncommon, while cholera, typhus, scurvy

---

[5] *The Statesman's Year Book* (1940), p. 1031.
[6] *A Manual of Eurasian Routes*, p. 97.
[7] *Two Lectures on the Mesopotamia Campaign* by Major J. E. Shearer, M.C., 15th Punjab Regiment, and *War Diary*, 41 Field Park Company S. & M.
[8] *A Manual of Eurasian Routes*, p. 97.
[9] Ibid.
[10] *Field Notes Mesopotamia*.

and heatstroke also occur. Sickness is spread by the insects, mosquitoes, sandflies and an incredible number of flies. There is an element of truth in the Arab saying, "when Allah made hell, he found that it was not bad enough, so he made Iraq and added flies."[11] Basra is the most malarious town in Iraq, due to the numerous creeks, seepages and flood waters. The high prevalence of fevers of the enteric group renders the provision of a pure water supply of great importance.[12] No man or animal is ever really free from diarrhoea, on account of traces of Epsom salts in the water.

Towns

Among the towns of Iraq, the most prominent ones are Baghdad, Mosul and Basra. Other towns of varying importance are Kirkuk, Khanakin, Karbala, Nejef, Al Qurna, Nasiriya, Hilla, Hit, Amara and Kut al Amara. The city of Baghdad is situated on both banks of the Tigris, nearly midway between Mosul and the Persian Gulf. It is the capital of Iraq, being situated in a very favourable position where the Euphrates and Tigris approach within forty miles of each other. From here traffic with the south is easy, and here converge the northern lines of Iraq's communications, which enter Iraq from the north-west, the north and the north-east. On the east bank of the Tigris lies the most modern portion of the town, with Government offices and the chief commercial and public buildings. On the west bank is the old town, enclosed by an extensive tract of orange and date groves.

Basra is the port of southern Iraq, which ocean-going steamers can ascend by the Shatt al Arab. It lies about fifty-six miles above the mouth of the Shatt al Arab in the Persian Gulf. The name Basra is generally taken to include a considerable area stretching from Maqil (which includes the dock area), through Makina and Ashar, to the old Basra City. Maqil and Ashar occupy about four miles of the river front on the right bank, and the whole comprises the Port Area. The dock area is confined to Maqil, whilst in the river opposite Ashar are a number of mooring buoys, where ocean-going steamers unload into river craft. Makina lies to the south of Maqil, about 1½ miles from the river.[13] The old Basra City lies two miles from the river, on a narrow creek, along which runs a fairly good carriage road. There was a Royal Air Force station at Maqil, while Makina contained a hospital and the Levy Lines.

The city of Mosul stands on the right bank of the Tigris, with

[11] *Two Lectures on the Mesopotamia Campaign*, by Major J. E. Shearer, M.C., op. cit.
[12] *Basra Recce. Report*, Appendices D, G and J.
[13] *Basra Recce. Report*.

the remains of Ninevah on the other bank. Being situated at a junction of the waterway and the roadway, Mosul is of considerable strategic and commercial importance. Kirkuk, picturesquely perched on a hill, owes its importance to the oilfields, while Khanakin is a strategic border town situated on the Baghdad-Kermanshah road.

Karbala and Nejef are pilgrim centres, which attract Shiahs from all parts of the Mohammedan world, chiefly from Iran and India. Nejef is also the starting point of a pilgrim route to Mecca. Of lesser importance as places of pilgrimage are Kufeh and Samarra. Al Qurna, Nasiriya, Hilla, Amara and Kut al Amara are important owing to their position on the water-ways or as centres of fertile districts. Hit is famous for its bitumen industry.

The Terrain

The physical features and the climate of Iraq are by no means ideal for carrying out military operations in that country. The terrain, in Lower Iraq particularly, does not provide satisfactory conditions for such activities. The first difficulty is the absolute flatness of the country and "nothingness of the landscape." With no features at all upon which to take compass bearings, or by which the troops can recognise their objectives, it is unbelievably difficult to write clear orders or to maintain direction in attacks. Mirage and dust add further to the difficulties. Mirage habitually distorts vision, so that even after months of experience it is impossible to trust one's own eyes. In the dry season, these difficulties are accentuated by dust storms, which blot out the landscape.

The low-lying country is often inundated by the flooded rivers. The floods are controlled to a certain extent by large earthen 'bunds'. Yet any breach in these 'bunds' leads to a rapid flooding of a very large area of the country. Heavy rain-storms during winter render the country impassable for wheels in a few hours, and reduce the speed of infantry movement to about one mile an hour, and that with great exertion. There is practically no drinkable water anywhere except in the main rivers. Thus, while far away from the rivers want of water makes operations difficult, nearest them the excess of water is almost as great a factor of trouble.[14]

---

[14] *Field Notes Mesopotamia.*

CHAPTER III

Communications and Economic Resources

Most of the misfortunes of the Mesopotamian Expeditionary Force during World War I were due to the backward economy of Iraq. Operations in those days had to contend against the difficulties of unsatisfactory means of communication, lack of port facilities, inefficient river transport and a general paucity of local supplies. Before the outbreak of World War II, however, Iraq had made considerable progress in various directions and had become a less difficult country to campaign through. The military operations in the second war, therefore, instead of dragging on for years, as during the preceding one, had a smoother progress and a speedier conclusion, and Iraq soon came to form an important base for the subsequent operations against Syria and Iran.

Port of Basra

Thus in September 1939, at the outbreak of war, Iraq already had an excellent port at Basra, which was a legacy of the British military occupation during First World War. Situated at Maqil, four miles upstream of the city of Basra, this port was capable of admitting ocean-going steamers, which could enter or leave the Shatt al Arab by the Rooka channel at all seasons of the year. A useful adjunct to the Port was a mid-channel anchorage, at 34 to 48 feet of water, in the Basra reach of the river.

As to loading and unloading facilities, Maqil had seven main wharves, three large jetties and several berths in stream. There were additional special wharves at Muftich, half way between Maqil and Ashar, for handling petrol, kerosene and oil fuel; and at the entrance to the Ashar Creek, which runs through the town proper of Basra and forms its main channel of transport, was the Viceroy's Pier, a substantial wooden jetty of 18,440 square feet in area, suitable for inland water vessels. There were also a number of less important subsidiary wharves at various other points.

The wharves, which were served by sixteen electric cranes and several steam cranes of the most modern type, ranging in capacities from 30-cwt to 60-tons, had an ample and carefully planned layout of sidings. Adjacent to, and running parallel with, the wharves were seven large transit sheds. Seven ocean-going vessels, up to 26 feet draft, could, therefore, be unloaded simultaneously at the main wharves, while unloading of five more could proceed at the same

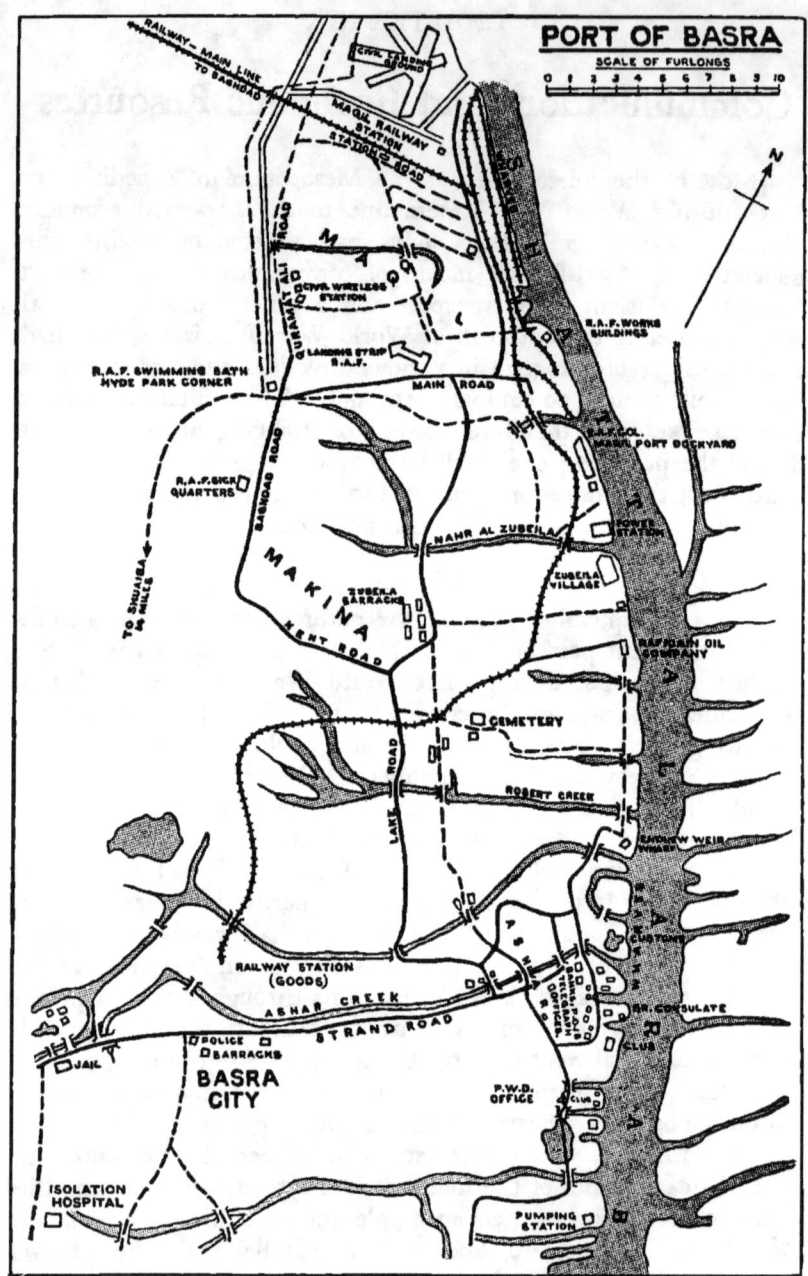

time in the mid-stream barges, for which ample additional wharves were available. Troop-ships could discharge an infantry battalion in four to six hours and a battery in about nine hours. Store ships would, however, take from two to seven days depending on the type of cargo. Personnel, ammunition and light equipment could be disembarked and unloaded at the seven main wharves, without causing any congestion.

The clearing capacity of the railway in the dock area, however, was not equal to the unloading or intake capacity of the docks. But the seven large transit sheds were capable of holding some 30,000 to 35,000 tons of overflow, and that allowed sufficient elasticity for overcoming the drawback. Mechanical transport, ammunition and stores could be loaded direct from the ships into the railway trucks, which were collected in the marshalling yard inside the dock area.

There was a Port Directorate Power Station at Zubeila which supplied the whole of the Basra area; and a water-filtration plant, with a maximum capacity of 105,000 gallons per hour, of which only half the output was enough for the entire population of Basra, Ashar, Maqil and Zubeila.[1]

Water-ways

The rivers of Iraq form an important line of the country's internal communications. The Tigris is the main line of communication between the sea and Baghdad. River steamers can progress up the Tigris as far as that city, but above Baghdad the navigation is usually only by rafts, though small steamers may go up to Samarra. Such navigation, however, depends as a rule, upon the seasons of a high and low water. It improves about the middle of November when rain causes the first rise in the level of the river. Then throughout January, February and March, the rain keeps the river fairly full, which is at its highest in April and May. The river then falls gradually through July and August, and is at its lowest in August, September and October.[2] On the whole, navigation by steamers of suitable size is possible throughout the year between Basra and Baghdad.

Unlike Tigris, the Euphrates is little used for navigation. The Hindiya Barrage virtually blocks all navigation of the lower Euphrates, about six miles below Mussaiyib, while, in some other parts the river is used mostly for the down-stream traffic only. Below the Barrage, however, it is navigable by the country boats of different sizes.

[1] *Radley Report*, pp. 1-2 and Appendix A; *Basra Reconnaissance Report*; *Plan for the move of Force Heron from Basra to Egypt*, Appendix B; *Report on the Persian Gulf Ports*, October 1941.
[2] *Field Notes Mesopotamia*, p. 97.

On the eve of the outbreak of hostilities with Iraq in 1941 there were altogether 86 steam and motor craft available. Of these, there were 6 paddle steamers, 6 paddle tugs, 67 screw tugs and 7 stern wheelers. There were in addition 33 motor bellums varying in size from 10 to 50 tons, and over 400 barges of capacities from under 100 tons to over 300 tons.

Mechanical transport vehicles could be transported on these barges but the number depended on the type of barge and whether it was decked over. As a rough guide it may be taken that a barge could carry up to eight 3-ton lorries or its equivalent in 30-cwt. trucks and motor cars.

Apart from the river steamers there was a total of nearly 5,000 registered country craft plying on the rivers of Iraq. These were mainly "Mahailas", approximately 550, with a capacity varying from 5 to 150 tons; and "Bellums", approximately 2,500, with a capacity varying from 1 to 80 tons.[3]

Railways

At the time of the commencement of hostilities with Iraq in May 1941, the Iraq State railway system consisted of a meter gauge line from Basra to Baghdad, a distance of 354 miles. There was another meter gauge line from Baghdad to Kirkuk, over a stretch of 201 miles, which was connected with the former by a wagon ferry across the river Tigris at Baghdad. This in turn was linked by a branch meter gauge line, which took off from Qaraghan (Jaloula) and continued up to Khanakin, an important town near the Iraqi-Iranian frontier. This line was about 17 miles in length. There was also a standard gauge line connecting Baghdad with Mosul via Baiji and Qaiyara, and still another length of a standard gauge line from Mosul to Tell Kotchek, where it connected with the Syrian railways.[4] The total stock of Iraqi railway, early in 1938, was 1,400 wagons and 53 engines. Considerable stock was then on order and had commenced to arrive in November 1938.

Roads

The principal roads before World War I were mostly in northern Iraq, to which well-frequented routes radiated from Baghdad. Since then much progress had been made in the construction of roads and about 4,000 miles of roads and tracks had been developed, which were fit for vehicular traffic. Of this total about 750 miles were metalled, complete with bitumen seal coat, about 150 miles were metalled without bitumen seal, and the remaining

---

[3] *Plan for the move of Force Heron from Basra to Egypt*, Appendix C.
[4] *The Statesman's Year Book* (1940), p. 1035; and *Radley Report*, p. 2.

were earth-roads and tracks. The bitumen sealed roads included the main road from Kirkuk to Mosul and a little beyond, the branches east from this road to the Iranian frontier, and the Kurdish province of Sulaimaniya, and also about 125 miles of the main road west from Baghdad towards the Syrian frontier.[5]

Baghdad was the centre of communications. It was connected with Basra by two roads, one winding along the Tigris and the other along the Euphrates. The Basra-to-Baghdad roads were in the 'bad road' area. The soil was alluvial and quickly became a morass after rain, since large areas were liable to inundation after rain, and little metalling for road construction was available. In the neighbourhood of the rivers the delta was intersected by many canals and irrigation channels while roads frequently ran along the top of narrow bunds, which could not be skirted. In dry weather these roads were passable throughout for a force of all arms including armoured cars and heavy mechanical transport. The surface was such, however, that after heavy rain the routes might be unserviceable from 4 to 7 days. Certain parts of them might remain unserviceable even for weeks.

Roads connecting Mosul to Baghdad were two, one going via Samarra and the other via Kirkuk and Erbil. The road via Samarra (distance 230 miles) was passable for wheeled traffic, though with difficulty. The track sometimes followed the floor of the Tigris valley, crossing not a few wadis, and sometimes ascended the low plateau or the hills around. The road via Kirkuk was better. The country through which it passed was for the most part populous, cultivated and well watered. Connected with this route were three important roads, one branching from Jaloula and passing through Khanakin to Kermanshah in Iran, the second connecting Kirkuk with Sulaimaniya and Penjwin, and the third starting from Erbil and passing through Rowanduz and Rayat to Tabriz in Iran. From Mosul the main road led into Turkey via Qamichliye.

Baghdad was connected with Haifa, in Palestine, by a desert route, which led through Habbaniya, Ramadi and Rutba to Transjordan and finally to Palestine. Except for the sixteen miles immediately east of Falluja, the route from Baghdad to Habbaniya, a distance of 60 miles, was a good two-way tarmac road, of bitumen layer on an earth foundation. It could stand up to much traffic. The iron bridge near Baghdad, the Falluja bridge and that over a canal half-way between Falluja and Habbaniya could carry any traffic. From Habbaniya the road led via Ramadi to Rutba, and thence along the pipeline to Mafraq in Transjordan, and onward

[5] *The Statesman's Year Book* (1940), p. 1035.
[6] *Plan for the move of Heron Force from Basra to Egypt.*

to Haifa on the Mediterranean coast. Water was available at Iraq Petroleum Company's stations at convenient stages, between Rutba and Mafraq but had to be dumped between Habbaniya and Rutba, as this stretch was waterless. Between Habbaniya and Ramadi the road was out of use for 15 to 30 days in April and May if the bund holding the Euphrates had to be cut. The route was good, hard desert going up to H-4, a station along the pipeline, whence it passed through 110 miles of the lava belt. Here the surface was hard but corrugated and bumpy. The lava belt route was a one-way road. The only serious drawbacks, which manifested themselves in wet weather, were the Wadi Hauran (which was being bridged in April 1938) near Rutba, and the Wadi Abu al Taraft, six miles east of H-4.[7] Connected with this main route was the road which branched off from Rutba via Sab Biyar to Damascus.

A second desert road connected Baghdad with Aleppo. It led through Habbaniya, Ramadi, Haditha, Abu Kemal and Deir ez Zor. Still another desert route connected Mosul to Aleppo via Al Badi and Deir ez Zor.

As to principal roads radiating from Basra, one led into Iran via Khurram Shahr and Ahwaz, while another, a desert track, led into Saudi Arabia via Kuwait.[8]

As regards mechanical transport, the use of motor vehicles had increased considerably in recent years, and motor transport was used for both passengers and stores on the overland routes connecting Iraq with Syria, Transjordan and Iran. Most of the mechanical transport in the country was based on Baghdad and engaged in the trans-desert service between Baghdad and the Mediterranean sea-board and in the Iraq-Iran service. In Basra itself there were only 70 commercial vehicles and these were in a very poor state of repair, though there was a large number of private cars. The reason for the shortage of commercial vehicles in Basra was that although the town had a number of roads, few of them led into the interior. Ignoring town facilities, there were a large number of 5-ton vehicles engaged in trade in the country-side, mainly in northern Iraq. Owners usually owned a fleet of three or four lorries only, many of which had been bought on the "hire purchase" system. In a military emergency, large numbers of these lorries might be drawn off the roads for a few weeks without causing serious dislocation, except during the grain transport season from June to December. About 600 of such vehicles might be obtained for use, if the rate of hire was sufficiently attractive to draw them off their normal work.[9]

[7] *Radley Report*, Part III, p. 1.
[8] *Military routes in Iraq*, G. H. Q. Paiforce (1943).
[9] *Basra Recce. Report;* and *Radley Report*.

Telephones, Telegraphs and Post Offices

On 31 December 1938, the line and wire mileage of Iraq's telegraph and telephone system came to 4,441 miles and 31,812 miles respectively. There were 159 post and telegraph offices in Iraq. Air mail service was operated by the Imperial Airways Ltd., the K.L.M., Air France and Ala Littoria air services. The transit period between Iraq and England by these services was three to four days and between Iraq and India about two days. Air mail communication with Syria was maintained by means of Air France and Ala Littoria twice a week, and with Palestine and Egypt by Imperial Airways, K.L.M., and Ala Littoria services. In addition to these there was also the Iranian State Air Line, which operated once a week between Baghdad, Kermanshah and Teheran.

Aerodromes and landing grounds

There were serveral aerodromes and landing grounds in Iraq, some of which were fairly large and had sufficiently good approaches and surface to enable the Royal Air Force aircraft to operate from there. Not all of Iraq's landing grounds were, however, equipped with runways. Those with runways in northern Iraq were Ain Zala, Haditha (K-3), K-1, K-2 and Qaiyara; in southern Iraq they were the Baghdad Airport, the Basra Airport, Habbaniya and Rashid. The rest of the landing grounds had no runways, which meant that they usually became unserviceable for one or two·days after heavy rain. All of Iraq's airfields, landing grounds, landing strips etc. may be conveniently divided into the following main classifications:

(a) *Northern area* (north of Baghdad exclusive)

   (i) Aerodromes and landing grounds suitable for or being made suitable for modern aircraft were at Ain Zala, Baquba, H-1, Haditha (K-3), K-1, K-2, Kirkuk, Mosul, Qaiyara, Shahraban, Tell Kotchek.

   (ii) Landing grounds capable of being made suitable for modern aircraft existed among others at Al Badi, Baiji, Erbil, Khanakin, T-1.

   (iii) Landing grounds suitable for old type aircraft only existed at Altun Kopru, Ana, Awasil, Diana, Faish Khabur, Halabja, Khurmal, Mandali, Penjwin, Samarra, Qaraghan, Sulaimaniya, Zakho.

(b) *Southern area* (south of Baghdad inclusive)

   (i) Aerodromes and landing grounds suitable or being made suitable for modern aircraft were mainly at Baghdad Airport, Basra Airport, Habbaniya, Rashid, Shuaiba, H-3, Diwaniya.

(ii) Landing grounds capable of being made suitable for modern aircraft existed at Karbala, Kufeh, Kut al Amara, Amara, Ur, Al Busaiya, As Salman, Shabicha.

(iii) Landing grounds suitable for old type aircraft only existed at Rutba, H-2, Hilla, Nasiriya, Hamza, Samawa, Al Aziziya, Shatra, Ali Gharbi, Badra.

Those aerodromes and landing grounds described as "suitable for use by modern aircraft" were large enough to enable R.A.F. aircraft to operate from there. They were not, however, in all cases, suitable for the Bredas and Savoyas with which some squadrons of the R.I.A.F. were then equipped.

Local Resources

The position as regards local resources about 1941 was much better than that during the war of 1914-1918. In 1941-42 fairly large quantities of local supplies were available and a proportion of military requirements might be possibly met from them. But difficulty might have been experienced in procuring supplies of cattle and wood. But the shortage of beef was compensated for by a surplus of mutton, while the shortage of wood was compensated for by unlimited supplies of fuel oil, which was used in Iraq for all purposes, including cooking.

On the whole, it was then estimated that the local supplies of consumable goods were sufficient to meet the requirements of Indian troops in Iraq during the war. Iraq's most valuable crop was dates, which accounted for three-quarters of the world's date trade.[10] Wheat, barley and rice were the principal crops of the country. A large variety of fruits and vegetables were also grown. Similarly large quantities of fish were procurable from Fao, and chickens were available in plenty, though supplies were scattered. From two to four million eggs were exported annually. Cattle were not available in large numbers and the condition of those at Basra was poor. Better cattle were available at Amara, Ali Gharbi and Kut. Sheep were bred throughout Iraq in large numbers. There were 10,000,000 sheep and 3,000,000 goats in Iraq in 1941. Potatoes were grown in very small quantities and were chiefly imported from Iran and India. Dairy Farming on modern lines had not been introduced in Iraq. There was no milk or butter turning plant in the country and there was only one dairy in Basra owning about a hundred head of cattle,[11] which was however run on "primitive lines".

[10] Richard Goold—Adams: *Middle East Journey* (1947), p. 99.
[11] *Basra Recce. Report.*

Oil Resources

No description of Iraq's economic resources is complete without an account of its abundant oil supplies. Iraq's chief oil-producing centre is Kirkuk. The Kirkuk Oilfield was first developed in 1927 by the Turkish Petroleum Company, whose name was changed in 1931 to the Iraq Petroleum Company, which was an international group. There was an oil pipeline from the oilfield to the Mediterranean coast. The line proceeded from Kirkuk to Haditha, where it bifurcated, the French section passing through Abu Kemal, Palmyra to Tripoli, and the British section passing through Rutba to Haifa. The total length of the two lines was 1,200 miles.[12]

A refinery had been built at Haifa in 1939 by British interests. At Tripoli was another smaller refinery operated by French companies. There were pumping stations at intervals along the pipeline west of Haditha. These were numbered according to the branch on which they were situated. Thus T-1 was the easternmost station on the Tripoli branch and H-5 the westernmost station on the Haifa branch. This latter pipeline was of vital importance to the British naval forces based on Malta and Gibraltar and to the Imperial Air Services to the east.

At Naft Khana, near Khanakin, was another Iraqi oilfield, which was operated by the Khanakin Oil Company, a subsidiary of the Anglo-Iranian Oil Company. The production was much smaller, hardly comparable with that at Kirkuk, the entire output being for local consumption. This oilfield had its refinery at Alwand, to which it was connected by a pipeline. The refined oil was distributed and marketed by an associated company, the Rafidain Oil Company, in all parts of Iraq, at cheap prices controlled by an agreement between the Company and the Government.[13]

The British Oil Development Company (Mosul Oilfields Ltd.) held a concession for oil, covering Iraqi territory west of the Tigris and north of the 33rd parallel of lattitude. Several wells had been drilled in this area but no oil had been marketed. Similarly, the Basra Petroleum Company had been granted a concession for oil covering the southernmost part of Iraq, roughly the old Basra Vilayet. Oil production in 1938 was 4,272,000 tons.[14] In 1939 another oilfield was discovered at Ain Zala, north of Mosul, but the threat of Axis invasion of Iraq in 1941 stopped further development.

The oil resources of Iraq, supplemented by those of Iran, were more than sufficient for the requirements of a British force of any size operating in Iraq or Iran. The Anglo-Iranian Oil Company exploited the Khuzistan fields of south-west Iran, which consisted

---

[12] A. G. Boycott: *Elements of Imperial Defence*, pp. 110, 113 and 295.
[13] *The Statesman's Year Book* (1940), p. 1034.
[14] Ibid.

of six oilfields—Masjid-i-Suleiman, Haft Khel, Gach Saran, Agha Jari, White Oil Spring, and Lali. Oil was first produced in 1908 at the Masjid-i-Suleiman field and then in 1928 at Haft Khel. The remaining fields came into production during or after World War II. A 150-mile long pipeline, constructed in 1910-13, connected Masjid-i-Suleiman to Iran's main refinery at Abadan, a port on Shatt al Arab.

There was another separate oilfield at Nafti-i-Shah, where oil was produced only for the local market of northern Iran. Crude oil from here was conveyed by a pipeline to a small refinery at Kermanshah.[15] This oilfield was being exploited by the Kermanshah Petroleum Company, a subsidiary of the Anglo-Iranian Oil Company.[16]

Thus the combined supply from the refineries producing high grade petrol at Abadan, Khanakin and Kermanshah was practically unlimited. The petrol from Abadan was received in Basra either in bulk or in tins, and the economic limit of supply from this source was Diwaniya by rail and Al Aziziya by river. All requirements of Iraq above this line were met from Khanakin.

---

[15] Fisher: *The Middle East*, pp. 227.
[16] *Tenth Army* O. 1. No. 30 dated 26 June 1942.

CHAPTER IV

Pre-war Defence Plans

Bastions of India's External Defence

The existence of oil in Iraq and Iran, although of vital importance to the British empire, was not the only interest Great Britain had in this part of western Asia. There was also a strategic aspect to her attitude towards Iraq in the late nineteenth and the early twentieth centuries. Iraq lay athwart Great Britain's air route to India and East Asia, forming as she did a landbridge between the eastern Mediterranean and the Persian Gulf. She was therefore an integral part of Britain's imperial communications. British naval security in the Indian Ocean also, to a degree, depended on her control of the head of the Persian Gulf. Therefore, it was not surprising that after World War I, Iraq should be recognised as forming part of Great Britain's scheme of strategic defences.

But how was India concerned in the defence of Iraq? Before 1939, a new principle had been developed that Aden, Iraq, Iran and the Persian Gulf region formed an integral part of the external defence of India. In March 1921, the Legislative Assembly of India had passed a Resolution defining the role of the army in India as "the defence of India against external aggression and the maintenance of internal peace and tranquillity."[1] For any other purpose, the obligations resting on India were to be optional and self-imposed, as they were in the case of the self-governing Dominions. This restricted definition of the role of the army in India was accepted by the Government of India and His Majesty's Government in the United Kingdom.

A new development, however, took place, when detailed military planning started with the Defence of India Plan of 1927-28. This plan was drawn up to meet the contingency of the Russian aggression against Afghanistan. The army in India, (which included British troops serving in India, and is to be distinguished as such from the exclusively Indian army proper), was to prevent the Russian forces from entering Afghanistan and invading India. This plan could be successfully implemented only if the army in India was assisted by a powerful British expeditionary force sent from the United Kingdom. The role of the army in India was, therefore, only to offer initial resistance to the invading force, pending the arrival of Imperial reinforcements. In accordance

[1] Paper 'F', F. 461.

with this plan, the British War Office inquired in 1929, whether, apart from the despatch of a force to Afghanistan, India would agree to send forces also to Iraq and Iran, in case those countries were attacked by Russia. The reply of India's Chief of General Staff to this rather embarrassing request was that the acceptance of such a proposal was bound to be hedged round with so many stipulations as to make the agreement hardly worth while, but that, in an emergency, "we should of course do our utmost to meet the immediate requirements of the situation."[2] This was the beginning of what a few years later crystallised into the axiom that India and the United Kingdom were mutually interdependent in the matter of defence, inasmuch as the army in India was not by itself strong enough to repel attack on India by a major power, while it was also not practicable for Great Britain either, to defend her eastern Imperial interests and outposts, without the aid of the armed forces of India. This principle was accepted and incorporated in the Garran Award of 1933. The primary role of the army in India was then described as follows:—

"The duties of the Army in India include the preservation of internal security in India, the covering of the lines of internal communication, and the protection of India against external attack. Though the scale of the forces is not calculated to meet external attack by a Great Power, their duties might well comprise the initial resistance to such an attack pending the arrival of Imperial reinforcements."[3]

India secured from the British exchequer an annual grant of £1,500,000 for this new role of her army as an Imperial Reserve. This was the official recognition of the principle that while the United Kingdom was to assist India in defending her territory against a major power, India was to assist the United Kingdom in defending her vital Imperial interests and outposts whenever a necessity arose.

A further development took place in 1938 when the Pownall Committee stressed the desirability of India playing a more important part in the defence of imperial interests and outposts. Emphasising the point that it would be in India's own interest, the Committee said:

"The changed strategical situation throughout the world, and the development of modern armaments, particularly air forces, have brought into prominence the need for India, in her interest, to play a more important part in the defence of the vital areas of our Imperial communications in the Middle and Far East."

A little later, when the Chatfield Committee reported on India's

[2] *D. I. Plan*, F. 498.
[3] *Garran Report*.

defence policy in February 1939, it made still more far-reaching recommendations. The localities that had till then been treated as Imperial outposts were now held by the Committee to be the bastions of India's own "External Defence". The Government of India and the British Government were thenceforth to be jointly responsible for defending not only the Indian frontiers but also certain outposts overseas, which, it was claimed, were essential for India's own security. The report further explained that "the obligation (of sending troops overseas) on the Government of India is no longer a contract to perform something outside the sphere of their normal duties; it becomes an integral part of those duties." Accordingly, the formations earmarked for duty outside India were no longer to be separated from the rest of the army in India as an "Imperial Reserve", but were to be treated as an integral part of India's army, and were to be known as the "External Defence Troops".

Plans before September 1939

Even in the early thirties, several years before the outbreak of war, India had made and kept ready, plans for the defence, among other things, of the Persian Gulf and the Anglo-Iranian Oilfields. Two schemes were so prepared: the one to meet possible local disturbances in the oilfield area, and the other to deal with a hostile Iran. The first scheme was prepared by the Air Officer Commanding the Royal Air Force in Iraq in 1930, and the second by the Joint Planning Committee in December 1932.

The aim of the first scheme was the protection of the personnel and property of the Anglo-Iranian Oil Company in case of a local disturbance. This was to be achieved, in the first instance, by despatch of an air force and naval landing parties, and later by bringing in an infantry battalion from India.[4] While reviewing the scheme on 29 June 1931, the Committee of Imperial Defence considered that the provision of one battalion from India was inadequate and suggested that India should raise her contribution to a whole brigade.[5] The defence scheme was accordingly revised in June 1933. The Indian brigade was to be utilised as follows: one battalion for the defence of the oilfields and the pipeline, the second for the defence of Ahwaz and the third to be allotted in accordance with the prevailing situation.[6]

In the meantime a new situation had arisen, which led to the preparation of the second scheme. A dispute had been going on

---

[4] *The Defence Scheme for the Persian Oilfields*, General Staff, dated 14.3.1933, pages 1-4; *Policy regarding the despatch of reinforcements to Iran*, Part II, F. 266E.
[5] *Committee of Imperial Defence Note* dated 29.6.1931.
[6] *Committee of Imperial Defence*, File J.P. 102.

between the Anglo-Iranian Oil Company and the Iranian Government in which danger of a military conflict with Iran was not entirely ruled out. Hence a new scheme was prepared by the Joint Planning Committee in December 1932, for the protection of the Company's property against a hostile Iran. It would not be possible in such an emergency to protect the oilfields and the pipeline, since the Iranian Government maintained a considerable garrison at Ahwaz and could concentrate in the early stages a force of some 15,000 to 20,000 men, with 60 to 70 guns, in the area of the oilfields. Therefore, initial action would have to be confined to Abadan where there was the main refinery, and to the protection of the Company's property at that place. For that limited purpose, two battalions could be moved from Egypt to Abadan. But if, after initial retaliatory measures, such as capture of the Iranian gun-boats, seizure of the Iranian customs and occupation of various points along the Persian Gulf, further action was needed, then at least two more divisions would be necessary for such wider military operations, and for the ultimate re-capture of the oilfields. The Joint Planning Committee suggested that, in such an eventuality, India should provide either one or both of the two divisions thus required.

In 1935, both the above defence plans were reviewed and re-cast under the authority of the Air Officer Commanding Iraq, and were finally approved by the Chiefs of Staff in the latter part of 1937.[7] They were subjected to a further re-examination before 1939, as some parts of the two plans were considered to have gone out of date. No occasion arose for the implementation of either of the plans, since the danger of local disturbances had disappeared by 15 June 1939. The Bakhtiari tribes, from whom trouble was apprehended, had been disarmed and many of them were employed by the Company. The dispute between the Government of Iran and the Oil Company, too, had been brought to a peaceful settlement.

Schemes for the defence of the Persian Gulf

The above two plans had in view only the security of the Anglo-Iranian Oilfields. While they were on the *tapis*, the broader aspect of the defence of the whole of the Persian Gulf region, also, came up for consideration. Sir T. Fowle, the Political Resident in the Persian Gulf, in a memorandum dated 17 January 1938, raised the important issue of the possible military commitments in the greater part of the Persian Gulf region and stressed the importance of safeguarding various other imperial interests in that region in addition to the oilfields of Iran. Those interests, according to him, were:

(i) *Communications*. The Cable and Wireless Limited operated the only cable linking India with Iraq, which ran

[7] Letter from Air Ministry to India Office, 17 June 1938, File J.P. 102.

from Karachi to Fao via Muscat and Bushire. A second cable ran from Bushire to Fao, and a third linked Bushire with Bahrein. The company also operated a wireless station at Bahrein, which could communicate with Basra, Karachi and Aden. The Royal Air Force operated a wireless station at Muscat and there were Imperial Airways stations at Sharja and Gwadar.

(ii) *Naval Bases.* The base of the Persian Gulf Division of the Royal Navy was at Bahrein, with a small advanced base at Khor Khawi, in Muscat territory, at the mouth of the Gulf. There were seaplane anchorages at Yas Island, Dibai, Ras al Khaima, Muscat, Khor Jarama and Murbat.

(iii) *Air Bases.* The Air France and K. L. M. Air Lines operated along the Iranian side of the Gulf. The Air France made a night stop at Jask and landed at Bushire for mails and passengers. The Imperial Airways used the Arab side of the Gulf. There was another purely military air route from Muscat to Aden. The Persian Gulf had become the Suez Canal of the air. There were aerodromes and landing grounds at Kuwait, Bahrein, Yas Island, Abu Dhabi, Sharja, Kalba, Muscat, Shinas, Ras al Hadd, Umm Rasas, Shuwairima, Murbat and Salala.

(iv) *Oil other than Iranian.* The chief oil interests in the Gulf area were of course the Anglo-Iranian Oil Company's refinery at Abadan and their oilfields inland. But there were other oil interests also, outside Iran. There was, for example, on the Arab side of the Persian Gulf, a large and flourishing oilfield at Bahrein; and of lesser importance were those at Kuwait, Qatar, on the Trucial coast and at Muscat.

Sir T. Fowle was of opinion that, from the political and strategic point of view, the Iranian side of the Persian Gulf, with the exception of the above oil area, was not so important as the Arab side, and he, therefore, suggested that in the event of a major war Bushire and Bandar Abbas should be evacuated and defence schemes made for the Arab side of the Persian Gulf only. The Admiralty and the Air Ministry, on the other hand, were of opinion that no defence need, at all, be organised in the Persian Gulf region against possible naval or air attacks, whether from the Arab side of the Gulf or the Iranian side; and that schemes for local defence and internal security only ought to suffice.[8] These schemes were prepared before the end of April 1939 by Major

---

[8] *M.D.I., Defence of the Persian Gulf,* 12 January 1938; *Possible commitments in the Persian Gulf.*

Price, who was detailed for this purpose by the Air Officer Commanding Iraq.[9]

Force 'Heron'

It would not be out of place here to give a brief description of another plan having no direct bearing on the protection of the Persian Gulf region but incidentally underlining its importance as an area of great strategic value. On 26 January 1938, the War Office issued a directive to Lieut.-Colonel H. P. Radley to reconnoitre a route through Iraq to Egypt with a view to its being used as an alternative route for the despatch from India to Egypt, in an emergency, of a force equal to a brigade group. This force, which had the code-name Heron, was to consist of one British and two Indian infantry battalions, one field artillery brigade, one field company of Sappers and Miners, some ancillary units and a Royal Air Force contingent.[10]

The reconnaissance was duly carried out. Lieut.-Colonel Radley, acting under the direction of, and in close co-operation with, the Air Officer Commanding Iraq, remained busy from 10 March to 7 May 1938. In his report he expressed the opinion that the despatch of the proposed force by this route would be a practicable operation only under certain conditions. These conditions were that the Government of Iraq should furnish facilities as envisaged in Article IV of the Anglo-Iraqi Treaty of Alliance, the Euphrates tribes should not offer any serious opposition, the road in Transjordan should be improved and sufficient water receptacles be available for dumping water between Habbaniya and Rutba.[11] He also mentioned two other factors which might delay the progress of such a force. First, until bridges were constructed over the Wadi Hauran at Rutba and the Wadi Abu al Taraft, six miles east of H-4, the force in question would be liable to a delay of five days in the event of a spate. (A bridge over the former was under construction at the end of April 1938). Secondly, during the flood season of April and May, the Euphrates bund was sometimes cut at Ramadi to allow the surplus flood water to drain out into Lake Habbaniya. That action normally made the road Habbaniya—Rutba impassable for about one month and would therefore very seriously delay the passage of any force using that route.[12]

In January 1939, the Government of India made two suggestions to the War Office regarding Heron. First, while agreeing to the proposal of sending that force by land, the Government of India

---
[9] D.M.O. and I. dated 12 June 1939; *Commitments in the Persian Gulf*.
[10] War Office Directive No. 16 (Heron), 26 January 1938.
[11] Radley Report.
[12] Ibid.

expressed concern over this route being used as a permanent line of communication in view of its insecurity and non-availability of hired transport.[13] Secondly, they proposed an all-British force, i.e. three British battalions instead of one British and two Indian.[14] The War Office realised the dangers inherent in the scheme but thought that there was no alternative to developing that route. Nor would they accept the proposal for an all-British force, since they could not provide the necessary ancillary units.[15]

Soon afterwards, the War Office deputed Colonel Barry[16] and the Government of India deputed Lt.-Col. Key[17] to co-operate with the Air Officer Commanding Iraq, in preparing a plan for the movement of Heron. The plan was ready on 27 March 1939. Its chief features were that Heron consisting of one infantry brigade group was, in the first instance, to be moved from Basra to Baghdad, using the road, rail and river communications, after which it was to proceed to Haifa, via the desert staging posts of Habbaniya, L.G.5, H-3, H-4, and Mafraq. The main consideration in preparing the plan was to produce a continuous flow in the movement of troops. Therefore the Force was to move from Habbaniya in six groups, each group being one day's march behind the one in front of it. Two conditions were necessary for the success of this scheme, the neutrality of Iran to ensure the passage of the Shatt al Arab, and friendly relations with Iraq for the movement of the troops through that country. The plan was therefore worked out on the assumption that neither Iraq nor Iran would be hostile.

The need for putting this scheme into effect at the outbreak of the war, however, did not arise, but it came to the fore again in 1940, when Italy entered the war and the Red Sea route was threatened. This led to a revised scheme, known as 'Basloc' being prepared by the General Headquarters, Middle East.

---

[13] Tel. No. 52814 of 7 January 1939 from Troopers to General Staff and No. 52852 of 13 January 1939—Heron, 222B.
[14] Tel. No. 113 of 11 January 1939 from General Staff to Troopers—Heron, 222B.
[15] General Staff Branch, 16 January 1939, 222C.
[16] Tel. No. 52886 of 16 January 1939 from Troopers to General Staff, p. 7—Heron, 222B.
[17] From War Office dated 19 January 1939, p. 26—Heron, 222B.

CHAPTER V

Defence Plans (1939—June 1940)

Scheme for the despatch of a force to Iran

In August 1939, when war seemed imminent, the War Office ordered Army Headquarters, India, to prepare schemes for the despatch of a force to Egypt, Singapore, Iran or elsewhere, for meeting any emergency that might develop in one or more of these theatres, during the next three months. Accordingly, the General Staff in India prepared appreciations of the administrative problems involved in such moves. One of these related to the move of a force to Iran, designated K-3, which was to consist of an infantry brigade group and was primarily intended for the security of the Anglo-Iranian oilfields.

The first problem to be solved in connection with the move of K-3 was the selection of a "base" for the landing of the troops and subsequent operations. Three alternatives were suggested, Abadan, Basra and Bandar Shahpur. Abadan, it was found, could maintain an infantry brigade group and could therefore meet the initial needs of the force K-3. But any considerable expansion of the force would entail a corresponding expansion of the base for which Abadan was unsuitable. In that case, Basra was the obvious choice. As a base, Basra would not only meet the initial requirements of the force K-3 but was also capable of expansion. Another advantage of selecting Basra would be that in case it was not considered desirable for the British and Indian troops to enter the Iranian territory, on political grounds or otherwise, they might be held in Basra to cross the border at short notice. The third alternative of Bandar Shahpur as a base was ruled out as it had few port facilities. It was also hot and malarious and navigation was difficult. The conclusion arrived at, therefore, was that Basra alone would answer the purpose.[1]

Threat of Russian aggression

The scope of K-3 was considerably expanded in March 1940, when fresh plans were made for the despatch of a force of no less than three infantry divisions for operations in Iraq and Iran. The plans were drawn up against the eventuality of an attack by Russia on those countries. The Russo-German Pact of August 1939, which pledged the two countries to mutual peace and friendship, had

[1] *Force K.3—Administrative appreciation*, 1089 H.

roused the apprehension that, while the German forces marched against the "Western Democracies", the Russian forces would be launched against Iraq and Iran on the one hand, and Afghanistan and India on the other. There were already several German agents in Afghanistan who, together with the Soviet representatives, were undermining British influence in that country. Consequently the British Government felt it necessary to remain in readiness for a military intervention in Afghanistan. As a result, the General Staff in India drew up a "plan for the assistance of Afghanistan." It was known briefly as Plan 'A' and was submitted to the Secretary of State, in May 1940. It provided for the employment of a Field Army of one armoured division, composed of one armoured and two motor brigades, and five infantry divisions.

The problem of the possible Russian attacks on Iraq and Iran had begun to receive attention as early as December 1939, when the General Headquarters, Middle East, prepared a memorandum on the "Military Policy in the Middle East", for submission to the War Cabinet. This memorandum pointed out that in the event of Russian aggression it would be necessary to operate air striking forces from Iraq and Turkey against objectives in Caucasia, where was centered practically the entire Russian oil production. A Russian advance on this front, it was argued, ought not to be allowed to penetrate far enough to deny to the British the requisite air bases in Eastern Turkey and Iraq. As for Iran, the Russian attack might take the form of an advance on Tabriz with five or six divisions, or a seaborne expedition across the Caspian, with Teheran as its objective, or a combination of both these courses. That would bring the Anglo-Iranian oilfields within reach of Russian bombers, against which it would be necessary to provide the necessary fighter and anti-aircraft defences. A minimum of one fighter squadron was deemed to be necessary in the neighbourhood of Abadan. Further, since Russian air action, combined with their propaganda, might cause disaffection against the British, both in Iraq and Iran, it was necessary to take steps to ensure the security of the oilfields and the port of Basra. For that purpose, at least one division was considered to be necessary in the first instance.

A further Russian advance, except perhaps for a minor diversion across the Iraqi frontier at Rowanduz, would have to follow the Hamadan—Kermanshah road towards Iraq or the Trans-Iranian Railway towards Abadan. The progress along these lines would be necessarily slow and the communications would severely limit the size of the advancing forces. But, on the other hand, such an advance would compel the British to deploy large forces on the Iraqi frontier in order to defend air bases in the Iraqi plains, and to

Gen. Sir Archibald P. Wavell

Lt.-Gen. Sir William Platt

Maj.-Gen. A. G. O. Mayne

Maj.-Gens. L. M. Heath and N. M. de la P. Beresford-Peirse

(c) to ensure free and unhindered use of the Shatt al Arab as far as Basra.

Abadan, it may be mentioned here, is situated on the Iraq-Iran border, on river Bahamanshir, which branches off the Karun river before the latter joins the Shatt al Arab. It is 32 miles south-east of Basra and is the seat of the main oil refinery of the Anglo-Iranian Oil Company.

The necessity for implementing Trout would arise only if Iran showed an attitude of hostility towards Britain. At that moment, however, the policy of the Shah of Iran seemed to be genuinely one of neutrality and it did not appear that he would abandon it willingly. But he might be forced to do so by Soviet pressure; or, alternatively, a threat to Abadan might develop through actual Soviet invasion. In either case there would, it was expected, be some warning of the approaching crisis and in such a case Trout would have to be moved to Iraq and kept ready at Basra to take the necessary counter-measures.

Composition of the First Echelon of Trout

Were Iran to turn hostile, the opposition which the first echelon of Trout would meet was estimated to consist of:

(i) The Iranian Navy based on Khurram Shahr, having a strength of two sloops and four gun-boats, which would have to be neutralised in the initial stages. Its efficiency, however, was reported to be low. Khurram Shahr stood at the junction of the rivers Karun and Shatt al Arab.

(ii) Regular Iranian force of the *6th Division* based on Ahwaz. Although its standard of equipment and training was not considered to be very high, it was likely to derive some strength from the activities of the local tribesmen. Ahwaz, on the Karun river, is 110 miles upstream of Khurram Shahr.

(iii) Units of the Iranian Air Force, based on Ahwaz. These were negligible in quality but steps for neutralization would be necessary. Should Trout move after the Soviet penetration into Iran, enabling the establishment of Russian air bases forward, the anti-aircraft defence would present a serious problem. In such an eventuality, the inclusion of an anti-aircraft cruiser or sloop in the naval escort would be essential, and anti-aircraft formations, which would have to come from England would have to accompany the first echelon of Trout.

(iv) The existing strength of the Iranian army in Abadan—Khurram Shahr area, believed to consist of only a few small detachments, but capable of being increased.

Thus the initial opposition which Trout would meet on landing was not much and could be overcome by a force of under two infantry brigades. The strength of the assaulting force of Trout, that is Part 'A' of its first echelon, was accordingly fixed at:

    Headquarters 9th Indian Infantry Brigade and Signals
    One Mountain Battery, Indian States Forces (150 animals)
    One Field Company, Sappers and Miners
    Four Indian infantry battalions
    300 pack animals for carriage of machine-guns, ammunition, tools, medical equipments etc.
    Medical, Veterinary, Supply and Ordnance units.

The Part 'B' which was to follow up the assaulting force was to consist of:—

    Divisional Headquarters and Signals
    One (Motor) Cavalry Regiment
    One Field Regiment R. A.
    One Field Park Company, Sappers and Miners
    One Bridging Section, Sappers and Miners
    Base Development staff and units.

It was clear that this echelon, if opposed, would not be able to achieve more than the initial objects of Trout, namely to land the portion 'A' of the first echelon and to secure Abadan and the free use of the Shatt al Arab as far as Basra. If, however, the situation at the time of the mobilization of Trout was such as to require immediate protection of the entire oilfield area, with a high degree of probability of opposition, then it would clearly be desirable to include in the first convoy, or to follow it up a few days later with, at least one more infantry brigade and a second Field Regiment, and preferably also with a third infantry brigade.

Air and Naval support for Trout

The naval forces to be provided for supporting the first echelon of Trout, were:

(i) An ocean escort, as necessary, of cruisers and armed merchant cruisers, to be detailed by the Commander-in-Chief East India's Squadron.

(ii) A river escort for escorting the transports up the river, consisting of 3 vessels or China gunboats armed with two 4-inch guns and a number of light machine-guns; 2 minesweepers (tugs) with one 12-pounder gun each; and four Iraqi river gunboats, each with one 3.7-inch howitzer, two 3-inch mortars and four machine-guns.

As for the co-operation by the Royal Air Force, the Report suggested that the allotment for Trout of one General Purposes

Squadron, one Fighter Squadron and one B. T. Flight, was not sufficient and should be increased by one Bomber Squadron. All these squadrons were to operate from Shuaiba aerodrome, 17 miles west of Basra.

Plans for Trout: movement and landing

It was planned that the convoy consisting of the 1st Echelon of Trout would move straight through to the head of the Persian Gulf, where the ships containing the assaulting force would proceed to what was known as the "Examination Anchorage" outside the mouth to the Shatt al Arab, about 20 nautical miles from Fao, while the remainder of the convoy would proceed to the Kuwait anchorage. Should there be danger of air attack from Soviet aircraft, then part 'B' of the 1st Echelon would have to anchor at Bahrein.

It was assumed that the strength of the hostile force on the Abadan island would not exceed one regiment of infantry (three battalions), with some supporting artillery plus a few hundred tribesmen, and that not more than one battalion, with a battery of artillery, would be located in the southern portion of the island opposite Fao or thereabout. Any opposition in excess of this would make a forced landing on the east bank of the river too hazardous an operation to attempt, and if there was the possibility that the passage up the river to Basra by British ships would be disputed by gun fire, then the move would probably have to be abandoned or delayed.

If Soviet aircraft would intervene from the Iranian bases within 400 miles of Abadan, then an anti-aircraft sloop, or preferably a cruiser, would be required for anti-aircraft protection, till the arrival of Part 'B' of the 1st Echelon, which was to include one anti-aircraft regiment for the protection of Abadan, and another for the protection of Basra port and base.

Apart from Abadan, where an opposed landing was not feasible, there were two other points along the Iranian coast which gave a reasonable chance of effecting an opposed landing. These were the two stretches along the east bank, one of two miles along the Kasba and the other of 4½ miles in the centre of which stood Khosroabad,[5] a new oil delivery point of the Anglo-Iranian Oil Company. The latter had two advantages. There were three new jetties at which ships could berth, two complete and one under construction, and a good metalled road to Abadan, a distance of about 17 miles.

Along both these stretches there was deep water right up to the banks, one of which was entirely open for some three hundred

---

[5] Khosroabad is situated in the Abadan Island, 17 miles below Abadan town.

yards south of Khosroabad. This would much simplify the problem of landing, as large self-propelled craft could be used right up to the banks.

If opposition was expected, there would be no hope of surprise in a day operation. It would therefore be necessary to move upstream by night. The best site for landing in that case would be the Khosroabad stretch. It was however likely to be guarded by an Iranian force. It was therefore considered inadvisable to confine the efforts to this stretch only and hence the Kasba Reach was also to be invaded simultaneously.

It was necessary to prevent the Iranian Navy from interfering with the landing operations. Since the Iranian Navy had its base at the mouth of the river Karun, just opposite Khurram Shahr, steps were to be taken to watch the junction of the Karun with the Shatt al Arab. That was to be done by one escort vessel, which would move up the river before dark, ahead of the convoy. If any Iranian gunboats were at Bandar Shahpur, the entrance to this port up the Khor Musa would also have to be guarded. A third possible line of action by the Iranian ships existed down the Khor Bahmanshir. In World War I, '*Odin*', one of the ships, came down that way from Abadan, although later the mouth of this river was believed to have silted up. Yet it was desirable to post a watch there also. It was the task of the ships of the ocean escort to watch these two river mouths. The Royal Air Force bombers were to try and locate the Iranian ships at dawn and deal with them,[6] which it was believed they would be able to do without much difficulty.

Plans for Trout : Operations

Hardly had the plan for the movement and landing of Trout been finalised, when steps were taken to prepare the ground for the ultimate stage of actual operations. This was done at a conference of officers, held in Bombay from 21 to 24 June, where an outline plan for the seizure of Abadan was given a careful consideration. Amongst the officers who attended the conference were Major-General L. M. Heath, Commanding Rainbow and Major-General G. de la P. Beresford, Commanding Trout.

The conference decided that a silent *coup de main* would be the most suitable line of action for the capture of Abadan, if damage to the oil refineries, through fighting, was to be avoided. Two methods were considered to secure this end. The first was to tranship troops from transports to warships at the Examination Anchorage of the Shatt al Arab, after which the warships would move upstream by night and attack at first light. This method, however, suffered from certain defects. In the first place, at least

[6] *Report on Trout Reconnaissance*, April 1940, F. 1034.

four destroyers, each carrying 500 men, or two 'C' class cruisers, each of which could take 1,000 men, would be necessary for the purpose. But the use of this number of warships would preclude surprise, once they were seen approaching the jetty, where the landing was to be effected. Moreover, even if a single Iranian automatic weapon were in position, heavy casualties might ensue on the tight-packed decks. Further, except at the main jetty (No. 4), the rapid disembarkation of troops was not feasible, since the remaining jetties were mostly designed for the delivery of oil, and were long and narrow, making it impossible for men to leave their ships rapidly. Even after getting ashore, the men would have to advance along a cramped and confined line of approach. On the other hand, a disembarkation at points other than the jetties was more or less out of question as the river front had high, sloping, concrete banks all along, topped by a strong wire fence.

The second method was to move a ship or ships in the normal way up the river, carrying ostensibly labour and stores for the Anglo-Iranian Oil Company, but actually containing troops. The usual procedure of the notification of the arrival of the ship to the Iranian port authorities would have to be followed, and the customs and other port officials coming aboard would have to be overpowered as silently as possible; but otherwise the ship would not disclose her warlike intentions, till in position and tied up along No. 4 jetty. The troops disembarking from these ships, would be dressed to look like Indian labourers, with their arms concealed. A minimum number of high Anglo-Iranian Oil Company's officials would be informed of this and they would help by having guides available to lead the troops to the vital points for seizure. This second method was considered to be preferable as it held out the best hope of success. But the success of this plan would depend largely on the possibility of achieving a complete surprise, which might be lost through some accident. Much would depend on the extent to which Iranian suspicions had been aroused, and on the extent to which they had taken measures for the defence of Abadan against occupation.

It will be recalled that, earlier, Captain Wilson and Colonel Messervy had prepared plans concerning landings at 'A', the Khosroabad stretch, and at 'B', the Kasba Reach. They had then ruled out the landing at Abadan as being of a doubtful practical value. The Bombay conference, however, came to the conclusion that a *coup de main* at Abadan also offered a reasonable chance of success. They therefore decided to superimpose the *coup de main* at Abadan on the plans for landing at 'A' and 'B' Beaches, and to allot one of the reserve battalions with one section of the Field Company and a detachment of the Field Ambulance, for the former operation. One of the China gunboats would also be detailed to arrive on the scene in support of this battalion as soon as possible, moving downstream from opposite Khurram Shahr.

The conference therefore finalised the following outline plan of operations for Trout:—

    (a) Seizure of Abadan by a *coup de main* at dawn on DI day. Troops—one battalion, one section Field Company, detachment Field Ambulance, with one China gunboat in support.

    (b) Landing at Beach 'A' and seizure of Khosroabad. Troops—one battalion, supported by one China gunboat and two Iraqi gunboats (if available).

    (c) Landing at Beach 'B'. Troops—one battalion, to be supported by two Iraqi gunboats (if available).

This beach was a date-palm grove bank and flat trajectory guns would be able to give little support.

Other troops allocated were:

    (i) Reserve for 'A' and 'B' Beaches—one battalion (floating reserve).

    (ii) Artillery support available for landing either at Abadan, if *coup de main* was successful, or at Khosorabad—one mountain battery, Indian States Forces.

    (iii) Anti-Aircraft defence—one anti-aircraft sloop in the area just below 'A' Beach.

    (iv) R. A. F. Co-operation—One General Purposes Squadron, under the command of the Assaulting Force, and one bomber squadron under the command of Rainbow.

Thus there were to be three almost simultaneous attempts to land. If the *coup de main* gained a footing then the rest of the Assaulting Force would advance, some by road from Khosroabad and the remainder by ship, entailing two hours' steaming. If the *coup de main* failed but the landing at 'A' Beach succeeded then the Assaulting Force, less the *coup de main* battalion, would land at Khosroabad and push on to Abadan, astride the road. If the *coup de main* and the landing at 'A' Beach both failed, there was still the third and longest string to the bow, namely, the landing at 'B' Beach where opposition was least to be expected, since the Iranians would not anticipate a landing along that more difficult stretch.

Report on reconnaissance of the A.I.O.C. Area

The operational plan for Trout, put forward by the Bombay conference in June 1940, envisaged the securing of Abadan by British and Indian forces against a possibly hostile Iran. But there was yet another, and much vaster, problem to be tackled in this

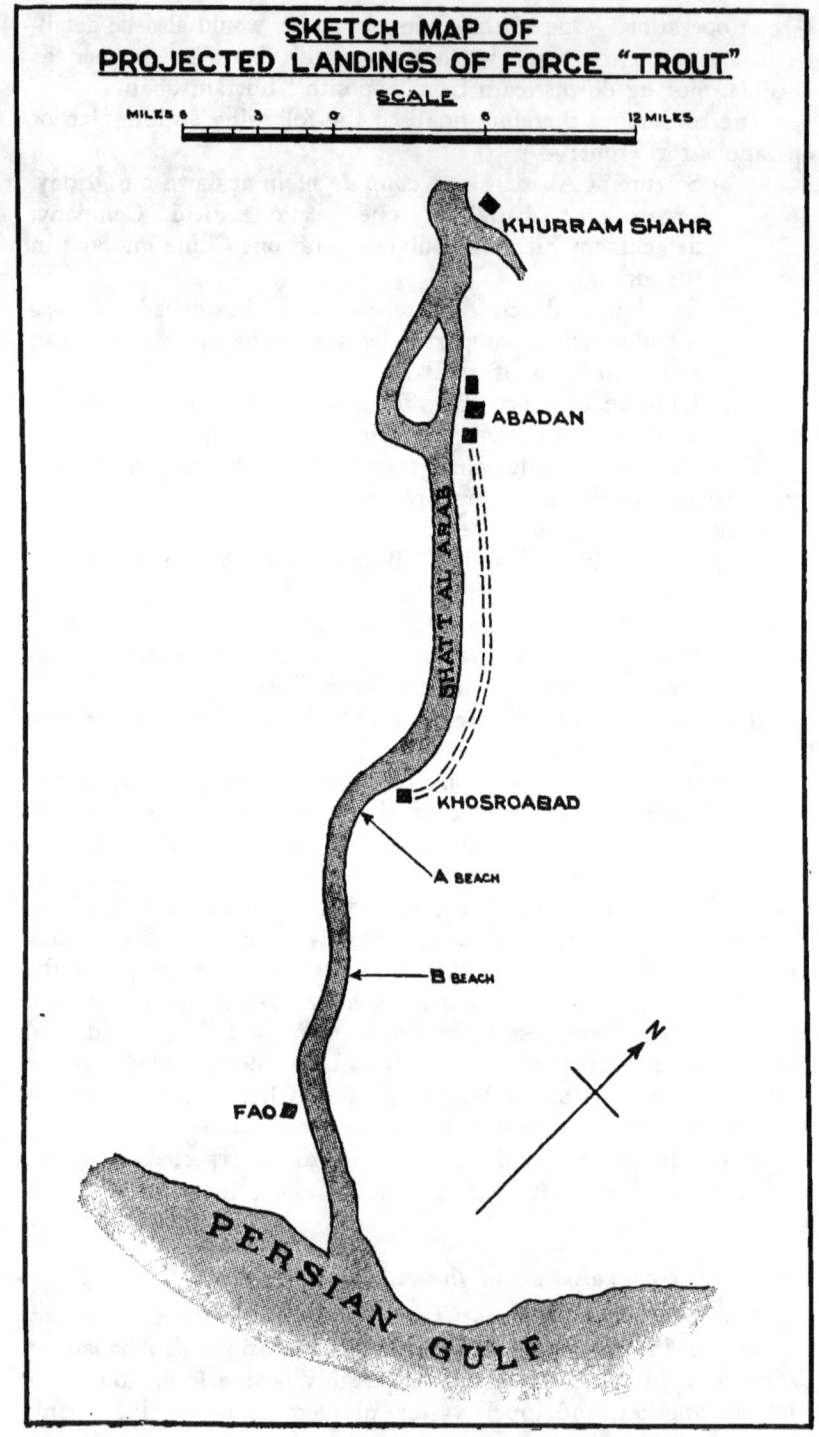

connection, namely that of protecting the Abadan oilfields in case of a Russian invasion of Iran, a circumstance not to be entirely overlooked in those days. This problem had been dealt with a month earlier by Mr. H. W. Lane, in his report on the reconnaissance of the oilfield areas of the Persian Gulf. The situation assumed by Mr. Lane in his report was that of an advance of a hostile force (presumably Russian) through Iran to occupy the oilfields.

The report dealt with two aspects of such a problem: (i) protection of the property of the Anglo-Iranian Oil Company and (ii) checking the advance of the hostile force.

The protection of the property of the Company against sabotage or bombardment by hostile aircraft was not an easy thing. The Abadan refinery, and its vital key-points, were extremely vulnerable to attack by hostile aircraft. The key-points were the main Power Station, the main water pumping stations and the major process units which were so huge that no amount of camouflage could in any way conceal them, and in fact any attempt to do so might direct attention towards them. The whole refinery system, so to say, constituted one large fire hazard, inasmuch as large process plants with their high pressure vessels and pipelines, carrying highly inflammable liquids and gases, were spread over the entire refinery area. A direct hit on one of these plants would start a fire of such immensity that it would undoubtedly envelop other units in a very short time. However, the report made certain suggestions for the protection of the properties of the Company. These properties were the Abadan refinery; the Mashur Development Area; miles of pipelines; and the oilfields of Lali, Masjid-i-Suleiman, Haft Khel, Agha Jari, Gach Saran and Naft-i-Safid. There was a total of 35 producing wells in all the fields: 19 in Masjid-i-Suleiman, 11 in Haft Khel and 5 in Gach Saran.

The pipeline system consisted of three 12-inch lines from Masjid-i-Suleiman; two 12-inch lines from Haft Khel to Wais; one 12-inch line from Salamieh to Wais; two 12-inch lines from Haft Khel to Kut Abdullah and one 12-inch line from Gach Saran to Abadan via Mashur. The lines from Kut Abdullah to Abadan varied in number and size but might be taken to be five 12-inch lines. The Mashur Development Area lay at the head of the Khor Musa, about 12 miles from Bandar Shahpur. It was at that time under construction and was intended to be a terminal loading point.

After considering all the relevant points, Mr. Lane's report made suggestions for the protection of the vulnerable key points in the oilfields area, namely, producing wells, production plants, pipelines, pumping stations, water and power supplies, refinery installations, wireless, and telegraph and telephone systems etc., against sabotage and bombardment by hostile aircraft.

The best protection of the wells, it was argued, lay in the fact that only certain widely spaced wells were vulnerable and in the assailants' difficulty of finding out which these were. There were, for example, 250 wells in the Masjid-i-Suleiman field, of which only 19 were in use; while in the Haft Khel field there were 50 wells, with 11 in use. These, distributed over various areas of the fields, made a very confusing target for any attack. It would be possible to enhance this confusion by developing a dummy producing system, complete with flames and pipelines, which would draw fire, while the key wells remained concealed.

As to the very vulnerable pipelines, the difficulty of camouflaging them was offset by the ease with which they could be repaired. The pumping stations, on the other hand, which were also very vulnerable points, would have to be protected by sand-bag emplacements. These could be erected round the stations and anti-aircraft defence installed at suitable points. The greatest difficulty would however be encountered in devising measures for the protection of the refinery. Some protection would be obtained by the erection of splinter-proof walls and roofs, and sand-bagged walls, but the only adequate protection, it was suggested, lay in an extensive air defence.

A second aspect of Mr. Lane's investigations concerned the checking of the advance of an invading force from the north. Such a force might approach the oilfield area from any of the following routes:

(i) Through Iraq, between the Tigris and the Pusht-i-Koh. This involved the defence of Iraq itself.

(ii) Down the Khurramabad road. This was the most favourable route for the invader.

(iii) Down the Iranian railway. Any troop movement would undoubtedly make use of this railway, although the capacity was limited, as it was a single track railway.

(iv) By the caravan route from Isfahan. This track was only possible for pack transport.

(v) By the Basht—Shiraz road. This road entered the oilfield area in the Gach Saran area, and for 30 miles east of this point (as far as Basht), was passable for light motor transport. The road was however incomplete and not suitable for heavy mechanical transport.

(vi) By the Kazerun—Mishun track. It was only possible for pack transport.

(vii) By the Shiraz—Bushire—Ganeweh road. It was incapable of carrying more than a very limited weight of mechanical transport.

Thus the only satisfactory routes into the oilfields areas, from the point of view of the invaders, were the Iranian railway and the Khurramabad road.

The terrain in the oilfield and refinery area was of three main categories:
- (i) the mountainous country to the north and east,
- (ii) the foothills, in which the oilfields were situated, and
- (iii) the desert, across which the pipelines traversed to Abadan on the Shatt al Arab.

In view of this terrain and the main lines of approach open to an invading force, the following plan of operations was recommended:

An Expeditionary Force, using mechanised transport and cavalry, was to advance from Basra on Khurram Shahr and Ahwaz, simultaneously. At the same time, naval units would establish control in Khurram Shahr, while the Royal Air Force would evacuate women and children from the threatened areas to Abadan, and land detachments of troops at Asiab Yamaha, Haft Khel, Dizful, Ahwaz, Kut Abdullah, Gach Saran and Agha Jari, for their protection. After occupying Ahwaz, the Expeditionary Force would push forward, up the road and railway, towards Dizful and Dar-i-Khazineh, and a strong defence line would be constructed north of Dizful. Meanwhile, mechanised cavalry would have established patrols on the right bank of the Karun to protect the flanks of the Expeditionary Force.[7]

No further action was taken on this report, as there was no immediate necessity for making an operational plan to meet such a contingency, namely that of a hostile force marching through Iran towards the area of the Anglo-Iranian Oil Company. But meanwhile planning for Trout was continuing.

Administrative Base for Herring

It will be recalled that Trout was only a part of the much wider scheme Herring. Accordingly, while steps were being taken to give shape to Trout, work had also been taken in hand for planning an administrative base for Herring. Reconnaissance to this effect had been carried out as early as April 1940 and a report had been submitted to the authorities recommending the formation of a base at Shuaiba, for maintaining a force of three infantry divisions, capable of being expanded to meet the requirements of six divisions, if necessary. This plan was still awaiting implementation when Germany invaded France and Italy entered the war in June 1940.

---

[7] *Reconnaissance of A.I.O.C. area,* 17 May 1940, F. 518.

CHAPTER VI

Defence Plans (July 1940—April 1941)

The role of Trout or Sybil

The plan for Trout had a limited objective—the protection of the Anglo-Iranian oilfields against a hostile Iran. It was based on the assumption that the only threat to those oil regions emanated from Iran or Russia, or from the Axis fifth columns. The possibility of an invasion of Iraq (and then of Iran) from Syria, was left out of account, since Syria was then administered by France, an ally of the United Kingdom. However, the situation had changed before the end of June 1940. France had capitulated to Germany after a successful invasion by the Axis forces and, with that, Syria had more or less passed under the influence of Germany. It was now feared that the Vichy French in Syria would collaborate with the Axis and invade Iraq, or stir up a revolt there with a view to undermining the British influence in that country. Simultaneously, the Shah of Iran, too, might, under Axis instigation, turn hostile to the British. In view of these new developments, coupled with the uncertain attitude of Iraq and Iran towards the cause of the Allies, the Chiefs of Staff in England issued a fresh directive to India, on 10 July 1940. It defined the role of Trout as including not only the establishment of a bridgehead at Basra for protecting the Anglo-Iranian oilfields, but also the task of strengthening the morale of the friendly government of Iraq, and deterring hostile Iraqi elements from interrupting the line of communication overland to Palestine.[1]

The role of Sabine

There was no immediate necessity for implementing the new role of Trout, since the Axis were too preoccupied with the Battle of Britain to turn their attention to the Middle East. However, towards the end of the year, the threat to Iraq became more imminent and consequently in December 1940, the War Office elaborated the role of Herring, which was now redesignated Sabine.[2] The role of Sabine was to check Axis attack on Iraq through Turkey or Syria, and prevent internal disturbances in Iraq

---

[1] *Role of Force Sybil*, File *Sabine*, 48 W.
[2] On 12 July 1940, the code-name of Trout was changed to Niblick. By 16 August 1940, further changes took place—Sybil in place of Niblick and Sabine in place of Herring. *Code-Names*, p. 33, F. 720.

and in the area of the Anglo-Iranian oilfields in Iran. In other words, the force Sabine was to be trained, organised and equipped to meet a powerful Axis attack.[3]

As the scheme Herring was supplanted by Sabine, so was its component Trout replaced by Sybil (the new code-name for Trout). India, as already described, was necessarily interested in the defence of Iraq and Iran, and was anxious to have all the relevant plans ready. In order to expedite the planning of Sabine and Sybil, General Auchinleck, then Commander-in-Chief in India, made certain proposals, on 5 February 1941, to General Wavell, then Commander-in-Chief in the Middle East. General Auchinleck felt that it was necessary to get down to details without losing time. He urged an early completion of such preliminaries as laying down the object for the Force, appointing a Force Commander with a nucleus staff to draw up detailed plans in consultation with divisional commanders, and installing a Base Commander and a small staff to continue administrative planning.[4] He made it plain that he was worried over the slow progress in the drawing up of the plans, and that he felt the time was getting short and the situation in Iraq looked threatening. Realising, however, the preoccupations of General Wavell and his staff in North Africa, he decided to make what contribution he could in solving the problems. He accordingly directed his General Staff to re-examine the plans and prepare a detailed appreciation of the situation in Iraq.

Appreciation by General Staff, India

The appreciation, when ready, was incorporated in a Memorandum and was forwarded to General Wavel on 21 February 1941.[5] It was drawn up against the eventuality of an attack by the Axis and the Russian forces. The view taken was that the Axis forces would advance from Rumania and invade Iraq, either by overrunning Turkey or by moving north of the Black Sea into Caucasia. Taking advantage of the weakness of the Allies, Russia too might attack via Turkish or Iranian territories, after advancing through Caucasia. Even were it not to be so, there was still the possibility of Iraq herself turning hostile to the Allies. In that case, she could make her air bases available to the Axis and Russia and such a situation would seriously endanger the Allied position in the Middle East. The best way of avoiding such a possibility would be to have a friendly government in Iraq. Thus it was necessary to keep two separate objects in view, namely maintaining friendly governments in Iraq and Iran, and being ready to

[3] *Role of Force Sabine*, p. 7, Sabine, 48 W.
[4] *Minutes of a meeting*, 5 February 1941, p. 14, Sabine, 48 W.
[5] *Memorandum on the operational role of Force Sabine*, Sabine, 48 W

meet major external aggressions against them. The first object would be attained, it was believed, by merely sending a force of mechanised troops or airforce from Palestine to occupy Habbaniya, and to threaten Baghdad. The threat to Baghdad from Palestine would, it was considered, be sufficient to overawe any hostile Iraqi government. But for securing the second object, namely checking Russian or Axis aggression against Iraq and Iran, it was absolutely necessary to establish a bridgehead at Basra for carrying out large-scale operations in those two countries.

The plan for Sabine had these two aims in view. Its principal object was to deny air or land bases in Iraq to any hostile power, and to that end it was suggested that it should be carried out in the following three stages:

(i) To land a force in southern Iraq and establish a bridgehead in the vicinity of Basra, as well as a base at Basra; and in the event of Iran proving hostile, to secure the Shatt al Arab and the Anglo-Iranian oilfields.

(ii) To establish forces in the Baghdad-Habbaniya area.

(iii) To establish further forces beyond Baghdad in Upper Iraq, and beyond Habbaniya in the direction of Syria.

Difficulties in occupation of Basra

This plan, however, suffered from certain defects. The occupation of Basra and its vicinity presented the following difficulties:—

(i) Although the Iraqi and Iranian regular forces were not formidable, they could effectively oppose the initial landing. The blocking of the Shatt al Arab was not a very difficult operation and was considered to be well within their capabilities.

(ii) Army opposition from either bank of the Shatt al Arab, until overcome, would render it unusable. In that case any landing at Basra would be out of question, and it would be necessary to carry out the initial landing, either at Umm Qasr in Iraq, or at Bandar Shahpur in Iran, and to overcome opposition with forces based on those places. This would involve considerable delay, for neither Umm Qasr nor Bandar Shahpur had any landing facilities comparable to Basra.

(iii) Many difficulties would be encountered in moving rapidly an adequate force from Karachi to Iraq. The shipping problem was very acute. Depth of water over the bar at Fao and in the Shatt al Arab imposed limitations on the ships that might be used. To move a division from Karachi to Basra required about 36 ships, and more would be required for base units. The journey took about 8 days, so that, allowing 5 days for unloading, it would be three weeks before ships again returned to Karachi. It was unlikely that sufficient shipping would be available to move a division, with adequate base installations, in one echelon and to maintain it for five weeks in active operations. The limitations of shipping thus imposed the necessity of despatching, at the start, only the first echelon, in sufficient operational strength to hold its own against possible opposition and with sufficient supplies and stores to maintain itself for a minimum of five weeks. Even when one division had been established at Basra with the necessary maintenance, the construction of a permanent base for the remainder of the force and the stocking of that base would take from six to nine months. A temporary base could be generally stocked in three to five months.

In view of these difficulties, certain suggestions were made for the move of the force to Basra. It was recommended that the leading division of the Force should be prepared and tactically embarked for an opposed landing. The force, while at sea, should be convoyed and efforts made to attain a surprise landing. The initial objective would be to secure Basra and its vicinity and the safe passage of the Shatt al Arab. Umm Qasr would have to be developed in advance and facilities for convoy anchorages ascertained beforehand. The leading echelon of the force would have to be sufficiently strong to maintain itself after landing, until reinforcements might arrive, and should be sufficiently well-equipped to enable it to carry out an opposed landing, without having recourse to the use of local craft. It would have to take with it at least five weeks' supplies of all descriptions. Adequate air force, for co-operation with convoys, was to be established in the Persian Gulf, prior to the despatch of the force, together with sufficient troops for aerodrome protection. The leading echelon would need reinforcements soon after landing and arrangements would have to be kept ready to that end. Subsequent to the occupation of Basra alternative plans would be needed, according to whether the further advance was going to take place in Iraq or south-western Iran.

Should it however not be a case of Iraq or Iran being invaded by any major power but merely that of their turning hostile, then, as a first step, Habbaniya and Baghdad might be occupied by a force from Palestine. But even in that case it would be necessary to have additional forces in Basra, well provided with mobile troops (including armoured fighting vehicles) for line of communication protection, since the Palestine forces would have to be maintained from India via the Persian Gulf.

Besides indicating a plan for Sabine and making concrete suggestions regarding its move to Basra, the appreciation of the General Staff also discussed the problem of the control of operations. As the defence of Iraq and Iran was now recognised to be a part of the external defence of India, and the bulk of the troops were to be provided and maintained from India, it was argued that the control of operations in these parts should also rest with India. To that end it was thought necessary that:

(i) The commanders and staffs should be provided by India.
(ii) The planning by these commanders and staffs should start as soon as possible, under the control of the Commander-in-Chief, India, subject to the general direction of the Commander-in-Chief, Middle East.
(iii) The operational control in Iraq, the south-western Iran, and the Persian Gulf should vest initially in the Commander-in-Chief, India, subject to the general direction of the Commander-in-Chief, Middle East, but that
(iv) The provision of air forces with troops employed in this theatre must be made by the Air Officer Commanding-in-Chief, Middle East, since India could not provide any air force for that purpose.

Mideast—India Conference at Cairo

In forwarding the Memorandum to General Wavell and to the Chief of the Imperial General Staff, General Auchinleck explained his point of view and emphasised the necessity of his delegating to the Army Headquarters in India the task of occupying Basra, and of appointing for that purpose a Corps Headquarters, which might begin the necessary detailed planning[6] forthwith.

On 8 March 1941, General Wavell signalled to General Auchinleck that he had discussed his Memorandum, in Egypt, with General Dill, Chief of the Imperial General Staff, who was then on a visit to that place. They agreed that the planning should be done in India and that the initial control of operations in Iraq should also rest with India.[7] The Chief of Imperial General Staff also accepted the proposal that General Auchinleck should deal with the War Office direct, and not through normal channels, the Viceroy to the Secretary of State.[8] A few days later, on 13 March 1941, General Wavell followed up his reply with critical comments on the details of India's appreciation. He generally agreed that the occupation of Basra was the first step necessary to safeguard

---
[6] Letters from Auchinleck to Dill and to Wavell, 21 February 1941, *Sabine*, 48 W.
[7] Tel. No. 58228 dated 25 March 1941 from Troopers to Armindia and Tel. No. 613-8 dated 28 February 1941 from S.S. to Viceroy, *Sabine*, 48 W.
[8] Ibid.

Imperial interests, and that the Anglo-Iranian oilfields, though very important, ranked as the second.⁹

As a result of this acceptance of India's view-point, both by the Middle East and the War Office, it was decided to hold a conference of the representatives of India and Middle East for discussing the planning of Sabine. The venue of the conference was Cairo, where the Indian Commander-in-Chief was represented by his Chief of the General Staff, Major-General T. J. Hutton. Before leaving for the conference, General Hutton was briefed at a meeting on 15 March 1941, by General Auchinleck, who explained his attitude on the subject, stressing it as follows: "I am most anxious to gain a foothold in Iraq. The sooner we begin to get control, militarily, in Iraq, the better. It is very necessary to gain the Euphrates tribes on our side."[10]

However, after reviewing the existing political situation in Iraq and Iran, the Cairo Conference arrived at a decision which turned out to be fundamentally different from the plan originally suggested in the appreciation of the General Staff, India. The latter had stressed the importance of having a bridgehead at Basra and had suggested that, after that had been secured, it would be open to the British and Indian forces to advance from Basra, either towards souh-west Iran for the occuption of the Anglo-Iranian oilfields or towards Baghdad, for controlling the government of Iraq. The conference, however, came to the conclusion that the better plan was to have forces avilable in Palestine instead of Basra, to be moved without delay for the occupation of Baghdad, in order to intimidate a hostile Iraqi government or to establish one that would be friendly to the Allies. In thus departing from the previously accepted plan of the General Staff of India, the Conference appears to have been influenced by the view that a force from Palestine could enter the borders of Iraq in far less time than one from India. The anti-British elements in Iraq, it was argued, would hesitate to come into conflict with the British Government if they saw even a reasonable likelihood of a swift retribution falling on them. The arrival of a British force from India would take much longer than of one from Palestine. It was essential, therefore, that strong British and Indian forces should be immediately available and so placed as to constitute an obvious and vital threat to a hostile Iraqi government. Baghdad was the centre of government, the stronghold of the Iraqi army as well as of the anti-British elements, and the point to which all Iraqis turned. Whoever dominated Baghdad controlled Iraq. A threat against

⁹ *G.H.Q. Mid. East Comments on the Memorandum*, 8 March 1941, *Sabine*, 48 W.
[10] *Delhi Conference*, 15 March 1941, 27 W.

Baghdad would be infinitely more effective than the one against Basra.

Further, while safeguarding Imperial interests, it was necessary that the British Government should not give the impression that they intended, as so many Iraqis then believed, to take over the political control of the country. The unnecessary or premature entry of considerable forces from India into Iraq, through a landing at Basra as urged by India, would undoubtedly have this effect.

Besides these political factors, the Conferenc also kept in view certain strategic considerations. The war situation in the Middle East was likely to develop rapidly and to require the greatest fluidity in the movement of the reserves. To tie up any force in Iraq, unless absolutely necessary, would be a grave error. If the British Government could obtain their object without force, or without committing any of their formations, there was every advantage in doing so. Therefore, a striking force operating from Palestine with the object of securing Baghdad would, it was thought, be preferable to a large force to be despatched from India, necessarily at a much earlier date, for establishing the Basra bridgehead.

In Iran, though the government and the people may be anti-British, they were afraid of Russia. The Shah was aware of his precarious position between the two great Powers and was not likely to precipitate a conflict by challenging either of them. The only vital British interest in Iran was the oilfields area. Intervention in that vital area, however, might be forced on the British Government by circumstances beyond their control, such as widespread sabotage provoked by Axis agents, attempts by the Shah to impose prohibitive terms on the Anglo-Iranian Oil Company, a Russian invasion of northern Iran, or air attacks by the Axis, should the latter be successful in obtaining the use of aerodromes in Syria. This last was indeed the most likely and the most serious threat. However, taking all these various possibilities into consideration, the Conference came to the conclusion that there was no immediate threat to the oilfields. The immediate problem, in fact, was to take steps to protect the Royal Air Force bases and the air route through Iraq, the Kirkuk oilfields, the pipeline to Haifa, and to control all land communications from Basra to Haifa and from Turkey into Iraq. It was therefore essential to ensure the presence of a government in Baghdad that was willing to co-operate with the British Government. This could be achieved either,

(i) by supporting a friendly government against subversive influences, or

(ii) by intimidating a hostile government, or

(iii) by ejecting a hostile government by force and installing one, likely to prove friendly, or
(iv) by taking over the government themselves.

The above alternatives were in order of preference, and if the British Government could achieve their aims by the first two only, it would obviously be most unwise to employ the other more radical methods, and thereby promote a conflict, the end of which could not be foreseen, and which would inevitably absorb a very large proportion of their war effort in men, material and shipping. Such an action would, in fact, be playing the game of the Axis.

The view of the Conference, therefore, was that the policy to be pursued should be:

(i) To open the line of communication from Basra to Transjordan, if and when political conditions allowed or military necessities demanded; and to take that opportunity to install sufficient guards at both Basra and Habbaniya to ensure the retention and control of these places.
(ii) To prepare reinforcing schemes to supplement (i).
(iii) To provide a striking force, so situated, that it could, with the greatest facility, strike at the centre of the government of Iraq and its military resistance, if and when it should become necessary to do so.

The Plan

The Cairo Conference, therefore, arrived at the conclusion that the objective for the striking force should be Baghdad, and that this force should be located in Transjordan. Although its strength would necessarily be limited, it would be in a position to strike swiftly, whereas a force starting from India would take three to five months before it exerted anything more than a remote influence on the situation at Baghdad.[11]

Clash of views: India and Middle East Command

The view of the Cairo Conference, namely that priorty in men and material should go to a striking force to be located in Transjordan, undoubtedly ran counter to the appreciation made by the General Staff in India. The irony of the situation was that Major-General Hutton, who had gone to the Conference to represent India's views about the urgency of having a bridgehead at Basra, himself became a convert to the new theory. After having ascertained, as he put it, "the considered and unanimous opinion of all those authorities," he felt compelled to change his

---

[11] *Appreciation of the problem of safeguarding British interests in Iraq and Iran,* 27 W and 48 W.

view-point. He further informed General Auchinleck that General Wavell was definitely of the opinion that the best contribution that India could make towards the safety of the British interests in Iraq and Iran, was to undertake the commitment of providing the proposed striking force, to be located in Transjordan, besides the Sabine.[12]

This communication was disconcerting to General Auchinleck, who was plainly "disturbed by this tendency to depart from the object which was decided after careful consideration and agreed to." While accepting the contention that an early occupation of Baghdad, concurrently with the occupation of Basra, might facilitate the latter operation, he was strongly of opinion that it was secondary in importance and ought not delay the occupation of Basra, which was essential to enable operations to be carried out both in Iraq and Iran. The Cairo proposals, he thought, also involved considerable increase in commitments, which could not be met, unless equipment and trained technical personnel of all categories were supplied from the United Kingdom. Further, since Middle East would not be able to maintain the Indian force in Palestine from the Indian administrative units then with them, the proposals also involved the sending of the 10th Indian Division to Transjordan, with many of its base and ancillary units which were fundamental parts of Sabine. This would inevitably delay the readiness of Sabine. Last but not the least, the Government of India did not want Indian forces to be sent overseas, unless they were adequately equipped, particularly with a sufficient number of anti-tank and anti-aircraft units.[13]

Accordingly, General Auchinleck signalled to Middle East, on 3 April 1941, that the Cario Conference proposals seemed to him to imply a radical change in the policy suggested by him and previously agreed to both by General Wavell and the Chief of the Imperial General Staff. He, therefore, wished Major-General Hutton to return to India so that he could discuss with him this "changed strategic conception.[14]" In the meanwhile events in Iraq took a serious turn and put a stop to all controversy, since immediate steps had to be taken to retrieve the situation.

Until now, little, if any, progress had been made in the preparations for the despatch of Sybil and Sabine to Iraq. The orders of battle for these forces had, however, been practically finalised. Sabine, according to these, was to comprise the 10th, 8th and 6th Indian Infantry Divisions and force troops, plus base

---

[12] Tel. No. 0/52632 dated 29 March 41 from Mideast to Armindia, pp. 53-4, *Sabine*, 31 W; and Tel. No. 53613 dated 2 April 41 from Mideast to Armindia, p. 55(a), *Sabine*, 31 W.
[13] Tel. No. 3300/G dated 1 April 1941 from Armindia to Mideast, *Sabine Planning*, 31 W, p. 55.
[14] Tel. No. 3389/C from Armindia to Mideast, p. 56, 31 W.

and line of communication troops for all the three divisions.[15] Out of these Sybil was to have the 10th Indian infantry Division, the force troops and base and line of communication troops for that division alone.[16]

The 10th Indian Division was to comprise:
H.Q. 21st Indian Infantry Brigade
(4th Battalion 13th Frontier Force Rifles, 2nd Battalion 4th P.W.O. Gurkha Rifles and 2nd Battalion 10th Gurkha Rifles).
H.Q. 24th Indian Infantry Brigade
(1st Battalion Kumaon Rifles, 2nd Battalion 6th Rajputana Rifles and 5th Battalion 5th Mahratta Light Infantry).
H.Q. 25th Indian Infantry Brigade
(1st Battalion 5th Mahratta Light Infantry, 2nd Battalion 11th Sikh Regiment and 3rd Battalion 9th Jat Regiment).

The 8th Indian Division was to consist of:
H.Q. 17th Indian Infantry Brigade
(1st Battalion 12th Frontier Force Regiment, 5th Battalion 13th Frontier Force Rifles and 1st Battalion 5th Gurkha Rifles).
H.Q. 18th Indian Infantry Brigade
(3rd Battalion 10th Baluch Regiment, 1st Battalion 2nd K.E.O. Gurkha Rifles and 2nd Battalion 3rd Q.V.O. Gurkha Rifles).
H.Q. 19th Indian Infantry Brigade
(1st Battalion 1st Punjab Regiment, 3rd Battalion 8th Punjab Regiment, and 2nd Battalion 6th Gukha Rifles).

The 6th Indian Division was to consist of:[17]
H.Q. 26th Indian Infantry Brigade
(1st Battalion 1st K.G.O. Gurkha Rifles, 1st Battalion 19th Hyderabad Regiment and 1st Battalion 9th Gurkha Rifles).
H.Q. 27th Indian Infantry Brigade
(4th Battalion 8th Punjab Regiment, 1st Battalion 10th Baluch Regiment and 5th Battalion 12th Frontier Force Regiment).
H.Q. 28th Indian Infantry Brigade
(2nd Battalion 1st K.G.O. Gurkha Rifles, 2nd Battalion 2nd K.E.O. Gurkha Rifles and 2nd Battalion 9th Gurkha Rifles).

All the troops of Sybil and Sabine, on reaching Iraq, would come under the designation "British Troops in Iraq," which often used to be referred to, simply, as the "Iraq Force."[18]

---

[15] See Appendix 1.
[16] See Appendix 2.
[17] *Formation—Base Sabine and Basloc*, 8187 H.
[18] Tel. No. 66601 dated 14 May 1941 from Troopers to Mideast, p. 53, *Sabine*, F. 720.

The readiness of Sabine for operations overseas was dependent on the supply from the United Kingdom of equipment, weapons and those ancillary units which India could not provide and for which the War Office had accepted responsibility.[19] On the basis of the time that would necessarily pass before all shortages were made good, it was calculated that the Force Sybil would not be ready to go overseas until 1 September 1941.[20] Matters in Iraq, however, came to a crisis much earlier than expected—as early as April 1941—with the result that immediate despatch of a force to Iraq became imperative, and India, took action in time to grapple with the unexpected situation, at a moment when neither the United Kingdom nor the Middle East was in a position to avert the danger.

---

[19] Tel. No. 2028 dated 5 April 1941 from Defence Department, New Delhi to S.S., *Sabine Planning*, 31 W.
[20] Ibid.

CHAPTER VII

The Developments in Iraq—1941

Political Developments

King Feisal, the first ruler of independent Iraq, had died in September 1931. His successor was the young King Ghazi to whom fell the difficult task of controlling the turbulent elements in the country, which had never allowed Iraq to settle down in peace ever since the inauguration of his late father's regime. The task had by no means been completed, when, in April 1939, King Ghazi died in a motor accident and was succeeded by King Feisal II, a minor, who was only about four years of age at the time of his accession. The responsibility of ruling the country, therefore, devolved on a cousin of Ghazi, Emir Abdul Illa, who became the Regent. The Regent, as well as Nuri es Said, Iraq's Prime Minister, continued to maintain the tradition of friendly relations with the British Government, and on the outbreak of war in September 1939 agreed to carry out the provisions of the Anglo-Iraqi Treaty of 1930. In keeping with that spirit, the Government of Iraq decided to close the German Legation in Baghdad and to intern the German subjects residing in Iraq.

In April 1940, however, the political scene of Iraq underwent one of its periodical changes and Rashid Ali el Gailani became the Prime Minister, supplanting Nuri es Said, who became the Minister of Foreign Affairs. Soon afterwards, in June 1940, while Rashid Ali was still the Prime Minister, Germany invaded France and Italy entered the war. In view of Italy's having ranged herself against the Allies, the British Government requested the closure of Italian Legation and the internment of Italians living in Iraq, as had been done in the case of Germans. But Rashid Ali was unwilling to comply with that request. The chances of Allied victory, at that critical time, were extremely problematical, and it was understandable that the Government of Iraq was anxious not to be drawn into the conflict or to give offence to the Axis. Consequently, the Italian Legation in Baghdad continued to function, and the question of compliance with the British request for its closure continued to be put off on one pretext or another. Shortly afterwards Nuri es Said resigned, since his policy to break off diplomatic relations with Italy was not accepted by Rashid Ali. The latter also, however, did not long remain in power for he, too, resigned in January 1941, when Taha el Hashmi became the Prime Minister. Rashid Ali, it would seem, was merely waiting for an opportunity to regain power. If so, he had not long to wait. For, by April 1941, he was back at the helm of Iraq's affairs, not as a constitutional Prime Minister but as a virtual dictator, in consequence of a *coup d'etat* which was as successful as it was subtle and bloodless.

Axis infiltration

The chief factor which helped Rashid Ali in seizing power by a *coup d'etat* was the Axis propaganda, which had weakened British influence in Iraq. The growth of Arab nationalism offered an opportunity to the Axis to undermine Britain's political position in the Middle East. The pan-Arab movement had taken strong roots in Iraq. The extreme pan-Arabs believed in an Arab Federation stretching from the Mediterranean to the Persian Gulf, and considered Britain, with her vital interests in the Middle East, as the chief obstacle in the attainment of this goal. The letter, dated 20 January 1941, written by the ex-Mufti of Jerusalem to the Fuhrer of Germany may be an example of the anti-British views of some leaders of the pan-Arab movement.[1]

Iraq's importance to the Axis was indeed very great. The occupation of Iraq could give them enormous strategic advantages over the Allies. It would lead to the dislocation of British Imperial communications and seriously jeopardise the overland despatch of reinforcements from India to Egypt. It would also enable the Axis to gain control of the Abadan oilfields, thus denying to the British Navy their most important requirement, without which they would be more or less immobilised. From Basra, the Axis might hinder British shipping in the Persian Gulf and coerce Iran into allowing the use of her territory to their forces to attack India through Afghanistan. Faced with the threat of invasion, India would turn from an asset into a liability for the British Government.

The Germans had begun to interest themselves in Iraq as early as 1933. The earlier dream of a Berlin-Baghdad railway, for a political link with the east, had given place to the subtler scheme of infiltration into Iraq and eventual domination of Baghdad. The Germans had gained considerable influence in various spheres of activity—commercial, cultural and political. In 1939, the ex-Mufti of Jerusalem, who had played an important part in organising the 'Arab Revolt' in Palestine during the years 1936-39, arrived in Baghdad, accompanied by a number of Syrian and Palestinian adherents, and started work on behalf of the Axis. The main plank of their propaganda was that, whereas Hitler was the sworn

[1] See Appendix 3.

enemy of the Jews, the British Government supported the Jews against the Arabs in Palestine.

The ground for this sort of work had, in some measure, been prepared by Herr Grobba, the German Minister in Baghdad, and his agents, who had been, for some time, carrying on a subtle propaganda by radio and leaflets, supplemented by subsidies to the pan-Arab movement and to the Arab leaders. This work hardly suffered an interruption when Iraq broke off diplomatic relations with Germany at the outbreak of the war, since the Italian Legation at Baghdad practically played the same role. It became a centre of Axis propaganda, and through it some of the Iraqi leaders established contacts with von Papen at Ankara. The Japanese, who had established a Legation in 1939, also co-operated with the Axis and greatly reinforced the anti-British activities and propaganda.

The chief weakness of the British position in Iraq lay in the fact that the Iraqi army, led by a clique of militarists, was anti-British in its outlook. The senior officers of the Iraqi army and air force were mostly extreme pan-Arabs. Rashid Ali's position was considerably strengthened by the support he received from the army, and particularly from a group of four very prominent army officers. These were Colonels Salah ed Din Sabbagh, Kamil Shabib, Fahmi Said and Mahmud Salman. These officers were working as a team which came to be known as the 'Golden Square'. Salah ed Din Sabbagh was the commander of the 3rd Division, Kamil Shabib of the 1st Division, Fahmi Said of the Mechanised Force, and Mahmud Salman of the Air Force.[2]

Rashid Ali's coup d'etat

The growing influence of the 'Golden Square' was probably being watched closely both by the Regent and the British Ambassador. For, on 21 March 1941, the Regent is said to have informed the British Ambassador that he proposed to press the Prime Minister, Taha el Hashmi, to deal firmly with this anti-British military clique. The Prime Minister, who apparently had no difficulty in seeing the Regent's view-point, ordered the transfer of certain prominent military officers, known for their anti-British attitude, with a view to weakening the influence of the 'Golden Square' through their dispersal. At this the 'Golden Square' took the most unexpected and audacious decision to defy the government by refusing to obey or implement the transfer orders. This led to a first rate crisis during the night of 1/2 April 1941, when troops under the control of the 'Golden Square' picketed the main buildings

[2] Hammerton: *The Second Great War*, V, p. 1679; *Political Situation, Iraq*; *Sabine* I, 46 W, Appendix A, p. 73.

and roads in Baghdad.³ The Regent fled to Habbaniya, where he hoped to establish, "in a congenial atmosphere of tribal loyalty," a coalition cabinet of sufficient strength to command the confidence of the country. The attempt was by no means successful and the situation deteriorated daily. The military clique had acted with energy and Rashid Ali had been prompt in seizing power. Taha el Hashmi, the Prime Minister, felt compelled to resign, and on 3 April, Rashid Ali took over control of the government as "Chief of the National Defence Government". Sherif Sharaf, another member of the Royal family, was elected Regent by a 'National Assembly', dominated by the adherents of Rashid Ali. Meanwhile, the ex-Regent, Emir Abdul Illa, accompanied by Jamil Madfai, an ex-Prime Minister, fled farther south from Habbaniya to Basra where, on 4 April, they took refuge in a British gunboat. The British Government helped them to proceed to Transjordan, whose ruler was the Emir Abdulla, the uncle of the Regent.

Reactions of the British Government

The British Government was much perturbed by Rashid Ali's *coup d'etat*. The pro-British Regent was ousted from power and the anti-British military clique had assumed control over the government of the country. It would give a dangerous turn to the war in Western Asia if Iraq slipped from Allied control and threw her weight on the side of the Axis, particularly as at that time the situation facing the Allies in Europe and Africa was none too favourable. In Europe, France lay prostrate and crippled, with the Vichy Government not only co-operating with the Axis but showing signs of being inimical to the Allies. Britain, herself, had been exhausted by the terrible ordeal of the Battle of Britain. The Axis had already brought Rumania and Bulgaria under their control; and on 6 April 1941, soon after Rashid Ali had installed himself in power in Iraq, the Axis simultaneously invaded Yugoslavia and Greece. In North Africa, General Rommel had, only a few days back, launched a strong attack on the British forces at El Agheila, and was threatening Benghazi and Tobruk. In view of the unfavourable position of the Allies, it was natural for the British Government to take a very serious view of the turn the events had taken in Iraq. The British Government could not let Rashid Ali and the anti-British Iraqi military clique further undermine British influence in the Middle East.

The British Ambassador in Iraq, at this time, was Sir Kinahan Cornwallis. By an unfortunate coincidence, he stepped into his new appointment on the same day (2 April 1941) on which Rashid Ali

---

³ *Political Situation, Iraq; Sabine* I, 46 W, Appendix A, p. 73.

staged his *coup d'etat*. However, Cornwallis, who had previously for several years been the Political Adviser to King Feisal I, knew the country well enough to be able to take a firm grip of the situation without any loss of time. He proposed to have no official relations with the existing unconstitutional government of Rashid Ali; and was therefore unable to present his credentials or legitimately claim privileges pertaining to the office of an ambassador. Rashid Ali, however, in order to legalise his position as much as possible seemed to be ready to deal with him on a semi-official basis at least, should establishment of full diplomatic relations become impossible through the procedural scruples of the new British Ambassador.

Immediately after Rashid Ali had seized power by his *coup d'etat*, the British Government had asked General Wavell, Commanding Middle East Forces, to indicate the troops he would be able to spare for a military intervention in Iraq.[4] Sir Kinahan had also been sounded as to the prospects of successful resistance in Iraq to Rashid Ali's government. The British Ambassador had replied that much depended on the initiative of the Regent, but that the general public was anxiously waiting for a definition of policy by the British Government. He however emphasized that "at any moment, His Majesty's Government may have to decide between the alternative of seeing Iraq passing rapidly under Axis influence, or having to give armed help to the Regent's cause."[5] By 5 April, that is barely three days after his arrival, Sir Kinahan felt himself in a position to advise the British Government, more firmly, on the possible courses of action that might be needed in Iraq. By this time the Regent had fled to the safety of a British gunboat and Rashid Ali had gained control over Iraq. Cornwallis considered that the chances of the Regent once more coming into power, without the help of the armed forces of the British Government, were remote. There were, in his opinion, three courses open to the British Government.

Firstly, that the situation should be restored by armed intervention. Such an action, if taken quickly, would only have to be directed against the hostile portion of the Iraqi army. If however it was delayed, Rashid Ali would obviously do his utmost to strengthen his hold upon the country, by intimidation and bribes; and if he was allowed to do this for the next few months, operations on a much more comprehensive scale would be necessary to restore the situation.

Secondly, that Rashid Ali should be informed that the British

---

[4] Tel. No. 242 dated 4 April 1941 from S.S. to Ambassador, p. 5(a), *Iraq situation*, April 1941, F. 687.
[5] Tel. No. 274 dated 5 April from Cornwallis to Foreign Office, p. 6, *Iraq situation*, F. 687.

Government would have no official dealings with his regime. At the same time efforts should be made to 'squeeze' him as much as possible. Sir Kinahan, however, had been too short a time in the country to predict the result of such an attitude, but he thought that the British failure to support the Regent would reflect very unfavourably on the British prestige. In that case, he expected to see Iraq fall rapidly under the Axis influence.

Thirdly, that the regime of Rashid Ali should be recognised. This course was ruled out as Rashid Ali was known to be an Axis agent.

Of the above three courses, the British Ambassador favoured the first, although he realised that it might not be possible to spare the forces necessary for an armed intervention, and that the British policy in Iraq must be subordinated to wider issues.[6]

The Foreign Office took note of these three courses but awaited General Wavell's opinion. There followed, after this, discussions betwen Rashid Ali and the British Ambassador, in which it appeared that both of them were playing for time. Sir Kinahan kept countering Rashid Ali's proposal for recognition of his regime by the British Government until the situation should clarify sufficiently for a clear-cut decision.

In the interval certain steps were taken by Rashid Ali's administration which left no doubt as to the changed temper of the new regime. On 6 April, orders were passed preventing the Royal Air Force personnel from passing between Habbaniya and Baghdad. At about the same time wireless transmitting sets of the Air Liaison Officers, at Sulaimaniya and Mosul, were confiscated.[7] On 10 April, Cornwallis gave it as his opinion that Rashid Ali had considerably strengthened his power and that consequently nothing short of armed intervention could dislodge his regime.[8]

Forces available for intervention in Iraq

Meanwhile, the War Office had received, on 7 April, a reply from General Wavell regarding the troops that might be despatched to Iraq. General Wavell's reply was not encouraging. All that he could do was "in the case of most extreme urgency" to move one British battalion by road from Palestine to Iraq and utilise Royal Air Force aircraft in Iraq. Rather than take a military action of unpredictable value, he suggested a strong declaration of policy, reinforced by an air demonstration. This, he thought, might have some effect. If it failed, British prestige would, of course, be

---

[6] Tel. No. 281 dated 5 April 1941 from Cornwallis to Foreign Office, *Iraq Situation*, F. 687.
[7] Tel. No. 286 from Cornwallis to Foreign Office, dated 6 April, F. 687.
[8] Tel. from Cornwallis to Foreign Office, dated 10 April, F. 687.

damaged, but there was no other alternative. The restoration of the situation by force, with inadequate resources, was not advisable.[9]

Having tried one avenue and found it a *cul-de-sac*, the Imperial Chiefs of Staff turned their attention to another. On 8 April, a "most immediate" telegram was sent to the Viceroy by the Secretary of State for India, in which he stated that the situation in Iraq was critical, and that everything depended on British ability to make a show of force in support of the Regent, even if it was only to hold Basra and Shuaiba. Moreover, the Americans were very keen on a great air assembling base being formed at Basra to which they could ship direct. The Secretary of State inquired if the Government of India would make available a suitable force for occupying Basra.[10]

The Government of India rose to the occasion by offering to divert to Iraq a convoy, which was originally meant for Malaya, but which was then still at Karachi in the process of embarking. It consisted of one infantry brigade and one field regiment with ancillary troops.[11] They also proposed to send approximately 400 British infantry by air to Shuaiba, with twelve light machine-guns, six Vickers guns and two anti-tank rifles. The Government of India were strongly of the opinion that the land force, in and around Basra, should be brought up, as soon as possible, to an equivalent of at least one division. They accordingly proposed to follow up the first brigade group by two further brigade groups and base units for Sybil.[12] The offer was accepted by the British Government on 10 April 1941.

The convoy sailed from Karachi for Basra, on 12 April 1941. On board were, Headquarters 10th Indian Division, 3rd Field Regiment R.A., Headquarters 20th Indian Infantry Brigade, 3rd Battalion 11th Sikh Regiment, 2nd Battalion 7th Gurkha Rifles, 2nd Battalion 8th Gurkha Rifles and certain ancillary troops. In command of the force was Major-General W. A. K. Fraser, C.B., C.B.E., D.S.O., M.V.O., M.C., Commander 10th Indian Division.[13]

As this convoy had originally been prepared for despatch to Malaya, it had not been embarked with a view to immediate tactical employment on arrival at destination; and in view of the necessity for speed there was no time left to readjust the loading of the units. Consequently a risk was accepted in diverting it to Iraq without readjustment, where an opposed landing was by no means impossible.

[9] Tel. No. 54836 dated 7 April 41 from Mideast to Troopers, *Sabine 1*, 46 W, p. 55.
[10] Tel. from S.S. to Viceroy, 8 April 41, *Sabine 1*, 46 W, p. 59.
[11] Tel. from Viceroy to S.S., *Sabine 1*, 46 W, p. 61.
[12] Tel. No. 3628/C dated 10 April 41 from Armindia to Mideast, *Sabine 1*, 46 W., p. 61 and p. 65.
[13] General Sir A. P. Wavell's *Despatch*: Operations in Iraq, Syria and Persia (May 1941—January 1942).

Major-General Fraser was instructed to occupy the Basra-Shuaiba area, on arrival of the convoy at Basra, in order to ensure the safe disembarkation of further reinforcements and to enable a base to be established in that area. Should disembarkation be opposed, he was to overcome the opposition by force. Care was to be taken, however, not to infringe the neutrality of Iran.[14]

Ambassador's objections to landing in Basra

The despatch of the troops was to be kept a closely guarded secret in order to surprise Rashid Ali, and to give him as little time as possible to organise any effective opposition to the landing. But on 11 April, Sir K. Cornwallis, the British Ambassador, sent a telegram to the Foreign Office, advising deferring of the action for securing the Basra-Shuaiba area.[15] He then held that the secret and the unheralded arrival of the troops would be difficult to justify. Rashid Ali would certainly represent the measure as an act of British aggression. He would thus exploit the situation to rally the country against the British Government. In his speech to the Senate on 10 April, Rashid Ali had declared that the national movement (i.e., his *coup d'etat*) was entirely an internal affair, having no connection with any foreign power. He had declared his intention of honouring international law and obligations, and had emphasised his resolve to carry out the terms of the Treaty of 1932.[16] By this speech, he had placed himself in a very favourable position, since the British Government now could not use the *coup d'etat* in Iraq as an excuse for intervention, namely to protect their treaty rights, which Rashid Ali had emphatically declared he would honour. Sir Kinahan was of the opinion that the British Government must have a clear-cut issue with which to justify to the people of Iraq the despatch of the troops. Hence he requested that he should be allowed to test Rashid Ali's sincerity by telling him that the military situation outside Iraq required the rapid passage of the troops through Iraq to Palestine, and that in accordance with the treaty rights, the British Government were opening the lines of communication at once, and that the movement of the troops would begin on a date to be named. If Rashid Ali refused, the British Government would have a perfect right to take any action they thought fit. If he agreed, the British would gain a military foothold in the country without an armed clash and be in a better position to retain their grip over Iraq. The Imperial Chiefs of Staff accepted this suggestion to delay the sending of the troops to Iraq.

[14] Directive to Fraser dated 11 April 1941, *Sabine I*, 46 W, p. 102.
[15] Telegram from Ambassador to Foreign Office, dated 11 April 1941, *Sabine I*, p. 93.
[16] Tel. No. 312 dated 11 April from Cornwallis to Foreign Office, *Iraq situation*, F. 687, p. 36.

They signalled to India on 12 April that the departure of the airborne troops should be suspended and that the convoy, which had already sailed, should be held at Bahrein or elsewhere en route.[17]

India's criticism of the Ambassador's proposal

This counsel of procrastination was not to the liking of General Auchinleck, or to that of the Government of India, who protested in no uncertain terms against the Ambassador's advice. They held that the disclosure of the Ambassador's proposals to Rashid Ali would, at once, rob the operation of its element of secrecy and surprise, on which they had so far relied for success. If Rashid Ali was given time to organise defence, they could not agree to undertake the operation, without completely recasting the plan, so as to give an opposed landing a reasonable chance of success. This might take some weeks to prepare and might involve the reloading of the ships and the provision of landing crafts etc. General Auchinleck held to his belief that it was essential for the British to establish themselves in Basra, with the minimum delay, so as to secure its use as a base. The possession of a base at Basra might make a difference between success and failure to the British, in the Near and the Middle East, during the next six months. This being so, General Auchinleck felt compelled to express his disagreement with the decision of the Imperial Chiefs of Staff. He was of opinion that the time for diplomatic parleying had passed; and that there was a grave danger of Rashid Ali using the breathing space, now to be made available to him, to consolidate his position and probably to invoke Axis aid, which might take the form of provision of air assistance to Iraq and even of air-borne troops. He, therefore, urged bold action to prevent the deterioration of the situation not only in Iraq but also in Asia generally, and especially in Turkey, Iran, and Arabia.[18] After this strong representation, those in charge of military strategy in England could not escape the responsibility of re-examining their decision. The whole problem was reviewed by the Defence Committee and, on 13 April 1941, the British Government decided that the expedition to Basra should, after all, proceed as planned.[19]

---

[17] Tel. No. 4030 dated 12 April 41 from S.S. to Defence Deptt., *Sabine I*, 46 W, p. 115.
[18] Auchinleck's letter dated 12 April 1941, *Sabine I*, 46 W, p. 114a; *Tel.* G.G. to S.S. dated 13 April 1941, *Sabine I*, 46 W, pp. 127-29.
[19] Tel. from S.S. to G.G. 13 April 41, *Sabine II*, p. 23.

CHAPTER VIII

Plans for an Opposed Landing

The next step, after the decision to let the expedition to Iraq proceed as planned, was to achieve a successful landing in Basra. Much depended on whether the landing would meet with opposition or not. This, in turn, depended upon such factors as whether Rashid Ali would honour the terms of the treaty without hesitation, or whether he would try to back out by a legal quibbling over their interpretation. Sir Kinahan, an able diplomat, would undoubtedly do his best, but there was the Axis influence to be countered and he had already given the warning that, should Rashid Ali be looking for an excuse to back out of the treaty obligations, the secret and unnotified arrival of a military convoy at Basra would supply him with a very plausible pretext. In case the Government of Iraq decided against permitting a peaceful entry to the Indian troops, it may be interesting to speculate on the likely chances of success of the Basra expedition. For that, it would be necessary to look into the quality, strength and disposition of the Iraqi troops, which the 20th Indian Infantry Brigade would have to face on landing.

Iraq Army and Air Force

Iraq's army and air force had been equipped and trained largely through the efforts and co-operation of the British Government. The latter had not only provided an Inspector-General and a military mission, but had also given facilities to a number of Iraqi officers for receiving military education in England. The Iraq army consisted of four infantry divisions. The *1st Division*, with its headquarters at Baghdad, was composed of two infantry brigades, one Field Artillery brigade, one Mountain Artillery brigade and one Divisional Cavalry Squadron. This division, less the Mountain Artillery brigade then at Diwaniya, was concentrated at Baghdad with, however, its cavalry squadron at Jaloula and one infantry brigade at Mussaiyib. The *2nd Division*, with its headquarters at Kirkuk, had three infantry brigades, one Divisional Cavalry squadron, two Field Artillery brigades, and one Mountain Artillery brigade. This division was concentrated at Kirkuk, with the exception of one infantry brigade and the Mountain Artillery brigade located at Mosul, and one infantry battalion stationed at Erbil. The *3rd Division*, with its headquarters at Baghdad, was, like the 2nd, composed of three infantry brigades, one Divisional Cavalry squadron, two Field Artillery brigades, and one Mountain Artillery brigade. The Divisional Cavalry squadron was at Jaloula, while one infantry brigade had a battalion each at Baghdad, Jaloula and Mansourat al Jebel, respectively. The *4th Division*, with its headquarters at Diwaniya, was composed of three infantry brigades (one 1st line and two 2nd line) and one Mountain Artillery battery, plus the Mountain Artillery brigade from the *1st Division*. Of these, one infantry brigade, and the Mountain Artillery brigade of the *1st Division*, were located at Diwaniya. The second infantry brigade was posted in or near Basra, less one battalion at Amara, where also was located the Mountain battery. The third infantry brigade (less one battalion at Samawa) was stationed at Nasiriya. Besides these four infantry divisions, there was also a mechanised brigade, with its headquarters at Baghdad.

The river flotilla of the Iraq navy, consisted of four Thornycroft gunboats, each of 100 tons displacement, and each armed with a 3.7-inch Howitzer, one 3-inch Mortar and four machine-guns There were also three other vessels—'*King Feisal I*' a pilot vessel with a 4-inch gun, '*Alarm*', a minesweeper with one 12-pounder gun and '*Alert*' a control vessel with no armament.[1]

The Iraqi air force (as on 15 November 1940) consisted of seven squadrons and aircraft of the Flying Training School. One squadron was located at Mosul and another at Kirkuk, while the rest were at Rashid, near Baghdad. Out of a total of 116 aircraft, only 57 were said to be in a serviceable condition.[2]

Rival Forces in the Basra area

Of all the military forces of Iraq, variously disposed from Mosul to Basra, those that mattered most to the 20th Indian Brigade were the troops in and around Basra and therefore in an immediate position to offer resistance to its landing. It was this part of the Iraq force that the Commander of the 20th Indian Brigade had to take into account in his plans for landing, which were made on 15 April while the convoy was still at sea. It will have been seen from the foregoing account of the disposition of Iraqi troops that there were at least two battalions in or at Basra and several more in the immediate vicinity. Accordingly Brigadier D. Powell, the Commander of the 20th Indian Brigade, based his landing plan on the assumption that there would be 300 infantry at Fao, two infantry battalions at Zubair, one battalion in Tanuma and two battalions at Zubeila.

---

[1] For Iraqi land, sea and air forces see Appendices 4 and 5. See also 20 Bde. 0.1 No. 1 dated 16 April 1941 and *Infantry Organisation, Iraq Army, War Diary* 20 Ind. Inf. Bde.
[2] *Royal Iraqi Air Force as at 15 November 1940, War Diary* 20 Ind. Inf. Bde. See also Appendix 5.

The artillery in the Basra area was estimated to consist of one Mountain Battery 3.7-inch Howitzers in Zubeila, and another Mountain Battery 3.7-inch Howitzers plus one Field Battery 18-pounders at Zubair. These the Iraqis could reinforce with one Mountain Battery 2.75-inch from Amara and the whole Mountain Artillery brigade located at Diwaniya.[3] As to the air opposition there were three Iraqi Vincent aircraft, based on Maqil Airport. Although Iraq possessed 57 serviceable aircraft, the majority of them were in Baghdad. But these might, if necessary, be moved to and operated from Maqil Airport.[4] The Iraqi naval forces available for opposing the landing of the Indian troops at Basra would comprise the three vessels—'*King Feisal*', '*Alarm*' and the '*Alert*', besides one gun boat at Fao and three more seven miles upstream from Maqil.

As opposed to these Iraqi forces in the Basra area, there were, in the convoy, the headquarters of the 20th Indian Brigade, 2/8 Gurkha, 3/11 Sikh, 2/7 Gurkha, 3rd Field Regiment, R.A., and ancillary units. The naval forces available to assist the landing of these troops at Basra were H.M.S. *Seabelle* and H.M.S. *Yarra* escorting the convoy, H.M.S. *Falmouth*, H.M.S. *Cockchafer*, being sent to meet the convoy at the mouth of the Shatt al Arab and H.M.S. *Emerald*, anchored in the dock area at Basra. 400 officers and men of the 1st Battalion the King's Own Royal Regiment, were to be flown from Karachi to Shuaiba, to land there 16 miles south-west of Basra, almost simultaneously with the landing of the 20th Indian Brigade. In addition to these was No. 244 Bomber Squadron R.A.F. which was located at Shuaiba. Possible reinforcements would come from the Middle East and Habbaniya, the latter however possessing negligible land force and purely training types of aircraft. Therefore, the only reinforcement that the 20th Indian Brigade might count upon immediately on landing was one company of the Iraq levies at Shuaiba and another such company at Basra.

The Plan

Before making his plan for the landing of the troops at Basra, Brigadier Powell had an appreciation of the situation prepared. According to that, the Indian troops might meet opposition either at Fao (at the entrance to the Shatt al Arab), or at any point up the river or at Basra. In view of the threat of an opposed landing, there were three courses open to the Indian forces, viz., to land at Kuwait and move north; to land at Fao and advance both via land and sea; or to move along the Shatt al Arab to the dock area. The proposal of a landing at Kuwait and a subsequent move

---

[3] *Order of Battle of Iraqi Army, War Diary* 20 Ind. Inf. Bde. See also Appendix 6.
[4] 20 Bde. O.I No. 1 dated 16 April 1941, *War Diary* 20 Ind. Inf. Bde.

north suffered from certain serious defects. It involved a march of 112 miles, with little water en route. The route though parallel to Shatt al Arab was at a distance from the waterway, with the additional disadvantage that the line of communication might be cut by a hostile force infiltrating through this gap. The proposal of a landing at Fao, or further north, and advance both by land and sea also had some serious drawbacks. Any advance by infantry on the road Fao—Basra would be rendered difficult by the numerous water channels running along the date-palm groves, which would obstruct the movement of the troops and make progress exceedingly slow. Therefore the course approved by Major-General Fraser was to move up the Shatt al Arab to the dock area, and after landing to secure that area.[5] On 16 April, the Commander of the 20th Indian Infantry Brigade, made the following plan of operations:[6]

> The initial landing was to be made by 2/8 Gurkha, with 200 men, in the R.A.F. Cantonment area. The remainder of the battalion was to follow up at the first opportunity and help to secure the entire dock. The extent of ground to be secured in this initial landing was the Basra dock area and the area enclosed by the R.A.F. Cantonment—Main Road—Quramat Ali Canal—Civil Landing Ground. A detachment of 2/7 Gurkha was to deal with the Iraqi opposition at Fao. They were to land with the help of lifeboats, capture Fao, disarm the Iraqi garrison and re-embark. If no opposition was encountered, they were to resume their position in the convoy. On landing at Basra, 2/7 Gurkha was to take over the portion of the dock area from 2/8 Gurkha, from R.A.F. Cantonment to and including the Civil Wireless Station area. After that 2/7 Gurkha was to extend the cordon so as to include the Nahr al Zubeila. 3/11 Sikh was to be in reserve in a locality to be chosen. All the battalions were to be prepared to land self-contained, with food and water for 48 hours. None of the battalions had any transport. The 3rd Field Regiment R.A., as it happened, was temporarily "divorced from its guns." Its role in the landing was, therefore, merely to assist the Navy in producing the necessary covering fire. It was accordingly to be prepared to send one troop to the vessel *Jalladutta*, to operate guns from the deck, and also to send forward observation officers ashore with the battalions. The disembarkation both at Fao and Basra was to be covered

---

[5] *Appreciation by Commander 20 Ind. Inf. Bde. on 15 April 1941*, pp. 31-37, *War Diary* 20 Ind. Inf. Bde.
[6] 20 Bde. O.1 No. 1 dated 16 April 1941.

by the fire of the automatic weapons from the ships and the naval guns. The 26th Field Ambulance was to open an Advanced Dressing Station in the dock area.

The landing

As it turned out, all these plans and preparations for a hypothetical opposed landing proved superfluous, the Government of Iraq having decided to permit the landing. It will be remembered that the Indian troops had sailed from Karachi on 12 April 1941. The convoy composed of eight transports and escorted by H.M.S. *Yarra*, was met at sea, on the morning of 15 April, by H.M.S. *Seabelle* from Basra. Later in the day the escort was reinforced by H.M.S. *Falmouth*, and on 17 April, the convoy, joined by H.M.I.S. *Lawrence*, proceeded towards the entrance of the Shatt al Arab.[7]

In the meanwhile, on the evening of 16 April, Sir Kinahan, the British Ambassador at Baghdad, announced to Rashid Ali that it was the intention of the British Government to avail themselves of the facilities granted under the Treaty for the passage of the troops through Iraq, and that a disembarkation of troops at Basra would take place shortly.[8] At the same time, it is said, Major-General G. G. Waterhouse, Inspector-General of the Iraqi army and head of the British Military Mission in Iraq, set to work to avoid a 'show-down', and finally succeeded in persuading the Iraqi Chief of the General Staff, Major-General Amin Zaki, to secure from Salah ed Din, an influential member of the 'Golden Square', an order that no opposition should be offered to the landing of the Indian troops at Basra. Thus the threatened crisis was averted and the Indian troops landed at Basra, without meeting any opposition. The 2/8 Gurkha occupied the area allotted to them, namely the R.A.F. Quay—R.A.F. Hospital—Wireless Station—Civil Aerodrome—Maqil Quays.[9] Disembarkation of the Indian troops was completed on 19 April, when the headquarters of the 20th Indian Brigade was established at Makina.[10] During the week, beginning 17 April, 400 officers and men of the 1st Battalion King's Own Royal Regiment were also flown from Karachi to Shuaiba,[11] where they were deployed to protect the aerodrome. The part of the Iraqi territory that thus went under British occupation consisted of the area enclosed by, and inclusive of, the R.A.F. Cantonment—Main Road—Quramat Ali Canal and Civil Landing Ground. This was in addition to the R.A.F. stations at Habbaniya and Shuaiba, which were already British and whose garrison was now merely reinforced.

[7] General Wavell's *Despatch*.
[8] *Sabine II*, Page 104.
[9] *War Diary* 2/8 G.R.
[10] *War Diary* 20 Ind. Inf. Bde.
[11] *War Diary* the King's Own Royal Regiment.

Despatch of further troops to Iraq

Soon after the landing of the 20th Indian Brigade, Rashid Ali, through his Adviser to Ministry of Interior, informed the British Ambassador that he had agreed to the disembarking of that force on the understanding that the treaty facilities would be used by it merely for a rapid passage through Iraq and not for staying on indefinitely in the country. Thereupon arose sharp differences over the interpretation of the treaty clauses, Rashid Ali contending that under the treaty, he was bound only to provide facilities for a passage through Iraq; and that he would not permit a military occupation of his country by Indian and British troops on the pretext that such troops were necessary for the protection of Base, lines of communication or installations, which might remain in existence indefinitely. He, therefore, officially informed the British Ambassador on 18 April that if the British Government wanted to retain the goodwill of Iraq, they would have to conform to four conditions regarding the working of the Anglo-Iraqi Treaty. These were: (*i*) the British and Indian troops then in Iraq should be moved through to Palestine at once, (*ii*) other troops should not arrive, until after their departure, (*iii*) in future, timely notice would have to be given of the arrival of troops, who would have to arrive in a manner that would enable them to pass through Iraq quickly, and (*iv*) at no time should the British and Indian troops in Iraq exceed one mixed brigade.[12]

At this, there took place an exchange of views between Sir Kinahan, the Government of India and the British Government. The British Ambassador seemed willing to make some concession to Rashid Ali's argument. He, therefore, proposed retaining in Iraq enough troops for the protection of the lines of communication and the Base of Basra and for strengthening Habbaniya, and then despatching the rest of the Sabine to Palestine as future reinforcements. The Government of India, on the other hand, seemed to be frankly of the view that merely opening the line of communication to Palestine was not what the troops in Iraq were for. The Indian Government was preparing to dispatch a second brigade group, with Base units, about the second week of May, and the remaining troops to complete one division and Base, about the beginning of June. The disposition of troops that it would have liked, therefore, was:[13]

(*i*) One brigade group at Basra.
(*ii*) One brigade group in the area Baghdad-Habbaniya, ostensibly for line of communication duties, and

[12] Tel. from Cornwallis to Foreign Office dated 18 April 1941, *Sabine II*, p. 169, 46 W.
[13] Tel. No. 4261/G dated 20 April 1941 from Armindia to A.O.C. Iraq, *Sabine II*, p. 183, 46 W.

(*iii*) One brigade group, apparently, as a floating reserve; eventually to be sent to Palestine, "but this must await development of Line of Communication."

The British Government agreed with the Government of India and even went further. It decided on 23 April 1941, that one division was the minimum force for Iraq; and that, in fact, the Basra Base should be developed to receive further Sabine divisions. The disposition of the brigade groups, as suggested by the Government of India, was, in its view, politically desirable; but the security of the force itself, of the Basra Base, and of the Royal Air Force Station at Habbaniya would require priority in that order, over the opening of the overland route.[14]

Rashid Ali, on his part, seemed resolved not to permit what looked to him like a British military occupation of Iraq in the guise of opening the lines of communication to Palestine. He was confident of Axis support, and the Chiefs of Staff in London considered him "hand in glove with the Axis powers". Earlier, in March, hopes of German help had been held out to the Grand Mufti, and Rashid Ali was also told that "the German Government was in full sympathy with his action and would do everything possible to help him."[15] By raising a rebellion in Iraq the Axis hoped to strengthen the anti-British forces in the Middle East, cut the British lines of communication and tie down British troops and ships at the expense of other theatres of war. Fortified by the knowledge of Axis intentions Rashid Ali became bolder, so that when, on 28 April, Cornwallis informed him of the impending arrival, the next day, of a convoy of three transports carrying Indian troops, the latter refused to agree to their landing and was quite adamant in his refusal.[16] Thus the political situation in Iraq suddenly deteriorated and a military clash seemed imminent.

Plan for the defence of Maqil

As the situation looked threatening, steps had to be taken for the protection of the convoy now about to touch the port of Basra, as well as for the defence of Maqil. The Royal Navy was providing escort for the convoy up the river to Basra. The convoy was to arrive at Rooka Float at 0500 hours on 29 April and was to proceed up the river in the following order: H.M.S. *Cockchafer* and *Nevasa*, H.M.S. *Yarra* and *Bandra*, H.M.S. *Falmouth* and *Esperance*, at half mile intervals. Low and high angle armament and machine-guns were to be ready in all ships, but unobtrusively manned. Air

[14] Tel. No. 4538/G dated 23 April 1941 from Armindia to Fraser, *Sabine II*, p. 24, 46 W.
[15] *The Mediterranean and the Middle East*, Vol. II, p. 185 and p. 194.
[16] Tel. No. A 388 dated 28 April 1941 to Mideast, *Sabine III*, p. 104 and Tel. No. A 389 dated 29 April 1941 from Iraq, *Sabine III*, p. 122.

General Sir Edward Quinan

Major-General W. A. K. Fraser

Gateway to Iraq

Indian Troops arrive at Basra Dock

escort was to be provided.[17] At the same time, the 20th Indian Infantry Brigade Group was to protect the Dock—Maqil Camp—Makina—Civil Airport area.

The Commander of the 20th Indian Brigade detailed 3/11 Sikh for the defence of this vital area. 2/7 Gurkha and 2/8 Gurkha were held in reserve. The Iraq Levies, approximately one and a half platoon, with medium machine-guns, were to move for the defence of the Power Station and Marine Dock Yard area, if required to do so. The rest were to defend the R.A.F. Station area. The 3rd Field Regiment R.A., less one troop, and the naval guns were to support the defence by observed fire.[18] The disposition of the four companies of 3/11 Sikh was: one company to defend the Makina Camp; the second to provide protection for the dock area; the third to patrol the area Quramat Ali Canal—railway crossing, and the fourth to guard the 3/11 Sikh camp at Maqil.

Outbreak of hostilities

The convoy of three transports, carrying additional Indian troops, arrived at Basra and disembarked without incident on 29 April.[19] These were only ancillary troops for Sybil, and not the second brigade which the Government of India was preparing to despatch early in May. No opposition was offered to the landing of these troops, in spite of Rashid Ali's firm refusal to permit it, because the Government of Iraq gave up the idea of defending Basra and decided, instead, to hold Baghdad and prevent the establishment of any large British force there. This placed the lives of British residents of Baghdad in danger and led to the women and children being evacuated in R.A.F. transport, on 29 April, from Baghdad to Habbaniya and Basra. At the same time, on the same day as the landing of the Indian ancillary troops, Iraq military forces began their own troop movements with a view to carrying out tactical dispositions. Accordingly, at about 2330 hours, on 29 April, Iraq troops estimated to be two infantry brigades, supported by artillery and mechanised units, marched from Rashid camp, near Baghdad, westward towards Habbaniya, and by dawn on 30 April, were established on the high ground which closely overlooked the British aerodrome and the cantonment there.[20] The same day, another Iraq force, estimated to consist of one brigade, occupied Ramadi, 14 miles west of Habbaniya, with the object of preventing British reinforcements from Palestine reaching Habbaniya. The Iraqis had also occupied the oilfields of the Iraq

[17] Tel. from S.N.O. P.G., *Sabine III*, p. 99.
[18] 20 Inf. Bde. O.O. No. 1 dated 28 April 1941, *War Diary* 20 Ind. Inf. Bde.
[19] Tel. A 399 dated 29 April 1941 from A.O.C. Iraq to Mideast, *Sabine III*, p. 123.
[21] *Despatches-operations Iraq*, F. 830.

Petroleum Company at Kirkuk, and had cut off the flow of oil thence to Haifa, diverting it at the same time to Syria, via the Tripoli pipeline, which had been closed since the collapse of France. Thus the British Government lost the oil from Kirkuk, which went to the Vichy French in Syria, then under German domination and collaborating with the Axis.

Next, the Commander of the Iraqi force, which had taken up its position on the high ground overlooking the Habbaniya airfield, sent a note, at 0600 hours on 30 April, to Air Vice-Marshal H. G. Smart, Air Officer Commanding at Habbaniya, to the effect that he had occupied the high ground overlooking Habbaniya for purposes of training, and that he prohibited any "flying from or the going out of any force or person from the cantonment". The note further contained the threat that "if any aircraft or armoured car attempts to go out, it will be shelled by our batteries and we shall not be responsible for it". The tone of the note and the threat evoked from Air Vice-Marshal Smart the prompt reply that he would not cease training-flying, and that if any aircraft was fired on, immediate reprisals would follow. A few hours later, however, the Iraqi messenger returned to re-assert that no training by the British aircraft would be permitted. Air Vice-Marshal Smart took this opportunity to gain some time and informed the Iraqi Commander that he was awaiting a reply from the British Ambassador to a political question which he had raised, and that in the meanwhile it would be desirable for the Iraqi troops to withdraw from the high ground which they had occupied. The reply to this was that such a withdrawal was not possible without specific orders from Baghdad, but that there was no intention on the part of the Iraqis to attack, unless the British themselves did so. Accordingly, the Iraqis refrained from any hostile action on 1 May, and, indeed, until the British attacked. In the meanwhile, a communication was received from the Foreign Office, both by the Embassy and the Air Officer Commanding Habbaniya, giving full authority for air attacks on the Iraqi forces, should they be deemed necessary. At that Air Vice-Marshal Smart decided to bomb the Iraqi force out of its position before the first light on 2 May 1941.

The operations that followed that decision passed through three phases. In the first phase, which lasted from 2 May to 7 May, was fought the Battle of Habbaniya, while, at the same time, Indian troops secured their hold over the Basra—Shuaiba area. In the second phase, from 8 May to 26 May, the Iraqi air force was practically eliminated, while a force from Palestine had reached Habbaniya and preparations were afoot for that force and the Indian troops at Basra to converge on Baghdad. In the third phase, which lasted from 27 May to 31 May, the Indian troops, advancing from

Shuaiba towards Baghdad, reached Ur while the Palestine force, advancing from Falluja was on the point of entering Baghdad.

Objects of the force operating in Iraq

On 2 May 1941, at the commencement of the first phase of operations in Iraq, Army Headquarters, India, issued a directive to Lieut-General Quinan, Commander designate of the force operating in Iraq, outlining his duties and responsibilities and stating the objectives to be achieved. According to that directive General Quinan was to command all British Empire land forces in Iraq and was to develop and organise the port of Basra for use as a Base or as a port of entry by Allied forces operating in the Middle East. To that end, he was to secure control of all means of communication, including all aerodromes and landing grounds in Iraq, and develop these to the extent requisite to enable the Port of Basra to function to its fullest capacity. He was also to begin planning a system of defences, to protect the Basra Base against an attack by armoured forces, supported by strong air forces, and was to be equally ready to take special measures to protect the Royal Air Force installations and personnel at Habbaniya and Shuaiba, the lives of the British subjects in Baghdad and elsewhere in Iraq, and the Kirkuk oilfields as well as the pipeline to Haifa. He was also to make plans to protect the Anglo-Iranian Oil Company's installations and its British employees in south-west Iran, if necessary. He was informed that it was the intention to increase the force under his command up to three infantry divisions, with possibly an additional armoured division, as soon as these troops could be despatched from India.[21]

Operational control of Iraq

The point about the operational control in Iraq had always proved difficult to settle. On 8 March 1941, General Dill, Chief of the Imperial General Staff, had agreed that initial control of the operations in Iraq should rest with India. On 11 April 1941, however, just as the convoy of first troops for Iraq was to leave India, the Government of India informed the War Office that it would not be possible for Army Headquarters, India, at that stage, to assume responsibility for Habbaniya or Baghdad, that is for northern Iraq. They suggested, therefore, that Major-General Fraser, commander of the force due to arrive at Basra on 18 April 1941, should exercise command under the Commander-in-Chief of India over all military forces in the Basra-Shuaiba area only, commencing from the time of arrival, the limit of the command being the Basra-Division.[22]

[21] Directive to Quinan, 2 May 41, *Directive to Commander Iraq Force*, F. 700.
[22] Tel. 3706/C dated 11 April 41 from Armindia to Troopers, p. 1, F. 702.

The Imperial Chiefs of Staff agreed to this and decided that Major-General Fraser would take over from the Air Officer Commanding Iraq as soon as India found it convenient to undertake responsibility for the whole of Iraq. Accordingly, Major-General Fraser assumed command of all military forces in the Basra-Shuaiba area on 18 April 1941, when the Indian troops landed at Basra, which he extended to the whole of Iraq on 29 April 1941.[23] This, however, did not last long. For, on the outbreak of active hostilities with Iraq, on 2 May, the War Office requested General Wavell to resume, temporarily, the operational command of Iraq,[24] which the latter did, after a little hesitation, taking over the control of northern Iraq on 5 May and of southern Iraq on 9 May 1941.

---

[23] Tel. C/47/G dated 30 April 41 from Mideast to Armindia, pp. 19 and 21, F. 702.
[24] Tel. No. 64676 from Troopers to Mideast, dated 2 May 41, *Command of Operations*, p. 23, F. 702.

CHAPTER IX

Battle of Habbaniya

Preparations
   Some time before the outbreak of active hostilities in Iraq, preparations had begun for the defence of the British air base at Habbaniya. The air base at that time comprised nothing more than No. 4 Service Flying Training School, R.A.F., and was neither on a war footing nor adequately provided for engaging in air warfare even in its own defence. It was then under the command of Air Vice-Marshall H. G. Smart, A.O.C. Iraq and had 78 aircraft. But almost all of these were the training types, the Oxfords, Gordons and Audaxes, which were fast becoming obsolete. Amongst these, however, there were about fifty-six which could be made fit for use in operational tasks by careful alterations, and the matter was taken in hand. But of the pilots to fly them, there were only thirty-five available and not all of these were fit or experienced enough for carrying out operational duties. The majority of them, in fact, were instructors, who had done nothing but circuits and landings for some time past, while some others had done only a negligible amount of flying, or were in need of rest, or had been returned from their squadrons as being unsuitable for operational flying. As to Observers and Air Gunners there were only two of each. Of the seventy-eight aircraft with which the School was equipped there were 3 Gladiators and one Blenheim I.
   As the crisis in Iraq deepened, steps were taken to increase the bomb-carrying capacity of some of the aircraft, and to fit bomb-carrying racks to such training aircraft as did not have any. Thus the Audaxes were fitted with two racks each carrying two 250-lb. bombs, although the authorised war load of an Audax was eight 20-lb. bombs only. Likewise the Oxfords, which were not intended to carry any big load, were improved to carry eight 20-lb. bombs each; while the Gordons, which were mostly doing the target-towing jobs, were successfully altered and made fit to carry two 250-lb. bombs each. The result of this work was to provide about fifty-six aircraft for operational emergencies. Twenty-seven of these were Oxfords, seven Gordons and twenty-two Audaxes. In addition, one Wellington bomber and six Gladiators had arrived on 19 April as reinforcements from the Middle East.[1] Thus the total number of Gladiators at Habbaniya on 19 April was nine. All these aircraft

[1] *The Defence of Habbaniya*, Iraq Papers, Vol. II, pp. 123-36.

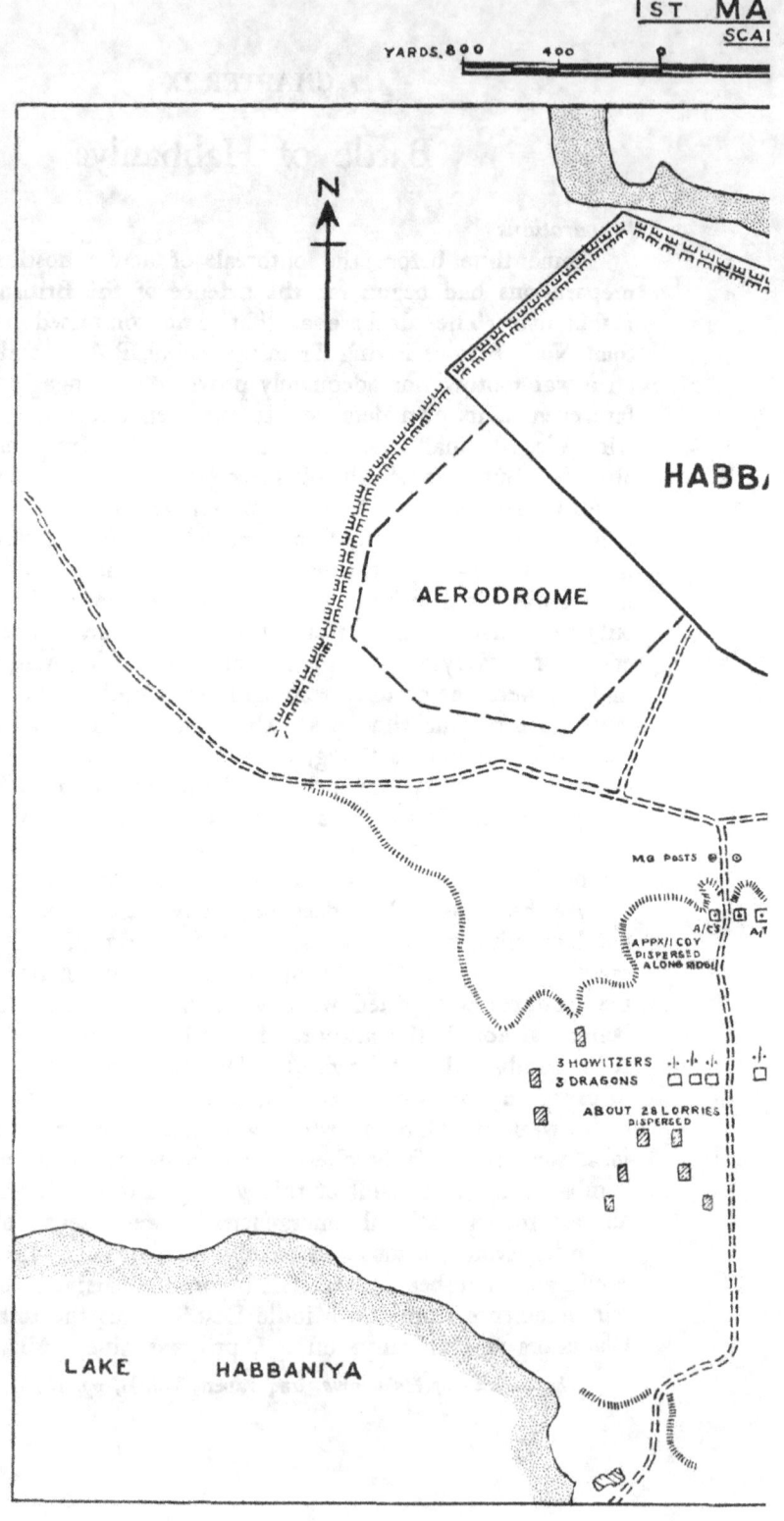

TROOPS AT HABBANIYA
Y 1941

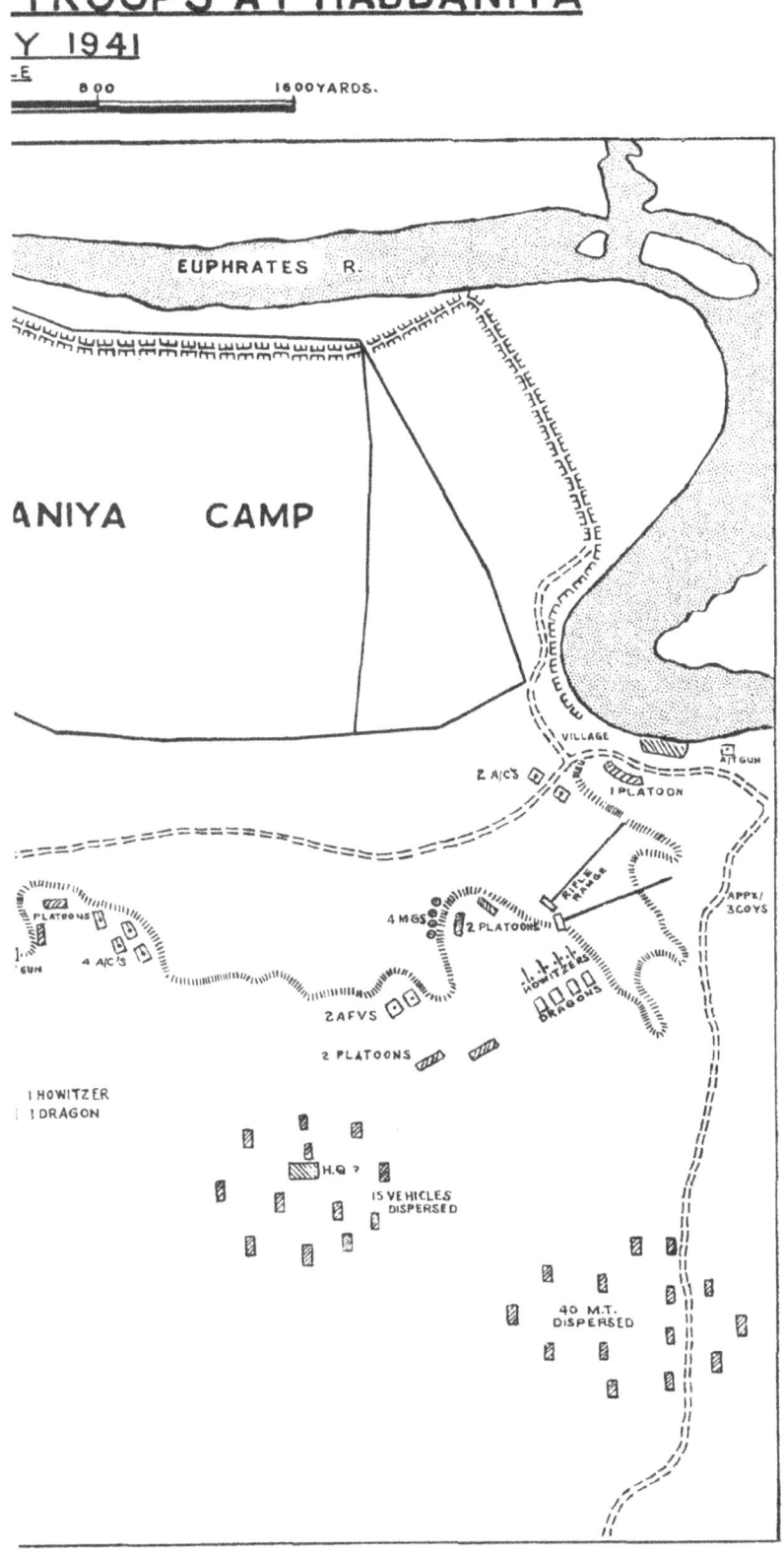

were organised into five squadrons and one flight. Further, there was also No. 244 Bomber Squadron (Vincents) at Shuaiba, which could co-operate in the defence of Habbaniya, if required.

As to the ground forces for the defence of the aerodrome, they numbered 2,000 and were composed of the 1st Battalion the King's Own Royal Regiment (who moved by air from Shuaiba to Habbaniya on 29 April), the Iraq Levies and a company of R.A.F. personnel organised as infantry. All these were placed under the command of Colonel O. L. Roberts, G.S.O. I, 10th Indian Division. The Eighteen Royal Air Force armoured cars provided patrols on the road to Falluja.

The Iraqi Force

As opposed to these forces, the Iraqi force, roughly a brigade in strength, was supported by artillery and some armoured cars. There were also some fifty-seven serviceable aircraft at their disposal. The Iraqi infantry had one great advantage over the British force opposite to them, in that they had taken up a tactically advantageous position on the high ground overlooking the airfield. There, on the plateau, they had mounted their guns and covered the whole of the main airfield and cantonment, at point blank range. At the same time, their armoured cars had taken up positions only about five hundred yards from the edge of the airfield, and their guns were so positioned that they could fire at British aircraft in the act of their landing.

Outbreak of hostilities

Such was the state of affairs on 1 May, when Air Vice-Marshal Smart, after consulting the War Office and the British Ambassador at Baghdad, took the decision to bomb the Iraq force out of its position on the plateau. The Air Officer Commanding-in-Chief ordered eight Wellingtons of No. 70 Squadron to go from Egypt to Shuaiba, to be followed by ten of No. 37 Squadron. The bombing commenced at 0500 hours on 2 May, the attack being made by three squadrons of bombers and one of fighters (Gladiators). The Wellingtons from Shuaiba also co-operated in the attack. It took the Iraqi artillery five minutes to get into action, after which there commenced a furious shelling of the British camp. At first the flashes of the Iraqi guns gave away their positions, which proved easy targets for the British bombers. The pupils of the S.F.T.S., who were acting as bomb aimers and rear gunners, proved surprisingly accurate with their attacks in spite of their lack of experience, and the Wellingtons, with their front and rear guns, were able to take a particularly heavy toll of the Iraqi gun positions and vehicles. But the Iraqi ground fire was both intense and accurate, and soon several British aircraft had bullets through their wings and cockpits, and a number of personnel were wounded. The Wellingtons suffered rather badly; so also the Gordons, which being on the hangars nearest the plateau, had to take the brunt of the Iraqi shelling. In addition to shelling, the Iraqis also bombed the airfield spasmodically. Their Northrops could not be caught by the Gladiators owing to the former's superior speed. The British casualties for the day were two aircraft destroyed in the air and three on the ground, and many others damaged through anti-aircraft fire. A total of 22 British aircraft were out of action. Casualties in personnel were 13 killed and 29 wounded. The Iraqi casualties were very likely much heavier, specially in guns and vehicles.

The main objectives of the British aircraft, for this first day of the Battle of Habbaniya, were the Iraqi guns, armoured cars and armoured fighting vehicles on the plateau. The other objectives were Iraqi aerodromes, road convoys and concentration of Iraqi troops at other places. No. 244 Squadron from Shuaiba, on this first day, co-operated by flying sorties by some seven aircraft, which bombed and cut the railway line at Gubaishiya, 39 miles north-west of Shuaiba, and also destroyed some machine-gun nests.[2]

During the whole of the next day, on 3 May, the British aircraft at Habbaniya, which had been reinforced by the arrival there of four Blenheim IVs from No. 203 General Reconnaissance Squadron, kept up their bombing, while the Iraqi shell fire became less intense. This was no doubt due to increasing casualties among the Iraqi guns. After dark, however, the heavier Iraqi guns opened up and fired intermittently throughout the night. On the same day, three Wellingtons from Shuaiba raided the Rashid aerodrome, south-east of Baghdad, dropping 7100 lbs. of bombs on Iraqi magazine and petrol dumps,[3] and machine-gunning aircraft on the ground. Next day, on 4 May, the Iraqi guns opened up again at dawn, but were soon silenced by the British aircraft taking to air. Throughout that day, the Iraqi air force remained inactive. The British air activity outside Habbaniya, for that day, was an attack on the Rashid aerodrome by eight Wellingtons from No. 37 Squadron which unloaded about 15,700 lbs. of bombs on hangars, workshops and dispersed aircraft.[4] Blenheim fighters of No. 203 Squadron made low-flying machine-gun attacks on Rashid and Baghdad airfields. Six Swordfish of No. 814 Squadron, operating from Shuaiba, bombed a railway bridge four miles above Samawa.

On 5 May, the Iraqi gunners ceased fire altogether except for some intermittent anti-tank and machine-gun fire. That day, the

---

[2] Tel. No. A 462 from Air H.Q. Iraq to Air Minister dated 4.5.1941, *Sabine VI*, p. 40, F. 830.
[3] Tel. A462 dated 4.5.41 from Air H.Q. Iraq to Air Ministry, p. 40, *Sabine VI*, F. 830.
[4] Ibid.

British aircraft maintained continuous air patrols over Iraqi positions, and further bombed and machine-gunned Iraqi gun positions, mechanical transport and personnel.[5] The same day, the King's Own Royal Regiment sent out a fighting patrol of one platoon to deal with an Iraqi post at Sin el Dhibban, four miles downstream of the cantonment, where a river-crossing was being used by the Iraqis for ferrying troops across the Euphrates. The patrol did not achieve any substantial result but succeeded in inflicting some casualties and damaging a few lorries.[6]

Next morning, 6 May, it was discovered that the Iraqi forces had withdrawn from the high ground overlooking the Habbaniya airfield. But the Iraqi post at Sin el Dhibban still remained to be dealt with. The 'D' Company of the King's Own Royal Regiment was ordered to proceed on foot to the village Sin el Dhibban and occupy it. At 1015 hours that morning, the leading troops of the company ran up against some skilfully concealed machine-gun nests, and were obliged to withdraw. They were soon reinforced by a mortar and medium machine-gun detachment of Iraq Levies, and were instructed to attack again in conjunction with the 'B' Company who were to attempt at the same time to take the position from the rear. About two hours later the 'B' Company supported by armoured cars crossed the plateau, from where the Iraqi troops had recently withdrawn, and attacked the position behind Sin el Dhibban at 1450 hours. Thus the Iraqi troops were compelled to retire and the mopping up was in progress when, at 1600 hours, an Iraqi convoy of armoured cars, cavalry and infantry was seen moving from Falluja in the direction of Sin el Dhibban, either to reinforce it or to reoccupy the plateau. This convoy was caught on the road by the R.A.F. and bombed most thoroughly. The bombing lasted about two hours and was so successful that the road became a solid sheet of flame, with ammunition exploding and cars burning by the dozen. The Iraqi column, frustrated and unable to disperse, withdrew in confusion to Falluja and Ramadi suffering very heavy casualties.

This practically ended the fighting at Habbaniya. The plateau overlooking the airfield was taken possession of by the British troops and a serious threat to the British airfield was thus removed, at least for the time being. The airfield, however, continued to suffer for some time from bombing by a handful of Axis aircraft which made a belated appearance a few days later and tried ineffectually to retrieve the situation.

---

[5] Tel. A 469 dated 5.5.1941 from Air H.Q. Iraq, *Sabine VI*, p. 69, F. 830.
[6] *War Diary* 1 King's Own Royal Regiment.

CHAPTER X

Defence of the Basra-Shuaiba area

Shuaiba and the Maqil dock

While the British troops were fighting at Habbaniya, the Indian troops were busy consolidating the Basra-Shuaiba area. When the hostilities broke out on 2 May, Brigadier D. Powell, Commander of the 20th Indian Infantry Brigade Group, decided to concentrate on strengthening his hold over Shuaiba and the Maqil dock area, and to defer the occupation of Ashar (the town part of the port of Basra), till the arrival of reinforcements, which were expected shortly. Shuaiba was important because of its R.A.F. Station and Maqil because of its docks. Accordingly 2/8 Gurkha was posted for the protection of Shuaiba, and 3/11 Sikh for that of Maqil. 2/7 Gurkha was held in reserve. Of these, the task of 3/11 Sikh was more difficult, as there was a certain amount of unrest in the Maqil area. The Sikh battalion was disposed thus:[1]

A Company—Docks; one platoon at post on the river bank, on a corner of the Airport (Civil Landing Ground); and one section at the main Wireless Station.

B Company—Maqil Camp.

C Company—One platoon Makina; one platoon Quramat Ali creek crossing; one platoon Airport.

D Company—Maqil Camp defence; two sections at the Wireless Station.

The Indian troops did not meet with any serious opposition from the regular Iraqi troops in their occupation or garrisoning of Maqil or Shuaiba; nevertheless, some incidents were created in Maqil by the hostile attitude of the people and the civil authorities, who showed their resentment in diverse ways during the whole of the first day of the outbreak of hostilities. Thus, at 1130 hours on 2 May, three R.I.A.S.C. drivers were attacked in the dock area by an Iraqi mob and a lorry was damaged.[2] At 1200 hours, a detachment of 2/7 Gurkha, on protection duties in the docks, was threatened by a yelling crowd, and at 1500 hours, a mob was seen moving from the Zubeila Barracks towards the Maqil Camp, led by the Iraqi troops, and had to be dispersed by the guns of the 3rd Field Regiment R.A., which were then located in the

[1] *War Diary* 3/11 Sikh.
[2] *War Diary* 2/7 G.R.

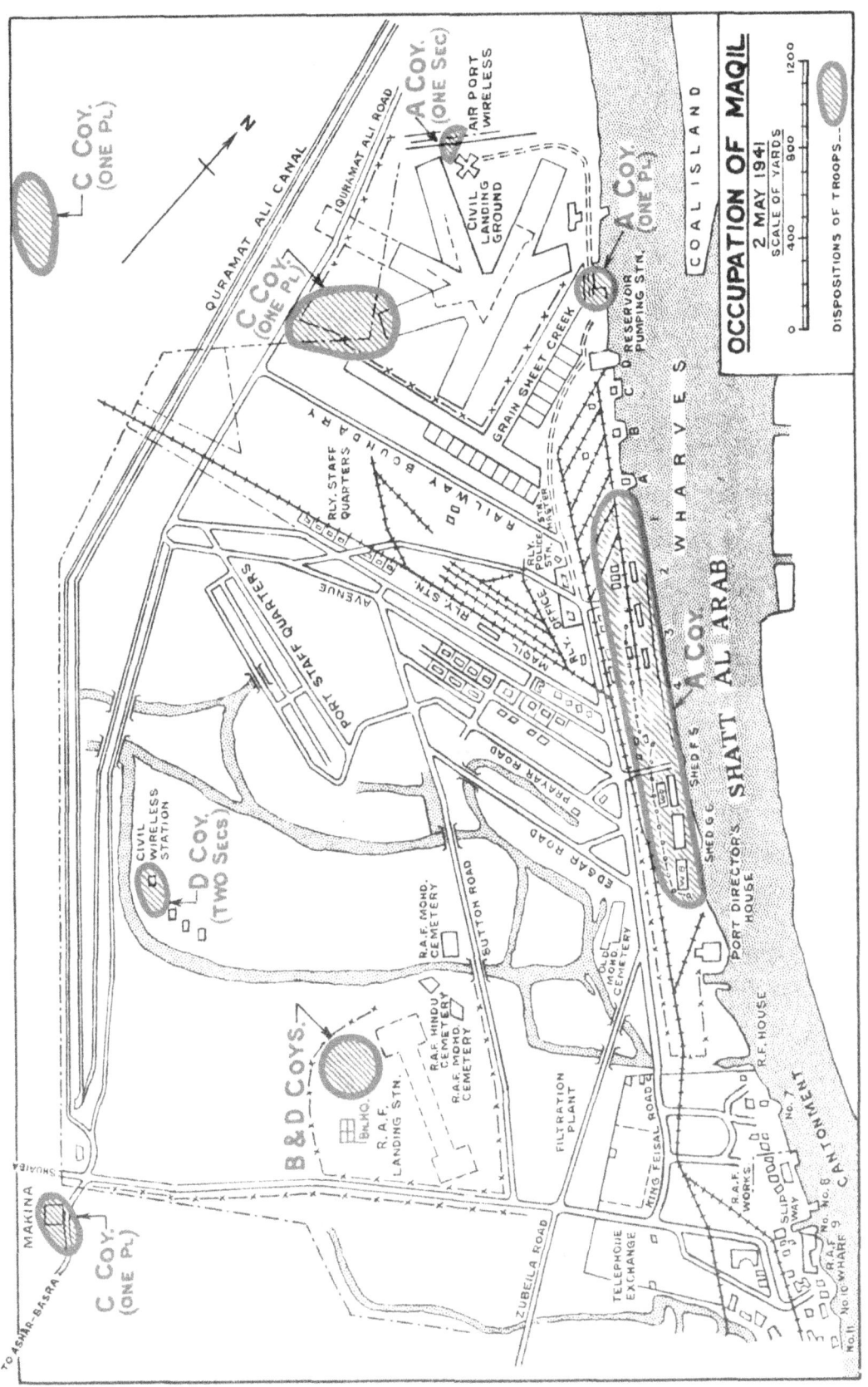

compound of the Makina hospital. The same day, at 1530 hours, the Iraqi Railway Police at the Maqil Railway Station (about fifty rifles) became truculent and surrendered only after some three armoured cars were sent to the Railway Station area to co-operate with a small detachment of 2/7 Gurkha already there. Then, again at 1605 hours, two Vincent aircraft, R.A.F., had to be sent up to bomb the Iraqis, who were in position near the Quramat Ali creek crossing, and who fired at the aircraft, one of which was hit by rifle fire and crashed. In the evening, an Iraqi armoured train was captured by a detachment of 3/11 Sikh, and at 1910 hours the Iraqi Police in the dock area became truculent and had to be disarmed.[3] After this the civil authorities and the population of Maqil gave up resistance and became reconciled to the occupation of their area by the Indian troops. No trouble was experienced in securing Shuaiba, but the bigger problem of securing the control of Ashar still remained to be tackled.

Plan for the occupation of Ashar

On 6 May 1941, the 21st Indian Infantry Brigade, consisting of 4th Battalion 13th Frontier Force Rifles, 2nd Battalion 4th Gurkha Rifles and 2nd Battalion 10th Gurkha Rifles and ancillary troops, arrived at Basra as further reinforcements, and as part of the 10th Indian Division. With the arrival of these troops it was now possible to occupy Ashar.

Major-General Fraser, Commanding British Troops in Iraq, at 1700 hours on 6 May 1941 ordered the 20th Indian Infantry Brigade to secure Ashar. As the brigade had only one battalion (2/7 Gurkha) available for this operation, 3/11 Sikh and 2/8 Gurkha being engaged at Maqil and Shuaiba respectively, the 21st Indian Infantry Brigade was ordered to send one battalion (2/4 Gurkha) to hold the north approaches to Ashar to be ready to support 2/7 Gurkha. The remainder of the 21st Indian Infantry Brigade, as soon as it disembarked, was to hold itself in readiness to reinforce the occupation of Ashar if necessary. 2/7 Gurkha was instructed to occupy the Iraqi naval and military headquarters in the town, as well as the Police Barracks, the Government offices, the Post, Telegraph and Telephone Exchange Offices, and the Eastern Bank, the Ottoman Bank and the Imperial Bank of Iran. The police were to be disarmed. The Rafidain Oil Company depot was already held by one platoon of 2/7 Gurkha.

The battalion plan was for 2/7 Gurkha, with half a section of armoured cars under command, to move against Ashar in two columns—one by the river, consisting of Battalion Headquarters, H.Q. Company, and B and C Companies; and the other by the

[3] *War Diary* 3/11 Sikh and *War Diary* 20 Ind. Inf. Bde.

Lake road, consisting of A and D Companies with three armoured cars. As regards the river column, B Company was to secure the wharf, and C Company was to pass through with all possible speed to secure the first three bridges over the Ashar Creek. Simultaneously, C Company was also to secure and place guards at the three banks and at the Post and Telegraph Offices, and to block the road leading to Basra. The road column, in the meanwhile, was to secure the Power Station and the Government offices and was then to be ready to despatch A Company and armoured cars to capture the Police Station. The arrival of the battalion at Ashar was to be so timed that the river-borne troops would disembark at 0400 hours on 7 May and those moving by land would arrive there soon after.

The following craft were available for the river-borne troops: *Yenan, Rose, Enterprise, Pinnace* and Launch No. 43. *Emerald* and H. M. S. *Falmouth* were to remain in readiness for supporting the operation should there be opposition, the latter occupying a position covering the Ashar Creek. Royal Artillery's Observation Post at Makina Hospital was to maintain continual observation over roads approaching Makina from the direction of Ashar, from 0400 hours on 7 May. Aircraft patrols were to operate over the Ashar area from 0400 hours to 0500 hours and from 0600 to 0700 hours on the same day, and 2/4 Gurkha was to stand in reserve for supporting 2/7 Gurkha,[4] if required.

Occupation of Ashar

2/7 Gurkha moved to Ashar at 0200 hours on 7 May. The object of these operations was to secure the various strategical points before the first light, so that the inhabitants should wake up to find a *fait accompli*. But this plan was based on extremely inaccurate intelligence. Contrary to expectations Ashar proved to be full of sniper's posts, located on the roofs of buildings commanding all principal roads and approaches. The Iraqi troops had anticipated the arrival of the battalion by road, and had posted two Iraqi trucks with light machine-guns to guard the main approach to Ashar from Zubeila. Consequently, although the river column completed its task without opposition, the road column was subjected to considerable fire from the Iraqi trucks. The trucks however managed to escape the heavy fire of the Indian troops and the road column completed its task of occupying the Power Station and Government buildings and compelling the Iraqi police, thirty-two men and two officers, to surrender.

It was, however, found impossible to counteract the fire from the city, along the whole of the Ashar Creek front. Most of this

[4] *War Diary* 20 Ind. Inf. Bde.

fire came from inside the houses and from the roof tops, and could not be countered without a systematic search of all the houses commanding the route, an operation which demanded more troops than were available at that time. Major-General Fraser, therefore, tried to bring the situation under control by getting into touch with the Iraqi officer in charge of Ashar, who was doing his best to stop the sniping. But the efforts of the latter were, at best, only slightly successful, and now and then a fresh burst of firing showed that the snipers had by no means been conciliated. Major-General Fraser, therefore, decided to adopt a sterner attitude and issued an ultimatum that unless firing ceased, orders would be given for the bombardment of the city. His instructions to his troops were to send a feeler patrol into the city, after some time, to test the effect of the ultimatum. Should opposition be met, the patrol was to withdraw immediately, when certain localities would be shelled. This process was to be repeated until a patrol could move into the city without opposition. The first patrol, exclusively of armoured cars, went into the city at 1210 hours and met with no opposition. Next an infantry company went in at 1230 hours and moved through the city without being sniped at or otherwise opposed. The patrolling was repeated at 1600 hours again, with the same result. The occupation of Ashar was then completed without any difficulty. The casualties of the Gurkhas, for the entire action, were 4 killed and 9 wounded.[5]

In order to prevent a recrudescence of trouble the 21st Indian Infantry Brigade was now ordered to reinforce 2/7 Gurkha in Ashar and clear up the outskirts. C Company of 4/13 Frontier Force Rifles moved to the Rafidain Oil Company Depot and took over the defences from 2/7 Gurkha. A few hours later, that is at 2130 hours, the Company Commander received a call for help from Andrew Weir's Wharf, where a disturbance had broken out. Two platoons were ferried across and the third was left at Rafidain Oil Company Depot. The two platoons arrived at Andrew Weir's at about 2300 hours, and while they were landing, five shots were fired at them but no damage was caused. The situation was then quickly brought under control, without any incident.

In order to strengthen the occupation still further 2/4 Gurkha was embarked at Maqil on H. M. S. *Cockchafer* and *Yennan*, at 1430 hours on 7 May, and landed at Gray Mackenzie's Wharf, Ashar, at 1530 hours, entering the city at 0430 hours the next day. The remainder of the 21st Indian Infantry Brigade, consisting of the Brigade Advanced Headquarters, 4/13 Frontier Force Rifles less one company, 2/10 Gurkha, and one company 3/11 Sikh under command, moved to the Zubeila Barracks to clear up the area west

[5] Ibid.

of Ashar. The operation was completed by 1200 hours, a number of Iraqis being arrested for looting.

As the situation in Ashar improved, the 21st Indian Brigade withdrew to Maqil at 1300 hours on the same day (8 May), leaving a detachment of one platoon of 4/13 Frontier Force Rifles at Rafidain Oil Company Depot and one company of 2/10 Gurkha in the Zubeila Barracks.[6] Thus by 8 May the situation in Ashar had been brought fully under control. A day earlier, Lt.-General E. P. Quinan, C.B., D.S.O., O.B.E., had arrived at Basra by air from India, and had taken over command of all the British land forces in Iraq from Major-General Fraser, who resumed command of the 10th Indian Infantry Division.

This marked the end of the first phase of the operations in Iraq, lasting from 2 May to 7 May, during which the Iraqi forces threatening Habbaniya had been routed and the Indian troops had secured a firm hold over the Basra-Shuaiba area.

---

[6] *War Diaries* 2/10 G.R., 2/4 G.R., 21 Bde., 20 Bde, and 10 Div.

CHAPTER XI

Advance of Kingcol to Falluja

The first phase of operations which lasted from 2 to 7 May decided nothing. It is true that the Iraqi force had been driven from Habbaniya and the Indian troops had strengthened their hold over the Basra-Shuaiba area. But this was very nearly the same position as had prevailed before the commencement of the hostilities, and what the operations had achieved was more or less to restore the *status quo*. In fact, the situation had now taken a turn for the worse since there was an open armed conflict between the United Kingdom and Iraq. The question that faced the British Government now was: What was to be the next step? Would it be prudent to be satisfied with the occupation of Habbaniya and Basra or would it be more advisable to proceed further and complete the occupation of the major part of Iraq including Baghdad? General Wavell from the Middle East Command favoured the former course and General Auchinleck the latter, both basing their views on the strategic and tactical necessities in the wider context of winning the World War II. The second phase of operations in Iraq thus started with this controversy and lasted from 8 May to 26 May, during which time the Axis airforce tried to intervene in Iraq and British troops from Palestine began an advance towards Baghdad.

Clash of views between India and Middle East Command

It may be recalled that on the outbreak of hostilities with Iraq on 2 May, the War Office had decided that since the situation in Iraq was not what had been visualised, when India assumed responsibility, the operational command should pass temporarily to the Middle East, whence alone immediate assistance could be given.[1] At the same time the War Office had requested General Wavell to take steps to secure the Basra-Habbaniya line of communications, if possible, by getting the Euphrates tribes to rise in rebellion against Rashid Ali.[2] But General Wavell was by no means happy to have additional responsibilities thrust upon him, and he took the occasion to express his views about the policy that ought

---

[1] Tel. No. 64676 from Troopers to Mideast dated 2.5.1941, *Command of Operations*, p. 23, F. 702.
[2] Tel. No. X 914 from Air Ministry to Middle East dated 2.5.1941, *Sabine II*, p. 1, 21 W.

to be followed in Iraq, in a telegram dated 3 May addressed to the Chief of the Imperial General Staff. He had then estimated that at least a brigade group, with the strongest support of artillery and armoured fighting vehicles, would be required for restoring the situation in Iraq. But he was short of guns and armoured vehicles, and, since it would not do to send forward weak or unsupported forces of cavalry or infantry, he had suggested avoiding military commitments in Iraq and making efforts to establish a friendly government, instead, by direct negotiations.[3] He had also offered to help the negotiations, so far as lay in his power, by creating an impression that a large force was being organised in Palestine for operations in Iraq, so as to induce the Government of Iraq to come to terms quickly.[4] His opinion seemed to be that matters ought never to have been brought to a head by making premature landings in Basra. The War Office had replied to that telegram on 4 May, stating that they felt that a commitment in Iraq was inevitable, and that even if Indian forces had not been sent to Basra, Rashid Ali would still have created trouble,[5] under the instigation of the Axis.

In the meantime, on 3 May, the Turkish Government had made a formal offer of mediation in the Anglo-Iraqi dispute.[6] On 4 May, the British Government had advised the Turkish Government to point out to the Government of Iraq that even if they hoped for Axis armed assistance it would only make matters worse. Iraq would be turned into a battle ground; its cities, and Baghdad in particular, would not escape bombing to which the cities of the belligerent countries had been subjected. Their public works, e.g. the great irrigation works, which had added so greatly to Iraq's prosperity during the past twenty years, would be destroyed. Their great oil industry would receive a serious set-back. Their overseas trade would be completely cut off and their country would relapse into weakness and poverty.[7] The British Government further added that the Turkish Government should realise the absolute necessity of keeping open the lines of communication through Iraq. For that purpose it was essential for the Indo-British troops to remain in Iraq, for protecting the Base and the lines of communication.

The Government of India, under the inspiration of General Auchinleck no doubt, had always favoured a strong line of action

[3] Tel. No. 0/61267 from Middle East for C.I.G.S. dated 3.5.1941, *Sabine II*, p. 10, 21 W.
[4] Tel. No. 0/61447 from Mideast to Troopers dated 3.5.1941, *Sabine II*, p. 12, 21 W.
[5] Tel. No. 65023 of 4 May 41 from Troopers to Mideast, p. 27, F. 702.
[6] Tel. No. 1048 of 3 May 41 from Ambassador Ankara to Foreign Office, p. 26. *Sabine II*, 21 W.
[7] Tel. dated 4 May from S.S. to Viceroy, p. 27, *Sabine II*, 21 W.

in Iraq. Their view-point, as expressed by General Auchinleck, was that any suggestion for negotiations with the Iraq Government, at that stage, would be "hailed as a sign of weakness" throughout the Middle and the Far East and would have a disastrous effect on British prestige in India. They did not think that any Iraqi authority, with whom the British Government might negotiate, would emerge until the British Government had extended their control probably to Baghdad.[8] The Government of India, therefore, opposed mediation by Turkey, in a signal to the War Office, on 5 May, and the idea of mediation was eventually dropped whether for that reason or otherwise.

On the same day, General Wavell once again gave expression to his views about the urgency of resolving the imbroglio in Iraq by negotiations. He solemnly warned the British Government against the prolongation of fighting in Iraq, which he believed would seriously endanger the defence of Palestine and Egypt and produce political repercussions leading to internal troubles all over the Middle East. He, therefore, urged that "settlement should be negotiated as early as possible". At the same time he informed the War Office that, as desired by it, he was arranging to assemble, at H-4, near the Iraq-Transjordan frontier, a force, comprising an incomplete mechanised cavalry brigade, with one field regiment less one troop, fifteen R.A.F. Armoured Cars, three Squadrons of the Transjordan Frontier Force and 1st Battalion the Essex Regiment. He warned, however, that the force would not be ready before 10 May and could not possibly reach Habbaniya till two days later, even if no Iraqi resistance was met at Rutba or elsewhere.[9]

By this time, 7 May, the Iraq air force as well as infantry had suffered a severe reverse at Habbaniya and the first phase of the operations had ended. At the same time General Wavell had assumed operational control over northern Iraq, and was preparing to take over also in southern Iraq. It seemed to General Auchinleck, now, that in conformity with his views, General Wavell would avoid taking a strong line of action in Iraq, which would give enough time to Rashid Ali to recover from his surprise and to the Axis for organising an intervention. Although no longer in the picture, due to his not being in command of operations in Iraq, he decided to continue to impress his views on the Chief of the Imperial General Staff. Accordingly, on 9 May, he represented that although the operational control of Iraq had passed to the Middle East, it was

---

[8] Tel. No. 2729 from Defence Department to S.S. dated 5.5.1941, *Sabine II*, p. 24, 21 W.
[9] Tel. No. 0/61872 from Mideast to Troopers dated 5.5.1941, *Sabine II*, p. 31, 21 W.

impossible for India "to dissociate herself from the formulation of policy in that area". Not only was "success or failure in Iraq vital to the safety of India, but most of the forces and material employed in that theatre, must come from India". In his opinion, British control of Iraq was necessary to avert an ultimate threat to India. Hence he deprecated a mere passive defence of Basra and advocated a more forward policy. He emphasised the fact that, at that moment, the Iraqi forces had suffered a serious set-back at Habbaniya, were short of ammunition and indecisive of purpose, and that it was therefore a rare opportunity for carrying out a bold and vigorous policy of military occupation of Baghdad, Mosul, Kirkuk and other key points, so as to be able to resist any attack, internal or external, by the Axis. Only by such a policy of effective occupation of Iraq would the security of Egypt and Palestine be assured and oil supplies saved.[10]

In opposition to this view was that of General Wavell, which was once again expressed on 10 May in no less emphatic terms. To General Wavell, whose time and attention were then being monopolised by the vital campaigns in Africa, the fighting that had started in Iraq was a distraction and a nuisance; and he could hardly conceal his irritation at India's advocacy of bolder action in Iraq. He declared that at that critical moment, it was essential for him to concentrate his limited resources on really vital military interests. In Iraq there were only four such interests, (*i*) avoidance of a major conflict with the Arabs, (*ii*) security of the oil supplies from Iraq, (*iii*) safety of Abadan and (*iv*) maintenance of the air route to India. All these were of minor importance as compared with the security of Egypt and Palestine. The policy advocated by the Government of India, he feared, would lead to a large-scale Arab uprising against the British in Iraq. That would have repercussions in Palestine, Aden, Yemen, Egypt and Syria, which might absorb a very large proportion of the Middle East Force in maintaining internal order. Nor would that policy achieve its primary aim of preserving the supply of oil to Haifa, since that depended on the goodwill of Iraq. At that time, the Iraqis were in a position to destroy the refineries and cut off the oil supply, and it would be an illusion to imagine that a long and vulnerable line of supply would be secured by a military occupation of Iraq. The security of the Abadan refinery, likewise, depended on a strong anti-aircraft defence of Abadan and the Shatt al Arab, which was difficult to provide. As to India's anxiety about its own safety, General Wavell pointed out that the air route to India had been already made secure by the occupation of Habbaniya and Basra; and the

[10] Tel. No. 5412/G from Armindia to Troopers dated 9.5.1941, *Sabine II*, p. 58, 21 W.

threat of invasion of India by the Axis was too remote a possibility to be considered seriously, especially in view of the strained relations between Germany and Russia. Even granting that the Axis succeeded in securing a passage through Turkey, it was more likely that it would use that facility to invade Palestine and Egypt via Syria, rather than move toward India via Iraq. The occupation of Baghdad offered no worth while tactical or political advantage to the Allies, except that of being able to establish a more friendly government in Iraq, and even then that aim would be more easily achieved from northern Palestine than from Basra, which had the additional disadvantage of having vulnerable lines of communication passing through tribal territories.[11] General Wavell, therefore, advocated avoidance of heavy military commitments in non-vital areas and recommended that a political solution be sought by all available means. He was even in favour of coming to an agreement with Rashid Ali or the Iraq army provided they agreed (*i*) to release the British Ambassador and staff, who had been virtually imprisoned in the Embassy grounds,[12] (*ii*) to rehoist the British flag there, (*iii*) to honour the Anglo-Iraqi treaty, (*iv*) to the occupation of certain key points by the British, and (*v*) to hand over all aviation petrol then in their hands.[13]

The views thus expressed by General Wavell had been forwarded to the Government of India for their reactions and had reached them the same day as they reached the Chief of the Imperial General Staff. On the following day and the day after, the Government of India came out with a fresh expression of their views which were more or less a re-elaboration of their earlier statements. They, generally, declared themselves as being against any negotiation with, or recognition of, Rashid Ali whom they suspected to be an agent of the Axis Powers. They held that, on military grounds, the maintenance of Rashid Ali in power would prove a serious menace to India, as that would facilitate Axis control not only of Iraq but also of Iran and Afghanistan. Nor would it improve matters even if a pro-British government was installed in Iraq. For, an Arab government in Iraq, however friendly to the British Government in the beginning, could not be relied upon to stand firm against the methods of subversion and penetration so successfully practised by the Axis in other countries, unless closely watched and supported by the British Government at all important strategic points.[14]

After considering the divergent views expressed by Generals

---

[11] Tel. No. 0/63234 from Mideast to Troopers dated 10.5.1941, *Sabine II*, p. 76.
[12] John Bagot Glubb: *The Story of the Arab Legion*, p. 299.
[13] Tel. No. 0/63340 of 10 May 41 from Mideast to General Basra, *Sabine II*, p. 78.
[14] Tel. No. 2850 of 12 May 41 from Defence Simla to S.S., *Sabine II*, p. 86.

Wavell and Auchinleck the British Government adopted a course of action which was more in conformity with India's views. They rejected the idea of coming to terms with Rashid Ali, and at the same time it was suggested to the two commanders that they should meet in a conference at Basra to discuss their differences and evolve a common plan of action. But due to the preoccupations of one or the other commander the meeting did not take place till 24 May. In the meanwhile it was decided that a British force should move from Palestine to Habbaniya and thence, if the situation permitted, to Baghdad; while at the same time, the Indian troops should secure the Base at Basra and endeavour to establish good relations with the tribes, in preparation for a move to Baghdad at a later date.

The Striking Force from Palestine

On resuming operational control of northern Iraq on 5 May 1941, General Wavell had ordered General Headquarters Palestine and Transjordan, to prepare a mobile force, to be known as 'Habforce', for operations in Iraq. The force was to consist of a mechanised cavalry brigade, three mechanised squadrons of the Transjordan Frontier Force, a Desert Patrol of the Arab Legion, 1st Battalion Essex Regiment, one Field Regiment less one troop, and attached troops.[15] The move to Habbaniya involved a march of five hundred miles across the desert, which called for an entirely motorised force. But such a force could not easily be raised. The 1st Cavalry Division which was engaged on internal security duties in Palestine had been denuded, not only of vehicles, but also of supporting arms, and even of signals for operations in Greece and North Africa.[16] However, General Sir H. M. Maitland Wilson, who assumed command in Palestine and Transjordan on 7 May, acted with resourcefulness and energy, and succeeded in assembling a fully mobile force—the Habforce—under the command of Major-General J. G. W. Clark, which consisted of Headquarters 1st Cavalry Division, 4th Cavalry Brigade (commanded by Brigadier J. J. Kingstone, D.S.O.), a mechanised regiment of the Transjordan Frontier Force, the Arab Legion, the 1st Battalion of the Essex Regiment, 60th Field Regiment R. A. less one troop, a Squadron of Armoured Cars R. A. F., and other troops.

A flying column, commanded by Brigadier Kingstone and known as Kingcol, was detached from the Habforce and made to go ahead so as to reach Habbaniya, as quickly as possible. This column consisted of Headquarters and Signals 4th Cavalry Brigade, the Household Cavalry Regiment, two companies of the Essex

---

[15] Tel. No. 0/61872 from Mideast to Troopers dated 5.5.1941, *Sabine II*, p. 31.
[16] *Wavell*, File 9537, p. 112.

Regiment, a carrier platoon, a battery of the 60th Field Regiment R. A., an Anti-Tank Troop R. A., a troop of Cheshire Field Squadron R. E., and ancillary troops.

Rutba

The immediate objective of Kingcol was the fort of Rutba, which it was essential to capture for clearing the way to Habbaniya, the destination of Habforce. Rubta was attacked on 9 May and captured on the 11th, but not without a disproportionately strong effort, considering that it had a garrison of only about a hundred Iraqi policemen. The preparations for the attack had started on 5 May with movements of detachments of Kingcol, first to H-4 and then to H-3. When the attack was put in finally, on the 9th, it was supported by four Blenheim bombers and two Blenheim fighters and had the co-operation of a detachment of the Arab Legion, under the command of Colonel John Bagot Glubb, known to the Arabs as Glubb Pasha. The attack was ineffective. Three British aircraft were damaged by Iraqi rifle fire, and in spite of about 200 men of the Arab Legion, who had established a base about three miles from Rutba, the garrison of the fort succeeded in getting a reinforcement in the shape of a relief column of 40 trucks, armed with machine-guns, and filled with Iraqi police and followers of Fawzi Qawukji, a reputed guerilla leader and an old opponent of the British. On the morning of 10 May, Fawzi Qawukji's men fought an indecisive action outside the walls of Rutba against the armoured cars of the Kingcol, after which they evacuated the fort during the night which was occupied by the forward detachments of Kingcol on 11 May.[17] The rest of the Kingcol followed up during 13-14 May, and the move towards Habbaniya was resumed, with the main body of Habforce coming behind to take over the line of communication as far as Rutba.

At this stage, the Government of Iraq decided to flood the countryside in an effort to cut the way between Rutba and Habbaniya. The Euphrates and the Tigris were in high flood during this part of the year, and the Iraqi engineers made full use of the season to produce inundations across the vital roads, by cutting the river bunds at various places. The road to Habbaniya lay via Ramadi, but Ramadi was now completely isolated by water and the road Rutba—Ramadi—Habbaniya had become impassable, the more so because of the bridge at Suttaih, midway between Ramadi and Habbaniya, having been effectively blown up. There was, however, an alternative route to Habbaniya, across the Mujara canal,

---

[17] John Bagot Glubb: *The Story of the Arab Legion*, pp. 258-67.

which, though also under floods, due to the engineers having opened a floodgate known as the 'Mujara cut', was still capable of being bridged. The work of bridging was entrusted to a section of 10th Field Company, Q. V. O. Madras Sappers and Miners— approximately sixty men, who were specially brought there by air on 10 May. The idea was to keep the bridge ready before the arrival of the Kingcol at that spot, so as to avoid delay in crossing. The construction of the bridge proved a very difficult job due to the swiftness of the current of water in the Mujara canal. The work was nevertheless completed in time and the bridge was ready by 17 May, when the head of Kingcol arrived at the spot.

Advance to Habbaniya

Kingcol had left Rutba for Habbaniya, on 15 May, the Arab Legion leading the way. The destination was 'Kilo 25', a point about 15 miles west of Ramadi. On the way it was machine-gunned and bombed by German aircraft, which attacked with impunity as the column possessed no weapons for dealing with that form of attack.

After reaching Kilo 25, it became necessary for the column to leave the Haifa—Baghdad road and move south-east along a track fit for heavy transport. But after the column had moved a little further along that way, it found itself in difficulty due to heavy lorries sinking in the soft sand. These had to be dug out with great effort, in a temperature which was about 120° in the shade, and it seemed as if, with further progress, the column would either get wholly 'bogged' or not be able to complete its march in the scheduled time. This latter circumstance threatened to wreck the whole operation since the supplies of water and fuel were sufficient only for 36 hours, at the end of which the column would have had to return to Rutba or run the risk of being stranded in the desert without food and water. Fortunately for Kingcol, a patrol of the Arab Legion, carrying out reconnaissance, discovered a more suitable route on 17 May, and on the 18th the whole force crossed the Mujara bridge and arrived at Habbaniya. Only one incident had occurred on the way: the tail of the column had been machine-gunned by German aircraft, resulting in a few casualties. The arrival of Kingcol was a welcome relief to the garrison of Habbaniya, for although the latter had driven out the Iraqi force on the plateau, the threat to Habbaniya had not been altogether eliminated. An Iraqi brigade which had established itself in a menacing position up the Euphrates at Ramadi still remained to be dealt with; and there was also a considerable Iraqi force downstream at Falluja.

Preparations for the capture of Falluja

The capture of Falluja was an essential preliminary to the capture of Baghdad, since it controlled the road to the latter city. After the arrival of Kingcol at Habbaniya, on 18 May, preparations were made for an advance on Baghdad, and it was decided to take the main road from Habbaniya which followed the west bank of the Euphrates and led by a steel-girder bridge to Falluja, from where Baghdad was only thirty miles away. But the Iraqi engineers had cut the dykes of the Euphrates, and flooded the country around Falluja, thus creating difficulties in the way of Kingcol advancing towards Baghdad. These dykes or bunds had been originally built to prevent the flooded waters of the Euphrates from overflowing into the surrounding country. One of these was the Hammond Bund and the second the Takiya Bund and there were also two regulators—at Saqlawiya and Notch Fall—for controlling the overflow. The Takiya Bund and the Saqlawiya Regulator had been opened up to flood the main road Habbaniya-Falluja and a wide breach had been made in Hammond's Bund to cut the road Haifa-Falluja. Fortunately, the Iraqis did not demolish the steel-girder bridge over the Euphrates, which gave access to Falluja, which was possibly due to their policy of restricting the demolitions to easily repairable structures only.

Colonel Roberts, who had assumed command of the Habbaniya garrison, had prepared a plan for the capture of Falluja, which was put into effect on the arrival of Kingcol at Habbaniya. Major-General Clark, Commanding Habforce, had arrived at Habbaniya on 18 May, flying from his advanced headquarters at H-4, and taken command of the operations. Air Vice-Marshal H. d'Albiac, the successor to Air Vice-Marshal Smart (who had been wounded in a car accident on 15 May), also arrived on the same day to find everything ready for an advance on Falluja. It was now vitally necessary to prevent the Iraqis from destroying the steel-girder bridge and, therefore, it was decided that the troops should move under cover of darkness at night and attack and capture the bridge as well as the town, subsequent to a heavy air attack. As to the obstacles created by the flooding of the country around Falluja, two steps had already been taken to overcome the difficulty. Firstly, a ferry had been constructed at Sin el Dhibban village, four miles downstream of the Cantonment, by a section of No. 10 Field Company, Q.V.O. Madras Sappers and Miners, so that a force might cross to the left bank, pass through the village of Saqlawiya and attack Falluja. At the same time boats, which were used for rowing and sailing on the Habbaniya lake, were brought to the Hammond's Bund for negotiating the gap, which had been created by the flood waters.

Plan of Operations

The attack on Falluja was to be carried out by five detachments of the British force, which also included a company each from 2/4 Gurkha and the King's Own Royal Regiment. These detachments were to be in position before 0500 hours when the air offensive was to begin. A force, organised into three columns, 'A', 'S' and 'L', was to cross by the Sin el Dhibban ferry to the left bank and attack Falluja from that direction. This force comprised a company of the Iraqi Levies, a company of 2/4 Gurkha, R.A.F. armoured cars and some 3.7-inch howitzers. The objectives of column 'A' were firstly the Saqlawiya Regulator and secondly the high ground to the north of Falluja, covering the exits from the outskirts of the town. 'S' column was to move behind 'A' column, as a possible reinforcement. 'L' column was to establish a ferry across the Notch Fall Regulator and thus provide a line of withdrawal, in case of emergency. In addition to this force operating on the left bank of the Euphrates, a company of the King's Own Royal Regiment, comprising 'V' column, was to be flown to a position, across the track leading from Falluja to Notch Fall Regulator so as to give cover to the main road to Baghdad. The frontal advance was to be made by 'G' column, under the command of Captain A. Graham. This detachment, comprising a company of the Iraq Levies and a battery of 3.7-inch howitzers, was to cross the gap in Hammond's Bund by boats and be in position in a palm grove, adjoining the main road, about a mile from the Falluja bridge, which it was to seize intact. Each column was to have a detachment of Queen Victoria's own Madras Sappers and Miners.

Finally, a detachment of the Royal Engineers from 'Kingcol' was to assist the Indian Sappers and Miners in maintaining the Sin el Dhibban ferry, in reconstructing Hammond's Bund where breached, and in providing ferries at Saqlawiya and Notch Fall Regulators.[18]

Attack on Falluja

The preliminaries to the attack on Falluja began on 18 May 1941, the Royal Air Force bombing various points in the town of Falluja and on the Baghdad—Falluja road beyond. The first movement of the troops began at dusk. The 'G' column successfully crossed the gap in the Hammond's Bund, though some vehicles were "ditched", and took up its position in the palm grove adjoining the main road, at a distance of about a mile from the Falluja bridge. The company of the King's Own Royal Regiment was also flown to its appointed position according to schedule. However, the columns 'A', 'S', and 'L' failed to be in position in time, due

---

[18] *War Diary* 1 King's Own Royal Regiment.

ATTACK ON

18–23 MA

SCAL

MILE 1 0 1

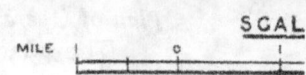

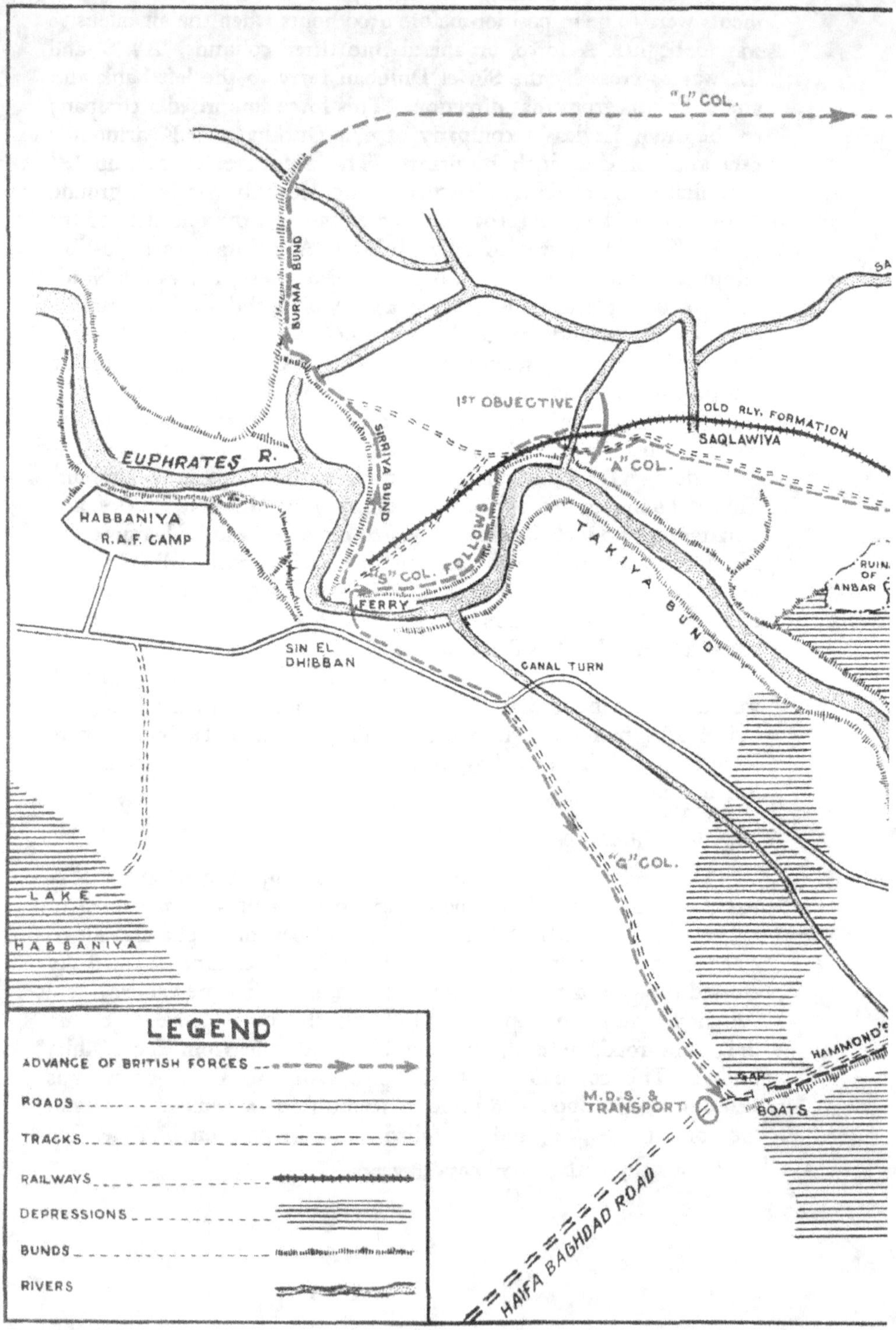

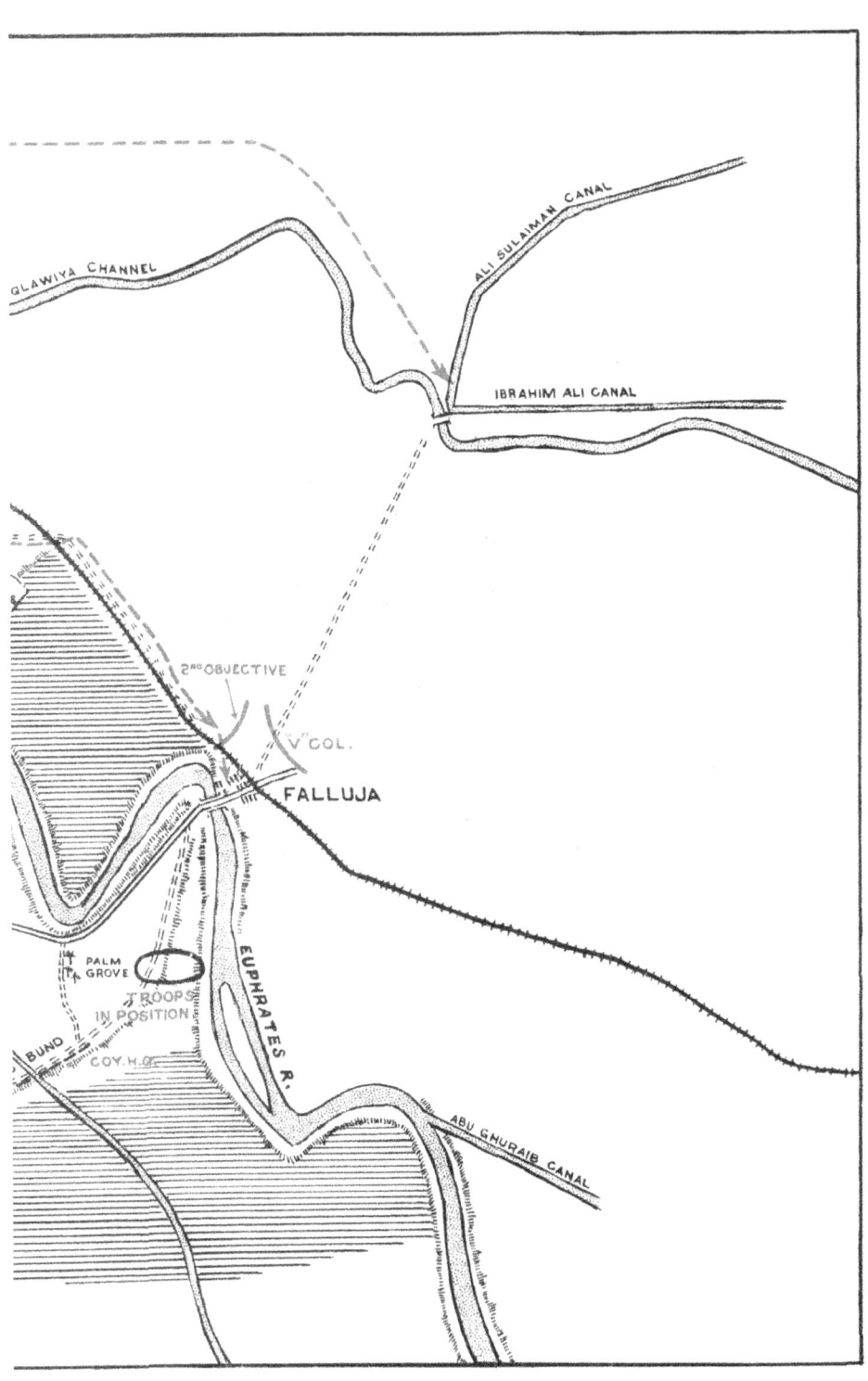

to delay caused by their having to cross several canals and irrigation channels. This force which was to operate on the left bank of the Euphrates, therefore, arrived too late in its position to take part in the action.

The attack by the Royal Air Force, in and about Falluja, commenced at 0500 hours on 19 May as scheduled, and was sustained until 0900 hours. After a lull, there was another heavy air attack at 1445 hours. All air operations ceased at 1500 hours, after which the 'G' column was ordered to attack the bridge, which was captured without any opposition, and the column entered the town where it began to dig in. Iraqi resistance had been largely broken by the air attacks.

The Iraqi troops now made determined efforts to recover Falluja. A brigade of infantry moved out from Baghdad and came into action on the morning of 22 May. It attacked the company of the King's Own Royal Regiment on the north-eastern side of the town and forced it to seek shelter in houses. Two Iraqi light tanks, which entered the streets, were however put out of action, and the situation was restored when the 'G' column counter-attacked and drove back the Iraqis. The latter repeated their attack at first light the next day, this time against a second company of the King's Own Royal Regiment, which had been brought up earlier into Falluja, and which was occupying a position to the south of the first company. This attack was heavier than the previous one and at first the British troops had to yield some ground. But the situation changed as the British columns re-organised and stiffened their resistance. Finally, the Iraqi troops withdrew from Falluja on 23 May, thus uncovering the road to Baghdad.

CHAPTER XII

Axis Intervention

The second phase of the operations in Iraq, which lasted from 8 May to 26 May, was marked not only by the advance of Kingcol from Palestine and capture of Falluja, but also by Axis intervention in Iraq and a movement of Indian troops towards Baghdad.

The Vichy French in Syria had allowed the Axis full use of their aerodromes. As a result a few German aircraft arrived at Mosul sometime between 8 and 10 May, which were later reinforced by more until they totalled about fifty. They began bombing and strafing the British camp at Habbaniya from 13 May and, as we have seen, had also paid some attention to Kingcol during its advance from Transjordan to Falluja. Before the arrival of the German aircraft, however, the Royal Air Force had struck hard at the Iraqi aerodromes of Baquba, Rashid, Shahraban, Washash, Musaiyib and Mosul, and had destroyed and damaged so many aircraft that the Iraq Air Force had practically ceased to exist as an effective fighting force. It was therefore all the easier for the Royal Air Force to deal with the German aircraft when the latter made their appearance in northern Iraq. Thus, while the Axis aircraft turned their attention to the Habbaniya airfield, the Royal Air Force directed their attacks mainly against Mosul, Erbil and Rashid, which served as bases for the Axis aircraft. At no stage was the German intervention in Iraq very effective. This was possibly due to the fact that Major Axel von Blomberg, who had been sent to Iraq to organise air operations, was killed when an Iraqi tribesman fired at his aeroplane as it was landing at the Baghdad aerodrome. From that time on, the Axis air activity in Iraq had remained at a low level. The highest number of sorties by the German aircraft, on any one day, it is said, did not exceed six and the average per day was only about one and a half. The total number of their aircraft was never more than fifty. It is not to be wondered at, therefore, that after attacking Habbaniya a few times, and causing the maximum damage they could, they finally withdrew from Iraq on 2 June 1941, abandoning the field to the British.[1]

Operations of the 10th Indian Division

The capture of Falluja by Kingcol and the defeat of the Axis

[1] Air Ministry Weekly Intelligence Summary No. 104 of 1941.

air force brought to a conclusion the second phase of operations in Iraq. In another sector, the Indian forces had established a base at Basra and made it secure by occupying the strategic areas in its vicinity. This force consisted of the 20th and the 21st Indian Infantry Brigades and Headquarters of the 10th Indian Division. Henceforth the activities of the 10th Indian Division were mainly concerned with the defence of the Basra-Shuaiba area, which also included the town of Ashar. The main object of the division was to mop up the remaining pockets of Iraqi resistance and to guard all roads of approach against a possible attack on the area of occupation by the Iraqi army or the tribal forces. Fear of attack from any other source was rather remote.

The area to be defended was divided between the 20th and 21st Indian Brigades by a demarcation line running from Maqil to Zubeila via Makina and Ashar. Roughly, the 20th Indian Brigade was responsible for the defence west of this line and the 21st to its east.

Defence of Shuaiba

The defence of Shuaiba was the task of the 20th Indian Infantry Brigade. The most important point to be defended in this area was the R.A.F. enclosure. The Brigade set about to prepare an all round defensive position consisting of a barbed wire perimeter around the R.A.F. enclosure and the landing ground. This perimeter, which had a radius of about one mile, was garrisoned by 2/7 and 2/8 Gurkha Rifles and the 3rd Field Regiment R.A. (less one battery). On its external periphery, it was protected by seven medium machine-gun posts of which three also had two anti-tank guns each. The anti-tank guns were mostly on the western periphery where the defences were the strongest, due to the fear of an atatack by the Iraqi army from that direction. Inside the defended area there were three more barbed wire fencings, one enclosed the area of 3rd Field Regiment R.A. and the Brigade Headquarters, and another covered the western flank of the R.A.F. enclosure; while the third, running north to south, provided an extra barrier on the west of the R.A.F. enclosure, in case the western periphery be broken through. A further precaution against such a contingency was the provision of eight additional anti-tank guns inside the defended area.

The whole perimeter was divided into two sectors. The northern sector was assigned to 2/7 Gurkha and the southern to 2/8. The 3rd Field Regiment R.A. (less one troop) was positioned between the two, so as to be able to support the defence of either by observed fire. The 2/7 and 2/8 Gurkha were to keep a minimum reserve of one company each for use within the defended area; and

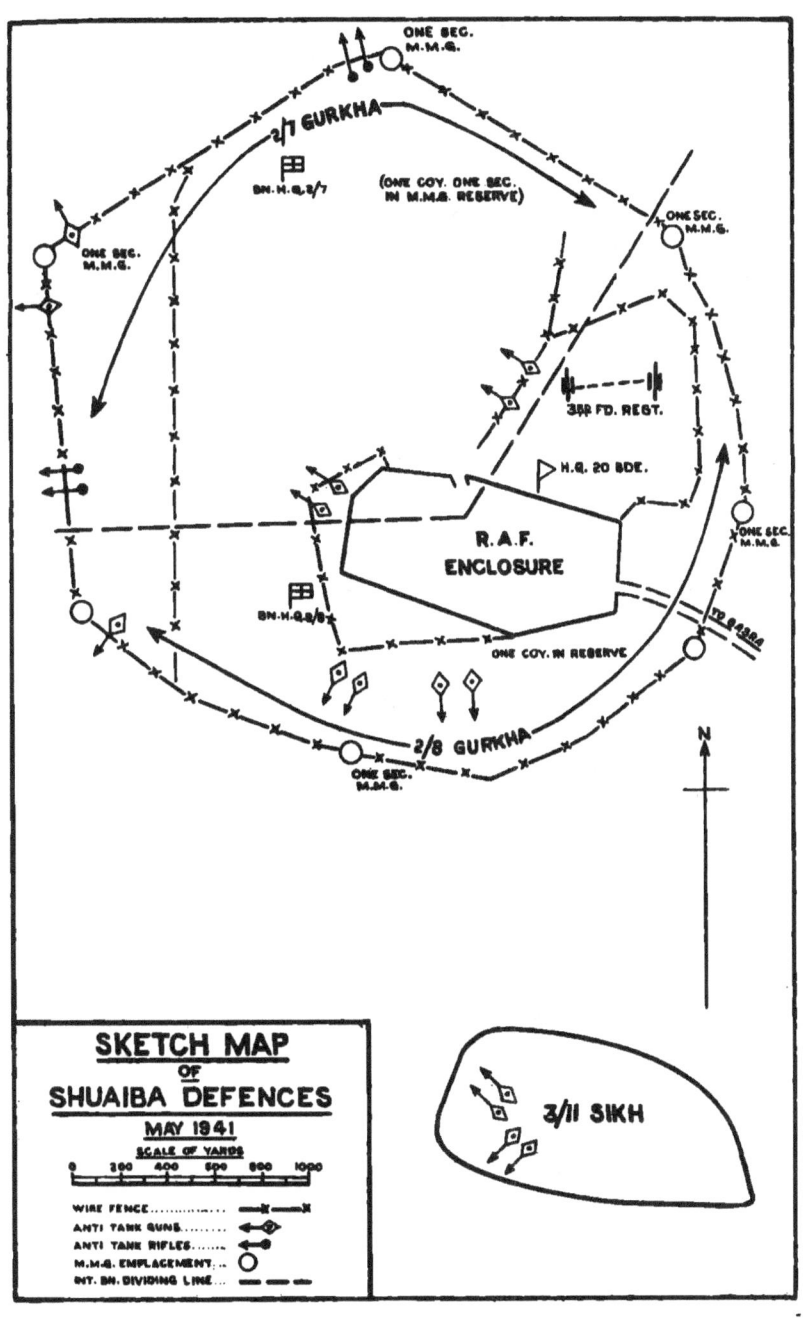

personnel of all other units were, likewise, to be available as local reserves in their own vicinity. The rest of the forces, except in an emergency, were apparently not to remain confined to the perimeter area but might be employed elsewhere.

Outside this main defended area was another defended locality occupied by 3/11 Sikh. This position was 1000 yards south of the main position, which was also prepared for an all-round defence, with two anti-tank gun emplacements on the western edge and two to the south. The Sikhs were to play a mobile offensive role; hence their location outside the main defended area.

To complete an all round defence of Shuaiba it was also necessary to guard against surprise Iraqi attacks from outside the perimeter, across the open and vulnerable territory from At Tuba to Kuwait, which was easily passable by mechanical transport. A part of this territory was occupied by a belt of tamarisk groves, extending from Chuwaibda to Al Najmi on the Kuwait road. Hence the importance of controlling these two places. To the west and south of these groves the country was open and flat and passable for mechanical transport. But it was waterless, except for some water-holes near Safwan. The only feature here of any prominence was the Jebel Sanam, eighteen miles south-west of Zubair. This hill afforded a clear observation and also guarded the water-holes of Safwan. Hence it was necessary to occupy both Safwan and Jebel Sanam. Another place in this part of the territory which also had to be occupied was Ar Rafaiya, an Iraqi police post with a wireless telephone set and one or more machine-guns, situated on one of the approaches to Shuaiba. It was capable of being reinforced by Iraqi troops and therefore dangerous. Much further north, to the north-east of At Tuba, was Ar Rumaila, which also had to be guarded to prevent the Iraqis from damaging the railway line.

All those places, Jebel Sanam, Chuwaibda, Safwan, Ar Rafaiya and Ar Rumaila, were occupied without opposition. Jebel Sanam was taken over by a patrol of two companies of 3/11 Sikh, on 14 May, with one section medium machine-guns, three armoured cars and ancillary units. The same day Chuwaibda was occupied by a large reconnaissance party of 2/7 Gurkha consisting of two motorized companies, a detachment of Royal Engineers, 26th Field Ambulance and one company Iraq Levies. Next day a platoon from the detachment of 3/11 Sikh at Jebel Sanam established itself at Safwan. The occupation of Ar Rafaiya followed three days later, when a detachment of two companies of 2/8 Gurkha left Shuaiba at 0430 hours on 18 May, and took possession of the locality and of the police post which had been evacuated a day earlier.

BASRA AREA

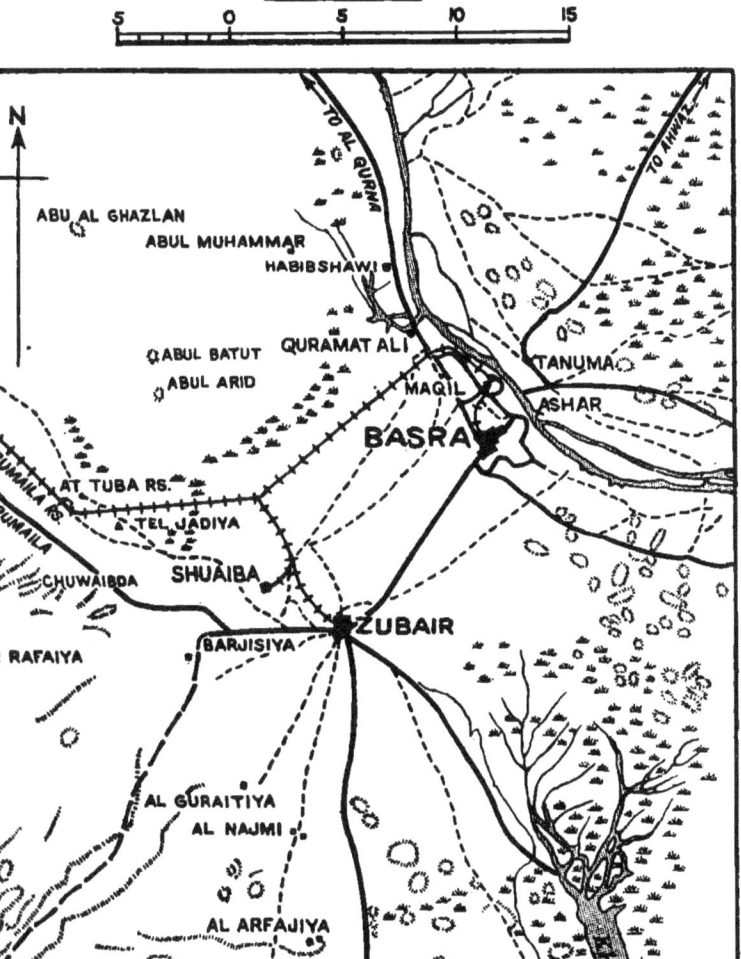

Defence of Basra

According to the division of the areas of responsibility mentioned earlier, the 20th Indian Infantry Brigade was responsible for Shuaiba and the area to its west, and the 21st for Basra and its vicinity. To guard against surprise Iraqi attacks in the Basra area, the 21st Indian Infantry Brigade found it necessary to clear up two points, the Tanuma Barracks and Habibshawi, not far from the town. Iraqi troops were suspected to have retired from Basra to the Tanuma Barracks, across the Shatt al Arab. However, they vacated the barracks on the approach of the Indian troops. A fighting patrol of 2/10 Gurkha, one company of 4/13 Frontier Force Rifles, one troop 65/75 Field Battery and a mortar detachment of Iraq Levies, embarked in *Yomah, Rose* and other barges at Maqil at 0400 hours on 16 May and occupied Tanuma Barracks at 0645 hours. The troops re-embarked at 1130 hours on the same day and returned to Maqil.[2]

In case of Habibshawi, however, opposition was met with from about a hundred men of Iraqi police who were garrisoned in that place. The threat which this position was holding out to Basra became clear when a patrol of one platoon of 2/4 Gurkha was sent to the Broken Bridge in the Habibshawi area, as an escort for a Royal Engineer, who was to reconnoitre the bridge. The patrol came under heavy fire some three hundred yards south of the bridge and suffered two casualties.[3] Since the road was also under flood water further advance was not possible, and the patrol retired without completing its mission. Thereupon Major-General W. J. Slim, who had succeeded Major-General Fraser in command of the 10th Indian Division, ordered Brigadier C. J. Weld, commanding 21st Indian Infantry Brigade, to attack and disperse the Iraqi police and troops in Habibshawi. The latter detailed 2/4 Gurkha for this task, who were also to have a sub-section of armoured cars, a troop of 157th Field Regiment R.A., and Royal Engineer and Field Ambulance detachments under command. The plan was to land river-borne troops in the vicinity of Habibshawi Creek and at the same time to make a holding attack by road on the area round the Broken Bridge. The object of the operation was to clear up the area to the north and south of the Habibshawi Creek and capture the Broken Bridge.[4] Thus B Company, one platoon and one section of 2/4 Gurkha, one sub-section armoured cars, one section 157th Field Regiment R.A., a detachment of Royal Engineers and a detachment of Field Ambulance, constituting the 'Landforce' was to advance north from the Girder Bridge at 0300 hours on 24 May

---

[2] *War Diaries* 4/13 Frontier Force Rifles and 2/10 G.R.
[3] *War Diary* 2/4 G.R.
[4] The operation was given the code-name 'Scoop'.

ATTACK ON HABIBSHAWI

24 MAY 1941

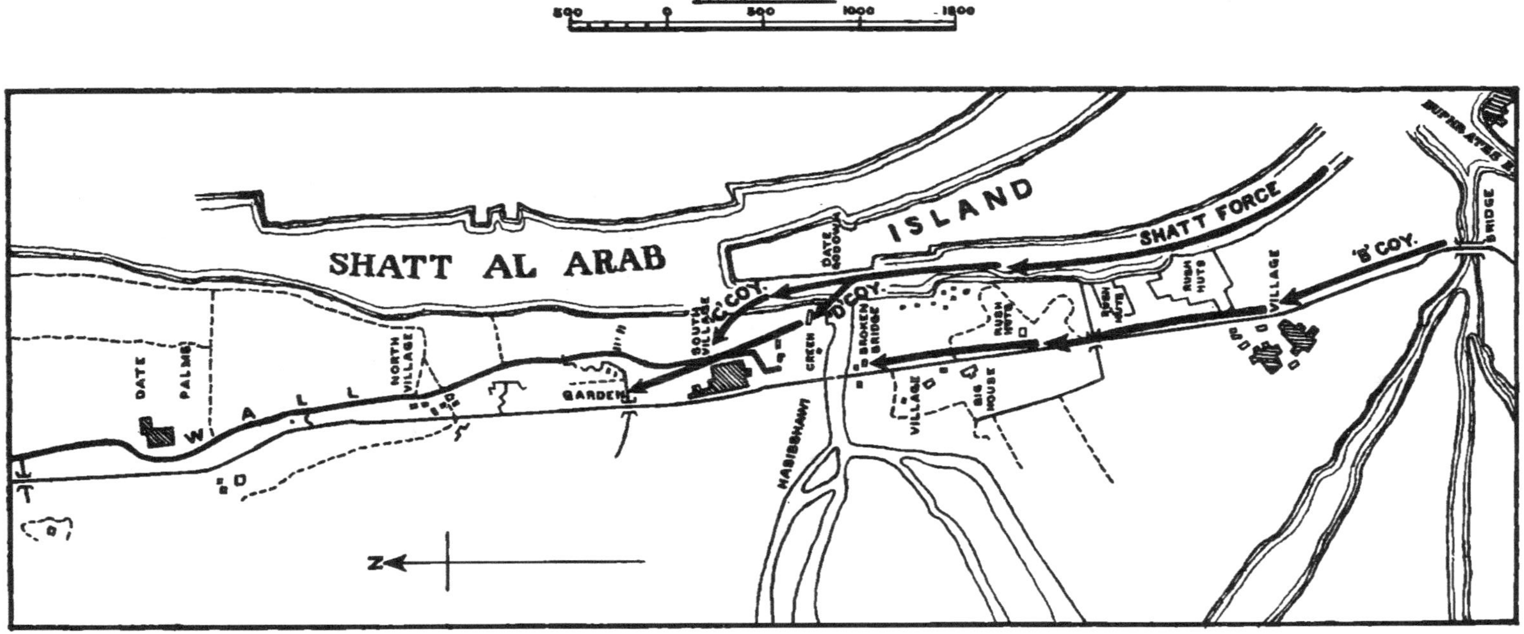

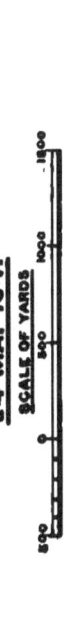

and reach the area south of Habibshawi Creek by 0400 hours. Almost simultaneously, a flanking attack was to be made on Big House by 'Shattforce'—the river-borne troops. H.M.S. *Yarra*, assisted by the tugs *Souriya* and *Shamal*, with one pontoon and R.A.F. Motor Launch, was to carry C and D Companies of 2/4 Gurkha and two sections machine-guns, up the river from Maqil. En route, it was to take up a position in the stream between Big House and Date Godown, from 0400 hours to 0415 hours. Immediately on the cessation of fire, at 0415 hours, it was to land D Company and one section machine-gun for capturing the Big House and the Godown. A little later, at 0440 hours, it was also to land C Company and one section machine-gun for occupying the South Village. These two landings were to the south of Habibshawi Creek. The landings to the north of the Creek were to be made soon thereafter. For this H.M.S. *Yarra* was to be in position opposite Garden, at 0530 hours, prepared to engage any firing heard in North Village or Date Palms. At the same time, it was to land D Company, which was to attack and capture the Garden, with C Company (otherwise in reserve) covering the initial stages with light machine-gun fire. The Officer Commanding 'Landforce' was to be ready to embark a rifle company, less one platoon, from the south shore of the Creek, if called on to do so, after 0500 hours. The 244th Squadron R.A.F. was to provide sorties from 0415 to 0615 and from 0815 to 1015 hours.

The operations started according to the plan, with 'Landforce' advancing at 0300 hours, on 24 May, from Girder Bridge towards Big House. As it drew nearer to its objective, it was fired on by two Iraqi machine-guns, from the area of the Broken Bridge. On account of the flood water on both sides of the road, there was not much cover from fire, and consequently, the leading troops suffered casualties, 5 being killed and 9 wounded. The armoured car of the column had been "ditched" prior to the advance, with the result that it could not go forward to deal with the Iraqi machine-gun fire.

'Shattforce' however fared better. That part of it which was to make a landing to the south did not meet with opposition as the Iraqi garrison had crossed the Creek to the north and taken refuge in the North Village and the Date Palms beyond. H.M.S. *Yarra* bombarded the area round Date Godown and the Big House according to plan, and at 0415 hours landed D Company and a section of machine-guns who captured the two objectives without opposition. C Company then occupied South Village also without opposition, and D Company pushed forward north up to the Garden without meeting any resistance. However, when patrols of D Company advanced further north to occupy the

North Village, they met with some desultory fire from the Date Palms. This was soon silenced by the artillery sending off a few rounds whenever the Iraqi small arms fire became brisk. After the Iraqi fire had died down completely, Shattforce began its withdrawal at 0745 hours and returned to Maqil Air Port and Dock area by 1040 hours the same day. Troops of the Landforce had also returned by that hour, except two platoons of B Company, which had been left behind to extricate the "ditched" armoured car in the neighbourhood of the Girder Bridge. Only one Iraqi body was found in a house beyond Date Godown. It could not be ascertained whether gun fire had inflicted any more casualties, as no trace of other dead or wounded was visible.[5]

[5] *War Diary* 2/4 G.R.

CHAPTER XIII

Advance on Baghdad

The Basra Conference

The third phase of the operations, which lasted from 27 May to 31 May, was preceded by a conference between General Wavell and General Auchinleck, which was held at Basra on 24 May to decide upon the future course of action. The discussions at this meeting revealed a sharp difference of opinion regarding the policy to be followed in Iraq. Both were agreed that the object of the British military intervention in Iraq was to prevent the acquisition by the Axis Powers of the land or air bases in Iraq. General Wavell thought that this object would be best attained by merely holding Basra and Habbaniya, and securing the Baghdad—Haifa line of communications against a small-scale land or air attack by Axis forces, and for the rest, trusting to a friendly government to be set up at Baghdad. The Axis, he thought, were more interested in Syria than in Iraq. Their plan seemed to be to seize Crete, close the Aegean, and establish themselves in Syria, from where they would be in a better position to interfere with his campaign in North Africa, than from Iraq. The occupation of Syria would bring them closer to Suez and Palestine and enable them to threaten Turkey from the south, so as to prevent Turks from throwing their weight on the side of the Allies. Syria also had the added attraction for the Germans in so far as it was ruled by the Vichy French who could not be regarded other than hostile to the Allies. Since the Axis had no direct land communication with Syria, it was likely that the initial landings in Syria would be by airborne troops and at a later date from the sea. In view of these possibilities, Britain, he thought, ought not to get more deeply involved in Iraq. He was therefore in favour of regarding the Kirkuk oil as lost for the time being since about five or six divisions would be required to regain it. He did not think the use of airborne troops for this purpose advisable, as it would be difficult to reinforce and maintain small detachments in that isolated area. He regarded the chances of taking Baghdad as being not more than even each way, and was therefore opposed to its military occupation. In short, General Wavell was of the opinion that, although his main task—the defence of Egypt and Palestine—would be made more difficult by the Axis control of Iraq, it would not yet be so badly jeopardised as it would were the Axis to establish themselves in strength in Syria.

General Auchinleck was unable to see the force of these arguments. He regarded Iraq as an absolutely vital outpost for India's defence. He was of the opinion that the Axis, who had at that date already established air bases in Iraq, would soon establish land bases also. He was firmly convinced that no Iraqi government, however well disposed, could keep the Axis out, without the support of the British forces in Iraq. Were the Axis to get into Baghdad, they could move into Northern Iran and thereby outflank the Indian forces at Basra. General Auchinleck was therefore in favour of occupying Baghdad and controlling the whole of northern Iraq.[1]

The problem of the operational control in Iraq was also discussed at the Conference. Middle East Command was fully occupied with the Western Desert campaign, defence of Crete, danger to Syria and Cyprus, and the East African campaign. Troops in Iraq were mainly Indian. Maintenance was from India and administration could more easily be done from India.[2] On the other hand, from the political point of view, it was better that all Arab affairs should be under one control, which could only be Middle East. Moreover, if Iraq became the line of communication to Turkey, there were advantages in the control remaining with the Middle East.[3]

The final result of all these discussions was that General Wavell and General Auchinleck arrived at two important decisions. First, that "Habforce", which was then on move towards Baghdad, should be allowed to occupy Baghdad at the earliest possible date, and that the Indian troops should open up communications between Basra and Habbaniya;[4] second, that in view of her greater interest and greater stake in Iraq, India should resume control of operations in Iraq, as soon as possible.[5]

Operation Oakley

For opening communications between Basra and Habbaniya, it would be necessary for the Indian troops to make a general move in the direction of Habbaniya. Such a move commenced on 25 May 1941, the next day after the Basra Conference, when Lieut-General Quinan ordered Major-General Slim, Commanding the 10th Indian Division, to capture Ur, on the Euphrates road to Baghdad, no doubt as a first step towards a further northward advance. The objects of the operation, which was designated Oakley, were to locate and destroy all Iraqi forces between Shuaiba

---

[1] *Notes on the Conference held between C-in-C Mideast and C-in-C India on 24 May 1941 at Basra, Sabine VI*, pp. 3-7.
[2] Tel. No. 0/67273 of 25 May 41 Mideast to Troopers, *Sabine IV*, p. 45.
[3] Ibid.
[4] Tel. No. 2436 from Force H.Q. Palestine to General Basra dated 24 May, *Sabine IV*, p. 50.
[5] Tel. No. 0/67273 from Mideast to Troopers dated 25 May, *Sabine IV*, p. 45.

and Ur (inclusive), specially in the areas Jaliba and Tal al Lehm; to cover the repairs of the railway between Ur and Basra; and to repair the landing grounds at Ur and Jaliba. The intention was thus to open up the line of communication as far as Ur and to form a base there, from which special service officers might operate among the Diwaniya and the Muntafiq tribes to incite them to rebel against Rashid Ali's regime. The 244th Air Squadron was to co-operate in these operations and report the presence of Iraqi troops or tribesmen in the area Tal al Lehm—Gubaishiya railway station—Chabda.[6] If it was found for any reason, such as lack of water, that the force could not remain at Ur, it was to move further north, to Al Khidhr. Reconnaissance was to be carried out as far as Nasiriya and Al Khidhr.[7]

The latest information on 26 May 1941 indicated that small Iraqi police detachments might be in the area Jaliba and Tal al Lehm. It was probable that about six hundred Iraqi troops would be met with in the Ur area. Major-General Slim ordered the 20th Indian Brigade Group, consisting of 2/7 and 2/8 Gurkha, one battery 3rd Field Regiment R.A., a section of armoured cars and ancillary units, to be established at or near Ur junction, by the morning of 29 May 1941.[8]

The plan was for the armoured cars to move independently ahead of the Column, leaving Shuaiba at 0730 hours on 27 May, and to report the presence of any Iraqi troops at Luqait. They were then to leave Luqait at 0500 hours, the next day, and report Iraqi position at Jaliba and Tal al Lehm. Two armoured cars were to remain at Tal al Lehm to watch the routes from Khamsiya, Nasiriya and Ur. They were also to locate the position and report the estimated strength of the Iraqi force at Ur. The R.A.F. was to arrange continuous reconnaissance sorties from 0500 hours to 1300 hours to report hostile movements in the Tal al Lehm—Ur—Nasiriya—Khamsiya area, whether on water or on land.[9]

The armoured cars left Shuaiba at 0730 hour on 27 May, for Luqait, followed by the main column, an hour's distance behind. The road leading from Shuaiba to Ur was found fit for the heavy mechanical transport. There were some sandy patches between At Tuba and Jaliba, but these were easily passable. A number of soft patches were also encountered between Jaliba and Tal al Lehm, but these did not hold up the heavy vehicles either. The supplies carried by the 20th Indian Brigade Group were ten days' rations and 14,500 gallons of water. Petrol, oil and lubricants were calculated at

[6] South Iraq Operation Instruction No. 1 dated 25 May 1941, *War Diary* 10 Ind. Div.
[7] O.O. No. 1 dated 26 May 1941, *War Diary* 10 Ind. Div.
[8] Tel. No. 0/67273 from Mideast to Troopers 25 May 1941, *Sabine IV*, p. 45.
[9] 20 Bde. O.O. No. 7 dated 26 May 41, *War Diary* 20 Ind. Inf. Bde.

a 150-mile radius, plus a reserve. There was water in the Hor al Hammar, approximately two to three miles from the Luqait railway station, but no other supply was available further north up to Ur. At Ur, however, reconnaissance for water led to the discovery of approximately 16,000 gallons of drinkable water. In addition, the canal water was made fit for human consumption.[10]

The armoured cars, which had left Shuaiba, at 0730 hours on 27 May, reached Luqait at 1400 hours the same day, without any incident. The tail of the main column following them was in by sunset. The advance was resumed the next day at 0515 hours, and met with no opposition until the armoured cars began approaching the village Ur, when they were fired upon by an estimated Iraqi strength of 100 rifles and 3 machine-guns. On this report of resistance being encountered, the Brigade Group assembled about one mile from Ur, and 2/7 Gurkha, supported by one battery from 18/65th Field Regiment R.A. and the armoured cars, prepared to attack and capture the village. The attack was arranged to commence at 1430 hours the same day (28 May), after half an hour's artillery preparation. The plan for the attack was for the armoured cars to come up on Ur from the left, while 2/7 Gurkha would be attacking frontally with artillery support. The guns commenced ranging on Ur at 1400 hours and continued doing so for thirty minutes. This had the effect of dispersing a large party of Iraqis, who had been observed displaying flags and demonstrating on a high ground outside the village, just before the commencement of the artillery fire. The demonstrators disappeared after a few shots, and small parties of Iraqis were thereafter observed evacuating the village and moving northwards. They were further harassed by fire from armoured cars and an Iraqi lorry was hit. By 1445 hours, the village was clear of all resistance, the leading companies of 2/7 Gurkha reached the outskirts of Ur without a single shot being fired at them, and by 1510 hours the battalion was in full occupation of the whole area.[11] Patrols were then sent out, during the next two days, to reconnoitre the neighbouring area, Nasiriya—Al Khidhr—Khamsiya, for any Iraqi troops that might need to be engaged.[12]

The Advance of Habforce on Baghdad

While the 20th Indian Infantry Brigade was consolidating Ur, Habforce was making big strides towards Baghdad. Soon after the occupation of Falluja, it had begun an advance on Baghdad from

---

[10] *Report on operation 'Oakley'* by the Brigade Commander, *War Diary* 20 Ind. Inf. Bde.
[11] *War Diary* 10 Ind. Div.
[12] *War Diary* 20 Ind. Inf. Bde.

two directions—Brigadier Kingstone's column moving out from Falluja along the direct road to Baghdad, and Lt.-Colonel A. H. Ferguson's column crossing the Euphrates at the Sin al Dhibban ferry, and then taking a track which led to the Mushahida railway station, and down the Mosul-Baghdad road, to the same objective via Al Khadimain. Kingstone's column (Kingcol) consisted of one squadron of Household Cavalry, two companies of the Essex Regiment, three armoured cars and a troop of 25-pounders. Ferguson's detachment consisted of the Household Cavalry Regiment less one squadron, a troop of 25-pounders, three R. A. F. armoured cars and the Arab Legion.[13] Both the columns had air assistance.

Kingcol moved out from Falluja at 0430 hours on 28 May. The armoured cars going ahead of the main column discovered Iraqi troops entrenched at Khan Nuqta, about 17 miles from Falluja. As this position was protected by a canal, which could not be crossed by the vehicles, the men of the Household Cavalry Regiment dismounted their trucks, crossed the obstacle on foot and after overcoming the feeble resistance offered by the Iraqi police post of Khan Nuqta, cleared the area for a further advance. But the progress thereafter was slow as the region ahead was irrigated by dykes and canals and the flood water covered the road in places. The column finally came to a halt in the evening, about twelve miles from Baghdad, on discovering that the bridge over the Abu Ghuraib canal had been blown up and there were, besides, Iraqi troops on the further bank in well entrenched positions.

These Iraqi positions were bombed by the Royal Air Force and shelled by the guns of Kingcol on the morning of 29 May. There was hardly any opposition when later at noon a troop of the Household Cavalry Regiment crossed the canal to the other side. Then the bridge over the canal was completed and the advance to Baghdad resumed the next day (30 May). The next obstacle was the Washash Canal, the bridge over which was guarded in strength. This second bridge was of great importance since it gave direct access to Baghdad, and its defences were also correspondingly elaborate. There was a wide anti-tank ditch, protecting the approach to it, and in a belt of trees close by were machine-gun posts screening the royal palace, the Palace of Roses. As the leading troops of Kingcol arrived within three miles of that bridge, the armoured cars went forward to reconnoitre, but soon had to withdraw under heavy machine-gun fire. Then the Iraqi guns, from the banks of the Tigris away to the left, shelled the trucks of the Household Cavalry Regiment, which streamed back down the road to get behind cover.[14] Soon after, however, the British 25-pounders

[13] John Bagot Glubb: *The Story of the Arab Legion*, p. 287.
[14] Ibid., p. 89.

engaged the Iraqi guns and the machine-guns; and the men of the Household Cavalry Regiment advanced on foot slowly from dyke to dyke, across a region which was irrigated and partly flooded, so that, by evening, they were still about a mile from the anti-tank ditch.

While Kingcol was thus nearing Baghdad, Ferguson's column too had been making steady progress. Led by the Arab Legion, which had already reconnoitred the route of march between Samarra and Al Khadimain, the column crossed the Euphrates on the evening of 27 May. Next morning, the Arab Legion set off in advance, and cut a few lengths of the railway line near the Mushahida railway station, after which the main column crossed to the other side and turned southwards down the main Mosul—Baghdad road. Some opposition was met three miles south of the Taji station, and later the progress became slow, the column finally coming to a halt about four miles from Baghdad in the Brickfields outside Al Khadimain, due to heavy artillery and rifle fire from the vicinity of the railway station.[15]

Armistice

Thus on 30 May the whole of Habforce was concentrated on the outskirts of Baghdad—Kingstone's column to the west of the Washash canal and Ferguson's in the brickfields of Al Khadimain—when, in the evening, the Lord Mayor of Baghdad and Lt.-Colonel Nur-ud-Din, Chief of Iraqi Military Operations, who had assumed command of the Iraq army, called at the British Embassy and asked for an armistice. Rashid Ali had fled from the country; so also the ex-Mufti of Jerusalem, the officers of the Iraq army known as the Golden Square and some Germans and Italians who had been working as Axis agents.

Two important factors had led to the collapse of the Iraqi resistance. First was Rashid Ali's anxiety to leave Iraq before all the avenues of his escape got blocked. This anxiety increased as Ferguson's column approached Baghdad from the north, thus cutting off his retreat to Turkey and Syria. The only paths of escape still open to him, then, were the road and railway to the east of Baghdad, connecting it with Iran. He, therefore, abandoned the struggle and fled on finding that Habforce was about to cross the Tigris, which would cut off also this last remaining line of retreat to Iran. Secondly, he did not get as much Axis support as he had expected, nor in time. The German air support did not arrive during the first eight days and, thus, much valuable time was lost. This was probably due to the Axis preoccupation with preparations

[15] Ibid., p. 291.

for the invasion of Crete and the need to rest units after the operations in Greece.

The armistice was signed at Baghdad on 31 May 1941. The Iraq army was permitted to retain its arms, equipment and munitions, but all units of the army had to proceed to their normal peacetime stations. British prisoners of war were to be released and Axis service personnel were to be interned. The town and vicinity of Ramadi were to be vacated by the Iraq army by 1200 hours on 1 June. All facilities were to be accorded immediately to the British military authorities for unimpeded through communication by rail, road and river. Iraqi prisoners of war were to be handed over to the Regent.

The Regent, Emir Abdul Illa, entered Baghdad on 1 June and on the next day Jamal Madfai headed the new Iraq administration. friendly to the British Government.

CHAPTER XIV

Iraq as an Operational Base

Occupation of northern Iraq

After its occupation, Iraq came to fulfil a role which was by no means intended for it during any of the stages of planning or despatch of the Basra expedition. It became a base for the invasion of Syria and Iran in turn. The operations in these two countries have been dealt with separately and, therefore, will only be touched upon briefly here to show how Iraq became an important operational base for their execution.

For a few days after the signing of the armistice, the situation in Baghdad and on the lines of communication along which reinforcements would have to proceed, remained insecure. Anti-Jewish rioting in Baghdad itself resulted in 2,000 deaths, and proportions of the Iraq army at Amara and Al Qurna appeared to disown or resist the armistice.[1] It was essential to get Indian troops forward from Basra to Baghdad and Mosul, to secure the lines of communication and to relieve Habforce, which was required for operations in Syria. The 20th Indian Infantry Brigade had not been able to advance beyond Ur and Nasiriya, as the Iraqis had done considerable damage to the railway track, and the roads had become impassable owing to the extensive flooding of the area ahead of them.

Activities of Habforce

Until it was possible to move the Indian troops to Baghdad, it fell to the lot of Habforce (less Ferguson's column which had returned to Habbaniya) to occupy places of strategic importance in upper Iraq and to check the activities of Fawzi Qawukji, the guerilla leader, on the Iraq-Syria border. On 31 May 1941 the Defence Committee had informed General Wavell that large Axis forces were concentrating against Russia. Under this threat there was a possibility that Russia might agree to certain concessions, which might be injurious to the Allies. The British Government would be able to put pressure upon Russia to resist the Axis demands if they could secure Mosul as a base for destroying the Baku oil. It was, therefore, decided to secure Mosul. The 2/4 Gurkha was flown from Habbaniya to Mosul on 3 June 1941, escorted

---

[1] Lieut.-General Quinan's *Despatch*.

by six Blenheims.[2] Also a small mobile Habforce column (called 'Gocol'), consisting of one squadron Household Cavalry, two 3.7-inch howitzers and six R.A.F. armoured cars, left Baghdad by road on 2 June and arrived on 3 June at Mosul, which was secured without opposition.[3]

On 6 June a small detachment of Habforce (called 'Mercol'), consisting of a squadron of the Household Cavalry Regiment and two 4.5-inch howitzers, left Habbaniya for Haditha, for checking the hostile activities of Fawzi Qawukji.[4] This column engaged Qawukji's force of five hundred well-armed men at Oseba, two miles south-east of Abu Kemal on 9 June, and drove it across the Syrian frontier.[5] At the same time, during the night of 7/8 June, 'Gocol' moved from Mosul to Tell Kotchek, where the railway crossed the Syrian border. It arrived there at dawn on 8 June, and finding no sign of hostile activity returned to Mosul. The British force at Mosul was reinforced by the 1st Battalion King's Own Royal Regiment, who left Baghdad on 7 June and arrived at Mosul on 8 June 1941.[6] On 9 June a small detachment of Habforce consisting of one squadron, less one troop, of the Household Cavalry Regiment and two R.A.F. armoured cars left Baghdad 'to show the flag' at Kirkuk.

Preparations for advance of Indian troops

In the meantime, preparations were being made for the move of the Indian troops to Baghdad. Reconstruction of the damaged railway track was carried out rapidly and the Basra-Baghdad line was re-opened to traffic on 9 June 1941. It was then possible for the Indian troops to advance from Basra to Baghdad, especially as further reinforcements had arrived from India. The 25th Indian Infantry Brigade consisting of the 3rd Battalion 9th Jat Regiment, 2nd Battalion 11th Sikh Regiment, 1st Battalion 5th Mahratta Light Infantry, and ancillary troops had arrived on 30 May; and the 17th Indian Infantry Brigade, consisting of the 1st Battalion 5th Royal Gurkha Rifles, 5th Battalion 13th Frontier Force Rifles, 1st Battalion 12th Frontier Force Regiment and ancillary troops, arrived on 9 June. On 10 June 1941, the 20th Indian Infantry Brigade left Ur by road and rail for Baghdad. On 12 June, the 21st Indian Infantry Brigade (less 2/4 Gurkha flown to Mosul and 2/10 Gurkha left behind at Basra) proceeded by river from Basra to Kut al Amara, and thence by motor transport to Baghdad.

[2] *Sabine XII*, 830, p. 8.
[3] *Sabine XII*, 830, p. 10 and XI, p. 830.
[4] *Sabine XII*, 830, p. 28.
[5] *Sabine XII*, 830, pp. 28, 33, 43 & 97.
[6] *War Diary* 1 King's Own Royal Regiment.

Advance of the 20th Indian Infantry Brigade

The advance of the 20th Indian Infantry Brigade from Ur to Baghdad began on 10 June, under the command of Brigadier Powell. It had the following troops under command:[1]
>2nd Battalion 8th Gurkha Rifles
>Detachment 13th Lancers
>3rd Field Regiment R.A.
>10th Field Company, Sappers and Miners
>26th Field Ambulance
>Detachment 1st Field Hygiene Section
>20th Brigade Transport Company
>L.R.S. 28 (M) Workshop Company
>Section 16 (M) Workshop Company
>48 Field Post Office
>Detachment Armoured Car Section R.A.F. and
>Mechanical Transport 2/4 Gurkha.

The move was carried out by road and rail. The road convoy moved in three stages: from Ur to Samawa (60 miles), from Samawa to Hilla (107 miles) and from Hilla to Baghdad (68 miles). A detachment of 13th Lancers, with some armoured cars of the R.A.F. under command, moved ahead of the road column. One company of 2/8 Gurkha, with a section of medium machine-guns, formed the Reconnaissance Group. 2/8 Gurkha less one company, one troop 3rd Field Regiment R.A., two Motor Ambulances 26th Field Ambulance, and the reconnaissance party of 10th Field Company, Sappers and Miners, formed the Holding Group and moved in rear of the Reconnaissance Group. Then came the Main Group in the following order of march:
>Headquarters 20th Indian Infantry Brigade
>3rd Field Regiment R.A., less one troop
>3/11 Sikh Mechcol, less Detachment
>Section 16 (M) Workshop Company
>10th Field Company, less Reconnaissance Party
>26th Field Ambulance, less ambulance car detachments and marching personnel
>Mechanical Transport 2/4 Gurkha
>20th Brigade Transport Company
>Two Ambulances 26th Field Ambulance
>L.R.S. 28 (M) Workshop Company
>48 Field Post Office

Detachment 3/11 Sikh Mechcol formed the rear party. The starting point for the road column was a ruined village, immediately south of the railway at Ur. 3/11 Sikh less Mechcol, 2/7 Gurkha,

---

[1] 20 Bde. O.O. No. 8 dated 7 June 1941, *War Diary* 20 Ind. Inf. Bde.

detachment 1st Field Hygiene Section and marching personnel of the 26th Field Ambulance moved by rail from Ur to Baghdad.

The road party had to encounter many difficulties on the way, especially on the night drive from Samawa to Hilla. Several vehicles were "ditched" and had to be recovered later. The crossing of the river Euphrates by a boat bridge at Samawa took 7½ hours, one company being deployed for the defence of the bridge. There were two staging posts on the route, one at Ur and another at Diwaniya.[8] Ultimately, the 20th Indian Infantry Brigade concentrated at Taji camp, about 5 miles north of Baghdad, on 12 June 1941.

Major-General Slim arrived the same day by air, with an Advanced Headquarters, having been instructed by Lt.-General Quinan to take over from the Habforce so as to release the latter for operations in Syria.[9] At that time the troops of Habforce were holding Mosul, Kirkuk, Baghdad, Habbaniya and the Abu Kemal-Haditha area, and all of these had to be relieved.[10] The task was completed by 17 June, when the last units of Habforce left Habbaniya for Syria.[11] On the following day the control of operations in Iraq passed from the Middle East to India. Lt.-General Quinan assumed command of all land forces in Iraq while Major-General Slim was appointed to command northern Iraq.[12] The latter was instructed to prepare three landing grounds in the Mosul district and make administrative arrangements for the maintenance of four R.A.F. squadrons in that area. He was to retain the minimum number of troops in Baghdad or its vicinity, and to keep them in a mobile role so as to give the Iraqis an impression that the British and Indian forces were more numerous than they really were. He was also to station detachments at the oil stations T-1, H-1, H-2, H-3 and K-3 (Haditha).[13]

Advance of the 21st Indian Brigade

The 21st Indian Infantry Brigade under the command of Brigadier Weld, commenced its move towards Baghdad on the same day that the 20th Indian Infantry Brigade reached the outskirts of that city. This force which proceeded up the river Tigris towards Kut al Amara, comprised the following:

    Headquarters 21st Indian Infantry Brigade and Signal Section
    Detachment 10th Indian Division Signals

---

[8] *War Diary* 20 Bde. Tpt. Coy.
[9] Iraq Force O.I. No. 3 dated 12 June 1941, Appx. J/12/A, *War Diary* Iraq Force.
[10] *War Diary* Iraq Force.
[11] *Sabine VI*, 21 W, p. 48.
[12] General Wavell's *Despatch*.
[13] Iraq Force O.I. No. 5 dated 18 June, Appx. J/18/B, *War Diary* Iraq Force.

Two troops 13th Lancers (eight armoured cars)
One troop (four guns, 4.5-inch Howitzers) 157th Field Regiment R.A.
4/3 Frontier Force Rifles
One section 9th Field Company Sappers and Miners
One company 29th Field Ambulance
Detachment 16 Mobile Workshop Company
21st Infantry Brigade Transport Company

The total strength of this force was approximately 1,500 personnel and 210 vehicles. There were two important reasons for opening the river route. The Marsh Arabs, who lived along both banks of the Tigris were turbulent by nature, as the British had found in 1914-1918. Further, although an armistice had been signed, it was by no means certain what the reactions of the Iraqi regular troops in Amara would be to the British use of the river as a line of communication. Thus this operation was intended to check these two possible sources of danger to the British line of communication.[14] Preparations for the advance of the Tigris had been made in advance. All available barges and steamers had been collected. The barges were 'decked' to take motor transport, guns and armoured cars. The convoy, which was accompanied by a naval officer, consisted of the sloop *Falmouth* (as far as Al Qurna), the gunboat *Cockchafer* and the R.A.F Launch No. 43. There were 11 towing craft in it, towing 22 barges. The five larger towing craft were armed with one 3-pounder gun each, and some others with automatic weapons. In addition, eight of the barges carried one armoured car each, guns of which were available for protection. Defence against air attack was provided by the commanding officers of the ships arranging with the officer commanding of any troops on board or in barges alongside to dispose any Bren or other automatic anti-aircraft guns to the best advantage. Force Headquarters was arranging for daily air reconnaissance ahead of the convoy.

Anchors were weighed at 0420 hours on 12 June, and the convoy was moored again just above Aburuba at 1850 hours the same evening. Next day it resumed the move at 0420 hours and tied up again at 1530 hours, about six miles below Amara. At the end of the third day's journey, the convoy had reached a point one mile below Ali Shargi, and two days later its advanced party was in Kut al Amara with the rest of the vessels following up.[15]

The force then moved by road from Kut al Amara to Baghdad on 19 June. Having passed through Baghdad, the convoy proceeded to Taji Camp, where it arrived at 1530 hours the same day.

[14] This operation was given the code-name 'Regatta'.
[15] *War Diary* 4/13 Frontier Force Rifles.

Military occupation of Iraq

While the 20th and 21st Indian Infantry Brigades were moving to Baghdad, fresh troops were arriving from India. The 17th and 25th Indian Infantry Brigades had already arrived before 9 June, as mentioned earlier, to which, on 16 June, was added the 24th Indian Infantry Brigade comprising the 2nd Battalion 6th Rajputana Rifles, 1st Battalion Kumaon Rifles, 5th Battalion 5th Mahratta Light Infantry and some other troops. The general disposition of Indian troops on 20 June 1941, when the military occupation of Iraq was completed, was two brigades of the 10th Indian Division (the 20th and 21st) in north Iraq, the 25th en route from Basra to Baghdad, and the remaining two, the 17th and 24th (now under command of the 8th Indian Division), in the Shuaiba—Basra area. These last two were engaged in improving transit facilities, and, in addition, the 17th Indian Infantry Brigade was earmarked for the protection of Abadan refinery if required.[16]

Plans for operations against Syria[17]

As soon as the military occupation of Iraq was completed by 20 June, preparations were begun for the despatch of Indian troops to Syria. An Allied force consisting of British, Indian, Australian, Free French and Transjordan troops, had begun the invasion of Syria on 8 June 1941. The main advance was from Palestine to Damascus jointly with a parallel advance along the coast to Beirut. Damascus fell on 21 June but this did not end the hostilities in Syria. The Vichy French still held about four-fifths of the country including the ports of Beirut and Tripoli and the entire railway line north of Damascus. It was at this stage that Iraq came to be used as a base for attacking Syria from the east. On the same day that Damascus fell, Habforce crossed the Syrian border with Palmyra as its objective. At the same time Lt.-General Quinan ordered Major-General Slim to concentrate a force at Haditha as soon as possible with a view to moving up the river Euphrates to Aleppo, in order to establish a threat to the rear of the Vichy forces holding Beirut. Major-General Slim ordered the 21st Indian Infantry Brigade Group, the striking force, to capture Deir ez Zor and advance towards Aleppo; the 25th Indian Infantry Brigade Group was to protect the lines of communication from Haditha to Baghdad. A mobile column was to advance from Mosul to Fadrhami and Souar to distract the attention of the Vichy troops from the move of the 21st Indian Infantry Brigade Group up the Euphrates to Deir ez Zor. In addition, a column under Head-

---

[16] *Sabine VI*, 21 W, p. 122. See also Appendix 7.
[17] A detailed account of the operations in Syria has been given separately.

quarters British Troops in Iraq, was to operate independently on the northern flank of the 10th Indian Division towards Tell Kotchek, Qamichliye and Hassetche.[18]

Habforce captured Palmyra during the night of 2/3 July. The 21st Indian Infantry Brigade Group captured Deir ez Zor on 3 July and Raqqa on 5 July. By then the mobile column operating from Mosul had also completed its task of creating a diversion and patrolling to Al Badi, Fadrhami and Souar, as also the third column moving towards Tell Kotchek. Tell Kotchek was occupied on 5 July, and Tell Aalo, Qamichliye and Hassetche within the next three days.

In the meantime, Australian troops, advancing up the west coast, were pressing towards Damour, which they captured on 9 July, thus opening the way to Beirut. The terrific bombardment of the Vichy positions in the coastal sector by the Royal Navy, the extremely heavy toll taken of the Vichy aircraft by the Royal Air Force and the vigorous Allied thrusts up the coast, Damascus, Palmyra and Deir ez Zor contributed to the defeat of the Vichy French. The armistice terms were signed on 14 July.

Plan for defence of Mosul aerodrome

Sometime before the end of hostilities in Syria, a plan had been drawn up for the defence of the Mosul aerodrome by Indian troops against the possibility of an attack either by the Vichy forces from Syria or the Iraq army garrison, quartered in the Ghazlani Barracks, on the ridge overlooking the aerodrome. This aerodrome which lay to the south of the Mosul city was shut in between the river Tigris on the one side and the Ghazlani Barracks ridge on the other, and only its southern face therefore needed defending. Although the British were no longer at war with Iraq, the local population was not wholly friendly, being affected by the events happening outside the frontiers of Iraq, while the Iraqi garrison on the ridge, if anything, was even more truculent. Consisting, as it did, of one infantry brigade and one mountain artillery brigade, this garrison was a distinct menace to the safety of the aerodrome. But owing to political considerations its existence had to be put up with, and the best that could be done under the circumstances was to keep a plan ready for containing it in the event of local or external trouble. The preparation of such a plan was the task of the Commander of the 20th Indian Infantry Brigade, who announced its completion on 29 June 1941. His appreciation was that attack on the Mosul airfield might take the form either of dive-bombing attacks followed by a landing by parachute and air-borne troops

[18] No. 102/29/1/GHQ, B.T.I., Basra, 19 June 1941, Appendix J/19/C, *War Diary Iraq Force*.

or an advance from Syria by a land force. To guard against these dangers it was recommended that the available troops should be so disposed as to provide the following defensive arrangements:

(i) Outer defences designed to prevent any advance into the area by land forces.
(ii) Inner posts sited to cover the landing ground area for dealing with parachute and airborne landings.
(iii) A mobile reserve capable of moving quickly to occupy positions on the ridge. It was also to be capable of counter-attacking hostile penetrations, dealing with parachute and airborne troops within the defensive area, or otherwise moving out (self-contained for fortyeight hours) as ordered.
(iv) Artillery sited to support the defences, both inner and outer, and able to engage armoured fighting vehicles which might penetrate the landing ground area.
(v) Anti-Aircraft and Light Machine-Guns so sited and manned as to be ready to engage all hostile aircraft within their range.

The strength of the British and Indian troops located at Mosul was expected to vary from time to time. Initially that scheme was based on the following force being available:

Two infantry battalions
One Field Regiment less two troops
One Field Company, Sappers and Miners
One Brigade Transport Company
One Workshop Company (for detachment)
One Field Ambulance
Two sections Armoured Cars, R.A.F.

The Mosul aerodrome area was divided into two battalion areas—'A' area north and east, and 'B' area south and west of the landing ground. Inside the 'A' area were situated the R.A.F. buildings and works, the close defence of which was the responsibility of the R.A.F. Within the areas of the two battalions were located the Field Regiment less two troops and all other units. The position of defensive posts is shown in the sketch. The object of these posts was to dominate their respective areas, e.g. areas 4 and 5 dominated Mac's Wood cum Pumping Station, and Nos. 9 and 10 dominated the ridge. The posts were not purely for passive defence. The garrisons were to seize every opportunity to take the offensive against small hostile parties in their respective areas.[19]

[19] *Mosul Defence Scheme*, June 1941, *War Diary*, 20 Ind. Inf. Bde.

Protection of air and sea routes

In addition to the above mentioned plan for the defence of the Mosul aerodrome, tentative plans were also discussed concerning the protection of the air and sea routes between India and Iraq. In this connection the Political Resident, Bushire, submitted a memorandum to the Government of India, on 8 June 1941, regarding the protection of these routes. According to him, on account of the British hold on southern Iraq, the Arab coast of the Persian Gulf might well be regarded as secure and the air bases on it safe. But it was different in the case of the air bases on the Iranian coast of the Persian Gulf, which were still in danger of falling into the Axis hands, especially in view of the uncertain attitude of Iran.

This danger was aggravated by the fact that Iran was falling under German influence. The major portion of Iran's trade was with Germany and there was a large number of German experts, engineers and technicians in Iranian railways and industries, besides doctors, merchants and teachers and numerous employees of the commercial concerns carrying on trade with Iran. General Wavell, in his despatch to Lt.-General Quinan, dated 29 July 1941, estimated the number of Germans in Iran at "two to three thousand persons, all of whom may be counted as active fifth columnists". If Iran turned hostile or allowed the Axis and pro-Axis Powers the use of her aerodromes and landing grounds, particularly near the Persian Gulf, a serious situation might be created. Effective hostile bases e.g. that at Bushire, could close the Persian Gulf, as the bases on the Arab coast would be too far away to counter them. The Germans had pilots familiar with the Bushire aerodrome, since this was the terminus of the former Junkers' Teheran—Bushire air route. Owing to navigational requirements, all India-Iraq shipping had to pass close to the Iranian coast, until approach of the Shatt al Arab was gained. Diversion of that shipping along the Arab coast would not only be hazardous but would also fail to take the ships off the range of air action from Bushire. It was therefore necessary to mark out the aerodromes and landing grounds on the Iranian littoral which must be denied to the Axis in order to prevent the Persian Gulf from being closed to shipping.

The existing Iranian aerodromes and emergency landing grounds on the Iranian littoral were as follows:

Aerodromes
  (a) Ahwaz
  (b) Abadan
  (c) Gach Saran
  (d) Ganeweh
  (e) Bushire
  (f) Jask

MOSUL AERODROME AREA DEFENCES
29 JUNE 1941

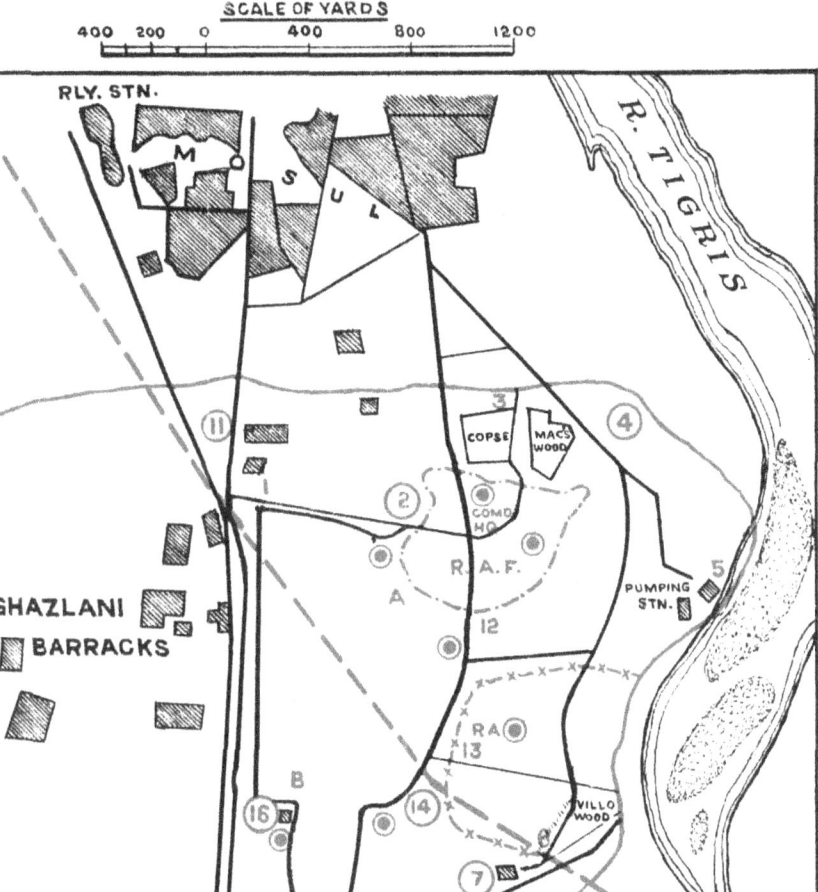

Landing Grounds
(1) Bandar Asalu
(2) Lingeh
(3) Bandar Abbas
(4) Basidu
(5) Salagh (Qishm Island)
(6) Chahbar
(7) Iranshahr
(8) Kwash
(9) Shiraz

As the whole coast line could not possibly be held, it was necessary to decide which of the above mentioned air bases would have to be held in case a necessity arose for their occupation. The aerodromes at Ahwaz, Abadan, Gach Saran and Ganeweh were absolutely necessary for the defence of the Anglo-Iranian oilfields. Since Bushire was ideally situated for hostile bombers, it would have to be held and denied to the Axis. Shiraz, Kwash, Iranshahr and Asalu were inaccessible to Axis aircraft and might be neglected. Lingeh would be useful but Bandar Abbas was preferable, though it was more accessible to the Axis. Basidu and Salagh would present the Axis with difficulty and might be neglected. Jask and Chahbar, which had some shelter for sea planes, could be easily held with the aid of the friendly Baluch tribes.[20]

Defence of the Persian Gulf

On 24 June 1941, the Government of India instructed Brig. F.E.C. Hughes, who had been appointed Commander Designate of the Persian Gulf Force, to carry out, along with the representatives of the Senior Naval Officer, Persian Gulf, and Air Officer Commanding, Iraq, a detailed reconnaissance of the defence requirements in the Persian Gulf.[21]

This reconnaissance was carried out in July 1941 and Brigadier Hughes made some recommendations for the defence of the Persian Gulf. According to him the ports of Bushire and Bandar Abbas held the key to the situation. Bushire flanked the sea route and formed an ideal potential base for operations by hostile dive bombers against shipping, and against the Bahrein refinery. It also threatened Basra, Abadan and Shatt al Arab. Were Bushire to be held by the British, it would constitute a valuable base for the interception of Axis attacks from the air bases south of Teheran. It would also prove of value in defending the shipping in the Persian Gulf and the Bahrein refinery, and would also aid British air

---

[20] Tel. No. 601 dated 8 June 1941 from Political Resident Bushire, *Defence of the Persian Gulf.*
[21] Directive to Hughes, 24 June 1941, *Defence of the Persian Gulf,* pp. 35-39.

counter-offensives against Axis penetrations south and east. The place was difficult to attack from sea or from land, and any force once in possession, whether British or Axis, would be difficult to dislodge. The position of Bandar Abbas was similar to that of Bushire. Its possession was important in order to protect shipping in the Straits of Hormuz. Brigadier Hughes, therefore, recommended that in the event of a close Axis threat to the Iranian coast, the main bases of Bushire and Bandar Abbas should be occupied as a precautionary measure to forestall any hostile penetration of that area. As to the requirements of troops for the defence of this area, his recommendations were as follows:[22]

> (i) Sporadic bombing of the Bahrein refinery being a possibility, heavy and light anti-aircraft guns would have to be provided for its defence.
>
> (ii) Whenever an advance of Axis forces into northern Iran was apprehended, Bushire would have to be occupied by about two infantry companies. There would have to be about eight heavy and four light anti-aircraft guns, and one company infantry, for the protection of the Bahrein refinery.
>
> (iii) If further Axis penetration southwards was apprehended, the garrison of Bushire would have to be increased to two infantry battalions less two companies, and one light anti-aircraft battery less one troop. No increase in the Bahrein garrison would be necessary but one company infantry would have to be provided for the protection of Bandar Abbas.

The necessity for implementing this scheme, however, did not arise as the situation changed radically in the next month. Iran was invaded jointly by Britain and Russia in August 1941, after which the security of the Persian Gulf ceased to be a problem.

Operations against Iran[23]

The reasons that led to the invasion of Iran may be stated here briefly in conclusion. Britain's anxiety about Iran's oil, and about the safety of India and the Middle East, were no doubt the main considerations on the British side; and Russia's desire to remove the German menace from its rear was undoubtedly the prime motivating factor on the Russian side. But it was not on these questions that the two Powers went to war against Iran. The immediate cause of the invasion was a simpler question, namely that of the expulsion of the German nationals from Iran.

[22] Tel. 12330/G dated 2 September 1941 from Armindia to Troopers, *Defence of the Persian Gulf*, p. 91.
[23] Operations in Iran have been discussed in a separate part of this narrative.

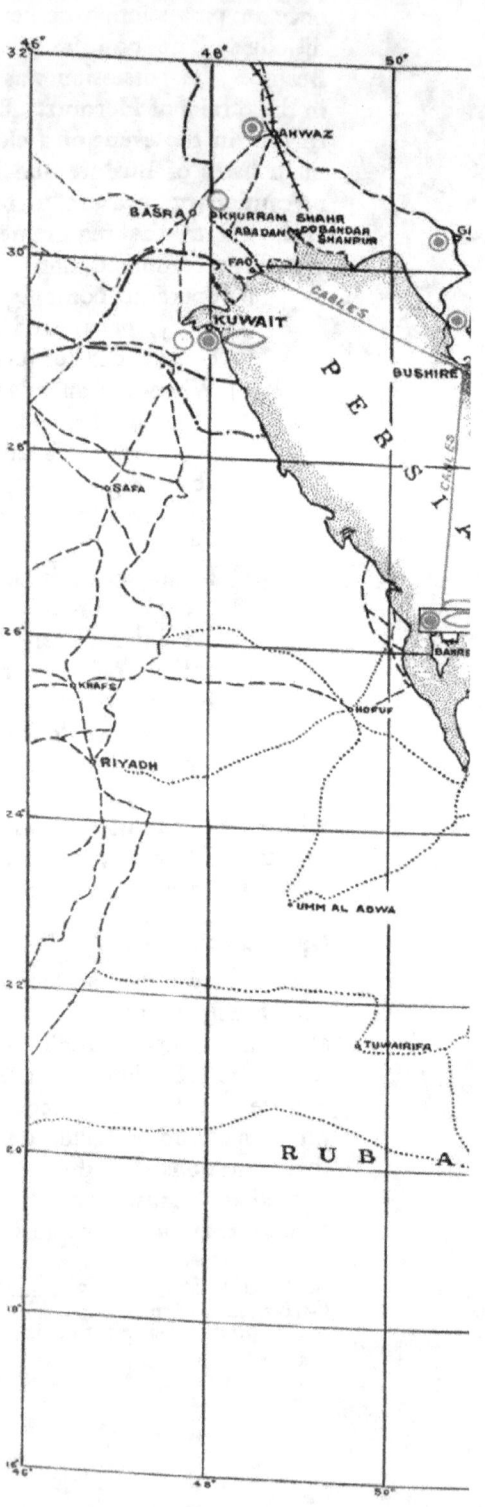

PERSIAN GULF
SHOWING DEFENSIVE LAYOUT

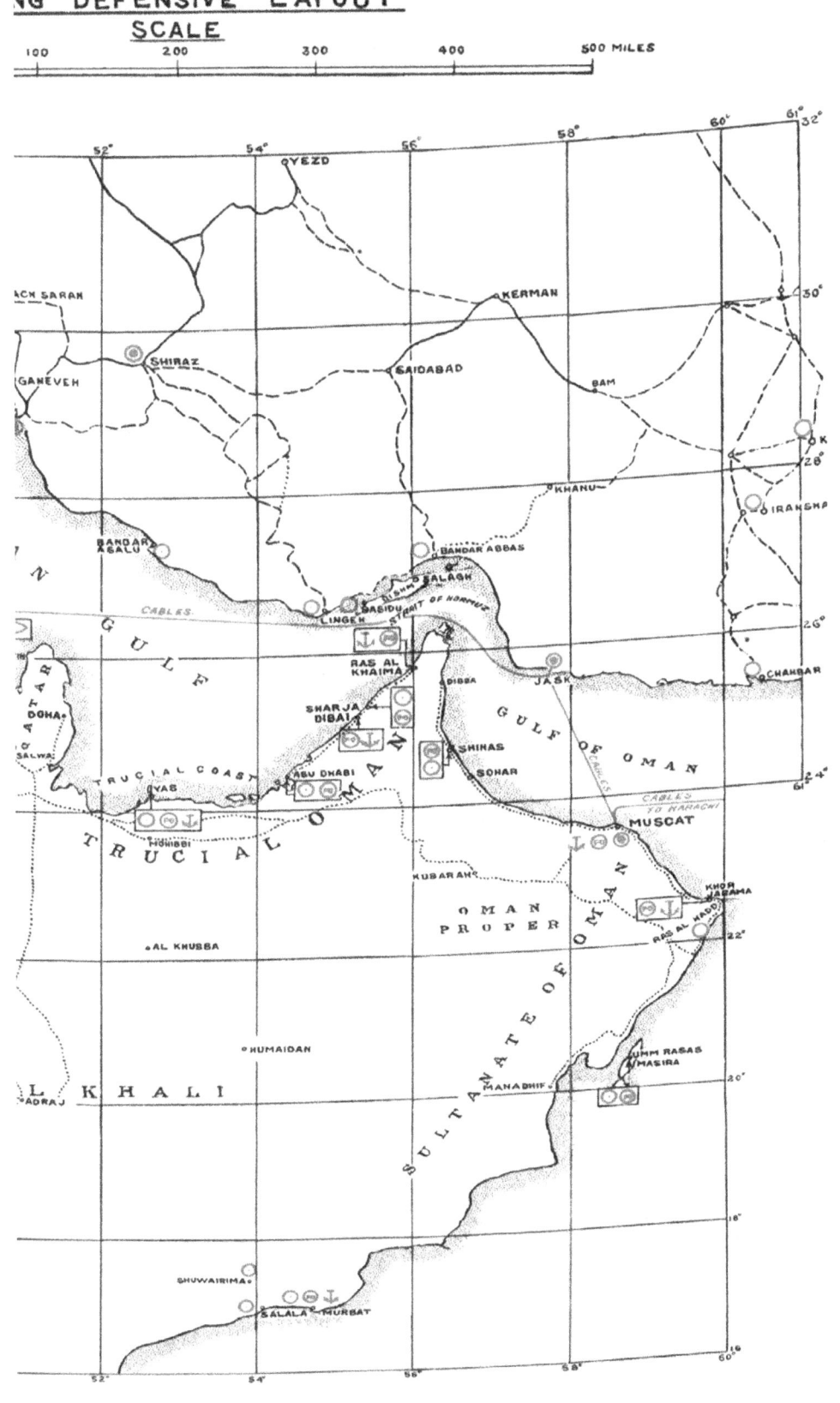

For a long time both Britain and Russia had been greatly perturbed by the existence of a large number of Germans in Iran. With the outbreak of the Russo-German war on 22 June 1941, the problem became more acute and intriguing. The Allies felt that unless early steps were taken to rid Iran of this increasing Nazi influence, the Germans might occupy the country, thus depriving the Allies of the Middle East oil, and endangering the safety of India,[24] Egypt and the Caucasus. As in the case of Iraq, the Government of India had played an important part in influencing the policy of the British Government in this matter, from the earliest stages. The Governor-General of India had repeatedly represented to the British Government the need to take energetic steps for the expulsion of Germans from Iran, whose stay there was, in his view, the "most dangerous threat to India's security".[25]

At last on 22 July, the General Headquarters, India, informed Lt.-General Quinan that the British War Cabinet was considering measures to secure this end. On 24 July he was further informed that the British Government had approved a proposal for the application of the Anglo-Soviet diplomatic pressure on the Iranian Government in order to secure the expulsion of Axis nationals from their country. If diplomatic pressure failed, force was to be used. The joint Anglo-Soviet note was to be presented on 12 August, and meanwhile Lt.-General Quinan was to complete the preliminary concentration of a striking force near the Iranian frontier in the Basra area. The note was delivered on 17 August, and as the reply to it was deemed unsatisfactory, it was decided to proceed against Iran on 25 August. On that day the Russians invaded Iran from the north across the Caucasian border, and the British and Indian troops from the south and west across the borders of Iraq.

---

[24] File No. 601/8181/H.
[25] File No. 830, serial 1.

CHAPTER XV

Initial Plans to Meet Axis Threat

Axis threat to Caucasia

Hostilities in Iran ceased on 29 August. The Iranian Government accepted the final terms of armistice on 9 September, after which the country became the occupied territory of the Allied forces. The occupation of Iran, together with that of Iraq and Syria, gave the Allies the control of an entire block of Middle East countries stretching from the Eastern Mediterranean to the Caspian Sea. This was no doubt made possible by the initial occupation of Iraq which, in an unintended way, had served as a base for the invasion of Syria on the one hand, and of Iran on the other. On the completion of that role, Iraq had yet another important part to play, namely to serve as a pivot of serveral schemes of defence for the whole of the Middle East block.

These schemes related, in particular, to Palestine, Syria, Iraq and Iran and were aimed at defending those countries against an Axis attack from the north, that is from Anatolia or Caucasia. Due to the uncertain attitude of Turkey, the threat from Anatolia was always there, but it was not so serious or immediate as that developing in Caucasia which had come into existence with the invasion of Russia by Germany and was growing daily with the rapid advance of the German troops along the northern margin of the Black Sea.

By July 1941, just about the time that General Auchinleck was taking over the command of the Middle East from General Wavell, the situation had begun to look somewhat alarming. The German advance was bearing down rapidly towards Caucasia, against which the Russian opposition seemed ineffective and evanescent. Apprehensive of a sudden collapse of the Russian resistance, General Auchinleck began to think of measures to be adopted against the possible emergence of the Axis on his northern front.[1]

On 7 July 1941, he sent to the War Office his appreciation of the situation with certain suggestions. He had two alternative lines of defence in mind: one, far up in the north, intended to defend the whole of the Middle East block comprising Syria, Iraq and

---

[1] On 5 July 1941, General Sir Claude Auchinleck, who until then had been Commander-in-Chief, India, became Commander-in-Chief, Middle East Forces, in succession to General Sir Archibald Wavell, who took up the appointment of Commander-in-Chief, India, on 11 July 1941.

Iran; another, lower down in the south, for holding only the vital belt covering Palestine, the Basra area and the Iranian oilfields. Of the two, he recommended the latter as the more dependable course of action. Were the former course to be adopted, it would be necessary to retain in hand the aerodromes in northern Syria and northern Iraq and deny them to the Axis. But to do this it would be necessary to enter Turkey and forestall the Axis in southern Anatolia, a proposition not easy to achieve without the willing collaboration of Turkey,. Were that co-operation lacking, the Allies would find it difficult to hold the northern frontiers of Iraq and Syria against a heavy attack such as was to be expected, and would find themselves in the unhappy predicament of having to fight delaying actions on increasingly divergent lines in Iraq and Syria. Anxious to avoid such a situation, General Auchinleck counselled the adoption of the other course, namely the line of defence in the south. With that object, he wished to have positions in the south reconnoitred and prepared in advance, in the areas Baghdad and Tripoli-Homs, to which the Allied forces might withdraw under pressure. At the same time he wanted an early completion of the final lines of defence which were to cover the Basra bridgehead and northern Palestine. These restricted defensive positions were apparently intended to do no more than enable the Allied troops to maintain a foothold against heavy odds.

War Office Appreciation

The War Office replied to General Auchinleck's appreciation with a more detailed appreciation of their own. They agreed that the Axis forces might reach Caucasia by mid-August, and after organising their defences of the Caucasian oilfields might attempt to deny to the British the use of the northern Iraq aerodromes. But the action to oust the British from the forward aerodromes was not likely to commence till late September. It would be mid-September by the time the Axis established enough long and short range bombers in Caucasia with corresponding fighter defences for the area. After that the air offensive would start, more as a preliminary to the main attack by land and would therefore be fairly heavy in Mosul, light in Baghdad and spasmodic in the Basra area. Granted favourable conditions, namely Iranian co-operation, the aerodromes of northern Iran would be occupied at about the same time. The land attack could then begin and would be aimed at Iraq either from southern Anatolia or from Iran. But the weather would seriously curtail activities from December to March. The attack on Iraq was more likely to come from Anatolia than from Iran. In case Iran was the base, the attack would emanate from Hamadan and Tabriz, and it might be made by about five divisions, one operating from Tabriz and four from Hamadan. But the rail and road communications of Caucasia being very limited, especially in winter, it would not be possible to concentrate so many divisions in Iran till the end of the season. Therefore, according to the estimate of the War Office the attack from Caucasia via Iran was not likely to develop before April 1942.

But as regards the threat from Anatolia it was a different matter. The Axis would have an overwhelming advantage in attacking Syria and Iraq, if Turkey collaborated. Their first objective in that case would be to secure the Aleppo railway and control northern Syria. The attack would no doubt be preceded by air operations which would prepare the ground for the main offensive. The air activities would commence by September, and the Axis would probably be having five divisions on the southern frontiers of Turkey by 1 November, with sufficient maintenance capacity for increasing the strength to nine divisions by 1 December and to fourteen thereafter, assuming that sufficient rolling stock was available for working the Aleppo railway to its maximum capacity. In addition it would be able to maintain three more divisions by the Turkish roads.

Against this vast strength, which might be launched simultaneously against Syria and Iraq, it would not be possible for the Allies to put up an effective defence. The War Office, therefore, agreed with General Auchinleck's appreciation that there was no point in defending northern Iraq which it would be best to evacuate, the main system of defence in such a case being based on the area west and north of Baghdad and the mountains running southeast from Kermanshah. This plan offered certain advantages. It provided a good natural obstacle besides depth for land and air defence. The lines of communication were not unduly stretched and could be protected. Moreover, mobile forces working north of this defensive area would enable the British to keep the aerodromes of northern Iraq in use, until attacked by the Axis in strength. The War Office was silent on the plan for the defence of Syria which probably meant that General Auchinleck's suggestion regarding the Homs-Tripoli defence line had been accepted. It also seemed to accept by implication the suggestion for a final defensive position covering northern Palestine and the Basra bridgehead. But it made additional suggestions for the seaward defences of the Persian Gulf area. It recommended that in the organisation of those defences, the emphasis should be on adequate mine-sweeping facilities and anti-aircraft escort for the ships, since Shatt al Arab was difficult to keep open against even the light-scale air-mining possible from northern Iran. For that reason, it was considered prudent to have in readiness an alternative port linked by rail and road to Basra, and it was recommended that the port of Umm Qasr should be developed to answer that purpose.

The main conclusion from the appreciation of the War Office, therefore, was that the target for the administrative planning should provisionally be accepted as ten divisions and thirty air squadrons. This was however a long range target and was not to interfere with the short-term plan for a maximum scale attack on Caucasia as soon as possible. The air forces for the long term plan were to amount to fifteen squadrons by October 1941 and to twenty-five by April 1942, increasing to thirty at a later period. The twenty-five air squadrons for April were to consist of five heavy and six medium bomber squadrons, nine short range and one long range fighter squadrons, two Army Co-operation squadrons and two transport squadrons.

General Wavell's criticism

It will not be difficult to see that this appreciation of the War Office, with which General Auchinleck seemed to be in agreement, was based on a rather alarmist view of the Russian situation. It was left to General Wavell to point this out and restore the perspective. On 26 July 1941, he expressed his opinion that the Axis were unlikely to reach Caucasia by mid-August 1941. In other words, he did not agree with the view of the War Office, which presupposed complete Russian collapse at an early date and compliance on the part of Turkey with the Axis demands for the passage of troops. Nor was he ready to subscribe to the view that in face of superior Axis forces, it would be difficult to defend northern Iraq and Syria and that therefore the best course would be to base the main system of defence in the area west and north of Baghdad and the mountains running south-east from Kermanshah. He rather thought that such a system of defence would spell disaster, as it would leave the rear of the Allied defences exposed to Axis air attacks. He argued that if the Axis succeeded in establishing air bases in northern Iraq and northern Iran, within effective range of the port of Basra and of the shipping in the Persian Gulf, it would be able to disrupt the lines of communication, dislocate the Basra Base and strike at the other vulnerable ports, as well as at Abadan and the Anglo-Iranian oilfields. To guard against such a mischance, it was essential to hold northern Iraq and northern Iran, or at least prevent the Axis forces from establishing themselves there.

Thus maintaining, contrary to the War Office appreciation, that the defence of northern Iraq was more important than that of the Basra area, General Wavell made certain suggestions for the defence of the former. He proposed taking steps to prevent the Axis from securing control of the Aleppo railway, by persuading the Turks to permit a limited advance of Allied forces into Anatolia. He also suggested keeping suitable forces ready in Iraq to forestall an Axis attack developing from the east, that is via Rowanduz gorge, or from Hamadan or along the railway Teheran-Ahwaz. If, however, the Allies did get driven back on the Baghdad line (which was to be the next successive line of defence), armoured forces would be required to cover withdrawal over the desert and to prevent the line being turned by Axis mobile forces, and these would have to be provided somehow. In brief, the essence of General Wavell's criticism of the War Office appreciation was that once the Allied troops were forced out of Baghdad, it would not be of any value to hold the bridgehead at Basra. At best, it might be regarded as a last stand to enable troops to be evacuated. But, provided the necessary armoured force and air support were forthcoming, there was no reason why the attacks from Rowanduz, Hamadan and Teheran, and also probably from Diyarbakir, should not be held.[2]

To this criticism the War Office replied on 15 August that the object of their appreciation was not to review or indicate to him the British strategy in the Middle East.[3] The aim was rather to arrive at a basis for administrative and maintenance planning for the future. Certain factors in the situation, such as the strong or weak resistance of Russia to Axis forces, did not, therefore, materially affect the main conclusion of the appreciation which was that the target for administrative planning should be taken as ten divisions and thirty air squadrons.[4] General Wavell's suggestions for controlling the Aleppo railway and defending northern Iraq were acceptable to the Chiefs of Staff, who also agreed that the "main defence of the Persian Gulf area must, if possible, be in Anatolia and northern Iraq".

Directive to Lieut.-General Quinan

Thus, after an exchange of views between General Wavell, General Auchinleck and the War Office, it had been decided that the defence of the Persian Gulf area must begin in Anatolia and northern Iraq. Earlier on 29 July, General Wavell had issued a revised directive to Lt.-General Quinan, who was instructed to hold northern Iraq against any Axis attack developing through Turkey or Iran or both, and to develop facilities for the maintenance and employment in Iraq of a force which might in certain circumstances amount to ten divisions (some armoured), and thirty squadrons of

---

[2] Tel. 9924/G dated 26 July 1941 from Armindia to Troopers, pp. 32-36, *Appreciation of threat to Iraq*, F. 945.
[3] The control of operations in Iraq, it will be recalled, had passed from the Middle East to India on 18 June 1941 and remained so till 12 Jan. 1942.
[4] Tel. 84292 dated 15 August from Troopers to Armindia, pp. 55-9, F. 945.

the Royal Air Force. Full-fledged plans were to be got ready to that end; but the construction of permanent defences in those areas was to be confined only to denying, where possible, the main lines of approach to armoured fighting vehicles into Iraq from Turkey or Iran, with the object of slowing down an Axis advance and forcing it into unsuitable country. Plans in detail were also to be prepared for an Allied advance into Turkish or Iranian territory in order to seize defiles, suitable for fighting delaying actions and for carrying out extensive demolitions. Aerodromes were to be constructed in northern Iraq to enable a force of thirty squadrons of the Royal Air Force to operate from that area against northern Iran, Caucasia or Turkey. Finally, a suitable force was to be held in readiness, to enable the occupation of Abadan and Naft-i-Shah to be carried out at short notice. The Basra Base was to be developed for the maintenance of all the ten divisions and thirty air squadrons, and Umm Qasr and Kuwait were to be developed as subsidiary ports.[5]

CHAPTER XVI

Planning in India, Iraq and the Middle East

It may be recalled here that on 5 July 1941 there was a change in the Middle East Command. General Wavell who was until then the Commander-in-Chief, Middle East Forces, became the Commander-in-Chief of India, in succession to General Auchinleck who assumed command of the Middle East. A little earlier, there had also been a change in the control over Iraq. On 18 June the operational control in Iraq had been transferred to the India Command, in view of India being the base of supplies for operations in Iraq and her larger stake in the safety of the Persian Gulf. Thus, when General Wavell assumed command in India, Iraq was the responsibility of India and, anomalous though it may seem, the construction of defences in Iraq was being directed and supervised by the India Command.

It has been seen that on 29 July, General Wavell had issued a directive to Lt.-General Quinan, Commanding the Iraq Force, instructing the latter to prepare plans for holding the northern frontier of Iraq against an Axis advance across Anatolia or Iran. At the same time he had also set his General Staff and Air Staff in India to produce another plan from their point of view. General Quinan was ready with his plan on 1 September and the Staffs in India by the 10th. Suggestions from the two plans were then incorporated in a third plan which was approved by General Wavell on 29 September. As regards Syria, which was not the responsibility of India, a separate plan was being prepared by the General Headquarters Middle East; it was completed on 9 September.

General Quinan's Plan.

The plan made by General Quinan was based on two considerations: one, that the aim of the Axis would be to clear British troops out of Iraq and capture Basra; two, that the Axis after securing the oilfields of Iraq might ignore Basra and move towards Egypt, turning the defences of Palestine from the east. The invading troops would be mostly those freed from the campaigns in Russia and they would advance against Iraq either across the eastern Anatolia or via Iran. In the first contingency they would enter Iraq from the valleys of the Euphrates and Tigris; in the second, by the passes on the north-eastern frontier, starting from Tabriz. It was not improbable that both the operations might be attempted simultaneously, in which case they would be well supported by *Luftwaffe* and the armoured forces. Any plan for the defence of Iraq would therefore have to provide for the defences of the Iranian and Anatolian frontiers of Iraq and for the safety of Basra.

It was to be expected that no attempt would be made by the Axis at invading Iraq, unless the invasion was properly supported by superior air and armoured forces. The British plan, therefore, would have to accept inferiority in the air and greater inferiority in armoured fighting vehicles. Hence it was essential to find tank-proof positions, or positions that might admit of being rendered tank-proof and from which easy withdrawal might be possible. These positions were to be so sited as to prevent the Axis forces from crossing the mountains of Kurdistan on the north-east or of Turkey on the north-west; and that purpose could be better served if the Allies were in possession of important aerodromes to be able to bomb the mountain routes. Taking these factors into consideration General Quinan suggested the following plan:

On the north-west—in Turkey

(a) All preparations to be made for a rapid advance by an armoured force and the 10th Indian Division to the area Elaziz, for action in conjunction with the troops from Palestine and Syria.

(b) Positions to be prepared in the rear:
   (i) At Zakho, covered by the rivers Khabur Su and Tigris.
   (ii) On the Dohuk and across the river Tigris to Ain Zala.
   (iii) On the line Aski Mosul—Was Sufa—J. Ishkaft—J. Sinjar and the river Khabur Su.
   (iv) Along the river Little Zab—Tigris—Jebel Mak Hul.

On the north-east—in Iran

Positions to be prepared:
   (i) On the frontier east of Rowanduz.
   (ii) On the frontier east of Sulaimaniya, in the Penjwin area.
   (iii) In the area Kermanshah-Karind.
   (iv) In the Eilam area.
   (v) In the area of the gorge, north-east of Dizful.

As for the defence of Basra, General Quinan's plan laid down that a depth in front of the base of Basra was essential for the security, both of the line of communication installations and aerodromes. It was also very desirable for the above reasons, as well as for the Iraqi morale, that Baghdad and the Iraqi plain should not be overrun. General Quinan therefore ordered the building of a separate and specially well-prepared position south-west of Baghdad, as the last line of defence of Basra. This position, among other things, would involve the use of extensive inundations on the west and would utilise the river Tigris to protect the eastern flank. Withdrawal to this position would mean abandoning Baghdad and evacuation of all installations to Basra for embarkation. Besides the inundations, it was intended to make the maximum use of demolitions also, to delay the Axis advance wherever possible.[6]

Appreciations by General and Air Staff

The planning by the General and Air Staffs in India was based on a detailed study of the various factors involved, such as the condition and capacity of the roads and railways, the length of the frontiers to be defended, the air and infantry strength which the Axis might be expected to muster on the borders, the weather conditions in Caucasia and Anatolia, and the probable date of invasion. In view of the extreme weather conditions prevailing both in Anatolia and Caucasia from November to April, it was felt that unless an Axis attack developed by October 1941, it was not likely to commence until about May 1942, though some minor preparatory moves might take place in the meantime. By May 1942, under the most favourable circumstances (i.e. in the case of Russian capitulation), the Axis might be able to bring up and maintain ten divisions in the Tabriz area and five on the general line Teheran—Hamadan—Kermanshah.

As regards the attack through Anatolia, it was estimated that the total land forces which the Axis would be able to bring against northern Iraq, through Turkey, by May 1942, would be about nine divisions. This estimate was based on the probable capacity of the road and rail communications. The capacity of the main railway line Samsun-Sivas-Malatya-Diyarbekir was taken as eight trains each way per day, that is an equivalent of 2,000 tons, or the requirements of five divisions. There was also an additional railway line linking Malatya to Nisibin via Aleppo, with a capacity of four trains per day. But this was not taken into consideration as it could only be used at the expense of the Samsun-Diyarbekir sector. As regards road communications, the maximum capacity of the roads (*i*) Ordu—Elaziz—Diyarbekir (*ii*) Trabzon—Erzurum—Mus—Diyarbekir and (*iii*) Trabzon—Erzurum—Bayazit—Maku—Khoi—Tabriz, was not known, but it was presumed that it would be possible to

[6] 297/G.H.Q., Iraq Force dated 1 September 1941, *Defence Policy Iraq and Iran*, F. 688.

maintain at least one division on each of the above systems, in addition to those maintained by rail.

As for the air force, it was estimated that the Axis would be able to direct from 1,000 to 1,200 aircraft for use in Turkey and Caucasia, if the Russian front stabilised. There were sixteen aerodromes fit for heavy bombers in Trans-Caucasia, five in northern Iran and six in eastern Anatolia. In addition, there were numerous landing grounds capable of expansion.

Thus by May 1942 the Axis might be expected to bring up fifteen divisions for an attack through Turkey, besides operating 1,000 to 1,200 aircraft.

But for opposing this rather formidable strength the Allied forces were not believed to be as numerous. It was understood that the Russians had provided in north Iran: 3 infantry divisions, 2 cavalry divisions and 1 armoured brigade. In Iraq-Iran the British had 3 infantry divisions and 1 armoured brigade, which force, by the spring of 1942, was expected to be increased to 5 or 6 infantry divisions, 1 armoured division and 1 heavy armoured brigade. The total Anglo-Russian joint force would not therefore amount to more than 12 miscellaneous divisions. As regards the air force, the War Office had already envisaged for Iraq 15 squadrons in October 1941, increasing to 25 in April 1942. The Russian contribution in air power was problematical and, in any case, was not likely to amount to much. On an overall view, the Allies were likely to be numerically inferior to the Axis both on land and in the air.

The frontage which was to be defended by these comparatively inferior numbers extended from Baku, in the east, to the region of Deir ez Zor in the west, a total distance of some 700 miles. Roughly about half of this was to be defended by the Russians. In view of the inadequacy of infantry and armour for holding such a wide front, it was not considered possible to adopt any linear system of defence. To the General Staff, India, it appeared that the whole defensive system would have to be based on the static defence of certain vital areas as self-contained "Fortresses", i.e. areas organised for all-round defence, which, even if by-passed by the Axis, could still exert effective pressure, owing to armoured and air forces which they would contain. Having regard to the necessity for depth, they recommended that the defensive areas should be organised, approximately about Mosul, Baghdad and Basra. Getting down to specific details, the General and Air Staffs of General Wavell made the following suggestions for the defence of Iraq:

(i) If Turkey was willing to co-operate, then British and Indian troops should get forward on to a line in the mountains, covering thereby the main communications southwards. Subject to reconnaissance, such a line was to be Bitlis—Mus—Elaziz—Malatya. Owing to the uncertainty of the Turkish attitude, however, such a position was regarded only as a forward zone, without obviating the necessity for a secure position in the rear in northern Irq.

(ii) If Turkey vacillated, then there was no alternative to starting work on the defences in northern Iraq at the earliest opportunity. In that case, it was suggested that three divisional areas should be established near and about Mosul: one north-east of Mosul, covering the Rowanduz approach and linking with the Russians, the second northwest of Mosul, and the third round Mosul itself. Each of these defensive areas was to include the operational aerodromes. They were to be constructed for all-round defence and to be stocked with at least 60 days' supplies in each case. Supporting these defensive areas, and probably located in the vicinity of Mosul, was to be one armoured division and a heavy armoured brigade. In order to maintain touch with the forces in Syria and prevent the left flank being turned in the early stages, a desert base for an armoured division was required in the area Deir ez Zor or Abu Kemal.

(iii) In addition to these forward defences, a defensive system in the Baghdad area might also be necessary. This system was to link up with the Russian system in the general area Kermanshah-Hamadan, and might require at least two infantry divisions and some armoured force. In the event of a complete Russian capitulation, however, the British might be prepared to hold Tabriz, with one infantry and one armoured division, in addition to the divisions mentioned above. For without such a force it might be impossible to prevent the Axis from establishing aerodromes in north Iran and infiltrating southwards, thereby threatening the oilfields.

If the main Axis attack developed against northern Syria, the forces from Deir ez Zor or Abu Kemal would have to be directed towards the flank of any such attack, and would have to be replaced from Baghdad by similar other forces.[7]

General Wavell's Plan

The appreciation and plans of General Quinan, as well as those of the Air and General Staffs in India, were examined by General

---

[7] *Appreciation by General Staff and Air Staff*, 10 September 1941, F. 688.

DEFENCE
1ST SEPTEMBE
SCALE O
50
0
PROPOSED DEFENSIVE
A
ELAZIZ (KHARPUT)
MUS
BITLIS
DIYARBAKIR
KHABUR SU
NISIBIN
B
ZAKHO
QAMICHLIYE
RAS EL AIN
J. AIN ZALA
DOHUK
C
TEL KOTCHEK
DOHUK R.
GREAT ZAB
HASSETCHE
D
ASKI MOSUL
JEBEL SINJAR
MOSUL
J. ISHKAFT
TEL AFAR
R. KHABUR
E
AL HADHR
LITTLE ZAB
DEIR EZ ZOR
JEBEL MAKHUL
MAYADINE
I R A
R. EUPHRATES
ABU KEMAL
R. TIGRIS
HADITHA
K
RAMADI
RUTBA
KARBALA

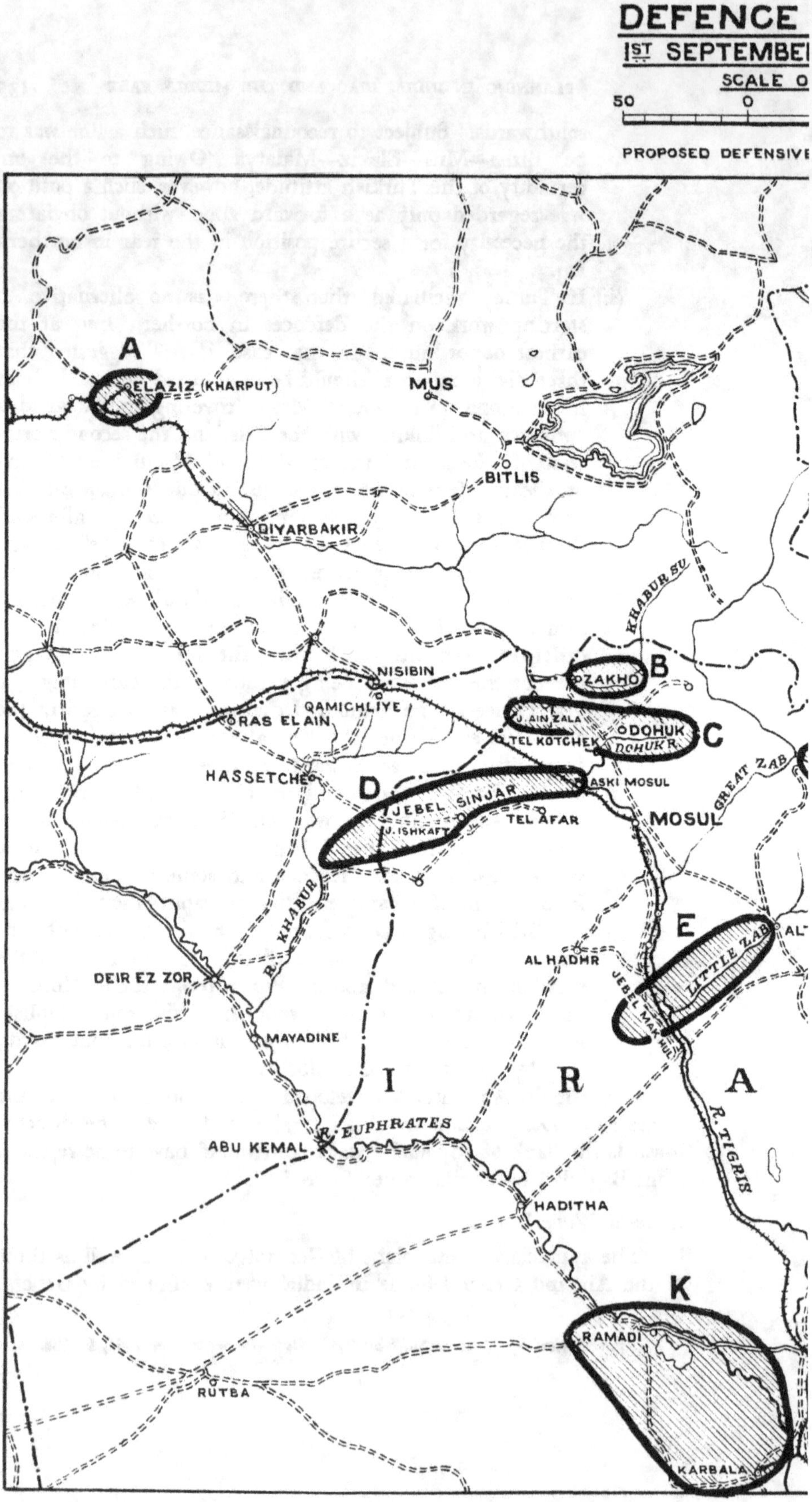

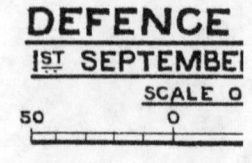

OF IRAQ
R 1941 – PLAN
F MILES
50
100
POSITIONS
K
CASPIAN SEA
KHOI
ARDEBIL
TABRIZ
F
ROWANDUZ
I R A N
ZENJAN
BIJAR
G
PENJWIN
TUN KOPRU
SULAIMANIYA
KIRKUK
HAMADAN
Q
H
KHANAQIN
KERMANSHAH
KARIND
IRAQ
I
DEILAM
BAGHDAD
J
DIZFUL

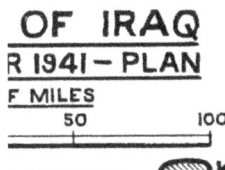

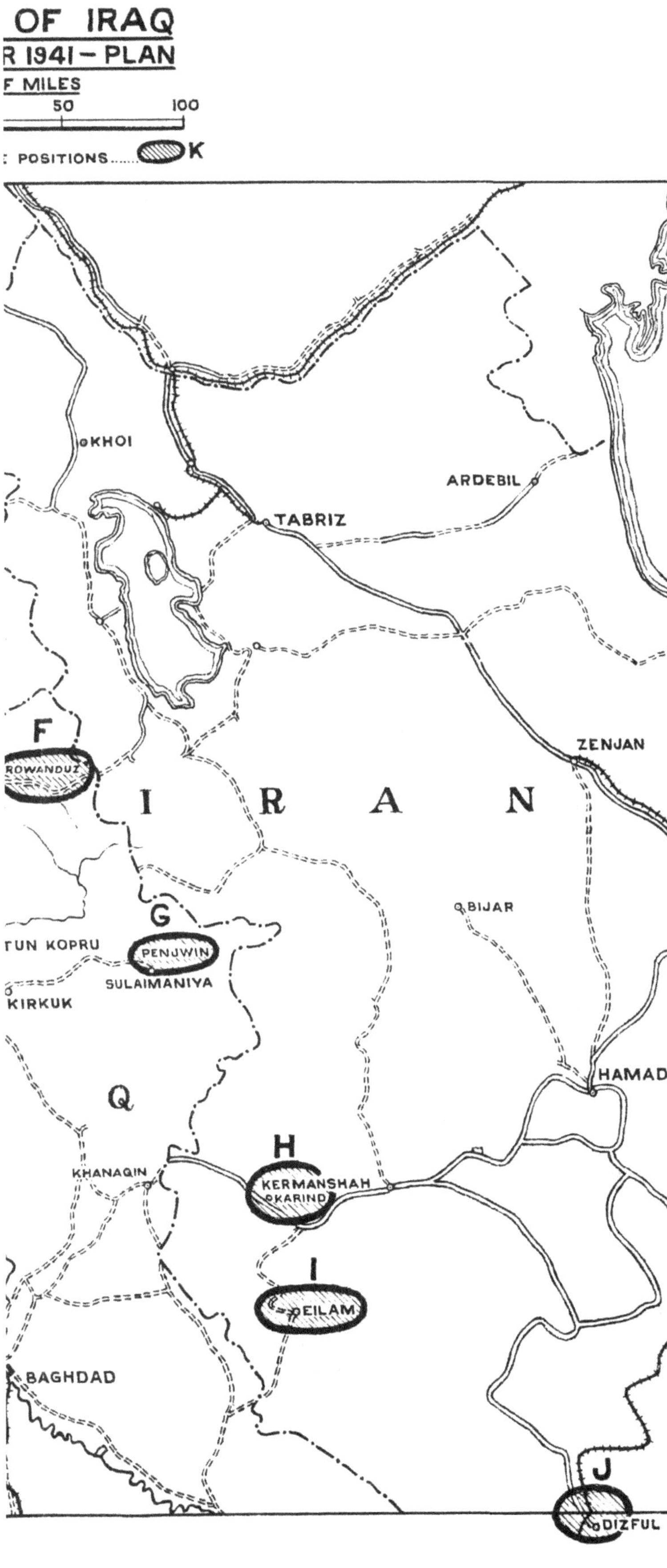

Wavell, who, as stated earlier, approved a final plan containing suggestions from both. He agreed with the suggestion of his Staff about the unsuitability of the linear defence and the necessity for a system of defence by manoeuvres. For a force inferior in numbers and armour there was no suitable area in northern Iraq that might not easily be turned. Defence, in the circumstances, would necessarily have to be by manoeuvre from within an area not easily admitting of being attacked or turned by the invader without his exposing himself to counter-attack at a disadvantage. For getting the best results, the troops would of course have to be mobile and skilfully handled. Such an area had to be selected and a suitable one was available just east of the Tigris, well positioned for defending Mosul, Baghdad, North Iraq and to some extent Syria. It was enclosed by the stretch of the river Tigris, from Baghdad to the area Faish Khabur—Zakho; by the mountainous country on the Iraq-Iran frontier; and by the Diyala river up to Baghdad, with an extension south of Baghdad, made by flooding, to protect the flank, against an advance on Baghdad along the west bank of the Euphrates.

This area, as defined above, had the advantage of providing facilities for meeting Axis threats, both through Anatolia and Caucasia. As mentioned earlier, an Axis attack through Anatolia might develop down the Euphrates and Tigris valleys and in the Jezireh between them; while an attack through Caucasia could develop along the routes Tabriz—Rowanduz and Pahlevi—Kazvin—Hamadan—Khanakin. A really mobile force, supported by a strong air force and assisted by fortifications at certain points, might by skilful manoeuvres be able to prevent the advance south, of any strong Axis force from either of those directions.

Thus, if the Axis advanced through Iran, defences of the main defiles and attack by air force would make their progress slow and difficult, and give opportunities for a counter-stroke. Similarly, an advance from Anatolia, east of the Tigris, might be checked at the Faish Khabur—Zakho position, and at the Great Zab and Little Zab rivers. If the Axis advanced west of the Tigris, their line of communications would be exposed to attack provided the British had the means of rapidly crossing the river by fortified bridge-heads. An attempt by the Axis to turn the area west of the Tigris, by a wide movement down the Euphrates, would similarly be met by the flooding of the ground between lake Habbaniya and Karbala and between the Euphrates and Tigris.

Stated briefly, the final plan approved by General Wavell provided for two separate systems of defence for Iraq, one in the north and the other in the south. The largest possible concentration of troops was to be in northern Iraq in the area of manoeuvre defined above, while only the necessary minimum was to be established in southern Iraq. This latter force was to be so deployed as to ensure the security of the Base and the lines of communication from Basra to Baghdad, the protection of the Anglo-Iranian oilfields, and the defences of the defiles on the Khuramabad—Ahwaz route. The principal defences in the north would be the Faish Khabur—Zakho defile, the bridgehead at Mosul, the main crossing of the Great Zab and Little Zab rivers, the selected defiles on the routes through Iran and bridgeheads on the Tigris. Preparations were also to be made for inundations west of Baghdad, and for demolitions, minefields, obstacles etc. designed to delay the Axis advance. The role of the Royal Air Force in support of this plan still remained to be considered.[8]

Plan for the defence of Syria and Palestine

Besides the above plans for the defence of Iraq, there existed, as mentioned earlier, a plan for the defence of Syria and Palestine also, which was prepared by the General Headquarters, Middle East. This provided for the British forces, in conjunction with the Turkish Army, to oppose the Axis advance in western Anatolia in case Turkey offered its co-operation. But if for any reason the British forces were unable to reach western Anatolia, it might still be possible and desirable to seize positions in southern Anatolia, either along the watershed south of Erzincan, reaching up to the Taurus mountains, or along the high ground Maden—south of Malatya—Gaziantep—Alexandretta. Alternatively, if the attitude of the Turks made it impracticable to advance into the hills of southern Anatolia, British troops might be moved forward to the northern limit of the plains, where they could hamper the Axis, debouching from the hills. In face of a superior Axis force, the British forces might withdraw from Anatolia on two divergent fronts—Syria and Iraq. In Iraq, they would join the previously prepared area of manoeuvre as described above, namely the area enclosed by the Tigris, the Diyala and the mountainous country on the Iran—Iraq frontier. In Syria they would withdraw to similarly prepared defended localities, sited to protect the main aerodromes and base installations in the areas, Baalbek—Rayak—Beirut and Palestine. The main idea was to take up positions in the mountainous area of southern Syria and northern Palestine for stopping a further Axis advance. The withdrawal to this defensive area was to be accompanied by comprehensive demolitions so as to deny to the Axis all facilities which would be of use to them, particularly oil, communications and food stocks. This plan of defence had

---

[8] *Defence of Iraq against attack from north* by General Wavell dated 29 September 1941, F. 688.

obvious advantages. The Axis would be forced to attack the British force in its prepared positions or to detach forces to contain British garrisons. Difficulties of maintenance would also slow up their advance and provide the British a favourable opportunity for counter-attack. Where possible, defended localities were to be sited in natural tank-proof areas, prepared for all-round defence and for protracted resistance. Offensive action against Axis communications was an essential feature of the defence plan for each locality.[9]

Résumé of the Plans

Thus plans were ready, by the end of September 1941, for defending Iran, Iraq and Syria against any invasion from the north, whether it came from Caucasia or Anatolia, or from several directions simultaneously. Briefly, the plan was to offer initial resistance in the Turkish territory of western Anatolia, provided there was enough co-operation from Turkey to justify that step. Failing that, this plan contemplated a forcible seizure of positions in southern Anatolia, especially if there were reasons to believe that Turkey was co-operating with the Axis or was succumbing to hostile pressure. In case the attitude of Turkey justified neither of the two alternatives, the Allied troops were to move up to the northern-most limits of the plains and deal with the Axis forces debouching from the hills. In face of the superior strength of the invaders, these troops were to withdraw fighting delaying actions, along two divergent lines, to Iraq and Syria respectively, where they were to join the previously prepared positions and make their first firm stand, in defence of Baghdad and the Persian Gulf on the one hand, and Palestine and Suez on the other.

---

[9] G.H.Q., M.E.F. and G.H.Q., India combined O.I. No. 1 dated 17 September 1941, *Defence Policy Iraq and Iran*, F. 688; G.H.Q., O.I. No. 101 dated 9 September 1941, F. 688.

CHAPTER XVII

Problems Connected with the Threat to Caucasia

General Wavell's plan for the defence of Iraq against Axis aggression from Caucasia and Anatolia was, as we have seen, ready by the end of September 1941. Much work however remained to be done on the administrative side before it could become a working reality. Administrative appreciations were being prepared in India by the General Staff and in the Middle East by the Joint Planning Staff.

Russian Forces

The General Staff India had made three appreciations of the situation concerning the Axis threat to Caucasia. The first one was on 24 July 1941, the second on 10 September and the third on 1 November. These were based on the doubt about Russian ability to check Axis advance on Caucasia. Russian land forces, excluding those engaged at Rostov, were believed, in the absence of official Russian information, to be four infantry divisions, six or seven cavalry divisions, and eight reserve infantry divisions in Caucasia; and one infantry regiment, one or two cavalry divisions, one armoured division, one tank regiment and one reserve infantry division in north-west Iran. There was lack of faith in their value as effective fighting forces owing particularly to their being mountain divisions with lower fire power. The reserve divisions were not believed to be of high quality. Ammunition production and reserves in Caucasia were also believed to be small, and supply of ammunition or replacement of equipment was deemed to be difficult. As regards their air force, it was estimated, again without Russian figures, that Russia had about 640 aircraft in Trans-Caucasia. Perhaps up to 300 more as reinforcements might be transferred from other Russian fronts, if the latter became sufficiently stabilised. The fighting value of the aircraft in Trans-Caucasia was difficult to estimate, but it might be prejudiced by a fair number of obsolescent aircraft. The Russian Black Sea Fleet, however, was a formidable force, greatly superior to any Axis naval force in the Black sea.

Axis forces

The Axis force threatening Caucasia was the Southern Army

Group, which consisted of four armoured divisions, thirty-eight infantry divisions, Italian and Rumanian contingents, and six hundred and fifty aircraft.

It was believed that the Axis would necessarily be in a hurry to attack Caucasia. As a result, the Southern Army Group, while still operating against the Russians, would have to find the forces necessary to overrun and possibly hold Trans-Caucasia at the same time. It was estimated that the maximum force to be thus spared by the Southern Army Group would be two armoured divisions, one motorised division and thirteen infantry divisions. The aircraft to be spared might come up to about 350 machines immediately and 250 more by early December.[1] A land and air force of that size was believed to be sufficient for seizing Trans-Caucasia.

Possibilities of Axis attack on Caucasia

Apart from the mountain tracks and two military roads (Georgian and Ossetic), which in mid-winter are under snow, the Caucasus is an impossible terrain for military operations. Three infantry divisions were considered to be the maximum that might operate over the passes, provided adequate arrangements for snow-clearance were made. Many more divisions could, however, be passed along the east and the west coasts.

On the east coast, the thousand metre contour was nowhere nearer than nine miles to the coast. The country was therefore generally open, although intersected by numerous streams and rivers which were not believed to be serious obstacles in winter. The roads were not surfaced but rainfall was low; and it was reasonable to conclude that a force of ten divisions, including two armoured divisions, might operate on this coast. As to the west coast, the thousand metre contour approached to within five miles of the coast. The main road was a modern motor road but rainfall was high and the country close. Consequently, the vehicles would have difficulty in moving off the road, although the infantry could operate across the country. Hence it was estimated that not more than three divisions could operate along this route.

Thus if circumstances were very favourable and Russian opposition on the other fronts was not stiff, the Axis might cross the Caucasus with a force of sixteen divisions, including two armoured and one motorised, enough for seizing Trans-Caucasia.[2] It was however doubtful if in view of the poor communications and winter conditions, the Axis would sustain the momentum as far as Makhach Kala, let alone Baku.

[1] Historical Section file No. 12183.
[2] Ibid.

In case of Axis advance on Tabriz and Teheran

If the Axis forces succeeded in securing a foothold in Caucasia, northern Iran, as far as Tabriz, would be overrun, for which they would exploit the facilities afforded by the Black Sea ports as well as by the existing road and railway communications. If the existing port facilities and the rail and road communications were fully utilized, and were not interfered with by demolitions or sabotage, it was estimated that the Axis would be able to maintain a maximum force of ten divisions in the Tabriz area. Administrative difficulties would increase thereafter if, for example, they tried to advance down south towards the general line Kermanshah-Hamadan-Teheran.

This advance would have to rely almost entirely on the road communications, there being no railway link between Tabriz and the areas Kermanshah-Hamadan and Hamadan-Teheran.[3]

The Iranian railway connected Bandar Shah with Teheran, Zinjan and Kazvin, but there was a gap of about 200 miles between Tabriz and Zinjan. That was a serious limitation on the utility of that railway. The capacity of that sector was two trains each way per day. The gauge was British standard, 4 feet 8½ inches, and was therefore a misfit with the Russian standard of 5 feet. It was estimated that three divisions might be maintained through the port of Bandar Shah, via rail, to the Teheran area.

In addition to the road and rail communications, there were the Trans-Caspian Sea routes, from Baku to the three Iranian ports of Pahlevi, Bandar Shah and Chalus. Pahlevi was the best port in the Caspian. It had six berths, and ten small Caspian steamers could unload simultaneously at its wharves. At the port of Bandar Shah, two ships could lie alongside the quay at the same time, and

---

[3] The following road communications existed:—
   (i) *Route A*—Tabriz-Zinjan-Kazvin-Teheran (distance 400 miles). It was the main road from the north into Iran—all-weather and fit for heavy lorries throughout, except for parts between Tabriz and Zinjan, which might be under snow for ten days at a time in winter (January-March).
   (ii) *Route B*—Tabriz-Senneh-Hamadan-Kermanshah (approximately 400 miles long). This route served the Kermanshah-Hamadan area. The road was good as far as Maragheh; thence it was an unmetalled second class road unlikely to stand up to continuous mechanical traffic, without heavy demands on maintenance repairs. It was liable to floods in the Lake Urmia area.
   (iii) *Route C*—Kazvin-Hamadan-Kermanshah (distances: Kazvin to Hamadan 148 miles; Hamadan to Kermanshah 125 miles). This was the main route into Iraq, all-weather, and used by heavy lorries.
   (iv) *Route D*—Pahlevi-Kazvin (distance 151 miles), a generally all-weather route.
   (v) *Route E*—Bandar Shah-Shahi-Teheran (distance 250 miles), a generally all-weather route.
   (vi) *Route F*—Chalus-Meshed-i-Sar-Shahi (distance 90 miles to Shahi and 250 miles to Teheran) was also an all-weather road.
   (vii) *Route G*—Chalus-Teheran (distance 130 miles) was of very little strategic value.

there was a ship-repairing yard capable of dealing with ships up to 1,500 tons. The Chalus harbour required an enormous amount of dredging, for which facilities were poor, and the use of this port was therefore always below its potentialities. Road and rail facilities existed from these three Caspian ports to the Teheran—Kazvin area.

It was estimated that the maximum force which the Axis might be able to maintain under the most favourable conditions would be five divisions:

(i) Teheran area—three divisions through Bandar Shah by rail,
(ii) Kazvin area—one division by road from Pahlevi, and
(iii) Hamadan—Kermanshah area—one division by road from Tabriz.

With more mechanical transport available, the Axis might make a more intensive use of both the road routes—from Tabriz to Hamadan and Kermanshah, and Chalus to Teheran—which would enable further divisions to be maintained in the areas Kermanshah-Hamadan—Teheran.

Air transport was another important factor. Landing grounds existed at Tabriz, Zinjan, Kazvin, Hamadan and Kermanshah, and working on an average 'useful load' of 1½ tons per aircraft, the requirements of a division would mean 200 sorties. That was by no means an improbable employment, and, if available, it might be used to maintain additional forces in the Hamadan-Kermanshah areas and so save considerable mechanical transport.[4]

Directive to Lieut.-General Quinan

As the threat to Caucasia increased, with the German forces nearing Rostov, General Wavell issued a new directive to Lt.-General Quinan, on 15 November 1941. He was ordered to assume command of all Imperial land forces in Iraq, the Persian Gulf and Iran, up to and including Bandar Abbas, Kerman and Bandar Shah (Caspian). He was also to command any forces which might be sent to northern Iran or Caucasia. The directive gave details of the reinforcements he might expect up to June 1942. The 6th, 8th and 10th Indian Infantry Divisions were already in Iraq and Iran. Reinforcements were to include the 14th, 17th and 18th Indian Infantry Divisions, five battalions of the Indian States Forces and three additional infantry battalions as well as the 50th British Infantry Division and the 1st Indian Armoured Division. The non-divisional units of the various divisions would not be provided to

---

[4] *G.H.Q., 'Q' Appreciation dated 24 July 1941; German maintenance through the Caucasus; A Manual of Eurasian Routes,* (Naval Staff Intelligence Department), March 1920.

full scale until the late summer of 1942. A Corps Headquarters was to be provided early in 1942.

The primary task of Lt.-General Quinan was to defend Iraq and Iran against an Axis advance from Anatolia or from Caucasia. In the defence of Iraq he was to act in the closest co-operation with the Commander, Ninth Army (Palestine and Syria). He was also to be prepared for operations in Anatolia, in co-operation with the troops of the Middle East Command and possibly the Turkish army, and was to co-operate with the Russian army in the defence of Caucasia or North Iran. The operations were to be supported by the Royal Air Force under the command of the Air Officer Commanding, Iraq. Lt.-General Quinan was to prepare for the maintenance of ten divisions and thirty squadrons R.A.F. for employment in Iraq, and from four to six divisions in Iran. He was also to take such steps to develop road, rail and river communications as were necessary to ensure the maintenance of this force and the maximum possible delivery of supplies to Russia.

Administrative Problems of Defence

The ambitious target of ten infantry divisions and thirty R.A.F. squadrons for the defence of Iraq presented certain administrative difficulties. Already on 10 October, General Headquarters, India, had made a detailed appreciation to determine the administrative provision necessary to maintain a force of this size in Iraq, of which 50% might be operating in Anatolia and 20% in northern Iran. In this appreciation particular attention was paid to road, rail and port facilities and the provision of supplies.

The ports of Basra and Umm Qasr had inadequate facilities for handling the estimated 9,000 tonnage per day. It was necessary to provide more cranes, and to increase the number of wharves at Basra from seven to eleven, so as to enable that port to clear about 5,400 tons daily. Umm Qasr could clear an additional 600 tons per day. Another new port was necessary to clear the residual tonnage of 3,000 tons per day.

The transportation facilities in Iraq were also insufficient. It was estimated that the daily lift between Basra and Baghdad would amount to 7,500 tons. The maximum possible capacity of the single existing Basra—Baghdad railway line was however only 4,000 tons per day. The residue of 3,500 tons per day would therefore have to be carried by increased facilities for Inland Water Transport. For this, it was necessary to have a separate Inland Water Transport Port, as it was most wasteful in manual effort and in rail traffic to move goods from ocean-going steamers to Shuaiba base, and then move them back to the river for onward journey to Baghdad by the inland water system.

As regards movement of goods by road, it would take 1,680 lorries, each carrying 5 tons, to lift 1,000 tons per day, making allowance for repairs, maintenance and loss of days due to prolonged hold-ups by the seasonal floods. That would not be an impossible feat if the road Basra—Baghdad was improved. The improvement of the road was also desirable for tactical reasons. But it would not solve the whole problem of lifting 3,500 tons per day, except with a large expenditure of time and money. Since time was short there were only two alternatives: either a second railway line, or an Inland Water Transport lift up to 3,500 tons per day.

As to the railway line, it was not only the Basra—Baghdad line that was inadequate. The same was true of the Baghdad—Mosul—Turkey and the Baghdad—Kirkuk lines. The maximum capacity of the railway Baghdad—Mosul—Turkey was approximately 3,000 tons a day, whereas the total traffic for Turkey was estimated to be 4,800 tons per day. That surplus traffic could only be handled by using the road transport, in addition to the railway. Similarly, the maximum capacity of the railway Baghdad—Kirkuk was approximately 1,000 tons per day whereas the estimated lift was 1,200 tons per day. Therefore it was necessary to provide extra transportation facilities, such as a railway line from Kut al Amara to Baquba.

Besides the road, rail and water transport facilities, the problem of administrative bases for maintaining the force also received attention. Two alternatives were taken into consideration—to expand the Base at Basra-Shuaiba, or to hold reserves within fortress areas. The latter alternative was favoured, as it would give greater mobility to the troops in the forward localities. But large reserves concentrated in forward areas were liable to be lost through hostile action; hence it was decided to adopt a system of dispersal whereby each commodity might be distributed between two separate depots, the various items in each depot being further split up into mixed dumps. Such fortress areas, together, were to hold 100% reserves for four divisions, i.e. for two divisions in the Mosul—Kirkuk areas and two more in a southern area yet to be chosen.

This would be in addition to the six divisions which the Shuaiba base could maintain without any expansion. Khosroabad would be a transit area only for the change from steamers to the barges. Kut al Amara was also to be a similar transit area, but was to be expanded to an Advanced Base, if the forces to be maintained increased to more than six divisions.

As regards mechanical transport, it was estimated that a

maximum of 58 General Purposes Transport Companies would be required to maintain ten infantry divisions and thirty squadrons R.A.F. between the army, the line of communication Basra—Baghdad, and the R.A.F; and a stock of 4½ million gallons of petrol, being a reserve for three months.

Arrangements for the evacuation of casualties were also likely to add to the transport problem, the maximum force envisaged being thirty-three Field Ambulances, twenty Motor Ambulance Sections, fifteen Casualty Clearing Stations, six metre and two standard gauge ambulance trains, one hundred and twenty staging sections and ten British General Hospitals.[5]

Liaison between India and Middle East Command

Closest co-operation between India and the Middle East was necessary for planning for the defence of Syria, Palestine, Iraq and Iran against Axis threat through Anatolia or Caucasia. With this end in view an officer from General Headquarters, India, was posted to the Joint Planning Staff, Middle East, during September. At a conference held at Baghdad on 26 September 1941, and attended among others by General Auchinleck and General Wavell, it was decided that the Joint Planning Staff should study the problem of the Axis threat in all its aspects.[6] This facilitated liaison between India and Middle East Command for the drawing up of plans for the entire range of the northern front countries, namely, Palestine, Syria, Iraq and Iran.[7]

Aid to Russia

In view of the Axis threat to Caucasia, the British Government began to take into consideration the question of a suitable offer of help to Russia, and an interesting exchange of views took place between General Wavell, General Auchinleck and the War Office on the form the assistance should take. The question was whether Russia would be best helped by their sending a British force to operate on the southern Russian front, or by the despatch of supplies and equipment only. The first alternative was mooted towards the end of October 1941. The British Government proposed to send the 50th and 18th Divisions to help strengthen the Caucasus front,[8] to which General Auchinleck was agreeable, provided only that the Russian Government permitted the British representatives to carry out a reconnaissance of the aerodromes, base facilities and

---

[5] *Administrative Appreciation dated 10 October 1941*, Forward Planning, F. 5058.
[6] *Record of conference at Baghdad on 62 September 1941*, F. 688.
[7] General Auchinleck's *Despatch*, 5 July 1941—31 Oct. 1941.
[8] Tel. No. 98465 dated 29 Oct. from Troopers to Armindia, *British reinforcements to the Caucasus*, p. 6, F. 741.

communications in Trans-Caucasia.⁹ But the Russian Government did not react favourably to the British offer of Staff conversations[10] and the matter was not pursued further. On 14 November 1941, however, the War Office informed General Auchinleck that in their view it was not advisable to cease preparations for the despatch of the proposed force. They rather wished the preparations to continue as before, so that in case the situation deteriorated and the Russian Government showed willingness to accept the help, there would be no delay in sending it across. The force, consisting of a Corps of two infantry divisions—the 18th and the 50th—plus an Armoured Car Squadron, six fighter and one bomber squadrons, was to be available for operations by the end of March 1942. A part of it was to be made available even earlier should necessity arise. Evidently the War Office was attaching great importance to this form of aid to Russia.[11] Later, however, it changed its view-point due, in some measure at least, to the forceful representation of the other side of the case by General Wavell.

General Wavell, declared himself opposed to the idea of sending the proposed force to the Russian front, on the following grounds:—

(i) The movement and maintenance of that force in Caucasia by April 1942 would strain transportation resources to the utmost, and would mean that supplies to Russia by that route would practically cease. It was, therefore, a choice between sending the force or sending the material which Russia required.

(ii) The main weight of the Axis attack was likely to be directed on Baku from the north. In that area, between the Caspian Sea and the hill country, there was an average width of ten to twenty miles entirely suitable for the use of armour. Most of the country between the Caucasus range and northern Iran, and the greater part of northern Iran itself, were also good tank countries. Therefore, it would be most unwise to commit forces in northern Iran and Caucasia without an adequate armoured component.

(iii) The despatch of infantry forces was not the only means of securing facilities for reconnaissance and of stiffening the Russian morale, unless the Russians themselves asked for that type of help. On the other hand, the supply of material and technical units was likely to achieve that purpose even better.

⁹ Tel. O/22183 dated 4 Nov. 41 from Mideast to Troopers, p. 29, F. 741.
[10] Tel. 51682 dated 14 Nov. 41 from Troopers to Mideast, p. 82, F. 741.
[11] Tel. 51682 dated 14 Nov. 41 from Troopers to Mideast, p. 82, F. 741.

General Wavell, therefore, held that it was necessary to decide whether their limited transportation resources in the Persian Gulf area were to be used to provide supplies, equipment and air support to the Russians, or to send them infantry forces at the expense of those vital necessities.[12]

At this stage (18 November), General Auchinleck once again represented his views to the War Office. He agreed with General Wavell that if the effort of the British force to stabilize the Trans-Caucasian front failed, it would be defeated in detail. The British Government could ill afford the loss of two divisions which would be invaluable in the main areas of resistance, i.e. in Iraq-Iran. In spite of those obvious drawbacks, however, General Auchinleck felt that it was necessary to send a British force to the help of Russia, provided preliminary staff talks were held, reconnaissances made and an assurance given by the Russian Government that at least one Russian armoured division would be ready to support the British force in Caucasia.[13]

In the meantime, the 50th Division (less one Brigade Group) arrived in Iraq (14 November) and was later concentrated in the Kirkuk area.[14] With the outbreak of war with Japan on 7 December 1941, however, a new situation developed. The 18th Indian Division, then *en route* to the Middle East, was diverted to Bombay for the Far East. The Russian recovery during the same month further underlined this welcome change, which freed the 50th Division for a move to other theatres of the Middle East Command. The move commenced on 12 January 1942, after which preparations for sending a force to Caucasia ceased altogether. Assistance to Russia was, thereafter, to take the form of supply of materials, equipment, technical units, etc. The occupation of Iran had opened the way for this and the 'Aid-to-Russia' scheme began to make a satisfactory progress.[15]

---

[12] Tel. 18111 dated 17 Nov. 41 from Armindia to Troopers, p. 94, F. 741.
[13] Tel. 0/28044 dated 18 Nov. 41 from Mideast to Troopers, p. 103, F. 741.
[14] General Wavell's *Despatch*.
[15] For details consult the last pact of this narrative, entitled 'Paiforce'.

CHAPTER XVIII

Mosul and Baghdad Defences

Mosul Area

The Aid-to-Russia scheme was one aspect of the defence of Iraq. It aimed at defeating the invader in southern Russia so as to prevent his reaching the borders of Iraq. The other aspect concerned itself with the internal defence of Iraq, that is, with the construction of fixed defences for fighting the invader at or inside the Iraqi frontiers, in case he was not stopped in Trans-Caucasia. We have seen that General Wavell had issued a directive to Lt.-General Quinan to prepare plans for constructing such defences. The directive was issued on 29 July when the threat to Iraq was not so serious as it was at this later stage. Lt.-General Quinan had therefore been enjoined to carry out permanent constructions on a large scale but to confine them, for the time being, to denying to the Axis armoured vehicles the main approaches into Iraq, from Turkey and Iran.

Conforming to that directive, Lt.-General Quinan had submitted his plans to General Wavell on 1 September; and on 12 September had detailed the 8th Indian Division for siting and constructing defences in the Mosul area. The Divisional Commander, Major-General C. O. Harvey, assigned the task to Brigadier D. D. Gracey, commanding the 17th Indian Infantry Brigade which was then at Mosul. Brig. Gracey carried out a detailed reconnaissance and submitted specific proposals. These were to establish defensive positions at Halaila—Mosul West, to the west of the Tigris; at Ninevah-Yarimjah, to the east of the Tigris; in the Qaiyara area, about fifty miles south of Mosul; and in the area Aski—Mosul— Abu Maria (and at Faidah), to the north and north-west of Mosul. These proposals aimed at fortifying the approaches to Mosul from all sides, and included the preparation of the following defensive positions:—

(a) *Halaila—Mosul defensive position*

One division, less one brigade group, was to be responsible for the defence of this position west of Mosul. The role of the garrison was to prevent the capture of this important area guarding the western bank of the Tigris; to take offensive action against the airborne Axis troops landing in that area, and to be ready to assume the offensive in co-operation with the armoured division at Qaiyara.

MOSUL AND SURROUNDING AREA

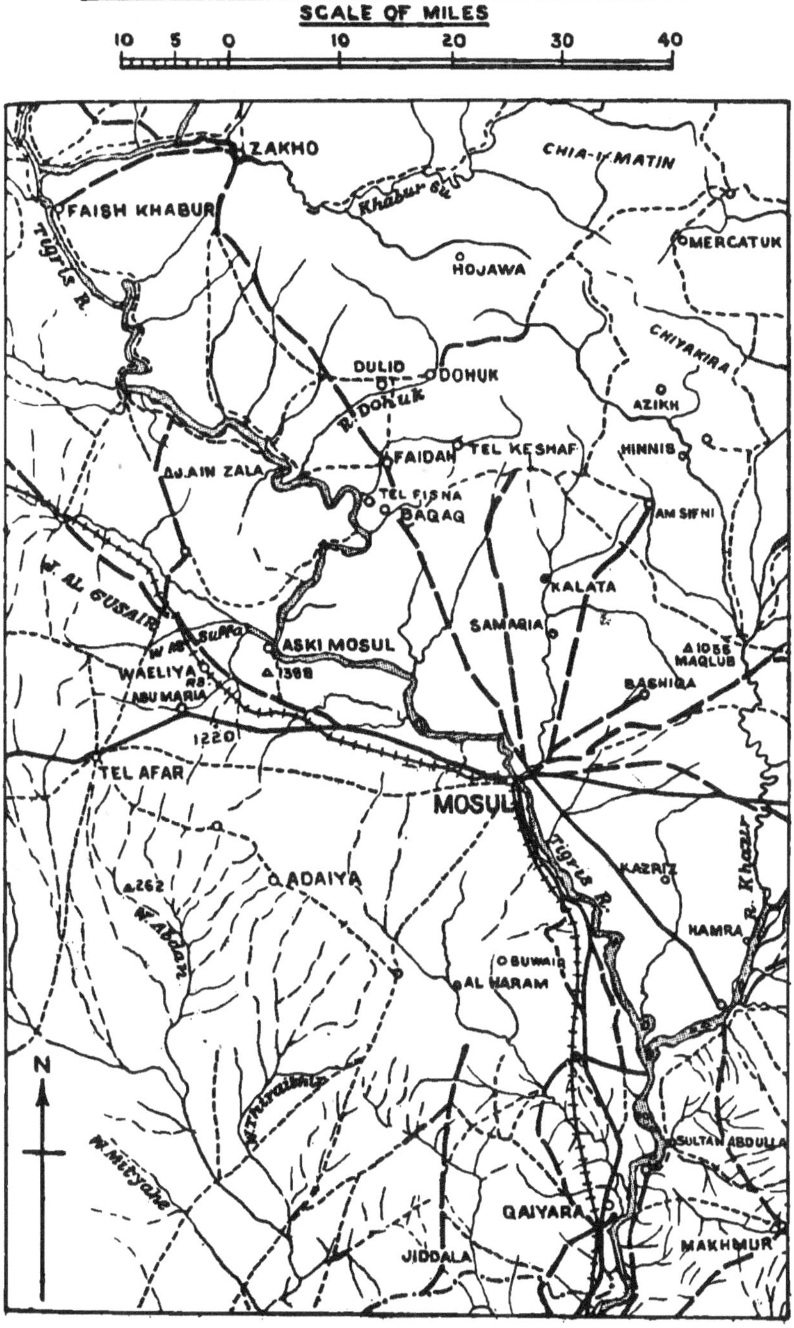

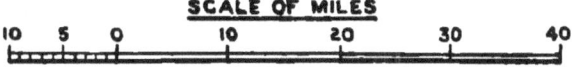

The Forward Defended Localities included the line of the Wadi Halaila from the junction with the Tigris to its source on the northern slopes of the Jebel Atshan—southern slopes of Jebel Atshan—track junction north of Dibbachah—thence the line of the track to the crest of Jebel Nuwaigit. An 'I' Tank Battalion harbour was to be dispersed and concealed in the lower foothills. This area had strong natural defences and with a little improvement, the Wadi Halaila, between the Tigris and the railway line, could be turned into a good anti-tank obstacle.

(b) *Ninevah-Yarimjah defensive position*

One division, less two brigade groups, was to be responsible for the defence of this area to the east of Mosul. One of the roles of the garrison was to act as a mobile reserve, but its primary task was to take action against airborne attacks on the aerodrome or other military targets in the vicinity of Mosul, particularly the main Mosul bridge.

(c) *Aski Mosul-Abu Maria defensive position*

One infantry brigade group was to hold this position to the north-west of Mosul. The role of this force was:—

(i) to ascertain the strength of the Axis force advancing from Tell Kotchek, and to delay it in conjunction with the Royal Air Force and by planned demolitions,

(ii) to support the action of the armoured division when operating westwards from Qaiyara, and

(iii) to be prepared, on the arrival of additional troops, to assume the offensive via Tell Afar or Adaiya.

Forward Defended Localities included the line of the Wadi Kisk Keupri from (excluding) Tell ar Rim to (including) Al Mazra Pt. 1220—Tell as Saman and the western slopes of Pt. 1388. Outposts were located on the line Al Waeliya railway station—Palu Tepe—Abu Maria—Pt. 1210—Al Butaishah and Pt. 1388.

The northern section of this line had strong natural defences, but in the southern section, the Wadi as Saman and the Wadi Kisk Keupri needed strengthening with anti-tank ditches.

(d) *Faidah defensive position*

One infantry brigade group was to hold this second position to the north of Mosul and to the south of Dohuk. Its role was:

(i) to prepare demolitions in Zakho defile and on bridges over Khabur Su,

(ii) to delay any Axis advance in the area Zakho—Faish Khabur, and

(iii) to hold the main defended area Faidah—Chia-i-Dakhan. Strong forward detachments were to be located in prepared positions along the Rudbar Dohuk (at about Dulid) and in the forward delaying positions in the area Zakho—Faish Khabur.

(e) *Qaiyara defensive position*

One armoured division and one infantry brigade group were to hold this defensive position about fifty miles south of Mosul. The infantry brigade group was to be the mobile reserve of the force. Its primary tasks were the defence of installations and the aerodrome against airborne attacks, and reinforcements to the Support Groups of the armoured division. The static defence of the aerodrome was to be carried out by Iraq Levies and one sub section of the R.A.F. armoured cars.[1]

The approved Plan

The above plan for the defence of Mosul underwent considerable modification before it was accepted by General Wavell. That was partly owing to a drastic cut in the resources that were to be made available to Lt.-General Quinan in the winter of 1941-42, and partly because, on 29 September, General Wavell had approved a plan for the defence of the whole of Iraq. The Mosul plan had therefore to be modified to fit into the general plan.

General Wavell visited Mosul on 18 October 1941, and reconnoitred the sites of the proposed defences. After consultation with Lt.-General Quinan he decided to rely for the defence of Mosul on the area of manoeuvre, which was the main feature of his plan of 29 September, together with certain bridgeheads for increasing the mobility of the troops and one or two static defensive positions of a restricted nature. Accordingly, he proposed constructing a defensive position between the river Tigris and the hills at Faidah, south of Dohuk. As to bridgeheads, he ordered one to be established on the west bank of the river at Mosul and another in the Qaiyara area, about fifty miles south of Mosul. The outpost positions at Faish Khabur-Zakho and at Aski Mosul (north-west of Mosul) were to be constructed if time and material permitted. But otherwise the basis of the general plan for the defence of northern Iraq was to be the area of manoeuvre, between the western bank of the Tigris and the eastern side of the Iranian hills, with the northern end of that area resting on the defensive position south of Dohuk, and the southern end on the Baghdad defences.

[1] *War Diary* 17 Ind. Inf. Bde.

Inside that area were to be kept the larger bulk of the fighting forces, fully mobile, and capable of moving rapidly to reinforce any threatened point, making use of the Mosul and Qaiyara bridgeheads to cross the river for the purpose. For that reason communications inside the area were to be improved to the maximum. Preparations were also to be made to block approaches to Baghdad, between the Tigris and the Euphrates, mainly by inundations; and a possible turning movement west of the Euphrates was to be prevented by flooding the ground between lake Habbaniya and Karbala. Positions were also to be prepared, as otherwise provided in the general plan, for defending the main routes from Iran into Iraq.

The force required for the defence of whole of Iraq was estimated to be one armoured division, one heavy armoured brigade and six infantry divisions. The allocation of these troops was, one infantry division for the protection of lines of communication and internal security in Iraq, one for Iran, two infantry divisions and one heavy armoured brigade for the defence of the Faidah position and Mosul bridgehead, and one armoured division and two infantry divisions to be available as a mobile force. Of the latter, one division was to be stationed in the Baghdad area.[2]

Revised Instructions by Lt.-General Quinan

Following the above change in the plan, Lieut.-General Quinan issued fresh instructions to his troops, on 20-21 October 1941, concerning the construction of defensive positions in their allotted areas. The immediate role of the Iraq Force, that is until the arrival of reinforcements, was defined as follows:

> The 8th Indian Division was to be responsible for the construction of defensive works at Mosul West (area west and south-west of Mosul), and for carrying out preliminary work at Ninevah (area east of Mosul) and at Faidah (north of Mosul) until relieved by the 6th Indian Division in January 1942. It was also to carry out reconnaissance of defensive positions in the area of the two rivers (between Khazir and Great Zab), until relieved by the 50th British Division from the Middle East. The 2nd Armoured Brigade, under it, was to be responsible for the construction of defensive works at Qaiyara and the reconnaissance of the Erbil area.
>
> The 10th Indian Division was to be employed on defences Ramadi—Falluja—Mujara, and in the Karbala area. In addition, it was to carry out reconnaissance of defensive positions in the area between the two rivers of Kirkuk, with

---

[2] Tel. No. 15872 dated 23 October 1941 from Armindia to Troopers, *Defence of Iraq Planning*, F. 746.

a view to protecting Kirkuk. The 6th Indian Infantry Division was to be responsible for the protection of Khanakin and Naft Khana and for the construction of defences at Pai Tak Pass and Pul-i-Tang.[3]

With the arrival of all expected reinforcements, it was assumed that the dispositions of the Iraq Force, as on 15 February 1942, would be approximately along the following lines: the 8th Indian Division would be responsible for the defence of Mosul west, the 2nd Armoured Brigade for that of the Erbil area, the 10th Indian Division for the area between the two rivers and Kirkuk, the 6th Indian Division for Faidah, Ninevah, Qaiyara and the two rivers, the 17th Division for the defence of Khanakin and Iran and the 34th Division for Mujara—Falluja—Hindiya—Baghdad and the line of communication.[4]

Construction of defences in the Mosul area

On 20 October 1941, Commander 8th Indian Division ordered the 17th Indian Infantry Brigade to prepare a bridgehead at Mosul West for a complete division, including three field regiments, one anti-tank regiment, one anti-aircraft regiment, one medium battery and one machine-gun battalion. The defended area was to be based on the general line Wadi Halaila—Shaikh Yunus—Tell al Hallab.[5] Administrative units were to be located at Ninevah and the Zab triangle.[6]

On 24 October 1941, the 2nd Indian Armoured Brigade left Iran for Qaiyara where it was to be assisted by the 20th Indian Infantry Brigade in its task of constructing defensive works in that locality.

The 50th British Infantry Division (less one Brigade Group) arrived in Iraq on 14 November 1941 and was concentrated in the Kirkuk area by 8 December 1941. Throughout the winter of 1941/42 units of the 8th Indian Division and of the 2nd Indian Armoured Brigade at Qaiyara worked incessantly at the construction of the defensive positions. Long stretches of the anti-tank ditch had to be cut through solid rock, and the Sappers and Miners were hard put to it.

Moreover Mosul experienced its coldest weather for many years. For some twelve days the thermometer never went above the freezing point by day or night. In spite of all precautions, such as emptying out the water from the radiators, over three hundred

---

[3] Table A, No. 309/G dated 21 October 1941 from H.Q. Iraq Force; 21 B, Forward Planning 8058 H.
[4] Table B, Forecast of approximate dispositions on 15 February 1942, 21 A, 8058 H.
[5] 8 Div. O.I No. 2 dated 20 October 1941, *War Diary* 8 Ind. Div.
[6] Triangle formed by the rivers Khazir and Zab and the road Mosul-Erbil.

lorries had cracked cylinders, and on account of shortage of welding material the division became unfit for mobile operations for some months.

Then came the thaw and passage over unmetalled roads became impossible. The 17th Indian Infantry Brigade at Faidah had to be supplied by artillery tractors, no other form of transport being able to reach them.

The Indian troops, particularly the Madras Sappers and Miners and the Mysore Transport Company, who had never before seen snow or frost, suffered great hardship but stuck to their work with admirable fortitude, and much progress on the defensive positions had been achieved before once again the plans were altered.

Defences in the Hindiya Barrage area

As for the construction of defences outside the area of manoeuvre, the 10th Indian Division arrived from Iran at Habbaniya, the 25th Indian Infantry Brigade moved to Ramadi—Mujara area to cover the controls of possible inundations, the 21st went to Karbala to lay out a fortress area for protecting further controls necessary for flooding that region, while the 20th Indian Infantry Brigade, as already mentioned, went to Qaiyara to assist the 2nd Indian Armoured Brigade in its task of fortifying Qaiyara and reconnoitring Erbil.

Defence of Baghdad

After a reconnaissance of the Mujara area, Lt.-General Quinan decided, on 12 November 1941, that the area Ramadi—Karbala—Habbaniya could not be developed into a fortress area. The Royal Air Force would, therefore, have to evacuate Habbaniya in the event of an Axis land force establishing itself within a striking distance. The best that could be done with that area was, by means of floods controlled at Mujara and Hindiya, together with a weir to be constructed in the Suttaih breach, to turn that area into a vast water obstacle against any Axis advance towards Baghdad. The obstacle, the controls, the Suttaih breach etc. would have to be guarded and the following points were, therefore, to be prepared and garrisoned for their defence:

Mujara Cut Regulator	Garrison—one Rifle Company and Anti-Tank detachment.
Hindiya Barrage	Garrison-Brigade Group.
Falluja Bridge	Garrison-one Rifle Company and Anti-Tank detachment.

The positions at Mujara and Falluja were intended only for defence against destruction by saboteurs, air-borne troops or light armoured forces. They were therefore located in the immediate vicinity of the Regulator and the Bridge. The Hindiya Barrage was, however, to be a fortress area and was intended to offer prolonged resistance to a full-scale attack by modern forces.[7]

Early in December, the 10th Indian Division moved to Erbil to carry out the second task allotted to it, namely the reconnaissance of the Erbil area with a view to its use by the 2nd Indian Armoured Brigade.

Defences in the main defiles from Iran into Iraq

Construction of defences to control the main defiles from Iran into Iraq was the responsibility of the 6th Indian Infantry Division. The defences were designed against hostile armoured fighting vehicles trying to cross the main defiles, so that a counter-stroke, closely supported by air forces, might be delivered with full effect. The defiles in question were those at (*i*) Pai Tak—Karind (*ii*) road Shahbad—Gilan (*iii*) road Shahbad—Eilam and (*iv*) Pul-i-Tang—road Dizful—Khurramabad.[8]

Most of the above defences were expected to be completed before 31 March 1942. Faidah, Mosul and Ninevah were to be ready before the end of January 1942, Qaiyara by 28 February and Hindiya by 31 March. By this last date, it was hoped, the completed defences would be in a position to withstand direct attacks.

As regards the remaining positions, viz. Pai Tak Pass, two Rivers (Great Zab and Khazir), Mujara—Falluja, and Pul-i-Tang, the actual dates of completion depended to a large extent on the supply of stores and plant. But it was anticipated that the field defences and anti-tank obstacles would be ready early in February, and the concrete works in March 1942.[9]

---

[7] No. 309/G.H.Q. Iraq Force to 8 Div. and 10 Div., 12 November 1941, p. 32; *Forward Planning "F" areas*, 8058 H.
[8] Iraq Force O.I. No. 14 dated 4 October 1941, Appx. O/4/3, *War Diary* Tenth Army.
[9] No. G/778 dated 18 December 1941, H.Q. British Troops Iraq, Appx. O/19/5, *War Diary* Tenth Army.

CHAPTER XIX

Plan "Wonderful"

The work of constructing defences in Iraq was proceeding as planned when Japan declared war on 7 December 1941. This extension of the conflict had its repercussions in Iraq in two ways. First, it led to a change in its operational command; next, it caused the whole of the defensive programme to be greatly modified.

At the time of the outbreak of the war with Japan, Iraq was the responsibility of the Commander-in-Chief of India, who now had to shoulder the additional burden of having to resist the Japanese aggression. The British Prime Minister was anxious that the former task should not prejudice the latter. He therefore proposed to re-transfer Iraq to the Middle East Command so as to leave the India Command free to devote all its energies to the prosecution of the war in the Far East. This was done on 12 January 1942 when Iraq passed back to the Middle East Command.

As regards modifications in the defensive programme of Iraq, it will be remembered that the layout of the defences, on which work was then proceeding, was as approved by General Wavell on 18 October 1941, when he inspected the proposed sites of the Mosul defences. Now that Iraq had been re-transferred to General Auchinleck's command, a certain measure of modification in the layout and policy was unavoidable, since General Auchinleck was not in agreement with General Wavell on all points of policy and appreciation. In any case, a change was called for otherwise also, since supplies and troops promised for Iraq were now required for the Far East, and Iraq had to fill the gap by reorganising its defences and re-distributing its manpower. As a result the defence scheme of Iraq underwent further modifications.

Creation of an Indian Corps

The first important step taken by General Auchinleck in this direction was to reorganise the fighting forces. He introduced changes on the highest level. One of these was to create an Army Command; and another was to form an Indian Corps with two Indian divisions and an Indian armoured brigade. Accordingly the IV Indian Corps came into existence on 13 January 1942 when Lieut.-General T. W. Corbett assumed command of the 8th and 10th Indian Divisions and the 252nd Indian Armoured Group. The Corps was responsible for the operational planning and training in northern Iraq. It was to be under an Army Command, to be known as the Tenth Army. The latter started its work on 1 February 1942, on which date Headquarters British Troops in Iraq became Headquarters Tenth Army with Lieut.-General Quinan as the Army Commander. The IV Indian Corps passed under its command on the same day; and the work of revising the defensive plan and redistributing the fighting forces was taken in hand at about the same time.

The Tenth Army consisted of the following[1]:—

- 8th Indian Division ⎫
- 10th Indian Division ⎬ IV Indian Corps
- 252nd Indian Armoured Group ⎭
- 6th Indian Division
- 151st Infantry Brigade Group (51st British Division), and ancillary units.

Of the above troops, the 151st Infantry Brigade Group was due to leave the Iraq-Iran theatre shortly, as mentioned earlier. This left the 6th Indian Division as the sole formation outside the IV Indian Corps. This formation was then in Iran and was allowed to remain there; and Iraq became the undivided responsibility of the newly-formed IV Indian Corps.

Construction of defences at Kirkuk

Lt.-General Corbett now turned his attention to defensive planning. It may be recalled that earlier General Wavell had marked out a defensive area which was to be the key-area for the defence of northern Iraq. This locality was to the east of the Tigris and north of Baghdad. General Wavell had called it the area of manoeuvre, since the idea behind it was to defend northern Iraq from there, by a rapid despatch of troops to threatened spots rather than by manning static defences built at a great cost and requiring vast manpower to hold them. This idea was not to the liking of General Auchinleck, who had all along been in favour of a defensive system more to the south and, in an earlier communication to the War Office, he had advocated the holding of a line in the area Baghdad—Tripoli—Homs.

The plan of defence evolved by General Corbett seemed to be a compromise between the two. In General Wavell's plan the emphasis was more on the defence of the area round Mosul. In General Corbett's plan, it was now on Kirkuk. General Corbett's idea was probably to afford greater protection to Baghdad and thereby bring his plan into greater conformity with General

---

[1] Tenth Army Order of Battle—1 February 1942, Appendix F/1/1, *War Diary Tenth Army*. See Appendix 8.

Auchinleck's views, without causing a considerable alteration in General Wavell's plan. If such was the idea, Kirkuk was the right area for holding the bulk of his forces. A force held at Kirkuk could move to the support of the Mosul area, or to the defence of Baghdad, or towards Rowanduz to check an Axis advance from Iran—all with equal facility. General Corbett, accordingly, decided to place his main reserves in the Kirkuk and the Fatha areas, and intended so to lay out his defensive system as to provide pivots of manoeuvre for the defence of northern Iraq and, at the same time, a substantial depth for the defence of Baghdad. With this view, he instructed Commander 8th Indian Division to prepare defensive positions at Altun Kopru, Dibis, Kirkuk and Fatha.

Altun Kopru was to be held by one infantry brigade group. The object was to use the area as a pivot of manoeuvre for the armoured and motorised forces in the vicinity, to defend the bridge at Altun Kopru, and to stop any hostile advance towards Kirkuk by denying to the Axis the use of the road Altun Kopru—Kirkuk. Dibis was to be held by an infantry battalion group for an almost identical purpose, except that (*i*) the battalion was, in addition, to protect the water-pumping plant which supplied Kirkuk, (*ii*) the bridge there was not yet in existence but was to be shortly erected on the Lesser Zab. Like Dibis, Kirkuk, too, was to be defended only by a single infantry battalion group. The vital points to be protected here were the oil stabilization plant, the supply dumps, and the defile through which the road Altun Kopru—Kirkuk passed over the Kani Domlan hills into the interior of Iraq. Fatha was to be held by a brigade group whose assignment was to defend a bridge to be built over the Tigris, to protect the supply dumps, and to provide a pivot of manoeuvre for armoured and motorised forces, operating on the right or the left bank of the Tigris.

In addition to the above positions to be held by the 8th Indian Division, it was also to select and prepare, in due course of time, a brigade position in the Baquba area. This task was assigned to the 18th Indian Infantry Brigade. The Divisional Headquarters itself, which was located at Kirkuk, had a mobile divisional reserve of one infantry brigade group (less one battalion), located in the same area.

The Baquba position was to form a vital part of a general line of defences covering Baghdad, to the west of which, on the Tigris, other positions were being prepared by the 10th Indian Division, at Taji, Falluja and elsewhere.² Broadly speaking, in the scheme of defence contemplated by General Corbett, the 8th Indian Division was to garrison the eastern half of Iraq and the 10th the western.

² 8 Div. O.I. No. 3, dated 11 February 1942, and No. 4 dated 28 February 1942, *War Diary* 8 Ind. Div.

Defensive posts in the Habbaniya area

In the sector of the 10th Indian Division, the areas of importance, besides Taji and Falluja, were Ana, Habbaniya, Ramadi, Suttaih Weir and Mujara. Of these, Habbaniya was comparatively the more important, since a defensive position there would be of use not only in protecting the aerodrome but also in checking an Axis advance on Baghdad from the west. General Corbett directed the 10th Indian Division to prepare defences at all these places.

The object of the defensive post at Ramadi was to delay the Axis advance eastwards, on the right bank of the Euphrates, protect a bridge to be built east of the Ramadi ferry, and to provide a pivot of manoeuvre for any armoured or mobile force operating in the vicinity. In the event of an attack on a heavier scale, the bridge was to be destroyed, the position vacated and the garrison, which was to consist of one infantry brigade group, was to be withdrawn to Suttaih Weir. The object of the defensive post at Suttaih Weir was to defend the western entrance into Habbaniya Base, and protect the Royal Air Force and supply installations, as well as the bridge to be built at Sin al Dhibban ferry and the northern end of the Burma Bund. The garrison was to consist of one infantry brigade group. The post at Falluja was to defend the bridge and to protect the eastern approach to the Habbaniya Base. The garrison was to consist of one infantry battalion group, less two companies; the two companies being posted at Mujara to protect the Mujara Regulator and the road across it, and to give warning of any Axis attempt to cross the Mujara Cut.

The defensive post at Taji was intended to prevent an Axis advance southwards on Baghdad, on the right bank of the river Tigris, the garrison consisting of one infantry battalion group and one troop static anti-tank (8-pounders).[3]

Before any further planning for the defence of Iraq—Iran could take place, the IV Indian Corps left Iraq for India, towards the end of February 1942. This, coupled with the intensive fighting in Libya, and the developments in the war with Japan, necessitated a further review of the defence policy, resulting in some more changes in this constantly fluctuating plan for the defence of the Iraq-Iran theatres of the Middle East Command.

General Auchinleck reviews the Situation

This weakening of the northern front, due to the diversion of troops to Libya and the east, caused considerable anxiety to General Auchinleck, since it appeared to him practically certain that the Germans would resume their Russian campaign in spring, and

[3] IV Indian Corps Operation Instruction No. 2 dated 7 February 1942, *War Diary* IV Corps.

possibly attack northern Iran or Turkey about the middle of May 1942. Reviewing the situation, on 23 February 1942, General Auchinleck estimated that after providing for the security of the western front, namely North Africa, there would remain only four infantry divisions, and at the most four infantry brigade groups, to meet the requirements of the Ninth Army,[4] the Tenth Army and the G. H. Q. Reserve. Such a small force would be too inadequate to stop an Axis attack in strength, through Iran and Syria, against the Persian Gulf and the Suez Canal. It was therefore necessary to revise the plans for the defence of the northern front, so as to re-group the forces more economically.

The new policy now adopted by General Auchinleck was built round the idea of imposing the greatest possible delay on the Axis advance, with the object of gaining time to enable reinforcements to arrive. This was to be done by supporting Turkey, were she willing to resist the Axis advance; by fierce Royal Air Force attacks on the vulnerable communications of the Axis through Turkey; by a thorough demolition of communications, and all oil stocks and installations; and by a series of delaying actions on well selected ground, terminating eventually on previously prepared positions on the general line Dizful—Pai Tak—R. Little Zab—Ana—Abu Kemal—Damascus—Baalbek—Tripoli.[5]

In conformity with this policy, General Auchinleck issued instructions for carrying out the essential tasks. Defences were to be completed on the general line Dizful—Tripoli; and bases of supply for mobile striking forces were to be got ready at or near Fatha, Haffa and Qatana, and in the Jebel Druse and the Lava Belt areas. Bridges necessary for ensuring mobility were to be built at Raqqa, Haffa and Fatha, and a defended staging post was to be established around Rutba, and if possible, at Al Gaara, for the same reason. In addition, positions were to be reconnoitred in southern Iraq and southern Palestine, in each case for a force of two infantry divisions and attached troops.[6] These were to be used for a last stand in front of the Basra bridgehead and the Suez Canal respectively, in case the Dizful—Tripoli line was breached.

Lieut.-General Quinan's Plan

In the light of these instructions, Lieut.-General Quinan, on 28 February 1942, allocated the various tasks to the Tenth Army, which, besides the 8th and 10th Indian Divisions, comprised at this stage the 31st Indian Armoured Division and six

---

[4] The Ninth Army was formed in September 1941 and was responsible for Palestine and Syria.
[5] General Auchinleck's *Despatch*.
[6] G.H.Q., M.E.F. O.I. No. 112, 23 February 1942, Auchinleck's *Despatch*.

Indian infantry battalions, of which three were unbrigaded and the rest were from the Indian States Forces. The 31st Indian Armoured Division, consisting of the 252nd Indian Armoured Brigade, the 3rd Indian Motor Brigade and one Army Tank Brigade, was to stay in the Mosul area, with a view to its initial employment offensively west of the Tigris, in conjunction with the troops of the 8th Indian Division. The latter, together with detachments of the Iraqi army, would have to operate in that case north of Mosul and subsequently east of the Tigris, in an offensive role, basing itself on positions previously prepared for occupation near Altun Kopru and in the vicinity of Fatha. West of the Tigris, it would be for the 10th Indian Division, with detachments of the Iraqi Army, to cooperate with the 31st Indian Armoured Division and hold Haffa as a base of supply for that division, as well as for the G. H. Q. Reserve and the supporting air forces. If forced to withdraw, the Indian forces were to retire to the positions to be prepared in the general area Baquba—Taji—Falluja, in order to cover Baghdad and the base at Mussaiyib. The final positions to be held would be Pul-i-Tang and Shuaiba-Basra.

The various tasks assigned to the Tenth Army by Lt.-General Quinan may be briefly summed up as follows: the 8th Indian Division was to complete defences on the general line Pul-i-Tang—Pai Tak—Little Zab—Haffa, and to reconnoitre in detail the area required for the close defence of the bridge at Baquba. The 10th Indian Division was to complete the defences in the area Baquba—Taji—Falluja and was to prepare the defended staging post at Rutba, and if possible also at Al Gaara. The 6th Indian Division, which was in Iran, was to reconnoitre positions for the close defence of Abadan and for opposing Axis attacks on Ahwaz or the Basra area; and the Headquarters of the line of communication area was to reconnoitre a position in the area of Shuaiba—Zubair—Basra to be held by two infantry divisions and attached troops. The defensive arrangements on the line Pul-i-Tang—Pai Tak—Little Zab—Haffa, were to be completed by 1 May 1942.[7]

Role of the Iraqi Army

The Iraqi Army was to help in the defence of Iraq. General Nuri es Said Pasha, Prime Minister and Minister of Defence, Iraq, had agreed to make available, for use within the Iraqi frontiers only, a force of ten infantry brigades (each of two battalions), one lorried battalion (nucleus of projected motorised brigade), three horsed cavalry regiments, eighteen batteries 18-pounders, five batteries 4.5-in. howitzers, eight batteries 3.7-in. pack howitzers

---

[7] Tenth Army O.I. No. 19 dated 28 February 1942, Appendix F/28/7, *War Diary* Tenth Army.

(two mechanised), and certain engineer, signal and ancillary troops. The roles which the Iraqi Army would play had been planned out previously.[5]

Plan 'Wonderful'

By the end of May 1942, when the fighting was growing intense, both in Russia and in North Africa, Lieut.-General Quinan had finalised the plan for the defence of Iraq. It was assigned the code-name "Wonderful" and the forces available for its implementation were expected to be a little more than those which he had at the end of February 1942, when the IV Indian Corps had just left for India. They were:

Tenth Army
   (a) XXI Indian Corps consisting of:
      31st Indian Armoured Division
      Chinkara (a force of two armoured car regiments with detachments of infantry and artillery, as may be decided upon by the XXI Indian Corps)
      8th Indian Division
      10th Indian Division
      One regiment medium artillery
   (b) 6th Indian Division (less one brigade group)
   (c) Three unbrigaded infantry battalions
      Three Indian States Forces battalions
   (d) Iraqi Army, and

G. H. Q. Reserves consisting of:
   One armoured division
   One armoured brigade group
   One army tank brigade and
   One Indian division.

The Plan "Wonderful" was based on the estimate that, in their attack on Iraq, the Axis would be able to employ up to seven or eight divisions, supported by strong air forces. The invading force, it was supposed, would advance from southern Anatolia, in several columns on a wide front, in order to outflank the Allied mobile forces and defended areas. Their primary objective was supposed to be Zakho, Mosul, Kirkuk and Baghdad. It was to be expected that they would attempt to secure intact the Mosul bridge and railway tunnel as a preliminary to a rapid advance, on the one hand to Kirkuk, and on the other to Baghdad. But at the same time, the possibility of their approach down the Euphrates, (from Aleppo) and by the river Khabur, was also there, and could not be overlooked as it might even prove to be the main thrust.

[5] No. G/501 dated 20 February 1942 from H.Q. Tenth Army, Appendix F/20/6, *War Diary* Tenth Army. See also Appendix 7.

The plan "Wonderful" aimed at opposing these anticipated moves by holding two successive lines. These were the Mosul—Tell Afar line and the Little Zab—Fatha—Ramadi line. It was for the Tenth Army to ensure that the Axis were not allowed, in any event, to establish themselves south of the latter line.

The general plan of operations which was to achieve this result was that Chinkara, a particularly mobile force, was to give the start to the operations by attacking or resisting the Axis north of Nisibin in Anatolia, as soon as the latter reached that point. This it was to do in co-operation with the air striking force and an army component from the Ninth Army. It was then to fight back slowly to the general line Mosul—Tell Afar. In this delaying action, it was to have the maximum of co-operation from the 31st Indian Armoured Division (based on Tell Afar) and the 8th Indian Division (based on Mosul); while in the meantime, the 10th Indian Division (based on Al Hadhr) was to secure the Mosul-west defended area and be ready to support the 31st Indian Armoured Division and Chinkara. Having reached the Mosul—Tell Afar area, all these formations were to make a further fighting withdrawal towards the prepared and stocked positions on the line Little Zab—Fatha—Ana. An important function of the Tenth Army was to prevent the Axis forces establishing themselves south of the general line Little Zab—Fatha—Ana.

To prevent the Axis establishing themselves south of the general line Little Zab—Fatha—Ana, the 8th and 10th Indian Divisions, (with varying numbers of Iraq brigades), were to withdraw fighting, when forced to do so, into previously prepared and stocked positions, the former occupying Altun Kopru, Dibis, Tell Ali and Fatha and the latter the Ramadi—Habbaniya area, the Mujara Cut, Safra, Taji and Falluja. Later, one Iraqi Brigade was to operate under the 10th Indian Division on the line of communication, Ramadi—Haditha, excluding Abu Kemal.

The 6th Indian Division (less one Brigade Group in the area Khuzistan—Basra), would, with one Iraqi brigade under command, be responsible for the line of communications Kirkuk—Baghdad, both inclusive. It was to be ready, if required, to occupy the previously prepared brigade group positions at Baquba and Hindiya. For this, the Baquba position was to be prepared and kept ready by the 8th Indian Division and the Hindiya position by the 10th.

While the Kirkuk—Baghdad line of communications was to be the responsibility of the 6th Indian Division, the rest of the line of communications in Iraq were to be operated by the Iraqi troops. Thus two independent brigades of the Iraqi Army were to operate, protecting the Euphrates line of communications. One Iraqi battalion, based on Amara, and four Iraqi gunboats, were similarly to protect the inland water transport on the Tigris and the Shatt al Arab.

The combined Army Royal Air Force Headquarters at Latifiya, and the advanced base at Musaiyib were to be the responsibility of two battalions of the Tenth Army Reserve, with about four armoured cars under a selected command. The Tenth Army units were also to prepare a defended staging post in the Rutba area, which was to be held by an Indian States Forces battalion.[9]

Air action by R. A. F.

The role of the Royal Air Force in "Wonderful" was both offensive and defensive. The Royal Air Force aircraft were to attack Axis communications and strategic objects so as to impose maximum delay on their advance, and were later to give support to the operations of own troops by striking at targets in the battle areas. In their defensive role, they were to protect the line of communications, ports and oil installations from air attacks, and watch over the Allied shipping in the Persian Gulf.[10]

Demolition Schemes

An important item in the plan "Wonderful" was the provision of well thought out and far-reaching demolition schemes. The idea behind these schemes was to delay the advance of the Axis forces by a thorough demolition of all types of communications, and all oil stocks and installations in south-east Anatolia, north-east Syria and northern Iraq, as well as by the early removal, to the south of Baghdad, of such war and other materials as might, otherwise, prove of operational value to the Axis. Under these schemes, which were ready by the end of June 1942, the destruction of communications and resources in the Tenth Army area was grouped under two main heads: (i) destruction of communications and (ii) devastation of resources and supplies. To enable this to be done, the Tenth Army area was divided into demolition zones and devastation areas. The responsibility for effecting demolitions and devastations, in their respective areas, rested with the fighting divisions and the L of C Commands concerned.[11]

Denial of oil resources to the Axis

Destruction of the oil stocks and installation was the major

---

[9] See Appendix 9.
[10] G.H.Q., M.E.F., O.I. No. 117 dated 29 April 1932, Auchinleck's *Despatch*; 18 Bde. O.I. No. 3 dated 6 April 1942, *War Diary* 18 Ind. Inf. Bde.; Tenth Army O.I. No. 21 dated 25 May 1942, *War Diary* Tenth Army.
[11] Tenth Army O.I. No. 30 dated 26 June 1942 and Tenth Army O.I. No. 29 dated 27 June 1942, *War Diary* Iraq Force.

item under the devastation programmes. It was of vital importance to deny to the Axis the facilities for obtaining and refining oil, and five oil-denial schemes were accordingly prepared to ensure the complete destruction of the oil resources of both Iraq and Iran. The first of these schemes was concerned with the destruction of the British Oil Development Company's properties and the Iraq Government's Refinery at Qaiyara. The second concerned the destruction of the Iraq Petroleum Company's property (exclusive of the water supply plants on the Little Zab river and at Kirkuk) and the Tinning plant at Kirkuk. This scheme included also the K-1 pumping station. The third scheme dealt with the most far-reaching of all the demolitions—the destruction of the Iraq Petroleum Company's pipeline for taking oil from Kirkuk to Haifa and Tripoli; the pumping stations involved being K-2, K-3, T-1, H-1, and included also the K-3 Topping Plant and pipeline siphons under the Tigris and the Euphrates. The two other schemes related to Iran. One embraced the destruction of the Khanakin Oil Company's Refinery at Alwand, the Khanakin Oil Depot at Khanakin, the Naft Khana Oil Fields, and the Naft-i-Shah Oil Field, with the topping plant, the pipeline and the pumping stations. The range of this scheme covered also the Pai Tak area. The other scheme was concerned with the destruction of the Kermanshah Petroleum Company's Refinery at Kermanshah, the pipeline Pai Tak to Kermanshah and the pumping station at Shahabad.[11]

Had these schemes been carried out, there is no doubt that both Iran and Iraq would have been amongst the unhappiest victims of the Second World War.

---

[11] Tenth Army O.I. No. 30 dated 26 June 1942, *War Diary* Tenth Army.

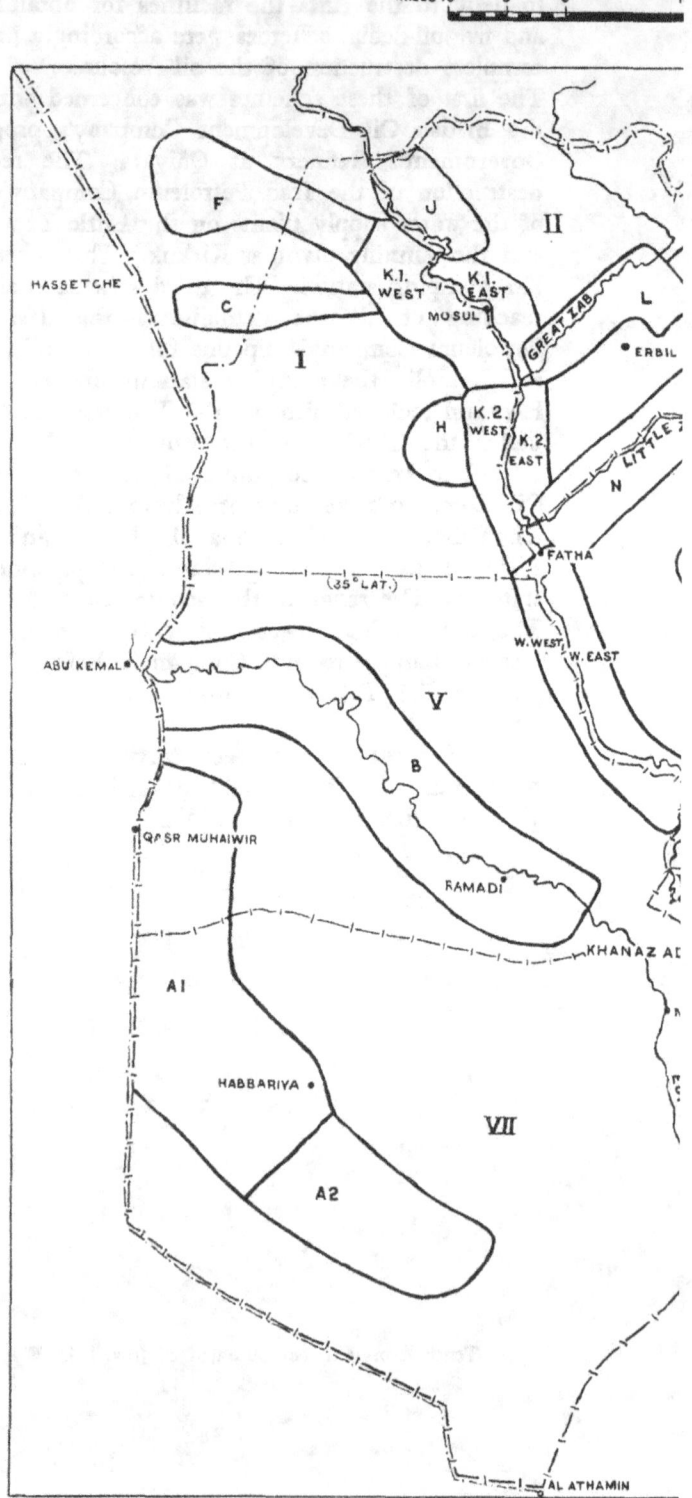

"...NDERFUL"
...DEVASTATION AREAS IN IRAQ & IRAN

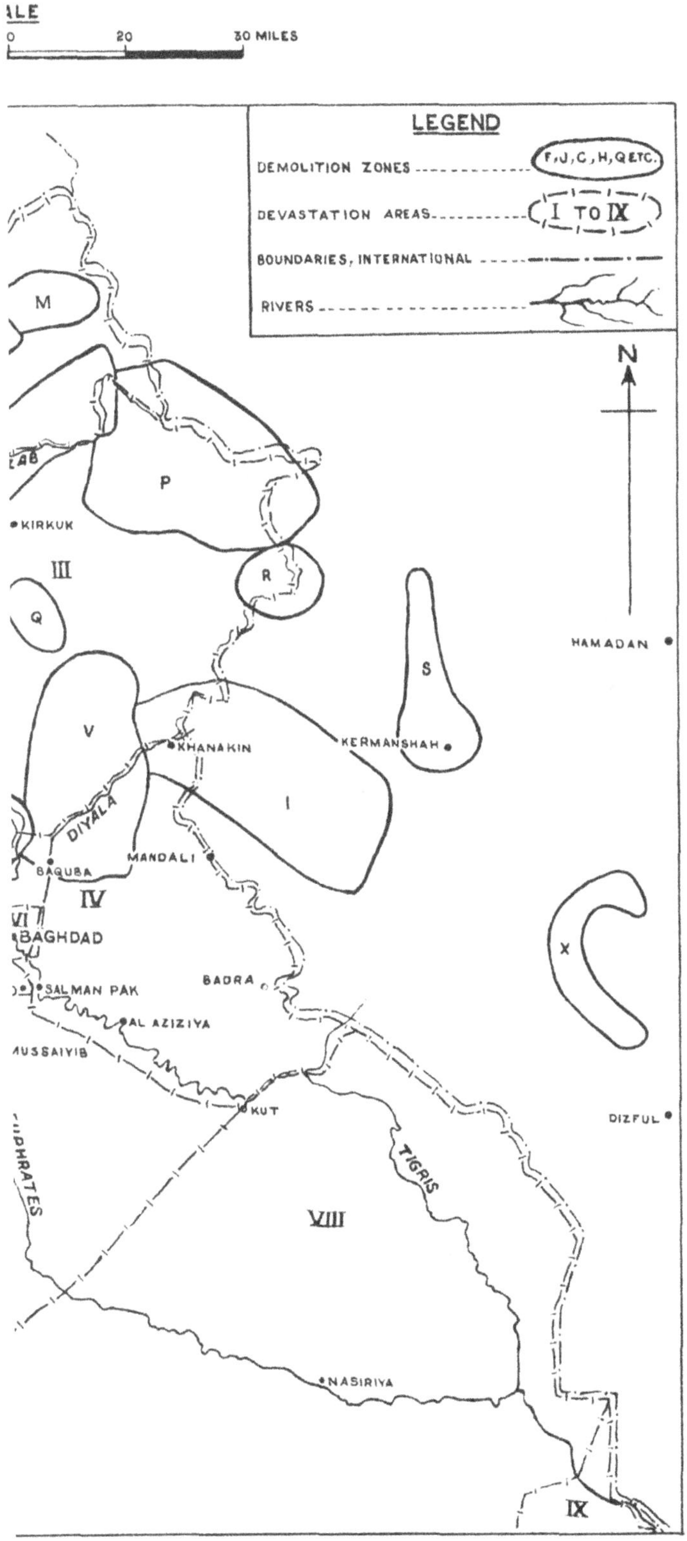

...LE
0   20   30 MILES

LEGEND
DEMOLITION ZONES ---------- (F,J,C,H,Q ETC.)
DEVASTATION AREAS --------- (I TO IX)
BOUNDARIES, INTERNATIONAL -----
RIVERS ----------

N

Zones and areas shown: M, P, R, Q, S, V, I, X, IV, VI, III, VIII, IX

Cities: KIRKUK, HAMADAN, KERMANSHAH, KHANAKIN, BAQUBA, MANDALI, BAGHDAD, SALMAN PAK, BADRA, AL AZIZIYA, MUSSAIYIB, KUT, DIZFUL, NASIRIYA

Rivers: DIYALA, EUPHRATES, TIGRIS

CHAPTER XX

Formation of a New Command

Axis offensive

Preparations for the defence of Iraq, Iran and Syria went on steadily throughout May and part of June 1942. Meanwhile, on 26 May, General Rommel launched his third counter-offensive in the Western Desert which made a phenomenal progress during the next month. Ultimately, the Allies made a stand at Alamein and the German offensive came to a halt; but the losses suffered by the Eighth Army in achieving it were very considerable, and more troops were required to consolidate the position. In June, this compelled General Auchinleck to withdraw most of the remaining troops from the northern front. The Ninth and Tenth Armies were thus denuded of men and transport, and were not even in a position to impose any serious delay on the Axis, were the latter to attack through Anatolia or Caucasia.

The danger of such attacks had by no means decreased. In fact it increased substantially after early July, when the Axis launched fierce attacks against the Russians on either side of Kharkov, and began a thrust towards the Don and the important Moscow-Rostov railway. Rostov fell on 14 July and the Axis forces pressed southward towards Caucasia. By the middle of August 1942 the Axis vanguards had reached the foothills of the Caucasus, and it seemed that only the fact of Stalingrad holding out and threatening their flank would prevent them from pushing into Iran.

At this stage, the Middle East Defence Committee felt itself called upon to make a decision whether to continue to concentrate all their efforts on defending Egypt from the west, or to divert the greater part of their resources to protect the Iranian oilfields against an attack from the north. The Committee referred the matter to the Defence Committee in London. It was evident that the two fronts might be defended simultaneously if further reinforcements were promptly available. But the British Prime Minister declared himself as being unable to provide any before the end of October 1942, and in the meantime wished the Middle East to concentrate on defending Egypt. He pointed out that there was no need to assume that the Axis could invade Iran in force before that time, and added that the best way to find the needed reinforcements for the defence of the northern front would be to inflict a decisive defeat on the Axis in North Africa. The advice was accepted and eventually it proved to be the correct one. All efforts were concentrated on the operations in North Africa, and the northern front was left to its own expedients for the time being.[1]

Pibas and Paiforce

It was now necessary to make up for the inadequacy of manpower by increasing the fighting efficiency of the troops in hand. General Auchinleck felt that if General Quinan were freed from the heavy administrative and political responsibilities, which he was discharging as Commander of the Tenth Army, he might be able to concentrate more effectively on the military problems of his theatre. Accordingly, on 22 July, he issued a letter proposing a reorganisation of the commands in Iraq and Iran. Iraq and Iran were hereafter to have three commands, instead of two, together with a specially created administrative organisation. The three commands were to be the Ninth Army and the Tenth Army as of old, and Pibas—a new command to be set up shortly. The specially created administrative organisation, which was intended to take over some of the administrative burden of the three commands, was to consist of an echelon of the General Headquarters Middle East forces, under an Inspector-General of Communications for Iraq and Iran, who was to work directly under the Lieut.-General incharge Administration, Middle East.

Broadly speaking, the Tenth Army in Iran, and the Ninth Army in Iraq, were to form a continuous area along the Anatolian frontier, embracing north Iran and north Iraq and covering the sub-areas Teheran, Kermanshah, Kirkuk and the district of Mosul. This more or less ensured the security of northern Iraq. As to southern Iraq, the responsibility was that of Pibas, which included the sub-areas, Baghdad, Shuaiba and the Persian Gulf. The dividing line between the north and the south was the general line Khanakin-Ramadi which was included in Pibas. The functions of the Inspector-General of Communications, subject to a general supervision by the General Headquarters Middle East, was to control all ports, rail and inland water-transport movements. He was also to be responsible for the general administrative agencies, depots etc, and for the maintenance to rail and water-transport heads, or to Army Depots, of all troops in Iraq and Iran.[2]

An important result of this re-adjustment of the commands was that it simplified co-operation between the various army and airforce commanders, which until then had been a complicated process due to an overlapping or other maladjustments of the boundaries of some of the commands.

[1] General Auchinleck's *Despatch*.
[2] See Appendix 10.

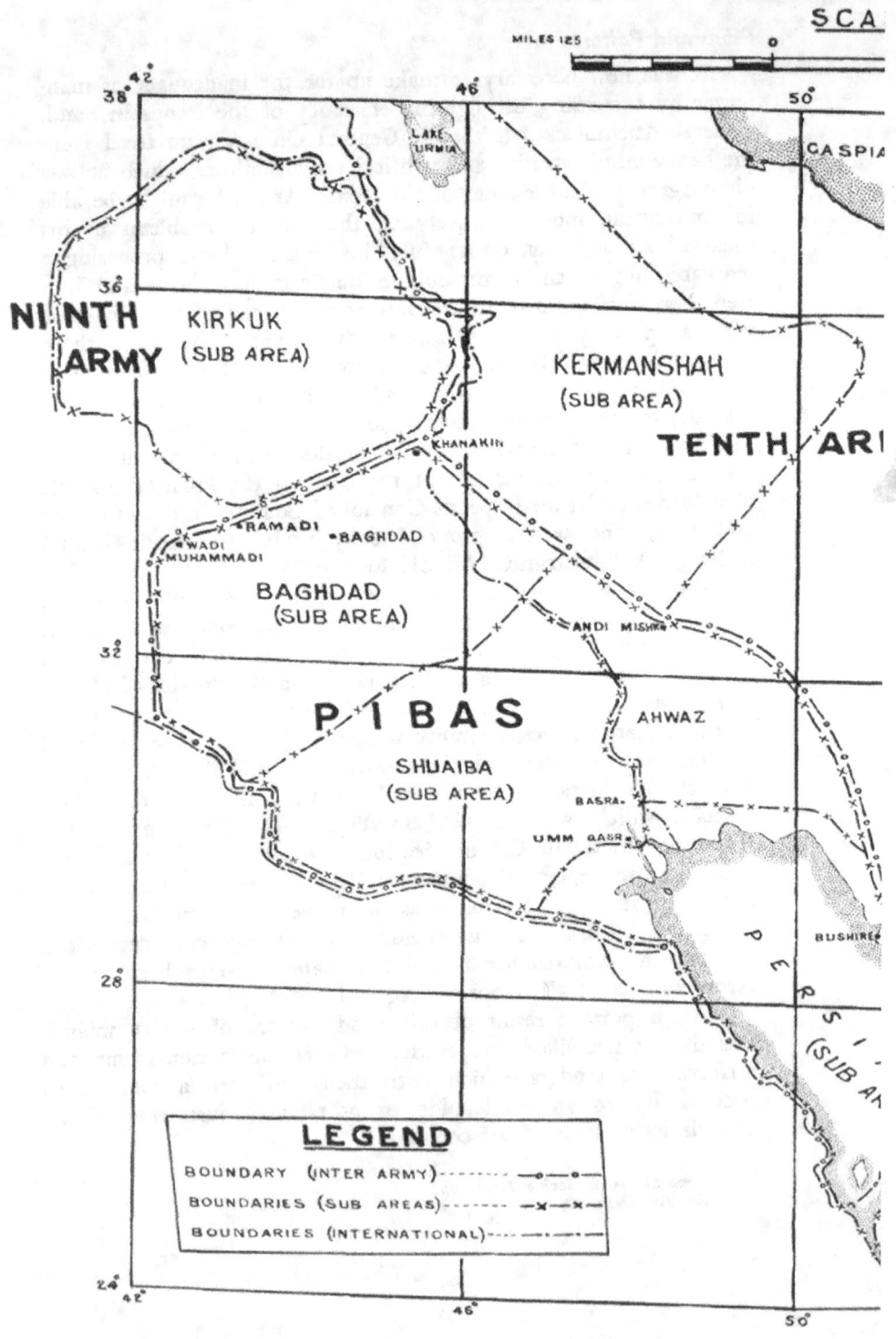

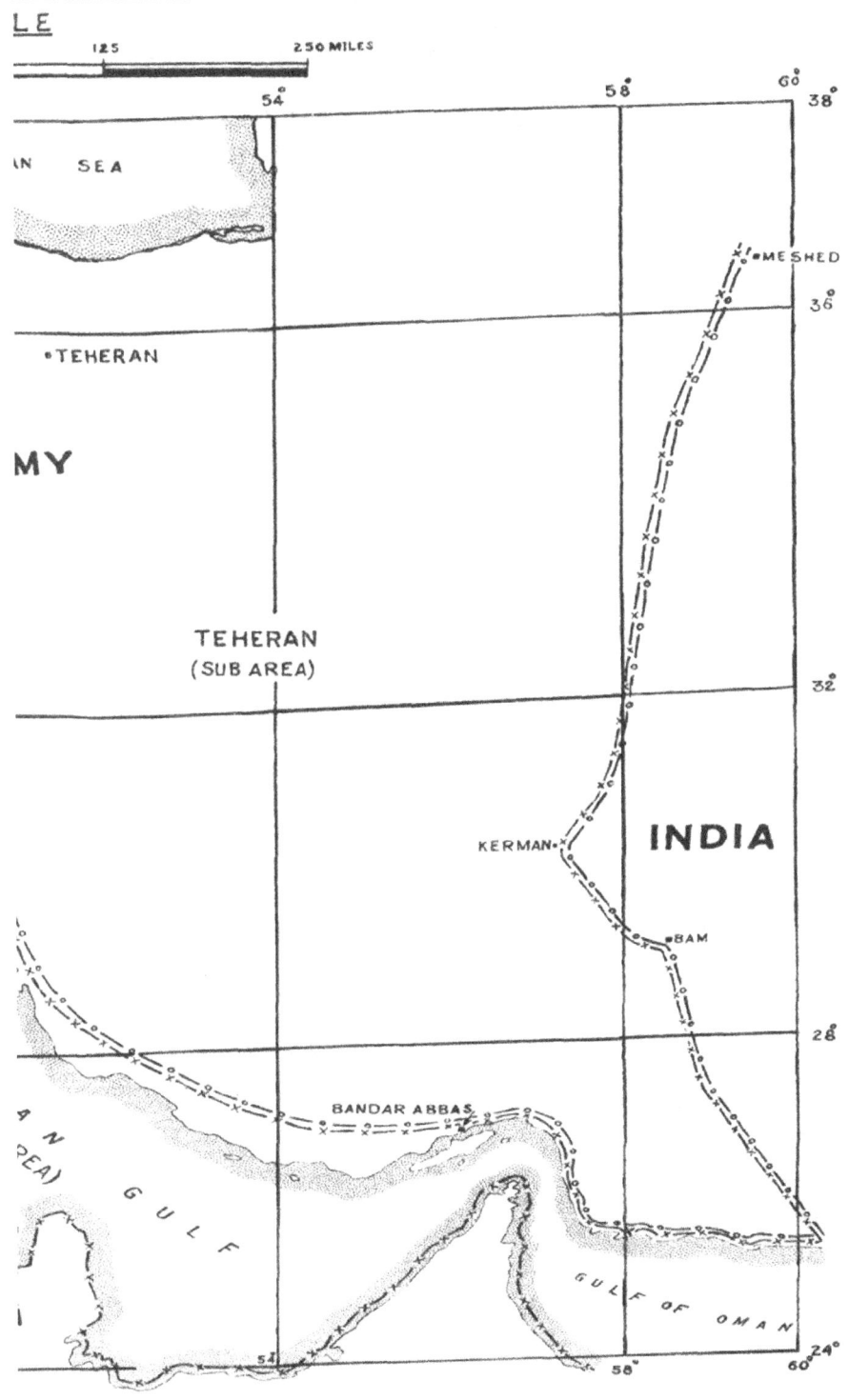

Creation of Paiforce

The above-mentioned reorganisation of commands was to come into effect from 15 August 1942. But about a week earlier, the British War Cabinet decided to make changes in the Middle East Command, which also affected the Ninth and Tenth Armies in Iraq and Iran. At about that time, the British Prime Minister, Mr. Churchill, and Chief of the Imperial General Staff, General Sir Alan Brooke, were in Egypt. They had flown to Cairo on 6 August and had discussions with General Auchinleck on the situation in the Middle East. Next day they toured the Eighth Army front and on the following day (8 August), General Auchinleck was informed by the Prime Minister that it had been decided to introduce certain changes in the various commands of the Middle East. The Middle East Command and the Eighth Army were to have new commanders, and Iraq and Iran were to be formed into a separate single command to function directly under the War Office. This latter command came to be known as Paiforce or Paic.

At this date General Auchinleck was still shouldering the twofold responsibilities of Commander-in-Chief, Middle East and Commander, Eighth Army. General Sir Harold Alexander was appointed to relieve him of his former charge and Lieut.-General Montgomery of the latter. Apparently, because General Auchinleck's attitude towards threats from the north had always been one of great alertness, he was offered the command of the Paiforce, which he was informed, would function independently of the Middle East Command. This offer he declined after a careful study of the proposed set-up extending over many days, on the ground that in his opinion, the new command was not well suited, strategically and administratively, to withstand the shock of a serious invasion from the north.

By 15 August, General Auchinleck had relinquished both his military commands and had left the Eighth Army headquarters. Pibas commenced functioning the same day but did not last for more than a few days as it was soon replaced by Paiforce. About a week later, it was announced that General Sir Henry Maitland Wilson had been selected as Commander-in-Chief, Paic (Persia and Iraq Command). General Wilson took up his appointment on 21 August and his General Headquarters opened in Baghdad on 15 September 1942. Henceforth the history of the activities of Indian troops in Iraq became a part of the history of the Paiforce.

SYRIA

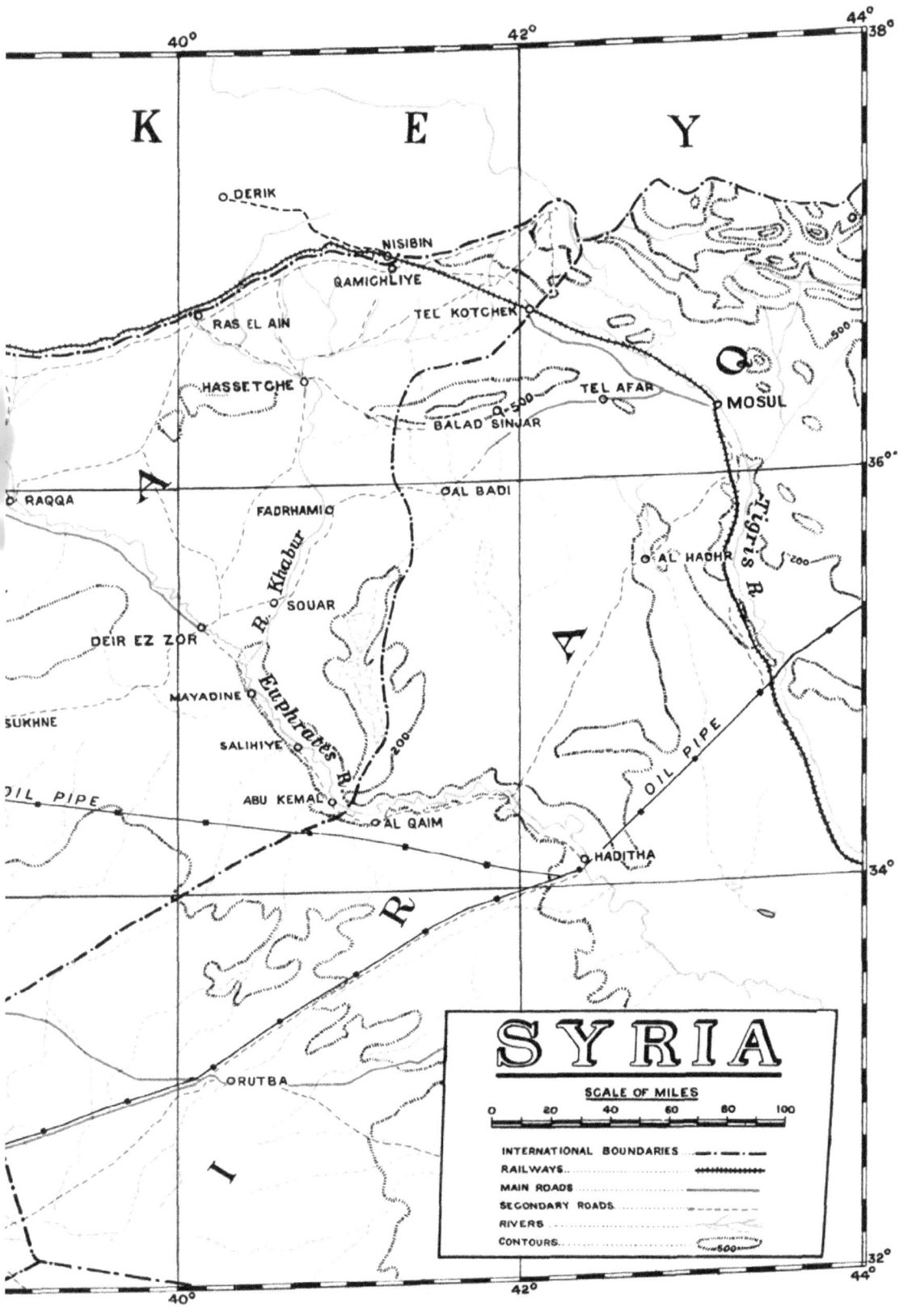

CHAPTER XXI

Physical Features and Historical Survey

Syria

Before World War I the name Syria was applied to a wide area, stretching from the Taurus mountains in the north to the Sinai Peninsula in the south, and from the Mediterranean sea on the west to the Syrian Desert on the east. After the First World War, this area was split into two political divisions—the northern area comprising Syria under the French Mandate, and the southern area comprising Palestine and Transjordan under the British Mandate. In the pages below the name Syria is used only for the northern area under the French Mandate.

Topography

The territory of Syria is bounded on the west by the Mediterranean, on the south by Palestine, Transjordan and Iraq, on the east by part of Turkey and Iraq, and on the north by Turkey. Broadly speaking, there are five natural zones of Syria: the western coastal belt; the highland zone immediately behind it; the central depression; the eastern highlands; and gradual transition to the steppe and the desert towards the east and the south-east.

The western coastal strip is an irregular stretch of land, which is narrow in the north but increasingly broadens out towards the south. For the most part it is rocky and at places leaves room for only a narrow road along the shore. The coastal region has a number of famous ports: Latakia, Tripoli, Beirut, Sidon and Tyre.

To the east of the coastal strip is a highland belt comprising Jebel Ansariya, rising to some 5,000 feet and the Lebanon, whose highest peak is just over 10,000 feet.

Further to the east of the highland belt is the central depression. East of Jebel Ansariya is the lowland rift (called the Ghab), 50 miles long and 10 miles wide, through which flows the Orontes river.[1] The valley, whose floor is 3,000 feet below the summits of Jebel Ansariya, is flooded in winter and turned into a malarial swamp in summer. Further to the south, lying between the Lebanon and the Anti-Lebanon ranges is the Bekaa valley, whose gently sloping floor rises gradually towards the centre, the Baalbek ridge(3,000 feet high), which forms the watershed between the Orontes and the Litani rivers. The eastern highlands lie to the east

[1] Fisher: *The Middle East* (1950), p. 373.

of the central depression. The Anti-Lebanon range emerges from the plain of Hassiya-Homs. Its highest peaks are just over 8,000 feet. South of Anti-Lebanon is Mount Hermon, whose culminating peak is over 9,000 feet.[2] Further to the south, in south-eastern Syria, near the Transjordan border is the extensive mass of Jebel Druse, covering an area of 13,000 sq. miles.

There is a gradual transition from the eastern highlands to the steppe and the desert. The northern plateau (to the north-east of the Anti-Lebanon range) slopes gently to the valley of the Euphrates. The eastern flanks of the Anti-Lebanon lead down to a barren steppe (called the Syrian Desert), which is interspersed by numerous oases.

There are three important rivers in Syria. The Baalbek ridge forms the watershed between the Orontes and the Litani, the former flowing north and then west, and the latter south and then west. Rising in Turkey, the Euphrates flows through the north-east of Syria towards the Iraq frontier.

Climate

Climatic conditions vary considerably in Syria. The coastal zone has a Mediterranean climate—cold winters, moderately hot summers and abundant rainfall. In the mountain zone there are extremely cold winters, pleasant summers and heavy rainfall. The lowland troughs (Ghab and Bekaa) have fairly cold winters, hot summers and moderate or deficient rainfall. In the steppe zone temperatures are more extreme and rainfall is scanty.[3]

Communications

When the Allies invaded Syria in June 1941, the country had a simple railway system. A railway line from Transjordan passed through Deraa and Ezraa to Damascus, and thence through Homs and Hama to Aleppo. A little to the north of Aleppo this railway line forked east and west, the western branch going to Turkey and the eastern through Turkish Kurdistan and north-east Syria to Iraq. Three branches from this line ran westwards to the Mediterranean sea ports, one from Deraa to Haifa, the second from north of Rayak to Beirut, and the third from Homs to Tripoli.

Syria possessed fairly good roads. The coastal road from Palestine passed through Tyre, Sidon, Beirut and Latakia, from where it forked east and north, the eastern going to Aleppo and the northern to Turkey. Damascus was the centre of communications; from here roads branched off in all directions. A road passing west of lake Tiberias ran through Rosh Pinna and Jisr Benett Yacoub to

---

[2] *The Middle East* (1948)—(Europa Publications Limited), p. 255.
[3] Fisher: *The Middle East*, pp. 384-9.

Damascus. (A motorable track skirting the edge of the lake joined this road at Kuneitra). Another road from Transjordan ran through Deraa, Sheikh Meskine and Sanamein. Damascus was connected with cities on the western coast, Beirut, Sidon and Acre. A road connected Damascus with Aleppo via Homs and Hama. A track ran from Rutba (in Iraq) via Sab Biyar to Damascus. Another road (partly track) connected Abu Kemal with Aleppo via Deir ez Zor.

Syria did not possess good ports. Latakia was undeveloped; Tripoli (the terminus of an oil pipeline from Iraq) lacked adequate harbour works; only Beirut had been developed by the French into a fine modern port.[4]

Area and Population

The total area subject to the French Mandate was estimated at 58,000 square miles; the total population (1935 census) at 3,630,000 composed mainly of Muslims of Arabic origin, the majority being of the Sunni sect. Other elements composing the population were Turks, Turkomans, Kurds, Circassians, Armenians, Iranians and Jews. Christians (Maronites, Greek and Armenian, Melkites, Protestants and those of the Orthodox Church) totalled over 500,000. The principal towns were Damascus, Aleppo, Beirut, Homs, Hama, Tripoli, Antioch, and Latakia.[5]

Economic Resources

Syria was mainly an agricultural country. Its chief products were wheat, barely, maize, millet, oats, olives, sesame, chickpeas, cotton and tobacco.[6] Silk rearing was an important industry. Sheep and goats were bred in large numbers. The most important fruit trees were olive, vine, mulberry, lemon, banana and orange.

Syria was poor in mineral resources; its industries were also not much developed. Textiles, metal working and preparation of foodstuffs were the principal industries. Many towns had small industries for the extraction of oil, cigarette making and distilling of brandy.

Early history

From the dawn of history Syria has felt the impact of foreign influences. It was conquered successively by the Egyptians, the Assyrians, the Hittites and the Persians. Then the Macedonian Greeks under Alexander the Great conquered the country in the fourth century B.C. The Greek rule, which lasted for three hundred years, left a deep impress on the language and culture of the people. The Romans conquered Jerusalem in 63 B.C. and

[4] Hourani, A. K.: *Syria and Lebanon*, p. 88.
[5] *The Statesman's Year Book* (1940), pp. 913-14.
[6] Dudley Stamp: *Asia* (1948), p. 132.

shortly afterwards Syria came to form a part of the Roman Empire. Remains of Roman occupation are found in many places in Syria, notably Baalbek and Palmyra. From 394 A.D. till the coming of the Arabs about 650 A.D., Syria formed part of the Byzantine Empire. Under the Arab rule of the Omayyads, Damascus became the capital of the Caliphate, and Syria's splendour and prosperity increased considerably. In 750 A.D. the Omayyads were succeeded by the Abbasid Caliphs, who made Baghdad the capital of the Caliphate. This was a cruel blow to the prosperity of Syria. In 1086 A.D. the Seljuk Turks from Central Asia established their control over Syria. The Seljuk State was split into two dynasties, at Aleppo and Damascus. At the end of the eleventh century and the middle of the twelfth century A.D. the crusading armies from western Europe conquered a part of Syria but failed to retain it. At the end of the thirteenth century Syria passed under the control of the Mamluke Sultans of Egypt. During their rule, which lasted for about two centuries, Syria was ravaged by the Mongols.[7]

Syria as a part of the Ottoman Empire

In 1516 the Ottoman Turks conquered Syria, which remained under their rule till the end of World War I. The first three centuries of Ottoman rule were a period of stagnation and economic decay. In the nineteenth century, however, Turkish Syria felt the impact of strong influences from the west. The attempt by Napoleon I to conquer Syria at the close of the eighteenth century met with failure. In 1831-32 Ibrahim Pasha (son of Muhammad Ali, ruler of Egypt) occupied Syria but was soon afterwards driven from the country by the intervention of European Powers. Besides these political factors, religious influences were also at work. European traders and missionaries were increasing their influence in Syria. The religious disturbances were largely responsible for the movement towards the autonomy of Lebanon. In 1841 the civil war between the Maronites and Druses resulted in the grant of some autonomy to Lebanon; the country was divided into two districts, one of which was to be administered by a Christian and the second by a Druse governor, both to be appointed by the Turkish Government. In 1860 further fierce disturbances (resulting in the massacre of thousands of Christians) led to the intervention of European Powers and the grant of autonomy to Lebanon, which was to be administered by a Christian governor appointed by the Turkish Government (with the consent of the European Powers) and responsible to it.[8]

[7] Richard Goold—Adams: *Middle East Journey* (1947), pp. 146-51.
Hourani: *Syria and Lebanon*, pp. 15-27.
[8] Ibid, pp. 28-33.

The chief features of the administrative system, which had been introduced early in the nineteenth century, were that the Ottoman Empire was divided into *Vilayets* i.e provinces administered by *Walis*—governor-generals; the *Vilayet* was sub-divided into *Sanjaqs* i.e. counties administered by *Mutasarref*—lieutenant-governors. There were however a few independent *Sanjaqs*, whose *Mutasarref* dealt directly with Constantinople and not through the *Wali*.[9] On the eve of World War I, Turkey's Arab possessions included Egypt, Syria, Iraq and the Arabian Peninsula. Syria was divided into the *Vilayets* of Aleppo, Beirut and Damascus, and the independent *Sanjaqs* of Lebanon and Jerusalem.[10]

During World War I, Turkey threw her weight on the side of Germany. This gave an opportunity to many discontented Arab nationalists to strike a blow for their independence and to throw off the hated Turkish yoke. Great Britain, too, realised the importance of harassing the Turks by organising the Arab revolt. The negotiations between Sir Henry McMahon, the British High Commissioner in Egypt, and the Sheriff Hussein, the Arab leader, were embodied in a series of letters, known as the McMahon Correspondence (July 1915—January 1916). The British Government, in return for the Arab support for the Allies, undertook to support Arab independence in Arab territories, from which certain areas were, however, to be excluded. On 16 May 1916 a secret agreement, known as the Sykes-Picot Agreement was made between the British, French and Russian Governments. Under this agreement Russia was to have, besides Constantinople and a strip of territory on either side of the Bosphorus, the greater part of the four Turkish provinces adjacent to the Russian frontier, while the Arab territories were to be shared by Great Britain and France as follows:

(*i*) An international zone in Palestine.
(*ii*) A British zone of Basra and Baghdad.
(*iii*) A French zone of Syria (and Cilicia).
(*iv*) An independent Arab state or federation between the British and French Zones divided into British and French spheres of influence.[11]

The Sykes-Picot Agreement, by which the Arab territories between the Mediterranean and the Persian Gulf were to be carved out into British and French spheres of influence, was quite contrary to the British Government's agreement with Sherif Hussein. A further complication was added by the Balfour Declaration in November 1917: in return for the support of the Jews to the Allied

---

[9] Clare Hollingworth: *The Arabs and the West*, p. 4.
Haddad George: *Fifty Years of Modern Syria and Lebanon*, p. 1.
[10] Clare Hollingworth: *The Arabs and the West*, p. 4.
[11] Reader Bullard: *Britain and the Middle East*, p. 70.

cause the British Government agreed to settle a large number of Jews in Palestine. Out of the conflicting claims of the Jews, the Arabs, the British and the French to a share of the Arab territories of the Ottoman Empire were to be born the complexities of the Middle East problems after World War I.

Though the Arab revolt had begun in June 1916 the decisive battle in Palestine began in September 1918. Damascus fell on 1 October and at the end of October when the armistice with Turkey was signed on the island of Mudros, the whole of Syria as far north as Aleppo had been occupied. After the armistice the Emir Feisal (son of Sherif Hussein) was left to administer Syria; Lebanon was held by the French; Palestine was left to the British; all the areas were under the ultimate control of General Allenby, the British Commander-in-Chief.[12]

The French Mandate

The Emir Feisal, representing the Arab case at the Peace Conference at Versailles, was disappointed to find that neither Great Britain nor France was willing to agree to his proposal for the Arabs to be united under one government. The King-Crane Commission—an entirely American mission—was however sent to Syria and Palestine to study the problem and submit its report. The Commission recommended that Great Britain should receive a mandate over Iraq and the United States a mandate over Syria—Palestine. In case the mandate could not be assumed by the United States it was to be assigned to Great Britain. The Commission found themselves unable to recommend a French mandate. The Commission further recommended that the Emir Feisal should be the king of Syria and another Arab sovereign, to be chosen by a plebiscite, should rule over Iraq.[13] The recommendations of the Commission were ignored, for the French were not prepared to forego their claims on Syria. "They were in a strong position, because they had no responsibility for the McMahon correspondence and, on the other hand, they held under the Sykes-Picot agreement two cards which interfered seriously with the British plans: Mosul and a share in a small internationalized Palestine. It was mainly these two cards which enabled the French to obtain a free hand in Syria. In return France gave up Mosul in favour of Iraq, and withdrew her claims in respect of Palestine.[14]" By a decision of the Supreme Council of Allied Powers at San Remo in April 1920, France was assigned the mandate for Syria and Lebanon and Great Britain the mandate for Iraq and Palestine. These decisions, so fundamentally at variance

[12] Ibid, p. 74.
[13] Clara Hollingworth: *The Arabs and the West*, p. 7.
[14] Reader Bullard: *op. cit.*, 82-3.

with the promise of Arab independence, caused deep resentment amongst the Arabs, particularly in Syria, where Feisal had been ruling as king under British supervision since the end of the hostilities. After heavy fighting around Damascus the French compelled Feisal to leave Syria. The decision of the San Remo Conference was confirmed by the League of Nations in July 1922.[15]

French rule in Syria began in an atmosphere of great mistrust. In order to prevent the growth of a united front against their rule in Syria, the French resorted to the expedient of encouraging separatist tendencies, and established several indigenous governments. Thus, in September 1921, an independent state of Greater Lebanon was set up. As it had a small Christian majority, it was never so hostile to the French administration as Muslim Syria. The latter was split up into the territory of the Alawis[16] round Latakia, Jebel Druse,[17] and the states of Damascus and Aleppo, the latter containing the *Sanjaq* of Alexandretta.[18] In June 1922, Aleppo, Damascus and the Alawis formed a federation. The experiment proved a failure and the federation was dissolved in 1923. From the beginning of 1925 a new administrative arrangement was made by which Damascus and Aleppo were united to form the state of Syria with its capital at Damascus. Now the mandated territories consisted of four political units: the State of Greater Lebanon, the State of Syria, the State of the Alawis (known from 1930 as the Government of Latakia) and the Government of Jebel Druse.[19]

"This extension of the 'divide and rule' principle enabled the French authorities to favour and try to obtain the support of the various minorities in Syria. The plan worked to some extent, but it did not lessen the hostility with which the Mandatory was regarded—a hostility sufficiently strong to obscure the quite considerable natural benefits a French administration brought to the territory."[20] In July 1925 the Druses rose in revolt and defeated a large French force. The Syrian nationalists also secured some control over Damascus. The French retaliated by the bombardment of the city. By the end of 1926 the French brought the situation under control. Ten years later nationalist feeling in Syria again came to a head. This time the French tried to conciliate the Arab nationalists. On 9 September 1936, the Franco-Syrian treaty was initialled; this was followed by the Franco-Lebanese Treaty initialled in November 1936. The governments of Jebel Druse and

---

[15] *The Middle East* (1948)—(Europa Publications Ltd.), pp. 258-259.
[16] It was given the name of 'State' in July 1922.
[17] The independence of Jebel Druse was proclaimed in April 1922.
[18] Hourani: *Syria and Lebanon*, p. 172.
[19] Ibid, p. 173.
[20] Clare Hollingworth: *The Arabs and the West*, p. 14.

Latakia were to be united to the State of Syria. The Franco-Syrian Treaty providing for peace, friendship and alliance between France and Syria was to come into force when the French Mandate ceased and Syria was admitted to the League of Nations. The treaty provided for the consultation by both the governments on all matters of foreign policy, affecting their common interests; the transfer to the Syrian Government of the rights and obligations resulting from agreements made by the French Government in the name of Syria; mutual aid in case either government was involved in a conflict; the Syrian Government's responsibility for providing to the French Government all requisite assistance and facilities, including the use of communications; and the Syrian Government's responsibility for maintaining order and defending its territory as well as protection of French air routes crossing Syrian territory. There were a number of subsidiary agreements by which France was to have two airfields; a Syrian army was to be formed with the help of a French military mission; French troops were to be maintained for five years in the districts of Jebel Druse and Latakia; and the Syrian Government was to provide facilities required by the French forces and to permit the use of Syrian waters and ports by French vessels. The treaty was to last for 25 years. After the treaty was formally approved, France was to move the League of Nations for the abolition of the Mandate, for the recognition of Syria as a sovereign state and its admission to membership of the League. The Franco-Lebanese Treaty was in principle similar to the Syrian Treaty with one notable exception, namely, that no limits were to be imposed upon the employment of French forces. The treaties were ratified by the Lebanese and Syrian Chambers in November and December 1936, respectively.[21] By a decree of December 1936, Jebel Druse and Latakia were formally annexed to Syria (in 1939 they were again given almost complete autonomy). The Arab nationalists were, however, embittered, for the treaties were not ratified by the French Chamber. Their anger was still further aroused when by agreement between France and Turkey the *Sanjaq* of Alexandretta was ceded to Turkey in July 1939. Thus, on the eve of World War II, the French rule in Syria was not broad-based on the support of the Arab nationalists.

---

[21] Hourani: *op. cit.*, 200-203.

CHAPTER XXII

The Plan for the Invasion

How Syria was drawn into the War

After the conclusion of the Franco-German armistice in June 1940, Syria continued to be ruled by the Vichy French. At first, it was outside the orbit of the Axis influence, at least ostensibly. This state of affairs however did not last long. The British Government's policy was to avoid entanglements in Syria but to resist occupation of that country by any hostile power. Axis influence gradually increased in Syria. An Italian Armistice Commission assumed control of ammunition dumps and petrol supply, and German agents increased their activities. Matters came to a head in April/May 1941 when Syria felt the impact of events in the neighbouring country of Iraq. Early in April 1941 the pro-British Regent of Iraq (Emir Abdul Illa) was ousted from power and the anti-British military clique led by Rashid Ali assumed control of the country. The British Government was much perturbed by Rashid Ali's *coup d'etat*. Events moved fast. Hostilities in Iraq commenced on 2 May and lasted till the end of the month.[1] The Axis helped Rashid Ali by sending aircraft to operate from the Syrian aerodromes and from Mosul in Iraq. For this purpose General Huntziger, War Minister in the Petain Government sent instructions in early May to General Dentz, the Vichy High Commissioner in Syria, to allow the use of the air bases in Syria to the Axis for the passage of German aircraft to Iraq. He was also ordered to send war material to Iraq.

The first Axis aircraft arrived in Syria on 7 May. A few days later, more aircraft landed at Mezze, Palmyra and Aleppo and went into action in Iraq, particularly in the Habbaniya area. Their number was estimated at the time to be sixty-six military aircraft and forty transport aeroplanes.[2]

In addition to offering the landing grounds, the Vichy authorities also allowed the use of the Syrian railways to the Axis for sending aviation petrol, arms and ammunition to Mosul. Since these goods passed through Turkish territory they were disguised as French and it was declared that they were being sent to meet the threat of an alleged Kurdish rising.[3]

---

[1] See the account of Iraq campaign in the earlier chapters.
[2] R.A.F. Narrative—The Campaign in Syria, p. 7.
[3] Ibid, p. 8.

At the same time German agents intensified their activities. A German emissary, Herr Otto Bahn, travelling under the pseudonym of Renouard, arrived in the country. He was followed by Colonel von Manteuffel, an air technician.

On 15 May, Mr. Anthony Eden stated in the House of Commons that the Syrian airfields were being used by the Axis and warned the Vichy Government of the consequences. The French declared that the Axis had used the Syrian airfields only in the case of forced landings. Meanwhile, British aircraft had started attacking airfields suspected to be in Axis use and similar other targets in Syria.

Axis intervention in Syria carried with it strategic implications which could not be easily ignored. From bases in the Dodecanese islands, Axis aircraft were striking at the Suez Canal and an airborne expedition to Syria was a serious possibility. By occupying Syria the Axis could disrupt the Allied strategy in the Middle East. An Axis occupied Syria would be a powerful threat not only to Iraq and the Iranian oilfields but also to Palestine, Suez and Cyprus, three positions of vital importance in the eastern Mediterranean. To meet this contingency the British Government acted with prompt energy and instructed General Wavell, Commander-in-Chief, Middle East Forces, to be prepared to send a force to Syria—an operation to be called 'Exporter'. On 31 May, General Wavell ordered General Sir H. M. Wilson, General Officer Commanding the British Forces, Palestine and Transjordan, to be ready to move a force into Syria with the object of securing Damascus-Rayak-Beirut, and (if the situation permitted) Homs—Tripoli.[4]

Topography

The Vichy forces had the advantage of the terrain. Apart from a narrow coastal strip, the Allied advance into Syria and Lebanon could be only through mountainous country, or by wide turning movements through the eastern desert. "All routes from the south were commanded by steep hill-sides and knolls of which the defence could—and did—make full use. Precipitous ravines made the cross-country use of vehicles and Bren carriers impossible in many areas."[5]

Three phases of the operations

Operations started on 8 June 1941 and lasted till 11 July 1941. They were carried out in three stages, each stage following the other in quick succession.

Stage 1—The main advance from Palestine and Transjordan

---

[4] G.H.Q. Middle East Instruction to General Wilson, 31 May 1941.
[5] *Active Service with Australia in the Middle East*, p. 60.

to Damascus, jointly with a parallel advance along the coast to Beirut.

Stage 2—An advance from Iraq in the direction of Palmyra.

Stage 3—An advance from Iraq towards Aleppo, and a second advance from Mosul to Hassetche and Qamichliye.

Vichy Forces in Syria

Vichy military forces at this time in Syria were estimated to be thirty-five thousand men, remnants of General Weygand's army, mostly well trained and experienced soldiers. Their great advantage was that they had about ninety tanks whereas the Allied forces were comparatively weak in armoured vehicles. The Vichy forces had also 120 field and medium guns. However it was doubtful if the bulk of these French forces were willing to fight for the Axis. Nor were the French-trained Syrian troops, *troupes speciales*, any more enthusiastic. On the other hand, there were two factors calculated to produce considerable resistance. One was the anxiety of at least some of the French troops to retrieve the honour of the French arms from the disgrace it had suffered at the fall of France, and the other was the general misgiving among the Vichy French that if the Free French succeeded in establishing themselves in Syria, they would supplant them in their jobs and positions of authority.[6]

Vichy troops were mainly concentrated on the Palestine and Transjordan frontiers, Jebel Druse, Damascus and Beirut. On 3 June 1941, the dispositions of the Vichy troops were known to be as follows:[7]

(a) *Damascus area*
   Five infantry battalions
   One group cavalry
   Three batteries 105 mm guns
   One anti-aircraft battery

(b) *Beirut area*
   Four infantry battalions
   Three squadrons cavalry
   One group armoured fighting vehicles
   Two batteries artillery
   Four anti-aircraft batteries

(c) *Jebel Druse area*
   Two infantry battalions
   Four squadrons cavalry
   Some armoured cars

---

[6] R.A.F. Narrative, (Hist. Section), p. 3.
[7] Order of Battle of French Troops in Southern Syria (as known on 3 June 1941), *War Diary* 5 Ind. Inf. Bde.

These troops were distributed at the following places:
  (i) Soueida—Possibly one infantry battalion
      One squadron cavalry
      Two troops armoured cars
  (ii) Salkhad—One infantry company
  (iii) Chahba—One infantry company
      One squadron cavalry
  (iv) Rhariye—One squadron cavalry

(d) *North Palestine Frontier Area*
  Four infantry battalions
  Four squadrons cavalry

(e) *Transjordan Frontier Area*
  Bosra—One company Senegalese Troops
  Deraa—One company Levant Troops
      Two squadrons Moroccan Spahis
      Two 75-mm and one 47-mm guns (anti-tank role)
      (with outposts at Nassib 25 Moroccans),
      Yadoude (34 Moroccans), Mzerib (20 Moroccans), Tell Chehab (30 Moroccans)
  Ezraa—One company Levant Troops
      One company Sappers
  Sheikh Meskine—One battalion Senegalese
      One section 75-mm guns (two)
  Kuneitra—One battalion Senegalese
      One company Foreign Legion
      One group 25-mm anti-tank guns or rifles
      One squadron Light Tanks
      One squadron armoured cars
      One battery colonial artillery (two 65-mm guns and two 105-mm guns)
      (with outposts at Fiq (one company Senegalese), Jisr Benett Yacoub (one section of Senegalese), El Allega (one section of Senegalese), Nerane (one company Senegalese), Ain Ziouane (probably two companies Senegalese), and Tell Abou Nida (artillery from Kuneitra in position).

Total available aircraft of all types for use by the Vichy Air Force was ninety-two (this does not include a small number of civil transport aircraft which were in Syria at that time).[8] Throughout the campaign a steady flow of reinforcement aircraft continued into Syria, and by 16 June 1941, it was estimated that, allowing for

---

[8] R.A.F. Narrative, *op. cit.*, p. 17.

losses, the Vichy Air Force strength had been increased to nearly one hundred and fifty-nine aircraft of all types.[9]

A part of the Vichy Air Force was based at Rayak with small forces at Damascus, Plamyra, Aleppo and at the seaplane base of Tripoli.[10]

Allied bombing of Palmyra airfield and that part of Nerab airfield, which was occupied by the Axis, caused them to confine themselves to the use of Aleppo. Allied bombing of the Syrian aerodromes caused the Axis to withdraw their aircraft and personnel from Syria. The main reason for this action was the Axis impression that their oil and aviation petrol stocks would be destroyed as a result of the Allied bombing. The Axis confined their activity to attacks on British shipping and on the naval base at Haifa from Dodecanese bases.

The Vichy war vessels based on Beirut comprised two destroyer leaders, three submarines, one patrol craft, one net layer and one sloop.

Allied Forces

The Allied troops available for this operation (Phase 1) were:
7th Australian Division (less one infantry brigade)
5th Indian Infantry Brigade Group
A Free French Division
'C' Battalion Special Service Brigade (Commando)
Scots Greys and Staffordshire Yeomanry
Composite Regiment (Mechanised)
Cheshire Yeomanry (Horsed)
Transjordan Frontier Force
Certain ancillary and Engineer units.

Of the above forces, the Free French were in Palestine stationed at Qastina, to the south of Jaffa, under the command of General le Gentilhomme. They were organised as a division of two brigades, one with a battalion of the Foreign Legion and two battalions of Senegalese and the other with a battalion of Fusiliers Marins and two battalions of Senegalese. They were incomplete in transport and, in some instances, in weapons.[11]

The Australian division was new to battle, not having been engaged in the Western Desert. It had no tanks other than the light tanks of the Divisional Cavalry Squadron, no medium machine-guns, and troop-carrying transport for two battalions only.

The 5th Indian Infantry Brigade Group (4th Indian Infantry

[9] Ibid.
[10] Ibid.
[11] Lord Wilson: *Eight years overseas* (1939-1947), p. 111.

Division), veterans of Sidi Barrani and Keren, crossed the Egypt-Palestine border on 16 May 1941, and concentrated in the Irbid-Samakh area on 23/25 May. During the period 26 May to 7 June, they worked on the defences at Irbid, Samakh and Mafraq, three points on the Transjordan road running parallel to the Syrian frontier.[12]

Allied air force consisted of about 70 aircraft operating mainly from the aerodromes in Palestine. The Royal Navy, which was to cover the Commando landing and also to support the advance of the army along the coast road to Beirut, allotted for these tasks the 15th Cruiser Squadron (two light cruisers and ten destroyers).

Plan of operations (Phase I)

General Wilson's strategy in outline was to secure the chief objectives—Beirut, Rayak and Damascus. The advance along the coast towards Beirut was to be facilitated by operations in area Merjayun. Merjayun was also to serve as a springboard for the attack on Rayak. The advance towards Damascus was to be made via Deraa and Kissoue and the flank to be secured by the capture of Kuneitra. According to the plan of operations drawn up on 5 June by General Wilson the force which was to advance into Syria was organised into three groups, each operating direct under orders of Headquarters, British Forces in Palestine and Transjordan:

(*i*) 7th Australian Division and attached troops, including C Battalion Special Service Brigade (Commando);
(*ii*) 5th Indian Infantry Brigade Group;
(*iii*) Free French Force.

Major-General J. D. Lavarack commanded the 7th Australian Division. The troops at his disposal were two brigades and divisional troops of the 7th Australian Division and some additional units of the 1st Cavalry Division and the 6th Australian Division. His sector extended from the river Jordan to the coast. For operations in area Merjayun and for the thrust towards Rayak, Major-General Lavarack selected the 25th Australian Brigade and attached troops. This force was constituted as follows:

Headquarters 25th Australian Brigade
2/31st Australian Battalion
2/33rd Australian Battalion
3 troops Royal Dragoons (armoured corps)
One squadron 6th Australian Division Cavalry Regiment
One squadron Cheshire Yeomanry (horsed)
2/6th Australian Field Regiment
7th Australian Anti-Tank Battery
One troop 170th Light Anti-Aircraft Battery

---
[12] 5 Ind. Inf. Bde. in the Campaign in Syria, *War Diary* 5 Ind. Inf. Bde.

2/5th Australian Field Company
Composite Regiment from 6th Cavalry Brigade ('Todcol').

For the advance on Beirut (considered as the main operation) Major-General Lavarack considerably strengthened the 21st Australian Brigade, which was organised into three columns:
- (i) 'Doncol' was to advance by the route El Malikiya-Tibnine-Tyre. It comprised:
    2/16th Australian Battalion
    Two troops Royal Dragoons (armoured cars)
    6th Australian Division Cavalry Regiment (less two tank troops)
    2/4th Australian Field Regiment (less one battery)
    Two troops 6th Australian Anti-Tank Battery
    One troop 170th Light Anti-Aircraft Battery
    2/6th Australian Field Company (less one section).
- (ii) Cheshire Yeomanry (less one squadron) was to advance by the Aitaech Chaab track to Bennt Jbail, Tibnine, Srifa and thence to turn the line of the Litani river.
- (iii) 'Motcol' which was to advance by the coastal road comprised:
    2/27th Australian Battalion
    Two tank troops 6th Australian Division Cavalry Regiment
    One battery 2/4th Australian Field Regiment
    6th Australian Anti-Tank Battery (less two troops)
    170th Light Anti-Aircraft Battery (less two troops)
    One section 2/6th Australian Field Company. (A detachment of 2/14th Australian Battalion with an anti-tank gun was to follow 'Motcol' and act as garrison of Tyre. A special party of the 2/14th Australian Battalion was to be sent forward in advance to Iskandaroun, to prevent the demolition of the stone bridge).

The advance of the Australian division was to be assisted by a Commando landing from Cyprus on the northern bank of river Litani. The Royal Navy was to protect the advance along the coast from interference by the French war vessels based on Beirut and to give support by the bombardment of Vichy defences. The British naval forces engaged were under the command of Vice-Admiral E.L.S. King. They were organised as follows:
- (a) Force B consisting of two cruisers (*Phoebe*, flag of V.A. 15 Cruiser Squadron, and *Ajax*) and four destroyers (*Kandahar, Kimberley, Jackal, Janus*). There were four additional squadrons from 10 June—*Stuart* (Australian) *Jaguar, Griffin, Defender*.

(b) Force C consisting of Special Service Vessel (*Glengyle*), an anti-aircraft cruiser (*Coventry*) and four destroyers (*Ilex, Isis, Hotspur, Hero*).

(c) Fleet Air Arm Squadrons—No. 815 (12 Swordfish at Nicosia), No. 829 (5 Swordfish at Nicosia and 4 Albacores at Lydda) and No. 803 (12 Fulmars at Palestine).

For his advance on Deraa, Brig. W. L. Lloyd, C.B.E., M.C., commanding the 5th Indian Infantry Brigade, had at his disposal:

3rd Battalion 1st Punjab Regiment
4th Battalion 6th Rajputana Rifles
Transjordan Frontier Force (one horsed and one mechanised regiment)
1st Field Regiment R.A.
5th Indian Brigade Anti-Tank Company
One troop 171st Light Anti-Aircraft Battery
18th Field Company R. Bombay Sappers and Miners.

The initial objectives of the 5th Indian Infantry Brigade Group were:[13]

(i) the east-west railway line between Bosra and Hamamat (El Hamme),
(ii) the junction town of Deraa on this railway,
(iii) the Tell Chehab viaduct, where it crossed the railway.

Further objectives were Kuneitra, on the road Tiberias-Damascus, Fiq on its eastern branch, Sheikh Meskine on the road Deraa—Damascus, and Ezraa, half way up the railway to Damascus.

The capture of Sheikh Meskine and Ezraa would deprive the French of the use of the railway Deraa-Damascus and the two lateral roads from Salkhad, while the loss of Kuneitra would leave them only with the road Damascus-Beirut as an access to the Mediterranean.

For the operations, the Brigade Group was divided into four columns as follows:

'A' (Commander: Lt.-Col. L. B. Jones, D.S.O.)
4/6 Rajputana Rifles
One platoon Brigade Anti-Tank Company
One section 18th Field Company Sappers & Miners.

'B' (Commander: Brigadier W. L. Lloyd, C.B.E., M.C.)
Headquarters 5th Indian Infantry Brigade
3/1 Punjab
1st Field Regiment R. A. (less one troop)
Brigade Anti-Tank Company (less two platoons)
Two troops Light Anti-Aircraft Battery

---

[13] 5 Bde O. O. No. 1 dated 5 June 1941, *War Diary* 5 Ind. Inf. Bde.

18th Field Company Sappers & Miners (less two Sections)
One Company 14th Field Ambulance.

'C' (Commander: Officer Commanding C Company)
C Company 1st Battalion Royal Fusiliers
Detachment 18th Field Company Sappers & Miners.

'D' (Commander: Lt.-Col. A.D.G. Orr)
1st Battalion Royal Fusiliers (less one company)
9th Field Battery A.I.F.
11th Field Battery (less one troop)
One platoon Brigade Anti-tank Company
One section 18th Field Company Sappers & Miners (less detachment with column C).

Column A was stationed at Mafraq, B at Irbid, C and D at Samakh. Detachments of the Transjordan Frontier Force patrolled the frontier.

The operation was to be carried out in three phases:
Phase I—Capture of Fiq and Kuneitra and the encirclement of Deraa.
Phase II—Capture of Deraa.
Phase III—Capture of Sheikh Meskine and Ezraa.

The plan in outline was for Columns A and B to converge on Deraa from different directions, and for Columns C and D to be directed against Fiq and Kuneitra respectively. The detailed instructions for the carrying out of this operation were as follows:[14]

(i) Column A was to move via Ramtha, cross tracks southwest Mzerib station-Yadoude and secure by 0500 hours on D1 day a position about 800 yards from the outskirts of Deraa covering the line including track and railway Deraa-Rhazale to track and railway Deraa-Mzerib, and attack Deraa in conjunction with column 'B' on the conclusion of the artillery programme by the 1st Field Regiment R.A. For the capture of Deraa, the companies of 4/6 Rajputana Rifles were allotted various objectives. D Company was to secure area 800 yards north-north-east of Deraa, astride road Deraa—Rhazale. Its A company was to secure area 1,000 yards north of Deraa, astride road Deraa—Damascus. B Company was to secure area 800 yards north-west of Deraa, astride road Deraa—Yadoude. Battalion Headquarters was to be in the rear of A Company during operation.

(ii) Column B was to advance along route Irbid-Ramtha, and secure by 0500 hours on D1 a position about 800 yards

[14] 5 Bde O. O. No. 1 dated 5 June 1941 and Appendix 'A' *War Diary* 4/6 Rajputana Rifles.

Maj.-Gen. Mayne with some officers after the Amba Alagi victory

Italian prisoners of war march down from Toselli Fort
to the bottom of Tosseli pass at Enda Medani Alem

the withdrawal of 1 Worcesters lay along the narrow bare ridge which was completely overlooked by Italian positions on Little Alagi and Bald Hill. The forward troops therefore had to hold the ground they had gained until dark. They withdrew at 1800 hours. The battalion suffered a few casualties during the day, 8 being killed and 28 wounded. One company 3/2 Punjab which had captured Middle Hill continued to hold it.

Further Planning

The General Officer Commanding 5th Indian Division had ordered the 29th Indian Infantry Brigade to hold Middle Hill on 6 May, to enable him to consider plans for further operations. The alternative courses open to him were to continue pressing with the attack on the west flank or to try to break through in the Falaga Pass area.

In the Falaga Pass sector Fletcher Force had reported on 5 May that although the Italians were building sangars and showing general activity they appeared to be withdrawing some troops from that sector to the other flank. The Commander of Fletcher Force was confident of success in breaking through on that flank. General Mayne, however, thought that a force strong enough for a decisive break-through on this front was not available. He also considered it difficult to get the guns forward in a long advance on this front.

On the western flank the Italians were holding strong positions. Their machine gun and mortar posts were sited in dug-outs, cut deep down or into the face of the rock which in most cases had proved impossible to be knocked out by artillery fire. The 29th Indian Infantry Brigade had already occupied Pyramid, Whale Back, Elephant and Middle Hill. Movement by daylight on the last named feature or between it and Elephant would immediately draw accurate machine gun fire from Bald Hill, Little Alagi and Amba Alagi. The only approach from Elephant to Middle Hill was along the cart track on the east side of the saddle of low ground separating the two features and was in full view of and within close range from Bald Hill. The approach forward of Middle Hill towards Little Alagi was along a narrow ledge with precipitous drops on both sides. Just to the west of Little Alagi there was a drop in the ledge. Little Alagi itself, though a big feature, was completely dominated by Amba Alagi. Thus the problem of capturing Little Alagi and Bald Hill was a very formidable one. It was not possible to force a way into the position merely on the strength of superior numbers, because there was not room enough on the ledge leading to it for the employment of large numbers. Nor was there any scope for manoeuvre

Twelve H39 (light medium) tanks
Five light cars
Two guns (one 75-mm, one 65-mm)
One Anti-Tank rifle.

After the 5th Indian Brigade Group had accomplished its task of securing the line Sheikh Meskine-Ezraa, a mobile Free French Force, under the command of General le Gentilhomme, moving from Irbid, was to pass through the 5th Indian Brigade and advance on Damascus. The force consisted of:

Two battalions Senegalese
One battalion Foreign Legion
Two companies Battalion l'Infanterie de Marine (motorized)
One Company Fusilier Marines
One battery 75-mm guns (tractor drawn)
One anti-tank Company
One tank company (B echelon).

Role of R.A.F.

The task of the Royal Air Force at the beginning of the campaign was:[16]

   (i) to provide close and direct support for the army,
   (ii) to maintain protective fighter cover for the fleet (which was to co-operate with the coastal advance of Allied troops and to restrict the movements of Vichy shipping),
   (iii) to attack strategical objectives, including ports, shipping and oil installations, and
   (iv) to bomb hostile aerodromes in order to restrict the activities of the Vichy and Axis air force.

---

[16] R.A.F. Narrative, *op. cit.*, p. 23.

CHAPTER XXIII

Capture of Sheikh Meskine

The operations commenced at 0200 hours on 8 June as planned. While the 7th Australian Division operated in the coastal and Merjayun sectors, the 5th Indian Infantry Brigade Group operated in the area Kuneitra—Sheikh Meskine. Of the latter, the two columns (A and B) converged on Deraa, while C and D columns advanced towards Fiq and Kuneitra respectively.

Advance of column B to Deraa

The two columns (A and B) of the 5th Indian Infantry Brigade Group made good progress on the first day of the operations. Preliminary to the advance on Deraa, the Transjordan Frontier Force secured without opposition the railway line, except at Nassib where the Vichy troops succeeded in blowing up the bridge.

Advancing from Irbid through Ramtha, column B (3/1 Punjab) crossed the Frontier at 0200 hours. B Company's objective was to cut the telephone wire from the customs barrier and to capture the customs post. A and D companies, on the left and right respectively of B company, were to overcome any opposition likely to hold up B company. By 0400 hours B company had accomplished its task, having cut the telephone wires, attacking the customs post from the rear and completely surprising it. Then the column advanced and took up its position on a high ground outside Deraa. A pourparler party went in a staff car towards Deraa at 0530 hours. Just outside the town the car was fired on and severely damaged. The party continued the advance on foot. The request for the surrender of the town was rejected at 0530 hours. Thereupon the Punjabis waited for the arrival of Column A in order to deliver the attack.

Capture of the Tell Chehab viaduct

In its advance on Deraa, Column A met with some opposition. C company 4/6 Rajputana Rifles and one sub-section 18th Field Company Sappers and Miners left Mafraq as advance guard to Column A at 2100 hours on 7 June. The Column halted short of Ramtha village. The advance was resumed at 2330 hours. Reaching south of the border at 0025 hours on 8 June the column halted while C company and one sub-section 18th Field Company proceeded on its independent mission of securing Tell Chehab viaduct.

This detachment concentrated at 0400 hours in debussing area near the border. C Company Commander ordered one platoon and sub-section Sappers and Miners to lead the attack and secure the Tell Chehab bridge. The second platoon was to secure Mzerib station while the third was to secure the railway line roughly midway between Mzerib station and Tell Chehab bridge. The platoon which was to lead the attack on the Tell Chehab bridge left the debussing area at 0500 hours, accompanied by an officer of the Free French force as a guide. (The two other platoons had left the debussing area at 0140 hours). The platoon proceeded along the side of the Wadi Meidane as the going in the actual wadi was difficult. At 0130 hours two men from the sub-section Sappers and Miners were sent to cut the telephone lines on the railway and at 0145 hours civilians and camels were met by the leading scouts but went away to the south without discovering the presence of the Indian troops. The railway line was reached at approximately 0200 hours and the platoon proceeded in single file quietly along it under the tunnel. At 0245 hours, Tell Chehab village was reached and the platoon crept slowly past and below the Vichy outpost (Poste de Combat) without being observed. The bridge was visible and a light and sentry could be seen.

When the platoon was within a hundred yards of the bridge, the company commander ordered it to halt. He then went forward with the Company Havildar Major and a Free French Officer and instructed the remainder of the platoon to attack the bridge with bayonets if fire was opened. The party of three crawled up to the wire surrounding the Vichy post and, cutting the wire, charged the sentry and other men guarding the bridge. The rest of the platoon then rushed at the bridge on hearing the noise of fire. By 0300 hours, the bridge was captured and consolidated, Sappers of the 18th Field Company having cleared the demolition charges.[1] Machine-gun and rifle fire, however, continued throughout the night from the village and the Vichy outpost (Poste de Combat). The other two platoons secured their objectives without opposition.

Advance of Column A to Deraa

In the meantime the main column, which had halted near the border, had crossed the frontier at 0200 hours, and with D company leading advanced towards Yadoude. At 0315 hours, after the leading troops had turned east towards Yadoude, it was discovered that the column had split into two, one half led by a Sappers and Miners' truck having failed to turn off. It was cloudy and the track which was very faint could not be traced. A Vichy patrol encountered west of Yadoude was surrounded and captured by D company.

---

[1] Appendix 'B' to *War Diary* 4/6 Rajputana Rifles.

General Sir Claude Auchinleck

Indian Troops take a view of picturesque Damascus

Brigadier W. L. Lloyd

Brigadier C. J. Weld

Col. Jones ordered D Company to push straight past Yadoude without engaging the Vichy garrison at that place (estimated to consist of 30 cavalry—Syrian Arabs), as it was getting late and it was essential that the company should reach Deraa without further delay. A few shots were fired as the company passed through but no casualties were sustained. D company debussed at approximately 2¼ miles south south-west from the village and advanced along the railway line towards Derra, at about 0400 hours. A Vichy patrol of six men was captured and another party repairing the railway line was rounded up. Two Vichy armoured fighting vehicles were surrounded and captured with their crew. D company then continued its advance, leaving an escort for the two captured armoured fighting vehicles and prisoners. It arrived at its appointed area outside Deraa at about 0700 hours.

Meanwhile the missing portion of the column had also been making satisfactory progress. The Commander had decided to strike out across country as daylight was fast approaching and the Vichy garrison of Yadoude had to be by-passed because of the time factor. Debussing began about 2¼ miles south south-west from Yadoude. A few Vichy detachments and armoured fighting vehicles opened fire on the leading elements. These were engaged by carriers and A and B companies. One Vichy armoured car was knocked out by an anti-tank rifle. At this stage some of the Indian troops manned the armoured cars captured by D company and brought their machine-guns into action. Having overcome the opposition, A and B companies advanced to their appointed areas, mopping up small Vichy parties *en route* and arriving in position at approximately 0700 hours.[2]

Capture of Deraa

By 0700 hours, when 4/6 Rajputana Rifles had taken up positions, 3/1 Punjab was ready to launch the attack on Deraa. A, B and D companies attacked with artillery support. Immediately the Vichy garrison began to evacuate the town. By 0830 hours the town had been entered by the three companies, and 250 prisoners had been taken.[3] During this action the role of 4/6 Rajputana Rifles was to prevent the escape of the Vichy troops from Deraa. The carrier section with A company held up Vichy transport attempting to use the Damascus road; one Vichy tractor and gun and two lorries were engaged and set on fire by the anti-tank platoon. Another section of carriers engaged a train escaping from Deraa but failed to stop it.

After the capture of Deraa, 4/6 Rajputana Rifles concentrated

---
[2] *War Diary* 4/6 Rajputana Rifles.
[3] *War Diary* 3/1 Punjab.

about 1,500 yards north of Deraa, where mechanical transport was assembling for the advance to Sheikh Meskine. Vichy aircraft had been active over Deraa during the final phase of the attack, diving and hedge-hopping but only opening machine-gun fire occasionally and ineffectively on the advancing Indian troops.[4]

The Advance to Sheikh Meskine

After the capture of Deraa, 4/6 Rajputana Rifles resumed the advance towards Sheikh Meskine. At 1000 hours on 8 June, 4/6 Rajputana Rifles, one battery 1st Field Regiment R.A. and one troop Light Anti-Aircraft Battery, advanced from the concentration area about 1,500 yards north of Deraa. C company which had started earlier reached Atmane and found that a large bridge had been blown up. C company took up its position round the village and rounded up four of the demolition parties. The main column reached Atmane at approximately 1100 hours. The advance was not held up for long, for a diversion was soon found and the advance was resumed, C company following in the rear. Throughout the advance on Sheikh Meskine, the Rajputana Rifles encountered opposition from Vichy armoured cars. The anti-tank guns and carriers, forward with the leading D company, came into action on each occasion. By pushing on boldly and taking risks the column avoided excessive delay. At 1330 hours Vichy artillery opened up but D company, undeterred, debussed and deployed about 200 yards south of Sheikh Meskine. By 1400 hours they had edged forward and made contact about 700 yards from the southern defences. During the advance Vichy aircraft had been over the column on several occasions but the only casualties sustained through dive bombing and machine-gun attacks were 1 killed and 2 wounded. On one occasion one Indian soldier fired with the tommy gun at a range of hundred feet on a Vichy aircraft coming straight at him. Black smoke poured from its tail and it was seen limping away in obvious difficulty.[5]

The plan

Colonel Jones planned to concentrate the attack (at 1500 hours) on a limited front on the western defences and to exploit the success. A company on the left and B company on the right were to lead the attack. D company was to support by fire, working close up to overlap the left flank, under cover of artillery bombardment. C company was to be in reserve, prepared to exploit the success. The carrier platoon was to advance with the forward infantry and support the final assault. The attack on Sheikh Meskine was to be

[4] *War Diary* 4/6 Rajputana Rifles and *War Diary* 5 Ind. Inf. Bde.
[5] *War Diary* 4/6 Rajputana Rifles.

supported by artillery. Registration was to be carried out while A and B companies moved to the forming-up place (about 2,000 yards from the objective). The artillery programme, from zero hour until the forward companies had reached a point in line with the forward observation post (about 1,000 yards from the objective), was slow fire by observation, thereafter rapid for seven minutes or until the troops got too close to the objective.

Capture of Sheikh Meskine

The attack began according to plan but did not succeed due to stiff Vichy opposition. Both the leading companies (A and B) were held up by intense machine-gun fire from the right flank, about 600 yards from the objective. Two carriers received direct hits from Vichy 75-mm guns and were completely burnt out. It was obvious by 1600 hours that further progress on this limited front (western defences) was impossible. Therefore a change in the plan was made. At 1640 hours D company was ordered to make a wide turning movement and capture a ridge approximately 600 yards from the north-west corner of Sheikh Meskine. At 1650 hours, D company moved wide to the left flank coming on the Vichy long range machine-gun fire at approximately 1725 hours. It advanced steadily, wheeling on to the objective when about 1,500 yards due west. The attack was pressed home, supported only by the weapons of the company. When due to intense Vichy machine-gun fire the leading platoon was pinned to the ground, Naik Bhopal Singh, the commander of a reserve platoon, with incredible gallantry stormed the forward post, killing or wounding three Vichy machine-gun crew. He then turned to the right and assaulted a second machine-gun from the flank. Encouraged by his example, the other platoons climbed the ridge and mopped up the ramaining posts with tommy guns. Vichy artillery shelled the ridge causing casualties, and Vichy machine-gun posts and armoured cars operating on the north flank also kept up an intermittent fire. These were dealt with while consolidation was carried out. The night was spent in holding the position and patrolling the road Sheikh Meskine—Deraa.[8] Vichy aircraft had again been active during the day, bombing the gun area and machine-gunning mechanical transport.

The attack was to be pushed home at dawn on 9 June. A and B Companies were to attack the earlier objectives (the limited front on the western defences); C company was to be in reserve and was to be ready to attack from the same direction as D company. Carriers were to demonstrate on the east flank. Mortars were to support the attack as soon as possible by observation.

[8] Ibid.

4/6 Rajputana Rifles attacked Sheikh Meskine at 0430 hours on 9 June but, beyond a few stray shots, no opposition was encountered. The Vichy troops had evacuated Sheikh Meskine during the night. Total casualties in the whole operation against Sheikh Meskine came to 9 killed, 36 wounded and 1 missing. The Vichy lost 89 killed, wounded and captured, besides 10 machine-guns, two Bofor guns and considerable material and ammunition.[7]

Capture of Ezraa

At 0630 hours on 9 June, C company of 4/6 Rajputana Rifles, one section of carriers, the mortar platoon and two anti-tank guns set out along the road Sheikh Meskine-Ezraa to secure the latter town, a task which they accomplished without opposition at 0730 hours. The remainder of the battalion, less one company and one section carriers left to garrison Sheikh Meskine, followed up and arrived at Ezraa at 0930 hours.[8]

Achievements of the Indian troops

In two days the two columns (A and B) of the 5th Indian Infantry Brigade Group had accomplished their task of capturing Deraa and the Sheikh Meskine—Ezraa line. The capture of Deraa, Tell Chehab bridge, Sheikh Meskine and Ezraa reflects very great credit on 3/1 Punjab and 4/6 Rajputana Rifles. Their training, determination to succeed, good leadership and individual initiative made possible what would otherwise have been a difficult operation.

Capture of Kuneitra

'Groupment Collet' advanced from Samakh, before dawn on 8 June, to Fiq, El Aal, Khisfine, Sheikh Saad and concentrated west of Sheikh Meskine to provide left flank protection to the 5th Indian Infantry Brigade Group. In its rear, Column C (a company of the Royal Fusiliers) occupied Fiq-El Aal area. Column D (the main body of the Royal Fusiliers) moved up to Rosh Pinna, crossed the Jordan at Jisre Benett Yacoub and advanced to Kuneitra. A pourparler party preceded the column. It was somewhat delayed by road-blocks but reached the town by 1030 hours on 8 June. Although the summons to surrender was rejected, the party was not allowed to leave until 1300 hours. During the proceedings a Free French liaison officer was fired on by the Vichy French but not hit. The Royal Fusiliers delivered an assault at 1500 hours but stiff opposition was encountered. The Vichy troops remained in

[7] Ibid.
[8] Ibid.

possession of the town, but during the night of 8/9 June they withdrew from it. Kuneitra was occupied at dawn on 9 June.[9]

The operation by the 5th Indian Infantry Brigade Group was carried out smoothly and in a determined manner. The high standard of training of the troops concerned was very fully demonstrated. Casualties were light while 30 officers and 300 other ranks were captured from the Vichy side.

---

[9] 5 Ind. Inf. Bde. in the Campaign in Syria, *War Diary* 5 Ind. Inf. Bde.

CHAPTER XXIV

Capture of Kissoue

With the capture of Sheikh Meskine, the stage was set for the attack on Kissoue by the Free French Force under the command of General le Gentilhomme, preliminary to the attack on Damascus. The Free French Force passed through Sheikh Meskine at 1000 hours on 9 June to attack Vichy positions at Kissoue. Brigadier Lloyd placed at the disposal of General le Gentilhomme a battery of the 1st Field Regiment R. A. and a troop of the light anti-aircraft battery. At the close of the day the Free French Force had advanced to Ghabagheb and Taibe and had captured Khan Denoun and Deir Ali. In the meantime, while 4/6 Rajputana Rifles and 3/1 Punjab watched the left (western) flank, 'Groupment Collet' crossed in the vicinity of Sheikh Meskine to protect the eastern flank. They passed through Mesmiye, Boueidan and Blei. Outposts were established to guard against attack from Vichy forces known to be at Bourak.

Dispositions of the Indian Brigade

The layout of the 5th Indian Brigade Group on 10 June was as follows:[1]

Ezraa ...	4/6 Rajputana Rifles less one company
Sheikh Meskine	One company 4/6 Rajputana Rifles
Deraa	3/1 Punjab
	One light anti-aircraft troop
	One section 18th Field Company Sappers and Miners
Fiq	One company of the Royal Fusiliers
	Detachment 18th Field Company Sappers and Miners
Kuneitra	The Royal Fusiliers less one company
	One troop 1st Field Regiment R.A.
Atmane	Brigade Headquarters.

Dispositions of Vichy troops

There were two main Vichy positions astride the Damascus road.[2] The first line was formed by the Aouadj river (Nahr el Aouadj) from Deir Khabie to Kissoue, whence it ran south along

---
[1] *War Diary* 5 Ind. Inf. Bde.
[2] Ibid.

the Jebel Maani ridge to Deir Ali and was extended to the villages of Boueidan and Bourak. The second line ran along the Jebel Madani to Jebel Kelb ridges (organised in depth as far as Achrafie), and thence to Jebel Abou Atriz and Nejha, with the river as an obstacle in the foreground.

Failure of attack on Kissoue

The Free French Force attacked Kissoue on 11 June. One Senegalese battalion advanced from the south-east astride the lower slopes of Jebel Maani but was held up by stiff resistance. Another Senegalese unit however did not meet with any opposition and occupied the eastern finger of the massif called Jebel Badrane, and pushed patrols down the farther slope towards Hardjilli on the river.

'Groupment Collet', which was protecting the right flank of the Free French Force, had advanced on 10 June from Boueidan to Nejha but had fallen back on Tell Djornye. Here on 11 June they were attacked by tanks and armoured cars. Groupment Collet's solitary anti-tank gun (25-mm) however proved very effective and the attack was repulsed. On the left flank of the Free French Force, the single company of the Royal Fusiliers at Fiq joined the battalion at Kuneitra to strengthen its defences.

The Free French Force renewed the attack on Jebel Maani on 12 June. Although the highest points on Jebel Maani were secured, Kissoue was not captured. About noon on the same day a message was received by the Headquarters 5th Indian Infantry Brigade from General le Gentilhomme reporting that a Vichy Column of about a hundred vehicles was outflanking him on the east, and urgently asking for help. A force consisting of one company 4/6 Rajputana Rifles, one troop 1st Field Regiment and one independent Anti-Tank Troop was sent to his help. One more company of 4/6 Rajputana Rifles was ordered to stand by, in the event of further reinforcements being required. The alarm, however, proved to be false and was presumably occasioned by the movements of Colonel Collet's column, with whom the Free French Headquarters had been out of touch for two days.[3]

'Gentforce'

On the same day reorganisation of the force for the attack on Kissoue was carried out. One squadron of armoured cars, the Royal Dragoons, which had just arrived, came under the command of the 5th Indian Brigade, which in turn was placed under the command of General le Gentilhomme for the attack on Damascus. Thence-

[3] Ibid.

forward, the protection of the line of communication, inclusive Deraa to Sheikh Meskine and Ezraa, devolved on the Transjordan Frontier Force.[4] General le Gentilhomme, however, never assumed effective command, for he was wounded. He himself wished to continue commanding from hospital at Deraa. The impracticability of this was represented to Force Headquarters, Jerusalem, by Brigadier Lloyd, Commander of the 5th Indian Infantry Brigade, whereupon the latter was appointed to command both his own brigade and the Free French Force from 14 June. This combined force was called 'Gentforce'. Lieut.-Colonel Jones, Commander 4/6 Rajputana Rifles, assumed command of the 5th Indian Infantry Brigade on 14 June.[5]

Meanwhile on 13 June, one squadron of armoured cars, the Royal Dragoons (less one section), one independent anti-tank troop and one anti-tank platoon had been sent to join Colonel Collet's force on the right flank, while the remainder of the 5th Indian Infantry Brigade Group with one company of Royal Fusiliers from Kuneitra, moved up to Sanamein in readiness for the next offensive by Gentforce. The Royal Fusiliers (less one company) remained at Kuneitra.[6]

Topography

The object of the operations by Gentforce was to secure the line of the road Damascus-Kissoue on 15 June by attacking the left flank of Vichy forces as a preliminary to severing their communications with Damascus. The area of operations now lay north of the line Sanamein-Kuneitra extending westward to the Australian sector. This part of Syria was a plain. Its western portion was crossed by numerous streams, and the eastern portion was studded with hills and lava rocks. The area was crossed by a river, the Nahr el Aouadj, which flowed from west to east; and was covered with gardens, houses, orchards and wood. The two roads leading to Damascus were the road Kuneitra-Damascus and the continuation of the road Deraa-Damascus. On the east and west of the former road was a stretch of plain suitable for the deployment of armoured vehicles. This area lay roughly in the quadrilateral Katana-Artouz-Kissoue-Oumm ech Charatite. In contrast to this, the ground west and east of the road Deraa-Damascus was dotted with hills; on the west were the high features of Tell Kissoue, Tell Afair and Jebel Madani, and on the east from south to north were the heights of Jebel Maani, Jebel Kelb, Jebel Temouri and Jebel Abou Atriz. Of these, Tell Kissoue was a high rounded

[4] Ibid.
[5] Ibid.
[6] 5 Ind. Inf. Bde. in the Campaign in Syria, *War Diary* 5 Ind. Inf. Bde.

hill, free of lava on its lower slopes; Tell Afair lay to its north; Jebel Abou Atriz was almost precipitous, and its continuations Jebel Kelb and Jebel Temouri were boulder-strewn, precipitous hills.[7] Towns, hamlets and other points of operational importance along the road Deraa-Damascus were, from south to north, Khan Denoun, Kissoue (at the junction of the road and Nahr el Aouadj) and Moukelbe to the south-west of Kissoue.

Dispositions of Vichy troops

During the period subsequent to the actions at Deraa and Sheikh Meskine, the Vichy forces had been withdrawn to a prepared position running east and west through the village of Kissoue. A considerable number of Vichy troops was at Sasa on the road Kuneitra-Damascus. The Free French Force had been halted in front of the Kissoue position. Kissoue village itself was a strongly fortified position. The Nahr el Aouadj passed south of it, forming an obstacle across the line of advance of the Indian troops. The village was surrounded by strongly wired defended localities in front of which were considerable defence works. A number of posts were concealed on the outskirts, while inside the village, many little orchards were wired in and defended by machine-guns.

It was estimated that the dispositions of the Vichy troops in the Kissoue area were: *5th Moroccan Battalion* behind the village of Kissoue and one *Tunisian Battalion* in the Kissoue gardens; one *Foreign Legion Battalion* guarded Tell Kissoue and another Moukelbe.

The Plan

The operation was to be carried out in two phases:
Phase A—Securing of the area Tell Kissoue —Kissoue-Moukelbe by the 5th Indian Infantry Brigade.
Phase B—Securing of Jebel Abou Atriz and Jebel Kelb by the Free French (13th Brigade).

For carrying out Phase A the Battalion l'Infanterie de Marine (BIM), Free French, came under the command of the 5th Indian Infantry Brigade on 24 June. The brigade was to be supported by all available artillery. Phase A was to be concluded by 0800 hours on 15 June, after which the 5th Indian Infantry Brigade was to lose all artillery, except one battery (eight guns), to the Free French for Phase B, which was to commence at 0815 hours. Phase B was to be put into operation irrespective of the degree of success achieved by the 5th Indian Infantry Brigade.

---

[7] *The Tiger Strikes*, p. 131.

Simultaneously, with the opening of Phase B, Colonel Collet's force was to cross wadi about Nejha and move north of Jebels Abou Atriz and Kelb to cut the Vichy communications with Damascus in the area round Subeine and to prevent interference by Vichy reserves and tanks with the operations of Allied infantry. One brigade (Free French) in area Deir Ali-Ghabagheb, and one battalion (Free French) at Sanamein were held in reserve. There was no change in the location of the rest of the 5th Indian Infantry Brigade.

The objective of 3/1 Punjab was Kissoue village, including junction of nulla and projected railway. Tell Kissoue was the objective of 4/6 Rajputana Rifles. The forming-up place for the Punjabis was the ground west of the road with its head on the line Khan Denoun-Taibe; for 4/6 Rajputana Rifles it was the area west of the road near the gardens of Khan Denoun. On the capture of Kissoue by the Punjabis, 4/6 Rajputana Rifles was to move through them along the track north of Kissoue, to attack and capture Tell Kissoue.

One company of the Royal Fusiliers was to move forward with 3/1 Punjab so as to protect the latter's left flank against ground attack from the direction of Moukelbe. B.I.M. from Taibe area was to support the attack of 3/1 Punjab by fire directed on Vichy troops in the vicinity of Moukelbe. Artillery was to concentrate from 0415 hours to 0445 hours on the south slopes of Tell Kissoue and the woods east of Moukelbe, and thereafter on any targets presented from 0445 hours to 0600 hours. For the support of 4/6 Rajputana Rifles, all available artillery was to be controlled by observation on the gardens east of Kissoue, and the Vichy observation posts on Tell Kissoue. When Tell Kissoue was captured, B.I.M. was to attack and capture Moukelbe on orders from the 5th Indian Infantry Brigade.

The R.A.F. was to bomb selected targets, make low flying atttacks and provide fighter patrols. Zero hour for the Punjabis was 0315 hours. The 4/6 Rajputana Rifles was to fix its own hour.[8]

Attack on Kissoue

The attack on Kissoue started according to plan. Kissoue had considerable defence works in front of strongly wired defended localities. 3/1 Punjab had formed up west of the main road with its head level with the villages of Khan Denoun and Taibe. It moved forward with all the four companies up for a frontal attack

---

[8] Gentforce O. O. No. 6 dated 14 June 1941, Appendix 'C'; and 5 Bde. O. O. No. 2 dated 14 June 1941, Appendix 'D', *War Diary* 5 Ind. Inf. Bde.

on the village of Kissoue and on a stretch of the wadi to the east. C company of the Royal Fusiliers, detached from Kuneitra advanced simultaneously as the left flank guard. The 13th Free French Brigade also started moving east of the road Deraa-Damascus. The B.I.M. patrolled aggressively on the west towards Zakie and on the north-west towards Deir Khabie. The artillery covered the early stages of the attack as previously arranged.

The Punjabis made a strong attack on Kissoue. The right company established a bridgehead over the wadi, just east of the village of Kissoue, shortly before 0600 hours. The bridge had been destroyed but the attacking party was carrying thirty wooden ladders, made overnight by the 18th Field Company Sappers and Miners, thus enabling the ditch to be negotiated. On the south edge of the village, the right centre company fought a close quarter action in the garden and the houses. To the west, the left company, which had taken its objective 1,000 yards west of the village, wheeled in to help the left centre company which was fighting in the garden about 500 yards south-west of the village. There was hard fighting in this sector for some time, but by 0830 hours news had reached the Brigade Headquarters that Kissoue was captured. Desultory firing, however, went on until late afternoon, the Vichy French having left sniping parties in a mosque in the centre of the village, before retiring. Difficulty was experienced in ejecting the snipers from the mosque, as, out of respect for the feelings of the Punjabi Mussalmans of the battalion, the mosque had to be taken without damaging it.

Next, 4/6 Rajputana Rifles passed through 3/1 Punjab in Kissoue village at 0900 hours on 15 June, and attacked Tell Kissoue from the south-west direction. A and B companies led the attack. There was little frontal opposition but cross-fire from machine-gun posts sited on Tell Afair harassed them a good deal. After the capture of Tell Kissoue an attack was launched on Tell Afair, D company and Carrier Platoon moving round the west side of Tell Kissoue and C company advancing round the east side. Tell Afair was captured. During the afternoon, however, the two companies were heavily counter-attacked by Vichy tanks and forced to withdraw—D company to area on the main road, just north of the Kissoue village, and C company and Carrier Platoon to area about 800 yards south of Tell Kissoue.

On the extreme left, the B.I.M., assisted by C company of the Royal Fusiliers cleared Moukelbe village by 1130 hours. This completed Phase A of the operations.

Meanwhile, Phase B had started at about 1100 hours. The Free French took Jebel Kelb but were held up from Jebel Abou Atriz and could make no further progress.

On the extreme right, Colonel Collet's force was similarly held up by heavy artillery fire and tank attacks from Tell Soltan.

The Vichy troops not only pushed back 4/6 Rajputana Rifles from Tell Afair to Tell Kissoue, but also delivered fierce counter-attacks.

CHAPTER XXV

Vichy Counter-attacks

Fierce Vichy counter-attacks on Kissoue, Kuneitra and Ezraa created a serious situation. Disturbing news reached the Brigade Headquarters from Kuneitra, where the Royal Fusiliers reported that a strong Vichy force was advancing from Sasa. From Ezraa (22 miles in the rear of Free French Headquarters at Ghabagheb) came the news that the town had been recaptured by a Vichy force of two companies of Tunisian troops, who had advanced from Soueida with ten armoured cars, two 75-mm field guns and three anti-tank guns, the Transjordan Frontier Force garrison having withdrawn to Sheikh Meskine.[1] This latter loss represented a serious threat to the line of communication. 3/1 Punjab too was heavily counter-attacked in Kissoue.

Fall of Kuneitra

The Vichy counter-attack at Kuneitra took a heavy toll of the Royal Fusiliers (less one company) who were guarding this strategic village. The role of the Royal Fusiliers was to hold Kuneitra, to harass the Vichy French at Sasa, divert their attention from the Kissoue operations, and prevent reinforcements being sent from Sasa to Kissoue. The Vichy French realised fully the importance of Kuneitra, which was an important road junction with roads leading off to (i) Sheikh Meskine, (ii) Jisr Benett Yacoub, (Syria-Transjordan Frontier), and (iii) Banias, just south-east of Merjayun. The possession of Kuneitra would enable the Vichy troops to cut the line of communication on both the Merjayun fronts. This was the main cause of the vigorous Vichy counter-attack on Kuneitra.

During the night of 14/15 June, a company of the Royal Fusiliers, a section of carriers and two armoured cars had been sent forward from Kuneitra to hold a position some four miles south of Sasa. At about 0230 hours, on 15 June, a strong Vichy force with ten armoured cars sallied forth from Sasa and drove this party back on Kuneitra. The Vichy French spent the day of 15 June in bringing up large numbers of infantry. Reconnaissance was made with armoured fighting vehicles of the Kuneitra defences. Kuneitra was isolated by sending cavalry patrols to cut the Sheikh Meskine, Banias and Jisr Benett Yacoub roads. As soon as it was obvious that an attack with armoured fighting vehicles was in preparation,

[1] *War Diary* 5 Ind. Inf. Bde.

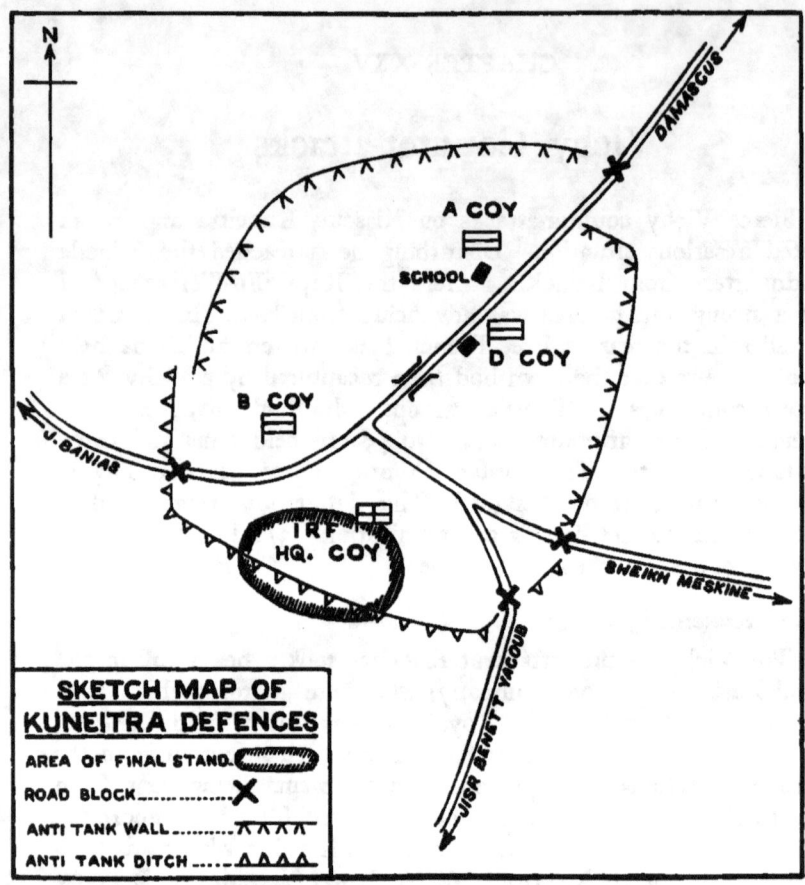

the battalion commander, Lieut.-Colonel Orr, sent an urgent message to the 5th Indian Infantry Brigade for the return of the battalion's anti-tank platoon of three Bofor guns (2-pounders) which, together with C company had been taken away to assist in the operations against Kissoue. The 5th Indian Infantry Brigade, however, was unable to spare these units, and it is doubtful if they would have succeeded in penetrating the beleaguered town or affecting the issue of the battle.

The struggle for Kuneitra started at dawn on 16 June. The strength of the Vichy force was estimated to be approximately:

> One battalion *17th Senegalese Regiment*
> One company the *Foreign Legion* (with mortars and heavy machine-guns)
> Two squadrons *Circassian Cavalry*

Eleven medium tanks
Ten armoured cars
One or two 75-mm guns.

In all, facing Kuneitra, on the Kuneitra-Damascus road, there were about 1,500 to 2,000 Vichy troops. Vichy armoured cars had been sent to cut the Sheikh Meskine and Jisr Benett Yacoub roads.

The garrison of Kuneitra consisted of the Royal Fusiliers (less one company) with B company greatly depleted by reverses during the earlier aggressive patrolling near Sasa, two armoured cars (Royal Dragoons) and one 20-mm Breda gun. The total garrison numbered about 575 men. The front held by A and B companies was about 1,000 yards. An anti-tank wall of stones, about 4 feet high by 3 feet thick, formed the principal defence. This had very numerous switches, with the result that (on A company's front at any rate) no reserve platoon could be formed and also not more than one section could support another by fire.

At 0430 hours the Vichy French pushed small parties of infantry over the ridge, about 400 yards outside the defence. These parties were met by small-arms fire and went to ground immediately. They contented themselves with sniping and small forward movements when possible. Vichy tanks made their appearance at 0445 hours and from that hour until 1030 hours they operated without infantry support. Their attack was principally directed against the right hand company, D. The Breda gun mounted on an armoured fighting vehicle near the Damascus road-block broke a spring after five rounds had been fired and had to be withdrawn because it could not be repaired. Thus practically without any serious opposition Vichy tanks knocked out the road-blocks with their cannon and pushed on over the debris into the town. Nothing could put them out of action. Boyes anti-tank rifles, even at five-yard range, and Molotov Cocktails and grenades made no impression on their thick armour.

At 1045 hours, a full-scale attack was launched by the Vichy French with tanks and infantry. The method followed was as follows: about five tanks were lined up nose to tail on the Damascus road and concentrated their fire, both machine-gun and cannon, on one section post. Armoured cars neutralised the fire of supporting sections. Under cover of this fire, Vichy infantry advanced along the line, with tanks threatening both sides of the wall and the infantry on the blind side. The Vichy troops closed up the section posts in detail, one by one. Consequently at 1200 hours the forward companies of the Fusiliers were ordered to withdraw to the Battalion Headquarters. Only twelve men each of A and D companies and about fifty men of B company managed to return. The

Vichy troops followed up this withdrawal so quickly that no cohesive defence plan was organised. As parties arrived back, they had to take up suitable positions in any of the houses, with the result that it soon became impossible to tell which houses were occupied by the British and which by the Vichy troops.

The most serious factor, however, was that the British troops were cut off from their reserves of ammunition, most of which had been dumped in section posts to be always within reach of the sections. The company reserve and the battalion reserve could not be reached owing to the distance to be covered in the open, where the Vichy troops could bring intense fire to bear on trucks at a range of about one hundred yards. Thus the only ammunition available was that in the men's pouches. During the afternoon, Vichy infantry infiltrated into the houses, and tanks continued to cruise about in the streets shooting at every available target.

At about 1730 hours, the Vichy French sent a flag of truce to the Battalion Headquarters demanding surrender. As the ammunition had been practically exhausted and further resistance would have involved unnecessary loss of lives, the commander of the Royal Fusiliers had no alternative but to surrender. The battalion surrendered at 1800 hours on 16 June.[2]

Situation retrieved

Meanwhile steps had been taken for retrieving the situation. Headquarters Gentforce had sent out orders at 1739 hours on 15 June for further operations during the night of 15/16 June and the following day. The 5th Indian Infantry Brigade, with one battery 1st Field Regiment R.A. in support, was to capture Jebel Madani and advance to Artouz and establish a position astride the road Kuneitra—Damascus.

The plan was for 3/1 Punjab to capture Jebel Madani, and for 4/6 Rajputana Rifles (on relief by a Free French Battalion at Kissoue at first light on 16 June) to pass through and seize line of the road from Jedeide Artouz to a little south of Artouz, where the track from Kissoue met the road. B.I.M. was to remain in Moukelbe until first light and was then to advance through Deir Khabie and co-operate with 4/6 Rajputana Rifles. All the operations thus planned were carried out with little opposition and negligible loss. At 0800 hours on 16 June, the 5th Indian Infantry Brigade Headquarters moved to Moukelbe and the day was spent in consolidation. At 1430 hours the B.I.M. near Artouz was attacked by Vichy tanks. This caused some confusion but the tanks were driven off by con-

---

[2] Statement by Captain T. P. Wilson M. C. 1st Battalion the Royal Fusiliers concerning the action at Kuneitra on 16 June 1941, Appendix E, *War Diary* 5 Ind. Inf. Bde.

centrated artillery and anti-tank fire. Shortly afterwards, at 1730 hours, five Vichy bombers escorted by fighters attacked them again and caused casualties. The same force of aircraft then bombed Kissoue. On that evening and for two or three evenings thereafter, regular French air patrols consisting of fifteen to twenty aircraft came over the Artouz—Kissoue area but did not drop bombs or cause casualties. These planes appeared to be operating from Homs. There was no sign of the R.A.F. but British anti-aircraft guns had some success.[3]

The 5th Indian Infantry Brigade spent 17 June resting and consolidating. A few brushes with Vichy tanks from Katana in the Jedeide—Artouz area took place. The same evening, the 2nd Battalion of the Queen's Royal Regiment who had been brought up as reinforcements, supported by a small force provided by Lieut.-Colonel A. S. Blackburn V.C., commanding the 2/3rd Machine-Gun Battalion, at Jisr Benett Yacoub retook Kuneitra with little loss, as the Vichy French had withdrawn.

The task of recapturing Ezraa had been entrusted to Colonel Jenin, commanding the 1st Brigade of Free French. He had put in an attack with a Senegalese battalion. The attack had been repulsed and Colonel Jenin had been killed. A small force from Sheikh Meskine led by Major Hackett, however, attacked Ezraa on the 17th and compelled the Vichy garrison to surrender.

Thus by 17 June the situation was retrieved, and preparations then commenced for the advance on Damascus on the night of 18/19 June.

---

[3] *War Diary* 5 Ind. Inf. Bde.

CHAPTER XXVI

Capture of Mezze

I Australian Corps

While the Gentforce had been advancing on the road to Damascus and was consolidating its position in area Kissoue, the 7th Australian Division had been developing powerful thrusts towards Beirut and Rayak. The main advance along the coast towards Beirut made considerable progress; the 21st Australian Brigade was held up by stiff resistance at the river Litani but the resistance was overcome by 10 June and the advance was resumed and Sidon secured by 15 June. The advance of the 25th Australian Brigade towards Rayak was however held up by fierce resistance in the difficult country of Merjayun. Though the Australians gained an initial success by capturing Merjayun, the Vichy troops launched a powerful counter-attack and recaptured it. The Australians made determined efforts to recapture Merjayun but failed in their efforts; they however successfully beat back the fierce Vichy counter-attacks on their position at Jezzine. Thus, although the main advance along the coast had made progress, the advance towards Rayak had been checked by stiff resistance in area Merjayun. It was felt necessary to reorganise the Australian force. On 18 June the Australian force was reorganised by the formation of I Australian Corps. Major-General A. S. Allen assumed command of the 7th Australian Division while Major-General Lavarack became the Corps Commander and assumed control of all operations from the Damascus area inclusive to the sea.

Vichy troops

While the reorganised Australian force under the command of Major-General Lavarack made vigorous prepartions for the advance towards Beirut and Rayak, Gentforce began the next phase of the operations with the advance towards Damascus on the night of 18/19 June.

The object of this advance was to capture Mezze and Kadem, preliminary to an attack on Damascus. Mezze was situated at the junction of the roads Kuneitra-Damascus and Damascus-Beirut, about two miles west of Damascus. Kadem stood on the Deraa-Damascus road about four miles to the south of Damascus. Between the two roads rose the hill Jebel Madani, dominating both the roads. North of this hill was a bare patch, beyond which the

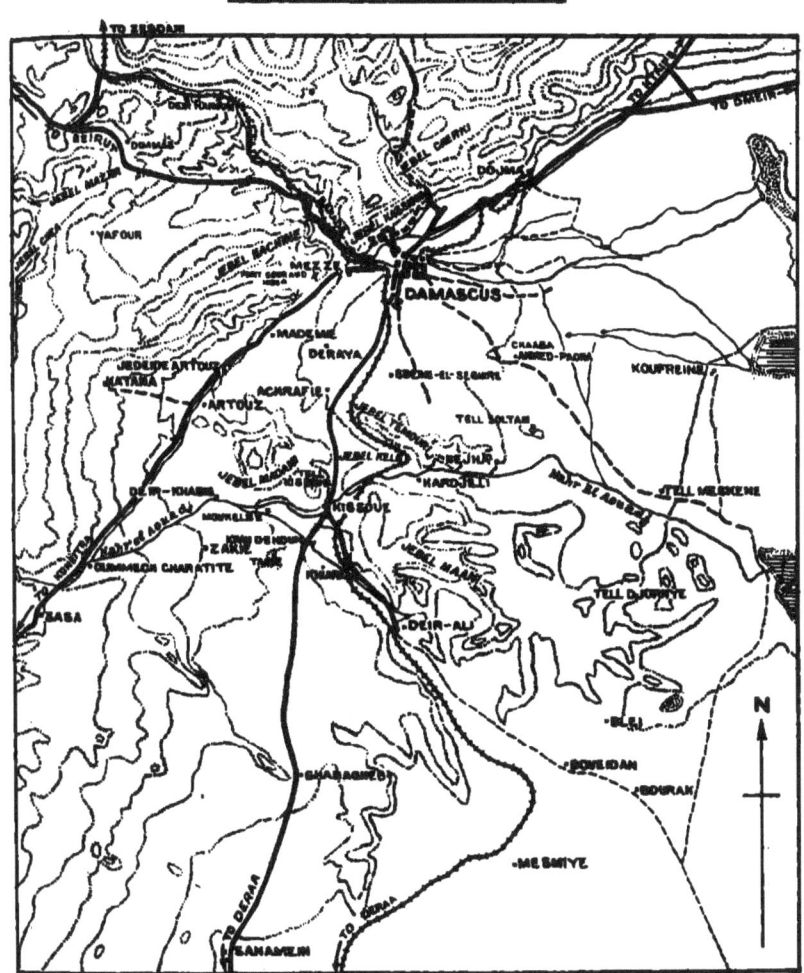

DAMASCUS AREA

country was covered with garden, orchards, cactus hedges, houses and a network of small streams and irrigation channels. Along the road Kuneitra-Damascus were the fortified hamlet of Mademie and the airfield of Mezze, both to the east of the road. To the west was a mass of hills surmounted by four forts at the northern extremity, which overlooked the low country round Mezze.

Vichy troops

It is difficult to say exactly what forces the Vichy French had in the area of contemplated operation. On 3 June 1941, they were known to have at Damascus:
- Five infantry battalions
- One group cavalry
- Three batteries 105-mm guns
- One anti-aircraft battery.

In addition to this, they had managed to withdraw a large proportion of their forces located in the area Kuneitra-Artouz-Kissoue-Deraa.

Plan of the operations

On 17 June the Commander of Gentforce issued instructions for the attack on Damascus: the 5th Indian Infantry Brigade was to capture Mezze and the Free French Force was to seize Kadem preliminary to entering Damascus from the south. To carry out these instructions the Commander of the 5th Indian Infantry Brigade made the following plan:

The main column was to consist of Advanced Brigade Headquarters, 3/1 Punjab (less B Company on Jebel Madani), 4/6 Rajputana Rifles, and 18th Field Company, Sappers and Miners (less one section). This force was to be followed by an armoured observation post, certain ammunition and signal trucks and the platoon of the Brigade Anti-tank Company, all under the Brigade Transport Officer.

The main column was to concentrate a little south of Artouz and advance (during the night of 18/19 June) along the road Kuneitra-Damascus, detaching one company of 3/1 Punjab to attack the fortified hamlet of Mademie. After securing Mademie the company was to rejoin the main column. During the advance of the main column a second company was to deal with any hostile defended localities which might be met on the way. When the main column reached the road and track junction south of Pt. 1085, one Punjabi company was to be detached to seize this feature while 4/6 Rajputana Rifles was to launch an attack on Mezze. On entering Mezze, 4/6 Rajputana Rifles was to take up positions blocking all roads entering the area. 3/1 Punjab (less three companies) and the 18th Field Company Sappers and Miners (less one section) were to remain in brigade reserve.

The 1st Field Regiment R.A. (less one troop) was to move to the area of the woods of Deraya by first light, escorted by six carriers of 4/6 Rajputana Rifles in order to support the advance of the infantry column.

Battalion l'Infanterie de Marine (B.I.M.), C company of the Royal Fusiliers, one troop of the 1st Field Regiment R.A., and one Light Anti-aircraft Battery (these two last in an anti-tank role) were to form a defensive flank on a line, inclusive Artouz-Jebel Madani.[1]

Capture of Mezze

3/1 Punjab less B company advanced at 2000 hours on 18 June from the forming up place in the vicinity of Kaoukeb farm in the following order—A, D, C companies, Battalion H.Q., H.Q. company. Following the track they concentrated a little south of Artouz, where the track met the road. They were shelled and also bombed from the air. Fortunately no casualties were sustained. After the rest of the column had concentrated south of Artouz, the advance began at 2045 hours on 18 July in the following order—3/1 Punjab leading as advanced guard, Brigade Headquarters in the middle, and 4/6 Rajputana Rifles as rearguard. The column advanced some distance along the main road and then marched across country to avoid the road-blocks, which were guarded by Vichy troops. On nearing the Mademie village, A company of 3/1 Punjab was detached to attack the village whilst the main column swerved round the village. The column was however subjected to terrific machine-gun fire from the village. The Indian troops at once laid themselves down on the ground and dispersed. Some casualties were sustained. After some time the firing stopped but there was considerable difficulty in finding the different companies as they had dispersed all round. The main column (less A and C companies of 3/1 Punjab and the transport column) resumed the advance. A company of the Punjabis was busy in overcoming the opposition at Mademie while C company went to the help of the section of Sappers and Miners and Brigade Transport, which advancing along the road had run into a road-block (near Mademie), guarded by Vichy troops with machine-guns and an anti-tank gun. Six trucks with ammunition, mortars and rations fell into the hands of the Vichy troops, before the latter were dispersed by C company of the Punjabis. C company remained as guard on the Brigade Transport till success signal from A company at about 0045 hours. Contact was made with A company and after a conference of all

---

[1] Appendix A to 5 Bde. O. O. No. 1 dated 5 June 1941, *War Diary* 5 Ind. Inf. Bde.

British officers present, it was decided to form one party of all who remained behind and to follow the rest of the brigade to Mezze. The advance was resumed along the main road to Mezze at 0200 hours on 19 June in the following order—C company 3/1 Punjab as advance guard, A company 3/1 Punjab, Sappers and Miners and Brigade Transport.

Meanwhile the main column had been advancing on Mezze. D company was detached to capture Pt. 1085, while 4/6 Rajputana Rifles advanced to attack Mezze. When the Rajputana Rifles neared Mezze at about 0430 hours, on 19 June, they were greeted with terrific fire coming from the pill-boxes on the outskirts of the village. A and C companies rushed straight for the village while D company cleared the right portion of the village. The advance of A and C companies was held up by Vichy tanks, which were however forced to retire by terrific anti-tank, rifle and small-arms fire. After about an hour of attack the Vichy troops were cleared from the village. About 40 Vichy French were taken prisoners. The companies were then put into defensive positions in the village, making road-blocks with stones, wood, some rolls of barbed wire and such things as they could lay hands on. The Brigade Headquarters, the two Battalion Headquarters, D company 3/1 Punjab, and D company 4/6 Rajputana Rifles were established in a large house (called Mezze House) and the adjoining garden.[2]

Attack on the Forts adjoining Mezze

While the main column succeeded in capturing Mezze, the rear column failed to capture the forts adjoining it. The two companies of 3/1 Punjab, 18th Field Company Sappers and Miners (less one section) and the Brigade Transport, which had been left behind, had been reorganised and had resumed their advance along the Mezze road at 0200 hours on 19 June. A road-block of motor vehicles was encountered and cleared and some prisoners taken. At 0400 hours on 19 June a Vichy machine-gun post at the aerodrome was engaged and dispersed. The advance continued towards Mezze along the left-hand side of the road without opposition. C company 3/1 Punjab attacked and captured the fort to the west of the main road on the lower ridge. This company then attacked the second fort but was held up due to heavy machine-gun fire on both the flanks. Hence it fell back and occupied the first fort. The company was however subjected to intense shell, mortar and machine-gun fire, causing several casualties.[3] So the fort was vacated and the company rejoined the rest of the force in the

---

[2] A personal account of the attack on Mezze by Captain S. N. Chatterji, I.M.S., War Diary 4/6 Rajputana Rifles.
[3] War Diary 3/1 Punjab.

nulla at the bottom of the hill. This was an exposed position, hence the column moved into the woods to the right of the main road. Not far from Kafr Sous a defensive position was taken up affording cover from Vichy tanks and aircraft.

Surrender at Mezze

The situation in the morning of 19 June was not very encouraging. Although the main column of the 5th Indian Infantry Brigade had occupied Mezze, the rear column had failed to capture the forts adjoining it (to the west of the Mezze road on a low hill) and had been forced to take cover in the woods south-east of Mezze (near Kafr Sous). The failure to join up with the troops in Mezze itself was a serious set-back, as the latter were thus deprived of their anti-tank guns. To make matters worse the Free French Brigade failed to carry out its task of attacking and capturing Kadem. One seemingly plausible explanation was offered for that. The attack on Kadem and Damascus was to be made with R.A.F. bomber support, but as the bombers could not be spared, the operation was postponed. So the Free French Brigade, which had been ordered to advance by the Kissoue-Damascus road, proceeded no further than the northern end of Jebel Kelb. Thus the original plan for a double-pronged attack on Damascus through Kadem and Mezze could not be carried out, leading to serious consequences. There is good reason to believe that the Vichy French, threatened by the cutting of their line of retreat by the thrust at Mezze, had begun to withdraw from Damascus; but the failure of the Free French to attack Kadem allowed the Vichy French to concentrate heavy forces against Mezze. Nor could relief be brought to the hard-pressed garrison by fresh Free French attacks during the morning of 20 June. The Free French could not mount a new attack until the afternoon of 20 June, when reinforced by some anti-tank guns they drove off the Vichy tanks which had been holding up the advance.

At 0900 hours of 19 June, a large number of Vichy tanks appeared and started firing at the Indian troops, who were engaged in making road-blocks. By 1400 hours the majority of these troops had been marched off as prisoners while the survivors rallied at Brigade Headquarters in the Mezze House, which was well suited for offering resistance. It was a double-storied house situated in a garden and enclosed by a wall. The house was completely tank-proof on three sides, surrounded as it was by a ravine. The front side was however insecure. The garrison made loopholes and gun embrasures through the wall and took up defensive positions along these posts. The Vichy infantry launched several fierce attacks on the house and the adjoining gardens under the covering fire of the tanks. The defenders fired anti-tank rifles at close range and threw Molotov cocktails at the tanks but without any effect. The defenders carried on the unequal struggle in trying circumstances. In defending their positions against countless attacks they had to fire almost continuously. They spared ammunition as much as possible. They tried their best not to fire a single shot uselessly. They collected all ammunition from the wounded and dead but in spite of this their ammunition position was critical. Rations and medical stores were completely exhausted. The fruits gathered from the garden were rationed out to the defenders, who were fatigued by the previous night's march and fighting throughout the day without any food or rest. By 2030 hours when the situation had become critical, Col. Jones sent a Jemadar with two officers to the rear Brigade Headquarters with a message for help. It required real nerve and courage to get out of that place, surrounded as it was on all sides by Vichy troops. But the mission was successfully accomplished; by 0500 hours on 20 June the message was delivered at the rear headquarters of the 5th Indian Infantry Brigade on the slopes of Jebel Madani. Succour however came too late to save the heroic garrison. Throughout the night and the next day wave after wave of attacks was made by the Vichy French. All of them were repelled. At about 1000 hours on 20 June, however, the Vichy tanks came very near and opened fire on the house. Shots came through the doors and windows. Still the heroic struggle continued. At about 1230 hours the Vichy French brought up some heavy guns and began shelling the house and the adjoining places. The garrison decided to leave the house and go into the open ground. But the Vichy tanks opened fire and the Vichy infantry scaled over the walls and hoisted a white flag. Further resistance was useless and the defenders surrendered at 1430 hours on 20 June.[4]

Failure to relieve the garrison

While the desperate struggle continued at Mezze, Brigadier Llyod made efforts to relieve the garrison. In the morning on 19 June, when the rear column had failed to join the main column in Mezze, Brigadier Llyod had decided to utilise the reserves. He despatched a small force under the command of Major Bourke (1st Field Regiment R.A.) to strengthen the rear column at Kafr Sous. Burke Force consisted of two companies of B.I.M, C company of the Royal Fusiliers, a Rifle company (composed of one platoon 3/1 Punjab, one platoon 4/6 Rajputana Rifles and one platoon mixed), one battery 1st Field Regiment R.A. and one platoon anti-tank company.

[4] A personal account of the attack on Mezze by Captain S. N. Chatterjee; *War Diary* 4/6 Rajputana Rifles.

Burke Force joined the rear column at Kafr Sous at about 2100 hours on 19 June.

At 0500 hours on 20 June, when Col. Jones' message for help was received at the rear headquarters of the 5th Indian Infantry Brigade on the slopes of Jebel Madani, Brigadier Lloyd (who, with the return of General le Gentilhomme to the command of the Gentforce, had resumed command of the 5th Indian Infantry Brigade that day) ordered the troops at Kafr Sous to relieve the hard pressed garrison. Thereupon the Burke Force advanced for the attack on Mezze while the rear column attacked the forts on the lower slopes to the west of the Mezze road (one of these was Fort Gourand). 2/3rd Australian Battalion (which had arrived in Syria from Palestine) was kept in readiness for strengthening the attack on Mezze. By 0700 hours on 20 June, A and C companies of 3/1 Punjab (rear column 5th Indian Infantry Brigade) had moved out of the woods of Kafr Sous to attack the forts on the lower slopes. C company occupied the first fort by 0900 hours under the covering fire from the battery of guns. A company then advanced and captured the second fort, consolidating its position about 1400 hours. At 1500 hours two platoons of C company then advanced and captured the prison. The Vichy troops immediately counter-attacked this position but were repulsed. Burke Force too worked its way into Mezze by the evening. The battery of the 1st Field Regiment played a notable part in this advance by destroying strong Vichy defences. The hard pressed garrison at Mezze however could not be relieved in time as the defenders had already surrendered at 1430 hours.

At dusk Brigadier Lloyd committed to action 2/3rd Australian Battalion to complete the capture of the forts on the high ground west of Mezze and to cut off the Damascus-Beirut road in the Barada gorge. The night attack was successful and the latter task was accomplished, resulting in the capture of many Vichy French prisoners. The Vichy troops however continued to offer resistance from the forts on the high ground. At 0300 hours on 21 June, a fierce Vichy counter-attack developed against Burke Force in Mezze and 2/3rd Australian Battalion on the high ground west of Mezze. This counter-attack was repulsed after fierce fighting. By 1100 hours on 21 June fighting had died down and Mezze was firmly secured.

Capture of Damascus

The fall of Mezze paved the way for the capture of Damascus. At nightfall on 20 June when the Vichy troops were still offering resistance at Mezze, two columns were trying to converge on Damascus. The first column consisting of the Free French Brigade, supported by a company of 2/3rd Australian Machine-Gun Battalion, had advanced from Jebel Kelb at 1730 hours on 20 June, but at nightfall it had not moved beyond Point 748 overlooking Achrafie. The second column comprising "Groupment Collet" had crossed the Aourdj near Tell Meskine and reached Karata at nightfall on 20 June. On 21 June, when Vichy resistance collapsed at Mezze, both the columns were able to make rapid advance and enter Damascus; the Free French Brigade pushing on through Kadem and 'Groupment Collet' advancing through Chaaba. The latter entered Damascus from the east at about 1430 hours on 21 June. General le Gentilhomme made a formal entry at 1600 hours. The capture of Damascus was essentially the result of skilled leadership of Brigadier Lloyd and the undaunted courage of the Indian troops of the 5th Indian Infantry Brigade.

The thrusts against Rayak and Beirut

After the capture of Damascus on 21 June a double thrust was made, one directed against Homs and the second against Rayak. The former task was entrusted to the Free French force and the latter to the 6th British Division.[5] The 5th Indian Infantry Brigade astride Damascus-Beirut road passed under the command of the 6th British Division, which had taken over the Kuneitra-Damascus road. The Indian brigade had suffered heavy losses at Mezze and therefore the task of advancing on the road Damascus-Beirut to Zahle area in order to capture Rayak aerodrome and cut off the Vichy forces fell to the 16th Brigade of the 6th British Division. The advance of the 16th Brigade was however held up by heavy opposition in area Jebel Mazar. As the Australians were also not making headway against fierce opposition in area Merjayun it was considered advisable to go on the defensive in this area and to develop a powerful thrust in the coastal sector towards Beirut. Consequently on 29 June the 6th British Division extended its sector by taking over the Merjayun sector from the Australian troops to enable the latter to be moved to the coastal sector for the main advance on Beirut. In spite of all efforts the 6th British Division failed to break through the strong Vichy positions in area Jebel Mazar. However the Free French Force advancing on the road Damascus-Homs made some progress. On 28 June they reached Nebek, about fifty miles from Damascus. Then they operated against the Baalbek-Homs road and railway. It was however on the coastal sector that substantial results were achieved. The Australian troops made determined efforts to break through the strong Vichy defences on the river Damour which

---

[5] Headquarters of this division had opened at Khan Denoun, south of Kissoue, on 19 June.

barred the way to Beirut. The formidable opposition was overcome and Damour was occupied in the morning on 9 June. With the capture of Damour the way was now clear for the advance on Beirut. But before the threat to Beirut could develop, the Vichy authorities in Syria opened negotiations for an armistice.

CHAPTER XXVII

Capture of Palmyra

An essential feature of the Allied planning was that though the main advance was to be made into south Syria from Palestine and Transjordan it was to be facilitated by keeping the Vichy troops in other sectors engaged by forces operating from Iraq. Iraq became in fact an important base of operations. The plan was to make a three-pronged attack—one directed against Palmyra so as to create a threat to Homs; the second directed against Deir ez Zor and Raqqa so as to create a threat to Alleppo; and the third directed against Hassetche and Qamichilye so as to liquidate Vichy opposition in the province of Bec du Canard in north-east Syria. The progress of the operations in south Syria has been already described. It is now necessary to give an account of the operations against Palmyra, Deir ez Zor and Hassetche.

On 13 June 1941, Major-General T. G. W. Clark, commanding Habforce, had received orders from General Wilson (G.O.C-in C, Allied Forces in Palestine and Transjordan) to advance into Syria from Iraq to occupy Palmyra and cut the Vichy communications between Damascus and Homs. At that time troops of Habforce were scattered at Mosul, Kirkuk, Baghdad, Habbaniya and in the Abu Kemal—Haditha area. On being relieved by the 10th Indian Division, Habforce was ready to advance on Palmyra. By 20 June the main body of Habforce had concentrated at H-3, the forward base of operations.

Rival forces

Habforce, which was to operate in Syria, consisted of the 4th Cavalry Regiment, the Royal Wiltshire Yeomanry, the Warwickshire Yeomanry, 1st Battalion of the Essex Regiment, No. 2 Armoured Car Company R.A.F., a battery of 25 pounders, an Australian battery of anti-tank guns, a battery of light anti-aircraft artillery and the Arab Legion Mechanised Regiment. Habforce suffered from one serious handicap—it had practically no air support. Vichy fighters and bombers had therefore almost a clear field of action.

Palmyra, the objective of Habforce lay in an oasis of the Syrian Desert, 1,300 feet above sea level. In ancient times it was an important caravan centre, being the meeting point of important trade routes, while in recent times its importance had increased

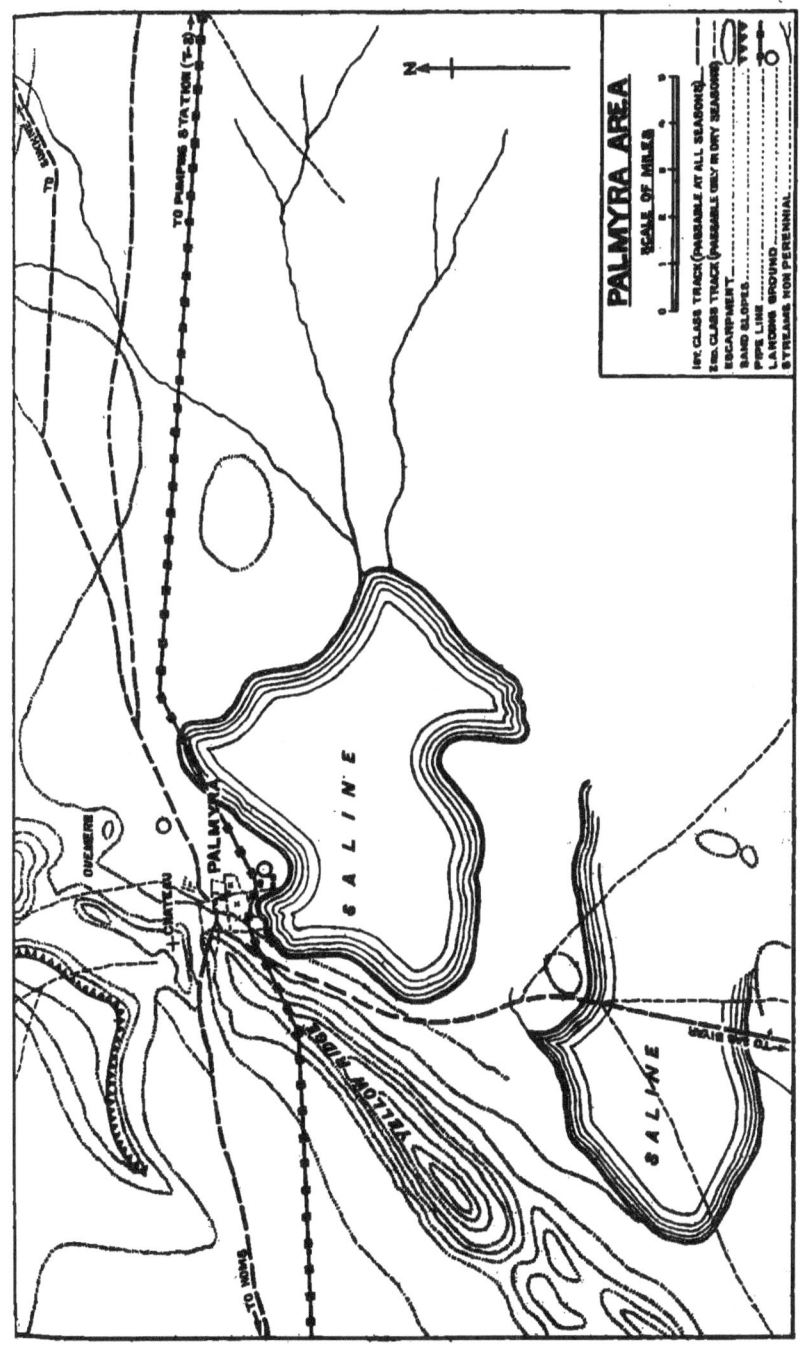

considerably due to the oil pipeline from Kirkuk to Tripoli passing through it.

The garrison of Palmyra consisted of two companies of the *Foreign Legion* and one *Light Desert Company*. The Vichy French had considerably strengthened its strong natural defences. The fallen pillars and masonry of the ruined ancient Roman city of Zenobia had been turned to good defensive purposes. The modern village built by the French (lying to the east of Zenobia) was protected by two forts (garrisoned by Vichy troops), situated further to the east on a flat plain. The open approaches to Palmyra were covered by tank traps, machine-gun posts and snipers' nests. In the north-west there was an old fortress called the 'Chateau'. To the south-west there were high rocky ridges (called the Yellow Ridge) and closely planted palm groves enclosed by a 18-foot wall forming a good natural obstacle. To the south of Palmyra lay the wide salt-pan, impassable to heavy vehicles. Thus Habforce was faced with the difficult task of overcoming the resistance of the Vichy troops in Palmyra, which had the advantages of terrain and strong natural defences.

The Plan of Operations

The plan was for the 4th Cavalry Brigade Group, under the command of Brigadier J. J. Kingstone, to advance from H-3 on Palmyra in three columns. The Royal Wiltshire Yeomanry, with three Armoured cars leading the way, was to cross the Iraq frontier by night on 20/21 June 1941, by-pass the salt-pan, and capture the Yellow Ridge and the Chateau. The Warwickshire Yeomanry, with three armoured cars leading the way, was to move east of Palmyra so as to reach the hills on the northern side, whence entry was to be made into the town. The Household Cavalry Regiment was to assemble at T-1 (to mislead the French into the belief that the main attack would be made up the Euphrates) and was then to move westwards along the oil pipeline towards Palmyra.

Operations on 21 June

The Syrian border was crossed early in the morning on 21 June. The Arab Legion and the armoured cars of the R.A.F. led the Royal Wiltshire Yeomanry, which was followed by Kingstone's Headquarters and the Warwickshire Yeomanry, the remainder of the 4th Cavalry Brigade Group being in the rear. After capturing a Vichy piquet at Juffa (25 miles south-east of Palmyra), the Wiltshire Yeomanry turned west and the Warwickshire Yeomanry to the east. But all hopes of a surprise attack on Palmyra vanished, for the British columns were observed by Vichy aircraft and, consequently, Habforce was subjected to attacks from the air. The Wiltshire Yeomanry by-passed the salt-pan and advanced under persistent air attack. By 1300 hours the advance was checked by machine-gun fire from the gardens and plantations near the Yellow Ridge. Later in the day, however, the patrols of the Wiltshire Yeomanry gained access to the Yellow Ridge. Meanwhile the Warwickshire Yeomanry advancing east of Juffa was held up south of the strongly fortified Vichy outpost at T-3. The British 25-pounders shelled the concrete pill-boxes without any effect. The Warwickshire Yeomanry was also subjected to air attack by several formations of Vichy aircraft. The Household Cavalry Regiment advanced before daylight from T-1 along the oil pipeline to the west. Leaving one squadron to watch T-2 (whose garrison surrendered in the afternoon) the regiment advanced towards T-3 but was held up east of this strongly fortified Vichy outpost. The regiment was attacked by nine Vichy aircraft and several vehicles were destroyed.

Thus, on the first day of the operations, some success was achieved because the Wiltshire Yeomanry gained a precarious foothold on the Yellow Ridge. But the Warwickshire Yeomanry and the Household Cavalry Regiment were held up by strong resistance from the Vichy outpost at T-3. Reinforcements were however at hand, for Major-General Clark had advanced from H-3 towards Juffa with the following troops:

        Headquarters 1st Cavalry Division Signals
        1st Battalion Essex Regiment
        Five troops Arab Legion
        Two sections No. 2 Armoured Car Company R.A.F.
        One section 2nd Field Troop R.E.
        One troop Australian Anti-Tank Battery
        One troop 237th Battery R.A.
        169th Light Anti-Aircraft Battery R.A. (less one troop).

Operations on 22 June

On 22 June an advanced Divisional Headquarters was established and supply dump formed in the Juffa area and Major-General Clark decided to intensify the attack on Palmyra. A troop of the Warwickshire Yeomanry was left near T-3 to contain the French garrison while the rest of the Warwickshire Yeomanry and the Household Cavalry Regiment advanced to the hills in the north of Palmyra to gain contact with the Wiltshire Yeomanry.

Operations on 23 and 24 June

Not much progress was made during the next two days. The Wiltshire Yeomanry was subjected to persistent cannon and machine-gun fire from Vichy aircraft and maintained with difficulty their precarious hold on the Yellow Ridge. The Household Cavalry Regiment was up against opposition in the high rocky ground about 1,500 yards north-west of Palmyra.

The Warwickshire Yeomanry failed in its efforts to establish contact with the Wiltshire Yeomanry. During the two days (23 and 24 June) not much headway was made against Vichy opposition. This was particularly due to the increased Vichy air attacks, which resulted in the destruction of large numbers of petrol lorries and water carts, thus increasing considerably the supply difficulties. The forward troops of Habforce did not succeed in closing around Palmyra; on the other hand the troops of the Warwickshire Yeomanry, who had been left behind in observation of T-3, met with disaster. Six Vichy armoured cars displaying a white flag drove up from the west to the Warwichshire troop, who were fired upon as they emerged from their shelters to parley. Twenty-two British troops were killed, wounded or captured. An R.A.S.C. ration convoy which had lost its way, had a narrow escape. It turned back just in time, losing a few officers and men, who were made prisoners.

Operations on 25 June

The prospects of the early capture of Palmyra were not bright. The Vichy French had absolute superiority in the air and naturally Major-General Clark did not want to risk any considerable movement of troops across the desert by daylight. The only notable event of 25 June was that the Vichy aircraft, which had so far concentrated their attacks on the British troops attacking Palmyra discovered the advanced supply dump at Juffa and attacked it heavily. The British crew of the Bofor guns shot down one aircraft and set another on fire.

Operations on 26 and 27 June

On 26 June the supply difficulties were eased to some extent for the Arab Legion secured without fighting the Vichy post at Sab Biyar (about 64 miles south-west of Palmyra), thus enabling Habforce to shift its base from H-3 to H-4, and ensuring a shorter and safer line of supply.

At night on 27 June the Wiltshire Yeomanry captured a Vichy machine-gun post on Yellow Ridge.

Operations on 28 June

On 28 June the prospects became brighter, for General Wilson had promised air assistance. R.A.F. bombed Palmyra and shot down six Vichy bombers. This was encouraging. The Wiltshire

Yeomanry succeeded in occupying Yellow Ridge in the teeth of opposition. The company of the 1st Essex Regiment, which had relieved the Household Cavalry, captured the 'Chateau' on the north-western side of Palmyra.

Operations on 29 June

Palmyra was now practically surrounded and the French garrison made fierce counter-attacks to retrieve the situation. On 29 June a Vichy counter-attack drove the Wiltshire Yeomanry from the Yellow Ridge. The attempt by the latter to recapture the Yellow Ridge at night met with failure but one of its squadrons found its way into the gardens on the south-western side of Palmyra. The ring was closing around Palmyra, for the 1st Essex Regiment was advancing towards the ruins of Zenobia. The advance of the Essex was checked by a ditch defended by anti-tank guns.

The Arab Legion had in the meanwhile been extending its activities in the region to the north-east of Palmyra. They occupied without opposition on 29 June the village of Sukhne, 45 miles away at a gap in the mountains on the route to Deir ez Zor.

Operations on 30 June

On 30 June the Vichy troops holding the Yellow Ridge were subjected to heavy artillery fire. At night the squadron of the Wiltshire Yeomanry, which had made its way into the garden adjoining the Yellow Ridge, safely withdrew from an exposed position. The 1st Essex Regiment made a spirited attack on the northern end of the ridge and captured it, retaining its hold in spite of heavy bombing attacks from the air. The fate of Palmyra was practically sealed.

While the ring around Palmyra was tightening, the Arab Legion was extending its activities. On 30 June the Arab Legion, who had handed over Sukhne to a squadron of the Household Cavalry in order to carry out a reconnaissance to the north and east, encountered and routed a Vichy mechanised column advancing along the road from Deir ez Zor. Five Vichy officers, 64 other ranks, six armoured cars, two trucks and 12 machine-guns were captured.

Fall of Palmyra

The victory at Sukhne led to important results. When the news of the destruction of the *2nd Light Desert Company* at Sukhne reached the *3rd Light Desert Company*, which was besieged in Palmyra, the latter refused to continue the struggle. Thus weakened, the garrison of Palmyra surrendered on 3 July 1941.

Next day, the garrison at T-3[1], which had held out, also surrendered. Habforce played an important part in the operations in Syria, for, with the capture of Palmyra, all the Vichy airfields in Syria were brought within the range of the R.A.F.

Advance towards Homs

On 5 July, General Wilson orderd Habforce to advance towards Homs. The 1st Essex remained behind at Palmyra while most of the 4th Cavalry Brigade Group pushed on and occupied Furqlus on 7 July. At the time of the 'cease fire' on 11 July the Habforce was thus operating in the neighbourhood of Homs.

---

[1] Petroleum Company's posts on the pipeline running to Tripoli were called T-1, t-2 *et seq*. Those on pipelines running to other places were similarly named, e.g. H-3 was post No. 3 on the pipeline to Haifa.

CHAPTER XXVIII

Plan for the Attack on Deir ez Zor

Operation 'Deficient'

While Habforce was directed on Palmyra, the 10th Indian Division made a thrust towards Aleppo. On 19 June Lieut.-General Quinan, Commander of the Iraq Force, received instructions from India that support in the operations in Syria took precedence over the defence of the Basra area and the protection of the oil centres. Hence on 21 June 1941, the latter ordered Major-General W. J. Slim, Commander of the 10th Indian Division, to concentrate a force at Haditha and advance up the river Euphrates to Aleppo, with a view to threatening the rear of the Vichy forces holding Beirut. Major-General Slim was to command the operation and establish his Advanced Headquarters in the first place at Haditha, when he was to come under the orders of the General Officer Commanding British Forces, Palestine and Transjordan. The Air Officer Commanding Iraq was to provide one fighter squadron for his support from the time that he reached Haditha. This squadron was to operate initially from Haditha and later from Deir ez Zor. Major-General Slim was further ordered to send 15 days' supply and petrol and as much ammunition as possible to Haditha, which was to serve as a supply base.[1]

The tasks allotted to the 10th Indian Division were:[2]
  (i) to advance from Abu Kemal and seize Deir ez Zor,
  (ii) to deal with any Vichy French garrison or troops encountered,
  (iii) to defeat and drive off any irregular opposition in the neighbourhood, such as the forces operating under the Palestine guerilla leader, Fawzi Qawukji,
  (iv) to prepare for a further advance via the line of the river Euphrates on Aleppo at the earliest possible date, and
  (v) to create among local tribes a friendly attitude for the Allied cause.

The 10th Indian Division, less the 20th Indian Infantry Brigade Group in the Mosul area, was to operate against Deir ez Zor from Abu Kemal. The 21st Indian Infantry Brigade Group

---

[1] Iraq Force O.I. No. 6 dated 21 June 1941, *War Diary* 10 Ind. Div.
[2] *Summary of the operations for the capture of Deir ez Zor and the Euphrates Province between 30 June and 12 July 1941* by Major-General W. J. Slim, Commander 10 Ind. Div., F 830.

was to be the striking force while the 25th Indian Infantry Brigade Group was to ensure the security of the lines of communication from excluding Haditha to including Baghdad (the 3rd Battalion 11th Sikh Regiment directly under the orders of the 10th Indian Division was to be responsible for protecting the pipeline including K-3 to including H-3 and of the line of communication from including K-3 to including Abu Kemal).³ This operation was given the code-name of "Deficient".³ᵃ

On the northern flank, 20th Brigade Group at Mosul was to send a diversionary column to demonstrate towards Deir ez Zor (with patrols advancing as far as Souar on the river Khabour, 30 miles north-east of Deir ez Zor). This demonstration was timed to coincide with the advance on Deir ez Zor.

In addition, a column under Headquarters British Troops in Iraq was to operate independently on the northern flank of the 10th Indian Division towards Hassetche and Qamichliye.

On the southern flank, Habforce was still surrounding Palmyra when the 10th Indian Division commenced operations.

Vichy Troops

The Vichy troops opposing the Indian troops were estimated to consist of three battalions of *"Troupes Speciales"* (a national army in which all ranks were native-born volunteers) with squadrons of cavalry and artillery groups. Up to 19 June 1941, the dispositions of the Vichy troops were believed to be as follows:⁴

Aleppo
'Troupes speciales'
4th Battalion *Levant Infantry*
4th Squadron *North Syrian Cavalry*
One battery 75-mm guns
2nd Group *Regiment Chasseurs d'Afrique* (Metropolitan)

Palmyra
'Regular troops'
15th Company 4th Battalion 6th *Foreign Legion*
'Troupes Speciales'
1st *Light Desert Company*

Deir ez Zor-Abu Kemal-Tell Abiad
'Troupes Speciales'
6th Battalion *Levant Infantry*
2nd *Light Desert Company*

---

³ HQ 10 Div to Brig. Powell dated 26 June 1941, Appendix 'AF', *War Diary* 10 Ind Div.; and 10 Div. O.O. No. 5 dated 26 June 1941.
³ᵃ See Appendix 12.
⁴ *French Forces in northern Syria—Location statement* up to 19 June 1941, *War Diary* 10 Ind. Div.

2nd *Light Mechanised Unit*
2nd Group 2nd *Levant Metropolitan Artillery*

Tell Kotchek—Qamichliye
'*Troupes Speciales*'
8th Battalion *Levant Infantry*
21, 23, 25, 28 *Light Squadrons Djejireh Cavalry.*

Air situation

The Vichy French had a relatively strong air force, equipped with modern planes and flown by their best pilots. Against this formidable air force, the only aircraft immediately available to the Indian troops was an improvised squadron of 4 Hurricanes and 4 Gladiators, manned by pilots with practically no training in fighter aircraft, and no experience of actual fighting. The 10th Indian Division had moreover no anti-aircraft artillery at all, and was seriously deficient in automatic weapons.[5]

Topography of the area of operations

The area over which the above operations were to be carried out was a plain, rolling desert. The river Euphrates cut through the middle of it, in a north-westerly direction, forming a belt of green vegetation across it. The Euphrates was joined by two main tributaries from the north, the principal of which was the river Khabour. The latter, in turn, was fed at its upper source by numerous small streams, all flowing from north to south and intersecting the entire width of northern Syria.

The Deraa—Damascus railway, which continued northwards across this area, divided into two branches at Aleppo. One branch proceeded west to Anatolia; the other east along the Turkish border and inside Turkey until it re-entered Syria near Qamichliye. After crossing the north-eastern tip of the country, this line emerged into Iraq, in the vicinity of Tell Kotchek to join the Baghdad—Mosul railway at Mosul.

The most important towns in this area were Aleppo, Deir ez Zor and Hassetche. Main roads and motorable and secondary roads from Deir ez Zor and Hassetche radiated in all directions connecting these three towns to the road system of the rest of the country.

The only outlet to the sea from this area was the very small and unimportant port of Latakia.

The oil pipeline from Haditha to Tripoli had pumping stations at intervals along its length. These were numbered T-1, T-2, etc., from east to west.

[5] Major-General Slim's Report.

Deir ez Zor, the principal town of east Syria, was situated in a plain on the south bank of the river Euphrates. It was overlooked from north and south by low lava-rock escarpments which, in the south, ran parallel to the Euphrates almost as far as Abu Kemal.

Four roads radiated from Deir ez Zor: one north-west to Raqqa and Aleppo; another north-east to Souar, Al Badi and Mosul; a third south-east to Abu Kemal; and the fourth south-west to Palmyra. Two river bridges spanned the Euphrates. One in the north-east of the town linked the town to the road system north of the Euphrates; the other in the north-west, over an inlet of the river, merely provided a convenient crossing from one part of the town to the other.

Deir ez Zor might be approached from Abu Kemal from two different directions by moving west along the Haditha-Tripoli pipeline to T-2 and thence due north.

A good fair-weather track ran along the south bank of the Euphrates until it reached a point near El Gata where it branched into two (both running parallel and converging on Mayadine), the right track proceeded via Salhiye to Mayadine, a small compact town, 52 miles from Abu Kemal. From here a good and hard track led to Deir ez Zor. The distance from Abu Kemal to Deir ez Zor was 84 miles. In addition to this, there was a secondary track running along the north bank of the Euphrates, with other stretches of secondary tracks on both the banks.

The road along the Haditha-Tripoli oil pipeline was a rough dry-weather desert track. From K-3 to T-1 (65 miles) there was no definite track. The going was extremely bad, and slow speeds were essential. From T-1 to T-2 (mile 65—mile 140) there was a clearly-defined track near harder desert. Going was very fair and speeds of 40 to 50 miles per hour might be kept up except at the wadi crossings. The road was flat or gently undulating throughout, and passed over gently rolling country. The first section, as far as T-1, was an earth and stony desert, grass-grown in spring, with occasional flat-topped hills. Movement off it was possible but was very rough for wheeled vehicles. From T-1 to T-2 a harder track led over stony, rolling grassland, cut by wide wadi beds, which were no obstacle in dry weather. Movement off the track was possible throughout. T-2 was the junction of several secondary tracks. Of these, one went due north to Deir ez Zor. The route ran across open desert and was closely defined the whole way. The track was suitable for all types of motor transport and provided good going throughout its length, having no sharp turns or steep gradients which might present any difficulty. The distance between Deir ez

Zor and T-2 by this track was 70 miles. Another track led from T-2 to Mayadine.⁶

For the advance of the 21st Indian Infantry Brigade Group two of these routes were used:

(i) the road Abu Kemal—Mayadine—Deir ez Zor along the bank of the Euphrates, hereafter referred to as the river route,

(ii) the road along the pipeline to T-2 and north across the desert, hereafter referred to as the desert route.

Three routes led from Haditha (the supply base) to Abu Kemal. The first route followed roughly the right bank of the Euphrates. Between Haditha and Ana (41 miles) the road, unmetalled but passable for mechanical transport, passed through broken hilly country, crossing many small wadis. From Ana, a long straggling town along the river bank, the track continued, mainly through broken country, to Al Qaim frontier police post (a distance of 51 miles), and thence over better going for 16 miles to Abu Kemal. The second route left Haditha in a westerly direction south of the Haifa pipeline. At about 19 miles from K-3, the track swung north to T-1, Al Qaim and Abu Kemal. The third route followed the Tripoli pipeline from Haditha to T-1, whence a track led to Al Qaim and Abu Kemal.⁷

Preliminary operations : Capture of Abu Kemal

Prior to the advance of the 21st Indian Infantry Brigade Group beyond the frontier post of Abu Kemal, it was necessary to organise the jumping off area, which was subsequently to be the line of communication area. During this period of preliminary operations the 3rd Battalion 11th Sikh Regiment was to come under the command of the 21st Indian Infantry Brigade. The jumping off area included Haditha (K-3), Abu Kemal, T-1, H-1, Rutba. The securing of these places was the task of 3/11 Sikh.⁸ On 22 June 1941, Major-General Slim ordered the Sikh battalion to advance from Baghdad to Haditha, pick up its garrison (A company 3/11 Sikh, A troop 3rd Field Regiment R.A., Squadron 13th Lancers, Detachment Field Ambulance, W/T Detachment and Light Aid Detachment) and move on to Abu Kemal, just over the Iraq border in Syria, to chastise the Palestine guerilla leader Fawzi Qawukji, who had entered Abu Kemal with 18 cars, armoured and others, on the previous day. The battalion left Taji Camp (Baghdad) at 1110

⁶ M.T. Routes in Syria (G.H.Q. Middle East Forces, 1942) and M.T. Routes in Iraq (G.H.Q. Paiforce, 1943).
⁷ Topography—latest route reports, *War Diary* 10 Ind. Div.
⁸ 21 Bde. O.I. No. 3 dated 27 June 1941, Appendix 46A, *War Diary* 21 Ind. Inf. Bde.

hours on 22 June and at 1830 hours arrived at Ramadi. While it camped one mile past the town of Ramadi, a squadron of 13th Lancers and fifty men from A company of 3/11 Sikh at Haditha demonstrated against Fawzi Qawukji. There was no opposition as the latter had left Abu Kemal early that morning. The demonstrating column returned to Haditha at 2300 hours.

3/11 Sikh left Ramadi at 0500 hours on 23 June and arrived at Haditha at 1330 hours and settled into a dispersed bivouac. The column consisting of a squadron 13th Lancers, A troop 3rd Field Regiment R.A., Battalion Headquarters, A company, D company, one platoon B company, detachment Field Ambulance, W/T detachment and Light Aid Detachment left Haditha for Abu Kemal at 0445 hours on 24 June. B company less one platoon was left at Haditha. One Mortar Platoon was sent to H-1. At 1030 hours the column arrived at T-1, where one platoon B company was posted in the Fort. The European quarters were found to have been badly looted by Fawzi Qawukji's men. The column left T-1 at 1200 hours and arrived at T-1 Pumping Station at 1300 hours. Here was posted one platoon A company, one section 4 (Sapper) Platoon, and one section 2 (Anti-Aircraft) Platoon. Sixteen miles further on was Abu Kemal, the objective of the column. The advance was continued and at 1500 hours the column arrived at an Iraqi police post near the Iraq—Syria frontier. Enquiries were made from a few Arabs regarding the situation in Abu Kemal. It was gathered that Fawzi Qawukji had left the place and that the inhabitants would welcome the column. An advance was then made to the outskrits of the village of Abu Kemal, three miles further on, and an iraq Petroleum Company's employee went in by car with a message, asking the village representatives to come out. This they did, and expressed themselves very pleased at the arrival of the Indian troops. The column then moved to a dispersal camp. A single aircraft flew over the camp; it could not be ascertained whether it was British or Vichy aircraft. The next day a British aircraft chased off a Vichy aircraft near the camp. In the afternoon of 27 June a detachment of the 2nd Battalion 4th Gurkha Rifles (B company headquarters and one platoon B company) arrived at the camp. For the next two days (28 and 29 June) the camp was bombed by Vichy aircraft and the Indian troops sustained some casualties.

The 21st Indian Infantry Brigade Group arrived in Abu Kemal on 30 June. Thereupon 3/11 Sikh with one troop 3rd Field Regiment R.A. left Abu Kemal for Haditha, leaving behind D company with one section anti-aircraft platoon and one section sapper platoon.[9]

[9] *War Diary* 3/11 Sikh.

Plan for the attack on Deir ez Zor

Due to administrative reasons it was not possible to utilise more than one brigade group for the operations forward of Abu Kemal. The 21st Indian Infantry Brigade Group—the striking force—was to be wholly mobile and mechanical transport was just sufficient for the purpose.

The composition of the 21st Indian Infantry Brigade Group was as follows:[10]

Troops
    Headquarters 21st Indian Infantry Brigade
    21st Indian Infantry Brigade Signals Section
    4th Battalion 13th Frontier Force Rifles
    2nd Battalion 4th P.W.O. Gurkha Rifles
    2nd Battalion 10th Gurkha Rifles

Under Command
    127 Fighter Squadron R.A.
    13th Lancers
    157th Field Regiment R.A.
    9th Field Company
    29th Field Ambulance
    Detachment 7 Motor Ambulance Section
    16 (M) Workshop Company
    21st Indian Infantry Brigade Transport Company
    17th Indian Infantry Brigade Transport Company
    25th Indian Infantry Brigade Transport Company
    35th General Purposes Transport Company.

To achieve surprise, Major-General Slim decided to keep the brigade in the Baghdad area until the last possible moment. Hence it moved from Habbaniya to Haditha only on 29 June and from Haditha to Abu Kemal area on 30 June. Owing to the length of the column and the indifferent roads, many of the units reached the Abu Kemal area late on 30 June, with the result that many of the men had little rest that night.

Major-General Slim arrived at Haditha by air on 29 June and approved Brigadier Weld's plan for the advance on Deir ez Zor on 1 July. This advance involved the move of a force containing nearly 800 vehicles over a distance of approximately 200 miles in two days. The basis of the plan adopted was the formation of three battalion groups, the bulk of the armoured car regiment being kept directly under brigade headquarters. Two battalion groups were to take Deir ez Zor by an enveloping movement and the third was to be in brigade reserve. The operations were to be carried out as follows:

---

[10] Composition of 21 Bde. Gp., Appendix 'A', *War Diary* 21 Ind. Inf. Bde.

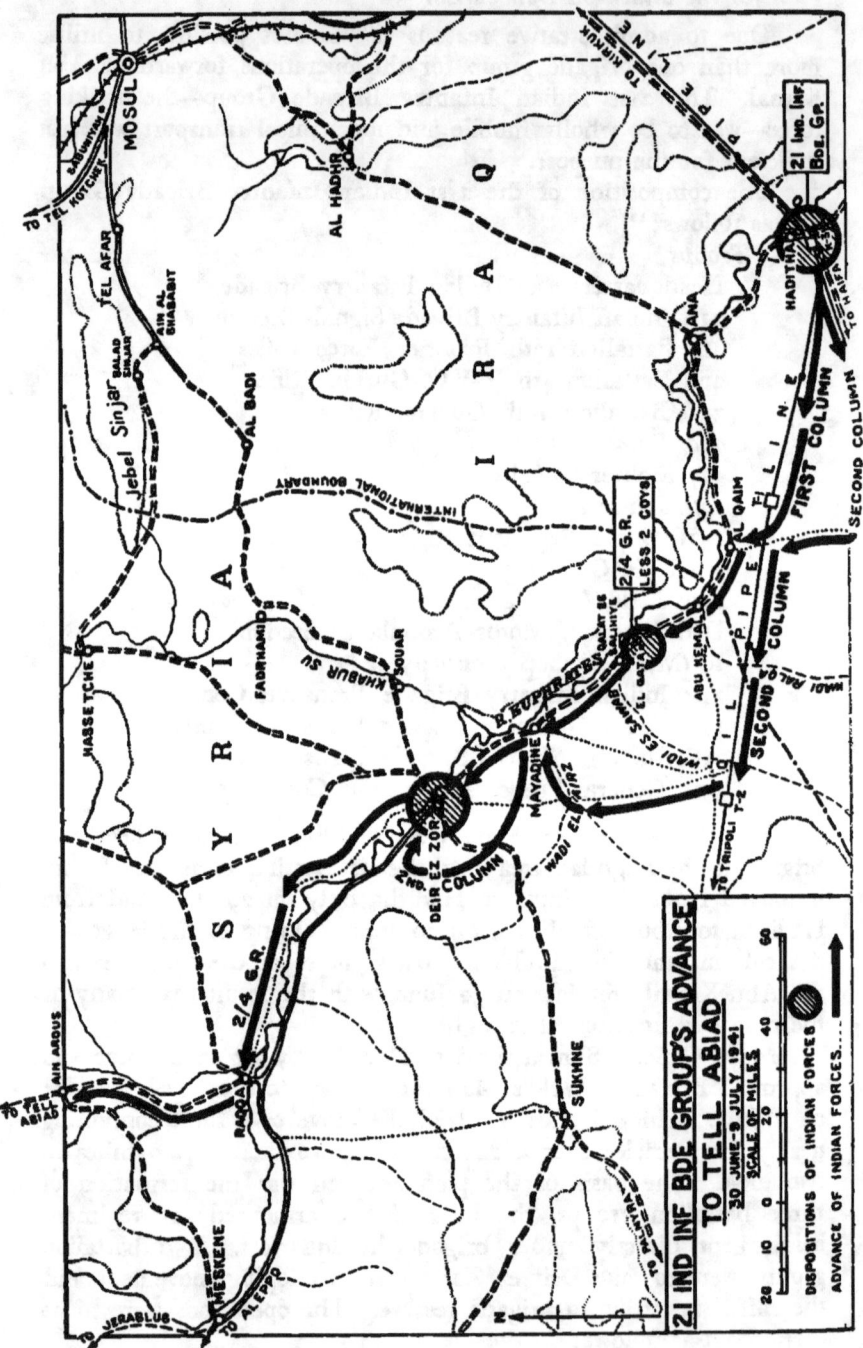

Phase I

On the afternoon of 30 June, 2/4 Gurkha less two companies, with under command a squadron of 13th Lancers, were to move out from Abu Kemal to the line of Wadi ez Sawab astride the road Abu Kemal—Deir ez Zor. They were to hold this position until the 21st Indian Infantry Brigade Group less detachments had passed through on 1 July.

Phase II

On 30 June three columns were to move forward of Haditha. The First Column[11] (Commander Lt.-Col. H.St.J. Carruthers) consisted of 2/10 Gurkha, one troop 4.5 Howitzers, 157th Field Regiment R.A. and ancillary units.

The column was to move by route K-3—Tripoli pipeline to T-1—Al Qaim—Abu Kemal. The starting point was the junction of the pipelines five miles south-west of K-3. The starting time was 0430 hours. The column was to be clear of the starting point by 0600 hours, and it was to halt dispersed north of Abu Kemal and clear of Wadi Ralqa (south of Abu Kemal) during the night of 30 June/1 July.

The Second Column[12] (Commander Lt.-Col. S.K. Furney, M.C.) consisted of 4/13 Frontier Force Rifles, 13th Lancers less one squadron, one troop 18-pounder, 157th Field Regiment R.A., and ancillary units.

The column was to move by route K-3—track running south of Haifa pipeline to mile post 168 (about 19 miles from K-3)—T-1—Tripoli Pipeline—T-2. The starting point was the road leading off south-west from the west gate and the time was fixed at 0600 hours. The column was to be clear of the starting point by 0730 hours. It was to halt for refill of water at T-1 before moving on to halt south of the pipeline in the vicinity of T-2 during the night of 30 June/1 July.

The Third Column[13] (Commander Major Rodwell, R.A.) consisted of two companies 2/4 Gurkha, troops 157th Field Regiment R.A. less one Battery, and ancillary units.

The starting point was the same as for the First Column. Starting time was 0815 hours. The column was to be clear of the starting point by 1000 hours and was to move to the vicinity of Abu Kemal by the same route as for the First Column. It was to halt dispersed behind the First Column during the night of 30 June/1 July.

---

[11] The First Column was called Nibe Column.
[12] The Second Column was called Puna Column.
[13] The Third Column was called Fund Column.

Phase III

On 1 July the above mentioned three columns were to move forward for the attack on Deir ez Zor. The First Column was to pass through 2/4 Gurkha position on Wadi ez Sawab, not later than 0530 hours. A squadron 13th Lancers was then to come under command. The column was to advance by the river route and seize Mayadine. Then it was to advance direct on Deir ez Zor.

The Second Column was to advance from T-2 by the desert route, taking the town of Deir ez Zor in flank and rear. This column was to remain slightly behind the First Column in reaching the objective. While directed on Deir ez Zor the Second Column was to be prepared on orders from the Brigade Commander to move towards the river Euphrates in case the First Column met opposition. Brigadier Weld's intention was to use the Second Column either to intervene on the flank of the First Column or to employ it in support of a turning movement by 13th Lancers less one squadron. The latter were initially to be in mobile reserve, but later in the day when the First Column had made a frontal attack on Deir ez Zor they were to attack on the rear.

The Third Column was to join up with 2/4 Gurkha less two companies at the outpost position on the Wadi es Sawab, after the First Column had passed through. The Third Column was to follow the First Column after an interval of one hour.

The Royal Air Force was to co-operate in the operations against Deir ez Zor. On 30 June, approximately one hour after the head of the leading column had passed T-1, a standing patrol of one Hurricane followed by two Gladiators was to be provided for a period of four hours. A standing patrol of two aircraft was to be provided from 1630 hours until dusk.[14]

Administrative arrangements

Preliminary to the advance, Haditha was stocked with fifteen days' supplies and with sufficient petrol and ammunition. Arrangements were made for the carriage of three days' ration and petrol for three hundred miles for every vehicle. Petrol was carried in vehicle reserve, in unit reserve and in the Brigade Transport Company. Water for the First Column moving along the river route presented no difficulty. For the Second Column moving by the desert route, it was hoped that it would be able to refill at T-1 and T-2.[15]

---

[14] 21 Bde. O.O. No. 9 dated 29 June 1941, *War Diary* 21 Ind. Inf. Bde. See Appendix 13.
[15] *Report on operations carried out by 21 Ind. Inf. Bde. Gp. between 30 June and 15 July 1941* by Brigadier Weld, *War Diary* 21 Ind. Inf. Bde.

CHAPTER XXIX

Capture of Deir ez Zor

Progress of the First Column

The operations for the capture of Deir ez Zor started on 30 June. The head of the First Column passed the starting point, five miles south-west of K-3, at 0445 hours. At 0745 hours the column extended into tactical formation and advanced in three lines with protective detachments ahead and on either flank. Owing to this disposition, control was difficult, and at certain places all vehicles had to return to the road owing to the nature of the ground. To improve discipline, regular halts were carried out. The column reached T-1 at 1400 hours. The road from T-1 to Abu Kemal was very poor at places. At 1600 hours the head of the column reached Abu Kemal and passed through to the bivouac area on the north-west side of the aerodrome.

A severe dust-storm, which blew for most of the day on 1 July, considerably slowed up movement. The advance of the First Column by the river route proceeded according to plan. Formed up in tactical formation it passed the starting point at the northern corner of the aerodrome of Abu Kemal at 0445 hours on 1 July. At 0530 hours a squadron of 13th Lancers was contacted at Qalat es Salihiye on Wadi es Sawab. Here the column halted for some time while the Lancers filled the machine-gun belts with armour-piercing bullets received from the brigade headquarters at 0600 hours. With the squadron of 13th Lancers leading the way, the column resumed the advance at 0715 hours. The road proved to be indifferent and in many places movement off the road was impossible. Bad ground and defiles made the tactical formation difficult.

In spite of these obstructions the column advanced in bounds, maintaining contact with cavalry at each bound and arrived at Mayadine at 1130 hours. The inhabitants were friendly. Four Vichy armoured cars had already left Mayadine for Deir ez Zor on the approach of the column.

At 1215 hours the forward vehicles were clear of Mayadine. For one hour the advance in tactical formation again proved impossible but at 1315 hours the column contacted the cavalry and closed up into formations. At 1400 hours it arrived at a point about seven miles from Deir ez Zor. Here on either side of the road were fields with dry irrigation channels, which made rapid deployment impracticable; but some two miles to the left (south-west) the fields ceased and there was a mile of good going between the fields and the escarpment, which ran parallel to the river. The commander of the column considered that it was unsound to continue motorised movement along the road and decided to move to his left flank where the going was good and where he hoped to progress forward more quickly and, with cover from his squadron of 13th Lancers, not to be caught embussed. During the progress of this movement, which due to numerous ditches and paucity of tracks (there being only one track) was very slow, the Vichy French opened artillery fire at extreme range from a high ridge south-east of Deir ez Zor. Vichy guns (75-mm) continued to shell the column at frequent intervals but many of the shells were either 'duds' or ineffective. During a period of about two hours the column suffered only one casualty. At 1600 hours, Brigadier Weld, who was up with the column, issued orders for the move in an easterly direction across the road to a bivouac area along the river bank and halt there during the night, resuming the advance the next day. The reason for this decision was that the First Column moving direct on Deir ez Zor was faced with an advance across an open plain, over which the Vichy French had good observation and could bring artillery and machine-gun fire to bear. As due to a dust-storm wireless contact had been lost with the Second Column, Brigadier Weld decided that it would be fruitless to allow the frontal advance to take place unsupported by the turning movement on the left flank. Hence he decided to halt the column near the river for the night.[1]

Progress of the Second Column

The head of the Second Column passed the starting point at 0600 hours on 30 June in the following order of march:

    13th Lancers less one squadron
    B company 4/13 Frontier Force Rifles
    'R' Group 4/13 Frontier Force Rifles and Forward Observation Officer
    R.A.F. Ground Party
    Section 9th Field Company
    A Company 4/13 Frontier Force Rifles
    'O' Group 4/13 Frontier Force Rifles
    One Troop 18-pounder 157th Field Regiment R.A.
    4/13 Frontier Rifles less three companies
    Detachment 21st Indian Infantry Brigade Transport Company
    Company 29th Field Ambulance
    Detachment Motor Ambulance Section
    D Company 4/13 Frontier Force Rifles.

[1] *War Diary* 2/10 G.R.

Water for the 140-mile-journey through the desert country presented a difficult problem. It was hoped that the column would refill at T-1 and T-2. But these expectations were not realised. Having found the journey hard and slow the column arrived at T-1 considerably later than was at first anticipated. As the drawing of water would have taken several hours, Colonel Furney decided to carry on without it and, at 1930 hours, he ordered a halt for the night as there was considerable chance of vehicles getting lost in the dark. The camp site was ten miles east of T-2. On the convoy's arrival it was found that a detachment of 2/4 Gurkha had erroneously become attached to the Second Column at T-1. The latter was ordered to return to T-1 the following day.

The Second Column directed on T-2 was unable to reach this pumping station by dark and halted nearly ten miles short for the night. It had thereby a greater distance to go on 1 July than was originally intended, and its task became more difficult owing to the severe dust-storm which blew for most of the day. A further difficulty was caused by the fact that the column had been unable to get water at T-1 and was subsisting on what the men carried in their water bottles or in 'Chaguls' when it moved out of its bivouac area at 0430 hours on 1 July. The column had a frontage of 1,800 yards and the dispositions were as follows:

Right Forward	D company and one section Medium Machine-Gun
Left Forward	A company, and one section Medium Machine-Gun and one section 18-pounders
Right Rear	C Company
Left Rear	B Company.

Between the above units in three lines was the rest of the column. Dust-storm made navigation and control of the column difficult, and to ensure that vehicles would not get lost the column had to close up considerably. At 1400 hours the head of the column halted near the Wadi el Airz awaiting orders from the brigade headquarters. Unfortunately wireless communications had broken down and were not established till about 1800 hours. The desert column had also run out of water as it had been unable to refill either at T-1 or T-2. Brigadier Weld, therefore, ordered it back to the river at Mayadine, since, contrary to the information previously received, it was not possible for the mechanical transport to get down from the escarpment (which ran parallel to the river) anywhere north of this town. The Second Column did not reach the escarpment above Mayadine till after dark and, being unable to find its way down in the dark, camped there for the night.

Wireless conditions were so bad that 13th Lancers made no contact with the Brigade Commander until the commanding officer reported to him personally at 2000 hours; he was ordered to camp near Mayadine. 2/4 Gurkha and brigade headquarters camped some four miles in the rear of the First Column.

Thus, late in the evening of 1 July, the First Column bivouacked near the river Euphrates about seven miles from Deir ez Zor, the Second Column on the escarpment near Mayadine and the Third Column about four miles in the rear of the First Column.

Review of the situation

Owing to the dislocation of the original plan, Brigadier Weld decided to modify his tactics. This was necessitated by the fact that the Second Column, which had to return to Mayadine on 1 July contrary to the original intention, had used more petrol than it should have done. A wide movement to enable this column to reach the rear of the Vichy forces would have brought it there with little or no petrol left. Thus, if the Vichy resistance proved obstinate, there was a danger of the armoured cars and the rest of the column being immobilised while in contact with the hostile force. To obviate this possibility Brigadier Weld decided to turn the enveloping movement into the flank of the hostile position instead of the rear. Accordingly he directed the Second Column to move in astride the Palmyra road and attack the Deir ez Zor from the west instead of going to the Aleppo road and advancing on Deir ez Zor from the north.

This alteration in the plan was, however, not approved by the Divisional Commander, who had gone forward to brigade headquarters on 2 July. He decided that it was worth taking the risk of petrol running short, in view of the fact that the Palmyra road approaches would almost certainly be strongly defended and the complete surprise hoped for from a really wide turning movement would thereby be lost.[2]

The final plan was that the First Column was to advance direct on Deir ez Zor making as much ground as possible during night of 2/3 July and infiltrate forward so as to be ready to advance at 0900 hours on 3 July when, it was hoped, the enveloping movement would be taking effect. One squadron of 13th Lancers with the column was to demonstrate on a flat plain to the south-west of the town.

The Second Column, which was to carry out the enveloping movement, was to start at 0415 hours on 3 July, move wide round the southern flank of the Vichy forces, gain the Aleppo road, and

[2] *Report on operations carried out by 21 Ind. Inf. Bde. Gp. by Brig. Weld.*

advance on Deir ez Zor from the north. The Third Column was to be in brigade reserve.

Thus, in the course of these operations, the Vichy French would find themselves surrounded on three sides, while the mobile diversionary column which was to demonstrate at Souar would advance to complete the encirclement from the fourth side.[3]

Frontal attack on Deir ez Zor (2-3 July)

Owing to the need for reorganisation and for replenishing petrol from the rear, the operations on 2 July were confined to 2/10 Gurkha pushing slowly and methodically forward with their right flank on the river. It was hoped to keep the Vichy attention fixed to this threat. This advance, which was opposed by Vichy artillery and automatic fire, was intentionally cautious and no risks were taken. At 1000 hours on 2 July, two fighting patrols were sent out—A to the left and B to the right of the main road—to obtain information of Vichy positions. At 1045 hours, the cavalry advanced along the road in support of the patrols but had to withdraw in face of heavy shelling. At 1130 hours advanced battalion headquarters was established near the main road 2,000 yards ahead of the camp. Spasmodic hostile shelling continued. At 1330 hours mortars and medium machine-guns moved forward, and, supported by these, A and B companies worked their way up and were in position behind a ridge about 3½ miles south of the Vichy position. At 1600 hours, the battalion moved forward to positions in support of A and B companies, and by 2100 hours the entire battalion was in position on the right side of the main road adjacent to the river. B company was forward on the right, A company on the left, C company in the middle, H.Q. company 800 yards behind and D company in reserve. B company advanced during the night of 2/3 July to the vicinity of the Block House situated at the east end of a large nulla with a 30-feet embankment in front, approximately 2,500 yards south of the Vichy's foremost positions. At 0430 hours on 3 July, advanced battalion headquarters moved to this forward position, and at 0530 hours the main body of 2/10 Gurkha was in position behind the embankment to the west of the Block House.

At 0600 hours on 3 July, 2/10 Gurkha moved forward for the attack on the Vichy positions. At 0715 hours they had occupied the forward positions, preliminary to the attack: advanced battalion headquarters and Gunners' Observation Post were established at Block House, while three companies occupied positions ahead with C company on the right, A company in the middle and B company on the left (D company being in reserve). During the advance to

[3] Ibid.

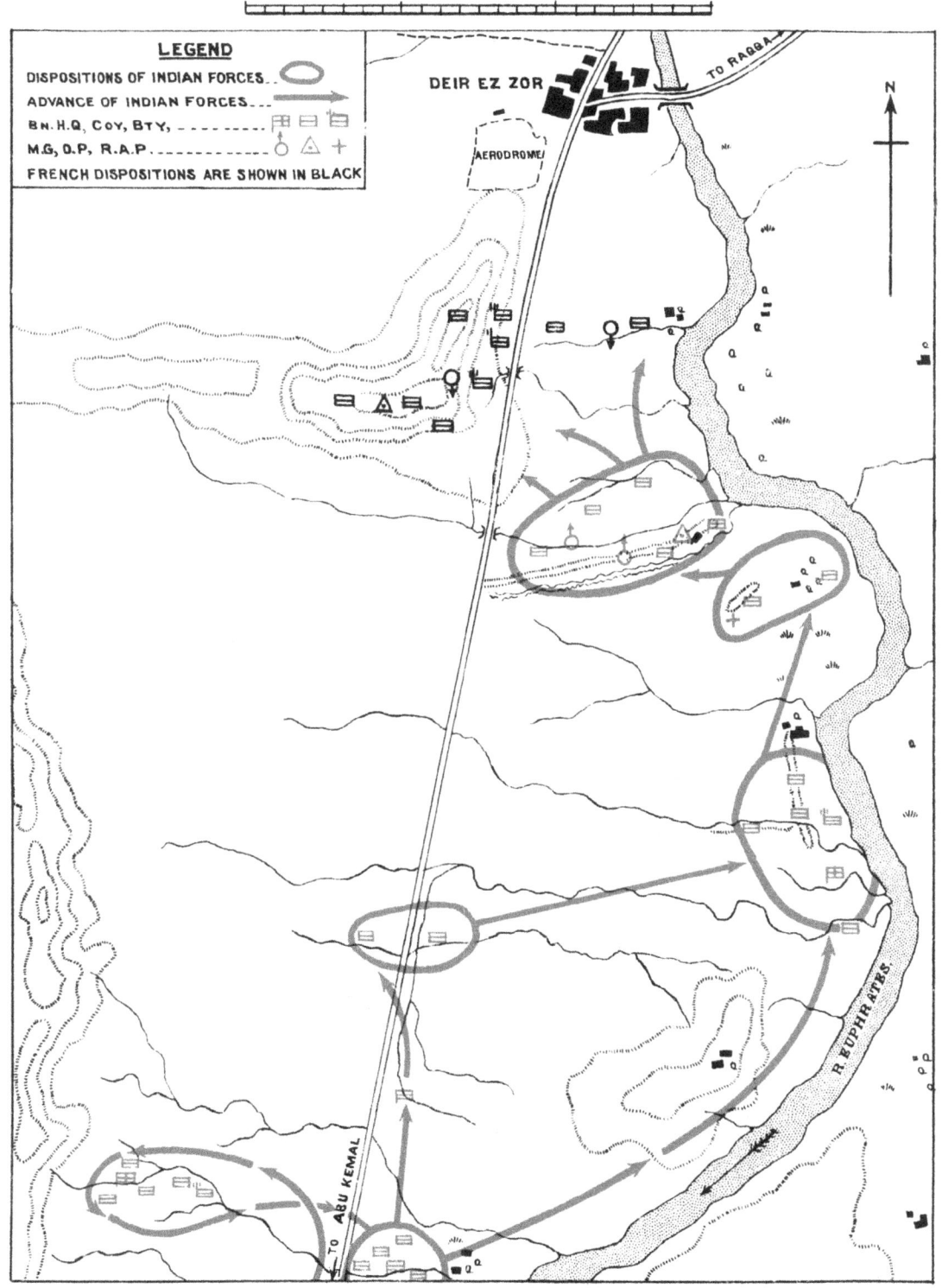

this forward position ahead of the Block House, the Vichy French commenced shelling; British guns replied and an artillery duel ensued. The forward companies came under occasional light machine-gun or medium machine-gun fire.

At 0730 hours on 3 July, Lt.-Colonel Carruthers ordered an attack on the Vichy positions. C company was to move out to the right flank and A company to the left flank, while B company was to take up position north-west of the Block House. D company was to be in reserve. The advance began with a small artillery duel. British guns were of necessity in exposed positions while the Vichy guns were behind the low hills covering Deir ez Zor. However, in spite of the accuracy of the Vichy fire, British guns remained in action, while the Gurkhas worked up close to Vichy position under gun, machine-gun and rifle fire. The squadron of 13th Lancers demonstrated on the left flank and even succeeded in getting within machine-gun range of the hostile guns. By 1045 hours the leading Gurkha companies were held up by Vichy machine-gun fire from well-established positions on the slopes of the high ground. It was at this time that ten large Vichy Bombers escorted by seven fighters appeared overhead and bombed the column, causing casualties to vehicles and men. The Field Ambulance suffered heavily, a stick of bombs falling through the main dressing station. At 1140 hours, after it had been observed that the Vichy French were withdrawing one or two of their forward guns, Lt.-Col. Carruthers ordered C, A and B companies to advance under supporting fire and seize the high ridge to the left of the road. At 1200 hours, the British gunners commenced heavy shelling of selected targets but soon afterwards the armoured cars of the Second Column were seen racing through the town, thus showing that the attack on Deir ez Zor from the rear had been successful. The threat from the rear had compelled the Vichy forces to abandon their positions south of the town. The Gurkhas pressed on, occupied the Vichy positions south of Deir ez Zor and met the Second Column in the town.[4]

Attack on Deir ez Zor from the rear

While 2/10 Gurkha made a frontal attack on Deir ez Zor, 4/13 Frontier Force Rifles carried out an enveloping movement in order to attack the town from the rear. The battalion moved out of the bivouac area on the escarpment near Mayadine at 0415 hours on 3 July. In front of the battalion on a broad front were the 13th Lancers. The battalion advanced on a two-company front—B and C companies leading and A and D companies in the rear. The battalion moved along the escarpment making a left flanking

[4] *War Diary* 2/10 G.R.

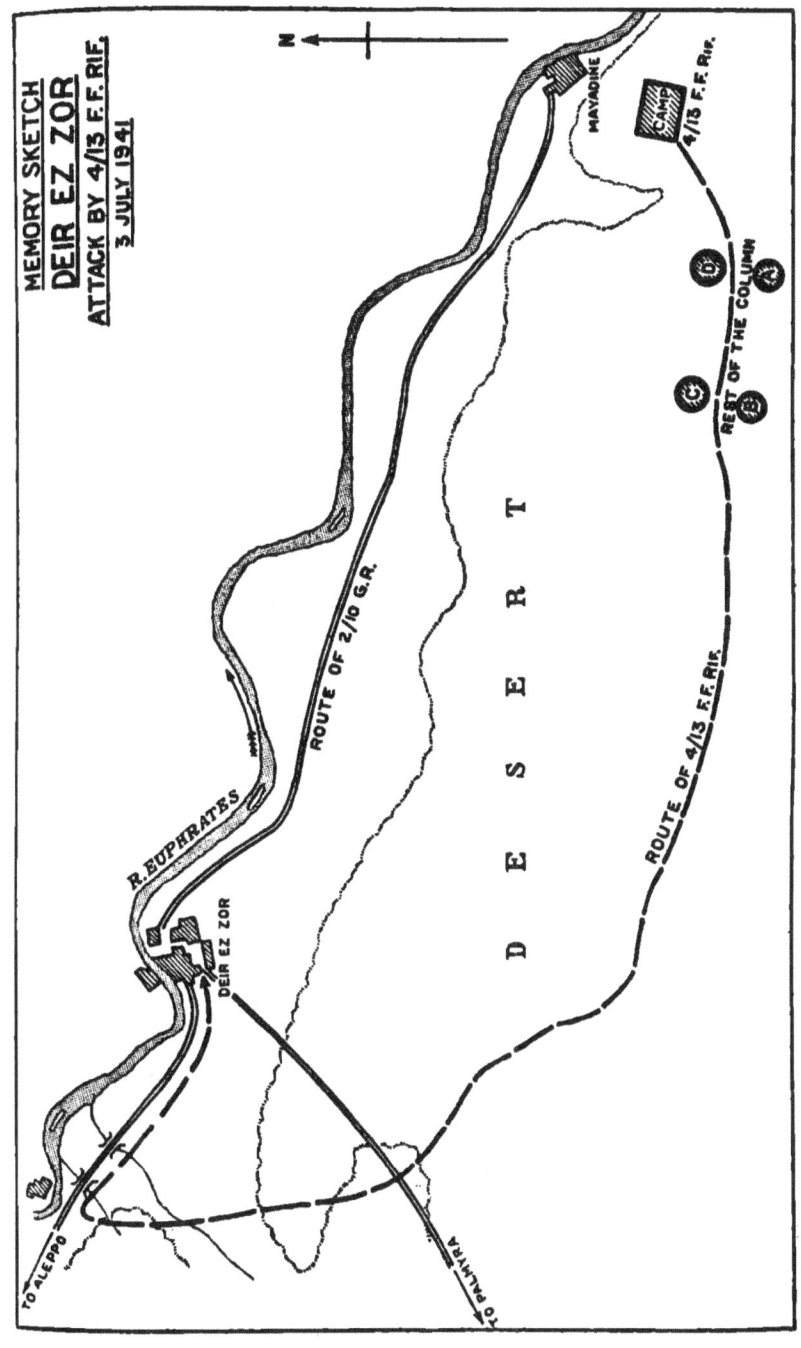

movement so as to reach the Deir ez Zor—Aleppo road north of Deir ez Zor. The head of the column arrived on the Deir ez Zor —Aleppo road at a point about six miles north-west of Deir ez Zor at 1015 hours. Armoured cars raced ahead towards the town. After they had successfully penetrated the outskirts of the town, two companies hurried forward to exploit the situation; C company to occupy the deserted French barracks at the entrance of the town and A company to follow up the advance of the armoured cars. There was some sniping and machine-gun fire in the town and a great deal of confusion in the narrow streets. The Vichy forces made an effort to cover the demolition of the Suspension Bridge over the Euphrates on the Deir ez Zor—Raqqa road. As a vehicle was drawn across the end of the bridge, the armoured cars found it impossible to advance further. A company then launched an attack on the bridge but its efforts to advance were checked by fire from several Vichy machine-guns well sited to protect the bridge. After several attempts to bring fire on the hostile positions it was decided to bring up two detachments of 3-inch mortars. These soon opened fire and with the 18-pounders firing on the far side of the bridge the Vichy guns were soon silenced. Spasmodic firing continued, however, and it was not till 1515 hours that it ceased altogether.[5] The last stray opposition inside the town was not overcome until 1530 hours. It was only then that Sappers of the 9th Field Company were ordered to remove the demolition charges from the suspension bridge, (which had been mined and fully prepared for demolition) and a detachment of 13th Lancers sent off in pursuit of the fleeing hostile forces. However, as these had the advantage of a long start and lighter vehicles, and as the pursuit was further limited by shortage of petrol in the armoured cars, the chase proved fruitless. A number of Vichy troops, mostly French officers in vehicles, and two guns (one 75-mm and the other 65-mm) escaped over the bridge. Only about one hundred were taken prisoners, as most of the Syrian troops changed into civilian clothes and hid themselves in the town or returned to their villages. However, much war material was captured, including nine guns, five aeroplanes, some fifty lorries, machine-guns; rifles and large stocks of artillery and small-arms ammunition, grenades, aeroplane bombs, petrol, supplies, etc.[6]

The operations against Deir ez Zor proved that considerable tactical advantage can be gained from the full and bold use of a completely motorised force. But to gain such advantage movement must be bold and risks must be accepted. Thus, had the turning movement at Deir ez Zor been directed merely against

[5] *War Diary* 4/13 Frontier Force Rifles.
[6] Major-General Slim's Report.

a flank down the Palmyra road it would have met with stubborn resistance; sent wide to the west and coming in from the north on the Vichy rear, it achieved complete surprise and led to the capture of almost the whole of Vichy guns, ammunition and transport.[7]

Vichy air attacks

After the capture of Deir ez Zor the British and Indian troops there were subjected to air attacks. At 1800 hours on 3 July, the Vichy air force delivered an attack inflicting casualties. The two long-range Hurricanes, whose pilots made a gallant attempt against superior numbers to drive off the attack, were shot down. During the next three days troops and transport were subjected to bombing attacks. During this period the remaining two Hurricanes were also shot down. On 5 July fourteen Vichy bombers bombed the fort which contained a large arsenal of shells, aerial bombs, explosives and small-arms ammunition, and a great quantity of petrol. The escorting fighters flayed the parade ground with bullets. "For two hours there ensued heavy explosions and the incessant crackle of exploding small-arms cartridges, and a great pall of smoke and dust rose ominously over the fortress."[8] C company 4/13 Frontier Force Rifles, who was guarding the captured remains of the French garrison in the fort, however, suffered only one casualty, for the deep slits which had been dug by the French afforded good protection. While the numbers of casualties inflicted were not many, the moral effect of the frequent bombing and machine-gunning from the air was serious. All units, British and Indian, were sometimes shaken by it; and certain administrative units, which were composed of recently enlisted men, only partially trained and often unarmed, were for some days hardly able to carry on. As however more suitable dispositions were assumed their morale gradually returned.[9]

Progress of the Diversionary Column

While 2/10 Gurkha made a frontal attack on Deir ez Zor and 4/13 Frontier Force Rifles attacked the town from the rear, the diversionary column (2/8 Gurkha) advanced from Mosul to Fadrhami and from there demonstrated towards Deir ez Zor with the object of inducing the Vichy French to believe that a strong column was advancing on the town. By these tactics it was hoped to induce the Vichy French to divert forces, especially armoured cars and aircraft, from the Deir ez Zor area.

[7] Ibid.
[8] Brigadier W.E.H. Condon: *The Frontier Force Rifles* (1953), p. 223.
[9] Major-General Slim's Report.

The column (under the command of Lt.-Col. F.D.Clarke) consisted of: 2/8 Gurkha (less one company and other details); one Section R.A.F. Armoured Cars; one troop—18-pounder, 3rd Field Regiment R.A.; and ancillary units. All personnel were motorised. Three days' rations were to be carried on unit vehicles and two days' in bulk in supply lorries.[10] Three gallons of water per man, excluding water bottles and 'chaguls', were to be carried in containers in unit vehicles. 4600 gallons of water was to be carried in supply lorries. Petrol sufficient for a 150-mile radius was to be carried in vehicle tanks and on vehicles, and that for another 350-mile radius, namely 6000 gallons, was to be carried in supply lorries.

The operations were to be carried out in the following four phases:

Phase I   The column was to advance on D1 (29 June) from Mosul to Al Badi (102 miles).

Phase II   The column was to advance from Al Badi to Fadrhami on D2 (45 miles) and demonstrate by reconnaissance patrols south-west towards Deir ez Zor.

Phase III   The column was to remain on D3 in Fadrhami area and demonstrate towards Deir ez Zor.

Phase IV   If the main operation was successful the column ws to return to Mosul on D4.

The road from Mosul to Fadrhami (150 miles) led to Kisk Keupri where it bifurcated—the right leading to Tell Kotchek and the left to Tell Afar. From this last place the road led to the south to Ain al Shababit, where it again bifurcated, the northern route leading to Balad Sinjar and the other to Al Badi and Fadrhami. The road from Mosul to the Syrian frontier ran west over an immense plain, which stretched away to the south as far as the eye could see. For the first nineteen miles from Ain al Shababit the road was rough and narrow, with an earth surface and numerous wadi crossings, which were impassable in the wet season. From mile 19 it became a desert track with a hard level surface, providing excellent fast going in dry weather. Except for dips into wadis, the road was flat throughout from Ain al Shababit.[11]

Advance to Fadrhami

The column moved out of Mosul at 0500 hours on 29 June. Only minor convoy difficulties were experienced. The force encamped by 1700 hours at Al Badi which it left at 0500 hours

---

[10] Isaac O.O. No. 1 dated 28 June 1941, *War Diary* 2/8 G.R.
[11] M.T. routes in Iraq.

on 30 June and crossed into Syria by 0730 hours. On reaching Fadrhami at 1100 hours a patrol of A company accompanied by two armoured cars went southwards to a distance of 26 miles along the river bank. Two armoured cars went north along the left bank to try and find a crossing across the wadi Jallal. No incident occurred. On 1 July a patrol consisting of C and D companies, one section R.A., Detachment Sappers and Miners, and two sections medium machine-guns, moved south along the left bank in search of a crossing and to test the Souar bridge. The main group of the patrol reached a point about 2,000 yards from the bridge, where the local inhabitants reported that it had been blown. Only two fords were discovered along the river bank, neither of them being of any great use. On 2 July a patrol, one company with armoured cars, reached the Souar bridge to find that it had also been blown. There was no incident and the whole column returned to Al Badi for the night, which it left at 0500 hours on 3 July, arriving in Mosul at 1600 hours.[12]

The demonstration towards Souar met with no opposition. It is difficult to estimate the importance of this operation but it seems probable that it played its part in diverting the attention of the Deir ez Zor garrison.

[12] *War Diary* 2/8 G.R.

CHAPTER XXX

Vichy Counter-attack on Raqqa

Capture of Raqqa

After the capture of Deir ez Zor it was learnt from the prisoners that some Vichy forces were at Raqqa. On 4 July, Brigadier Powell ordered 2/4 Gurkha and attached troops to occupy that place. The column (under the command of Lt. Col. Weallens) consisted of 2/4 Gurkha Squadron 13th Lancers, Troop 157th Field Regiment R.A. and ancillary units. The column was to move on Raqqa from Deir ez Zor at 0430 hours on 5 July. It was to advance along the road east of the river Euphrates. Fighter cover was to be provided from 0330 hours to 0700 hours during the passage of the column over bridges of Deir ez Zor and from 1000 hours to 1100 hours.[1]

At 0400 hours on 5 July the column moved from the camp outside the Aleppo road about two miles north of Deir ez Zor. Crossing the Euphrates by the suspension bridge it advanced over one mile of appalling road. Further on there was very good going on the desert road to Raqqa. Fully motorised, the column moved rapidly and widely dispersed on a wide front. The armoured cars entered Raqqa at 1000 hours and the rest of the column at approximately 1400 hours. The Vichy French had left Raqqa the previous day and the Arabs had looted the place.[2] From that day until the end of hostilities Vichy aircraft attacked the Indian troops at Raqqa at regular intervals. Air attacks were also made on supply columns proceeding to Raqqa, which were consequently compelled to move mostly by night.

Capture of Tell Abiad

On receipt of information on 8 July that the Vichy French force, being pressed by an Indian column advancing along the Mosul—Aleppo railway towards the north-eastern tip of Syria, was withdrawing along the northern frontier of Jerablus, Major-General Slim ordered 2/4 Gurkha and attached troops at Raqqa to cut them off at Tell Abiad, while one company of 4/13 Frontier Force Rifles was sent from Deir ez Zor to Raqqa with extra petrol and supplies to garrison that place. The column moved off at 2030 hours on 8 July, leaving a very small detachment (one platoon C

---

[1] 21 Bde. O.O. No. 11 dated 4 July 1941, *War Diary*, 21 Ind. Inf. Bde.
[2] *War Diary* 2/4 G.R.

company) to hand over to A Company 4/13 Frontier Force Rifles. The rest of the 13th Lancers less one squadron had already joined the column at 1900 hours. It was a fine bright night of full moon. On 9 July at 0200 hours D Company moved forward to occupy Ain Arous post and came under desultory rifle fire. This however turned out to be an Arab village "Homeguard". Firing ceased when the Arab guides accompanying the column shouted out from inside the armoured car revealing the indentity of the friendly Indian troops. The advance on Tell Abiad proceeded. A troop of armoured cars with D company led the column down the main road and entered Tell Abiad without opposition at 0430 hours on 9 July. They discovered that the Vichy French had passed through. The column was attacked by five Vichy Fighters at 1400 hours, and later at 1700 hours bombed by five Vichy Bombbers. At 1700 hours C company with a troop of artillery and section armoured cars moved back to Raqqa with a long convoy to bring up petrol and rations. On 10 July at 0500 hours a squadron of armoured cars and one platoon (A Company) of infantry in lorries were sent out in pursuit of the Vichy troops, whom they attacked with machine-gun fire as their rearguard crossed the Euphrates by the ferry at Jerablus. The Tell Abiad column was subjected to daylight air attacks but few casualties were caused, since all movements were carried out by night. The Vichy air attacks were nearly always directed against the armoured cars, and bullets from the cannon of their fighters easily penetrated their armour.[3]

Vichy Counter-attack at Raqqa

While 2/4 Gurkha secured Tell Abiad and was hot on the pursuit of the Vichy French rearguards near the ferry over the Euphrates at Jerablus, the small garrison at Raqqa was subjected to a severe Vichy counter-attack. A company of 4/13 Frontier Force Rifles (under command of Major Wemyss) escorting a convoy of supplies and petrol proceeded from Deir ez Zor to Raqqa by the desert route at 1430 hours on 8 July. This route was not easy to follow as there were many forks and some of the markings had been tampered with. The column did not reach Raqqa until 2345 hours. Lt.-Col. Weallens, while leading his column from Raqqa for the attack on Tell Abiad on 8 July, had left a small detachment (one platoon C company 2/4 G.R.) at Raqqa to hand over to A company 4/13 Frontier Force Rifles. The supply lorries were unloaded—the rations in the fort and the petrol in the tank ditch, the tins being then covered with earth. The lorries were then sent to their dispersal area to the south of the town. The new garrison

[3] Ibid.

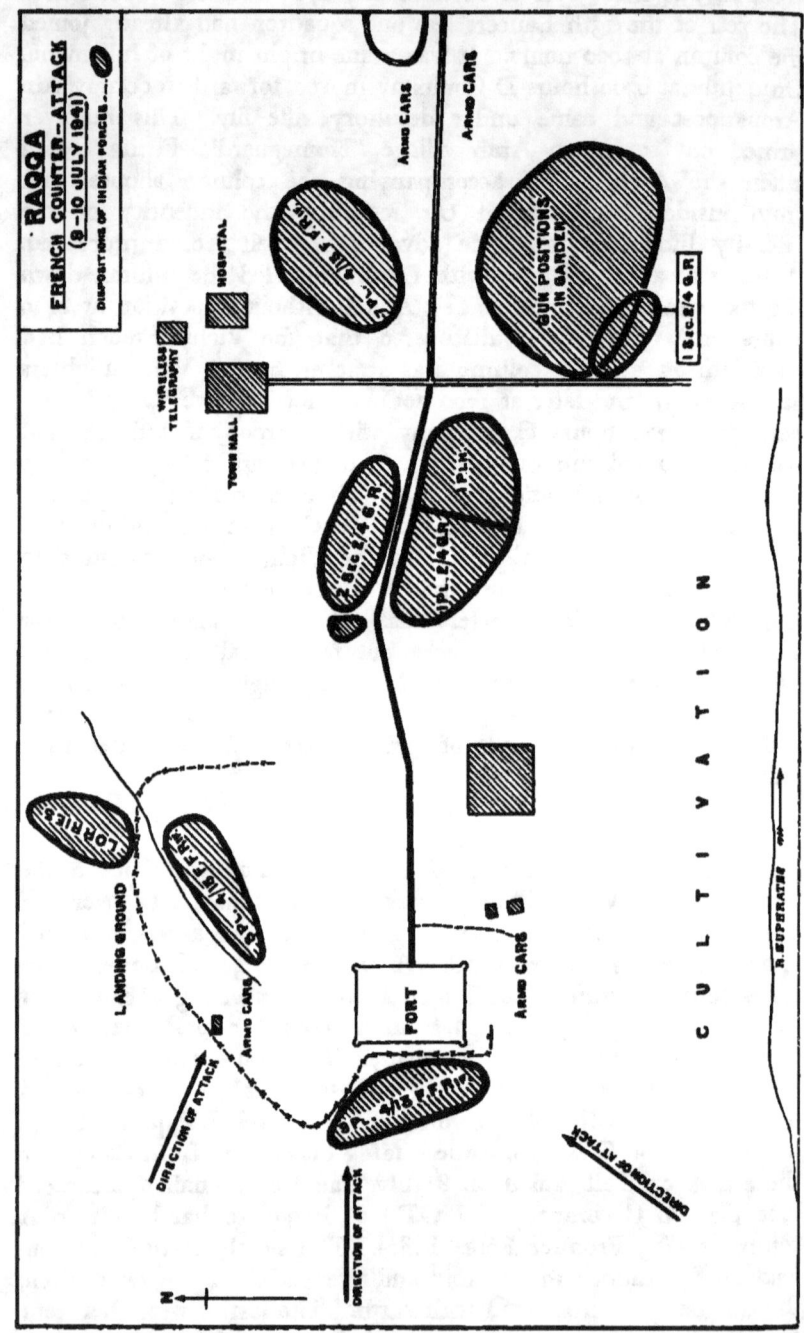

(A company 4/13 Frontier Force Rifles and a platoon of C company 2/4 G.R.) had hardly settled in when Vichy French artillery (two or three 75-mm guns) opened fire on them from the right bank of the river Euphrates on 9 July at 0500 hours and kept up a heavy and accurate fire for nearly one hour. Under cover of smoke from the shells, the troops (approximately 1 platoon made up of 4/13 Frontier Force Rifles and 2/4 G.R.) led by Major Wemyss withdrew from the Fort at 0510 hours and took up a position to the east so as to be ready to meet a ground attack in case it was launched. Shelling ceased at 0600 hours. The Vichy artillery had fired about one hundred and fifty shells. Every building in the Fort had been hit a minimum of three times, the main damage being the destruction of 1,500 gallons of petrol. Fifteen minutes after shelling had ceased, Vichy light bombers appeared overhead and commenced bombing the Fort Area and the area between the river and the town. Shortly afterwards at 0645 hours two Vichy Fighters appeared and proceeded to machine-gun the area. The 'all clear' was sounded at 0710 hours. The casualties due to the air attack were 1 killed and 5 wounded. Some difficulty was experienced in dealing with the casualties as the medical facilities of the Raqqa garrison was not up to the mark. Fortunately the local civilian doctor rendered invaluable aid and took complete charge, using his own drugs where necessary.

On 9 July at bout 1900 hours four armoured cars, one section 18-pounders, detachment Field Ambulance, C Company H.Q. plus a platoon of 2/4 Gurkha (the other platoon being already at Raqqa, while the third was on its way from Deir ez Zor to Raqqa), and an empty supply column arrived from Tell Abiad, with instructions from Lt.-Col. Weallens to fill up and return as 0400 hours on 10 July. The loading of this column had hardly been completed by midnight of 9/10 July when a determined attack was made by Fawzi Qawukji, supported by local tribesmen. They had automatics and were in possession of mechanical transport. They acted very boldly against the dispersed garrison and the situation became critical for a short period. At the time when the attack developed the dispositions of the Indian troops were: of 4/13 Frontier Force Rifles, No. 9 Platoon was to the west of the Fort just beyond the anti-tank ditch, No. 8 platoon was near the dispersal area of the lorries south of the landing ground, and No. 7 platoon was near the hospital. Of 2/4 Gurkha one platoon and two sections (and another platoon, presumably composite platoon) were to the east of the Fort, while one section was near the gun positions in the garden. The armoured cars were hidden in the narrow streets to protect them from being bombed by Vichy aircraft. The attack developed from three directions. Major Wemyss decided to send an armoured car to help No. 8 platoon, which was threatened by hostile action. It was however difficult to get the armoured car out of the narrow streets, and the one which managed to clear them and to get on to the landing ground was bogged across the anti-tank ditch, as the fire of the Vichy automatics had burst its tyres. Unsuccessful attempts were made to extricate it. By 0030 hours on 10 July, No. 8 platoon position had been overrun and it was not recovered until 0445 hours. No. 9 Platoon, however, held its position throughout the night, although completely isolated, and made two bayonet charges when the ammunition was running low. Touch was regained and supplies sent at 0420 hours, by using the armoured cars to cover the dead ground south and south-east of the Fort. The hostile force then withdrew to a position about 500 yards west of the Fort, and from there continued to harass until about 1030 hours when 18-pounders opened on their positions. About seven rounds were fired. One shell fell on or near a machine-gun post which was giving most trouble. Thereafter the Vichy force withdrew.[4] When Raqqa was attacked by Fawzi Qawukji's men, Major Wemyss had informed Brigadier Weld, who had ordered C company 4/13 Frontier Force Rifles, the supporting platoon and three detachments mortar platoon, to prepare to move out immediately from Deir ez Zor. The departure of the column was delayed on account of the late arrival of a petrol convoy, which was to accompany it. It was only at 1230 hours that the column moved out of Deir ez Zor. The Tell Abiad column returned to Raqqa on 11 July and hostilities ceased at midnight. In spite of this, Vichy French Fighters machine-gunned Indian troops at Raqqa on the morning of 12 July inflicting casualties.

Casualties

Throughout the period of operations the total casualties suffered by the 21st Indian Infantry Brigade Group were only 25 killed, 50 wounded and 10 missing, of which rather more than half were caused by air attack. Casualties to vehicles were heavy, but not excessive, taking into account the scale of air attacks, the lack of trained drivers and the distances covered over bad roads.

R. A. F. Co-operation

The part played by No. 127 Squadron R.A.F. deserves special mention. The squadron was very weak and consisted of only some eight aircraft, Hurricanes and Gladiators—all fighters. The role allotted throughout the operations was to provide fighter cover. This task was peculiarly difficult in view of the distance they were forced to operate from. Initially the landing ground was at T-1.

[4] *War Diary* 4/13 Frontier Force Rifles.

The range of the fighters was very limited except for two long-range Hurricanes, which were however shot down early in the operations. The operational landing ground was moved forward as soon as possible to a site 40 miles south of Deir ez Zor, but thereafter the Vichy French concentrated their attacks on Raqqa, which was in turn practically out of range of the British aircraft. In spite of these limitations, and though always heavily outnumbered, this R. A. F. squadron never failed to attack the hostile force wherever seen, and these attacks undoubtedly achieved a considerable effect on the latter, who were forced to drop their bombs quickly and clear off.

While reviewing the operations of 10th Indian Division in Syria, Major-General Slim wrote in his report that these operations provided two important lessons:

(i) It is unfair and unwise to push forward mechanised columns without adequate air support.

(ii) Troops must in peace training be accustomed to low flying attacks by real aircraft.[5]

Administration

The biggest problem in these operations was that of administration. Prior to the advance from Haditha 15 days' stocks of supplies had been accumulated at that place. A similar quantity of petrol and sufficient ammunition were also concentrated there. The 21st Indian Infantry Brigade Group was sent forward from Haditha with 8 days' rations and 7,000 gallons of petrol in the second line. Seventeen lorries and petrol were also sent forward with a brigade group to refill all tanks at Abu Kemal and a further 19,000 gallons were kept on wheels in the third line.

The ammunition and supply situation never caused any anxiety, but at one time (in the attack on Deir ez Zor) a shortage of petrol, forward with the brigade group, appeared imminent. This shortage was due to several causes—an unexpectedly high consumption, due partly to leakage and partly to slow going in the dust-storm and in the soft sand; the concentration of brigade transport vehicles too far forward resulting in uneconomic use of the brigade transport company; and the considerable greater distances covered by the enveloping column than were anticipated.

From 7 July regular convoys were running between Haditha and Deir ez Zor in order to accumulate sufficient stocks of petrol, supplies and ammunition at the latter place to enable the advance on Aleppo to be carried out.

Many of the drivers of the administrative units had had little training and were sent overseas much earlier than was intended.

[5] Major-General Slim's Report.

The successful running of convoys throughout the operation was under the circumstances extremely praiseworthy. The supply organisation had, in addition, to cater for the column which moved forward to Raqqa and Tell Abiad, although this movement had not been included in the original plan.

Medical arrangements had to be improvised, and offered considerable difficulties over a line of communications of about 400 miles. No casualty clearing sections or staging sections were available, and detachments were improvised from the field ambulances and the general hospital at Baghdad. Aircraft were available for evacuation of serious cases and the presence of well fitted hospitals at the pumping stations at K-3 and T-1 and the hospital at Deir ez Zor materially eased the problem. Fortunately casualties were few and the health of the troops remained good throughout the operation.

The vehicle repair organisation was perhaps the greatest problem of all. The Ordnance Mobile Workshops, though named mobile, were in point of fact the most immobile units in the division. They were all sent overseas ahead of schedule and were only partially trained. There were insufficient units to cope with the number of vehicles extending over such a very long line of communication. Further, few spare vehicles, particularly 3-ton lorries, were available and there was a very serious shortage of spare parts. Under the circumstances the number of vehicles kept on the road was very creditable, taking into account the heavy hostile air attacks, the bad state of the roads, the distances covered and the untrained state of the drivers and mechanics. As an example, the armoured car regiment, which had to operate over very great distances and was attacked from the air more than any other unit, ended the operations with only 5 cars not immediately repairable and 4 of these it was possible to replace from the reserve.

Communications

The problem of signal communications was a very difficult one. Land lines were out of the question over the vast distances involved, except where telephones already existed along the pipeline, and from Mayadine to Deir ez Zor. Later, lines of communication were established forward of Deir ez Zor to Hassetche-Raqqa and Aleppo.

The divisional wireless equipment supplemented by only two sets from Headquarters Palestine and Transjordan Force, had to provide, in addition to all the detachments in the area of operations, for communication of Palestine—Habforce—Baghdad-K.3-Rutba and the 20th Indian Infantry Brigade at Mosul. The divisional wireless resources were unable to cope with the demand, the most serious occasion being the lack of touch between the two advancing columns on Deir ez Zor on 1 July. If a set broke down mechanically or by enemy action, no spare set was available.

As in the case of every other unit in the force, the divisional signals suffered, perhaps more than any other unit, for having been sent overseas ahead of schedule and with untrained personnel. Several untrained officers reported only as the unit was about to embark at Bombay. In the circumstances the greatest credit was due to all concerned that communications were maintained so well.'

' See Appendix 14 and General Slim's Report.

CHAPTER XXXI

Advance to Tell Aalo

While the 10th Indian Division (less the 20th Indian Infantry Brigade Group in Mosul area) was directed against Deir ez Zor, the 17th Indian Infantry Brigade (8th Indian Division) was ordered by Lt.-General Quinan, Iraq Force Commander, to advance from Basra and pass through the 20th Indian Infantry Brigade Group at Mosul for operations in the province of Bec du Canard. One Battalion of the 17th Indian Infantry Brigade (which had already concentrated at Mosul on 28 June) was to carry out preliminary operations.

Lt.-General Quinan ordered Brigadier D. D. Gracey, Commander 17th Indian Infantry Brigade to clear the area, Qamichliye—Demir Kapou—Tell Kotchek—Hassetche, of Vichy ground forces with a view to securing the use of the railway Tell Kotchek—Tell Zouane (just east of Nisibin). Subsequently Brigadier Gracey was to establish such garrisons as might be necessary to ensure the working of the railway and withdraw the remainder of his force to Mosul.

Vichy Troops

Up to 19 June 1941, Vichy troops in area Tell Kotchek—Qamichliye were estimated to be:[1]

'*Troupes Speciales*'
8th Battalion *Levant Infantry*
21, 23, 24, 25, 28 Light Squadrons *Djezireh Cavalry*

The latest intelligence reports indicated that at Tell Kotchek there were 15 to 20 Assyrians and one officer, but the garrison of Tell Kotchek could be reinforced by 140 men guarding the railway bridge (reported to be mined) across the wadi at Tell Hadi. There were 130 soldiers at Tell Aalo. At Qamichliye there were one rifle company, one squadron cavalry and eight medium machine-guns while at Hassetche there were one infantry battalion, one battery Field Artillery and some aircraft.[2]

Topography

The province of Bec du Canard was a plain crossed by numerous streams (which were wadis when streams were dry)

---
[1] *French Forces in northern Syria—Location statement up to 19 June 1941,* War Diary 10 Ind. Div.
[2] Appendix A to Iraq Force O.I. No. 7 dated 4 July 1941; *War Diary* Iraq Force.

flowing from north to south to join the river Euphrates. It was studded with small hills and rocks. The principal elevations were to be found to the north-east and north-west of Hassetche.

A road (motorable track) from Mosul, which moved parallel to the railway Mosul—Aleppo, led to Tell Kotchek and Qamichliye. It ran through a wide open plain dotted with mounds and small villages. The high snow-covered peaks of the Turkish Armenian mountains could be seen all the way along on the north, and ridges of low hills ran a short way along the plain from time to time. The Tigris diverged gradually to the north and was fed by streams that flowed across the plain in winter and spring, but were mostly dry in summer and autumn. Grain was cultivated near the villages, but the greater part of the Jezireh plain was a desert waste, except in spring, when it was covered with grass and ablaze with flowers, and provided pasture for large herds of horses and cattle, and flocks of sheep and goats.[3] In general the road followed the railway; the greatest divergence being between Tell el Uwainat and Demir Kapou, where the road ran up to ten miles from the railway. From Mosul the road led to Sabuniyah railway station (16 miles). Just beyond the railway station the road forked; that to the left was the Tell Afar road for Deir ez Zor and to the right the Tell Kotchek road. There were several patches on the stretch of the road from Sabuniyah to Kisk Keupri (12 miles) which were impassable for several days at a time after heavy rain. Nine miles from Kisk Keupri was Tell el Hugnan, where the road was about 1,200 feet above sea level. The rise from Mosul (700 feet above sea-level) was gradual. From Tell el Hugnan to Tell el Uwainat (12 miles) the road hugged the railway and was fairly level. From Tell Uwainat to Bir Ugla, the Iraq frontier police post was a distance of 7½ miles. The road crossed the Syrian frontier at Tell Kotchek (11 miles). The French had made a good metalled road from Tell Kotchek to Demir Kapou (15½ miles). From Demir Kapou to Tell Zouane was a distance of 26 miles. From Tell Zouane to Qamichliye (15 miles) the road passed over gently rolling country; much of this part of the road was over 1400 feet above sea-level. The road from Qamichliye to Nisibin (2 miles) was poor.[4]

Qamichliye was a junction of four roads, one of which went to Hassetche. Of the several motorable and secondary tracks radiating outwards from Hassetche one went north-west to Ras el Ain.

Capture of Tel Kotchek

1/12 Frontier Force Regiment of the 17th Indian Infantry Brigade, which had advanced from Basra and concentrated at

[3] M.T. routes in Iraq.
[4] Appendix 'A' to Iraq Force O.I. No. 7 dated 4 July 1941, *War Diary* Iraq Force

Mosul on 28 June, was selected for the preliminary operations. On arrival at Mosul it came temporarily under the command of the 20th Indian Infantry Brigade. Brigadier Powell, the Commander, issued instructions on 1 July for the capture of Tell Kotchek. The code-word for the operation was 'Cotswold'. The force consisted[5] of two companies 1/12 Frontier Force Regiment, detachment Armoured Cars R.A.F., two detachments Mortar Platoon 1/12 Frontier Force Regiment, one section medium machine-guns, one section 3rd Field Regiment R.A., and ancillary units. The whole force was mechanised and its tasks were:—

(i) to occupy Tell Kotchek,
(ii) to seize intact the railway line up to Tell Kotchek with locomotives and rolling stock in that area, and
(iii) to prevent any looting in the railway station area.

The force was to advance from Mosul on 2 July and capture Tell Kotchek that day and remain in occupation until further orders. Patrolling was to be carried out in the direction of Demir Kapou and west of that place. R.A.F. sorties were to be flown over the column at varying periods during the day. Four days' rations were to be carried on unit vehicles. All water bottles, 'chaguls' and 'pakhals' were to be filled with water. It was reported that there was sufficient water for a brigade from one large and four small wells at Tell el Uwainat and a very limited output from two wells at Bir Ugla. There was a drinking water well at Tell Kotchek, and a storage tank (600 gallons) on the railway, two miles short of the station. Petrol sufficient for a 50-mile radius was to be carried in unit tanks and unit vehicles.[6]

The force left Mosul at 0800 hours on 2 July. On arrival at Tell Kotchek, the commander of the force deployed his guns in front of the village and sent a company round to each flank. He then informed the commander of the garrison that he had two battalions and a regiment of artillery and that resistance was useless. The garrison surrendered at 1830 hours; 3 French officers and 130 men of 3rd Battalion 8th *Levant Infantry* were taken prisoners.[7]

Capture of Tel Aalo

After the occupation of Tell Kotchek, reconnaissances were carried out towards Demir Kapou and Tell Aalo. At 0700 hours on 3 July, armoured cars (R.A.F.) reconnoitred to Demir Kapou, returning with reports about the road and of there being no signs of hostile patrols. At 1500 hours the armoured cars reconnoitred Tell Aalo Vichy post by the road running parallel to the railway line.

---

[5] H.Q. 20 Bde. to Major Clarke dated 1 July 1941, *War Diary* 17 Ind. Inf. Bde.
[6] Ibid.
[7] *War Diary* 17 Ind. Inf. Bde.

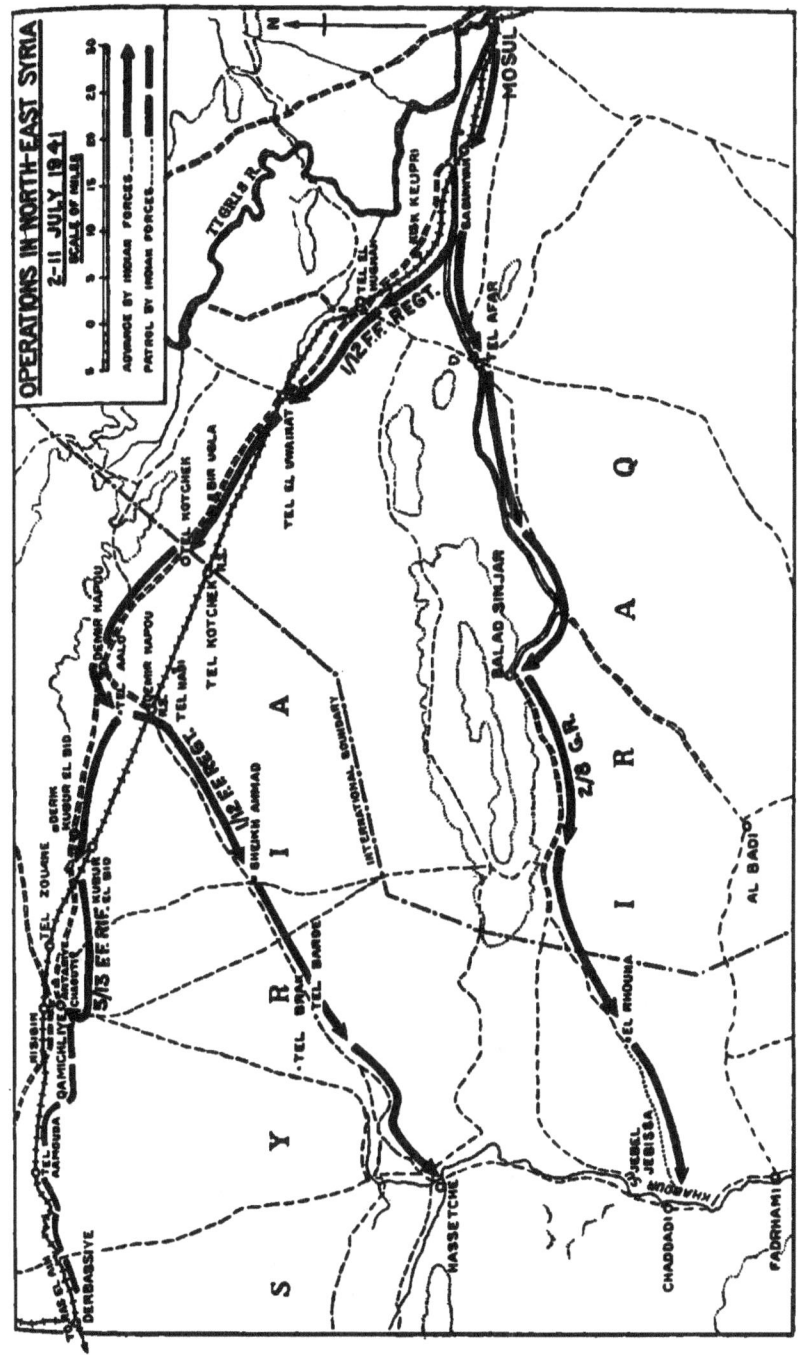

No hostile activities were observed. The day was spent in interviewing the local railway staff, the local sheikhs and informers who had come in from Tell Aalo, Qamichliye and other Vichy posts. They were all very friendly and said that there would be absolutely no resistance from the Syrian troops, though their French officers had orders to resist the Allied advance. At 0700 hours on 4 July, one platoon of B Company reconnoitred the road running along the railway to Tell Aalo post. The bridge at Tell Hadi, four miles south-east of Tell Aalo, which had been reported mined, was found to have been left intact with the mines removed. Approximately 25 men were seen standing on the roof of Tell Aalo fort.

While these reconnaissances were being carried out Brigadier Powell had ordered the remainder of the battalion to proceed on 4 July by road and rail from Mosul to Tell Kotchek. The object of concentrating the battalion at Tell Kotchek was to afford an opportunity for reconnaissance westwards to facilitate the advance on Qamichliye.

This part of the battalion arrived at Tell Kotchek at 1500 hours on 4 July. Lt. Col. L. E. Macgregor, Commander of 1/12 Frontier Force Regiment, then ordered three rifle companies (motorised) to occupy Tell Aalo post on the night of 4/5 July. At 1900 hours on 4 July, the commanding officer of the battalion proceeded to reconnoitre the road to Tell Aalo, dropping on the way one platoon of B Company to occupy Tell Hadi. Two columns of 1/12 Frontier Force Regiment moved out of Tell Kotchek during the night of 4/5 July to capture Tell Aalo. Column 'A' consisting of battalion headquarters, two rifle companies, one section R.A. and a medical detachment moved at 0100 hours on 5 July by the motorable track via Demir Kapou. Column 'B' consisting of improvised headquarters, one rifle company and a medical detachment, moved out at 0200 hours by the secondary road running parallel to and just north of the railway. This was a good route and shorter by six miles than the other road. At 0415 hours, 'A' Column took up a position about three thousand five hundred yards north of Tell Aalo. 'B' Column deployed east of that town at 0430 hours. At 0435 hours a local emissary was despatched to the Fort to ask the commander to give himself up. The commander refused to come out. He did, however, send his second-in-command to discuss terms. This officer refused to surrender but asked for permission to withdraw his force to Qamichliye. This was not agreed to and he was informed that if the Fort was not evacuated by 0615 hours it would be shelled. At 0615 hours, when the commander appeared in person for further negotiations, it became apparent to the Commanding Officer of 1/12 Frontier Force Regiment that the garrison was praying for time. The French Commander was detained and the garrison was given further 15 minutes to evacuate. The Syrian garrison now ran up a white flag but failed to leave the fort. Thereupon, one shell was fired well over the objective. This had the desired effect and the garrison swarmed out of the fort in all directions. A second shell put an end to these irregular movements. Those who had a white handkerchief tied it to their bayonets and the men marched back and laid down their arms. The fort was occupied at 0830 hours. Four French and three Syrian officers with ninety-nine other ranks were taken prisoners. During these operations, a patrol from the company protecting the rear of the troops ambushed a convoy consisting of four mule carts, two lorries and forty infantry. The convoy surrendered unconditionally.

Leaving one company and two platoons to garrison Tell Aalo, the battalion left for Tell Kotchek at 0900 hours on 5 July.

CHAPTER XXXII

Capture of Hassetche

Capture of Qamichliye

These preliminary operations paved the way for a double thrust towards Qamichliye and Hassetche by the 17th Indian Infantry Brigade. The brigade, less one battalion, with under command 32nd Field Regiment R.A. and ancillary units advanced from Basra on 4 July to pass through the 20th Indian Infantry Brigade Group at Mosul on 6 July and concentrate at Tell Aalo for the attack on Qamichliye. On arrival at Mosul, the 17th Indian Infantry Brigade came under the command of the Headquarters British Troops in Iraq.[1]

A column consisting of a composite company of 5th Battalion 13th Frontier Force Rifles (D Company) with a troop of 115th Battery (18-pounder) and three R.A.F. armoured cars moved out of Tell Aalo at 0500 hours on 7 July, and advanced by bounds through Kubur el Bid, Chaouti to Antariye in front of Qamichliye, where it deployed at about 1000 hours. One platoon 5/13 Frontier Force Rifles, which had been detached for capturing Tell Zouane station, accomplished its task without opposition. Two armoured cars with the column deployed in front of Qamichliye, proceeded to the entrance of the town and demanded surrender by 1100 hours. The demand was rejected. Thereupon the French commandant was informed that, unless he hauled down his flag by 1100 hours, the barracks and the trenches would be shelled. At 1100 hours as the Vichy French flag was still flying, the first round was about to be fired when a message was received that the commandant would pull down his flag at 1200 hours, if he was allowed time to escape with what garrison he could muster. As shelling the town would have caused suffering to the inhabitants the terms were accepted. The flag was eventually hauled down at 1220 hours and the town was entered ten minutes later. The fort was intact except for the wireless station which had been destroyed. Large quantities of stores of every description were found including arms, ammunition and engineering stores.[2]

B Company left Tell Aalo at 0710 hours on 8 July to reinforce D Company at Qamichliye. Kubur el Bid was occupied by one platoon B company. Another platoon of B company occupied

[1] *War Diary* 17 Ind. Inf. Bde.
[2] Ibid.

without incident, Aamouda, 15 miles west of Qamichliye. Next day (9 July) C company less one platoon with one section Field Regiment carried out reconnaissance from Tell Aalo towards Derik, with the object of arresting certain pro-Vichy persons. Derik post was found empty and clear of Vichy French troops. B company less one platoon carried out a reconnaissance from Qamichliye towards Derbassiye. The Indian troops were received everywhere with evident signs of satisfaction.[3]

Occupation of Hassetche

While 5/13 Frontier Force Rifles captured Qamichliye, 1/12 Frontier Force Regiment, concentrated at Tell Kotchek, was directed on Hassetche. There was a good metalled road from Tell Kotchek to Tell Aalo (Demir Kapou)—a distance of about 15½ miles. From here a motorable track proceeded to Hassetche via Tell Brak. The route from Tell Aalo to Hassetche (72 miles) was good and pleasant, passing over a plateau interspersed with a few wadis and frequent mounds about 300-feet high. From Tell Aalo to Sheikh Ahmad (20 miles) there was a good straight track, though deeply rutted in places. At Sheikh Ahmad there was a water splash, which required slow driving. For five miles beyond Sheikh Ahmad the route was bumpy, badly rutted and twisty. It had to make frequent diversions to avoid mounds. From this point as far as Tell Barde the route was fairly good. From Tell Barde to Hassetche the route was stony, but hard and level. Owing to the absence of ruts a high speed could be maintained.[4]

The mobile column for the capture of Hassetche consisted of C and D companies and No. 2 Platoon of 1/12 Frontier Force Regiment, half section R.A.F. armoured cars, a detachment of Sappers and Miners, and a detachment of workshop company. The plan was for A company 5/13 Frontier Force Rifles and one battery 32nd Field Regiment to proceed in advance from Tell Aalo to lay out a camp at Tell Brak. The mobile column was to follow, advancing to Tell Brak by day and moving to Hassetche by night so as to surround the town by first light.

The preliminary moves were made by A company 5/13 Frontier Force Rifles and a battery of 32nd Field Regiment R.A., which advanced from Tell Aalo at 0900 hours on 8 July, and occupied Tell Brak without opposition; small parties of Vichy cavalry retreated in the direction of Hassetche. The mobile column left Tell Kotchek at 1030 hours on 8 July. At 1600 hours when the mobile column was about five miles east of Tell Brak, it was met by the local Arab Sheikhs and representatives from Hassetche, who

[3] *War Diary* 5/13 Frontier Force Rifles
[4] M.T. routes in Syria.

said that the French had evacuated Hassetche that morning and that the fort was occupied only by the Assyrian troops. When the force reached Tell Brak at 1630 hours it was divided into two columns. The fast column leading the advance consisted of battalion headquarters, half section R.A.F. armoured cars and C company, while the slow column comprised No. 2 Platoon, detachment workshop company, detachment Sappers and Miners and D company. The fast column reached Hassetche at 1800 hours on 8 July. It was met outside the town by civil and police representatives, who said that it had been decided that no resistance was to be offered against the occupation of Hassetche. The occupation was completed the same evening. The fort was found in good condition but the wireless station had been completely wrecked. Large quantities of ammunition, petrol and stores had been left intact.[5]

Advance to Jebel Jebissa

The following day after the capture of Hassetche, Brigadier Powell, Commander 20th Indian Infantry Brigade at Mosul, ordered Lt. Col. Clarke, Commander 2/8 Gurkha, to lead a column from Mosul to Jebel Jebissa in order to intercept Vichy French forces withdrawing southwards from Hassetche. The column (whose code-name was 'Nobcol') consisted of 2/8 Gurkha (less one company and other details), one troop 3rd Field Regiment R.A. and ancillary units. From Mosul the road led to Sabuniyah railway station (16 miles). Just beyond the railway station the road forked; the right road leading to Tell Kotchek and the left to Chaddadi via Tell Afar and Balad Sinjar.

The operation ws to be carried out in three phases:

Phase I	Advance from Mosul via Tell Afar—Balad Sinjar—El Rhouna on D1 (10 July)—distance 110 miles.
Phase II	Advance from El Rhouna to Jebel Jebissa—Chaddadi area and withdrawal to El Rhouna on D2.
Phase III	Withdrawal to Mosul on D3.

During Phase I, the Reconnaissance Group consisting of one platoon D company was to halt on bounds until the arrival of the Holding Group and was to move to the next bound remaining in observation on the final bound. The Holding Group, consisting of D company, less one platoon, and one section medium machine-guns, was to move in the rear of the Reconnaissance Group.

---

[5] *War Diary* 1/12 Frontier Force Regiment and *War Diary* 17 Ind. Inf. Bde.

Next was to come the Main Group in the following order of march:

R Group 2/8 Gurkha
Detachment Brigade Signal Section
R Group Troop 3rd Field Regiment R.A.
R Group 10th Field Company Sappers and Miners
Battalion Headquarters (2/8 Gurkha)
B Company 2/8 Gurkha
Troop 3rd Field Regiment R.A.
C Company less one platoon 2/8 Gurkha
Section 10th Field Company Sappers and Miners
Detachment 26th Field Ambulance
H.Q. Company 2/8 Gurkha
20th Indian Brigade Transport Company
Detachment 28 (M) Workshop Company
One platoon C Company 2/8 Gurkha.

The Reconnaissance Group was to pass the starting point (junction main road—Mosul aerodrome road below the Iraqi Barracks) at 0500 hours on 10 July. The Holding Group was to move two minutes in the rear of the Reconnaissance Group. The head of Main Group was to pass the starting point at 0510 hours[6]

Operations

On the first day (10 July) the column halted for the night at a place where the Mosul—Jebel Jebissa road crossed the Syrian border. The road from this point to Jebel Jebissa, though marked on the map was non-existent. The column moved off at 0400 hours on 11 July and crossed a very steep-banked stream which caused some delay to B Echelon. The latter, under the protection of C company, remained at El Rhouna, while the remainder of the column advanced another sixteen miles to complete the task given to it. This was completed after some extremely hard work by the 10th Field Company, Sappers and Miners. The force started to withdraw to the previous night's area at 1530 hours on 11 July. Owing to the great difficulty in crossing the same steep-banked stream, the tail of the column arrived in camp at 2000 hours. The road from that camp to El Rhouna was not a well defined track. The column set out for Mosul at 0500 hours on 12 July and arrived in its camp areas at 1600 hours without incident. The three days of the column's advance were very tiring and a considerable amount of hard work had to be done by all ranks.[7] The column did not encounter any opposition.

[6] 2/8 G.R. O.O. No. 6 dated 9 July 1941. *War Diary* 2/8 G.R.
[7] *War Diary* 2/8 G.R.

Garrison Duties

The mobile column (1/12 Frontier Force Regiment) left Hassetche at 1330 hours and arrived at Tell Kotchek at 2000 hours on 10 July. Next day, 1/12 Frontier Force Regiment moved to Mosul. 5/13 Frontier Force Rifles remained behind in Syria for garrison duties. Brigadier Gracey ordered the following redistribution of the battalion:[8]

Group I	(Qamichliye)—Battalion Headquarters, H.Q. company less two sections, 4 platoon and three sections, 3 platoon and details, 1 platoon, B and D companies. (This group was to provide detachments of 1 platoon B company at Aamouda and 1 platoon B company at Kubur el Bid).
Group II	(Hassetche)—A company, one section 4 platoon, two detachments 3 platoon.
Group III	(Tell Aalo)—C company, one section 4 platoon and one detachment 3 platoon. (This group was to provide a detachment of one platoon C company at Tell Kotchek).

The garrisons were to be established at Qamichliye by 1600 hours on 12 July, at Hassetche by 1800 hours on 10 July and at Tell Aalo by 0800 hours on 11 July.

The role of these groups (garrisons) was to organise mobile columns for carrying out vigorous and intensive patrolling in areas as follows:—

(i) From Qamichliye in area Ras el Ain—Aamouda—Kubur el Bid—Hassetche.

(ii) From Hassetche in area Ras el Ain—Qamichliye—Tell Brak—Chaddadi.

(iii) From Tell Aalo in area Derik—Tell Kotchek—Tell Brak—Kubur el Bid.[9]

The primary object of the redistribution of the battalion was to defend the railway against any form of sabotage and to ensure its smooth working between including Tell Kotchek and excluding the Turkish border at Tell Zouane. The secondary object was to back up the local administration and to prevent disorder in the area Ras el Ain—Qamichliye—Derik—Tell Kotchek—Hassetche—Chaddadi.

Before the redistribution of the battalion was completely carried out, orders were received from the Brigade for the forward troops to cease hostilities with effect from 0001 hours on 12 July.

---

[8] *War Diary* 5/13 Frontier Force Rifles.
[9] O.I. No. 1 dated 10 July, Appendix 13, *War Diary* 5/13 Frontier Force Rifles.

The Armistice

On 11 July when General Dentz opened negotiations for an armistice the Allied forces had made considerable progress. The capture of Damour by the Australians after stiff resistance opened the way to Beirut. There was a serious threat to Homs—by the Free French force operating from Damascus and the Habforce operating from Palmyra. The capture of Deir ez Zor and the thrust towards Aleppo threatened to cut off the Vichy troops at Beirut. The capture of Hassetche and Qamichliye ended hostile opposition in north-east Syria. The Royal Air Force contributed their share to the Allied success. By 10 July the Royal Air Force had destroyed or damaged four-fifths of the hostile air force. It was a substantial achievement. The Royal Navy too played a notable part in the operations in Syria. In his report on 'Operations of the First Australian Corps in Syria,' Major General Lavarack paid a handsome tribute to the Royal Navy: " . . . . . there were two factors of the highest importance which contributed to the British victory—the bombardment provided in the coastal sector by the Royal Navy, and our superiority in the air." "The naval bombardments caused a great deal of destruction of enemy transport and armoured fighting vehicles on the coast road; engaged frequently with good effect the enemy's gun positions and last, but not least, caused considerable deterioration in morale amongst troops exposed, without hope of retaliation and small hope of protection, to the gruelling flank fire from the sea."

All these various factors—the terrific bombardment of the Vichy positions by the Royal Navy, the extremely heavy toll taken of the Vichy aircraft by the Royal Air Force and the vigorous Allied thrusts up the coast, Damascus, Palmyra and Deir ez Zor, contributed to the defeat of the Vichy French. As the situation had deteriorated considerably the Vichy authorities were compelled to end the hostilities. The Vichy representatives met General Wilson and the armistice terms were signed on 14 July at Acre in the barracks dedicated to the memory of Sir Sydney Smith, who had halted Napoleon's eastern advance in this town. According to the terms of the armistice, the Allied forces were to occupy Syria and Lebanon and the Vichy forces were to be concentrated in selected areas and granted "full honours of war". All Allied prisoners of war were to be set free. Until all were released an equivalent number of Vichy French officers and men might be retained as prisoners of war.[10] Some difficulty was experienced in implementing the terms of the armistice, especially in regard to the liberation of the Allied prisoners of war. By the end of July,

[10] See Appendix 15.

when 841 British and Indian officers and men had returned, it transpired that others had been sent out of Syria to France. The latter returned by 15 August while fourteen others who were in Italian hands at Scarpanto returned by the end of August.

Importance of the operations in Syria

The Indian troops played a notable part in the operations in Syria. The basis of the Allied planning was that the main advance should be made into south Syria and it should be facilitated by forces operating from Iraq. A careful review of the operations in south Syria highlights the achievements of the Indian troops. The capture of the strong Vichy position at Kissoue was no mean achievement and the heroic defence of Mezze, which paved the way for the capture of Damascus, redounds to their credit. The Indian troops operating from Iraq were less fortunate for they did not encounter fierce opposition and they did not get opportunities of covering themselves with glory. But that should not detract from their achievement, for they carried out the task allotted to them efficiently and energetically. They played an important part in hastening the end of the hostilities. The liquidation of opposition in north-east Syria and the thrust towards Aleppo were not a negligible factor in inducing the Vichy authorities to sue for peace.

The operations in Syria, though of short duration, were of great significance in the wider context of the Allied overall strategy. With the end of the hostilities in Syria, the Allies were not only able to exploit the resources of Syria but they also gained control over an area of great strategic importance. Allied planning for the defence of the solid block of territory (including Palestine, Transjordan, Syria and Iraq) against Axis attack was facilitated. There was only one chink—but a serious one—in the defensive armour, viz., Iran, which was under Axis influence. That problem remained to be dealt with. When the operations in Iran were concluded towards the end of August 1941, the Allies gained control over a vital strategic area, embracing Palestine, Transjordan, Syria, Iraq and Iran, for the build-up of their forces to check Axis attacks through Anatolia or Trans-Caucasia, and for opening up vital supply routes to stiffen the Russian resistance against the Axis forces. This is the significance of the operations in Syria in the context of Allied strategy.

IRAN

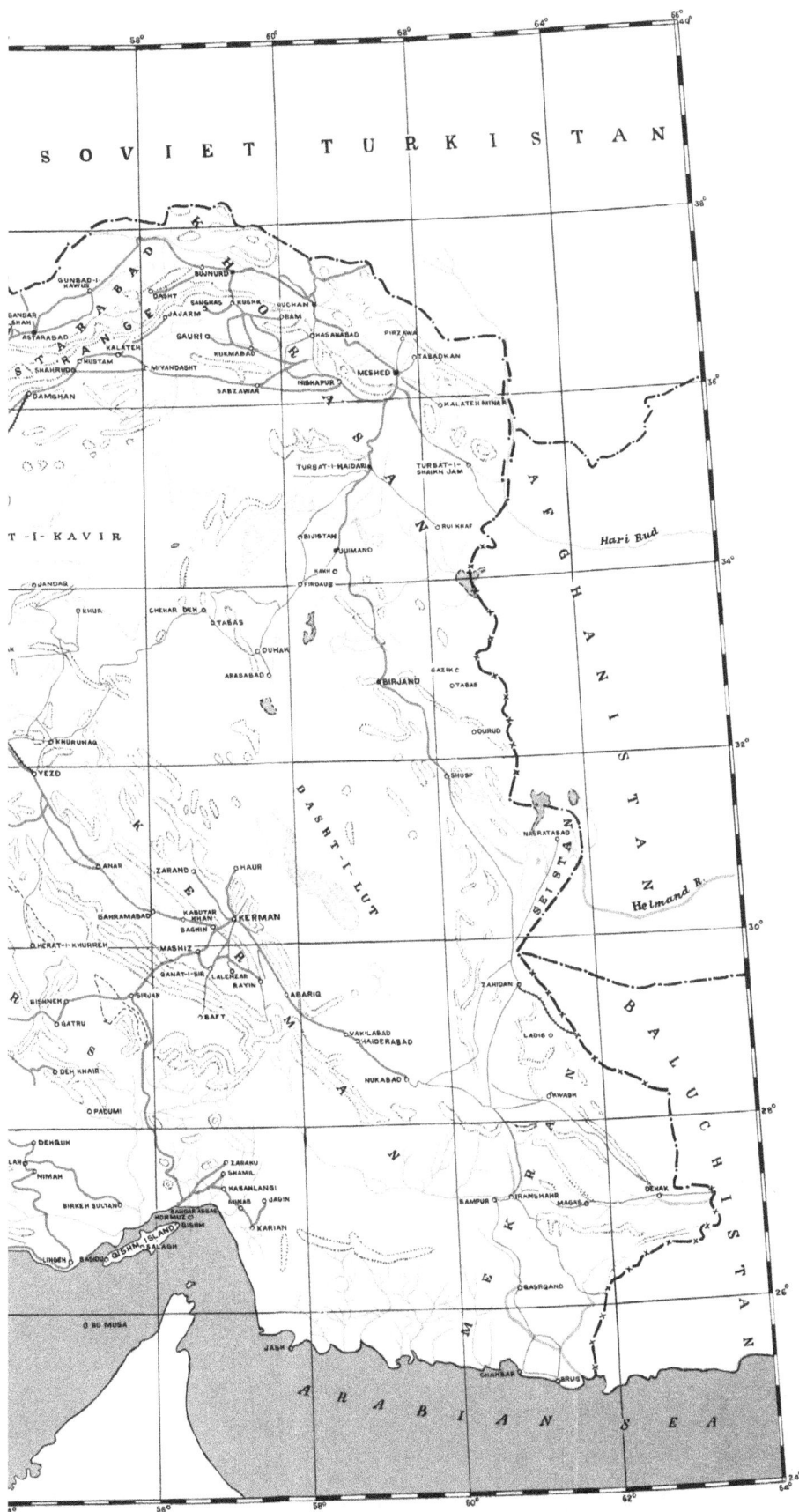

CHAPTER XXXIII

Geographical Survey

Persia or Iran

Iran,[1] the most romantic country of the east, the home of Zoroaster, Darius and Noshirvan, the birth-place of Firdausi, the author of the immortal Shahnama, the "glorious monument of Eastern genius and learning", of S'adi, the greatest moral poet, of Omar bin Khayyam, the renowned freethinker, and of Hafiz who gave to the world the "most perfect models of lyric composition"; and the land of supreme love, bubbling wine, bewitching beauty, melodious nightingales, sweet roses, nectarine fruits, magic carpets, luring light and captivating colour, the realm reminiscent of "Arabian Nights", and one of the few countries of the world which produced four rulers enjoying the title of the 'Great',[2] was drawn into the vortex of the second World War, but luckily it escaped with slight scars which were soon effaced.

Area and Boundaries

Iran is situated between 25° and 40° north latitudes and between 44° and 64° east longitudes. Its area is 628,000 square miles, twice as much as Turkey and five times that of Great Britain. The greatest length is nearly 1,400 miles and the maximum breadth slightly below 900 miles. About half the area is mountainous, one-eighth cultivable, and all the rest desert.

It was bounded on the north by Soviet Russia, on the west by Turkey and Iraq, on the south by the Arabian Sea and on the east by India and Afghanistan. The Caspian Sea, the Khorasan range and the Elburz in the north, the Hindukush in the north-east, the Arabian Sea and the Persian Gulf in the south, the Kurdistan hills and the Zagros in the west, and Mount Ararat and the mountains of Caucasia in the north-west, form the natural boundaries.

---

[1] The people of Persia call their country Iran and themselves Iranis, and since 21 March 1935, the country has officially been known as Iran. The term 'Persia' was used by Europeans and other foreigners. This word was derived from the classical Persia, which referred to 'Faras', the most typical part of the country. Today only two words have the old association, Persian language and the Persian Gulf.

In the military documents relating to World War II, Iran was almost everywhere called 'Persia', in order to avoid confusion with 'Iraq'. In this treatise, however, we have preferred to use its official as well as native name 'Iran'.

[2] Cyrus, Darius, Shapur, and Abbas.

The north, the north-west and the centre of Iran form one great plateau, in which are found all the big cities of the country. Its height varies from 3 to 5 thousand feet above the sea-level. The three northern cities of Tabriz, Teheran and Meshed are at an elevation of above 3,000 feet. Of the three central cities Isfahan is at an altitude of 5,000 feet, Yezd 4,000 feet and Birjand nearly 5,000 feet. Further south Zahidan, Shiraz and Kerman are from 3 to 5 thousand feet above the sea-level.

There are, besides, detached mountain ranges running in a south-easterly direction almost parallel to one another from Armenia to Fars. The important city in this area on the west is Hamadan, situated at a height of 6,200 feet. To the east, the great desert, which is completely barren, stretches across the plateau from the southern base of the Elburz mountains in the north to the Arabian Sea in the south. It is about 800 miles long, and varies in width from 100 to 200 miles. Its average altitude is 2,000 feet. Under most favourable circumstances it can be crossed only with sufficient supplies of food and forage, and one has to live on bad saline water. In the extreme north and south are the low-lying plains. The Caspian provinces of Gilan, Mazandaran and Astrabad enjoy pleasant climate and are covered with thick overgrowth of trees. The provinces of Khuzistan and a strip along the Persian Gulf suffer from intense heat and unhealthy climate.

Climate and Rainfall

Almost every variety of climate and every variation of heat and cold are found in Iran. Azarbaijan in the north has extremely bitter winter. There is a heavy snowfall on the uplands. Most of the plateau remains covered with snow for three or four months in the winter. In the plains, the temperature seldom falls below the freezing point. In spite of its severity the winter of Iran is considered as most delightful and invigorating. The provinces near the Persian Gulf have the hottest summer. In June the temperature at Shushtar in Khuzistan rises to 129° in the shade, the heat and glare nearly becoming unbearable. Travelling is mostly done by night but the cool hilly resorts are within a few hours' journey, and provide pleasing retreats. Spring and autumn are the best seasons. In spring there is greater rain than in autumn, but it seldom interferes seriously with the daily routine of the people. The rainy season lasts from December to March. The rainfall in the Caspian provinces exceeds 50 inches in the year, but nowhere else in the country does it exceed 13 inches. On the plateau the average rainfall is 8 inches. In the Urmia basin there is fairly good rain, but in Seistan it rains only 2 inches in a year. With the exception of the Caspian region, Iran is an arid country and the problem of irrigation and water often grows very acute. The general character of the country is barren, with vast uncultivated lands.

The climate in general is dry and hot. Its aridity can be realised from the fact that tree leaves, green and gay at six o'clock in the morning, fade, and are almost brown by nine. Water is the most valuable commodity and is diverted to gardens with great care and at considerable expense. The greatest economy is applied in its use. Only the sun drinks it up without payment, and unluckily it never appears satisfied. Owing to the position of the Mediterranean and Arabian Seas and the Iranian mountains, the winds blow with great regularity and uniformity. In spring and summer their direction is from south-east, and in autumn and winter from the north-west. Occasionally their speed becomes terrible, developing into a gale in Kerman, turning into furious hurricane in Seistan, with velocity varying from 72 miles to 120 miles an hour. The survival from such tempests, whether of man or beast, is always considered miraculous.

Rivers

On account of scanty rainfall, there are no big rivers in Iran. Most of the rivers are inland streams; only the Karun rising in the southern slopes of the Bakhtiari mountains reaches the sea. It emerges from the hills near Shushtar and is navigable for small crafts for about 50 miles up to Ahwaz, now called Nasiri. At this place the Trans-Iranian Railway crosses it by a fine steel bridge, over 3,000 feet long. Below this point it is navigable by medium-sized vessels. From Ahwaz its course down south is tortuous and tiresome. It joins the Shatt-al-Arab at Khurramshahr. There are numerous date groves at its mouth. About two miles above Khurramshahr, Bahmanshir, an old channel, bifurcates from the main stream and directly falls into the Persian Gulf.

Among the other important rivers are the Aras in the north, the Kizil Uzun in the north-west, the Zenda Rud in the centre, and the Helmand in the east.

Water Bodies

All the inland water bodies are saltish, some of them being as bitter as the Dead Sea. The most important of these is the Lake Urmia. It is situated in the north-west, over 4,000 feet above the sea-level. Its length from north to south is nearly 80 miles and width from east to west about 20 miles. There are numerous islands in it. The town of Urmia is 12 miles to its west and is believed to be the birth-place of Zoroaster.

The Persian Gulf washes the southern and south-western coasts of Iran. It is about 700 miles long and from 150 to 300 miles wide.

The Caspian Sea washes a part of the northern frontier of the country. It is nearly 600 miles long and 300 miles wide. The deepest water is in the southern part, but the harbours there were bad and shallow.

Flora

Due to the aridity of the country only one-twentieth of the area is under cultivation. The hills and plains are almost barren and the desert predominates. Vegetation is scarce. Trees and verdure are found only in the Caspian region, which is the greenest part of Iran, and in the irrigated uplands. Turf exists only in marshy places and in many parts even bushes are not to be seen. One tract along the Zagros starting from Shiraz, about 200 miles long and at some places nearly 100 miles broad, is covered with low oaks. In places where water is available many kinds of trees such as aspen, elm, ash, poplar, walnut and willow are grown. The cypress and pine are seldom to be found anywhere. The hill valleys abound with hawthorn and judas. In spring trees and plants are profusely laden with flowers, the commonest flowers being lilac, jasmine and roses. But spring comes with great suddenness and disappears with such rushing and rolling haste that flowers which should last for weeks have a short life. To-day it is a seed, tomorrow a plant, the day after a mass of flowers, and then nothing. In summer all is bare and brown.

Among the best products of Iran are fruits which are noted for their fineness, delicacy and deliciousness. Some of them vie in excellence with those of other countries. Such are the apples of Demavand, peaches of Meshed and Tabriz, pears of Natanz, sugar-melons of Isfahan and Kashan, figs of Kermanshah; and as regards grapes, nothing can surpass their elegance and softness. Almonds, pistachio and pomegranates grow best in the warmer climate; while dates, lime and oranges flourish in hot regions. Dry fruits, such as almonds, apricots, figs, peaches, pistachio, plums, raisins, walnuts and dates (last from south only), and also oranges (from the Caspian region), are exported.

Beans, barley, cotton, millet, oilseeds, opium, tobacco and wheat are the chief crops. Maize and rice grow in hotter parts and also in the Caspian provinces. Cabbages, cauliflowers, cucumbers, lettuces, potatoes and tomatoes are the main vegetables which are plentiful.

Fauna

There is no dearth of fauna in Iran. As regards wild animals, hyenas, jackals, leopards, lynxes and wolves are found in all parts of the country. Tigers, stags and roebucks are chiefly confined to the Caspian provinces. The fallow deer exists in the Zagros. Wild sheep and ibex abound in hills. Wild ass lives in plains. The wild pig swarms in the Caspian forests, low hills and along the rivers.

Among the domestic animals the horses of Iran have been noted for their power and endurance from time immemorial. The one-humped camel of Khorasan, massive in size and strength and with long hair, is very famous. He carries with ease a load of 700 pounds, just double that of the Indian camel. Buffaloes flourish in Khuzistan and the Caspian area. The fat-tailed sheep is seen everywhere. From a certain specie of goat the finest kind of wool is obtained.

Pheasant in the hills and partridges and sandgrouse on the plateau are common. Pigeon near cornfields and nightingale, the pet-bird, are plentiful in many parts. Poultry is good and abundant. Fish abounds in the Caspian Sea, Persian Gulf and in some rivers; but it is scarce in the interior of the country.

Minerals

Minerals, except oil, are not found in plenty in Iran. Due to the shortage of fuel and means of communication working of mines does not pay much, but coal mines at Teheran are worked. Copper is taken out at Sabzawar and Kala Zarri. Salt is obtained at Qishm, turquoise at Nishapur, red ochre at Bu Musa, Hormuz and Halul in the Persian Gulf, and sulphur at Lingeh. Iron, manganese and mercury are not worked. Many oilfields are found in the province of Khuzistan, all of which were leased to the Anglo-Iranian Oil Company. Another oil bearing area was found in the west near Kermanshah, which supplied the internal needs of the country.

Communications

Before the development of railway and motor transport, communications in Iran were very difficult. Entrance from the Persian Gulf was by the Bushire-Shiraz road which was extremely rough and inconvenient; and so was the approach from the west across Khuzistan, from the Caspian Sea on the north and through Baluchistan from the east. The whole country was cut into detached tracts by the desert. Travelling was done by camels, horses and mules. The construction of metalled roads began in 1924. In 1925 there were less than 1,000 miles of motorable road. In 1939 at the commencement of war, 15,000 miles of motorable roads existed, and 2,000 miles of new roads were being built every year. All Iranian roads are practically a succession of mountain passes of varying heights. From late November to February or March all the passes are liable to be blocked by snow. Every effort is made to keep the main roads open, but even so they are liable to blockade for several days at a time. For example, the Khanakin—Kazvin road gets blocked on the Pai Tak, Asadabad and Aveh passes. Similar is the case with the Shibli Pass between Mianeh and Tabriz. The railway is kept open by snow ploughs.

The greatest achievement of the country is the Trans—Iranian Railway which connects the Persian Gulf with the Caspian Sea. Plans for the building of this railway were drawn in May 1925, approved by the Parliament in March 1926, and the work commenced in October 1927. It was completed on 26 August 1938. Its total length in 1940 was 866 miles. The cost, about 30 million sterling, was met from the tax on tea and sugar, without any investment of foreign capital. Only technical help came from Europe. The British, French, German, Italian, Belgian and Danish firms were engaged under contract for the construction of its various sections. The railway runs through some exceptionally difficult regions in the mountains of Luristan in the south, and the Elburz Range in the north. In the former it rises to a height of 7,217 feet and in the latter 6,889 feet. Besides, there are narrow gorges, some about 300 feet deep, with swift rivers passing through them. In such places a number of viaducts, each 427 feet long and 82 feet high, had to be constructed. Tunnels there were many; one of which was two miles long with spiral curves of 656 feet in radius. The Trans-Iranian Railway was so planned as to avoid connection with the four neighbouring railway systems of Russia, Turkey, Iraq and India. With the exception of the capital it avoided also the main commercial centres of Iran itself. Several branch lines were under construction in 1941, connecting Kazvin and Tabriz, Qum and Yezd and Qum and Kashan.

Wireless Stations

The Government wireless stations had been established at Tabriz, Pahlevi, Teheran, Meshed, Kermanshah, Khurramshahr and Kerman. The Teheran Radio Station was established in 1940, and was equipped and operated by German technicians.

Population

A large part of Iran being a desert, the population is scanty, and the average comes to 24 persons per square mile as against 468 in Great Britain, 300 in India and 54 in Turkey. The total population is roughly estimated at 15 millions. Of this nearly 3 millions are nomads who depend upon pastures, about the same strength are the townfolk living on industries and trade, and the rest live in villages where the main profession is agriculture. From the religious point of view the division of the population was as follows:—

Muslims	Shias	14,000,000	
	Sunnis	800,000	(mostly in Azarbaijan, Kurdistan and Baluchistan).
Christians		80,000	
Jews		36,000	
Zoroastrians		9,000	

In spite of the religious differences the people in Iran have no communal bickerings, and all live peacefully together. There are no communal riots and no discord. The Iranian peasantry and nomad tribesmen possess a sound physique, and are sturdy and strong, but the dwellers of towns and cities are soft and delicate. The Iranians are not a warlike people and like to live harmoniously with their neighbours. Lovers of the soft ways of life as they are, they eat and dress well and are noted for their cheerfulness. They enjoy the best reputation in the East for wit, humour, eloquence, and love for beauty and poetry. Their fame for hospitality to strangers and guests is well known, and the country people are noted for killing their last sheep for a traveller. Few peoples excel them in virtues of the home. The parents display the utmost indulgence to children, and that affection is reciprocated by the greatest regard and respect. A son would seldom sit in the presence of his father, and nothing can surpass his reverence for the mother whose wishes are commands or even laws to him. In the household affairs the mother's will reigns supreme. The grandmother, the paternal uncle and the mother-in-law, all receive full obedience and esteem. The servants are well looked after and treated with great care and consideration. Iranians are not cruel by temperament, and are kind to men and animals alike. Being emotional they quickly seize upon new ideas and easily assimilate them. It is on that account that under Riza Shah in a short space of ten years Iran witnessed the emancipation of women, the adoption of European dress, and cessation of some religious practices. The Iranians have great capacity for adaptability, but at the same time they never lose their individuality.

CHAPTER XXXIV

Historical Background

The Aryans

The history of Iran like that of India has been a chequered one. The first historic people who occupied Iran were the Aryans. The country was called Ariana, " the land of the Aryans", from which the modern name 'Iran' has originated. It is believed by historians that the Iranians and the Aryans who settled in India had lived together in pre-historic times and formed a single people, thus introducing elements of similarity in religion, language, culture and character of the two peoples.

In the course of time, the people of Iran came to be divided into two groups, the Persians living in the south-east, in the modern province of Fars, and the Medes dwelling in the west. One of the famous rulers, Cyrus the Great, who belonged to the Persian branch, conquered the Medes about 550 B.C. He subjugated also the territory in the west (now comprised in Iraq), Syria and eastern territory up to Turkistan. His son Cambyses subdued Egypt. The greatest ruler of this dynasty was, however, Darius the Great (521-485 B.C.) whose dominions extended from the Indus to the Danube.

The Greeks

This family remained in power for two centuries and a quarter when it was overthrown by Alexander the Great. Iran was then Hellenized. The Greeks married Iranian women, and introduced their language, philosophy and science in the country.

The Parthians

The Greeks were subdued by the Parthians, who formed part of the Turanian tribe from Khorasan. They ruled the country for nearly 500 years. They had to bear the onslaughts of two conquering people, the Romans from the west and Scythians in the east, but they managed to hold their own. The middle Persian or Parthavi, which later came to be called Pahlevi language, came into being during this period and became the official language of the land.

The Sassanian Dynasty

The Iranian genius could not be suppressed for long, and the province of Fars brought into existence the Sassanian dynasty

(226-640 A.D.), which not only freed the country from foreign yoke but added greatly to its material prosperity and progress in art and learning. The two great kings of this dynasty were Shapur the Great and Noshirvan. The former seized from Rome five of her provinces, defeated the Huns, and at his death left Iran at the height of her glory and greatness. The latter is considered the most illustrious of the Iranian kings. He curiously combined in himself a peculiar blending of might and mercy. Not only did he win dazzling victories over the Romans and other foes, but he also displayed rare genius in the arts of peace. He established a strong standing army on fixed pay, reduced the scale of land-tax on peasantry, converted waste lands into smiling fields of corn, built roads and guarded them properly, attracted foreign visitors, enforced work on every man and woman, and punished mendicancy and idleness. He was a renowned scholar and read Persian translations of the works of Aristotle and Plato. A University was established at Gundisapur. Under his instructions a 'Book of the Kings', containing all the known history of Iran, was prepared, and the celebrated poet Firdausi based his famous Shahnama on this work. From India he introduced indigo, the game of chess, and certain literary works considered to be the precursors of Aesop's fables. During his regime Iran became a halfway house and a central emporium for the exchange of ideas and commodities between the east and the west. He dispensed justice so equitably that he is known as Noshirvan the Just. The Sassanian rulers had to fight against the Romans and the Huns constantly and vehemently. This warfare gravely affected Iran's manpower and material resources, and ultimately led to her conquest by the Arabs.

The Arab Conquest

In the first half of the 7th century A.D. Islam was established in Arabia. Islam gave the Arabs such fire and frenzy that they easily conquered all the countries in the neighbourhood of Mecca. The Arabs then turned their attention towards Iran. Under their famous leader, Khalid, they first took the outlying provinces of the Persian empire along the western coast of the Persian Gulf and the valley of the Euphrates. Afterwards they crossed the Euphrates near Babylon by a bridge of boats in 637 A.D., and called upon the Emperor of Iran to embrace Islam or pay tribute. The offer was spurned with disdain. In the fight that followed, the Iranians were defeated and the victor acquired vast booty. Each of the 60,000 men obtained about £500, which to the destitute dwellers of the desert meant wealth. In another engagement 100,000 horses were seized. Three years later Ahwaz and Shushtar were captured. Kerman, Kohistan, Seistan and Makran were soon reduced to subjection.

Another Arab army took Gurgan and Azarbaijan. Khorasan was conquered last of all. Thus Iran was occupied by the Arabs, who were alien in race, language and religion. "Hellenism", says Noldeke, "never touched more than the surface of Persian life, but Iran was penetrated to the core by Arabian religion and Arabian ways." A vast majority of the people embraced Islam. The Iranian nobles were reduced to the position of clients of Arabs. The hatred of the conquerers towards Iranians is shown by their contemptuous saying, "Three things only stop prayer: the passing of a client, an ass, or a dog". The Zoroastrians had to pay a poll-tax in order to have the liberty to follow their religion. Though Iran lost her independence for the time being, she soon asserted her intellectual supremacy over her rulers.

Adoption of Shia Faith

The Iranians accepted the Shia faith, which is associated with Hazart Ali, the cousin of Prophet Mohammed. He became the fourth Caliph in 656 A.D. and was assassinated five years later. His eldest son Hasan succeeded him, but he had to abdicate immediately after. The other son, Husain, lost his life in 680 A.D. at Kerbela in Iraq, in an engagement with the rival party. It is believed that Husain had married a daughter of the King of Iran who had previously been defeated by the Arabs. The Shias consider Ali, the first cousin of Prophet Mohammed, also his adopted son and son-in-law, and "perhaps the first male convert of the Prophet", as his rightful successor, both by right of birth and by the will of the Prophet, and reject the first three Caliphs as usurpers, in opposition to the belief of the orthodox Muslims known as the Sunnis. The authority of the Shia sect is invested in the twelve Imams, and the Shah of Iran is bereft of any religious power. The highest authority is vested in the *Mujtahid* who resides either at Kerbela or Najaf. The holiest places of the Shias are Kerbela, the place of Husain's martyrdom, Najaf where stands the tomb of Ali, both situated in Iraq, and Meshed, situated in Iran where Riza, the eighth Imam, lies buried.

For about 150 years, Iran was ruled first from Medina and then from Baghdad by Caliph's officers who imposed the official Arab language on the people. Afterwards the Iranians gradually began to regain their sense of nationality under the Abbasids who had risen to power largely with their help.

The Mongol Occupation

At the beginning of the 13th century, the Mongols began to spread westward and Iran was occupied by them. This was the worst period of foreign rule in Iran. Fire and sword were the only weapons of governance adopted by these ruthless invaders from the east. Their rule of about two hundred years brought to this country nothing but misery and misfortune. Then the Turks appeared on the scene and they seized a large portion of the country.

The Safavi Kings

The Iranian genius again asserted itself, and the kings of the Safavi dynasty (1502-1736), restored not only the unity of the country but also revived her culture. The greatest ruler of this dynasty was Shah Abbas the Great (1587-1629), a contemporary of Akbar and Elizabeth. He inflicted a crushing defeat on the Turks and recovered from them Azarbaijan, Kurdistan, Mosul, Baghdad and the sacred places of Najaf and Kerbela. His court was attended by ambassadors from England, Holland, Portugal, Spain, Russia and India. The decline of this dynasty was brought about by the Afghans of Kandahar, who invaded Iran in 1721, defeated and murdered the king, massacred the people, and took possession of Kerman and Isfahan. Nine years later they were expelled by Nadir Shah who crowned himself a king in 1736. He made many conquests and invaded India in 1739. His assassination in 1747 was followed by a period of anarchy lasting over half a century.

The Kajar Family

During this confusion the country was partitioned among many ambitious chiefs. The strongest of them was Muhammad Hasan Khan, the hereditary head of the Kajar tribe of Turkomans living to the south-east of the Caspian Sea. His son Agha Muhammad, a cruel despot, conquered a major portion of Iran. He established his capital at Teheran in 1796, but was murdered soon after. The Kajar period is marked by the growing influence of European powers in Iran, particularly that of Great Britain and Russia. King Nasir-uddin Shah (1848-96) visited Europe thrice. In 1873 he went to England, in 1879 to Russia, Germany, France, and Austria, and in 1889 to England and the principal courts of Europe. As a result of these visits the Shah made up his mind to develop his country with the help of foreigners. In 1888 he threw open to international navigation the Karun river from its mouth to Ahwaz. In the same year a Belgian Company built the first railway line from Teheran to Shah Abdul Azim, only 5½ miles long. In 1889 the English were permitted to establish a Persian State Bank "with exclusive rights of issuing bank-notes and working the mines of iron, copper, lead, mercury, coal, petroleum, manganese, borax, and asbestos."[1] In 1890 the Shah granted to a British Company the monopoly of tobacco. This was deeply resented by the people. Their religious

[1] *Encyclopaedia Britannica,* Vol. XXI, page 248.

leader, Haji Mirza Hasan, issued instructions to stop smoking forthwith. "Suddenly, with perfect accord", says Dr. Feuvrier, "all the tobacco merchants have closed their shops, all the qalyans (waterpipes) have been put aside, and no one smokes any longer, either in the city, or in the Shah's entourage, or even in the women's apartments. What discipline, what obedience!" The concession was withdrawn for a large indemnity. In 1895 the French Government was given the exclusive right to explore ancient sites. The Shah was assassinated in 1896 for his European inclinations.

He was succeeded by his son Muzaffar-ud-Din, who was absolutely in the hands of a corrupt set of courtiers. He very soon wasted all the treasures of his father. Then he wished to obtain a loan of one million sterling to clear off the arrears of pay of his army and civilian officers. The English firms offered it on stringent terms, hence the loan was secured from Russia. Between 1899 and 1903 the Shah borrowed £4,000,000, half of which was spent by the Shah on his personal pleasures, foreign travels and favourites. He visited Europe in 1900 and 1902, and formed a commercial treaty with Great Britain.

The misgovernment of the Shah and the daily growing influence of Europeans caused great discontentment. Led by the successful example of protest against the tobacco monopoly, the people organised a regular agitation, demanding representative institutions and a constitution, declaring that they would no longer tolerate an absolute monarchy. The Shah had to yield. By a rescript, dated 5 August 1906, he gave his assent to the formation of a National Council. It was to consist of the representatives of various classes such as clergy, landed magnates, tribes, Kajar family, nobles, merchants and agriculturists. Their number was fixed at 162, sixty for Teheran and 102 for the provinces. Right of vote was given only to Iranian male subjects of 25 or above, who could read and write Persian. No man was elected if he was an alien, below 30 or above 70, a Government employee, in the active service of army or navy, a criminal, or a bankrupt. The National Council met for the first time on 7 October 1906, and its president was elected. By another ordinance ministers were made responsible to the National Council. Special powers of finance and administration were given to this body. Its approval was necessary for any change in territory, state property, grant of concessions, contracting of loans, ratification of treaties, and building of roads and railways.

Muzaffar-ud-Din Shah died in January 1907, and was succeeded by his son Muhammad Ali Mirza. About this time keen rivalry had been going on between Great Britain and Russia for the commercial privileges in Iran. Finding the country in weak hands, and realising that their mutual differences would injure both, they came

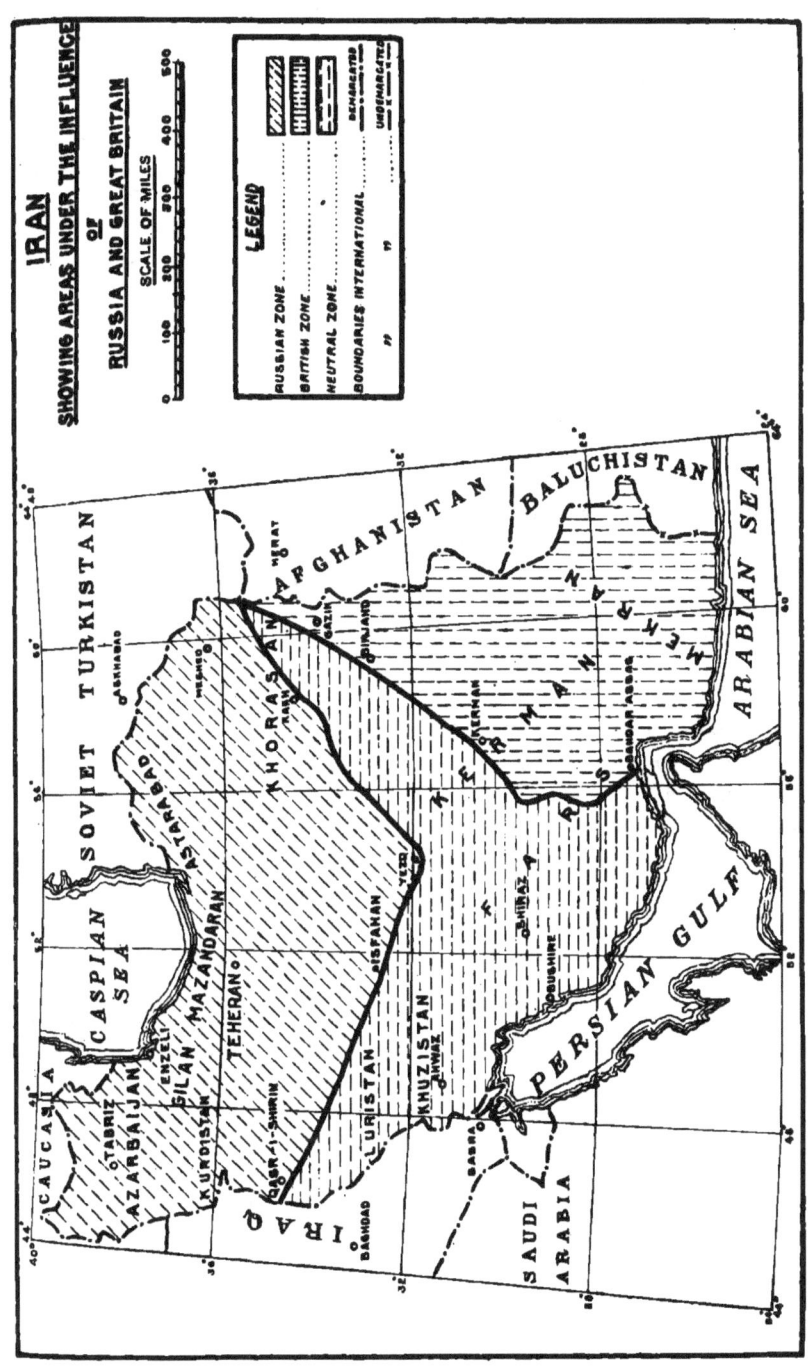

to an understanding and signed a convention on 31 August 1907. They decided upon their particular spheres of influence as if Iran were their subject territory. The whole country was divided into four zones. North of a line drawn from Qasr-i-Shirin, Isfahan, Yezd and Kakh to the junction of Russian, Iranian and Afghan territories was to be the purely Russian zone in which Great Britain "undertook to seek no political or commercial concession, and to refrain from opposing the acquisition of any such concession by Russia." A similar undertaking was given by Russia in the territory south of a line stretching from Bandar Abbas, Kerman, Birjand and Gazik to the Afghan frontier which was to be absolutely a British zone. The territory lying between these two zones was to be considered as a neutral zone in which both of them could secure any concessions. The Persian Gulf was outside the convention, and beyond Russian interests.

The Anglo-Russian Pact caused great indignation in the country against the weak government of the Shah. Certain modifications were demanded in the constitution, and the revised constitution was approved by the new King on 12 November 1907. According to it the Shah must belong to the Shia faith. The eldest son or the next male heir was to be his successor. His civil list amounted to £100,000. The executive government was to be under a cabinet consisting of seven or eight ministers, one of whom was to be the Prime Minister.[2] Soon after this the Shah endeavoured to crush the national movement, to overthrow the constitution and to revive his old dictatorial powers. Insurrections broke out at many places, the national agitation grew stronger and the Shah had to abdicate in July 1909. He was sent to the Crimea in exile on a pension. His son, Ahmad Shah, aged 13, became King with Asad-ul-Mulk, head of the Kajar tribe, as regent. The change brought about no improvement in the administration, and disturbances continued as before.

From 1911 to 1913, the ex-Shah made several attempts to regain his lost throne; but in the face of people's hostility it proved a vain effort. The condition of the country at this time was critical. The treasury was empty and there was no efficient army to suppress disorders. To add to the difficulties the Great War broke out in 1914. Iran declared her strict neutrality; but she had no means to have this position respected by the Great Powers. The country immediately became a battleground. The Russians entered from the Caspian Sea and the Caucasus. Germans and Turks made their way into it from Iraq which at that time formed a part of the Turkish empire. Three armies were raised in Iran by the rival powers.

---

[2] The present number of members of the National Assembly is 130 and the Cabinet consists of twelve ministers.

The Cossacks were trained by Russian officers in the north, the gendarmerie under Swedish officers with pro-German feelings, and the South Persian Rifles by the British. The official Iranian army existed in name only. The tribes rose everywhere for looting the natives, and to receive bribes from the foreigners.

About the close of the war the Czarist regime in Russia was overthrown and the Bolsheviks rose to power. The Anglo-Russian Treaty of 1907, therefore, automatically stood dissolved. At the end of the war the British found the field clear for exercising sole control over Iran, which was achieved by the Anglo-Persian Agreement of 1919. The entire civil and military administration was to be controlled by them, as also all the commercial privileges, including the concession for building a railway from the Persian Gulf to Teheran.

Rise of Riza Shah Pahlevi

The Anglo-Persian agreement could become valid only on its ratification by the National Assembly. Luckily many of its members had enough patriotic pride and national spirit to resist this move to subject the country to foreign control despite Ahmad Shah's favourable inclination towards the Agreement. And when it was being pushed through the Assembly, Mullah Zia-ud-Din assumed power and called upon the Cossack brigade, under the command of Riza Khan, for support. The latter immediately responded to the call, marched on the capital at the head of a few thousand men, and overthrew the old, corrupt government. He became a war minister in the new cabinet in February 1921.

This move had its reaction on Russian policy. "The Soviet Government reversed their policy and renounced with one gesture all the privileges they had held so far: the Persian debt was cancelled, the Imperial Bank of Russia was turned over to the Persian Government, and the Julfa railway was ceded to Iran. At the same time the Russians evacuated the occupied provinces."[3] The new government of Iran forthwith rejected the Anglo-Persian Agreement, and the same day signed a fresh Russo-Persian Treaty. Riza Khan became Prime Minister in 1923, and set himself to the task of administration in right earnest. Heretofore the foreigners had dominated almost all the departments of the government. The finance department was under the Americans, customs under the Belgians, gendarmeries under the Swedes, education and justice under the French, while the English controlled the Imperial Bank of Iran and the Anglo-Persian Oil Company. Gradually and slowly he tried to replace the foreigners by Iranians, and by his faith and devotion showed that the welfare of the country was dearest to his heart. He managed to win over the majority in the National

[3] Haas: *Iran*, page 141.

Assembly to his side. At his instigation Ahmad Shah of the Kajar dynasty was deposed on 31 October 1925, and a provisional government with himself at its head was established. On 13 December 1925, the National Assembly unanimously offered the crown to Riza Khan and his male descendants. He assumed the title of Riza Shah Pahlevi.

Riza Shah belonged to an Iranian family of Mazandaran. He joined the Cossack brigade as a soldier at a young age, and rose to the supreme position by virtue of his valour, diplomacy and statesmanship. He was nearly fifty-four at the time of his accession. As he had lived a hard life, he was strong enough to undertake the heavy burdens involved in restoring a weak, disorderly and poor country to peace and strength. To achieve this object he turned his attention simultaneously in three directions: building up a strong central government and a new model army, developing industries and communications, and bringing about educational and social reforms.

He reorganised the army with the help of a French military mission. A large and well-equipped force was created with an efficient air force and a small navy in the Persian Gulf. He retained the entire administrative powers in his own hands, and appointed and dismissed his ministers at will. He then turned against the tribes, and ruthlessly reduced most of them to subjection. To a large extent they were disarmed and forced to convert their swords into ploughshares, leading a settled life on land. Thus were put down lawlessness and brigandage. Titles were abolished. The Shia clergy were deprived of their independence. The dervishes were forbidden in the streets. Pilgrimage to Najaf and Kerbela was discouraged. The display of *taziahs*, the passion performance of Shias, was abolished. The land and property dedicated to religious shrines were appropriated by the Government and spent on public welfare. For example, the revenues of the sanctuary of Imam Riza at Meshed were utilized for a hospital, water supply of the city and industrial schemes. The religious law or the 'Shara' was substituted by secular laws. Roads and railways were built, and many local industries were established. Numerous schools and colleges were opened, and elementary education was made compulsory. About one hundred students were sent abroad every year, preferably to French speaking countries—France, Switzerland and Belgium, and some to America, England and Germany. The emancipation of women began in 1927. In December 1928 the traditional turban and cap were banned and wearing of western dress was made compulsory. In 1931 a law was passed by which all marriages and divorces were to be registered with a civil official instead of a religious priest. In 1935 purdah was abolished. No woman could go out in veil. The shopkeepers, bus conductors and taxi drivers were ordered not to attend to a veiled woman. Women were recruited as teachers, typists, clerks and nurses. Polygamy and child marriage were greatly restricted by law. Such peace and justice prevailed in the country that an Armenian said: "This Shah has done miracles. We owe it to him that our women no longer wear the Chadar, for he has made life safe for them. A Moslem can no longer run away with a pretty girl and not be punished."[4] The new laws of Riza Shah gave protection to all women, whether Muslim or non-Muslim.

Foreign Policy

In the realm of foreign relations the reign of Riza Shah was without any striking events. Among the Great Powers, Iran's immediate neighbour, Russia, was extremely busy with her plans of reconstruction. Germany was struggling hard to regain her lost position. The British had changed their diplomacy towards Iran. They found that their interest would best be served by a strong, independent Iran, and so they were on the whole co-operating with Riza Shah. The new Shah's foreign policy was, however, assertive. Iran had become a member of the League of Nations in 1919. The system of capitulations by which foreigners residing in Iran were beyond the jurisdiction of Iranian courts and were to be judged by their own consuls, was abolished in 1928. In 1932 the Anglo-Iranian Oil Company was compelled to revise the concession and more favourable terms were secured for Iran. In 1937 Iran became a non-permanent member of the Council of the League of Nations. The same year by the Treaty of Saadabad, a pact of friendship, consultation and non-aggression was formed between Iran, Iraq, Turkey, and Afghanistan. In 1939, Riza Shah married his eldest son, Muhammad Riza Pahlevi, the crown prince, to Princess Fowzieh, sister of the King of Egypt, and thereby united two Muslim countries by matrimony.

Thus, at the outbreak of World War II, the position of Iran had remarkably improved from that of 1914. This quarter of a century found her changed from an old, static state to a new and modernised country. She had been saved from falling "into the hands of the British Empire or the U.S.S.R.", and was now absolutely independent, and free to choose her allies. But she preferred to remain neutral as in 1914, and, on 6 September 1939, declared her neutrality in the European conflict.

Military Strength

At this stage it may be pertinent to take stock of the military

[4] Hawkes, p. 130.

strength of Iran. The state maintained, besides the army, a small air force and navy, but quite inadequate for the defence requirements of the vast country, for a large military force was beyond the means of Iran to maintain. Besides, national character and tradition were largely responsible for the peaceful predilection of the people.

CHAPTER XXXV

Military Resources and Organisation

Army

Iran's manpower being rather low, her armed forces were not very strong. Military service was compulsory. It began at the age of twenty-one, and the obligation lasted for twenty-five years—two years of active service, four years of active army reserve, fourteen years of general reserve and five years of supplementary reserve. The law of conscription was passed by the Parliament in 1925, and was enforced in February 1926. In May 1927, the pay of the conscript was raised from 7 Krans to 31 Krans per mensem. In 1940 the Iranian army comprised 9 mixed divisions, 5 independent brigades and independent regiments and an independent mechanized brigade consisting of anti-aircraft, tank and mechanized infantry regiments. The strength of the active army was approximately 3,200 officers and 116,800 other ranks. On 15 July 1941, the total manpower of the army was computed at 126,400. Defence expenditure in 1937-38 was estimated at 309,408,000 *rials*. The army was equipped with modern arms and weapons and the cadets were trained at the Military Academy Teheran. Students were also sent to France and Germany for technical instruction and to Italy for naval training. There was an arsenal at Teheran. The number of tanks was 100.

The Tribal Strength

Riza Shah's policy of repression and disarmament of the tribes had resulted "in almost completely breaking up the old tribal organisations". As a consequence the tribal armament and the number of fighting men were considerably reduced, so that the fighting strength of the powerful Bakhtiari tribe was believed to have "decreased in the last 15 years from 30,000 to 2,000."[1]

The British Military Attache at Teheran estimated the tribal strength as follows:

(1) Bakhtiaris, about 2,000 rifles, leaderless, reported hostile to the British and in touch with the Germans.
(2) Kungalu, about 1,000 rifles, dispersed and unimportant.
(3) Arabs, several hundred rifles, disorganised.
(4) Qashgai, about 2,000 rifles, leaderless, in touch with German agents.

---
[1] Wavell to Quinan, 29 July 1941.

(5) Tangistanis, perhaps 800 to 1,000 rifles, no German contact, possibly friendly.
(6) Baluchis, about 1,000 rifles, some organisation, not very friendly.[a]

Air Force

Aerial transport in Iran began in 1927, and in 1935 a national service was started. The National Aero Club was established in 1939, and soon had 250,000 members on its rolls. Pilots for military aviation were trained at the Military Academy, Teheran. There were aerodromes at Tabriz, Teheran, Hamadan, Kermanshah, Gach Saran, Ganaweh, Isfahan, Ahwaz, Abadan, Jask, Shiraz and Bushire, and landing grounds at Bandar Asalu, Lingeh, Bandar Abbas, Basidu, Salagh (Qishm Island), Chahbar, Iranshahr and Khwash. Aviation fuel was available at all the aerodromes. Flying schools existed at Meshed and Ahwaz. There was an aircraft factory. The air force was equipped with modern aircraft, mostly Hawker and De Havilland, purchased from the United Kingdom.

The total estimated strength of the Iranian Air Force in October 1940 was believed to be 200,[b] including 25 Fighters, 100 General Purpose Aircraft, and 75 Training Aircraft.

The operational aircraft, majority of which were serviceable and fitted with bomb racks and gun mountings, consisted of the following types:

Hurricane	1 (believed indefinitely unserviceable).
Fury	24
Audax	63
Hind	34
Oxford	3
Total	125

The operational aircraft were located at the following aerodromes:—

	Fighters	General Purpose	Total
Teheran Area	25	54	79
Ahwaz	—	18	18
Tabriz	—	14	14
Meshed	—	14	14
Total	25	100	125

[a] Case No. 33692/A, Part I, p. 20, dated 8 June, 1941.
[b] File No. 601/9758/H.

The Iranian Air Force had been further strengthened by the addition of:
  (1) Curtiss P40 (Tomahawk)—9, all of which were lying in their crates at the Ahwaz railway station.
  (2) Rearwin Cloudstar Trainers—25, of which 16 were reported to be in use. There were 300 trained pilots to operate these aircraft, 610 mechanics and 130 students.[4]

Navy

In spite of the fact that Iran is bounded by sea on two sides, the Iranians did not develop a seafaring spirit even in modern times. The reason probably is that on the north the Caspian Sea was dominated by the Russians, and the Persian Gulf in the south was almost a British lake. But Riza Shah laid the foundation of the Iranian navy. It consisted of two gunboats of 950 tons with 4-inch guns, five sloops of 350 tons with 3-inch guns and several tugs and motor patrol boats for service in the Persian Gulf. In the Caspian Sea there was an imperial yacht and several motor patrol boats, mostly built in Italy.

The principal ports on the Persian Gulf were Bandar Abbas, Bushire, Bandar Shahpur and Khurramshahr, and on the Caspian Sea, Pahlevi, Astara, Babul, Bandar-i-Gaz and Bandar Shah.

Gendarmerie

In addition to the regular army there was the Gendarmerie, maintained for guarding the interior and the frontiers. This force was organised into battalions, each consisting of four to six companies. For discipline and administration the force was under the supervision of the General Officer Commanding the division, in whose area it was stationed. For police administration work, it came under the local civil authorities. These men were armed with old pattern rifles of various makes, Russian, French and some English carbines, but they were not provided with most modern weapons. The Gendarmerie was composed of 7 independent mixed regiments and 15 mixed battalions, forming a corps.

Disposition of Iranian Forces

The disposition of the Iranian forces in August 1941 was as follows:

AHWAZ—ABADAN—KHURRAMSHAHR AREA

Ahwaz

  1st Infantry Regiment (1st Division)
  2nd Infantry Regiment (1st Division)

---

[4] AVM D'Albiac's Despatch; file F. 830; File No. 601/9758/H.

11th Infantry Regiment (15th Division)
8 light tanks armed with machine-guns and light arms
8 medium tanks armed with 3.7-mm guns and machine-guns
10 armoured cars armed with 3.7-mm guns and 1 machine-gun

Susangurd

Detachment 1st Infantry Regiment
Detachment 2nd Infantry Regiment
Detachment 11th Infantry Regiment

Qasr

4 aircraft
10 armoured cars
70 motor cars
60 requisitioned lorries
600 horses
10 guns
30th Infantry Regiment (6th Division)

Dizful

19th Infantry Regiment (6th Division)

Shush

9th Cavalry Regiment (6th Division)

30 miles west of Hawizeh

Detachments of troops, probably remainder of the 6th Division, strength about 2,000

Qasbat

One company infantry ⎫
Two batteries artillery ⎬ 6th Division
Transport ⎭

Abadan

11th Infantry Regiment (6th Division)
13th Infantry Regiment (6th Division)
Gendarmerie (6th Division)

Khurramshahr

One company infantry (less detachment 60 men at Manyohi)

Khosroabad

One pack battery

Between Khurramshahr and Abadan
    Sloop *Palang*
    Sloop *Babr*
    Gunboat *Karkas*
    Gunboat *Simorg*
    Gunboat *Shahrukh*

About to arrive in the area
    ½ regiment artillery (2nd Division)
    105-mm Skoda guns (short)

SENNEH—KERMANSHAH AREA

Senneh
    Headquarters 5th Kurdistan Division
    6th Artillery Regiment (mixed)
    22nd Muzaffar Infantry Regiment
    8th (I) Battalion Gendarmerie
    W/T Section

Sakriz
    14th Cavalry Regiment
    6th (I) Battalion Gendarmerie

Baneh
    24th Infantry Regiment

Merivan
    23rd Infantry Regiment

Nausud
    7th (1) Battalion Gendarmerie

Kermanshah
    Headquarters 12th (Kermanshah) Division
    23rd Cavalry Regiment
    38th Infantry Regiment

Qasr-i-Shirin and Naft-i-Shah
    14th Artillery Regiment (mixed)
    39th Infantry Regiment less one battalion

Pusht-i-Koh
    One battalion 39th Infantry Regiment
    5th Regiment Gendarmerie

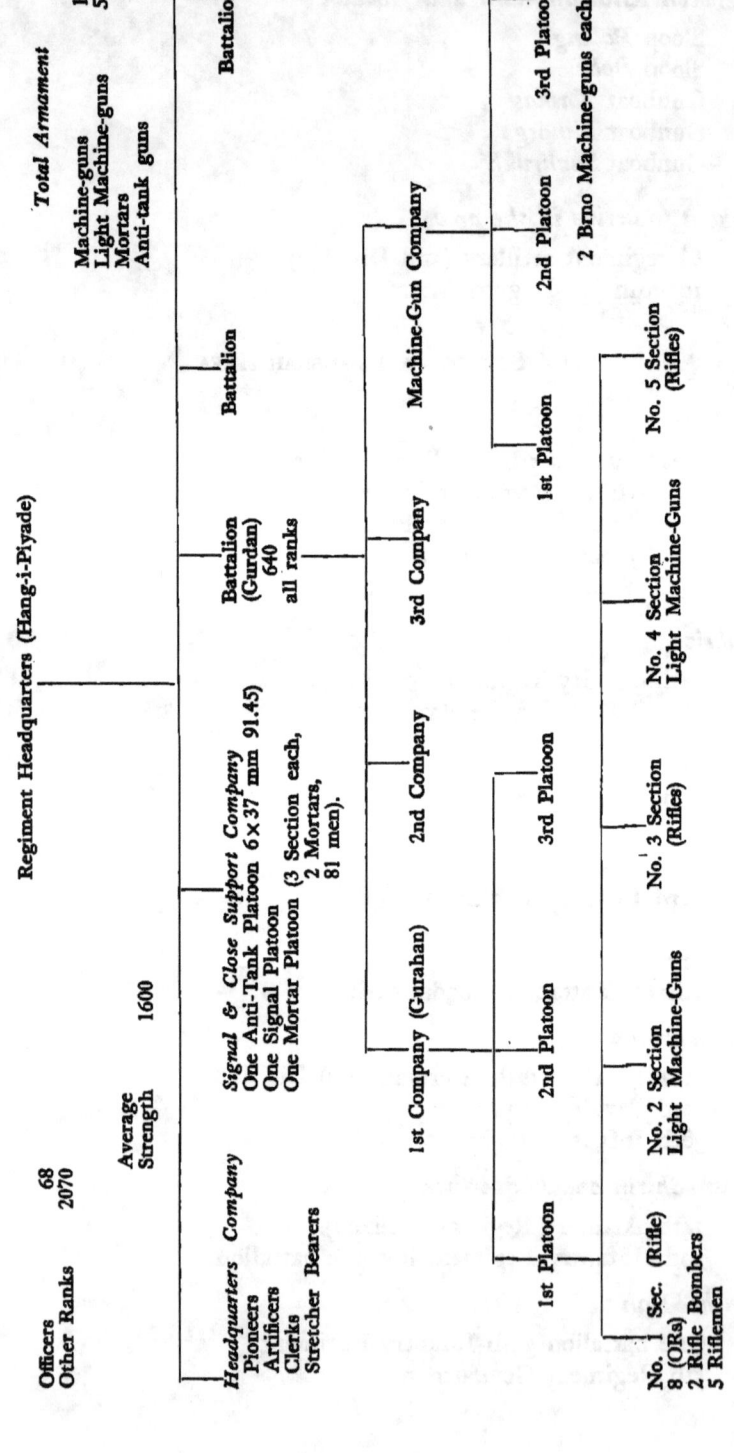

Throughout Area
   Detachments 8th Battalion Engineers

Reinforcements en route from Isfahan
   37th Infantry Regiment (13th Division)
   38th Artillery General Purpose

Reinforcements en route from Teheran
   (i) *From 1st Division (Teheran)*
       20th Infantry Regiment
       1st Artillery Regiment (Skoda 105 short)
       Batteries of mountain artillery.
   (ii) *From 2nd Division (Teheran)*
       6th Infantry Regiment
       21st Infantry Regiment
       1st Artillery Regiment (Skoda 105 short)
       Batteries of mountain artillery[5]

Organisation of a Cavalry Regiment (Hang-i-Savar)

The Iranian cavalry consisted of 22 regiments of horse and 3 regiments of camelry. The normal strength of a regiment was 720, all ranks, and its armament consisted of 8 machine-guns and 16 light automatics.

The following diagram shows the chain of command:

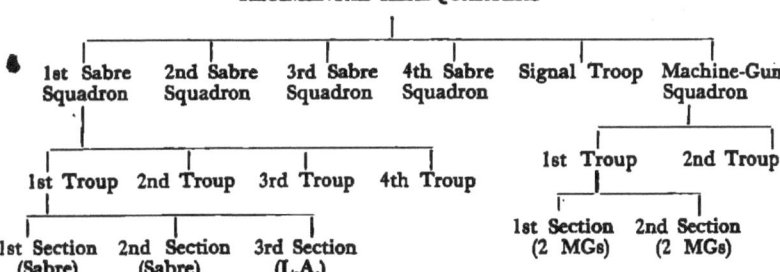

The Camel Regiments had similar organisation. All units were numbered and a few bore special names in addition.

Artillery Organisation

The Iranian artillery was organized into 94 four-gun batteries. The strength in personnel was 13,645 all ranks. Batteries were equipped as follows:—

[5] File 9758 and F. 830.

12 batteries equipped with skoda 105-mm guns (short)
18 batteries equipped with skoda 105-mm guns (long)
39 batteries equipped with Bofors 75-mm mountain field guns
6½ batteries equipped with Schneider 75-mm guns
4 batteries equipped with Schneider 75-mm guns
2 batteries equipped with Aboukoff 75-mm field guns
1 battery equipped with guns of British pattern
11½ batteries equipped with Bofors 75-mm anti-aircraft guns

The organisation of the artillery of the provincial divisions varied, but generally each had a regiment of three mountain batteries and 1 field battery. Six of anti-aircraft batteries formed part of the mechanized brigade and three were included in the 6th Khuzistan Division. Of the latter only one battery was in use, while the remainder were in store.

The guns of all mountain artillery batteries were carried on pack-mules while those of the mechanized brigade were drawn by Marmon Harrington tractors. The remainder of the artillery was horse-drawn.

The horse-drawn artillery of the Teheran garrison had heavy Hungarian horses which had been imported during recent years. The latest attempt to purchase more of these horses had failed and steps were being taken to collect locally-bred horses for the expansion of the artillery. It was doubtful if these could be procured locally in sufficient numbers.

Some coast defence artillery had been installed at places on the Caspian seaboard. The guns were probably 105-mm Skodas, but details of location were not available.[6]

UNITS EQUIPPED WITH A.F.Vs

General Organisation, Administration and Strength

All units equipped with armoured fighting vehicles and all mechanized units were organised into a mechanized brigade which formed part of the Teheran Central Garrison.

The organisation of this brigade was as follows:—

Headquarters

Four staff cars and one section of motor cyclists having sixteen 2-cylinder Harley Davidson motor cycles.

1st Regiment (anti-aircraft)

One battery	16 heavy 15-mm Besa machine-guns mounted on lorries with a crew of six.
Six batteries	75-mm Bofors anti-aircraft guns drawn by Marmon-Harrington tractors.

[6] File No. 601/233/WD.

2nd Regiment (armoured fighting vehicles)

One light tank battalion	50 Czecho-Moravska 3½-ton tanks armed with one light and one heavy machine-gun.
One medium tank battalion	50 Czecho-Moravska 7½-ton tanks armed with 3.7-mm gun and two machine-guns.
One armoured car battalion	19 Marmon Harrington (4-wheel drive) and 14 Marmon Harrington (6-wheel drive) armed with one 3.7-mm gun and two machine-guns and four Rolls Royce cars.[7]

3rd Regiment (Mechanized Infantry)

There were fifty armoured lorries, each carrying driver, relief driver, commander and 20 other ranks (infantry). Fifty motor cycle combinations of Belgian manufacture for the transport of machine-guns formed part of the 3rd Regiment. One Brno light automatic was mounted in front of the side-car. This was believed to be a temporary measure pending the arrival of the Browning Machine-gun.

Artillery Regiment

6 × 4 gun batteries—Bofors 105-mm (long).
The estimated strengths of the units were as follows:

1st Regiment	345
2nd Regiment	650
3rd Regiment	1,100

Tanks

The tanks were seldom seen except on the day of the Annual Review, when the brigade was smartly turned out. The personnel were indifferently trained and the tanks were badly driven across country, being frequently stalled at obstacles. A.F.V. personnel wore black leather jackets and a form of crash helmet. There were no heavy tank units. There was one battalion of medium tanks, consisting of fifty 7½-ton Czecho-Moravska tanks. There was one battalion of light tanks, which consisted of fifty 3½-ton Czecho-Moravska tanks. The tanks were, thus, of the following two types only:

	Weight tons	guns	M.Gs.	L.As.	Crew
Medium tanks—					
Czecho-Moravska	7½	1	2	—	3
Light tanks—					
Czecho-Moravska	3½	—	1	1	2

[7] *Ibid.*

Armoured Car Units

There was one battalion of 4 Rolls Royce and 33 Marmon-Harrington armoured cars (nineteen 4-wheel drive and fourteen 6-wheel drive).

Types of Armoured Cars

  (a) Rolls Royce (1919) equipped with one machine-gun and one light automatic.
  (b) Marmon-Harrington 4-wheel drive 12 speed equipped with one 37-mm gun and one machine-gun carrier.

Ammunition

Type of vehicle	37-mm Shell	MG. Ammn.	L.A. Ammn.	Remarks
Medium tanks—				
Czecho-Moravska	200	4,800	—	On each tank.
Light tanks—				
Czecho-Moravska	—	4,800	—	On each tank.
Marmon-Harrington armoured car	50	1,500	1,500	On each car.[a]

Efficiency and Morale

The Shah of Iran by his personal efforts had considerably raised the standard of efficiency of the Iranian troops and created loyalty of the army to the country and king; but he was so much handicapped for want of funds and the proper national spirit in the country that he could not achieve his object to the fullest degree. The general impression was that the morale and standard of training of the Iranian Army was low. A weekly Intelligence Summary, for the period ending 12 August 1941, stated that "the morale amongst officers and men is being very bad, the maintenance of tank units poor, and the foreign mechanics employed fully capable of deliberate sabotage. A shortage of ammunition for field guns was also reported, and that the supply then in hand was old and not of good quality." Another later report said that the defence of Iran "depended on demoralised modern army".

[a] 601/233/WD.

CHAPTER XXXVI

Events Leading to the Action

Foreign Relations

Riza Shah had formed ambitious schemes for the development of trade and industries of Iran, but this object was difficult to achieve without foreign assistance. Both Russia and Great Britain, though anxious to retain their influence in this country, offered hard terms in view of the weak financial resources of Iran. Nazi Germany was, however, prepared to offer trade and industrial facilities. Riza Shah in his eagerness to seek economic assistance from abroad turned to Germany, and was deeply impressed by the German offer of economic and financial advantages, and the courtesy and consideration extended to him. Consequently the major portion of Iran's trade was, immediately before the war, carried on with Germany. The trade figures for the year ending 20 March 1941, reveal this state of affairs:[1]

Germany	813,714,000 Rials
Russia	2,00,803,000 Rials
U.S.A. ...	... 196,641,000 Rials

In the scheme of industrialisation also Germany occupied the first place, and a large number of German experts, engineers and technicians, were employed.

On the other hand, Iran's relations with Great Britain were deteriorating. The spirit of nationalism engendered feelings of indignation against foreign exploitation. As a result, in 1932, the concessions granted to the Imperial Airways for the use of Bushire aerodrome were cancelled and they had to change their routes. The same year the Anglo-Iranian Oil Company (A.I.O.C.) was threatened with the cancellation of its concession, and it had to agree to a curtailment of its privileges. Besides, the Shah revived his long-standing claim on the Bahrein Islands controlled by the United Kingdom.

After the outbreak of the war in September 1939, Riza Shah adopted a policy of 'strict neutrality' and it was believed that he would not 'willingly abandon this attitude'.[2] A British despatch of 3 April 1940, stated that 'the Shah is tending to show a more friendly attitude towards the British Empire .... The Shah during his recent visit to Abadan actually sat down to tea at the General

[1] Hamzavi: *Persia and the Powers.*
[2] Report on a reconnaissance, carried out in April 1940 for Trout Plan.

Manager's House and conversed freely with the A.I.O.C. officials present. This was apparently an unprecedented act of grace'.[3]

British policy towards Iran had been conditioned by the trend of Russo-Iranian relations which were governed by the Treaty of 1921. One of its clauses authorised Russian forces to enter northern Iran if the troops of any third power made their way into southern Iran. Great Britain, therefore, scrupulously avoided giving any pretext to Russia to send her forces into the northern parts of the country. The German attack on Russia in June 1941, however, completely changed the situation. The main problem now was to organize the despatch of supplies to Russia, by using Persia as a channel for this purpose.[4] "Iran was not in a position to deny the route. The inability of Persia to resist Russian and British demands was well recognised, and it was therefore considered advisable in some (Persian) quarters to come to some agreement in regard to payment for the use of the railways and to guarantee eventual evacuation, rather than to offer resistance which could only be weak."[5] Economic difficulties, military weakness and bureaucratic inefficiency contributed to the general dissatisfaction and magnified the feebleness of possible resistance.

German Agents

At the moment that the Allies had need of Iran, the country had been the haunt of German agents whose number was variously estimated. A report of May 1940 stated that there were "700 resident Germans supported by some 2,000 tourists" including a number of German women who were married to British and Iranian staff of the Anglo-Iranian Oil Company.[6] A Belgian, who had spent six years in Teheran in the International Standard Electrical Corporation and had been employed in Belgian Legation since 1940, put it at 2,000, saying that "the German hold on communication system was complete."[7] Sir Reader Bullard, the British Minister at Teheran, thought it was 3,000, including women and children, of whom the number of men was about 1,000. The local papers gave the number as 1,690, employed in railways and industry. In addition there were doctors, merchants, teachers and employees in the service of certain companies. Lord Wavell's despatch to Lt-General Quinan, dated 29 July 1941, assessed the number of Germans in Iran to be "two to three thousand persons, all of whom may be counted as active fifth-columnists." An operation order of the Iraq Command, dated

---

[3] File 601/8180/H.
[4] 601/9758/H.
[5] Ibid.
[6] File No. 518.
[7] File No. 708, Serial 6.

8 August 1941, stated the number of Germans in Iran as "approximately 2,500."[8] On 22 August 1941, the Iranian Minister in Washington informed the press that the number of Germans in Iran did not exceed 700, and many of them had been there long before the outbreak of the war. Their number had been further strengthened by the German mission from Ankara and by the infiltration of some German malcontents from Iraq.[9]

Sir Reader Bullard had particular objection to three Germans, a doctor at Kermanshah, the Director of Technical School at Kerman, and a lecturer in the Agricultural College at Kerej, who formed centres of Nazi propaganda. He also did not like Germans working in arms factories, and on the railways.

Sir Reader Bullard's Protest

Sir R. Bullard, therefore, pressed upon the Iranian Government the necessity of taking proper steps against German activities in that country. On 1 July 1941, he had an interview with the Iranian Prime Minister and asked him to immobilise German ships at Bandar Shahpur by removing either the crews or essential parts of the machinery. The Prime Minister appeared to be vague about details and Bullard was told that the question would be examined. Bullard's impression was that the Prime Minister knew about the existence of the fifth column activities of the Germans, "but he is hampered by Shah's policy of industrial development which has filled Iran with Germans."[10] Bullard demanded that four-fifths of the Germans in the country must be expelled immediately.

Views of the Governor-General of India

The Government of India felt deeply concerned about the political situation in Iran. The reason was that the defences of Iraq and Iran were closely bound up with the external defence of India, and "the bulk of the troops were to be provided and maintained by India through the Persian Gulf line of communication". The Governor-General of India, therefore, exercised great influence in determining the British policy towards Iran, and was repeatedly pressing the United Kingdom Government to take strong and urgent action to expel German agents and eliminate German influence from that country. In a despatch to the Secretary of State for India, dated 9 July 1941, he wrote: "In our view positive policy to secure elimination of enemy centres in Iran is a matter of most vital importance." He also opposed the delivery of aircraft to Iran, which might result in making that country "considerably better equipped

[8] File No. 601/9758/H.
[9] File 830 Serial 7.
[10] File No. 708.

in air than India herself which at present has no fighters at all."[11] On 16 July, he again made a vehement protest: "We wish to protest in strongest terms against the apparent failure in spite of assurance given in your telegram No. 8169 of 15 July even to take into account our considered representations regarding policy in a country where we are most directly interested, and from which most dangerous threat to India's security may well develop."[12] To secure his object, the Governor-General advocated the expulsion of Germans. On 20 July he reiterated the view that "we do not believe that general public of Iran whose sentiments of national loyalty are still ill developed would long sustain deprival of items such as sugar, tea, piecegoods and cheap bazar articles, particularly if they could be made to understand that restoration of supplies depended solely on expulsion of German technicians and tourists."[13]

Iranian Prime Minister's Reply

On 27 July 1941, the Iranian Prime Minister informed Sir R. Bullard that to send away four-fifths of Germans would be contrary to their treaty with Germany and to their policy of neutrality. He also said that to ask such a thing from the Government of Iran was prejudicial to their sovereignty and declared that his government was conscious of the need for vigilance and they were doing their best to reduce the number of Germans. He supplied some details of the action then contemplated or taken. According to him "six Germans whose residence permits had expired, had been ordered to leave; the State Department would take over the radio station so that the two[14] Germans could leave; three Germans would leave from Pahlevi; ten more Germans would leave in ten days' time; efforts were being made to replace Germans by Iranians in Government and private factories as far as possible; at Tabriz strict orders had been issued for listing every German and the Director of Police had been summoned to Teheran; a gunboat had been posted at Bandar Shahpur and enemy vessels could not move." Sir R. Bullard repeated his request for the expulsion of the three Germans from Kermanshah, Kerman and Kerej, who, in his opinion, were particularly dangerous. The Prime Minister assured him that he was doing everything he could to find some jurisdiction for driving out two of them, and asked for ten days' time. But the British Ambassador did not regard these measures quite adequate.[15]

[11] File No. 830, serial 1.
[12] *Ibid*, serial 7.
[13] *Ibid*, serial 17.
[14] In 1940 secret agents of whom the most notable were Franz Mayer and Berthold Schaltze, were appointed to organise it.
[15] File No. 830, serial 52.

Pacification Measures by Iran

The Government of Iran had not opposed the British demand for the expulsion of Germans from the country; only they desired to adopt a cautious policy which would be in conformity with their attitude of neutrality and rights of a sovereign state. The British, on the other hand, were losing all patience for fear of a sudden German penetration into Iran or an unexpected change in the situation in that country. The Iranian Government took steps to satisfy the United Kingdom as much as possible. It was noted "that the Shah has also lately taken some inadequate steps to curb the influence of the highly organised German colony in his country."[16] Moreover information was received before 15 July that "the German women were leaving for Turkey."[17] Orders for the arrest of all Germans and German agents in the area of the Anglo-Iranian oilfields and refineries were reported to have been issued. On 11 August, Sir R. Bullard conveyed his opinion to the Secretary of State for Foreign Affairs that the Germans were "so closely watched by Iranian authorities" that "I do not think they could give serious trouble."[18]

On the same day the Secretary of State for India sent the following message to the Governor-General of India: "Not many Germans have left I believe, but there is no doubt that supervision by authorities is now very close. German archaeologist Eilers has been summoned from Isfahan and is closely watched there. Dossiers of all Germans are being re-examined by Teheran police. Police in oil area have orders to apprehend any German found there. Acting Minister for Foreign Affairs states that German residents in Tabriz number only 34 and this is confirmed by British Bank·Manager, Mr. Turner, who has just returned from Tabriz."[19]

The Governor-General, however, did not agree with these views. He severely criticised this attitude, saying it "gives us impression that Persians believe themselves to have Bullard in their pocket." He expressed the hope that "local complacency will not be permitted to divert H.M.G. from pressing home their demands on Persia."[20]

As regards refugees from Iraq who were regarded as odious by the British Government as the Germans, Sir R. Bullard sent to London on 12 August a message which stated that the Government of Iran had ordered Yunus Sabhawi and several other Iraqi refugees to leave Teheran for Zinjan. Others were also to be sent to

---

[16] No. 601/8186/H.
[17] No. 601/9758/H. Weekly Intelligence Summary No. 22 of 15 July 1941.
[18] File No. 830, serial No. 18; Weekly Intelligence Summary No. 26 of 12 August 1941.
[19] File No. 890, serial No. 18.
[20] *Ibid*, serial No. 23.

provincial towns. In his opinion, the "removal of reactionaries from Teheran is the first step in the right direction."[21]

This obdurate British attitude may be explained by the fear of sabotage by the Germans particularly in the Anglo-Iranian Oil Company's refineries at Abadan and Kermanshah and the oilfields in Khuzistan and at Naft-i-Shah. The Abadan refinery, the second largest in the world, was the most important as it supplied a large quantity of aviation fuel. Regarding its importance a despatch stated, "our only vital interest in Iran is the oilfields" and the protection of the oil refinery was a task "of the very highest importance." Hence it was naturally felt that unless early steps were taken to rid Iran of increasing Nazi influence, the Germans by occupying the country might not only cut the lines of supply to Russia and deprive the Allies of the Middle East oil, but also threaten the rear of the Russian army as well as endanger the safety of India and of the vital lines of communication.[22]

Attitude of the Neighbouring Muslim Countries

It was desirable for the British to take into account the attitude of the neighbouring Muslim countries, particularly members of the Saadabad Pact of 1937, in case military action was considered necessary against Iran. Of these, Afghanistan was friendly to Great Britain and Iraq was under British occupation. As regards Turkey, there was some criticism against the Shah's policy in the Turkish press; but the Turkish Ambassador in London stressed, on the Secretary of State for Foreign Affairs, the need for "attempting to seek collaboration of Shah. He hoped we should try to win him to our side."[23] Of the remaining countries Egypt was almost hostile to Iran. Hence it was clear that the Allied military action in Iran would not rouse any opposition in the Muslim countries, particularly in those which had previously entered into a treaty of alliance with Iran.

While representations were being made at Teheran and the Government of India was insisting on the expulsion of Germans from Iran, His Majesty's Government in the United Kingdom was considering the policy which might be adopted in this respect. On 22 July 1941, General Headquarters, India, sent a signal to Lieutenant-General Quinan, General Officer Commanding British and Indian troops, in the area, to the effect that the War Cabinet was contemplating application of pressure on Iran with Soviet co-operation with the object of compelling the Iranian Government to expel all Germans and Italians from their country. He was further asked

---

[21] *Ibid*, serial No. 41
[22] File No. 601/8181/H.
[23] *Ibid*, serial No. 36.

to be in a state of readiness to secure, as far as possible without any damage, the oil refinery at Abadan, and to occupy Naft-i-Shah and the Khuzistan oilfields. The plans for these operations had already been prepared. On 24 July intimation was received that the British Government had approved of the plan to exert Anglo-Soviet diplomatic pressure backed by a show of force. The joint Anglo-Soviet note to the Iranian Government was to be presented on 12 August, and, meanwhile, Lieutenant-General Quinan was to complete the preliminary concentration of a striking force near the Iranian frontier in the Basra area. For this purpose a boat bridge was to be constructed at Basra.

A rough plan of operations was drawn up. Forces were to remain in readiness to move into Iran in the second week of August, but the concentration of troops in the Basra area was not to be effected till further orders. The Russians were to make a simultaneous advance into northern Iran.[24]

On 8 August, Lt.-General Quinan submitted the following outline plan for action:

Army

(a) *South-West Iran*

The 8th Indian Division which was to move from Kirkuk to Basra was to be responsible for:

(i) Capture of Abadan Refinery at first light on the D 1 day by the 24th Indian Infantry Brigade Group, less one battalion, moving by the river Shatt-al-Arab and supported by the Royal Navy.

(ii) Taking of the Khurramshahr by one battalion of the 24th Indian Infantry Brigade, supported by one squadron Guides Cavalry, moving by land from Tanuma (opposite Basra).

(iii) Simultaneous advance by the 25th Indian Infantry Brigade Group and the 13th Lancers from Tanuma to Ahwaz, thence to Haft Khel oilfields with detachments to Kut Abdullah and Dorquain pumping stations.

(iv) All moves were to be supported by the Royal Air Force.

(b) *West Iran*

The 2nd Armoured Brigade was to be responsible for:

(i) Simultaneous seizure of Naft-i-Shah and Qasr-i-Shirin.

(ii) After capturing Naft-i-Shah advance was to be made to Gilan and Shahabad, preparatory to a general march on Kermanshah. The 9th Armoured Brigade was to participate in the latter move.

(c) Simultaneous capture of the port Bandar Shahpur, by two

[24] File No. 830, serial No. 40.

companies of the 3rd Battalion 10th Baluch Regiment, embarked on H.M.A.S. *Kanimbla*.

Lt.-General Quinan decided to place all the operations in the south under Major-General C. O. Harvey, Commander 8th Indian Division. Operations in the west were placed under Brigadier J. A. Aizlewood, Commander, the 2nd Indian Armoured Brigade, whose force was to consist of the 2nd Indian Armoured Brigade Group (less two regiments), two Indian infantry battalions and one medium battery.

Naval

The Senior Naval Officer, Persian Gulf, was given command of Naval operations. He proposed to carry the 24th Indian Infantry Brigade Group in a flotilla to Abadan, and seize shipping at Khurramshahr and Bandar Shahpur.

Air

The role of the Royal Air Force in all these operations was as follows:

(*i*) Direct support of the military and naval operations in the Abadan area and at Naft-i-Shah.

(*ii*) Strategical leaflet dropping and bombing operations against military objectives in Iran.

Memorandum Presented to the Government of Iran

Under instructions from the British Government, Sir R. Bullard presented a memorandum to the Government of Iran on the afternoon of 17 August 1941, a summary of which is given below:—[25]

"The Imperial Iranian Government on many occasions have affirmed their desire to maintain an attitude of most scrupulous neutrality; the British Government fully endorse this policy; they have no designs against Iran's political independence; their sincere desire is to maintain the policy of friendship and co-operation; as long as January last they brought to the notice of the Iranian authorities their grave concern in regard to excessively large number of German nationals who have been permitted to reside in Iran; since that date they have repeatedly warned Iranian Government of the potential dangers arising from activities of these Germans and asked for effecting a drastic reduction in their numbers; towards the end of July they instructed their representative at Teheran again to impress upon Iran Government the utmost gravity and urgency of the matter; Iran Government appear to recognise in principle the wisdom of our advice, but the number of Germans who have left the country is very small; they now wish to repeat in most formal and emphatic

---

[25] Summary of the memorandum—File No. 830, serial No. 53

manner their recommendation that Germans remaining in Iran should be required to leave the country without any further delay; if Iran should wish to retain temporarily a few German technicians employed in connection with Iran's industrialization projects, a complete list showing their names and the exact nature of their work should be communicated to their representatives at Teheran; they can endeavour to find suitably qualified British or neutral experts to replace German technicians; as regards the remaining Germans they should be kept closely informed of dates of their departure; no further Germans should be permitted to arrive in Iran; none of the German technicians to be retained should be employed on work connected with Iran-Syria communications, e.g. railways, roads, telephones, telegraphs and wireless; the German technicians to be retained should be kept under strict surveillance and their movements should be restricted; the activities of refugees who fled from Iraq should be strictly controlled."

No time limit was inserted in the memorandum as it was not desired to give it the character of an ultimatum. Sir R. Bullard was instructed to explain it orally that the reduction of 80 per cent asked for was to be effected by 31 August.[26]

A similar note was presented by the Soviet Ambassador on behalf of his Government on the same day.

The Iranian Replies

On 18 August, the Acting Minister for Foreign Affairs told Sir Reader that his Government was doing what they wanted "but in accordance with our own programme." He informed him that more than thirty Germans had left in three weeks, that greater results would follow in a week or two, and that the following week Mayer Gamotta, and Eilers would be sent away.[27] Again on 20 August, the Acting Minister for Foreign Affairs gave to Sir R. Bullard the following oral reply: "Three Germans mentioned in the memorandum, to leave within a week; at least 100 Germans to leave within a month from that day; thereafter elimination to be accelerated on basis of schemes being prepared in all ministries; no lists to be furnished but he might give him now and then names and jobs of Germans who had left; the Germans allowed to stay would be closely watched."[28]

The British Ambassador expressed his disapprobation at this reply. He criticised the expulsion of 100 Germans only as against 550 asked for, and he declared that lists were essential so that they might know exactly who had gone.

[26] File No. 830, serial No. 34.
[27] File No. 830, Serial No. 75.
[28] *Ibid*, Serial No. 83.

On 21 August, the written reply of the Government of Iran was handed to Sir R. Bullard. This was supplied in Persian only, and throughout the word foreigners was mentioned instead of Germans. The substance of this communication was that: "The Imperial Government was extremely glad at the declaration by H.M's Government of their intention to maintain friendly relations and at their confirmation of Iran's policy of neutrality; nothing had occurred to arouse anxiety about the residence of foreigners who were strictly controlled; H.M's Government would refrain from raising any question which might prejudice Imperial Government's policy of neutrality; foreigners in Government establishments who were no longer required or who could be replaced by Iranians, and other foreigners who had no special employment and whose presence was not necessary would leave the country; the number of foreigners in Iran had lately been specially reduced and their number would soon show a remarkable diminution; determination of superintendence and other minor matters of detail were the affairs of the Imperial Government who would take whatever steps they considered necessary; in respect of nationals of other states the Imperial Government could not take steps incompatible with their engagements and contrary to their treaties and which would lead to abandonment of their neutral course; they were ready to carry out any plan that they might consider necessary for safety of their country and protection of the legitimate rights of their neighbours, but they could not accept any proposal which was contrary to their policy of neutrality, or to their rights of sovereignty."[29]

A reply in similar terms was handed over to the Soviet Ambassador.

This reply to their memorandum was considered unsatisfactory. In the view of the Allies the presence of so many Germans in Iran constituted a grave menace to the Russian oilfields in the Caucasus, to the oilfields of the Anglo-Iranian Oil Company, and to the security of Syria, Iraq and Iran. They, therefore, decided to take a joint military action on 22 August, without presenting an ultimatum. But the D day was postponed to 0410 hours on 25 August, to enable the Russian forces to take simultaneous action from the north.

The Soviet and British Notes about Invasion

Immediately after the opening of the operations on the morning of 25 August 1941, Sir Reader Bullard and Mr. Smirnov, his Soviet colleague, presented to the Prime Minister of Iran two notes from their respective Governments. The substance of the Soviet note was: "The Soviet Government, guided by feelings of friendship for the Iranian people and by respect for the sove-

[29] File 830, Serial No. 100.

reignty of Iran, has always conducted a friendly policy; but German agents who penetrated into important and official positions in more than 50 Iranian institutions were trying to incite the peaceful Iranian people against the Soviet Union; German agents have arms and munition dumps at their disposal at different places in Iran, particularly in the neighbourhood of Migani; under cover of hunting they have created near Teheran a military training course for their accomplices; camouflaged as technicians and engineers, 56 German spies penetrated the Iranian war industry; since the invasion of the Soviet Union by Germany the Soviet Government has three times, on 26 June, 19 July and 17 August, drawn the attention of the Iranian Government to the danger threatening her from the espionage activity of the German agents in Iran; unfortunately, the Iranian Government declined to take appropriate measures and, in consequence, the Soviet Government has itself been forced to take the necessary measures and to avail itself of the right granted to it by the Russo-Persian Treaty of 1921 to despatch troops temporarily into Northern Iranian territory for the purpose of self-defence; these measures are in no way directed against the people, or the territorial integrity, or national independence of Iran, but solely against the danger created by the hostile activities of Germans in Iran."[30] The British note was similarly worded. It said: "During the past months His Majesty's Government have repeatedly warned the Iranian Government of the potential dangers arising from the presence in Iran of an excessively large German colony; the underground measures of Germans constitute a serious danger for the Iranian Government as well as for the British interests in Iran, India and Iraq; the British representations made at Teheran for many months past had remained without effect; towards the middle of July it was again pressed upon the Government of Iran as a matter of utmost urgency and gravity; the Iranian Government's reply showed that they were not prepared to give adequate satisfaction to their joint recommendations; it was clear that further friendly representations to the Iranian Government would serve no useful purpose, and that His Majesty's Government and the Soviet Government must have recourse to other measures to safeguard their essential interests; these measures would in no way be directed against the Iranian people and the independence and territorial integrity of Iran, but solely against the attempts of the Axis Powers to establish their control of Iran."[31]

Interview with Riza Shah

Just after the presentation of their notes to the Iranian Prime

[30] Hammerton and Gwynn: *The Second Great War*.
[31] *Ibid.*

Minister, the representatives of Great Britain and Russia were summoned by Riza Shah for an interview. Sir R. Bullard has given his impressions to the effect that: "The Shah looked old and rather feeble. We both gained impression he was taken aback by invasion, because he had supposed that everything was doing nicely, and we saw clearly that he had not been kept fully informed by his Ministers. . . . We spent much time in giving him information about the German menace in Iran and much of it seemed to be new to him. . . . Shah asked whether Great Britain and Russia were at war with Iran. I recalled passage in my communication of today 'these measures will in no way be directed against Iranian people.' "[32]

The decision to launch a joint military campaign by the British and Soviet Governments was actuated by the necessity of purging Iran of German influence and the reluctance of the Shah's government in taking action against the German nationals. The motive, therefore, was one of exerting pressure, and no hostility was involved against the people of that land. This factor determined the character and weight of the campaign, if campaign it may be called. The object was to impress the Shah and his government with the immense superiority of the armed might of the Allies and their keenness to employ it, when necessary, so that the purpose may be achieved speedily without shedding unnecessary blood. The plan of operations fully reflected this object.

---

[32] F. 694; No. 56032/MO4, Vol. II, Serial No. 200.

CHAPTER XXXVII

The Allied Plans

The Combined Plan

The combined plan of the Allies was carefully concerted between the Russian and British commanders. According to this, a simultaneous invasion of Iran was to take place from two sides—the northwest and south-west. The invasion from the north-west was the responsibility of the Russian armed forces; and General Novikov, their commander, was to send two strong mechanised columns: one down to the shore of the Caspian Sea moving on Kazvin, and the other crossing the frontier further to the west so as to converge upon Tabriz, and, after occupying points around lake Urmia, to advance upon Kazvin, as a preliminary to a combined attack upon Teheran, if it became necessary. On the other side, the British plan also was to advance in two separate columns, one against the oilfields on the western frontier near Khanakin and the other against the oilfields and ports of the south-west. The British forces were to be based on Khanakin and Basra respectively. Both the British and the Russian forces were ultimately to march against Teheran. The possession and control of the oil wells of the Anglo-Iranian Oil Company at Abadan was the primary consideration of the south-western operations, as possession of the oil resources was essential to the war effort of the United Kingdom. The Anglo-Iranian Oil Company had control over the oil producing area of the south-west (Khuzistan) and owned the Abadan refinery.

The local population of Khuzistan was composed of Iranians and about 200,000 Arabs attracted to the area by prospects of finding regular employment with the Oil Company. The population was comparatively more prosperous than in other parts of the country. But the intelligence reports and observations of foreign travellers indicated that the Arabs were in a state of unrest on account of the Iranian Government's policy of centralisation. The primitive tribal system was disintegrating and was being replaced by Iranian bureaucracy controlled from Teheran. It was therefore expected that the disaffected elements of Khuzistan would rather welcome the occupation of the area by British troops, if only as a corollary of being anti-Iranian. They respected the A.I.O.C. as a regular source of income, felt no hatred towards the Europeans, and disliked the Iranian Government's efforts to bring them under its effective control.

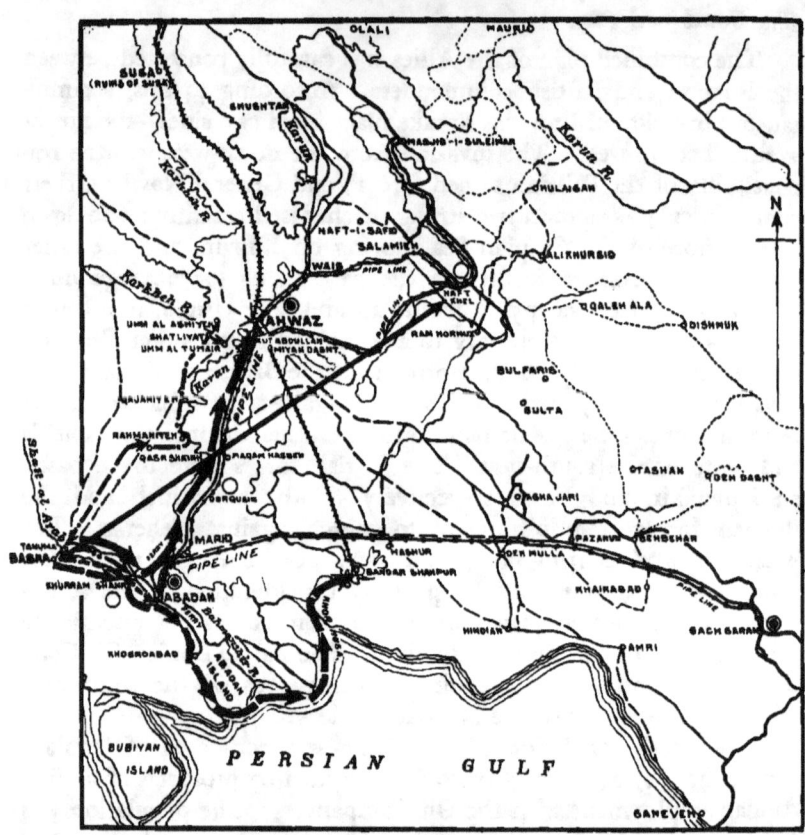

The British Plan of Operations in Khuzistan

The object of the British operations, as stated earlier, was to capture the oilfields area including the refinery and to push the Iranian troops away from the Gulf area. The 8th Indian Division under the command of Major-General Harvey was entrusted with this task. For this purpose the division was to concentrate at Basra from where the operations were to be launched on D1 day which, it was thought, would be in the second week of August. The whole scheme was given the name "Countenance." It was also arranged that if the seizure of the oil refinery at Abadan became necessary before the 8th Indian Division was concentrated at Basra, another smaller scheme called "Dover" would be put into operation as a part of the overall scheme "Countenance".

At the time when Major-General Harvey received orders—on 29 July 1941—to move his headquarters from Kirkuk to Basra in order to be ready to move his division into Iran, the 8th Indian Division consisted only of the 18th Indian Infantry Brigade, 11th Field Regiment and 7th Field Company Bengal Sappers and Miners. Other troops were to be collected from all over Iraq and certain portions of the 18th Indian Infantry Brigade had yet to arrive from India to complete a composite division. However, the troops started arriving in Basra from 5 August, and the whole division was concentrated at that place by 12 August, except for certain units which arrived from India on 23 August. After 12 August, when the division was concentrated at Basra, the smaller plan, Dover—with the limited object of capturing the refinery—was merged into the overall scheme, Countenance. The division now had under it the 18th, 24th and 25th Indian Infantry Brigades.

The original plan of Major-General Harvey was to make a surprise attack on D1 day simultaneously on Abadan, Khurramshahr and Ahwaz. But as the D1 day was postponed several times, and the concentration of the 8th Indian Division was completed by 12 August, the chances of achieving any measure of surprise were lost. In fact, the Iranian Government began to send reinforcements into Khuzistan. Some slight changes in the original plan were therefore made; and when definite orders came that operations were to begin on the night of 24/25 August, the plan of operations as finally adopted was as under.

The 24th Indian Infantry Brigade Group (less one battalion) transported down the Shatt-al-Arab from Basra in ships, motor launches and barges, etc. was to effect a landing at 0410 hours in the Braim Creek and on the jetties on the water front near the Abadan refinery which it was to capture. British ships were to seize or sink the Iranian sloops at anchorage. Two sections field artillery were to support them from the right bank of the Shatt-al-Arab at

Siba, and a third section field artillery and two 3·7" Howitzers were to follow the brigade down the river.

The 18th Indian Infantry Brigade (less one battalion) with one battalion of the 24th Indian Infantry Brigade, a squadron of Guides Cavalry (armoured wheeled carriers), and a battery of field artillery were to move from Tanuma, opposite Basra, to Khurramshahr, to mop up the opposition to the north and east and then establish a bridgehead across the river Karun, north of the Bahmanshir creek. The Royal Navy was to capture or sink the Iranian naval sloops and gunboats at their anchorage in the Karun river or at their naval base, and with the assistance of a small detachment of land forces, seize the naval station and barracks on the eastern bank of the Karun.

The 25th Indian Infantry Brigade with 13th Lancers (armoured cars) was to move to Qasr Shaikh, and to round up the Iranian forces located in that area, and then protect the northern flank of the 18th Indian Infantry Brigade.

One company of the 3rd Battalion, 10th Baluch Regiment, was to fly in six Valentias to Haft Khel with the object of protecting the oilfields and escorting the British and Indian women and children from the main fields at Masjid-i-Suleiman to Haft Khel.

The naval force with two companies of the 3rd Battalion, 10th Baluch Regiment, on board the armed merchant cruiser H.M.A.S. *Kanimbla*, was to capture or sink five German and three Italian merchantmen lying at anchor at Bandar Shahpur, and also the Iranian naval sloop and gunboats guarding these ships, and then to hold the port.

The 18th and 25th Indian Infantry Brigades, after finishing the tasks first allotted to them, were to advance on Ahwaz along the eastern and western banks of the river Karun, respectively. The 24th Indian Infantry Brigade after leaving one battalion as garrison at Abadan was to come into divisional reserve at Khurramshahr.

The Royal Air Force was to perform the following duties:—
 (*i*) to prevent hostile bombing of Abadan refinery;
 (*ii*) to support the 24th, 18th and the 25th Indian Infantry Brigades in their respective areas;
 (*iii*) to have air reconnaissance of naval operations at Bandar Shahpur, and Ahwaz area;
 (iv) to carry troops to Haft Khel oilfields.

In the event of Iranian opposition the targets were defined as:—
 (*a*) wherever 'T' was displayed by ground troops;
 (*b*) anti-aircraft guns immediately south of Bahmanshir ferry;
 (*c*) army barracks at Abadan;
 (*d*) naval barracks on the south bank of the river Karun at Khurramshahr;

(e) Iranian occupied defences immediately north of Khurramshahr; and

(f) troops and guns at Khosroabad.[1]

The Royal Air Force in this sector was to operate from Shuaiba under the command of Group Captain D. L. Thomson who was designated Officer Commanding, Basra Wing. It comprised: No. 261 (fighter) Squadron, No. 84 Blenheim Squadron, No. 244 (General Purposes) Squadron and No. 31 B.T. Squadron.

Some days prior to the commencement of operations in Iran, a flight of No. 2 Photographic Reconnaissance Unit, comprising two long-range Hurricanes (with one Lockhead Electra for service work) and personnel had arrived at Habbaniya to photograph possible strategic bombing targets in Iran. This was successfully achieved, and if strategic bombing had been ordered the results obtained might have proved of considerable value.

Advantage was also taken of the presence of the flight to obtain certain photographs of important areas required by the Royal Navy and army in connection with the operations. It was stated that these photographs proved of the greatest assistance.

Activities of the air force were restricted to a certain extent. The British Cabinet ruled that the bombing of Iranian troops would not take place unless there was evidence that the latter had adopted the offensive. "Unless Persians have opposed you morning of 26 August bombing of Pai Tak area will not be carried out this afternoon or tomorrow."[2] Similarly, bombing of Teheran was strictly prohibited.[3]

D1 Day

The D 1 day was initially fixed for 12 August 1941. But it was postponed on account of some technical objections raised by Russia. On 21 August, orders came that the move into Iran would be made that night. Just before the troops were to march off, instructions were received postponing the operations. Two more postponements came on 22 and 23 August. These repeated eleventh hour postponements proved considerably inconvenient to the troops who had to "stand to" all the time, make preparations each day for marching in the night, only to have the orders cancelled at the last minute. Ultimately it was on 24 August that the final orders came fixing the zero hour at 0410 hours the next morning, but by that time the Iranians had reinforced their defences.

Sunrise on 25 August was due at 0522 hours. There was no moon in the early hours as the new moon had appeared only on the

[1] 601/236/WD.
[2] No. 601/9758/H—Part I, Appendix M.
[3] F. 694.

23rd. The zero hour at 0410 was selected so as to give the troops the cover of darkness while marching and just sufficient visibility of the rising dawn to help them in exploitation. The rainy season being far off, the night was expected to be bright and starlit with a cool desert breeze blowing all the time.

CHAPTER XXXVIII

Abadan

Iranian Defences

The move south-west of Iran began on 25 August and the first target was Abadan with its oil refineries, the capture and control of which was the main objective of these operations. The Iranian Government had organised some defences of the area.

The last reports received by the 24th Indian Infantry Brigade at Basra on 19 August 1941 indicated that from the Karun river to Braim Creek, a distance of nearly eight miles, there were five military posts, two with machine-guns, almost at equal distances, controlled by fifty men. From Braim Creek to the neighbourhood of Jetty No 1 there were four posts, two with machine-guns maintained by less than fifty men. There were no posts at three Jetties, 1 to 3, but it was assumed that they were covered by two light anti-aircraft guns at Jetties 2 and 3. From Jetties 3 to 6 there was only one post and a patrol with a sergeant and six men. No. 7 Jetty had two posts and two patrols. There was no post at Jetty No. 8. Between Jetties 9 to 11 there was one post besides one patrol, while a gunboat, *Palang*, was stationed at Jetty No. 11.

Light anti-aircraft guns were known to be posted at six places. Two of them were also located at the aerodrome. An anti-aircraft battery was sited in the area between the date-palms lining the south bank of the Bahmanshir river and the north line of the oil tanks.

Police posts were located at six places, and the whole area of the refinery and tank farm was enclosed by a metal fence. Normally there were no troops inside the fence but, outside, the police maintained a continuous patrol. Search lights manned by troops existed at the north-east and north-west corners of the fence. It was estimated that in the Iranian barracks there were 2,000 soldiers.

The Invading Force

The operations in Abadan were to be conducted by the 24th Indian Infantry Brigade Group, which had only two battalions, 2nd Rajputana Rifles and 1st Kumaon Rifles, besides the brigade troops comprising the 3rd Field Regiment, 7th Field Company Sappers and Miners, a detachment of 3rd Baluch Regiment (M.G.), and 25th Field Ambulance. This force was to be transported, down the Shatt-al-Arab

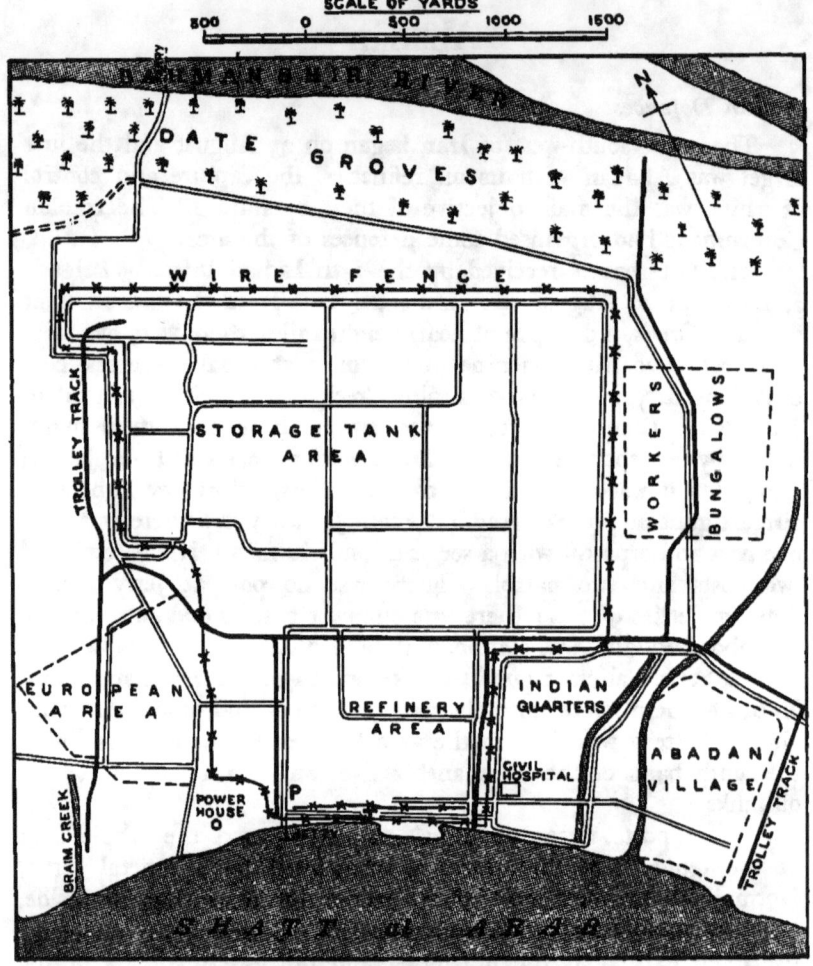

by a flotilla consisting of a sloop, an armed yacht, an auxiliary minesweeper, two river steamers, six eurekas (American motor boats) and three dhows.

Embarkation timings at Basra were fixed in conformity with the zero hour. The advance party of 1 Kumaon left the camp at dusk at 1845 hours to embark ammunition and stores. The rest of the battalion left at 1930 hours. A and B Companies and the Machine-gun Platoon embarked in *Ihsan,* and C and D Headquarter Companies and Battalion Headquarters in *Zenobia.* Both these were small river paddle steamers. *Ihsan* sailed at 2310 hours and *Zenobia* at 2320 hours. The other battalion, 2/6 Rajputana Rifles, moved in two sections, its C Company embarking at 2130 hours in two dhows and three eurekas, while D Company embarked at 2210 hours in three eurekas and one dhow. Two sections of 4·5 troop 3rd Field Regiment left Basra at 2000 hours and moved by road to Siba (Qutubaid), just opposite Abadan, so as to be in position to give covering fire from the other side of the Shatt-al-Arab. Other troops sailed in two ships, *Seabelle* and *Lilavati.* The former left at 0040 hours and the latter at 0045 hours.

Ihsan and *Zenobia* moved down the river without any incident and arrived opposite Abadan at zero hour. The smaller craft carrying 2nd Rajputana Rifles were to be seen nowhere. Some of these vessels did land soon after the zero hour; but one or two craft went aground, or lost their way and did not turn up till much later in the day. Both the companies of Rajputana Rifles were therefore late, and when they arrived they were below strength. These small craft were grounded because they were skirting too close to the shore for protection and moved into shallow waters. *Seabelle* and *Lilavati* reached Abadan in time.

Palang Set on Fire

At zero hour there was no sign of the Iranian soldiers anywhere, as most of them were fast asleep in their barracks. Absolute silence prevailed on all sides; complete surprise had been obtained. And then, at the appointed time, the stillness of the night was broken by the guns of the H.M.S. *Shoreham* which opened fire on the Iranian sloop *Palang,* lying off Jetty No. 11, and in a few moments reduced her to a blazing wreck. The firing awakened the opponents and the noise of the fighters buzzing in the sky frightened them so much that a large number of them escaped in lorries across the Bahmanshir river.

Braim Creek

At 0410 hours, *Ihsan* and *Zenobia* went into the Braim Creek. *Ihsan* was run ashore on the right bank and *Zenobia* was slightly forward on her left. One platoon of C Company of 1 Kumaon disembarked and formed a bridgehead on the right bank. D Company disembarked on the left side, secured the left bank and moved forward towards the aerodrome, which was captured including two aircraft by 0615 hours. C Company then turned to the north-east up the creek and secured the creek head and the northern bank. At 0420 hours A Company disembarked from *Ihsan* on the northern bank of the creek and entered the European section of the town. These three companies did not meet with opposition.

B company disembarked from the *Ihsan* at 0430 hours on the southern bank of the creek and moved southward to clear the area of small barracks and palm-tree woods 100 yards away. On entering the woods the company was heavily engaged by a force of about 60 to 70 Iranians. One hour and a half later the opponents were finally dislodged and driven back with the loss of 25 men and 10 prisoners. Having cleared the woods, B Company reached the area of the town. Their losses were two killed and one wounded.

European Bungalow Area

C Company of Rajputana Rifles was delayed on the way, and its first troops landed in the Braim Creek 10 minutes late. They passed to the European bungalow area. The company had been given to understand that all European and Indian employees of the Anglo-Iranian Oil Company would be in the refinery. But most of them remained in the European area, while some of the house roofs were occupied by the Iranians. The fighting was therefore made more difficult and it took much longer to clear the area than originally planned. The Manager blew the alarm siren prematurely and the employees began to move to their key positions in the refinery. Just at the time when the shooting started, an ambulance car of the oil company stopped near the office building. It did not bear any red cross, being forbidden by the Iranian Government to display a Christian mark. Immediately three men stepped out of the van in their blue uniforms. The Rajputs took them for Iranian soldiers, and instantly shot them dead, wounding the remaining seven who were inside. One post at No. 55 bungalow held on till 1730 hours. At this place the Iranians had nine heavy machine-guns, which kept on firing from very close range though without any serious effect.

Jetty No 1

D Company of the 2nd Rajputana Rifles was conveyed in three eurekas and one dhow. The eurekas arrived at 0415 hours and the dhow 10 minutes later. They were fired upon while landing and one soldier was killed while still in the boat. But the others moved on and the first post to be captured was the Central Exchange Telegraph building, where hard fighting took place. It was difficult to dislodge the opponents who had taken up their position behind parapets on high roofs. One regimental policeman did excellent work by scaling a ladder several times to throw hand grenades on a roof strongly held by the Iranians. The company was held up at two other posts, one of which was right on the quay, and the other in the vicinity of the Telegraph Exchange. But before the opposition was liquidated, D Company was required peremptorily to move to Jetty No. 7, leaving only a small party to deal with the resistance. Meanwhile B and C Companies of the Kumaon Rifles were pushed through palm trees to help the Rajputana Rifles in clearing the water front. They immediately came under heavy fire in the neighbourhood of the quarters occupied by European nurses. The immediate problem was to protect their right flank from a possible hostile advance from the barracks area and a platoon was sent off to guard the roads leading from that direction. The next task was to mop up the post holding up their advance, and it was accomplished by sending a party into a position behind the Iranians. Simultaneously another party advanced on the quay, and the Iranians gave in.

The Brigade Headquarters marched to clear the area beyond the Telegraph Exchange building up to Jetty No. 7. On their way they found a considerable number of Iranians, dead and wounded, lying in the streets and the Telegraph Exchange premises. They met with tough opposition at several places. The whole area from Jetties 1 to 7 was cleared by about 0945 hours. The D Company of Rajputana Rifles then took up defensive positions along the Jetties. In the afternoon they moved up with the Battalion Headquarters to artisan barracks, having left two sections to guard the Oil Company's hospital.

Jetty No 7

The Battalion Headquarters and A and B Companies of Rajputana Rifles were conveyed in *Lilavati*. They were due to arrive at 0415 hours, but the landing did not take place till 0430 hours. One platoon of A Company under the company commander landed first and proceeded straightaway to Jetty 7 to meet and help D Company advancing from Jetty 1. The platoon encountered heavy machine-gun and grenade fire and in the first few minutes the company commander was killed.

The remainder of A Company was immediately despatched to reinforce. This help did not, however, prove effective as the front on which they were advancing was very narrow, only about 15 yards wide. The only cover was a few railway wagons and some oil drums. Two platoons from B Company were then sent to the refinery to take the opponents in the rear; but they too could not get sufficiently close to do much damage. The main Iranian post at Jetty No. 7 was finally silenced by heavy machine-gun fire from the *Shoreham*.

The Iranians then started to fire with machine-guns from the east of Jetty No. 7. No reserves were available from the Rifle Companies, so the platoons from the Headquarters Company were detailed to deal with the Iranian guns. Meanwhile reinforcements from D Company were received. Ultimately they cleared the area and, with the exception of a few snipers, all was quiet by 0945 hours. The British and Indian casualties were 4 killed and 4 wounded. The Iranian casualties were estimated at 20 killed and wounded. Rajputana Rifles then advanced round the wire fence enclosing the distillery in co-operation with the Kumaon Rifles, who were to clear the west face of the distillery area. This task was accomplished by 1030 hours.

The Police Station

A Company of Kumaon Rifles which was to capture the police station came under light-machine-gun fire at 0512 hours. The surrounding area was cleared, but the police station held on in spite of the mortar fire. At 0900 hours, the company, less one platoon, was withdrawn to be used against an Iranian concentration on the Bahmanshir ferry. At 1430 hours, A Company with a section of 3·7 Howitzers was sent back to clear the police station. The opponents put up a determined resistance. A Company lost a rifleman, and one was wounded. The Howitzers shelled the police station from about 100 yards' range. At about 1800 hours A Company finally cleared the area.

The Bahmanshir Ferry

The Brigade Commander was informed at 0900 hours that the retreating Iranians were gathering to the north-west of the Tank Farm near the ferry on the Bahmanshir river. A reconnaissance was immediately made. The Kumaon battalion was concentrated to the north-west of Braim Creek to be in readiness for attack on the ferry. A company left one platoon in the town to continue resistance, and B company left one platoon to guard the headquarters and the prisoners. By this time the Anglo-Iranian Oil Company had collected a large number of trucks, cars and buses which were used by this battalion. It was also supported by one troop of 4·5 Howitzers. The former brought down accurate shelling on the ferry and the battalion advanced across the desert at 1240 hours, C and D Companies leading. At one time it was thought that the pipeline had been hit as a great column of black smoke rose in the air. This, however, only proved to be an Iranian ammunition lorry which had caught fire.

The Iranians did not wait for the attack to close in, but after a few shots retired across the river leaving only a small party on the southern bank. These were soon mopped up.

The Abadan Village

Fire was coming from the direction of Abadan native village. A reconnaissance was made as far as the M.T. Park where a platoon of the Rajputana Rifles was already in position to guard the flank. The troops were ordered to clear up the opposition in the streets leading north and west which was done.

Refinery Secured

In the street fighting of the Refinery area, the Iranian troops could not be easily dislodged without damaging the refinery buildings, and this was to be avoided as far as possible. The Iranian machine-guns could not be silenced by mortar or artillery fire without risking the safety of petrol tanks. Hence it took rather long to clear up these buildings by sniping. By 1630 hours, however, this area too was in possession of the Indian troops. The 24th Indian Infantry Brigade in its first action as a brigade had thus secured the greatest oil refinery in the world with only one week's loss of production. After capturing Abadan the brigade was required to get into touch with the 18th Indian Infantry Brigade at Khurramshahr. This was not possible as some part of Abadan including Bawarda remained to be cleared up.

During the night between 25 and 26 August, the troops bivouacked in a cordon round the refinery. The Kumaon Rifles took up a defensive position stretching from the river up the west face and along the north face of Abadan. The Rajputana Rifles held the east face joining up with the Kumaon's on the north. The Brigade Headquarters was in the centre close to the Central Telegraph Exchange.

The Iranian Barracks

On the 26th, early in the morning, the Rajputana Rifles less a piquet (left to guard the Camp area) went to capture the Iranian Barracks. Information was received that the opponents had fled across the Bahmanshir river. This was correct and the barracks were found evacuated except for a lot of stores, rifles and ammunition. The battalion moved into the barracks at night and used them as its headquarters.

Search for Iranian Troops in the South

On 26 August a battalion of Kumaon Rifles was ordered to march southward to clear the southern half of the Abadan Island. They moved off at 0759 hours in buses and cars, owned and driven by the Anglo-Iranian Oil Company's personnel. The Brigade Headquarters and one section of 4.5 Howitzers accompanied the battalion. The navy sailed down the river parallel to the road column and had fire support ready in case of need. They reached Khosroabad at 0930 hours. The Iranian garrison there had run away before the Indian troops arrived. The whole area was searched but no opponent was found. The Kumaon Rifles then advanced to Qasbat-un-Nisar further south. All this area had been vacated by the Iranians. The battalion returned to its headquarters on the western edge of Abadan at 1700 hours.

Episode of 500 Iranians

On 26 August, when a search column was returning from Khosroabad and Qasbat, an Iranian met it, and said that 500 Iranian soldiers with a couple of field guns had left Qasbat the night before and were hiding in the date-palm groves bordering on the Bahmanshir river at Tingeh and wished to surrender. A message was sent to them to move up the Bahmanshir river and hand themselves over at the ferry, the following morning between 0600 and 0700 hours. A and D Rajputana Companies were sent there early in the morning on 27 August. None except three envoys turned up. They were kept as prisoners. It was learnt that the 500 Iranians, having thrown away their rifles and artillery guns, had escaped to the north during the preceding night. Their arms were taken possession of by the neighbouring Arabs. The artillery guns and ammunition were recovered with the help of an Arab.

Guards left at Abadan

The whole brigade remained in Abadan on 26 August, while Hurricanes and Gladiators of 261 Squadron patrolled Abadan in the morning, and by 0900 hours they were ordered to "ground" but to remain on call. On 27 August, the bulk of the 24th Indian Infantry Brigade went to Khurramshahr some 10 miles away. Three Hurricanes and seven Gladiators of 261 Squadron were on patrol over Abadan area on this day.

The 2nd Rajputana Rifles less two companies were left in Abadan to deal with any local trouble, to restore peace and order in the island, and to ensure safety of the Oil Company personnel and plant. In the beginning of September the piquets were withdrawn and the battalion was formed into a mobile column. They recovered a lot of ammunition and many guns from the neighbouring Arab villages. One day, 4 mountain battery guns and over 50 boxes of ammunition were captured.

The 24th Indian Infantry Brigade, less one battalion of 2/6 Rajputana Rifles, which was left at Abadan, came into divisional reserve on 27 August on the northern bank of the river Karun at Khurramshahr, while the other two brigades of the division were advancing upon Ahwaz.

Khurramshahr

Major-General Harvey, the Divisional Commander, had initially planned for the simultaneous seizure of Abadan, Khurramshahr and Ahwaz on the same day. But owing to the delay in starting the operations, the Iranians had brought into that area a force of about two divisions. Hence, with the approval of Lt.-General Quinan, the plan was modified to achieve the object in two phases: Abadan and Khurramshahr being taken on one day in the first phase and the capture of Ahwaz to form part of the second phase. Hence, on the same day as the attack on Abadan, Khurramshahr also became the target of attack.

The divisional plan had allotted the 18th Indian Infantry Brigade (less one battalion), one battalion of the 24th Indian Infantry Brigade, one squadron of Guides Cavalry and one battery field artillery for operations in Khurramshahr. This force was to move from Tanuma in the night of 24/25 August so as to be in position on the road outside Khurramshahr at 0410 hours. The brigade was to exploit thereafter north and east and establish a bridgehead across the river Karun, north of the Bahmanshir river.

Iranian Defences

Khurramshahr was not very lightly held by the Iranians. Information received shortly before the commencement of the operations revealed that the *13th* and the *30th Infantry Regiments* and nearly 500 men from the *45th Infantry Regiment* were stationed at Khurramshahr. Besides the infantry, there were one anti-aircraft battery (Skoda), one pack battery, one machine-gun company, and seven light anti-aircraft machine-gun units. This brought the total defence forces to nearly 3,000. In addition to the land forces, there were between 1,000 and 1,500 officers and men of the navy. Two sloops and four gunboats lay moored on the east bank of the Karun river. The police force consisted of about 300 men armed with rifles. The town had been surrounded by two shallow trenches about 3 feet deep, 1½ miles west of Khurramshahr on the Basra road; a number of shallow trenches with low mud walls, about one mile west of the town on Basra side, and a ditch with water, 2 metres wide and 2 metres deep, extending from the Shatt-al-Arab to the north-west of Khurramshahr, 300 yards west of the wireless station.

Forces and Plan

To combat this force, Major General Harvey had detached the following troops for operations in Khurramshahr:

    (*a*) A company of the 3rd Battalion, 10th Baluch Regiment, whose business was to capture Iranian naval barracks;

    (*b*) Rapier Group comprising 5/5 Mahratta, A Squadron 10 Guides Cavalry, Battery Headquarters, one troop 18-pounder battery 3 Field Regiment, one section 7 Field Company, one section Sappers and Miners, 203 General Purposes Transport Company, and one company 25th Field Ambulance. This group was to move from Tanuma Camp and was to capture the town up to the northern bank of the Karun river, including all posts from the frontier onward.

    (*c*) The 18th Infantry Brigade Group Headquarters, 1/2 Gurkha Rifles, 2/3 Gurkha Rifles, 18th Brigade Transport Company, 9th Field Company, K Anti-Tank Battery, and 32nd Field Ambulance. This force was allotted the task of capturing the Wireless Station, Landing Ground, Police Post, Pul-i-Nao and Manduwan. They were also to support the advance of the Rapier Group, north of the various water obstacles and defensive positions, and were to be ready to advance on Ahwaz by mechanical transport.

Ships and Naval Barracks Seized

We shall first describe the operations in the Naval Barracks. This task was allotted to C Company of 3/10 Baluch. It left Basra at 1830 hours on 24 August, and arrived at the docks at 1900 hours and embarked in small boats. A platoon (13) boarded the H.M.S *Yarra*, while the company headquarters, 14 and 15 Platoons went by the H.M.S *Falmouth*. The ships left their moorings at 2359 hours and steamed down the stream. At 0415 hours on 25 August, when they neared the mouth of the Karun river, the ships opened fire. The Iranians replied with rifle and machine-gun fire. Just then British fighters appeared in the sky and without any bombardment struck terror into the hearts of the defenders. Under cover of fire two Iranian ships were boarded by the Baluch troops. Then 15 Platoon landed under heavy fire and took up its position at the appointed place, 14 Platoon came up on its right and 13 Platoon on the left. They then attacked a post protecting the main bank and silenced it. When the company advanced again, 14 Platoon came under fire from some buildings and the company commander was mortally wounded. However, the buildings were quickly seized. A patrol was sent to search and clear up the area up to 800 yards. The 15 Platoon searched the central buildings in front and seized thirty Iranian naval personnel, who were sent to the H.M.S *Yarra*. The 13 Platoon searched the remaining buildings and inflicted some casualties on an Iranian party. They had also occupied the date groves by 1300 hours. Thirty vehicles were captured from a garage and 400 rifles, 4 machine-guns, and a large quantity of clothing material and ammunition were recovered from a building at 1530 hours. Thereafter 13 and 14 Platoons returned to their ships. In the day's engagement the Iranian naval losses were 2 sloops sunk and 4 gunboats, 1 depot ship, 2 tugs, 1 floating dock for 6,000-ton ship captured. Admiral Bay Endor in command of the Iranian naval force was killed. "This officer had an English wife, and while giving full allegiance to the Shah was very friendly disposed towards us."[4] His death was much regretted, and he was buried with full naval honours the following day. The British naval losses were nil. In the night, 13 and 14 Platoons garrisoned the captured Iranian ships and patrolled ashore, while 15 Platoon posted a piquet on the roof of a lofty house 200 yards from the bank.

The Town Captured.

The next target was the town which task was allotted to the Rapier Group. The force arranged its men and vehicles for the move at 1800 hours on 24 August 1941. Each vehicle had a white towel tied at back to enable the vehicles in the rear to see it in the dark. The total number of vehicles was 157. Normal activity in the Camp was maintained by the battle replacements staying behind and all tents were left standing to mislead the Iranians. Then at 2015 hours the night march began on a bearing at 70°. The Cairn was reached in time without any mishap, where the column halted for three hours. At 2300 hours the frontier was crossed and a steady pace was maintained on a bearing of 90° for nine miles at a rate of 4 miles an hour. Lights from some Iranian piquets were seen to the north and south, but the force evaded detection. At 0145 hours the Rapier Group wheeled to 175° and after a halt went on for another four miles. The forming-up place was reached at about 0330 hours. The force had advanced 22 miles in the dark, but there was nothing to show that the force was at the right position.

At 0410 hours gun flashes were seen to the south-east. This was judged to be the landing by the 24th Indian Infantry Brigade at Abadan. At 0420 hours they detected gun flashes straight ahead, and conjectured that H.M.S. *Yarra* and H.M.S. *Falmouth*

[4] W/D 236.

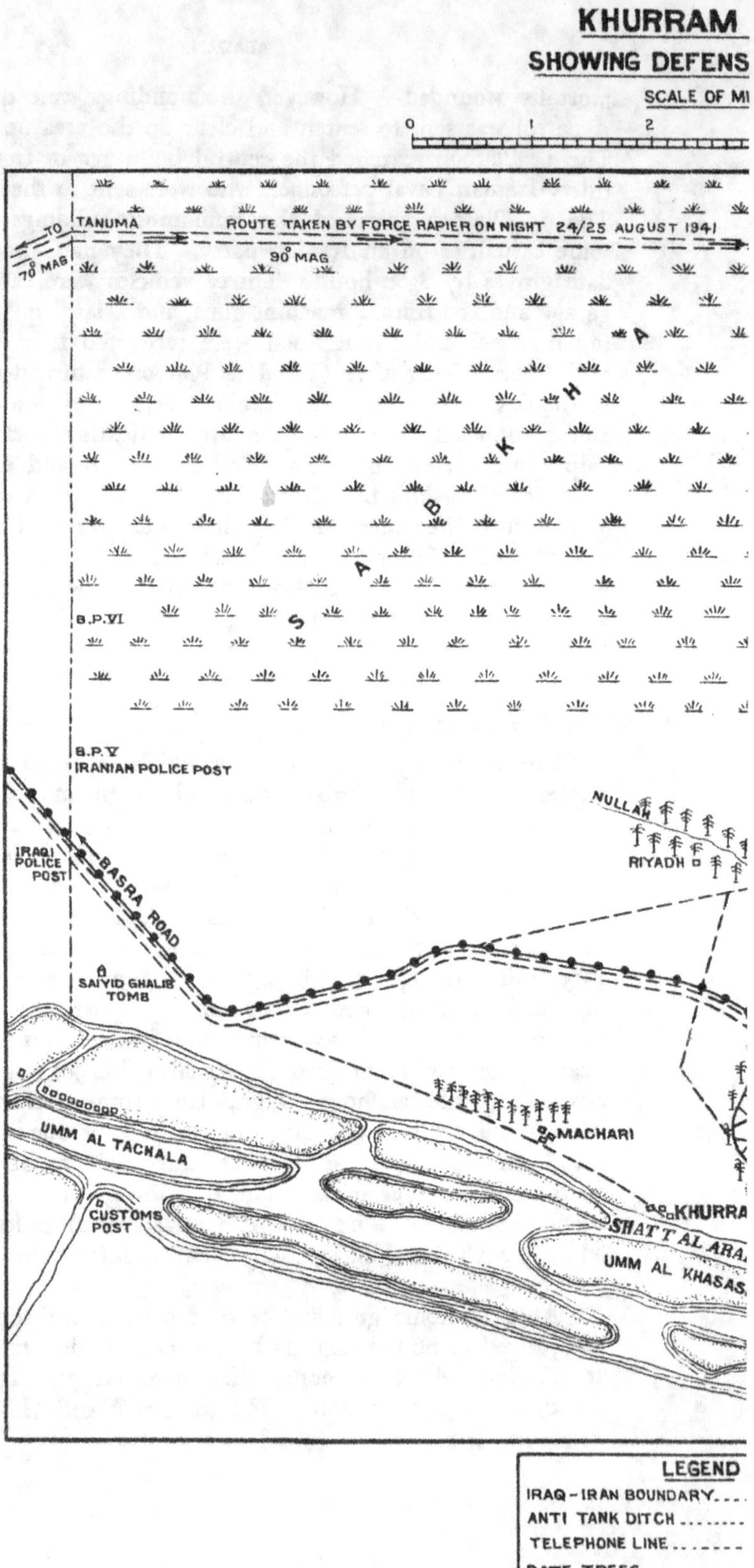

KHURRAM
SHOWING DEFENS[ES]
SCALE OF M[ILES]

ROUTE TAKEN BY FORCE RAPIER ON NIGHT 24/25 AUGUST 1941

TO TANUMA
70 MAG
90 MAG

SABKHA

B.P.VI

B.P.V
IRANIAN POLICE POST

IRAQI POLICE POST

BASRA ROAD

SAIYID GHALIB TOMB

NULLAH
RIYADH

UMM AL TACHALA

CUSTOMS POST

MACHARI

KHURRA[M]
SHATT AL ARA[B]
UMM AL KHASAS

LEGEND
IRAQ-IRAN BOUNDARY
ANTI TANK DITCH
TELEPHONE LINE
DATE TREES

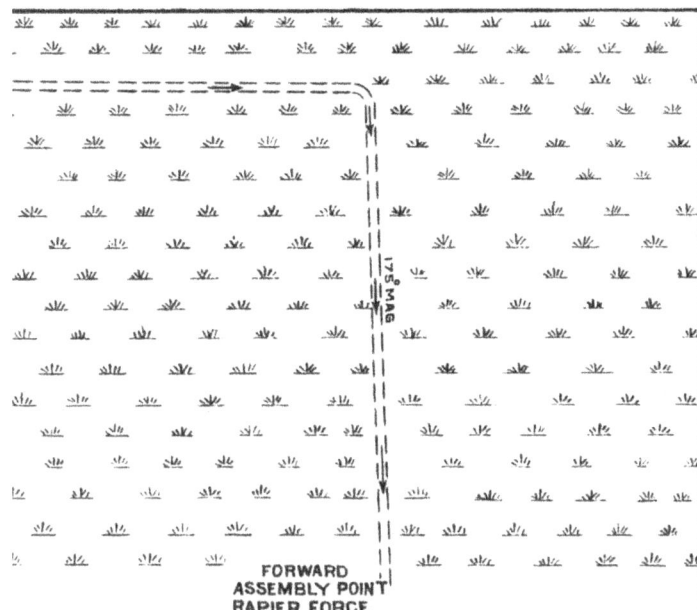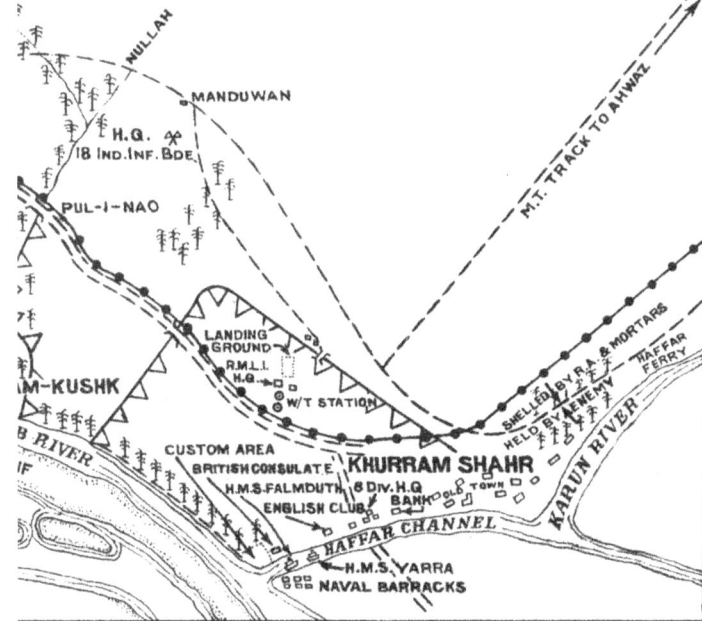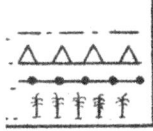

had started action on the Karun river. Judging from these flashes that the force was on the right line, order was given to advance. As the light increased the force opened out gradually to daylight formations. The cavalry immediately went ahead to brush aside the anti-tank obstacles surrounding the town, but while they were 500 yards from the obstacles, the Iranian troops opened up heavy machine-gun and rifle fire from the date groves, north of the town. The artillery, mortars and the machine-guns of the armoured cars were brought into action; while A and B Companies of 5/5 Mahratta debussed, about 100 yards from the Iranian positions and advanced to attack from the right flank. They met with weak resistance which was soon overcome and the town was captured with a loss of only one soldier. Fourteen Iranians were killed and eight captured.

Police Post, Manduwan and Pul-i-Nao

The third group also had easy success. It was split into two parties, 1/2 Gurkha Rifles and the 18th Brigade Transport Company forming one, and the rest the other. The first party left their camp at Tanuma at 2000 hours on 24 August, and crossed the frontier to the north of Duaiji at 0015 hours on 25 August. At 0400 hours they moved in the direction of the Manduwan Nullah, and approached the Police Post at 0645 hours. This had already been deserted by the Iranians, and only some secret documents and uniforms fell into the hands of Indian troops. Manduwan was then captured at 0800 hours without any resistance, as the Iranian troops had retired after discarding their uniforms as soon as they had seen the Gurkhas advancing. Many of them were however captured by 5/5 Mahratta. Next, Pul-i-Nao was seized at 0815 hours. Then 2nd Gurkha Rifles stayed at Manduwan until 1700 hours clearing the whole area from the frontier near Duaiji to Khurramshahr. A considerable number of Arabs "who are always glad of a little shooting before breakfast" joined in the affray, and made the task a little more difficult. The battalion however went to Marid after 1700 hours.

Wireless Station, the Landing Ground and Chasbi Nullah

The second party consisting of 2/3 Gurkha Rifles, 9th Field Company, K Anti-Tank Battery and 32nd Field Ambulance left the camp at 0200 hours on 25 August. They crossed the border before dawn, took the Wireless Station at 0614 hours, the Landing Ground at 0645 hours, and secured the Chasbi Nullah at 0650 hours. The area on the left bank of the Shatt-al-Arab was then cleared before 0700 hours.

In the Khurramshahr operations, the British and Indian troops captured 2 mountain batteries, a few machine-guns, and nearly 500 prisoners including several officers, besides some ships. The total loss on their side was only 3 killed and 3 wounded. The balance sheet was heavily in favour of the invaders.

Karun River Ferry at Marid

When the town had been captured at 0730 hours on 25 August, 9th Field Company Sappers and Miners was sent across the desert to Marid with B Company of 2/3 Gurkha Rifles, as a covering party, to reconnoitre a site for a ferry crossing over the Karun. At 1200 hours the covering party saw Iranian guns and transport from Abadan withdrawing across the river in the distance, but as sufficient troops were not available, they could not be intercepted. The earth-work for the ferry was begun on the right bank of the river, about ten miles above the confluence of the Karun and Shatt-al-Arab at Marid, and was completed by the evening. The ferry landing earth-work on the opposite bank was completed by 0830 hours on 26 August.

Dorquain

On 27 August at 0615 hours a report was received that Dorquain had been evacuated by the Iranians. The Indian employees at the pumping station of the place stated that 700 to 1000 Iranian soldiers with 4 guns had passed by that place during the two previous days towards Ahwaz. The 18th Indian Infantry Brigade arrived at Dorquain at 1130 hours and occupied it.

CHAPTER XXXIX

Qasr Shaikh

Preparation

The plan had provided for the simultaneous occupation of Abadan, Khurramshahr, Qasr Shaikh and Bandar Shahpur. The task of capturing the first two was assigned to the 18th Indian Infantry Brigade. The job had been well done, and in the course of less than two days Abadan, Khurramshahr and their neighbourhood had been cleared of the Iranians and all danger of resistance had been eliminated. The next objective was Qasr Shaikh which was the responsibility of the 25th Indian Infantry Brigade, which had to train itself for a night march over a terrain scarcely marked by any tracks. Their training continued over many days and experience was gained in movement by mechanised transport and attacking ill-defined objectives without loss to the transport.

The Brigade Operation Order of 21 August declared its object as destroying all Iranian troops in the Qasr Shaikh area and thereafter securing a defensive flank on the river Karun near Rahmaniyeh to protect the operations conducted by the 18th Indian Infantry Brigade, moving against Abadan and Khurramshahr. For this purpose, the 25th Indian Infantry Brigade and its attached troops were to be formed into several groups, each charged with a definite assignment. The cavalry part of the force comprising of 13th Lancers and anti-tank regiment formed one group. With it was attached one platoon of Royal Sikh. This group was to attack Qasr Shaikh from the north and was to operate as the spearhead of attack. The starting point for the brigade was Tanuma from where the advanced party, the mobile group, was to move to Saudiyeh which place was to be reached at 0630 hours. The rest of the force composed of the 25th Indian Infantry Brigade was divided into four groups, three of which were to move to Qasr Shaikh, advancing direct from Tanuma, following each other so as to be five miles south west of their objective at 0730 hours. The other two groups were to form the reserve at the Tanuma Camp.

The brigade plan had provided for a two pronged attack, from the north by the mobile group composed of 13th Lancers and from the south by the 25th Indian Infantry Brigade formed by 2 Sikh, 1 Maharatta and 3 Jat battalions with the artillery component and attached troops. The mobile group passed the starting point at 0330 hours and crossed the frontier at 0520 hours. Then an hour later they met four Iranian armed vehicles which soon retired. Meanwhile the other party was also on the move. Group I crossed the border at 0650 hours and soon after reached a gendarmerie post where they halted because one squadron of 13th Lancers was seen ahead. At this place information was received from the captured prisoners that Qasr Shaikh was held by a battalion. But immediately after, the air reconnaissance indicated that the town was covered by a line of trenches towards the south and possibly these were defended. This called for orders to alter the course of move to the west so as to arrive on the western flank of the Iranian positions. There were small sand dunes on the route which, together with a nullah on the way, slowed the progress of the advancing column. At the nullah, Group I came under artillery and long range machine-gun fire from the direction of Qasr Shaikh Fort, which was visible in the distance.

The Fort Taken

The 13th Lancers had reached Saudiyeh when they heard the sound of firing and immediately hurried towards Qasr Shaikh with C Squadron on the right and B Squadron on the left supported by B Troops 1 Anti-Tank Regiment. A Squadron, anti-tank guns, and 2/11 Sikh were left in reserve. Some armoured cars of C Squadron including the squadron commander's car got stuck in the sand close to an Iranian trench, and the squadron did not make much progress. A troop leader and an operator were wounded; but in spite of the severe battering the squadron commander's car escaped with only slight damage.

In the meantime B Squadron met with severe opposition and could proceed no further. A part of the reserve force was at once sent by a wide detour on the rear of C Squadron.

The remainder of the reserve force lay exposed to the heavy shell-fire from the guns located near the fort. Anti-tank guns, though not equipped for this type of fighting, opened fire on them. Leaving the guns in position 2/11 Sikh in their trucks were ordered to proceed straight to the fort. Two companies were up, C on the right and D on the left, with A in the right rear and B in the left rear. Two detachments of mortars were put under command of the leading companies and one section machine-guns was placed on the right flank to cover the advance. The move started at 0930 hours, and the force soon reached a place just south of the fort. The companies continued advancing although their commanders had been wounded. The battalion headquarters immediately moved on to the Pimples on which C company had formed up.

B Squadron of 13th Lancers was compelled to change the course of its advance, and by making a wide detour towards the west and

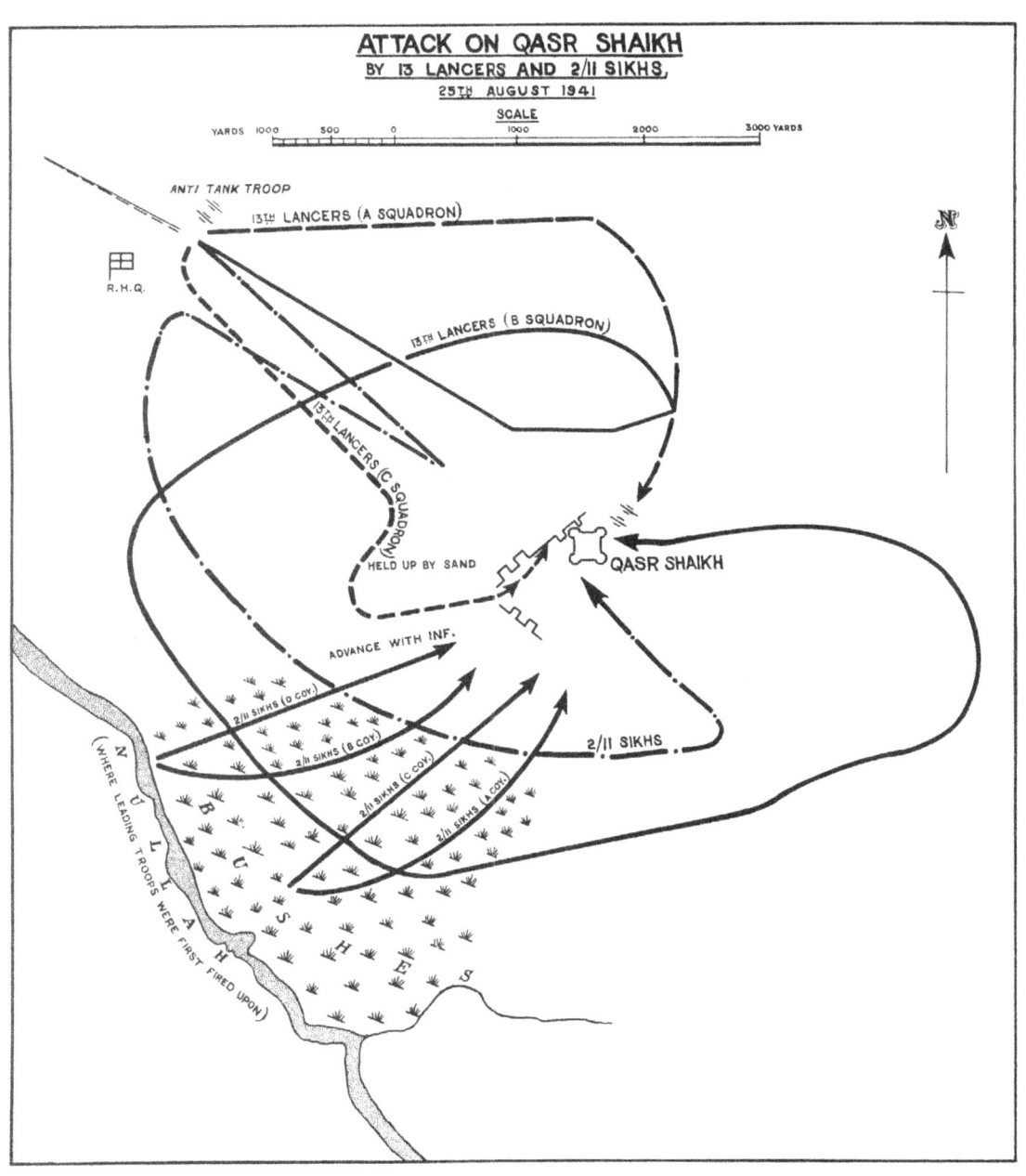

south appeared near the fort on the east. Meanwhile A Squadron moved to the east, and then both the squadrons launched an attack on the fort from the eastern side.

About this time, as mentioned earlier, 2/11 Sikh had also launched the assault on the fort from the south. All the four companies were making a parallel advance in two columns; D and B, one behind the other on the left, and C and A on the right. The Iránian machine-guns were firing heavily chiefly hitting the D Company whose further progress was almost brought to a standstill; but C Company was able to push on successfully. Just at this time A Company was ordered to swing to the right of C Company and exploit success. The artillery had fired only five rounds when it was ordered to stop, as the armoured cars of 13th Lancers had reached the neighbourhood of the fort, which was the target of artillery fire.

There was a gap between C and D Companies. This was a depression covered with scrub and long grass. The Iranians had dug trenches here and were heavily firing from their concealed positions. These trenches had not been detected and C Company was held up. B Company was ordered to push through the gap between C and D Companies straight down the middle of the depression and clear the opponents from the trenches. Battalion Headquarters also advanced with B Company. D Company was ordered to carry on mopping up operations. This company came on a concealed trench which was cleared by Thompson Sub-Machine-Guns, bombs and bayonets. One sepoy was killed and three were wounded, while the Iranian losses were 38 dead, 4 wounded and 6 prisoners. The trench contained two machine-guns and several light machine-guns. D Company then advanced a little further, but was held up by machine-gun and rifle fire from another trench in front. This was attacked by B and D Companies and was taken.

At 1115 hours B and C Companies of 2/11 Sikh and A and B Squadrons of 13th Lancers captured the fort. Nearly 200 men gave themselves up as prisoners. The Iranians fought well, and those in the front-line trenches opposing D Company died at their posts. After this action 13th Lancers went to Rahmaniyeh and the Brigade Group encamped between Saveh and Rahmaniyeh. Only 2/11 Sikh remained behind to clear the fort area.

AHWAZ

Reconnaissance of Ahwaz

The next step according to the divisional plan was to occupy Ahwaz and the oil installations in that vicinity, which was apparently the main objective of operations in the south-west sector. This task was assigned to the 25th Indian Infantry Brigade and the capture of Qasr Shaikh was a preliminary to it. Ahwaz was believed to be well defended and the Iranian *6th Division* was reported to be stationed there.

Originally the plan had provided for reconnaissance of the environments of Ahwaz by the 25th Indian Infantry Brigade for two days, viz 26th and 27th. Hence at 1845 hours on 25 August the brigade was ordered to reconnoitre the west of Ahwaz and to locate Iranian positions by means of contact columns from its positions at Qasr Shaikh. This involved a reconnaissance of a front of approximately 12 miles and an advance of about 24 miles in the face of Iranian armoured fighting vehicles, which were known to exist in the area. The most important feature was Hill 110 behind which tanks were suspected to be lurking. Recognising the futility of small patrols, it was decided that the entire 13th Lancers should be employed so that by means of their wireless communications they might present a co-ordinated picture of the whole position. Strict instructions were given to them not to be involved in any conflict as they could not expect support.

The 13th Lancers left Rahmaniyeh at 0620 hours on 26 August and proceeded along the road. In some places the road was very bad, and the speed of the advance was limited to only 7 miles an hour. Whilst this armoured unit was halting at Shatliyat a Vincent aircraft, which was co-operating with it, was shot down by mistake by one of the British Hurricanes then operating over Ahwaz. The pilot, though shot through the left thigh, brought off a good landing on rough country. The sergeant gunner was unhurt. The Lancers picked up the crew and sent them to the camp with two armoured cars. Umm-al-Ashiyeh was reached without opposition and the reconnaissance was carried out from there.

A Squadron reconnoitred the area to the south of Ahwaz. They found no opposition and advanced closer to the Iranian positions. B Squadron proceeded via Ghadir-uz-Zaid to Umm-al-Ashiyeh where they saw some Iranian vehicles (which retired) and tracks of tanks on the east bank of the Karkheh river. C Squadron went to Tell-i-Zibid and came under Iranian artillery, machine-gun and rifle fire. They also heard the sound of tanks.

The Lancers were withdrawn and went to Umm-at-Tumair via Shatliyat. At 1630 hours it was decided to return to the camp. Unfortunately the route selected was very bad, and after dark, sand dunes were encountered north of Qajaniyeh. Sand mats and digging had to be resorted to and the vehicles reached the camp at 0200 hours on 27 August.

The Divisional Commander visited Rahmaniyeh on 27 August, and wanted the Iranian defences to be reconnoitred in greater detail.

An infantry patrol containing officers from all battalions was therefore sent to Umm-al-Ashiyeh. They travelled in soft vehicles supported by one troop of 13th Lancers which had not taken part the day before. A company of Mahrattas and two troops of armoured cars went ahead. The Mahratta party got to a point within 1300 yards of the Iranian positions outside Ahwaz, but on the approach of the Iranian tanks they were ordered to retire to camp.

The information gained by the reconnaissance parties was of great value. It enabled the Brigade Commander to launch attack on Ahwaz from a direction which was undefended. It further confirmed the report that the Iranian positions extended from the south-east extremity to the river bend near Karaishan and that the Iranians had tanks and that their infantry was equipped with artillery and anti-tank guns. It showed further that an attack near the Karun river would be unprofitable on account of opposition and bad going.

The Plan

The 8th Indian Division had, as early as 12 August 1941, instructed the 25th Indian Infantry Brigade, to whom was allotted the task of capturing Ahwaz and the Anglo-Iranian Oil Company's installations in its neighbourhood, to reach Ahwaz as soon as possible after daylight on D 1 day. But in the course of the next few days, the plan had been modified so as to undertake Ahwaz operations only after the capture of Abadan island, Khurramshahr and Qasr Shaikh. Information had been further gathered about the strength of Iranian forces in the town or its vicinity, which revealed that no inconsiderable strength was maintained by the defenders there. All these led to the plan being revised so that practically the entire division was involved in the fight for Ahwaz. A two-pronged attack was planned, the 18th Indian Infantry Brigade moving by the eastern bank of the river Karun so as to emerge to the east and north-east of Ahwaz and the 25th Indian Infantry Brigade moving along the west coast of the river and attacking the cantonment from the west. The third brigade, the 24th Indian Infantry Brigade, was to be in divisional reserve to be used as the situation demanded in supporting the 25th Indian Infantry Brigade.

The advance on Ahwaz was to begin in the early hours of 28 August, the two brigades marching along the two banks of the Karun river. The bulk of the divisional artillery was to support the 25th Indian Infantry Brigade on the western side where the greatest opposition was expected. The 18th Indian Infantry Brigade was to hold Kut Abdullah and thereafter move the bulk of its forces round so as to launch the attack from the east and north-east of the town.

Order of March

The 18th Indian Infantry Brigade marched in the following order: the 3rd Gurkha Rifles moved on the left of the pipeline to take Kut Abdullah; the 2nd Gurkha Rifles preceded by a squadron of Guides Cavalry advanced on the right through a gap in the hills between Tubaiji Faris and Kot-i-Karaid, so as to cover the exits from Ahwaz to the east and north-east; two sections of 9th Field Company accompanied 2nd Gurkha Rifles in order to secure the railway crossing and the pipeline near the gap.

The fighting portion of the 25th Indian Infantry Brigade was divided into three groups in addition to the covering screen consisting of 13th Lancers and one troop anti-tank battery.

Group I
    1 Mahratta, one troop anti-tank battery, 3rd Field Regiment less one battery.

Group II
    3 Jat, one troop anti-tank battery.

Group III
    2 Sikh.

The 11th Field Regiment remained under divisional control, while the remaining artillery was put under the command of the respective groups.

Advance on Ahwaz

The 25th Indian Infantry Brigade commenced its move at 0515 hours on 28 August from its encampment west of the Karun at a point 25 miles south of Ahwaz. Its first objective was a hill feature, Point 100, which the divisional headquarters desired to be taken by 0700 hours. At 0530 hours a halt was made at Qurainat where the column had got strung out owing to unexpectedly bad going. Twelve Iranian light tanks were reported to have been noticed to the left, and the column was therefore shortened by moving Group II on to the left of Group I, and advance was resumed. The brigade reached Umm-al-Ashiyeh at 0715 hours, and got ready to attack the hill feature, Point 110, though visibility was bad and it was difficult to distinguish the hill.

Air Bombardment

Before we resume the description of the advance by land forces, it will be convenient to recount the preceding softening-up of the Iranian position by air bombardment, and also to take stock of the advance made by the 18th Indian Infantry Brigade in support of the operations of the other brigade. Ahwaz had been a special target of the Royal Air Force aeroplanes since the commencement of operations on the morning of 25 August. Consequently the morale of the Iranian troops had been considerably shattered by the time that the land forces started marching on it. Hurricanes of 261 Squadron made the first flight on Ahwaz aerodrome at 0542 hours on 25 August 1941, and, from a height of 6,000 feet, dropped 3,000 pounds of bombs, and successfully strafed three Hawker type Iranian aircraft which were warming up their engines on the ground. Six Blenheims of 84 Squadron carried on a second attack from a height of 2,000 feet and dropped 3,000 pounds of bombs on the aerodrome and the railway tracks, setting fire to the hangars. In both these attacks five Iranian aircraft were destroyed on the ground and two more were damaged.

On the morning of 26 August, two Iranian aircraft, believed to be Audax, took off from Ahwaz aerodrome. Hurricanes and Gladiators of 261 Squadron which were patrolling over Ahwaz, shot one of these aircraft which was forced to land in a field 5 miles southeast of Ahwaz emitting smoke. The other aircraft regained the aerodrome and made no further attempt to fly. This was the only occasion in the south-west in which Iranian aircraft took to air. In subsequent attacks on six aircraft at Ahwaz two were badly injured and four slightly. Anti-aircraft firing from Ahwaz aerodrome was more accurate than from the town.

A fighter patrol was maintained over Ahwaz on 27 August, until weather conditions deteriorated. Two photo-reconnaissance sorties were made by Blenheims of 84 Squadron on Ahwaz; but as visibility was poor in the afternoon, flying was cancelled.

On 28 August, seven Blenheims of 84 Squadron dropped 6,860 pounds of bombs on troop concentrations and barracks at Ahwaz from a height of 1,500 to 4,000 feet, at intervals of 20 minutes per flight, commencing at 0530 hours. The bombs fell on and among the barrack blocks and near small concentrations of vehicles. There was slight medium anti-aircraft fire from the town and machine-gun fire from troop concentrations. No Iranian aircraft were encountered. The aircraft returned to base, bombed up, refuelled and remained on call. Hurricanes and Gladiators of 261 Squadron provided continuous fighter cover over Ahwaz from 0600 hours. 244 Squadron provided tactical reconnaissance by five Vincents over each column on either side of the river.

On land across the river Karun, the 18th Indian Infantry Brigade, which was encamped at Maqam Hasbeh, started its march at 0400 hours on 28 August with the Brigade Commander at its head. At 0730 hours, 2nd Gurkha Rifles, 9th Field Company and 45 Troop of 18/62 Battery followed by Advance Brigade Headquarters made a swing to the right at Rahmaniyeh (No. 2) and crossed the railway at Miyan Dasht. A halt was made there to prepare for crossing the gap between the hills leading to Ahwaz and to be ready to launch an assault simultaneously with the 25th Indian Infantry Brigade on the other side of the river.

The Attack

We may now go back to the 25th Indian Infantry Brigade whom we left poised against the hill feature, Point 110. There, 1 Mahratta was ordered at 0810 hours to attack the eastern arm of this feature. The battalion advanced at 0835 hours, behind C Squadron 13th Lancers and followed by 3 Jat Reconnaissance Group. At 0900 hours, forward troops of 1 Mahratta moving embussed towards the south-east extremity of the point came under heavy fire from rifles, machine-guns and anti-tank weapons, at about 500 yards' range from the trenches in front of them. They debussed and went ahead under cover of artillery fire.

About this time one troop 1 Anti-Tank Battery with Group II opened fire on a party of Iranian cavalry on the left flank, at a range of 2500 yards. The party which might have been one of Arab looters broke up and galloped away. They appeared an hour later and were again dispersed.

A Squadron 13th Lancers was ordered to take its position just south of Tell-i-Zibid to the right of 1 Mahratta. The squadron reached there at 0930 hours and was joined by B Squadron whose eleven tyres had been burst by anti-tank and machine-gun fire. The Mahrattas were busy in fighting and in storming Iranian trenches in front. The Jats had just received instructions to clear another group of the opponent's trenches, when an Iranian envoy arrived with a large white flag on his car asking for an armistice. He was led to Major-General Harvey, Commander 8th Indian Division. The envoy delivered a message from his General saying he had received orders from the Shah to cease fire. He conveyed his General's desire to see Major-General Harvey to discuss terms. The Iranian resistance thus ceased at 1000 hours, but the 25th Indian Infantry Brigade remained in position until 1340 hours.

The 24th Indian Infantry Brigade was at some distance in the rear of the 25th Indian Infantry Brigade. The road which it followed was ill-defined and in parts very bad. The Brigade Headquarters had orders to move ahead and meet the General Officer Commanding at Umm-al-Ashiyeh. The 24th Indian Infantry Brigade was a little to the west of Umm-at-Tumair at 1200 hours, when a blue touring car with a white flag bearing an Iranian envoy asking for armistice approached it. The Brigade Commander received the envoy and led him to the Headquarters 8th Indian Division situated nearby in the rear.

On the other side of the river the 18th Indian Infantry Brigade was consolidating its position nearly 2 miles south of Kut Abdullah.

The 3rd Gurkha Rifles crossed the gap between the hills at 0940 hours and surrounded Kut Abdullah. The 2nd Gurkha Rifles and 45 Troop 18/62 Battery were preparing to move to this gap when, at 1056 hours, a message was received from the 3rd Gurkha Rifles that a car with a white flag came from Kut Abdullah with an Iranian envoy requesting for armistice and for the Brigade Commander to proceed to Kut Abdullah. The Commander left for Kut Abdullah with two platoons 2nd Gurkha Rifles and one section Sappers and Miners. The brigade remained in position and, at 1200 hours, the 3rd Gurkha Rifles reported that the Brigade Commander had left for Ahwaz to meet the Iranian General. At 1230 hours a message was received from the Brigade Commander ordering stoppage of all operations, but the troops to remain in their positions pending negotiations. At 1500 hours the brigade concentrated at Kut Abdullah.

The Iranian Surrender

On receiving the Iranian envoy asking for armistice Major-General Harvey sent Lieut-Colonel Galloway, Political Adviser, to accompany the envoy to Ahwaz to arrange for his arrival there. On their return Major-General Harvey entered Ahwaz and met General Muhammad Shahbakhti, commanding the troops in Khuzistan, and Mr. King, the British Consul at the Military Headquarters. The surrender ceremany was conducted in the house of the General Officer Commanding, and an Iranian Guard of Honour was provided to welcome him.

The Iranian General Officer Commanding agreed to the following terms:—

(i) Iranian troops to be confined to barracks on the west bank of the Karun for 24 hours.
(ii) Anglo-Iranian Oil Company personnel captured from Kut Abdullah and Masjid-i-Suleiman Oilfields to be released immediately.
(iii) The British forces to encamp on the east bank of the Karun north of the town.
(iv) No railway train to leave Ahwaz to the north till the armistice terms were settled.
(v) Any German and Italian found in Khuzistan to be arrested and handed over.
(vi) The property of the Anglo-Iranian Oil Company looted during the operations, such as transport, wheels, tyres, cutlery, carpets and clothing, as also a portable wireless set with transmitter aerial and masts stolen from Kut Abdullah, to be returned.

All Iranian soldiers captured were released on the spot. The Divisional Headquarters were installed in the Rest House and in the offices of the Anglo-Iranian Oil Company. The Iranian troops returned to their barracks, the British hurried off for tea, while the Indians rushed into the cooling water of the Karun, not caring for the sharks who infested the river, and many suffered heavily. The inhabitants of the town showed a friendly attitude towards the British, and they "appeared to have taken not the smallest interest in the affairs".

Message of Congratulations

The following order was issued by Major-General C. O. Harvey, at Ahwaz on 30 August 1941:

"The Divisional Commander wishes to congratulate all units belonging to and attached to the 8th Indian Division on the part they played in the successful operation just concluded, and to thank them for their loyal co-operation.

"On 25 August the 8th Indian Division was operating on a front of over 40 miles, both by land and water, and the fact that everything worked without a hitch reflects very great credit both on commanders and their staffs and also on the unit and sub-unit leaders who were responsible for leading columns and conducting local actions.

"On 26 and 27 August the work of the Sapper Unit in preparing and operating the ferry across the river Karun is worthy of special praise.

"Though the early armistice robbed us of the full fruits of victory, it was most gratifying that we were able to secure Ahwaz before it came into effect."

Haft Khel

One of the last places to be occupied in the south-west sector was Haft Khel, which was allotted to the 3/10 Baluch Regiment. This battalion was flown in from Shuaiba aerodrome, and landed on receiving a sign marked on the ground by the staff of the Anglo-Iranian Oil Company that all was safe. They were soon able to occupy the police outposts on the landing ground, the Iranian gendarmerie having fled to Ahwaz. Masjid-i-Suleman was also taken, and patrols were sent in the neighbourhood to clear the area of Iranian troops. Subsequently on 25 August the 18th Indian Infantry Brigade arrived from Kut Abdullah and established itself in Haft Khel.

CHAPTER XL

West Iran Operations

Plan of Operations

As mentioned earlier, the British plan of operations had provided for the invasion of Iran by two forces: one based on Basra was to enter from the south-west (the operations of which have just been described), and the other based on Khanakin was to enter Iran from the west.[1] On 22 July 1941, the possibility of sending troops into west Iran was first communicated by Lieut-General Quinan to Brigadier Aizlewood, commanding the 2nd Indian Armoured Brigade. On the following day the Brigade Commander carried out a preliminary reconnaissance at Khanakin. He then left for Kirkuk where details of the composition of the force were reviewed and the Brigade Commander's appreciation was prepared.

The armoured brigade reached Khanakin on 9 August, but on the 10th a message was received from Lieut-General Quinan that the operations intended for the 12th had been postponed by a few days. Some reconnaissance was carried out on land, as air photography was not allowed, and a fresh plan was prepared on 12 August.

The plan of operations as prepared by Brigadier Aizlewood was of a simpler nature than that for south-west Iran. It consisted of the following phases to be covered by the 2nd Indian Armoured Brigade:—

(i) A night march by 2/7 Gurkha Rifles in motor transport with one troop 25-pounders from Khanakin to Naft Khana, and to seize Naft-i-Shah by first light on 25 August.

(ii) A Column consisting of 14/20 Hussars less one squadron, 15th Field Regiment less one battery, Battery Headquarters and 1/5 Gurkha Rifles was to cross the frontier at first light on 25 August by the main Khanakin—Kermanshah road and seize Qasr-i-Shirin, reconnoitring subsequently the Pai Tak Pass area.

(iii) B Column consisting of a squadron 14/20 Hussars, a troop of 25-pounders, and a company of Gurkha Rifles was to march to Gilan at first light on 25 August and reconnoitre the country towards Shahabad. The composition of this column was later altered to include the whole of Warwickshire Yeomanry in place of a company of Gurkha Rifles.

---
[1] These two forces were, of course, in addition to the Russians who were to enter from the north.

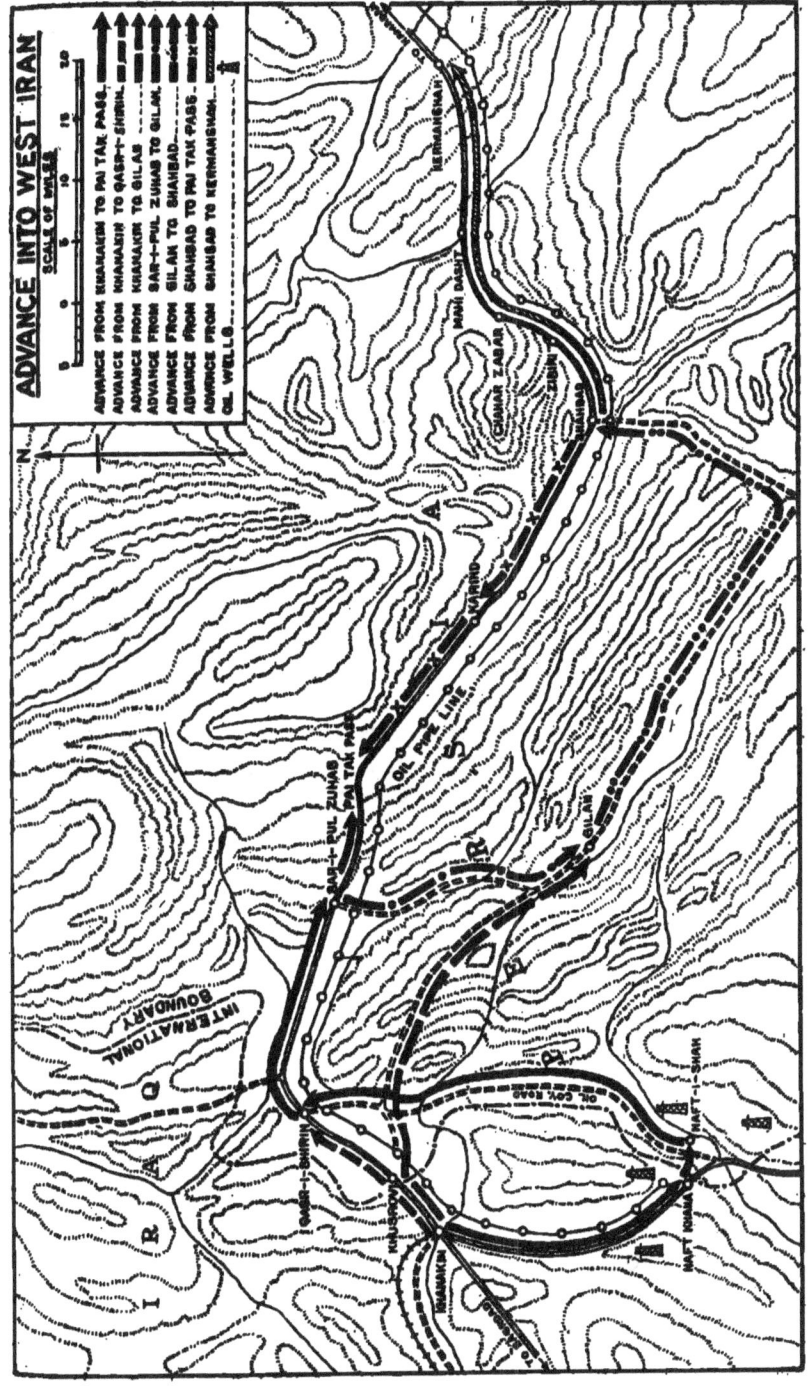

About 20 August, it was decided to increase the strength of this force in order to form, when required, a mobile element in addition to the infantry element. Another reason for its strengthening was the report of the Iranian concentration and their determination to hold the Pai Tak Pass.

On 22 August, the 9th Armoured Brigade arrived at Khanakin, and the plan was further amended. The combined brigades were then known as "Hazelforce".

On 23 August, a further change of plan was made according to which the 10th Indian Division was to take control of the operations of Hazelforce. Force Operation Instructions No. 12 of 24 August ordered Major-General W. J. Slim, Commander of the 10th Indian Division, who had just returned from India, to proceed forthwith to Khanakin and take command of the operations in west Iran. The 21st Indian Infantry Brigade Group (less one battalion) and the 157th Field Regiment at Habbaniya were placed at his disposal and ordered to move to Khanakin.

Major-General Slim, who arrived at Khanakin on the evening of 24 August, with a detachment of his headquarters, and who had had no time previously to study the details of the operations, decided to make no change in Brigadier Aizlewood's plan, that is to secure the oilfield at Naft-i-Shah, the Pai Tak Pass, the road to Kermanshah with all its strategic posts, and then to move northward to meet the Russian allies. He decided to employ the 21st Indian Infantry Brigade against the Pai Tak Pass. The force to be employed against the pass was named "Bedale", and its eventual organisation was as follows:[2]

Headquarters 10th Indian Division

21st Indian Infantry Brigade plus 157th Field Regiment plus 19th Medium Battery	Hazelforce
2nd Indian Armoured Brigade = (14/20 Hussars, 15th Field Regiment, 1/5 Gurkha Rifles, 2/7 Gurkha Rifles, 32nd Field Squadron Sappers and Miners)	9th Armoured Brigade (Household Cavalry, Warwickshire Yeomanry, Wiltshire Yeomanry, 2nd Cheshire Field Squadron, Royal Engineers)

[2] See also Appendix 18.

Royal Air Force

The operations in west Iran were to be assisted by the Royal Air Force based at Habbaniya, directly under the Air Headquarters, Iraq. The air force in this sector comprised:—

    No. 11 Squadron (Bombers)
    No. 14 Squadron (Bombers)
    No. 45 Squadron (Blenheims).

The plan provided for the ground forces to enter Iranian territory from Khanakin at dawn on 25 August. By the end of the day they were expected to have captured Naft-i-Shah oilfields, Sar-i-Pul Zuhab and Gilan. On 26 August, they were expected to have captured Karind and Shahabad (also named Harunabad) thus cutting off the Iranian troops in the Pai Tak Pass. By the evening of 26 August, the troops of the 10th Indian Division were expected to be 4 miles beyond Sar-i-Pul Zuhab and east of Sar-i-Mil. The R.A.F. was to bomb Pai Tak Pass positions on the afternoon of 26th and the morning of 27th after which the 21st Indian Infantry Brigade would attack the pass.

On the night of 24/25 August, when operations began in the south-west of Iran, simultaneously operations opened in western Iran as well, with their base at Khanakin, situated a little above 100 miles to the north-east of Baghdad, 7 miles from the Iranian border on the Iraq side. Khanakin formed the main gateway to western Iran. From there a route led across the Pai Tak Pass to Teheran, 600 miles further east, and thence on to the Russian border. Thirty miles south of Khanakin lay the oilfield of Naft-i-Shah on the Iranian soil which could be reached by the road running parallel to the oil pipeline. The northern column would move in a north-easterly direction from Khanakin to Qasr-i-Shirin. On its route lay Khusrovi, a customs and gendarmerie post in the Iranian territory. From Khusrovi onwards, there started a fine metalled road. The next gendarmerie post was located at Kaleh Shah Murj, $12\frac{1}{2}$ miles distant. The road from this point to Qasr-i-Shirin was rough, stony and narrow. It was very tortuous and undulating and made numerous sudden, short and steep descents into, and ascents out of, narrow, stony and dry nulla beds. At the 19th mile Qasr-i-Shirin was situated. It had a population of 3 to 4 thousand inhabitants and post, telegraph and telephone offices. Good perennial water was available in abundance from the river close by. Beyond this place the country was greatly broken up by numerous steep-edged nullas making movements off the road very difficult. Sar-i-Pul Zuhab stood at $39\frac{1}{2}$ miles. It had 500 houses with post, telephone and telegraph offices and a gendarmerie post. The village was dirty, with only a few good houses, the remaining being hovels. Water was plentiful, good and perennial from the Hulwan river, a quarter mile below. Next came the hamlet of Pai Tak, a village situated at the 49th mile. From this part began the ascent of the Pai Tak Pass. Near the peak of the pass there was a spring of good water. The summit of the Pai Tak Pass was reached at a distance of three and a half miles from the village. It had a gendarmerie post. Across the pass the road undulated sharply with ascents and descents. At the 66th mile the road reached a plateau at Sar-i-Mil. At 72nd mile began the orchards of Karind, which was situated at a height of 5,000 feet. In August the climate of Karind was cool and bracing in the day, but cold at night, and three blankets were needed to have a comfortable sleep. On the roadside existed a habitation of 50 houses, a small bazar, garages and tea houses. The main village was in a gorge two furlongs away. Plentiful, perennial and good water could be obtained from a stream flowing out of the gorge, half a mile below. Excellent apples and grapes were available in plenty and were cheap. Supplies of other food stuffs were abundant.

The Iranian Defences

The Iranian forces likely to oppose British advance were estimated to be as the following:

5th Kurdistan Division,
12th Kermanshah Division,
One composite division from Teheran,
One weak brigade group from the *13th Division* en route from Isfahan.

In addition to that, a patrol of the 21st Indian Infantry Brigade reported that 1,000 men of the infantry were posted at Gayara while another 1,000 were at Chinar with five pack guns.

The headquarters of the *12th Kermanshah Division*, was reported to have moved to Surrnadyza, east of the Pai Tak Pass. Some armoured cars were seen on Khanakin front. The Gilan—Shahabad road was reported to be defended in depth. Artillery and infantry had taken up positions near Tang Tarazat, 8 miles south of Shahabad. It was further learnt that a large number of lorries with anti-aircraft and field artillery were moving in this area. Between Pai Tak and Karind a number of troops were accommodated in huts on the hill sides, and these huts were effectively camouflaged. Another report gave out that the Iranian troops, estimated to be 10,000 strong with approximately 8 anti-aircraft guns and well concealed from view, were holding defensive positions on the Pai Tak Pass. But the morale of the troops was not high, and the troops had little desire to fight against the British. The morale of the Teheran garrison troops from which some of the troops in this area were drawn was, however, higher. The formations were the following:

General Sir Archibald Wavell

Major-General W. J. Slim

Detachment 1/5 Gurkha Rifles, Iran

Indian Armoured cars on patrol in Iran

20th Infantry Regiment
21st Infantry Regiment
6th Infantry Regiment
2nd Field Artillery Regiment
Skoda 105-mm. guns.

Naft-i-Shah

As approved by Major-General Slim, the plan of operations consisted in simultaneous attack on Naft-i-Shah, Qasr-i-Shirin and Gilan as preliminary to the capture of Pai Tak Pass which opened the way to Kermanshah and Iran. It has been mentioned earlier that operations were to be launched on 24/25 August simultaneously with those in south-west Iran against Abadan and Ahwaz, and Khanakin was to be the base of operations. The commander of the 2nd Armoured Brigade had previously reconnoitred Naft-i-Shah area from Naft Khana and Khanakin, in Iraq. At the appointed hour, the 2nd Battalion 7th Gurkha Rifles left Khanakin for a position opposite the Naft-i-Shah oilfields, which it attacked at 0430 hours on 25 August. Slight opposition was encountered and a few casualties inflicted. With this the Iranian resistance was over. A small garrison was then left in Naft-i-Shah, and at 1030 hours the battalion advanced embussed northward on Chicha Surkh whose garrison had fled eastward into the hills. At 1315 hours the Gurkhas continued their advance to rejoin the northern column (A column) which was at that time moving towards Sar-i-Pul Zuhab after clearing Qasr-i-Shirin.

Khusrovi

The northern or A column, before moving out in strength on the midnight of 24/25 August, ordered the B Company of the 1st Battalion 5th Royal Gurkha Rifles to seize the Iranian frontier police and customs post at Khusrovi. This company moved out of the camp at 2130 hours on 24 August, and cut off all telegraph and telephone lines between Khusrovi and Qasr-i-Shirin and attacked the former at 0400 hours on 25 August. Very feeble opposition was encountered and the place was captured. The Gurkhas kept one Iranian officer as prisoner, retained some arms and let off all other prisoners after disarming them.

Qasr-i-Shirin

Meanwhile the main body of the A column had left Khanakin at 0155 hours on 25 August for a rendezvous with the advance party, 3 miles south-west of Khusrovi. They crossed the Iranian frontier at 0515 hours and rejoined the B Company. The advanced guard was well ahead of the main body towards Qasr-i-Shirin. The 14/20

Hussars (less detachments) under command of the Gurkha Battalion had moved out during the night and at 0415 hours, after a difficult night march, had taken up position astride the main roads leading out north-west, north and east from Qasr-i-Shirin. The southern side was to be attacked by the Gurkhas. At 0505 hours B Company 1/5 Gurkha Rifles and advanced battalion headquarters, south of Qasr-i-Shirin, came under considerable Iranian fire. The battalion then debussed quickly and B Company was pushed out to hold tactical features to cover the deployment of the rest of the force. At 0730 hours A and C Companies attacked and secured two prominent hills south of Qasr-i-Shirin on either side of the road covered by B Company. No artillery support was available for capturing these hills as the light tanks of 14/20 Hussars were unable to co-operate owing to the damage done to their trucks by the small-arms fire of the Iranians. Qasr-i-Shirin was, however, effectively encircled by now, on three sides by the Hussars and from the south by the Gurkhas. The A and C Companies of the Gurkhas then moved towards the town closely followed by their battalion headquarters; while 14/20 Hussars attacked from the north-west with their armoured fighting vehicles. Seeing this the Iranian troops withdrew from the town and the Gurkhas entered it at 1000 hours. No further opposition was offered in the town itself and the inhabitants received the Indian troops warmly. During the whole engagement for the capture of Qasr-i-Shirin, the Gurkha battalion suffered only one casualty—a rifleman being wounded in the arm.

Soon afterwards, the battalion received orders at 1150 hours to push on towards the Pai Tak Pass which was to be reached as early as possible. The move began at noon, during the hottest part of the day, and the route was very dusty; to this difficulty was added an insufficient supply of water. However, by 1545 hours, the battalion had reached Sar-i-Pul Zuhab, five miles west of the Pai Tak Pass. Here it went into harbour facing the pass which was reported to be strongly defended. D Company of 1/5 Gurkha Rifles occupied a covering position east of the battalion harbour at 1630 hours and waited for its B Echelon with food and cooking facilities to arrive. Nothing arrived, however, and emergency rations were eaten. The failure of the administrative arrangements left the battalion without food or means of cooking it and with only sufficient petrol for a limited operation on the following day. This failure of the administrative services was probably due to a temporary strike of the civilian transport drivers employed by the military to drive lorries towards Rutba and Khanakin. Due probably to the same reason, the battalion did not receive any orders in the evening regarding the next day's tasks, and had to send an officer, back to the 2nd Indian Armoured

Brigade's headquarters, to get them. The officer returned to the camp by 2210 hours.

While the Gurkhas were encamped at Sar-i-Pul Zuhab, the main body of A column moved from Qasr-i-Shirin towards them in the night of 25/26 August. It was a difficult task to make the journey on the twisty road from Qasr-i-Shirin. In view of the absence of the Iranian Air Force in the sky, the General took the risk of according permission for the side and tail lights to be used. But shortly afterwards an "officious officer", driving towards Qasr-i-Shirin shouted to the drivers to put their lights out. This was done and a distance of twenty miles was covered in the dark. However, they were in harbour by 2345 hours. Slit trenches were soon dug, and the men who were pretty tired settled down to their night's rest, while 1/5 Gurkhas received orders to start early in the morning to move down south towards Gilan where B column was held up by strong opposition.

On 26 August at 1200 hours an officer was sent from the battalion column to the Brigade Petrol Point at Tang-i-Kora with an escort and two 3-ton lorries to fetch petrol in order that the battalion might proceed beyond Gilan if required; but no such Petrol Point was found to exist owing to a further breakdown of administrative arrangements. The battalion harboured at Gilan at 1430 hours and obtained sufficient petrol to last it till Shahabad.

Gilan

Meanwhile B Column, consisting of one squadron 14/20 Hussars, the Warwickshire Yeomanry, one battery of the 15th Field Regiment, Royal Artillery, and a troop of the 32nd Field Squadron, Sappers and Miners, left Khanakin direct for Gilan, about 25 miles south of Sar-i-Pul Zuhab on 25 August. This column advanced without meeting any resistance. At about 1215 hours it entered a village which was deserted. But then, stiff opposition was encountered from the west end of the Koh-i-Wazhlan ridge which held up the advance and resulted in some casualties. The battery of the 15th Field Regiment then came into action, but in spite of three attempts to advance with the support of tanks and artillery fire no progress was made, and the Iranian guns were not dislodged till the nightfall.

An attack was prepared for the morning of 26 August but the Iranians withdrew before the attack started. They left two antitank guns (3.7-mm. Skoda) and one prisoner was taken, while one Iranian soldier was found dead. By 1200 hours the valley was clear for further advance by the column, which was also expecting 1/5 Gurkha Battalion to reach Gilan in the afternoon.

According to previous information there was a road from Sar-i-

Pul Zuhab towards Karind and Shahabad between the main Gilan-Shahabad road and the Pai Tak Pass road, but no such road existed and the 2nd Indian Armoured Brigade at Sar-i-Pul Zuhab had to move by the Gilan road which was already occupied by B column, and along which the 9th Armoured Brigade was also to advance.

The 9th Armoured Brigade left Khanakin at 0500 hours on 26 August by the same route as B column. By 1000 hours the head of B column had reached the road junction west of Gilan where it had to halt till 1400 hours as the road was occupied by the 2nd Indian Armoured Brigade. When debouching from the hills into the Gilan plain, the advanced guard of light tanks was mistakenly fired on by a troop of Warwickshire Yeomanry who were guarding the pass, but no casualties occurred.

Meanwhile B Column had established by 1045 hours that the opponents had withdrawn from their position to the east of Gilan. The commander of Hazelforce reached Gilan and decided to re-organise his force. Up till now, though Hazelforce had existed in name, no separate command or staff had been formed, and the commander of the 2nd Indian Armoured Brigade was commanding both his own brigade and Hazelforce. An advanced guard was now formed with Warwickshire Yeomanry, one battery of artillery, and the 2nd Battalion 7th Gurkha Rifles with Royal Engineer and Medical detachments, under the direct command of Hazelforce. Advanced guard was followed by Headquarters Hazelforce, the 9th Armoured Brigade (less the Warwickshire Yeomanry), and then by the remainder of the 2nd Indian Armoured Brigade. Throughout the advance the attitude of the Iranian civilians was friendly, and the inhabitants who had left Gilan began to return after the place had been captured. According to local information the Iranian troops had been short of food and were not keen to fight.

The Hazelforce having covered a stiff hill journey of nearly 20 miles halted at Mille Chahar for a few hours on the 27th morning. The road took off about a mile from Mille Chahar village, turned sharply to the west and ascended the hill by a series of sharp, steep bends which the 25-pounders found difficult to climb. The road then ran east along the side of the hill to the top of Koh-i-Qaleh, 6000 feet above sea-level, from where it was well defined, and had good surface. The advance continued throughout the night. The leading elements reached Shahabad soon after first light, and the town was occupied without meeting any resistance at 0700 hours on 27 August. From Shahabad, a squadron of Household Cavalry was sent towards Karind and the Pai Tak Pass to cover the eastern approaches to the pass. At 1400 hours the main body of Hazelforce passed over Koh-i-Qaleh, and reached Shahabad at 1615 hours. The imperial Agricultural Estate at Aliabad was occupied and the troops harboured south of the sugar factory at Shahabad.

Pai Tak Pass

The 21st Indian Infantry Brigade had advanced towards the western approaches of the Pai Tak Pass during the night of 25/26 August, and spent the 26th in reconnoitring the pass. It was gathered from the local inhabitants that the pass was held by about 400 men. At 1130 hours on the 26th, a mountain gun sited near the top of the pass opened fire on the road. One of the patrols moving along the main road was fired on by a light machine-gun near the Pumping Station. One Blenheim of 45 Squadron reconnoitred Pai Tak Pass and made a photo reconnaissance of the road from Sar-i-Pul Zuhab to Karind. The Iranian positions in the pass were bombed by 12 Blenheims of 45 Squadron in the afternoon. One aircraft was heavily fired at by three or four light machine-guns in the hills, but the Iranian gun positions were effectively blasted.

On the morning of 27 August, local people coming down the road stated that the Iranian force had left the pass at midnight. The Brigade Commander decided to go up the road to the pass. Except for one or two very indifferent road-blocks there was nothing to oppose the advance. The Advanced Brigade Headquarters was at the top before noon and Major-General Slim arrived shortly afterwards. Although no equipment had been left by the Iranians, there was a considerable quantity of ammunition. A pursuit party of two companies and one troop artillery was ordered to be ready, and at 1300 hours a message was sent to Hazelforce that the 21st Indian Infantry Brigade was sending a motorised patrol through the pass towards Karind. Although this column entered the pass from the west, it was the move of the southern or Gilan column towards the rear of the pass from Shahabad which had induced the Iranians to evacuate it.

At the western outskirts of Karind this patrol from the 21st Indian Infantry Brigade met another patrol from Hazelforce which came from Shahabad, consisting of a squadron of the Household Cavalry Regiment and a troop of 15th Field Regiment.

Karind

The 21st Indian Infantry Brigade Group occupied Karind at 1505 hours on 27 August. A report gives out that "the local population seemed genuinely pleased at our appearance in place of the Shah's troops, and large quantities of the locally grown grapes found willing consumers". The Divisional Headquarters from Khanakin arrived at Karind the following day. A German engineer who was in charge of the construction of a hotel at Karind was arrested.

Zibiri

Reconnaissance from Shahabad on 27 August disclosed that the high ground overlooking the village of Zibiri, 25 miles east of Shahabad, on the route from Shahabad to Kermanshah, was held by Iranians. From this position the Iranian artillery intermittently shelled the road west of Zibiri. Consequently a little after their arrival at Shahabad on the morning of 27 August, C Squadron of the Warwickshire Yeomanry was sent out to cover the approaches to Shahabad from Kermanshah by blocking the road west of Zabiri, until the advance was resumed towards Kermanshah. On approaching Karim Harsada, the two leading trucks of this squadron came under light machine-gun fire from short range. This fire which was directed with skill and accuracy immobilised both the trucks and killed one British officer and one British other rank ; 3 British other ranks were wounded, and one British other rank was taken prisoner. The remainder of the squadron came into action but could not dislodge the opponents until a battery of the 15th Field Regiment, Royal Artillery, was brought in position and shelled the ridge. The Iranians then withdrew, and C Squadron was able to recover the two trucks with their contents intact. The high ground overlooking the village of Zibiri was occupied at 1800 hours. Shelling on both sides continued throughout the night. From first light on 28 August, one troop of the 15th Field Regiment, Royal Artillery, shelled the ground west of Zibiri at intervals of fifteen minutes. At 0530 hours on the 28th, the commander of Hazelforce visited the forward squadron and made a personal reconnaissance. C Squadron was ordered to send one troop in its trucks forward through Zibiri with the object of drawing Iranian fire. At 0645 hours this troop was shelled as soon as it came over the ridge. The Commander Hazelforce then withdrew the troop. The road west of Zibiri was also shelled by the Iranians with fair accuracy. An attack on the Iranian position east of Zibiri by one squadron 14/20 Hussars, the 2nd Battalion 7th Gurkha Rifles and the 1st Battalion 5th Royal Gurkha Rifles supported by guns of the 15th Field Regiment, Royal Artillery, was to start at 1000 hours ; but at 0915 hours on 28 August three Iranian cavalry officers carrying white flags rode out to stop the Iranian cavalry charge that was about to be delivered against the rear of the Hazelforce and made a request for a truce.

Lieut-General Quinan accompanied by two Russian Liaison Officers arrived at Zibiri at 1300 hours on the 28th, whilst Major-General Slim was still discussing terms with the Iranian Envoy. He lunched at the Advanced Battalion Headquarters of 1/5 Gurkha Rifles and instructed Major-General Slim to advance and occupy Kermanshah in order to secure the oil refinery and tinning factory.

Chahar Zabar

The Iranians were holding entrenched positions on either side of the road leading from Shahabad to Kermanshah at Chahar Zabar Pass situated to the east of Zibiri. They appeared to have a battery of mountain guns and some heavy artillery. On the 27th the Hazelforce and the 21st Indian Infantry Brigade were informed that an air reconnaissance would be made of the road and the Chahar Zabar area. This was done very ineffectively and wrong information was supplied regarding the opponents' position and strength. Preparations were being made for an attack on the Chahar Zabar Pass position, but at 0800 hours on the 28th, a white flag was flown from an Iranian post. Two cars carrying white flags and an Iranian Staff Officer came to ask for armistice. The following terms were offered for truce:—

(1) The Iranians to retire from forward positions at 1400 hours and withdraw from successive positions, the Allies to advance as they retired.
(2) Kermanshah to be surrendered at 0600 hours on 30 August.
(3) All Iranian troops to be beyond Bisitun by 1600 hours on 31 August.
(4) All British oil employees to be in the British lines uninjured on 28 August.
(5) Reply to be received before 1400 hours. If the reply was a refusal or there was any attempt to bargain, the attack would start.

After some attempts at higgling the Iranian emissary accepted these terms on behalf of General Muqaddam, General Officer Commanding Iranian Forces in the area. He was sent back with a British officer to report to his commander. At about 1400 hours the Iranian officer with his British escort returned and announced the acceptance of the terms by General Muqaddam. He also reported that a message had just been received by wire from the Shah ordering all resistance to cease. He was accompanied by the senior British official of the Iranian Petroleum Company in Kermanshah who reported that all British subjects in Kermanshah were safe and had not been molested in any way.

Shirwan

1/5 Gurkha Rifles had been previously ordered to continue advance towards Kermanshah from Zibiri at 1420 hours on 28 August. At 1500 hours the Gurkhas harboured at Shirwan, west of Mahidasht. They selected a good site for the camp, 5,000 feet above sea-level, on a hill covered with fine trees. The battalion put up strong picquets round the camp at 1730 hours as about 750 armed Iranian soldiers were camping in a nulla close by. 2/7 Gurkha

Rifles arrived shortly afterwards and harboured by the side of 1/5 Gurkha. The next day was spent at Shirwan in repairing and overhauling vehicles.

1/5 Gurkha Rifles left Shirwan camp at 0710 hours on the 30th, as part of the 2nd Indian Armoured Brigade column carrying out a flag march to impress the civil population of Kermanshah.

Kermanshah

Kermanshah is the largest town in western Iran. It is situated at a height of 4,000 feet. The mountains in its neighbourhood are above 10,000 feet high, and in winter are covered with thick snow. In spring snow begins to melt, and a large variety of wild flowers appear everywhere. The climate throughout summer is pleasant. In July the entire countryside is covered with multi-coloured flowers. Poppies are grown in abundance for opium. In summer numerous fine varieties of fruits, such as melons, grapes, pears, apricots and cherries are found in abundance.

On the afternoon of 28 August, Major-General Slim with Brigadier Aizlewood, two staff officers and an Iranian officer drove into Kermanshah, passing through the withdrawing Iranian troops on the way. The latter were in considerable numbers, with artillery, anti-tank guns and some motor transport. Their equipment, arms and clothing appeared to be brand new, and while there was a good deal of straggling, officers and non-commissioned officers were in control, and discipline seemed reasonably good. At Mahidasht the party passed a regiment of cavalry halting, with its horse lines laid out in peace-time style.

After visiting the Oil Refinery, the Divisional Commander with the other British officers motored into the city. They were received by General Muqaddam, General Officer Commanding, General Puria, Commander *12th Division*, the Civil Governor and other officials.

General Muqaddam again agreed to the terms imposed but as he had received an order from the Shah to keep the normal garrison (about 3,000 troops) in the city barracks, he was torn between his fear of the distant Shah and the adjacent British. To save his face he was given permission to retain two hundred officers and men in the barracks. The civil administration was ordered to carry on as before.

All British personnel in the Consulate, Bank and Oil Company were found to be well. It was arranged to hire from the Oil Company sufficient transport to maintain a brigade group at Kermanshah. A German with a broken leg was arrested. The refinery was occupied on 29 August by a detachment and, on 30 August, the remainder of the 2nd and 9th Armoured Brigades reached Kermanshah. 1/5 Gurkha Rifles entered Kermanshah at 1100 hours on

30 August. A large crowd gathered to watch the eight-mile-long procession of vehicles. Some persons waved and appeared pleased to see them, and some looked gloomy and unfriendly, but the majority indicated no emotions.

Among the captured material there were nine large lorries loaded with arms recovered about 70 miles from Kermanshah on the Hamadan road and four guns—two 105-mm Skoda (long) and two 105-mm Skoda (short).

Eighty soldiers who were in Kermanshah barracks moved out of them of their own accord, on the night of 30/31 August, and one squadron from the 9th Armoured Brigade took over the barracks which were reported to be capable of accommodating 5,000 troops. The main camp was fixed near a steep hill, 7,000 feet high, six miles from the city and three miles from the Anglo-Iranian Oil Company.

In the whole campaign total casualties, both British and Indian, were 20 killed and 50 wounded.

At the end of the operations in Iran General Wavell wrote in his despatch on 5 September 1941:—

"The Middle East Command owes a deep debt of gratitude to India. During the period of nearly two years while I was Commander-in-Chief, Middle East, I never made any request for men or material that was not instantly met, if it was within India's resources to do so."

The Russian Move

While the British and Indian troops were moving into Iran from Khanakin and Basra, the Russian troops were carrying out a simultaneous advance from two places. One of their columns moved from a base on the Caspian Sea towards Pahlevi and from there towards Kazvin. Another moved from Julfa, across the Russian border, towards Tabriz and from there through Mianeh to Kazvin. The plan was for both columns to concentrate at Kazvin, only ninety miles from Teheran, and later to move on the capital itself if necessary. They marched swiftly, meeting very little or no opposition and entered Kazvin on the fifth day of the campaign. A detachment of Indian troops was sent out to meet and establish contact with the Russians at Senneh. The Allied troops met there on 30 August, and later at Kazvin. At both places the Indian troops received a warm welcome from the Russians.

The Treaty

The four days' campaign in Iran cannot strictly be called a war or a military operation. Although some forces of Russia and the United Kingdom (including those of India) had entered Iran from two directions, the British and Russian ambassadors had continued to stay on in Teheran. The campaign was more in the nature of a police action to induce the Shah to get rid of the Germans and to organise the 'aid to Russia' programme. This limited objective was achieved easily, and with the minimum possible loss of life or property. A vast majority of the civilian population was not affected at all.

The Iranian Prime Minister had resigned even while the troop movements were continuing and his successor accepted the terms offered by the Allies, which included the closing of German, Italian, Hungarian and Rumanian Legations and the handing over of the Germans to the Allies or their expulsion from Iran. The Legations were closed but there was some delay in handing over the Germans. Meanwhile the Russians, who had stopped at Kazvin, about ninety miles from Teheran, began to march towards Teheran in order to expedite the handing over or expulsion of Axis agents from the country. This probably induced the Shah to abdicate on 16 September. Another result of this Russian move was that most of the Axis representatives also left Teheran by 18 September. The Crown Prince, Mohammad Riza Pahlevi, a young man of 23, was declared successor to the throne by the Majlis. The new regime co-operated with the Allies in a gradually increasing measure.

As the occupation was likely to disturb the Iranian economy, a result which would have been detrimental to the Allied interests also, the British Government agreed to change the status of occupation into that of a tripartite treaty. Negotiations were concluded by January 1942 and a treaty between Russia, the United Kingdom and Iran was signed. According to this, Iran promised to help in the passage of troops and supplies through the country by providing labour and other facilities. There was to be no military occupation, though Allied troops were to remain in Iran. The troops were to be withdrawn within six months after the end of hostilities.

With the cessation of hostilities, if hostilities they could be called, the Allied forces including those of Iran, began to devote themselves to the tasks of (*i*) feeding and clothing of the Iranian population, (*ii*) disarming and pacifying the tribes in whose hands a large quantity of German arms and ammunition had fallen during the confusion resulting from the short campaign, and (*iii*) the repair, maintenance and improvement of the lines of communication—ports, roads, railways etc.—for organising the aid to Russia. These tasks were now energetically taken in hand, with the co-operation of the Iranian Government, by the forces in the area which were organised, from 1 February 1942, into the Tenth Army. After some time, American technical troops also came into Iran and helped the Tenth Army, later constituted into the Persia and Iraq Force (Paiforce), in sending supplies to Russia and in running the railways and organising road convoys. The Paiforce (Persia and Iraq Force) was an independent command directly under the War Office. How this separate command came into existence in August 1942, and its activities, form the subject matter of the next part of this volume.

PAIFORCE

or

Persia and Iraq Force

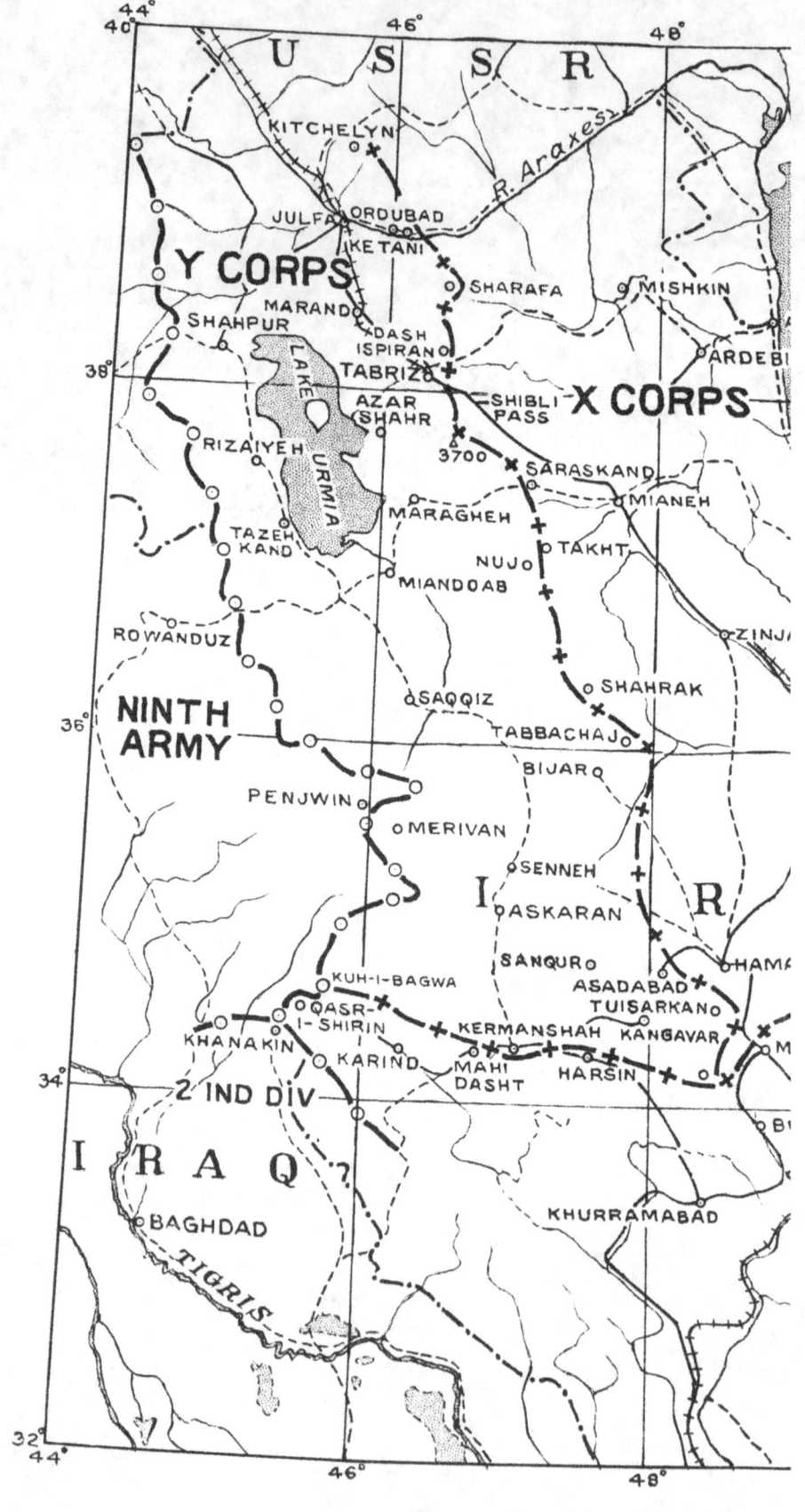

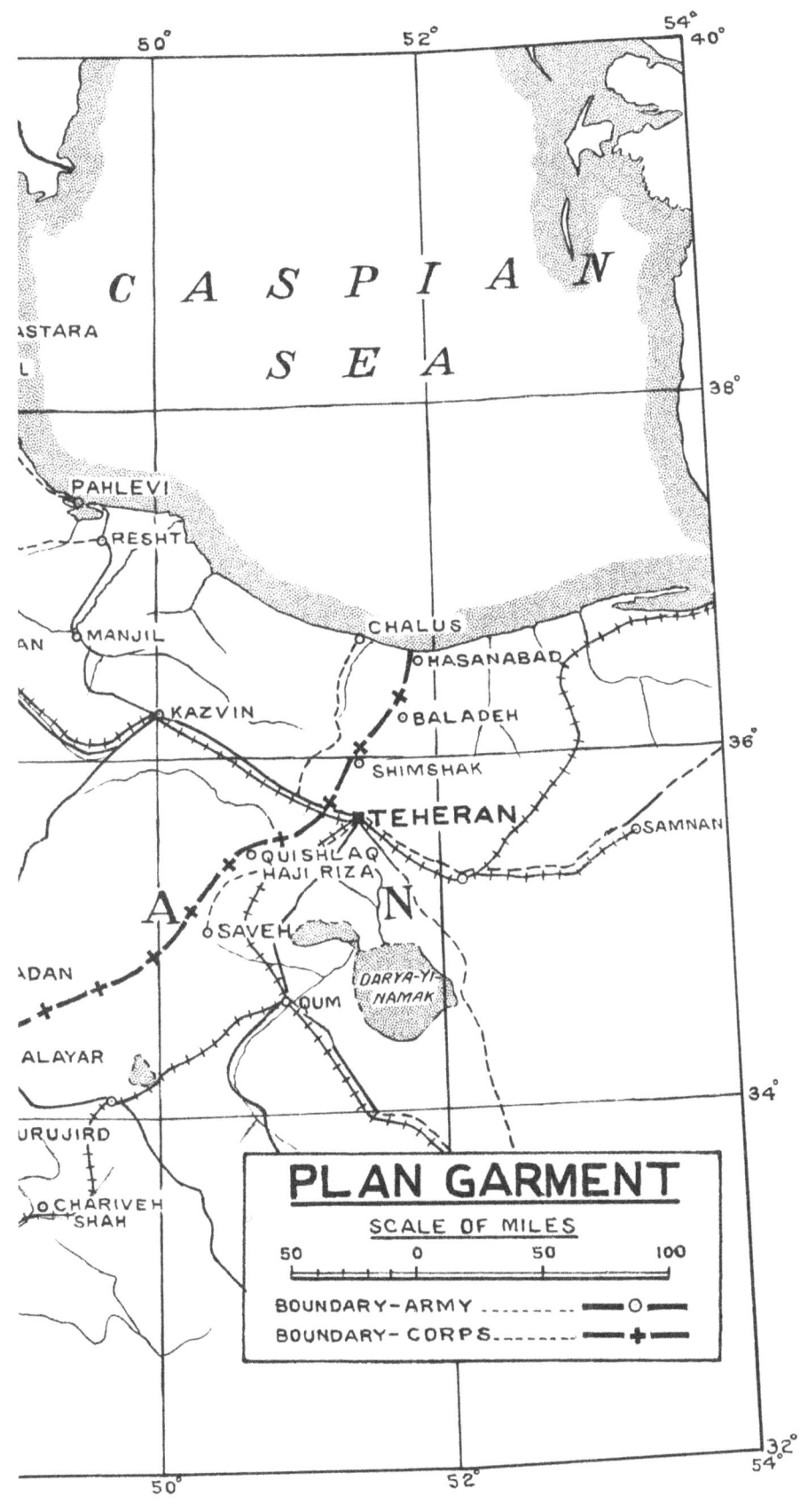

CHAPTER XLI

Paiforce and its Plans

Shortly before the outbreak of the Second World War, the Middle East Command had been formed in August 1939 with General Wavell as its General Officer Commanding-in-Chief. In peace-time, the area of the command included Egypt, the Sudan, Palestine, Transjordan and Cyprus. It was however laid down at the time of its formation, that, in case of an outbreak of hostilities, the area of the command would be extended to include all military forces in Somaliland, Aden, Iraq and on the shores of the Persian Gulf, in addition to the areas under it in peacetime. The war broke out soon after and the Middle East Command, with its headquarters at Cairo, became responsible for all the above mentioned areas.

After the entry of Italy into the war in June 1940 on the collapse of France, North Africa became an active theatre of warfare and the Middle East Command was engaged in fighting the Italians to protect Egypt. Thus, although this Command embraced many areas in Africa and Western Asia, North Africa became the most important region of its responsibilities from the military point of view. Thus, when troops from India were landed in Iraq in April 1941 their operational control was delegated to the Commander-in-Chief, India, initially, but when hostilities broke out there the operational control was transferred to the Middle East Command in May 1941. On the collapse of Rashid Ali's regime, operational control again reverted to the Commander-in-Chief, India, on 18 June 1941.

However, with the German attack on Russia in June of that year and the early successes gained by German arms against that country, the strategic importance of the countries of Western Asia suddenly increased. Plans and preparations had now to be made by the British forces in Iraq to meet any possible German thrust into Iraq or Syria through Anatolia and Iran.

Meanwhile, more troops and military units began to arrive in Western Asia and the tiny force in Iraq—known in the beginning as the "British Troops in Iraq"—began steadily to grow. In January 1942 the operational control of Iraq and Iran again passed from India to the Middle East Command, and a little later the force in that area was designated the Tenth Army. The expanded strength in Western Asia, and the more intense fighting in North Africa after the arrival of General Rommel on the scene, placed a great strain on the planning and administrative resources of the Middle East

Command. The need to split the command into two separate commands was thus making itself felt.

At the same time, certain internal administrative changes in the Tenth Army set-up were also contemplated. At this time, February 1942, the Tenth Army under Lieut.-General E. P. Quinan, consisting mostly of Indian formations, comprised the 6th Indian Division, 8th Indian Division, 10th Indian Division, 252nd Indian Armoured Group, and the 151st Infantry Brigade of the 50th British Division.[1] In July 1942, however, the necessity was felt of freeing Lieut.-General Quinan, Commander of the Tenth Army, from the heavy burden of administration of the bases and lines of communication in Iraq and Iran so that he might concentrate his attention on the operational tasks. Accordingly, General Auchinleck, the Commander-in-Chief of the Middle East Forces,[2] issued, on 23 July 1942, a letter proposing a reorganisation of the commands in Iraq and Iran. The main features of this proposal were:

(i) the control of the general administration of the ports, depots and communications behind the Tenth Army was to be vested in a senior Staff Officer of General Headquarters, Middle East, designated as the Inspector General of Communications;

(ii) there was to be created an area command, known as Pibase (Persia-Iraq Base) to deal with the internal security and local administration of the base and lines of communication area;

(iii) the zone of responsibility of the Commander of the Tenth Army was to be further reduced by transferring northern Iraq from the Tenth to the Ninth Army.[3]

New Command Created

This proposal, which was implemented on 15 August 1942, proved to be a temporary measure, for the British Cabinet decided to create in Iran and Iraq a separate command directly under the War Office. This command was known as Paiforce (Persia and Iraq Force) or Paic (Persia and Iraq Command). The creation of this separate command had become necessary owing to the fast changing situation in the Middle East. Axis thrusts towards the Caucasus had assumed significant proportions and there was danger that the Nazi forces would reach the river Araxes in north Iran before the close of October 1942. To meet this threat it was decided that a separate command directly under the War Office should control Iraq and Iran and devise effective measures for averting this danger. The

---
[1] The Tenth Army Order of Battle, 1 February 1942.
[2] General Auchinleck had replaced General Wavell at Cairo in July 1941.
[3] No. G/3043 HQ Tenth Army dated 23 July 1942, *War Diary* Tenth Army.

PAIFORCE AND ITS PLANS

command was first offered to General Auchinleck, who was to be relieved of his duties as Commander-in-Chief Middle East by General Alexander, but, on his refusal to accept it, General Sir Henry Maitland Wilson was selected as Commander-in-Chief Paic (Persia and Iraq Command). He took up his appointment on 21 August and his General Headquarters opened in Baghdad on 15 September 1942. However, the danger, to meet which the command had been created, never materialized, but it reduced the planning and administrative burden on the Middle East Command; and the Paiforce was used for other important functions described in the following pages.

With the formation of a separate new command under the War Office the Inspector General of Communications and his staff were merged into the General Headquarters. Major-General C. R. C. Lane, C.B., M.C., I.A., was appointed Deputy Quartermaster General, Bases and Lines of Communication, to exercise effective supervision over the development of ports, base depots and means of communication. As one commander was inadequate to exercise satisfactorily the entire responsibility for the local administration and internal security over the whole of the Base and Lines of Communication Areas of Iraq and Iran, the Base and Lines of Communication of Paiforce was divided into two, directly under the command of the General Headquarters viz., Iraq Area, and Persia (Iran) Area.

Each Area was divided into sub-areas:—

Iraq Area	Mosul, Sub-Area
	Baghdad Sub-Area
	Shuaiba Sub-Area
Persia (Iran) Area	Teheran Sub-Area
	Ahwaz Sub-Area

The Tenth Army was allotted one Sub-Area (Kermanshah) to assist in the local administration of the Army Area.[4]

As a result of this administrative arrangement Lieut.-General Quinan, Commander of the Tenth Army, was enabled to devote his attention to his operational task, for he was relieved of the heavy burden of administering the bases and lines of communication.

Tasks of General Wilson

On 15 September 1942, when the General Headquarters Paiforce opened in Baghdad, the Tenth Army was located as follows:[5]

Headquarters Tenth Army	Khurramabad
Headquarters III Corps	Kermanshah
Headquarters XXI Indian Corps ...	Hamadan
6th Indian Division (27th Indian Infantry Brigade Group)	Sultanabad Area
8th Indian Division (19th Indian Infantry Brigade Group)	Mosul-Kirkuk
31st Indian Armoured Division (3rd Indian Motor Brigade Group 252nd Indian Armoured Brigade Group)[6]	Bisitun

The IV Corps had by this time left for India. The 50th British Division also left Iraq. Thus the only operational troops at the disposal of General Wilson were two Indian infantry divisions (each of one brigade group) and one Indian armoured division. Reinforcements, however, soon arrived to strengthen the Paiforce. In September the 5th British Infantry Division started to arrive. It was followed by the 7th British Armoured Brigade and one independent motor brigade (the 10th Indian Motor Brigade). In November began the arrival of the 56th (London) Division. Moreover, the 3rd Carpathian Polish Division, which arrived in the Middle East, became the nucleus of the Polish Army in the East. Thus the Paiforce was considerably strengthened. Both the Indian infantry divisions had now two brigade groups each.

The primary task of General Wilson was to secure at all costs from land and air attack the oilfields and oil installations in Iraq and Iran. His second task was to ensure the transport from the Persian Gulf ports of supplies to Russia to the maximum extent possible without prejudicing the primary task.[7] These two commit-

---

[4] Tenth Army O.I. No. 40 dated 10 October 1942.
[5] Tenth Army Order of Battle dated 15 September 1942.
[6] For details see Appendix 20.
[7] General Wilson's Despatch on the Persia and Iraq Command, 21 August—17 February 1943.

ments—to plan for the defence of Iraq and Iran and to develop the ports and means of communications for speeding up supplies to Russia and to maintain the forces—engaged the attention of General Wilson. Although the Paiforce came into existence in September 1942, some measures for the development of ports and communications had already been taken in hand and, therefore, the word Paiforce (Persia and Iraq Force) is also loosely used for the Iraq Force. It is in this wider sense that the significance of its achievements can be truly appreciated.

Plan 'Wonderful'

The *raison d' etre* of Paiforce was its role in the defence of Iraq and Iran against Axis threat through Anatolia and/or Caucasia. The plan for the defence of Iraq had been worked out by the end of September 1941. But it was only at the end of May 1942, when the fighting had become intense both in Russia and in North Africa, that it was given its final shape and accorded the code-name of 'Wonderful'. This plan was based on the estimate that, in their attack on Iraq, the Axis Powers would be able to employ seven or eight divisions, supported by a strong air force. The invading force, it was supposed, would advance from southern Anatolia. The plan was based on two successive lines of defence, the Mosul—Tell Afar line and the Little Zab—Fatha—Ramadi line.[8]

Although this plan had been adopted in May 1942, steps had already been taken to lay down the target for the formations to be employed in the defence of Iraq and Iran. On 29 July 1941, General Sir Archibald Wavell, the Commander-in-Chief, India, had issued a directive to Lieut-General Quinan to prepare for the maintenance of ten divisions and thirty squadrons of the Royal Air Force for employment in Iraq. In November 1941, he was further instructed to prepare, in addition, for the maintenance of four to six divisions in Iran. He was also directed to take such steps to develop road, rail and river communications as were necessary to ensure the maintenance of this force and the maximum possible delivery of supplies to Russia. Thus Lieut.-General Quinan had been already engaged in the formidable task of improving the bases and the lines of communication for the maintenance of a large force for the defence of Iraq and Iran, an ambitious target of ten divisions and thirty squadrons of the Royal Air Force for employment in Iraq and from four to six divisions in Iran. The increased Axis threat to Caucasia in the summer of 1942, however, necessitated greater emphasis being laid on the defence of Iran than of Iraq. In order to appreciate the plan which was made for the defence of Iran, it is

---

[8] For details see earlier parts of this volume.

necessary to bear in mind the deteriorating Allied situation at the end of July 1942.

Deteriorating Situation

As the Axis threat through Anatolia loomed large in the British planning, greater emphasis was placed on the defence of Iraq rather than of Iran. But as the Axis forces scored, temporarily, victories in Russia in the summer offensive of 1942, especially in Caucasia, the threat to Iran became more imminent. The Axis forces swept on towards Egypt and Caucasia from two directions almost like an irresistible tide. The situation facing the Allies at the end of July 1942 was none too pleasant. On 27 May 1942, General Rommel had launched his offensive in North Africa and by 30 June had driven back the British and Commonwealth forces to the El Alamein positions. The threat to Egypt was very great indeed. The Germans had also secured notable gains in Russia. Their main offensive was launched on 28 June 1942, though preliminary operations had begun on 8 May, when the Nazis tried to secure control of the Crimea. On 13 May Kerch fell, and on 1 July Sebastopol. Thus by 1 July the Nazis had secured control over Crimea. The thrust towards Caucasia was significant: on 27 July 1942 Rostov fell, and the Nazis thus secured a springboard for their attack on Caucasia.

Plan 'Garment'

In view of the deteriorating situation, Lieut.-General Quinan, made a plan for the defence of Iran on 6 August 1942. It was given the code-name of 'Garment'. The plan envisaged the action to be taken by the Tenth Army in the event of an Axis attack through Caucasia on Iran. The object was to ensure the security of the British bases, ports, oil supplies and the connected plant in Iran. It was estimated that the Tenth Army would have the following troops available for the defence of Iran: three corps headquarters, two armoured divisions, one motor brigade group, two armoured car regiments, four infantry divisions and one army tank brigade. At the same time, the Ninth Army in Iraq would hold the Rowanduz and Penjwin passes. The General Headquarters reserve would consist of one armoured division, one armoured brigade group and one infantry division.

As regards the Axis force, it was estimated that the advanced elements of nine divisions, supported by a strong air force, would be able to advance to the river Araxes (the boundary between Trans-Caucasia and Iran) by about mid-October 1942. It was, however, felt that only a small force of five or six divisions would be able to advance further to the line Kazvin—Senneh. As regards the lines of Axis approach by road, it was anticipated that the main advance would take place from Tiflis and Baku. From Baku they would advance along the Caspian coast towards Teheran or Kazvin. From Tiflis they might go to Julfa and from there follow either of the two courses open to them, viz., capture Tabriz and then sweep forward towards Kazvin, or, advance astride lake Urmia towards Rowanduz or Hamadan. Of all these various alternatives it was considered that the most favourable axis of advance of the Axis armoured forces would be along the last mentioned route.

To counteract this threat the plan provided that the Tenth Army would engage the Axis forces north of the general line Pahlevi—Tabriz—Rizaiyeh, inflict the heaviest possible casualties and cover, for as long a period as practicable, the Royal Air Force aerodromes in the area Ardebil—Mishkin—Tabriz. In case the Tenth Army failed to hold this line it would fall back on the main defence line, Manjil—Zinjan—Bijar—Senneh—Merivan. The final stand for battle would therefore be made on this defence line.

In order to implement the plan the basic disposition of the troops was to be as follows:

(a) X Corps on the northern flank, with under command one army tank battalion, so as to establish one division in the general area of the Manjil and Chalus passes (in order to deny to the Axis forces the approaches to Kazvin and Teheran from the Caspian littoral) and one division in the general area Mianeh—Zinjan (to deny the approach from Tabriz towards Kazvin).

(b) Y Corps on the southern flank, with under command one army tank brigade (less one battalion) so as to establish
  (i) one division in the general area Askaran to deny the approaches to Kermanshah from the north (covering forces from this division to operate astride the defiles to the north and east of Senneh);
  (ii) one division in reserve, based on the general area Kangavar ready to co-operate with Z Corps, and in the ultimate issue, ready to deny the approach to Kermanshah from the east.

(c) Z Corps consisting of two armoured divisions and a motor brigade group to be located initially in a general area north-east and north-west of Hamadan and to be prepared to operate offensively with one or more of its formations as under:
  (i) in the area Senneh—Sunqur—Kermanshah connected with the formations at Askaran and Kangavar,
  (ii) in the area Tuisarkan—Malayar—Burujird—Kangavar, connected with the formation at Kangavar,
  (iii) in the area Bijar—Hamadan—Senneh.

(*iv*) south and south-east of Zinjan.

In face of the imminent Axis threat, X and Y Corps were to prepare rapidly to have covering forces, based on armoured cars and Royal Engineers, on the river Araxes. All the bridges over the river Araxes from the Caspian to the Turkish frontier, were to be destroyed and the maximum damage done to the railway. The light forces were to be backed by stronger forces designed to fight in favourable ground, unsuitable to the Axis armoured fighting vehicles, astride the main lines of advance of the Axis forces. The dispositions of these stronger forces, in support of the light forces, were to be:

(*a*) X Corps
  (*i*) A maximum of two brigade groups to cover the approaches to Ardebil from the east and to block the coast road running south through Astara.
  (*ii*) A covering force in the region of Shibli pass (discretion to be left to the Commander of X Corps as to whether this would be more than a mobile outpost to the Mianeh position).
  (*iii*) Commander of the X Corps to be prepared to detail a small force, lorry-borne and with local pack transport, to check infiltration through the mountains north-east and east of Tabriz.

(*b*) Y Corps
  (*i*) One brigade group in the area south of Marand to cover the approaches to Tabriz.
  (*ii*) One brigade group in the area south-east of Shahpur to cover the approach to Rizaiyeh.
  (*iii*) On being repulsed these two forward brigade groups would fall back and fight again, respectively, in the general areas Azar Shahr and Tazeh Kand, particularly to ensure that the British forces on either sides of lake Urmia were not cut off.

In case the Tenth Army failed to hold the first line of defence it would fall back on the general line of defence and the final stand for battle would be made as follows:

(*a*) *X Corps*
  (*i*) One division in the general area of the Manjil and Chalus passes, covering Kazvin and Teheran.
  (*ii*) Another division in the general area Mianeh—Zinjan, covering Kazvin and Hamadan.

(*b*) *Y Corps*
  (*i*) One division in the area Senneh—Askaran covering Kermanshah.
  (*ii*) Another division (in reserve) in the general area Kangavar.

(c) *Z Corps*
Two armoured divisions and a motor brigade group in reserve in the general area north-east and north-west of Hamadan.

This strategic deployment of the Tenth Army was intended to serve the purpose of covering all the Royal Air Force landing grounds in the area Teheran—Hamadan—Kazvin. In case the northern flank was turned by the Axis forces operating from the Caspian region and X Corps was seriously threatened, it might be withdrawn and one of its divisions might be located astride the Chariveh Shah and Sarwandar passes, and another division in army reserve in the area Khurramabad—Harsin.

The Tenth Army was then to adopt the role of covering all Axis approaches to the south on the general line Chariveh Shah—Kangavar—Askaran; but the landing grounds in the Teheran—Hamadan plain were not covered by this.

The air force in support of the ground forces which might be available at the commencement of operations was estimated to be approximately twenty squadrons for operation on the northern front viz. Iraq and Iran. That would be disposed as far forward as possible in northern Iran in the areas Tabriz, Ardebil and Kazvin in order to strike the advancing Nazi forces at the earliest possible moment at the maximum range. They would operate till the moment that the ground cover of the aerodrome could no longer be guaranteed. The air force might then be withdrawn to more southerly dispositions in conformity with the army plan of withdrawal. In case the Axis forces succeeded in securing aerodromes in the Kazvin—Teheran area it might be necessary to withdraw part of the air force to the dispositions at the head of the Persian Gulf for the defence of the installations at Abadan involving a consequent diminution in the close support of the ground forces operating in the north.

There was also a possibility that the Germans might try to operate surface vessels on the Caspian Sea in order to effect landings on its western shore, in the rear of the British forces on the northern flank. The question of providing a small naval force on the Caspian Sea to counter any such attempts in conjunction with the Royal Air Force, and to keep open sea communications, was already engaging the attention of the Commander-in-Chief, Eastern Fleet.

As regards demolitions, the general policy was to deny to the Axis the use of communications and supplies, which might otherwise assist their war effort in case they fell into hostile hands.

For the successful implementation of the plan it was necessary to have well prepared defended areas. These were in course of preparation at the following places:

Askaran	one infantry division

Kangavar	one infantry division
Chariveh Shah	one infantry division, less one infantry brigade group
Sarwandar	one infantry brigade group.

In addition to these it was laid down that the natural defensive positions at the Milamas and Gandarbat passes should be strengthened for occupation by a force of one infantry group at each of the two places. Moreover, defended areas would be developed at Mianeh, Manjil, and Chalus when the political situation improved.[9]

---

[9] Tenth Army O.I. No. 36 dated 6 August 1942.

CHAPTER XLII

Plan 'Gherkin'

The Situation in the Second Week of September

The occasion for implementing the plan 'Garment' did not arise as the situation facing the Allies had steadily improved. By 14 September 1942, it was evident that the Allies had weathered the storm. On 30/31 August 1942, General Rommel had launched a powerful attack on the British positions in North Africa. The Allied line, however, held firm and the attack was repulsed. On 3 September, General Rommel began to withdraw and the retreating Axis forces were hammered until 7 September when General Montgommery called a halt to his advance in order to reorganise his forces for a final trial of strength with his German counterpart. The situation in North Africa had thus considerably improved. The Allies had blunted the edge of General Rommel's attack and their forces were now poised for a final attack on the Nazi forces in North Africa. In Russia, on the other hand, the Axis forces had made substantial gains. Under the pressure of German attack the Russians had wrecked and abandoned the Maikop oilfields on 8 August. The Nazis followed up this success by capturing Krasnodar on 20 August and Mozdok (about 100 miles from the Caspian Sea) on 25 August. The Russians withdrew to Grozny. On 10 September, Novorossisk (a naval base on the Black Sea) fell into German hands. But here the tempo of the Nazi attack had slowed down and the situation showed no further deterioration. Nonetheless the possibility of an Axis attack, on a smaller scale, could not be ruled out as it might develop through Caucasia during the period 15 October—15 November 1942. To consider this new situation the Commander of the Tenth Army wrote an appréciation on 14 September, which served as a basis for a new plan, called 'Gherkin'.

Appreciation by the Commander of the Tenth Army

Plan 'Garment' was an ambitious scheme to check the progress of advance elements of about ten Axis divisions, supported by a strong air force. Plan 'Gherkin' was modest in its scope since it was designed to check the progress of only three Axis divisions. Therefore this plan differed from 'Garment' in as far as it presumed a lower scale of hostile attack. The plan was based on a comprehensive appreciation of the possible situation in Iran during the period

15 October—15 November 1942,[1] and it reveals to us a vivid picture of the difficulties and problems which then confronted the Tenth Army in fulfilling the formidable task of checking a likely Nazi attack through Caucasia.

The commander of the Tenth Army had based his plan on the presumption that, in case the Russian resistance in Caucasia proved ineffective, the Nazi forces would soon be established on the general line Baku—Tiflis—Batum; in the Baku area from the Grozny approach, in the Batum area from the Black Sea coast approach, and in the Tiflis area from either Baku or Batum or possibly by direct approach through the north Caucasus range. As the approach to Batum between the north Caucasus range and the Black Sea was more difficult, the greater probability was that the Nazi forces would be established first in the Baku area and at a later date at Batum and Tiflis. Having secured the general line Baku—Tiflis—Batum, the Nazi forces would sweep forward for attack on Iran. The approaches to Iran were basically two. From Baku they might advance by the coast road to Astara, from where three divergent routes would be available, viz., direct to Teheran via Resht, to Teheran via Shibli and Kazvin and to Kermanshah via Tabriz and Maragheh. From Tiflis the Nazis could advance to Julfa and thence to Teheran via Tabriz—Kazvin, or Kermanshah via Lake Urmia (east or west or both).

The appreciation further assumed that the Nazi forces would reach both Baku and Batum by 15-31 October 1942, but would not be in a position to mount a powerful attack on Iran without a long period of consolidation, reorganisation and administrative preparation. This would limit the weight of attack on Iran to a small force only, consisting of an armoured division, one motorised division and one mountain division.

The probable object of the Nazi attack might be to advance as far south into Iran as possible with a view to:—

 (i) securing suitable bases for their air force, from which they might launch air attacks on British installations immediately, and assume a major offensive early next spring;

 (ii) dislocating the British lines of communication through Iran and 'Aid to Russia' traffic;

 (iii) intimidating the Iran Government into a policy of active hostility against the British; and

 (iv) encouraging the disaffected tribal elements to cut off the British communications.

To counteract this move the object of the Tenth Army would be to break up and destroy the Nazi attack as far north as possible.

[1] Appreciation by Commander Tenth Army dated 14 September 1942.

Against three Nazi divisions it might be possible to deploy four infantry divisions and an armoured division. The Nazi armoured division, it was feared, would most probably be vastly superior to the British division in training and equipment, but as a counterpoise the British infantry division would be superior to that of the Nazis, both as regards its numbers and quality of its men and equipment. Therefore, the British strategy would be to avoid an armoured battle except under favourable conditions and to commit the British infantry as far as possible on a ground unsuitable for the Axis armoured force.

To meet the rival air force, it was apprehended that the British Air Striking Force would not have more than 12 to 20 squadrons of all types. This was likely to give the Nazis air superiority for a considerable time. Therefore, it would be desirable to increase the size and offensive power of the British Air Striking Force. It would be important not only to deny the Nazis the use of the landing grounds, Mishkin—Ardebil—Tabriz, but also to make full use of these.

In making his selection of the areas suitable for infantry engagements and armoured battles, the Commander of the Tenth Army took into careful consideration the nature of the terrain on the five main routes which might be followed by the attacking forces.

In his view the main axis of advance would be along the Caspian coast road from Baku to Resht and then to Teheran. This road crossed into the delta of the rivers Araxes and Kura at Salyani, an area intersected by numerous waterways. This terrain yielded pre-eminently to a programme of demolition of bridges and ferries, which would considerably retard the Axis advance to the south. But further to the south, at a point 36 miles north of Lenkoran, the route emerged into the southern tongue of the Mughan steppe, which in summer was excellent going for the armoured fighting vehicles. However, after rainfall in October, this area became boggy. Nonetheless, this area was not suitable for offering battle, though demolitions in the delta area might be useful.

From Lenkoran to the south the route ran between steep hills and the sea, through densely wooded country. There was no scope for the employment of armoured fighting vehicles or even for their movement off the road. The field of fire for infantry weapons was also restricted. The fighting, therefore, was likely to develop into a series of hand-to-hand skirmishes, making this area unsuitable as a ground for seeking decision in battle. But south of Resht, the road passed through the Manjil and Chalus gorges, where even weaker forces could hold up and defeat stronger ones. Hence in this region one division might be stationed to check the Axis forces advancing from Baku along the Caspian coast road to Resht and Teheran.

The second route led from Astara, an important road junction

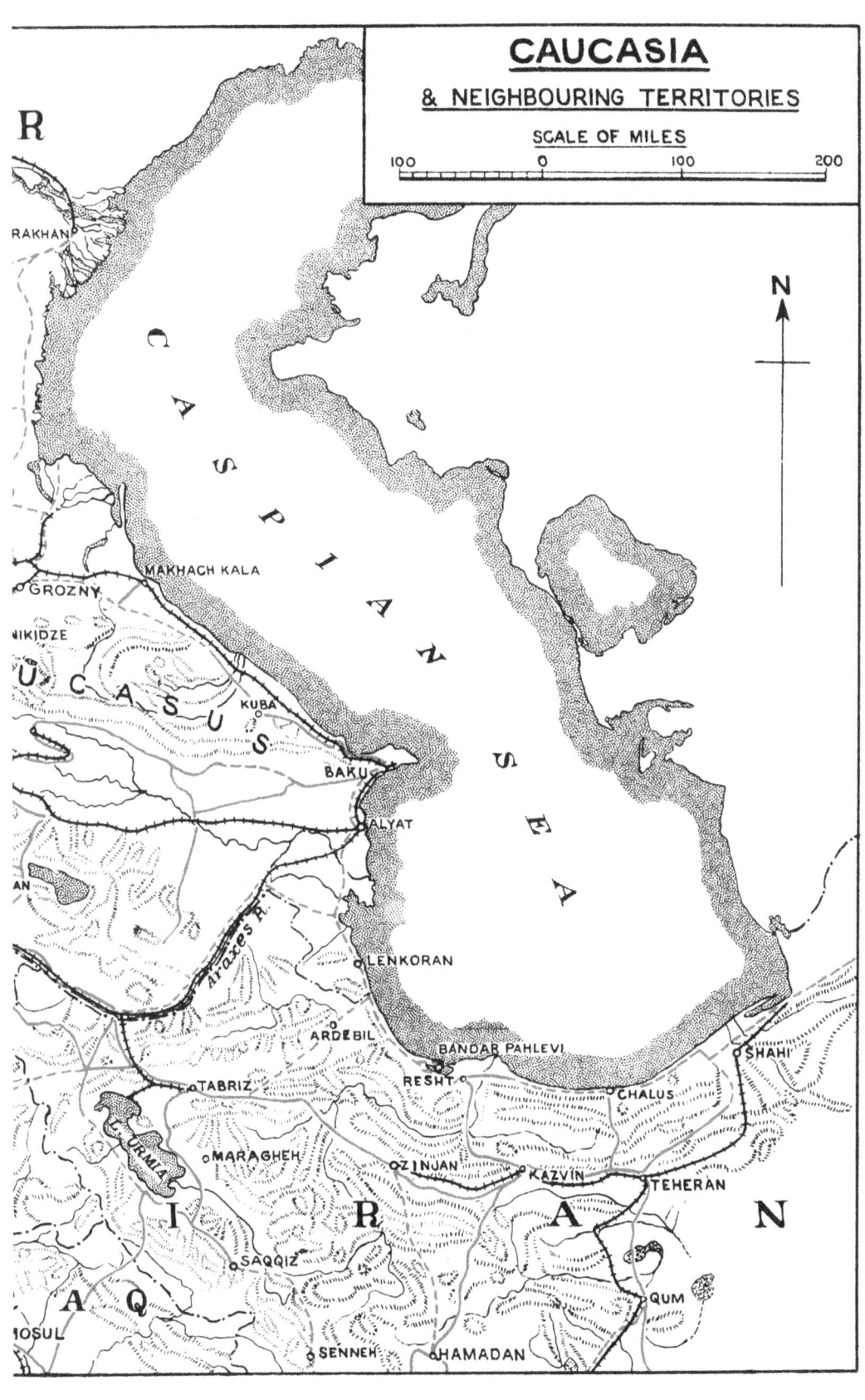

on the Caspian Sea to Tabriz. This road passed through the Ardebil pass, one branch leading via Mishkin and Ahar and the other via Shibli pass and thence to Teheran via Mianeh and Kazvin. The capture of the Ardebil pass, it was feared, would give the Axis one of the laterals, which gave access to the north and south roads astride Lake Urmia. On this line of Axis approach, Ardebil pass had an undoubted strategic importance, which might be denied to the hostile forces by placing a division there. In addition to these, there was the third road leading from Tiflis via Julfa—Tabriz—Kazvin to Teheran. There was no suitable area for giving battle between Tiflis and Julfa. Running from east to west the Kala Dagh mountains provided a barrier passable only to small bodies of specially trained and equipped troops. Not until Julfa, on the river Araxes, was reached did communications exist for the employment of normal formations. But it was not advisable to seek battle in the Julfa area, because it would be unfavourable to the British infantry while being favourable to the Axis armour. Along the road Julfa—Tabriz—Kazvin—Teheran, however, three good positions were available in which the infantry could fight and stop superior Axis forces. These positions were at Marand, Shibli and Mianeh. The first covered the forward landing ground area and was complementary to the Ardebil pass. It was suitable for the location of a brigade group, while Shibli pass could take another brigade group. On the western flank of this pass the ground was undulating and suitable for armoured action, and there the British armour might operate. Another strong position was at Mianeh which required a whole division to hold it against a sustained attack. There was an undeveloped road between Mianeh and Maragheh, which was fit for wheels and tracks, and was thereby a suitable location for the British armoured division, as from that place it could intervene, if required, either on the Urmia front, or support indirectly the action of the infantry in the area Mianeh—west of Shibli—Marand or on the axis Shibli—Ardebil.

The fourth road was the one, leading from Julfa via Khoi—Rizaiyeh—Mahabad to Rowanduz, the north-east gateway to Iraq. There were a number of strong positions on this road, where Axis forces might be opposed with good chances of success. But a formation, with responsibilities on both sides of Lake Urmia, would suffer serious dispersion and be forced to fight defensively and in penny-pockets. As this route was the shortest and most natural line of approach to the Rowanduz Pass, it was desirable to engage initially the Axis forces advancing west of Lake Urmia by forces drawn via the Rowanduz from the troops in Iraq. The last of the possible routes was the road leading from Tabriz via Maragheh to Miandoab. Following generally the eastern shore of Lake Urmia the mountain massif reached close to the lake only at Azar Shahr, where there was a strong position. Here, once again, an infantry brigade group might be able to fight with reasonably good chances of success. South of this position in the area Miandoab—Saqqiz—Bijar, the ground was well suited for the use of armoured forces. It might therefore be of great advantage to prevent the Axis armour debouching into this area.

On the basis of this review of the alternative routes and possible strong defensive positions on them, the Tenth Army drew the inference that, as the Axis forces were likely to reach Baku before Tiflis or Batum, the main attack would develop initially along the road Baku—Astara. To meet the threatened attack, demolitions were to be carried out at the Araxes, and every effort was to be made to deny to the Axis forces the Ardebil—Mishkin—Tabriz groups of landing grounds as also the lateral road Ardebil—Tabriz, for which airborne and parachute troops might be of considerable assistance. Moreover, holding the passes Ardebil, Manjil and Chalus in strength would retard the Axis advance southwards. A division would be needed at Ardebil and another for the two passes at Chalus and Manjil and if the British could retain control of the Tabriz—Mishkin and Ardebil landing grounds, the Axis forces would be hard put to get any support. The other conclusion was that strong ground at Marand, north of Tabriz, was complementary to the Ardebil pass for denying the landing ground area, and that the Ardebil—Tabriz lateral should be secured. Moreover, Axis advance west of Lake Urmia should be contested, and to avoid dangerous dispersion of the Tenth Army resources, the troops, to guard against this eventuality, should come from the Corps in Iraq (via Rowanduz). The Tenth Army also held the view that Axis armour should not be allowed to debouch into the country south of Lake Urmia, which was suitable for armoured fighting vehicles, and that Mianeh was the most suitable area in which to locate the armoured division at the start of the operations.

Based on these conclusions a plan was made which was incorporated in the Tenth Army Operation Instruction, No. 39, dated 15 September 1942. This plan was given the code-name of 'Gherkin'.

Plan 'Gherkin'

The following forces were estimated to be available for plan 'Gherkin':—

Tenth Army in Iran

III Corps	5th British Infantry Division
	56th British Infantry Division
XXI Indian Corps	6th Indian Division
	3rd Carpathian Division
	Afridi Commando

31st Indian Armoured Division	13th Lancers
	252nd Indian Armoured Brigade
	3rd Motor Brigade
Tenth Army reserve	7th Armoured Division
	10th Indian Motor Brigade
	6th Lancers

'W' Corps in Iraq
5th Indian Infantry Division ⎫ each of two
8th Indian Infantry Division ⎭ infantry brigades.

The maximum scale of Axis attack was estimated at one armoured division, one motorised division and one mountain division.

The intention was for the Tenth Army to engage and defeat the Axis forces as far north in the north-west Iran as practicable. The following was to be the mode of operation:—

(a) *Light Forces*
  (i) Parachute and Airborne troops would seize and hold bridge-heads at Salyani and Julfa, prior to the arrival of the earliest British ground forces.
  (ii) III Corps and XXI Indian Corps would move light forces with all speed to the river Araxes with the primary object of carrying out demolitions to the road and railway bridges in that area, between the Caspian Sea and the Turkish frontier.
  (iii) The light forces would be prepared to fight the reconnaissance elements of the Axis forces. For this operation the following troops were to be placed under command in order to relieve the Corps of the need to detach reconnaissance regiments from the divisions:—

XXI Indian Corps	6th Lancers
	One anti-tank regiment (less one battery)
III Corps	10th Indian Motor Brigade
	One battery anti-tank regiment.

  (iv) On completion of the task the 6th Lancers would concentrate at Ardebil and the 10th Indian Motor Brigade at Tabriz and come into Army reserve.

(b) *Main Force*
  (i) The light forces would be backed by the main force of the Tenth Army with the object of denying to the Axis forces the strategic area Mishkin—Ardebil—Tabriz and, in so doing, to destroy them. To carry out this task the XXI Indian Corps would establish one infantry division in the general area Ardebil and another in the general area Kazvin. The role of the former would be

(i) to hold the Ardebil pass and deny to the Axis the approach to the west from Astara, and (ii) to harass and destroy Axis forces attempting to use the coast road to Resht. The role of the latter would be (i) to be prepared to hold the Manjil and Chalus passes and deny to the Axis the approaches to Teheran from the Caspian littoral, and (ii) to be prepared to move on the axis Kazvin—Mianeh—Shibli.

(ii) III Corps would establish one infantry division in the general area, Tabriz, with one infantry brigade group in area Maragheh, and one infantry division in area Kermanshah in Army reserve.

If due to certain unavoidable circumstances it was found impossible to establish forces in the area Ardebil—Tabriz, then the III Corps and the XXI Indian Corps would direct their leading divisions to Maragheh and Mianeh respectively and assume control of the lateral communication Mianeh—Maragheh.

(iii) The 31st Indian Armoured Division would be established in the general area Mianeh, but north of the defile. Its task would be twofold viz., to be prepared to fight in the country west and north-west of the Shibli pass and move to Maragheh and intervene in the battle on that flank.

(iv) One British division in area Kermanshah and 7th Armoured Brigade at Zinjan would be held in reserve.[2]

This was Plan 'A' of 'Gherkin'. It was based on the supposition that the estimated strength of troops would be available for operations. In order, however, to be ready for all eventualities, two other intermediate stages were planned for, in case the troops required to implement 'Gherkin' were not available.

Plan 'B' was made to meet the Axis threat between 1—15 October 1942, approximately. It was estimated that only the following troops might be available:—

31st Indian Armoured Division (one regiment only of Stuart tanks but including armoured car squadrons of the 13th Lancers)
6th Indian Division (including 17th Horse)
One brigade group 5th Division
6th Lancers.

The object and the mode of operation of this plan were outlined as below:—

(i) To establish airborne and parachute troops at Astara and

[2] Tenth Army Operation Instruction No. 39 dated 15 September 1942.

to direct the 6th Lancers with strong anti-tank detachments to Astara in their support in order to harass and delay Axis advance on the coastal route.

(ii) To establish the 6th Indian Division in the Manjil and Chalus passes in order to deny the approaches to Teheran by the coastal route.

(iii) To direct the 31st Indian Armoured Division and one infantry brigade group (5th Division) to Mianeh in order to deny the approach to Kazvin from Shibli.

(iv) Iraq Corps to provide at least one brigade group to block the approach west of lake Urmia.

(v) Available portions of the III Corps (less one infantry brigade) to be directed to Senneh—Askaran or Kazvin.

(vi) Headquarters Tenth Army to be at Kazvin.

Plan 'C' was made to meet the Axis threat between 15—31 October 1942, and was based on the availability of the following forces to implement it.

31st Indian Armoured Division
6th Indian Division
5th Division
10th Indian Motor Brigade
7th Armoured Brigade
6th Lancers.

The Plan sought to place the troops in the following dispositions:—

(i) Airborne and parachute troops, the 10th Indian Motor Brigade and the 6th Lancers in the Araxes area.

(ii) The 6th Indian Division (less one brigade group) in Ardebil.

(iii) The 5th Division (less brigade group) in Tabriz; one brigade group in Maragheh.

(iv) The 31st Indian Armoured Division in Mianeh.

(v) The 7th Armoured Brigade in Kazvin.

Strength of the Paiforce

No need arose for implementing the plan 'Garment' or 'Gherkin' as the Axis forces suffered a crushing defeat in North Africa, and in Russia also their advance was arrested. In the battle of El Alamein (23 October—4 November 1942) General Rommel was decisively beaten and the pursuit of the *Afrika Corps* had begun. In Russia the Nazi advance was halted and the immediate threat of an attack on north Iran through Caucasia was removed.

It was fortunate for the Allies that the Russian front held firm and the Nazi forces failed to storm their way through Caucasia. It is difficult indeed to say how far the Paiforce would have succeeded in checking the Axis advance. The forces immediately available for General Maitland Wilson were not adequate to meet the threat, for when the General Headquarters Paiforce opened in Baghdad on 15 September 1942, General Wilson had at his disposal only two Indian infantry divisions and one Indian armoured division. The 6th Indian Infantry Division, consisting of the 27th Indian Infantry Brigade Group and ancillary troops, was concentrated in the Sultanabad area. The 8th Indian Division, consisting of the 19th Indian Infantry Brigade Group and ancillary troops, was concentrated in area Kirkuk—Mosul. The 31st Indian Armoured Division, consisting of the 3rd Indian Motor Brigade Group and the 252nd Indian Armoured Brigade Group, was concentrated in area Bisitun.[3] The infantry divisions were below establishment and were deficient in artillery, engineers and signals while the armoured division had no medium tanks. All the three divisions were short of transport. Thus the situation facing General Wilson was none too pleasant. Before he could hope to turn this small force into a balanced fighting force it was necessary for him to take steps to fill up the deficiencies, as, Corps artillery units, signals and administrative units were either short of requirements or lacking altogether.[4] To augment the forces under the command of General Wilson the War Office had earmarked two British infantry divisions (the 5th and the 56th). Further reinforcements were to come from India (the 7th British Armoured Brigade) and from the Middle East (the 5th Indian Division and the 3rd Carpathian Polish Division). Meanwhile the available units, though incomplete and often employed on administrative duties, were assigned fighting roles if necessity arose.

Early in October the following formations were under the command of the General Headquarters Paiforce:
Tenth Army
Polish Army in the East
8th Indian Division.

The troops available to Lieut-General Quinan (the Commander of the Tenth Army) for the defence of Iran were the 6th Indian Division (the 27th Indian Infantry Brigade Group), the 5th British Division (the 13th, 15th and 17th Brigades), the 10th Indian Motor Brigade and the 31st Indian Armoured Division (the 3rd Indian Motor Brigade and the 252nd Indian Armoured Brigade Group).[5] The Tenth Army was located as follows:—

Headquarters Tenth Army	Khurramabad
Headquarters III Corps	Kermanshah
Headquarters XXI Indian Corps ...	Hamadan

---

[3] Tenth Army Order of Battle dated 15 September 1942.
[4] General Wilson's Despatch on the Persia and Iraq Command, *op. cit.*
[5] Tenth Army Order of Battle dated 1 October 1942.

6th Indian Division	Sultanabad area
5th British Division	Kermanshah
10th Indian Motor Brigade	Malayar
31st Indian Armoured Division ...	Bisitun

Preparations Against the Axis Spring (1943) Offensive

It has been mentioned above that with the Allied victory at El Alamein (23 October—4 November 1942) and the heroic defence of Stalingrad, in addition to the dogged resistance of the Russians in the Caucasus, the Axis offensive in North Africa and Russia had been checked and the threat to north Iran during the winter months had for the moment disappeared. But he would be a bold man who could foretell that under favourable circumstances, the Axis might not launch a fresh offensive in the spring season (at the earliest by 15 April 1943). It was estimated that, at that time, the maximum force which they might possibly deploy on or south of the river Araxes would be five or six divisions.

However, in view of the lessening of the danger, General Wilson had decided to locate his forces in winter at places near the railway where they might be supplied without straining the transport resources. Moreover, as the troops were mainly located in the Iranian highlands about Hamadan and Kermanshah, it was desirable to move them to areas whose climate was not so severe. In view of these two considerations, General Wilson reduced the force in Iran to one division and one motor brigade (located at Qum and Andimishk respectively) and moved the rest of the force to winter training locations on the Iraq railway.

Meanwhile the arrival of reinforcements strengthened the Paiforce considerably. General Wilson had at his disposal two British divisions and one British armoured brigade; three Indian infantry divisions and one armoured division; and one Polish division.

Further, by an agreement with the Iraq Government, two Iraqi divisions were available for the defence of Iraq. Therefore, to meet the Axis threat in the spring of 1943, General Wilson proposed to reorganise his forces so that he might have at his disposal a balanced fighting force. This reorganisation of the forces for the spring of 1943 was to be as follows:—[*]

Tenth Army (for operations in North Iran)

Army Troops	31st Indian Armoured Division
	10th Indian Motor Brigade
III Corps	5th British Division
	6th Indian Division
XXI Corps	56th British Division
	8th Indian Division

[*] Organisation of forces for Spring 1943, Appendix A to Paiforce Operation Intelligence No. 3, dated 20 November 1942.

Lt.-General Sir Henry Maitland Wilson

Indian soldiers going through a pass in Iran on the 'Aid to Russia' route

Polish Army in the East[1]
  Army and Corps Troops (forming)
  3rd Polish Division
  5th Polish Division ⎫
  2nd Polish Army Tank Brigade ⎬ forming
  Polish Independent Infantry ⎪
    Brigade Group ⎭
G.H.Q. Troops
  5th Indian Division.

Thus adequate forces would be available for meeting the Axis threat in the spring of 1943. The Tenth Army was to operate in north Iran, while General Wilson would retain direct command of the Polish Corps and hold the remaining Indian infantry division in reserve. The role of the Polish Army in the East (assisted by troops of the Iraq Army[2]) would be to defend northern Iraq against an attack from Lake Urmia. The general plan for the defence of northern Iran was substantially the same as that described earlier. Similarly the general plan for the defence of Iraq (against the possibility of attack through Turkey), involving the employment of the Tenth Army in northern Iraq, remained substantially as before. But luckily the situation improved steadily and the danger of Axis attack on Iraq or Iran became a remote possibility. This easing of the situation enabled even the transfer of some formations (the 5th and the 56th British Divisions) to the Middle East Command (January/February 1943). When General Wilson left for Cairo on 17 February 1943, to take up his new duties as Commander-in-Chief of the Middle East, and was succeeded by Lieut.-General Sir Henry R. Pownall, he had the satisfaction of knowing that the danger of the Axis threat to Iraq and Iran, which had loomed large in 1942 had practically disappeared. Henceforth the main role of the Paiforce came to be to implement the 'Aid to Russia' schemes.

---

[1] Men were drawn from the Polish refugees, and the Carpathian Brigade in Palestine was expanded into a division, the 3rd Carpathian, with the additional personnel from the First Evacuation. Later, when this division moved to Khanakin area, additional personnel was drawn from the Second Evacuation, and the division developed into a Corps which was later designated the Polish Army in the East.

[2] The Iraq Government had agreed to deploy two divisions to guard some passes leading from Lake Urmia side into northern Iraq in case the Germans invaded Iraq from that side. General Wilson's Despatch in Supplement to the London Gazette of 27 August 1946.

CHAPTER XLIII

British Projects

We have described the operational role of the Paiforce to check any Axis attack through Anatolia or Caucasia on Iraq and Iran. The primary task for General Wilson was to secure at all costs from land and air attack the oilfields and oil installations in Iraq and Iran. His second task was to develop the ports and the means of communication in Iraq and Iran for the maintenance of troops and for speeding up the supplies to Russia. And in the implementation of this task, General Wilson had the benefit of considerable American support. By the joint effort of the two Powers, United Kingdom and United States, the otherwise difficult problem of developing the ports, the bases and the means of communication, as well as of despatching supplies to Russia was satisfactorily dealt with. Before General Wilson assumed command of the Paiforce, considerable administrative planning had already taken place and some progress had been made in implementing the plans. In this chapter an attempt is made to describe the chief features of the British administrative planning.

The Nokundi—Meshed route

The Axis attack on Russia on 22 June 1941, followed by rapid advance into the Russian territory created a situation equally alarming to the interests of the United Kingdom and of the United States. The collapse of Russia was bound to have grievous effects on the Allied war effort to defeat the Axis. For not only would the Nazi dictator have the undisputed use of the resources of southern Russia, particularly its oil, which would prolong German resistance, but the Middle East, Iraq and Iran would also be laid bare for his aggression and the route to India exposed. The Russian forces, without receiving adequate assistance in essential war material, could not be expected to successfully withstand the Nazi attacks, and with the collapse of the Russian front the whole Allied struggle in Western Asia might have ended in dismal failure. Hence it became an essential element of Allied strategy to render effective aid to Soviet Russia in materials, which were to be despatched by way of Iran.

Until the occupation of Iran by the Anglo-Soviet forces towards the end of August 1941, the Nokundi—Meshed road was the only possible supply route to Russia from India. Naturally the British Government turned its attention to the development of this route.

On 2 August 1941, the Secretary of State for India informed the Governor-General of India that the Soviet authorities wanted to send a trial consignment of 200 tons by the Nokundi—Meshed route and asked him whether there would be any objection to the policy of permanently developing this route to carry 2,000 tons of goods per month.[1] The Governor-General disapproved of this policy on strategic considerations. He was of the view that the development of this route would seriously affect the defence of the North-West Frontier of India. In the deployment of troops for the defence of that frontier till then, one determining factor was that there was little threat of invasion from the side of east Iran and Seistan, as the means of communication in that region were poor and undeveloped. But once the Nokundi-Meshed route was developed, the threat of invasion might increase considerably and the strength of troops guarding the North-West Frontier of India would have to be increased. In view of this strategic consideration, the Government of India opposed "any high development of the routes Herat—Kandahar and Meshed—Zahidan". It was in pursuance of this policy that they had already commenced removing the railway lines between Nokundi and Mirjawa, which had been earmarked for other projects. The Governor-General was of the view that the "most practicable and suitable line for supplying Russia" would be by the Trans-Iranian railway from Bandar Shahpur to the Caspian. "This route if selected would have no repercussions on the defence of India itself and could be destroyed comparatively easily whereas highly developed road communications on the immediate Western borders of India would be most difficult to destroy and might be far more valuable to the enemy than to ourselves".[2]

The objections against the scheme were considered by the Chiefs of Staffs on 29 August 1941, (immediately after the cessation of hostilities with Iran) and their decision was that the east Iranian lorry route should be developed in the first instance, upto the maximum carrying capacity of 2,000 tons per month only, and that the development beyond that point would raise the strategic question which would require further consideration.[3] Therefore it was decided that supplies to Russia should be despatched from India via the Nokundi—Meshed route.

Other Supply routes

But this route alone was not capable of transporting the large supplies needed by Russia. It was therefore necessary to develop other supply routes. Early in September 1941 the United Kingdom

[1] Tel. dated 2 August 1941 from S.S. to G.G. and tel. dated 3 August 1941 from S.S. to G.G., F. 698.
[2] Tel. dated 13 August 41 from Armindia to troopers, F 698.
[3] Tel. dated 29 Aug. 41 from S.S. to G.G., F 698.

Commercial Corporation was instructed to organise and operate all road routes in Iran except the Nokundi—Meshed route. It was authorised to enter into contracts with the local motor transport agencies to carry supplies for Russia. With a fleet of about a thousand trucks the corporation was soon in a position to carry supplies to Russia by the following three routes:—

(i) *Khanakin—Pahlevi*

The Russian—aid cargo imported through Iraq's chief port of Basra was carried mainly by the Iraqi railway to Baghdad (and partly by barges up the Tigris to Baghdad) and thence by rail to Khanakin. From this place the trucks of the U.K.C.C. carried it to the Russian zone.

(ii) *Andimishk—Pahlevi*

The Russian aid cargo was carried by the Trans-Iranian railway from Bandar Shahpur to Andimishk. Here the railway entered on its mountainous track and therefore the trains were broken up into two or three parts to enable them to climb up the steep gradient easily. Thus Andimishk proved to be the bottleneck. It was in order to supplement the volume of traffic borne by the railway that U.K.C.C. operated the route Andimishk—Pahlevi.

(iii) *Bushire—Pahlevi*

It was a very long and therefore an expensive route but there were possibilities of developing it.

Administrative Planning for the Defence of Iran (20 August)

Besides organising the supply routes to Russia the British planners turned their attention to the problem of the defence of Iraq and Iran against the possibility of an Axis attack through Turkey or Caucasia. On 29 July 1941, General Wavell, Commander-in-Chief, India, issued a directive to Lieut.-General Quinan, Commander Iraq Force, to hold north Iraq against any Axis attack through Turkey or Iran or both, and to develop facilities for the maintenance and employment in Iraq of a force, which might in certain circumstances amount to ten divisions (some armoured) and thirty squadrons of the Royal Air Force.[4] Planning for the maintenance of ten divisions and thirty squadrons R.A.F. started in India and was completed by 20 August 1941, when General Wavell reported to the War Office the essential features of his administrative planning. It was based on the assumption that seven divisions would be located north of Baghdad, two around Baghdad and one in Basra or Abadan area. This would involve unloading of a daily tonnage of 8,000 tons (including 1,000 tons for Turkey and 500 tons

[4] No. 55133/M.O.4, GHQ India, F 700.

of civil imports for Iraq) into Iraqi ports. The Basra docks were however only capable of clearing 3,600 tons daily. It was therefore necessary to increase the capacity of the docks at Basra as well as to develop a new port at Umm Qasr to handle the extra 4,400 tons in all. Hence the development of the ports of Basra and Umm Qasr assumed great importance.

It was equally important to develop the railway line between Basra and Baghdad. It was calculated that the daily lift from Basra to Baghdad would have to be 6,400 tons. The maximum lift of the existing metre gauge line, even when fully exploited, did not exceed 2,000 tons. Therefore it was necessary to double the line. In view of the inadequacy of the rolling stock and locomotives, orders had already been placed on the Indian Railways for 57 locomotives, 3,700 wagons and a number of specials as well as 90 miles of metre gauge track for use in bases. In order to double the line an addition of approximately 40 locomotives, 2,500 wagons and 350 miles of track was required. The last could be had only by partly tearing up the Indian lines and partly from India's steel rolling programme.

Besides developing the ports of Basra and Umm Qasr and doubling the railway line from Basra to Baghdad, it was also essential to develop the Inland Water Transport up the Tigris. The maximum lift by the through service during World War I was about 1,000 tons a day. It was unlikely that this figure would be reached because of the difficulties of the supply of river craft. The Government of India were requisitioning all available craft in India and Burma but they could not reckon on a greater lift than about 500 tons a day into Baghdad for a long time to come.

It was also necessary to commence work on the dry weather road from Basra to Baghdad, Mosul and the Turkish frontier. If this road were improved and about 1750 7-ton lorries made available, it might be possible to lift 700 tons a day into Baghdad. This would entail raising of eighteen Mechanical Transport Companies.

The Shuaiba base was being built for three divisions. It was desirable to extend the development of this base to six divisions and also to extend a new base at Umm Qasr up to four divisions.[5]

Modifications in the Plan

The War Office suggested certain modifications in the above mentioned plan. They were of the view that the strategical importance of connecting Basra to Turkey and Syria and later Egypt by standard gauge could not be overemphasised. Therefore they desired that in lieu of doubling the metre gauge, standard gauge should be laid in the sector Basra—Baghdad. They further pointed out that General Auchinleck, Commander-in-Chief, Middle East, had

[5] Tel. dated 20.8.41 from Armindia to Troopers, F 730.

raised the question of building a narrow gauge line (Baghdad—Rutba) with the object of providing a railhead on the Baghdad—Haifa line of communication. It was suggested that the line might start from Karbala to avoid a new crossing of the Euphrates.*

The Quartermaster General, India, who had gone to Iraq, discussed the various problems with Lt.-General Quinan. As a result of these discussions General Wavell rejected the suggestion of the War Office for the adoption of the standard gauge (Basra—Baghdad) for the following reasons:—

(i) It would result in great dislocation of the traffic during the period of construction.

(ii) Longer time would be required for construction.

(iii) Facilities would be required for the standard gauge marshalling yards at the port and terminus at Basra to receive the rolling stock needed for construction. There was no space available for this.

(iv) The layout of the port and base at Basra was such that a change over to the standard gauge would be exceedingly difficult. The probability was that the transhipment from the metre gauge to the standard gauge at either the port or the base would still be needed. The object of having a standard gauge would thus be defeated.

(v) No sleepers, locomotives or rolling stock for the standard gauge were available from India. The problem of shipping all such requirements to Basra would be serious. On the other hand considerable amount of metre gauge locomotives, rolling stock and sleepers were available in India.

In view of these considerations General Wavell recommended that the existing metre gauge line should be doubled. This would give a lift, if needed, up to 10,000 tons a day provided the additional 200 locomotives and 12,000 wagons were made available. But in addition to doubling the railway lines, General Wavell recommended that river facilities should also be developed to carry 2,500 tons of through traffic to Kut and that a single metre gauge line should be laid from Kut to Baquba, thus by-passing Baghdad. This rail link between Kut and Baquba would be necessary for being independent of the train ferry bottleneck at Baghdad. Thus it would be possible to lift 2,500 tons daily by Inland Water Transport to Kut, whence it might be carried by rail to Khanakin or Kirkuk. In short, the proposals of General Wavell, consequent upon the discussions between the Quartermaster General, India, and Lt.-General Quinan were:—

(i) the metre gauge line Basra-Baghdad should be doubled,

*Tel. dated 23.8.41 from Troopers to Mideast, F 730.

(ii) the Tigris line of communication should be developed to carry 2,500 tons a day,
(iii) a single metre gauge line should be laid from Kut to Baquba, and
(iv) the road Basra—Baghdad should be considered as a purely occasional route.[7]

Priorities for the Projects

On 6 September 1941, the War Office reviewed the problem of the priorities for the various projects in Egypt, Palestine, Syria, Iraq and Iran. They attached very great importance to the development of the Trans—Iranian railway for the transport of supplies to Russia. This railway was the only secure route for sending such supplies. Its rapid improvement was therefore of the utmost urgency as part of the general strategy of war. It must be developed at the earliest possible moment to its fullest capacity, short of doubling the line which might be too large a project to be practicable. Increase of rolling stock and the development of Bandar Shahpur would raise the transport capacity for Russia from 200 tons to between 600 and 750 tons per day. To raise the capacity to 12 trains a day, for which the line was constructed, would require further rolling stock, improvement of the water supply, further development of Bandar Shahpur, and organisation of the Inland Water Transport to Ahwaz. The railway would then be able to carry 2,000 tons per day through to Russia. It was of the utmost importance that the whole project should be completed by the spring of 1942. It was estimated that 168 locomotives and 3,800 wagons would be required to run 12 trains per day. These would be supplied by the War Office in stages. In the first stage 48 locomotives and 600 wagons would be shipped in the near future.

The War Office accorded the highest priority to the following projects:—
(i) Trans—Iranian railway up to 12 trains per day with parallel development of Bandar Shahpur and Inland Water Transport at Ahwaz.
(ii) Safaga port and Safaga—Qena railway (Egypt).
(iii) Haifa—Rayak standard gauge railway and Akaba—Maan road-rail link (Palestine).
(iv) Basra—Baghdad duplicate metre gauge, development of Basra and Umm Qasr ports, and improvement of the Inland Water Transport to 2,500 tons daily.

The following projects were accorded second priority:—
(i) Extension of Sudan's three-feet-six-inch railway from Wadi Halfa to Shellal.

[7] Tel. dated 5.9.41 from General Iraq to Troopers, F 730.

(*ii*) Arada—Diyarbekir railway (if the Turks agreed).

The Kut—Baquba railway project was accorded the third priority and the Karbala—Rutba railway, a lower one.

As regards the development of the roads the following two projects were accorded priorities[8]:—

(*i*) Mosul—Mardin—Diyarbekir.
(*ii*) Baluchistan—Meshed route.

As a result of these discussions General Wavell instructed Lt.-General Quinan on 17 September to proceed with the execution of the following projects with the greatest possible speed:—

(*i*) Development of the port of Bandar Shahpur to take 2,400 tons per day.
(*ii*) Development of the Trans—Iranian railway (locomotives, rolling stock and personnel were en route).
(*iii*) Development of the port of Basra to the extent of three berths, an extra lighterage wharf and repair of the existing berths in the R.A.F. area.
(*iv*) Development of Umm Qasr to take two berths and a lighterage wharf.
(*v*) Duplication of the metre gauge railway Basra—Baghdad.
(*vi*) Development of the Tigris river to carry 2,500 tons daily to Kut or 1,500 tons through to Baghdad.
(*vii*) Expansion of bases at Shuaiba and Umm Qasr to take ten divisions.
(*viii*) Necessary additions to the advanced base at Baghdad.
(*ix*) Development of the roads from Basra to the Turkish frontier.
(*x*) Development of the roads from the Turkish frontier to Diyarbekir (to be undertaken by the Turks).

Additional Projects

Thus, in september 1941, the projects were finally determined and their relative priorities settled. The list was not however exhaustive and attempts were made either to accord higher priorities to projects or to add new projects. General Auchinleck was not satisfied with the low priority accorded to the railway Karbala—Rutba. On 4 October 1941, he urged upon the War Office the desirability of keeping in mind the priority of this project, since this railway would assume far greater importance as an alternative line of supply through Basra in case the use of the Suez Canal ports was hindered. A higher priority would have to be given if such a contingency was likely to arise or if operations developed in Syria.[9] Similarly Lt.-General Quinan was not satisfied with the third priority

[8] Tel. dated 6.9.41 from Troopers to Armindia, F 730.
[9] Telegram from G.H.Q. MEF to War Office, dated 4-10-1941, F 730 p. 90.

accorded to the projected railway from Kut to Baquba. He urged on General Wavell the necessity of according a higher priority to this project, for he felt that half the value of the development of the Inland Water Transport on the Tigris would be lost if this line were not completed by the spring of 1942.

These attempts to change the order of priorities did not succeed. More fruitful was the effort to include new projects in the list. On 30 October 1941, Lt.-General Quinan urged on General Wavell the desirability of constructing the standard gauge line between Khurramshahr and Ahwaz. The main reason advanced for the construction of this line was that the necessity of increasing the Inland Water Transport capacity on the Tigris demanded the utmost economy of the river transport on the Karun. Further it was pointed out that this rail link would be of some help in carrying Russian-aid cargo. Thus as regards transit of stores to Russia this line could carry 600 tons a day which might be increased to 1,000 tons. The track and the means of construction were already available. The distance was 75 miles and the estimated cost was £5,000 a mile. The rail link would be completed in four months.[10]

On 1 November 1941, General Wavell replied that he fully realised the value of this railway line but he would like to have additional information before approaching the Chiefs of Staff for sanction as the latter had already laid down the priorities of railway construction. General Wavell wanted information on the following points:—

(i) An assurance that if this project was sanctioned neither labour, material, nor supervisory staff would be taken off the works for which priority had been sanctioned.

(ii) This project could not be completed before March 1942 and it was estimated that the first berth at Bandar Shahpur would be completed in May 1942 and the remainder in July 1942, after which the proposed line Khurramshahr—Ahwaz would lose much of its value.

(iii) The project would not increase the capacity of the Trans-Iranian railway as a whole as the real bottleneck would remain in the hill section beyond Ahwaz.[11]

Lt.-General Quinan replied on 9 November 1941. He assured General Wavell that neither labour, material nor supervisory personnel would be taken off the works which had received priority. He further assured him that the completion of the port of Bandar Shahpur would not diminish the value of the proposed line, for the base at Ahwaz could not be stocked and maintained via Bandar Shahpur except at the expense of the Russian traffic. Moreover, it

[10] Tel. dated 30.10.41 from General Iraq to Armindia, F 730.
[11] Tel. dated 9.11.41 from General Iraq to Armindia, F 730.

was undesirable to reduce the lift of the Inland Water Transport on the Tigris by its employment on the Karun.[12]

General Wavell, thereupon strongly recommended to the War Office to accord sanction to the immediate construction of this railway line, which would greatly assist the communication in southern Iran and be of particular value in the construction of the base and the maintenance of the British forces in that area.[13] On 13 November the latter sanctioned the construction of the standard gauge railway between Khurramshahr and Ahwaz.[14]

Another project which received the attention of the British authorities in India and Great Britain was the rail link between Bandar Shah (Caspian) and Krosnovodsk—Askhabad railway, viz. the Central Asian railway. On 21 November 1941, the Secretary of State for India asked the Government of India for an expression of their views on this project. The latter agreed in principle to this proposal and recommended that early steps should be taken with the Russians for the necessary survey of the route. They expressed the view that the advantages for supply to Russia and also for the maintenance of the Russian troops outweighed the disadvantages, such as differences in gauge and lack of rolling stock.[15] Accordingly on 27 January 1942, the British Government addressed the Soviet Government on the subject of linking the Iranian railway system with the Russian system in Central Asia (east of the Caspian Sea). They stated that they were aware that the Soviet Government were already improving transit facilities in northern Iran, particularly at the Caspian ports, but in order to avoid congestion when the Persian Gulf traffic was increased to a maximum, they suggested the construction of a railway either,

(i) from Bandar Shah (Caspian) or thereabout to a point near Krosnovodsk, or

(ii) from Shahrud to Sarakhs.

From a technical point of view they preferred the construction of the Shahrud—Sarakhs line, as some of the work east of Shahrud had already been started and the Iranian Government would probably be more likely to co-operate on this line than in the case of the line from Bandar Shah to a point near Krosnovodsk. They further stated that they would be prepared to provide rolling stock and locomotives for the standard gauge section of the new line. New railway construction material entering Iran from the Persian Gulf would however compete with the flow of other supplies to Russia. If the project was to be executed it was desirable that work should start from both ends, and it was particularly important that the

[12] Tel. dated 9.11.41 from General Iraq to Armindia, F 730.
[13] Tel. dated 11.11.41 from Armindia to Troopers, F 730.
[14] Tel. dated 13.11.41 from Troopers to Armindia, F 730.
[15] Tel. dated 7.12.41 from the Defence Department to S.S. F 730.

Soviet Government should press on with the construction work from the east.[16] The Soviet Government replied on 20 February 1942, that they were greatly interested in railway construction in northern Iran and the joining of the two systems. They stated that they were prepared to render every possible assistance to Iran in the completion of the Tabriz—Zinjan line and were contemplating other possible routes to link up the Trans—Caucasian railways with the Iranian railways. They preferred to join the two systems west of the Caspian rather than east of it, owing to construction difficulties and cost.[17] Thus this project was not included in the approved list.

Another project which received consideration was the rail link Zinjan—Tabriz. On 14 October 1941, the War Office informed General Wavell that they were considering whether the question of the completion of the rail link Zinjan—Tabriz should be taken up with the Russians.[18] General Wavell was asked to submit his views on this project. He was of the opinion that the link would be essential for the maintenance of the Russian forces in north-west Iran, British land forces employed in that area or British air forces. The question of the gauge however bristled with difficulties. Much could be said in favour of the standard gauge (in use by the Iranian railway) as well as the Russian gauge. In deciding on the gauge the most pressing problem would be the provision of the rolling stock. If the standard gauge was used the British would be called upon to provide all the standard gauge rolling stock, which was short everywhere, and which would further put a heavy strain on shipping. On the other hand, there would be no shortage if the Russian gauge was adopted, for the Russians might be able (before or during withdrawal) to provide or bring back the rolling stock and locomotives. The second problem was whether Tabriz or Zinjan would be more suitable for transhipping operations. If the standard gauge was continued to Tabriz it would have an advantage, for that town would be more suitable for transhipping operations. There might however be one disadvantage, namely that Tabriz would be more liable to air attack than Zinjan. The third problem was whether in the event of the Axis advance into Iran the break of the gauge at Tabriz or Zinjan would hinder the Axis advance. Here obviously Tabriz had the advantage. On the other hand there were several bridges on Tabriz—Zinjan line suitable for effective demolition which would retard the Axis advance. Lastly there was the problem of withdrawing the locomotives and the rolling stock in the contingency of an Axis advance. From this point of view the standard gauge was preferable for the rolling stock and the loco-

[16] Weekly Intelligence Summary No. 14 dated 6 February 1942, G.H.Q. India.
[17] Weekly Intelligence Summary No. 18 dated 6 March 1942.
[18] Tel dated 14.10.41 from Troopers to Armindia, F 730.

motives would be easily withdrawn. After considering these various factors the conclusion drawn was that to avoid delay it would be desirable to start work on the Russian guage from Tabriz and standard gauge from Zinjan.[19] A suitable location for the break of the gauge might be determined locally. It was estimated that the rail link would be completed in a year and a half.[20] Thereupon the War Office remarked that the link could hardly be justified on operational grounds for the most urgent problem was to meet the threatened Axis advance in the summer of 1942.[21] The rail link Zinjan—Tabriz was to be treated as a long term project.[22] On 20 February 1942, however, the Soviet Government informed the British Government that they preferred the project for the completion of the Tabriz—Zinjan line to the rail link between Bandar Shah and Krosnovodsk. Therefore the Zinjan—Tabriz project was accepted.

Target Import Tonnage of the Persian Gulf Ports

The administrative planning of 20 August 1941, based on the commitments in Iraq of ten divisions and thirty squadrons R.A.F., had envisaged the import of a daily tonnage of 8,000 tons into Iraq ports. It was, however, necessary to take into consideration the plan for the development of the ports of Iran. On 20 September 1941, the War Office impressed upon General Wavell the necessity for the development of the port facilities for Iran not only for supplies to Russia but also to maintain the maximum British force in north Iran. They were of the view that development should proceed at three places simultaneously, extension at Bandar Shahpur itself, new jetty at Mashur at the top of the Khor Musa with rail connection above the high water mark, and the development of Khurramshahr and its connection with Ahwaz by the river Karun, by road, and also possibly later by rail.[23] Further, on 13 October 1941, the War Office asked General Wavell to include in the administrative plan the maintenance of five or six divisions in northern Iran and Trans-Caucasia in addition to the ten divisions and thirty squadrons in Iraq.[24]

This additional commitment, as well as the supplies to Russia, were taken into account when early in November 1941 the Allied Supplies Executive reviewed the question of the capacity of the Persian Gulf requirements in relation to the estimated import requirements. Their estimate of the imports was 112,000 tons per

[19] Tel. dated 22.10.41 from Armindia to Troopers, F 730.
[20] Tel. dated 18.10.41 from BMA Teheran to Troopers, F 730.
[21] Tel. dated 24.10.41 from Troopers to Armindia, F 730.
[22] Tel. dated 25.10.41 from Armindia to BMA Teheran, F 730.
[23] Tel. dated 20.9.41 Troopers to Armindia, F 730.
[24] Tel. dated 13.10.41 from Troopers to Armindia, F 730.

month of which 40,000 would be required for the civil requirements of Iraq and Iran, 65,000 tons for the maintenance of the British forces and 7,000 tons for supplies to Russia. If the scale of supplies for Russia was increased the target of 250,000 tons might have to be reached or even exceeded. Later the imports might be increased to 565,000 tons per month, of which 50,000 tons would be for the requirements of Iraq and Iran, 265,000 tons for the British forces and 250,000 tons for supplies to Russia. In view of these estimates of imports, the Committee held that a minimum of 400,000 tons monthly should be the target to be achieved by the end of March 1942 and the maximum target was to be reached as soon as possible after March 1942. On 12 November 1941, therefore, the War Office asked General Wavell to report to them as to what extent, and by which earliest date, it would be possible for him to fulfil these commitments.[25] General Wavell informed the War Office that if the Persian Gulf ports, as well as the road and rail communications in Iraq and Iran were developed it would be possible to attain the target of 468,000 tons per month by August 1942. He estimated the total capacities in tons per day that might be imported through the Persian Gulf ports and carried forward by rail, road and Inland Water Transport as follows:—[26]

	Tons
Basra ...	5,500
Umm Qasr	3,000
Khosroabad and direct loading to I.W.T. ...	2,500
Total for Iraq ...	11,000 tons a day (or 330,000 tons per month)
Bandar Shahpur ...	3,000
Khurramshahr	1,000
Bushire ...	500
Bandar Abbas	100
	4,600 tons a day (or 138,000 tons per month)
Grand total Persian Gulf	468,000 tons per month.

In short, General Wavell expressed the opinion that it would be possible to achieve the ambitious target of 468,000 tons per month provided the projects for the development of the Persian Gulf ports and the schemes for the improvement of the means of communications in Iraq and Iran were vigorously executed and completed

---

[25] Tel. dated 12.10.41 from Troopers to Armindia, F 730.
[26] Tel. dated 23.11.41 from General Iraq to Armindia, F 730.

within the scheduled time. The outbreak of the war with Japan early in December 1941, however, upset all these calculations and fresh estimates had to be made. On 17 December the War Office informed General Wavell that their requirements to handle the target tonnage would not be met within reasonable period. Therefore, they had revised the figures for his planning of transportation development in Iraq and Iran. The revised figures in tons per month were as follows:—

(i) Civil requirements
    Iraq   20,000
    Iran   25,000 (this included a portion via Karachi—Nokundi)

(ii) Supplies for Russia   100,000 (excluding what could be sent over Nokundi—Meshed route)

(iii) Military forces   172,500
(iv) Supplies for Turkey   1,000

                Total   318,500 tons.

At least 200,000 tons capacity should be reached by 1 April 1942, and the balance as early as possible after that date. Thus the target for tonnage to be achieved by 1 April 1942, was reduced from 400,000 to 200,000 tons.[27]

---

[27] Tel. dated 17.12.41 from Troopers to Armindia, F 730.

CHAPTER XLIV

American Projects

The Wheeler Mission

By the end of December 1941 the British administrative planning had practically reached the stage of finality. Meanwhile planning of the American projects had also been making progress. The President of the United States of America had issued the Middle East Directive to the Secretary of War on 13 September 1941, to render lend-lease aid to the United Kingdom in the Middle East. On 6 October 1941, the War Office informed General Wavell that the U.S. War Department had suggested giving aid to Great Britain in the Middle East, Iraq and Iran. The Americans were anxious to initiate immediate action and proposed sending out a mission under General Wheeler, at the end of October, to examine the problems affecting those theatres. He was to be accompanied by military advisers and technical representatives and was authorised to take immediate executive action on points mutually agreed upon. To enable the U.S. War Department to issue general instructions to this mission before it left the United States, it was essential that General Wavell should inform the War Office of his views concerning the following projects for the American aid—(*i*) construction and maintenance of roads, (*ii*) development of ports and railway connection, (*iii*) maintenance of the American mechanical transport operated by the United Kingdom Commercial Corporation (U.K.C.C.) and (*iv*) development of the Inland Water Transport.[1]

On receipt of this telegram General Wavell asked Lieut.-General Quinan to express his opinion as to whether it would be desirable to recommend the repair, maintenance and construction of roads in Iran, as a suitable object of American aid. It will be remembered that America had not yet entered the war. Probably because of this reason General Wavell was of the view that it would not be desirable on military and political grounds to have small parties of Americans scattered about the British potential lines of communication. Preferably the American aid should be limited to well defined installations where they would not be mixed up with the British troops.[2] Lieut.-General Quinan replied that he would not

---
[1] Telegram dated 6.10.41 from Troopers to Armindia, F 747.
[2] Telegram dated 9.10.41 from Armindia to General Iraq, F 747.

object to the American road maintenance supervisors or workmen being located on the main roads from the south-west and west Iran towards the Caspian Sea. He further recommended the immediate installation of American workshops with American personnel at Ahwaz and Khurramshahr, not only for the existing transport vehicles on arrival but also for the subsequent repair and periodical maintenance.

Tentative List of the American Projects (16 October 1941)

On 5 October 1941, the War Office informed General Wavell that the Wheeler Mission would be shortly leaving the United States and that it would be desirable that General Wheeler should discuss the problems with him before going to Iran. The War Office added that they would be glad if the Wheeler Mission took over completely certain projects such as port construction, maintenance and construction of roads and maintenance of the American mechanical transport. They would, however, not agree to the American control of any line of communication or terminal, which might become an essential part of a theatre of war. On receipt of these instructions General Wavell informed the War Office on 16 October 1941, of the specific projects suitable for American aid. His conclusions may be summarised as follows:—

(i) It would not be desirable to hand over work already in hand, such as in Basra and Umm Qasr, to the Americans or associate them with the British in the same workshop. It was essential to give them definite jobs for which they would be responsible.

(ii) The construction and maintenance of roads should not be an American responsibility.

(iii) It was proposed to supply 3,000 3-ton trucks from the United States for U.K.C.C. American aid would be desirable for the maintenance and repair service of this fleet.

(iv) If the War Office proposed to place an order for a large number of locomotives in the United States for the Trans-Iranian railway then American aid would be valuable in maintenance and repair.

(v) Construction, operation and maintenance of the new port at Mashur would be a suitable subject for American aid.

(vi) Third-line workshop facilities, additional to those which India could provide, were required in the Basra—Umm Qasr area. It would not be desirable for these to be started under American aid arrangements as it would mean the mixing of British and American personnel in the same workshops and area, which might lead to difficulties.

(vii) If the War Office anticipated a large purchase of tugs in the United States for the Inland Water Transport, then a repair and maintenance organisation would be desirable. But on the whole it would be preferable to locate the major American installations for repair of tanks and mechanical transport in India.

(viii) Workshops should be located at Karachi for the overhaul of the American tanks.

(ix) Workshops should be established at Deolali for the repair of the American mechanical transport.

(x) Workshops should be established at some suitable place in India for the servicing and assembly of the signal and wireless equipment of United States design and supply.[3]

Other Projects

On 4 November 1941, the War Office informed General Wavell that it might not be practicable for the Americans to undertake simultaneously all the projects in Iraq, Iran and elsewhere. It was essential therefore to assess the priorities of these projects in relation to one another and the other British requirements under Lease Lend, including similar projects in other areas.[4] The tentative list of projects prepared on 16 October by General Wavell was, therefore, slightly modified. Development of the port of Maksur was ruled out. Further, on 1 November 1941, as a result of the conversation with Colonel Gillies, the U.S. Army railway expert on the Wheeler Mission, various projects were reconsidered. Colonel Gillies informed General Wavell that the Wheeler Mission's activities would be directed to assist to the fullest extent the development of docks and railways in Iraq and Iran. Two ships were already under charter to bring a contractor with 150 skilled personnel and equipment consisting of wooden piles, 80 to 85 feet, wharf construction equipment for 5,000 feet wharfage, decking and road work machinery. The ships were however not likely to arrive before early February 1942. Arrangements had also been made for the immediate construction of 50 steam oil-fired locomotives for Iran; but they were unlikely to arrive before May 1942. In view of these facts General Wavell informed Lieut.-General Quinan that the primary task for the American construction should be to take over a specific portion of wharf construction at Basra. He further suggested that in case the Anglo-Iranian Oil Company could not undertake the construction of the oil pipeline from Ahwaz to Andimishk this project should be undertaken by the Wheeler Mission.[5]

[3] Tel. dated 16.10.41 from Armindia to Troopers, F. 747.
[4] Tel. dated 4.11.41 from Troopers to Armindia, F. 747.
[5] Tel. dated 11.11.41 from Armindia to General Iraq, F. 747.

On 24 November 1941, General Wavell made a detailed report to the War Office about the problem of delivering mechanical transport to Russia. In view of the limited facilities which existed in Iraq and Iran or in the Persian Gulf ports, he was of the view that all shipments of mechanical transport vehicles should be made to Karachi where they would be assembled and from where they might be sent either by rail or road to Zahidan, supplemented by shipments to the Persian Gulf ports. From these areas they would be moved by road direct to Russia.

At the outset the delivery of the mechanical transport vehicles in Beta pack was essential in order to save time. General Wavell estimated that if the Beta pack assembly plant, which was being shipped to Iraq, was diverted to Karachi it would be possible to assemble at the rate of 3,000 3-ton vehicles a month. This figure might be doubled by improved arrangements.

General Wavell was further of the view that as C.K.D. (complete knock-down) plant was far more economical than Beta pack it would be desirable, as a long range policy, to aim at as much C.K.D. assembly as circumstances permitted. This would involve the provision of a special plant, which would have to be provided from the United States together with skilled supervisory personnel under the general arrangements for American aid. Unskilled labour (and some semi-skilled) would be found in India. If such a plant were established it would be possible to assemble 3,000 complete 3-ton vehicles per month with bodies built in India from Indian materials, provided chassis were all of one make. The production of completed vehicles assembled from C.K.D. might however be increased to 5,000 per month provided the plant was expanded to meet this output and bodies in knocked down condition were supplied. Thus a total of 11,000 vehicles might eventually be assembled per month.

It was estimated that 39,500 3-ton lorries would be required for the carriage of supplies. But the maximum number of vehicles which might be delivered was 6,000 by 31 March 1942, and 36,000 from 1 April 1942 to 30 September 1942, and thereafter 11,000 per month. All these estimates however depended on adherence to satisfactory shipping schedules. If the demand for 39,500 vehicles was to be met, deliveries of vehicles to Russia would be very seriously delayed. Hence it would be necessary to establish another Beta pack plant at the head of the Persian Gulf.[6]

Agreed List of American Projects (25 November 1941)

As a result of the discussions between General Wavell and General Wheeler the following agreement was arrived at regarding the American projects in Iraq and Iran on 25 November 1941:—

[6] Tel. dated 24.11.41 from Armindia to Troopers, F. 747.

(i) To establish immediately at Karachi a double unit pack assembly plant *en route* to Basra to deliver 3,000 to 6,000 motor vehicles monthly via routes in eastern Iran.

(ii) To establish at the head of the Persian Gulf, as soon as practicable, an additional double unit pack assembly plant to supplement delivery of motor vehicles via the central routes in Iran.

(iii) To establish at Karachi, as rapidly as possible, a complete knock down assembly plant for motor vehicles of one make, preferably Chevrolets or Fords, in that priority, to deliver 3,000 to 5,000 motor vehicles monthly via routes in Iran.

(iv) To develop docks at Umm Qasr. The British should carry on till the Americans were ready to take over.

(v) To develop the Caspian ports and the communications thereto. It was a work of the highest priority to avoid congestion at the northern Iranian rail and road heads. Obviously Russian co-operation was essential. General Wheeler would make direct approach to the Russians locally.

(vi) To develop the roads. The Wheeler Mission would undertake to develop and maintain initially 1,000 miles of road in Ahwaz—Hamadan—Khanakin area. The British would continue work at the highest pressure until the Americans were ready to take over.

(vii) To provide additional river craft for work on the Tigris and the Karun to develop the Inland Water Transport.

(viii) To provide personnel for the base repair shop at Agra for the radio and direction finding equipment manufactured in the United States.

(ix) To establish and run a repair shop at Deolali for 300 Chevrolet or Ford engines per week.

(x) To establish and run the base repair shop at Karachi for 148 tank-engines and 800 tank gear bodies and driving axles a month.

(xi) To establish a Base Ordnance Depot and workshop in northern Iran, probably at Teheran, to assemble, service and check up equipment to be handed over to the Russians.

(xii) The development of the dock at Kuwait was a matter for further consideration.

(xiii) It was not considered desirable that the Americans should undertake the construction of the oil pipelines as doubt existed as to whether this came within the terms of the Lease Lend Act.[1]

[1] Tel. dated 25.11.41 from Armindia to General Iraq; Tel. dated 24.11.41 from Armindia to Troopers, F. 747.

In addition to the above agreement the following plan was proposed by the United States for the despatch of aircraft and related equipment to Russia:—

(i) By ship to Basra with assembly there and flight to Russia. The estimated peak shipping requirements for the unloading at Basra were twelve ships of 10,000 tons monthly.

(ii) Assembly facilities to be given for the establishment of the assembly point at Shuaiba, with the capacity of at least 200 bomber and fighter planes per month. The assembly of the planes would be a purely American task under American military command and control. The requirements at Shuaiba would include an adequate airfield, hangar space and housing.

(iii) Delivery point—planes to be delivered to the Russians, preferably at Basra or Teheran or some other place in Iran. At delivery point the American personnel, adequate to meet all technical requirements, would be provided working facilities, and hangar space would be provided by the British.[a]

Aircraft Assembly and Delivery

Some modifications were made in the agreed plan subsequent to General Wheeler's visit to Iraq where he had discussions with Lieut.-General Quinan and the Air Officer Commanding in Iraq. The first modification related to the aircraft assembly and delivery. On 6 December 1941, General Wheeler signalled to Washington that the plan for the delivery of aircraft to Russia should provide for shipment to Abadan and assembly plant there, instead of Basra, because Basra and Shuaiba would be used to capacity as port and assembly plant for the erection of 300 planes per month for the British.

The Air Officer Commanding in Iraq had suggested that the Americans should take over from the Royal Air Force the assembly plants for the erection of 300 planes per month at Basra and Shuaiba, of which 200 planes per month might be delivered to Russia and only one hundred planes per month to the British. Neither General Wheeler nor Lieut.-General Quinan agreed to this suggestion, for they held that it would not be possible to develop assembly at such a rate for some time due to the existing demands upon the port of Basra. It was of vital necessity to relieve the port of Basra by diversion to other ports in the vicinity of all possible tonnage. The Air Officer Commanding in Iraq agreed with their views but felt it necessary to point out very strongly that the Abadan area would probably be the most important bombing target in the Middle East. If this site was selected it was essential that full consideration should

[a] Tel. dated 27.11.41 from Troopers to Armindia, F. 747.

be given to the provision of adequate fighter and anti-aircraft defence. As a result of these discussions General Wheeler had no hesitation in recommending Abadan as the site for the assembly of the American planes for delivery to Russia.[9] Lieut.-General Quinan too recommended to General Wavell that Abadan would be preferable to Basra and Shuaiba, for they should avoid any confusion resulting from the American aid scheme to Russia becoming mixed up with the Air Ministry erection scheme for aircraft for use by the British forces. Complications might result if the American and British personnel had both to be accommodated in the Shuaiba area.[10] Accordingly General Wavell recommended to the War Office to support the proposal.[11]

On 9 January 1942, the War Office informed General Wavell that His Majesty's Government had agreed to the establishment by the U.S. Government, as a purely American operation, of the base at Abadan for the assembly of bomber aircraft for Russia subject to the following conditions:—

(i) As the capacity of the port at Abadan was limited, aircraft must be broken down so that 15 to 30 could be carried on each ship.

(ii) The general cargo berths on which ships would be discharged would not be under exclusively American control since they would be required for the discharge of supplies for the Anglo-Iranian Oil Company also.

(iii) Oil jetties should not be used.

Pending the establishment of aircraft assembly base at Abadan the British Government agreed that bomber aircraft for Russia would be assembled by the Royal Air Force at Basra. They also accepted an offer of the Soviet authorities to ferry aircraft across Iran.[12]

Motor Vehicle Assembly and Delivery

Modifications were also made in the agreed plan (25 November 1941) as regards motor vehicle assembly and delivery. U.S. War Department had suggested to General Wheeler to use Bombay instead of Karachi for the assembly of the motor vehicles. General Motors had an assembly plant at Bombay capable of delivering 4,000 motor vehicles per month. This capacity could be doubled much more rapidly than if a new plant was established at Karachi. As a general policy the U.S. War Department believed it most advisable

---

[9] Tel. dated 6.12.41 from General Iraq to Armindia; Tel. dated 7.12.41 from A.O.C. Iraq to H.Q., R.A.F. Mid-east, F. 747.
[10] Tel. Q/418 dated 6.12.41 from General Iraq to Armindia, F. 747.
[11] Tel. 20633/Q dated 12.12.41 from Armindia to Troopers, F. 747.
[12] Tel. dated 9.1.42 from Troopers to Armindia, F. 747; Tel. dated 9.1.42 from War Office to India, F. 747.

to utilize the existing installations to capacity and limit the new ones to the absolute military necessity.[13] This proposal did not meet with the approval of either General Wheeler or General Wavell for the following reasons:—

(i) The port facilities at Karachi were more adequate than those at Bombay to handle without congestion the additional assembly capacity that would be required.

(ii) All vehicles assembled at Bombay must be shipped either to Basra or Karachi for forward transport by road or rail, thereby increasing the load on shipping and on the port of Basra.

(iv) Due to heavy rainfall at Bombay it would be necessary to have fully covered shelter for stocks and operations, whereas rainfall was negligible at Karachi, thus permitting storage and operations in the open, thereby conserving the building material.[14]

(iii) General Motors' output capacity of four thousand was the maximum which would be reached by 1 April 1942, and would be needed for requirements in India.

The U.S. War Department felt the weight of these arguments and concurred in the proposal for the establishment at Karachi of a Beta pack plant.[15] The proposal to establish a Beta pack assembly plant at Karachi was however not acceptable to the U.S.S.R., as that Government was averse to lorries being sent via the long Zahidan route and preferred that they should go via Tabriz. The War Office quite appreciated the undesirability of congesting the Persian Gulf ports with vehicle ships, but in view of the Russian reactions they thought it desirable to inform General Wavell that C. K. D. plant (being more economical than a Beta pack) might be established at Andimishk.[16] They asked General Wavell to consult General Wheeler and report his views to them. General Wheeler conferred with the Soviet authorities in Teheran and concurred in abandoning Karachi for the assembly of the motor trucks for delivery to the Russians. The best solution was to ship the cased trucks to Bandar Shahpur and rail to Andimishk, with the assembly plant at the latter point and delivery to the Russians by the highway.[17] At this turn of affairs General Wavell suggested that General Wheeler should come to India to discuss the questions of the highest importance affecting American aid in Iraq and Iran.[18] Accordingly, General Wheeler held discussions in India early in January 1942

[13] Tel. dated 1.12.41 from General Iraq to Armindia, F. 747.
[14] Tel. dated 26.12.41 from General Iraq to Armindia, F. 747.
[15] Tel. dated 12.12.41 from E. and Tn. Washington to C-in-C India; F. 747.
[16] Tel. dated 21.12.41 from War Office to C-in-C India, F. 747.
[17] Tel. dated 28.12.41 from General Iraq to Armindia, F. 747.
[18] Tel. dated 27.12.41 from Armindia to General Iraq, F. 747.

and a new list of the American projects was drawn up on 12 January 1942.

The Revised List of American Projects (12 January 1942)

General Wheeler informed General Wavell that the American projects would have to be reviewed since the Russians required through Iraq/Iran only 2,000 vehicles and 100 aeroplanes per month. They preferred that the bulk of the munitions of war should be sent by the northern route via Murmansk. They did not expect military stores or large quantities of raw materials via the Persian Gulf. They would receive limited raw materials from India via the Nokundi—Meshed route. This Russian proposal fundamentally altered the situation. So far planning had been based on the assumption that Karachi as well as the Persian Gulf would play an important part in the American aid to Russia. But the proposal for the employment of the northern sea route via Murmansk overshadowed the importance of the Persian Gulf. Consequently, after holding discussions with the Indian authorities, General Wheeler revised the list of 25 November 1941 as follows:—

(a) *Location of Assembly Plant*
  (i) The aircraft assembly plant should be located at Abadan.
  (ii) Two Beta pack plants ex U.S.A. should be located at Andimishk.
  (iii) A Beta pack plant, if obtainable from the Middle East, should be located at Karachi to supplement the existing arrangements of the Department of Supply.
  (iv) C.K.D. (complete knock-down) plant ex U.S.A. should be located at Karachi.
  (v) Approximately 1500 vehicles being shipped to the Persian Gulf should be routed to Bushire, the remainder to Karachi. U.K.C.C. would have to assemble lorries for Russia at Bushire.

(b) *Responsibility in general for Supplies to Russia*
  (i) The United States was responsible throughout for the delivery of supplies to Russia. This included onward transmission of assembled articles from Karachi.
  (ii) The United States was prepared to deliver vehicles to the Russians as far forward as Kazvin, assembling them at Andimishk and servicing them at Kazvin after the first 500 miles. The Russians wished to take delivery at Andimishk. This proposal was accepted, for there was a great shortage of drivers in Iran and the ferrying of vehicles might have caused the U.K.C.C. to go short of drivers.

(*iii*) Aircraft should be handed over to the Russians at Teheran, U.S. pilots to do the ferrying.

(*c*) *Roadwork*

Three American road operating groups had been allocated for the Persian Gulf. Half of these had already sailed. It was estimated that each group could construct one mile of road per day. The first priority of construction was to be given to the following roads which might be completed by the end of May 1942:—
- (*i*) Andimishk—Ahwaz—90 miles.
- (*ii*) Tanuma—Khurramshahr—Ahwaz—108 miles.
- (*iii*) Umm Qasr—Basra—50 miles.

The construction of the road Bushire—Shiraz was a long term project owing to the extremely stiff gradients, hairpin bends and the narrowness of the route. These difficulties might entail an entirely new alignment of the road.

(*d*) *Additional Base Ordnance Depot and Workshop*

This installation, which would include the C.K.D. plant, would also cater for the repair and overhaul of all American war-like stores for the whole Middle East. It would have advanced workshops at Cairo, Ismailia, Umm Qasr and Baghdad. The installation would be located at Karachi.

(*e*) *Responsibility for the Maintenance and Repair of U.K.C.C. Lorry Fleet*
- (*i*) The United States would establish a motor repair shop at Andimishk, which would take the place of the British third-line motor repair organisation in Iran and would serve both the British army and U.K.C.C. vehicles.
- (*ii*) The British would still have to be responsible for the repair of war-like stores in Iran.[19]

The Revised List of American Projects (1 July 1942)

The list of American projects approved in January 1942 was further modified in one important respect. On 15 April 1942, General Wheeler informed General Wavell that he had fresh instructions from Washington regarding the American aid installations at Karachi. The projects for the following American aid installations at Karachi were not approved:[20]
- (*i*) C.K.D. assembly plant,
- (*ii*) mechanical transport engine reconditioning plant and workshops,

---

[19] Discussion with General Wheeler dated 12 January 1942, F. 747.
[20] Record of a meeting dated 15.4.42, F. 747 p. 215.

(*iii*) ordnance depot.

Shortly afterwards General Wheeler handed over the charge of the U.S. Mission Iraq/Iran to Colonel Shingler. It marked the beginning of a new U.S. policy to shift the top priorities from Iraqi to Iranian projects. Thus work on the construction of the docks at Umm Qasr, the highway from Shuaiba to Maqil, and the railway from Umm Qasr to Rafadiyah was stopped.[21] The weight of the American effort was shifted from Iraq to Iran. Henceforth the United States played an increasingly important part in building up the supply line to the Soviet Union. Consequently the list of American projects approved in January 1942 was revised by 1 July 1942. The new list contained the following American projects:—

(*i*) Additional docks at Khurramshahr.
(*ii*) Highway Ahwaz—Andimishk.
(*iii*) Highway Ahwaz—Khurramshahr.
(*iv*) Road Khurramshahr—Tanuma.
(*v*) A 750-mile highway north from Andimishk.
(*vi*) A motor vehicle assembly plant at Andimishk.
(*vii*) Vehicle repair stations at Andimishk and Kazvin.
(*viii*) An aircraft assembly plant at Abadan.
(*ix*) A barge assembly plant at Kuwait.[22]

The Persian Gulf Service Command

The early American planning had been based on the assumption that Russia-aid cargoes would be sent mainly by the northern route via Murmansk. In fact the Russians had informed the Allies that their requirements via the Persian Gulf route would be restricted to 2,000 trucks and 100 airplanes per month. But three important events took place in the summer of 1942 which necessitated planning on fresh lines. Firstly, the Axis submarines and aircraft in the Arctic took a heavy toll of the Allied shipping with the result that it became increasingly difficult to supply Russia by the northern route. Secondly, the Axis swept forward in a triumphant wave towards Caucasia. Thirdly, the Axis pushed back the Allied forces in North Africa. Thus these three factors—the heavy losses sustained by the Allied shipping on the Murmansk route and the setback suffered by the Allied forces in Russia and North Africa—created a serious crisis. The Allied planners were confronted with the task of supplying Russia munitions of war through the Persian Gulf route. It was imperative that Russia should be strengthened considerably. As the British efforts were mainly turned to the build-up of the forces in Iraq/Iran to check a possible Axis thrust through Turkey or Caucasia, the Americans were called upon to

---
[21] *U.S. Army in World War II—The Persian Corridor and Aid to Russia*, p. 60
[22] Ibid, p. 84.

shoulder the responsibility for the supplies to Russia via the Persian Gulf. Thus, in September 1942, the Combined Chiefs of Staff assigned to the United States the direct responsibility for the supplies to Russia via the Persian Gulf. Consequently the United States Army prepared to take over from the British the major responsibility for the supplies to Russia through Iran. The take-over from the British in Iran was spread over a period of several months but was mostly completed by May 1943. The Persian Gulf Service Command under Major-General Donald H. Connolly, showed considerable vigour in developing in Iran a major supply route for Russia.

CHAPTER XLV

Development of Ports

Co-ordinating Authority

Having given an account of the various plans for the British and American projects it is now necessary to describe the steps taken to implement them. It was essential that there should be a single co-ordinating authority to deal with supplies to Russia by whatever route. Accordingly, on 15 October 1941, the Prime Minister of England issued a directive as follows:—

(*i*) The primary responsibility for the improvement and administration of the road and rail transport and for the development of the ports in the Persian Gulf area would rest with the War Office. The latter would keep in close touch with the Foreign Office in regard to negotiations with the Iran Government on transport matters. This did not however alter the fact that General Wavell was responsible to the War Office for the administration of Iraq and Iran. The War Office would not deal direct with these theatres but would pass all communications to him for action.

(*ii*) The prime responsibility of the Ministry of War Transport would be the arrangement and programming of shipments. The Ministry would maintain representatives in the Persian Gulf and Russian ports to watch over port arrangements and to improve port administration in co-ordinaton with the national authorities.

(*iii*) The Ministry of Supply would be responsible for obtaining locomotives and other stores as requested by the War Office in connection with the improvement of communications and ports in the Persian Gulf area.

(*iv*) The United Kingdom Commercial Corporation would act as agents for the Ministries of Supply and Food in dealing with the supplies for Russia. In running the local road transport services it would be under the control of the local military authorities.

(*v*) The work hitherto performed by the section of the Ministry of Economic Warfare dealing with the Russian trade would be transferred to the Ministry of Supply.

(*vi*) A new ministerial executive under the Ministry of Supply would take the place of the existing committee for the co-ordination of Allied supplies. It would be known as the

Allied Supplies Executive. This executive would determine the general priorities relating to the military and civil supplies to Russia and the Persian Gulf area, including the improvement of communications.[1]

In a further communication on 12 November 1941, the War Office informed the Government of India that the Commander-in-Chief, India, was responsible to the War Office for the following services in Iraq and Iran:—

(i) Transport services to Russia and the control of U.K.C.C. activities.

(ii) Clearance of goods from the ports and traffic by road and rail.

(iii) Maintenance and development of ports, railways, roads and Inland Water Transport, except for transport services to Russia.

(iv) Maintenance of U.K.C.C. lorry fleet, using existing and potential resources, including those at the disposal of U.K.C.C.

(v) Supply (through Allied commercial companies concerned) of petrol, oil and lubricants to railways and U.K.C.C. lorry fleet.[2]

The Persian Gulf Ports

Besides having a single co-ordinating authority for organising and regulating the imports into the Persian Gulf ports it was necessary to take steps to develop these ports. The administrative planning of 20 August 1941, based on the commitments in Iraq of ten divisions and thirty squadrons, had envisaged a daily tonnage of 8,000 tons into Iraq ports. Later, in November 1941, fresh estimates were made for imports into the Persian Gulf ports, viz., a target of 400,000 tons monthly to be achieved by 1 April 1942. This ambitious programme had to be modified as a result of the war against Japan in December 1941. The target for tonnage to be achieved by 1 April 1942 was reduced from 400,000 to 200,000 tons.

To achieve the target of 200,000 tons of imports through the Persian Gulf by 1 April 1942, it was necessary to develop the ports there, which had very limited capacity for discharge. Iraq had a good port in Basra (Maqil) which had six deep-water wharves, with a total capacity for discharge of about 3,000 tons per day. Maqil, however, could not cope well with the daily tonnage of 8,400 tons which was required to pass through Iraq. Hence the imperative necessity of developing some other port viz. Umm Qasr.

---

[1] Tel. dated 22-10-1941 from Troopers to Armindia, F. 730.
[2] Tel. dated 12.11.1941 from Troopers to Armindia, F. 730.

Iran had not a single good port. The following ports were however capable of expansion:—

Bandar Shahpur

The port, which was the Persian Gulf terminus of the Trans-Iranian railway, was situated on the Khor Musa, about 41 miles from the sea. The Khor Musa was lighted and safe for night navigation. Bandar Shahpur had safe anchorage for an unlimited number of ships of deep draught. The Outer Bar had a depth of 24 feet at the lowest lowwater and an average rise of tide of about 12 feet. The approach to the port was therefore satisfactory. It had only one jetty, about 800 feet long by 42 feet wide. It was capable of berthing two large ships at one time. The port capacity was limited to 800 tons per day.

Abadan

Abadan was situated on the Iranian side of the Shatt al Arab, 56 miles above the Bar and 32 miles below Basra (Maqil). The general cargo facilities at Abadan were designed to meet the requirements of the Anglo-Iranian refinery and oilfields (via Ahwaz) only. Apart from the oil loading jetties there was one general cargo wharf.

Khurramshahr

Khurramshahr was situated at the junction of the Karun river and the Shatt al Arab, 67 miles above the Outer Bar and 21 miles below Basra (Maqil). Shore facilities of this port were limited and the bulk of the cargo normally handled at Khurramshahr was discharged in the stream for lighterage up the Karun river to Ahwaz. It had one small concrete jetty and two lightly constructed jetties, which were suitable only for discharging barges. Though it was the nearest deep-water anchorage to Ahwaz, it had the disadvantage of being above the Karun Bar which limited ship's draft to 24' (neaps) as against 28' (neaps) at Abadan and below. The average capacity of the port was about 700 tons per day.

Ahwaz

Ahwaz was situated on the Karun river, 110 miles above Khurramshahr and 67 miles by rail from Bandar Shahpur. There were wharves at Ahwaz, but these could only be reached by barges plying on the Karun river.

Bushire

The port could probably handle consistently 500 tons per day, the limiting factor being the road clearance facilities (100/150 tons a day being the limit).

Bandar-Abbas

Subject to lighterage and labour being available, the port could handle 150 tons per day. The limiting factor was road clearance (75 tons per day being the limit).³

Ward's Report

With the exception of Basra (Maqil) the Persian Gulf ports were not well developed. It was necessary therefore to take steps to develop them. Early in September 1941, the Government of India appointed Mr. A. M. Ward, Chief Engineer, Calcutta Port Commissioners, as Consulting Engineer to the Commander Iraq Force. He was to advise Lt.-General Quinan on the following problems connected with the development of the Persian Gulf ports:—

(a) As regards the port of Basra it had already been decided to develop it to the maximum capacity of 8,400 tons per day and at least to a capacity of 6,000 tons a day by 1 April 1942. Mr. Ward was to advise as to the measures to be adopted to achieve this target.

(b) It had been decided to develop the Trans-Iranian railway from Bandar Shahpur to the Caspian Sea to carry 2,400 tons a day by the spring of 1942. The existing port at the southern end of the railway was at Bandar Shahpur, but the Anglo-Iranian Oil Company reported that in their opinion development would best be carried out at a place called Mashur further up the Khor Musa. Mr. Ward was to express his view as to whether Bandar Shahpur or Mashur should be developed.

Mr. Ward submitted his report in October 1942. He made many useful recommendations for the development of the port of Basra. But even with these improvements, this port could not handle more than 5,400 tons per day. As the total daily tonnage required through Iraq was estimated to be 8,400 tons, Basra port alone would not provide the facilities for handling this total tonnage. Hence, he advised that Umm Qasr should be developed to deal with this extra tonnage. This port was situated on the Khor Abdulla, about 36 miles due south of Basra, and the channel was navigable. Mr. Ward stated that there were no natural difficulties to be overcome in planning the layout for a number of berths which might be located at a reasonable distance from the bank without undertaking an undue amount of dredging. Further, it would also be possible to place the railway yard where it might serve the berths without any backward movement of stock. As Umm Qasr would be required to deal with the balance of 3,000 tons, Mr. Ward recommended that six berths

³ Report on the Persian Gulf Ports and Inland Transport Facilities and Organization by Mactier, dated 1 November 1941, F. 730.

should be constructed there and each berth should be fitted with six full portal electrically operated quay cranes capable of lifting 2 tons at 45-feet radius.

Mr. Ward inspected the Anglo-Iranian Oil Company's site for the new port at Mashur, situated on the Khor Musa about seven miles from Bandar Shahpur. He expressed the view that the development of Mashur was not practicable, hence Bandar Shahpur should be developed so as to make it capable of dealing with 2,400 tons of cargo per day. His recommendations provided for:

(i) the improvement of the old jetty (two berths) so as to make it capable of dealing with 300 tons a day at each berth	600 tons
(ii) three new berths, each capable of dealing with 400 tons per day	1,200 tons
(iii) a new lighterage wharf to deal with the cargoes from two vessels unloading overside into lighters, say 300 tons per steamer each day	600 tons
Total	2,400 tons

Mr. Ward further recommended that the new berths should be equipped with 18 full portal electric quay cranes, each capable of lifting two tons at not less than 45-feet radius. There would be difficulty in obtaining a floating crane to deal with heavy lifts. Mr. Ward therefore suggested that the crane then in use on the erection of the New Howrah Bridge at Calcutta, should be obtained from the Cleveland Bridge and Engineering Co., the contractors for the bridge, who would be prepared to part with it. This crane was capable of lifting (a) 60 tons at 40 feet radius (b) 33 tons at 60 feet radius and (c) 20 tons at 90 feet radius. Mr. Ward further recommended that the Khor should be deepened by about four or five feet to allow barges to enter at high water neap tides.

Mr. Ward was confident that if his recommendations for the development of the port of Maqil and Umm Qasr were carried out these two ports would be able to handle the total daily tonnage of 8,400 tons through Iraq.[4]

The Development Schemes

Lt.-General Quinan took steps to implement the recommendations made by Mr. Ward for improving the ports of Maqil, Umm Qasr and Bandar Shahpur. On 6 November 1941, he informed General Wavell that he had planned to have at Maqil a new lighterage wharf by January 1942 and one new deep-water berth per month (December 1941 to March 1942 inclusive), raising the capacity of

[4] Report on the Persian Gulf Ports by A. M. Ward, File No. 8110.

the port from 3,000 tons per day to 5,500 tons per day. The port of Bandar Shahpur was to be developed by the construction of a deep water berth by March 1942 and the additional two berths by June 1942. It was uncertain when the lighterage berth would be constructed. It was also uncertain whether the development of Umm Qasr would be taken in hand; much would depend on whether the supplies and the plant were made available.[5] The progress of the development of the ports was however not satisfactory. Thus by 1 April 1942, the capacity of the Basra port was only about 75,000 tons and that of Bandar Shahpur about 25,000 tons per month. The development of Umm Qasr had not been taken in hand.[6] But as a result of the mid-summer crisis of 1942 the Persian Gulf route assumed greater importance than before and the British and the Americans made serious efforts to improve the capacity for discharge at the ports. While the British were mainly concerned with the task of improving the ports of Basra and Bandar Shahpur, the Americans turned their attention chiefly to the development of Khurramshahr. The British made considerable improvement at Maqil which was the chief port for the supplies to the Paiforce. In addition it handled Russian-aid cargoes also. The latter arrived in considerable quantities during 1943 and 1944. It was estimated that in the period between June 1943 and November 1944, the Russian-aid cargoes received at Maqil totalled 446,430 tons.[7] The major part of this cargo was sent to U.S.S.R. via Khanakin and the balance to Teheran via Cheybassi (near Tanuma). In the latter half of 1944, however, the Khanakin trucking route was abandoned and the Russian-aid cargoes were discharged at the ports under the control of the Americans. Therefore, from November 1944 onwards, Russian-aid cargoes did not arrive at Maqil. In addition to the improvement of Maqil the British improved the port of Bandar Shahpur. The British firm of Braithwaite, Burns and Jessop had entered into a contract with the Tenth Army to construct a new jetty at Bandar Shahpur. This jetty was completed by August 1943, thus adding three berths.[8]

Development of the Ports by the Americans

It had been realised from the beginning that the British alone would not be in a position to improve the Persian Gulf ports. American firms acting as contractors to the U.S. Army, till the end of 1942, and, from January 1943 onwards the U.S. Army, took a leading part in the development of the Persian Gulf ports. They devoted

[5] Tel. dated 6.11.41 from General Iraq to Armindia, F. 730.
[6] Development Reports Iraq/Persia, F. 730.
[7] *The Persian Corridor and Aid to Russia* (United States Army in World War II), p. 415.
[8] Ibid, p. 395.

most of their energy to the development of Khurramshahr. Their main task was to construct additional wharfage. By the end of 1942, Folspen*—the American firms—had considerably improved the port, for they had constructed five wharf berths and completed one-fourth of a sixth berth.[10] A new phase began when the U.S. Army took over the operational control of Khurramshahr in January 1943. Considerable progress was made, for by May 1943 Sentab Jetty at Khurramshahr had seven berths.[11] In addition to this a lighterage wharf was constructed at Failiyah Creek by March 1943 to unload barge cargoes for placement upon railway cars.[12] The Customs Jetty was mainly used for commercial lighterage.[13] The Khumba wharf was used mainly for landing crated trucks.[14] The rail link and a modern highway connecting Khurramshahr to Ahwaz improved considerably the clearance capacity of the port. In January 1943, when the U.S. Army took over the operational control, the port discharged 41,421 tons of cargo. In July it touched the peak of 192,761 tons of cargo. Then commenced the decline in the importance of Khurramshahr. In August 1944 it discharged only 124,004 tons. In March 1945 it discharged 30,216 tons.[15] It had fulfilled its mission as a port for the Russian-aid cargoes.

At Bandar Shahpur also the Americans effected some improvements. It has already been mentioned that the British engineering firm had undertaken to build a new jetty. This jetty had been completed by August 1943, thus adding three berths. The Americans improved the port by constructing a large lighterage wharf at Khor Zangi by October 1943. This wharf was situated in deep water, thus enabling loads to be discharged directly from lighters to the railway cars. As a result of these improvements Bandar Shahpur discharged 71,000 tons in October 1943.[16] Henceforth its developed capacity was not fully utilised, for more and more shipping was diverted to Khurramshahr. In fact December 1944 marked the end of this port's Russian-aid commitments. In January 1945 it was handed back to the British.[17]

The small port of Cheybassi, about two miles from Tanuma, was taken over by the Americans from the British on 1 July 1943. The British had constructed in 1942 the standard gauge, single track, connecting Cheybassi with the main Trans-Iranian Railway. A meter gauge rail line connected Cheybassi and Maqil. This line ran over

* The firm of Spencer, White and Prentis, Inc. and the firm of Foley Brothers, Inc.

[10] Ibid, p. 123.
[11] Ibid, p. 392.
[12] Ibid, p. 393.
[13] Ibid, p. 393.
[14] Ibid, p. 393.
[15] Ibid, p. 410.
[16] Ibid, p. 411.
[17] Ibid, p. 411.

a bridge whose centre span sank into the river whenever it was necessary to make way for the ships. The port was primarily concerned with handling heavy cargoes like tanks, which were lightered to Cheybassi from Maqil and put on the flat cars of the Iranian railway to be taken to Teheran. Petroleum products and alkylate in bulk tins and drums were also lightered from Abadan to Cheybassi to be sent to the U.S.S.R. The performance of Cheybassi was not bad: 19,731 tons in August 1943 and 19,840 tons in December 1943. In the next eight months the landing ranged between 12,000 and 19,000 tons. Then the importance of Cheybassi declined, for the petroleum and alkylate shipments from Abadan were diverted to Failiyah creek[16] (Khurramshahr). On 5 October 1944 it was handed back to the British. During the period of fifteen months, when the port was operated by the Americans, the total landings were 235,000 tons. It has been calculated that the Persian Gulf ports handled about 7,900,000 tons of imports. This is an impressive record of the work done by the British and Americans to impove the ports so as to deal with the large tonnage required for the British forces (Paiforce) and the aid to Russia.

Organisation of Transportation and Movement Control

Besides the development of the Persian Gulf ports it was necessary to develop the railways and the roads in Iraq and Iran. The organisation of Transportation and Movement Control passed through several phases. In the beginning the Iraq Force had not a separate organisation for Movements and Transportation. Thus, at the end of May 1941, we find that Colonel F. G. Cangley, D.S.O., M.C., Assistant Director, Transportation, assisted by Lt.-Colonel J. N. Soden, Assistant Quartermaster General (M) and a Staff Captain (M) controlled movement. Under their command were three officers— Deputy Assistant Director Transportation, Deputy Assistant Quartermaster General (M) and a Staff Captain Transportation. These officers were in charge of four main sections—Base Sub Area, Rail Head, Line of Communication and Military Forward Organisation. The personnel for the last two sections had not however been provided. Rail Head Section was under the control of Staff Captain Transportation and Deputy Assistant Quartermaster General (M), who were assisted by three Railway Traffic Officers. Section—Base Sub Area—was under the control of Deputy Assistant Director Transportation and Deputy Assistant Quartermaster General (M). The section was divided into two sub-sections—one of these had six Embarkation Staff Officers who dealt with embarkation, disembarkation and emplanement. The second sub-section was controlled by a Staff Captain (M) who was assisted by a Railway Traffic Officer

[16] Ibid, pp. 412-415.

(Docks), a Railway Traffic Officer (base marshalling yard) and two Railway Traffic Officers (Base Depot, Shuaiba).[19]

On 19 June 1941, the War Office suggested to the Commander-in-Chief, India, the desirability of appointing a senior officer with transport experience as a Director of Transportation on the staff of the Iraq Force. They suggested for this appointment the name of Colonel Sir F. Carson, who had been General Manager of the North-Western Railway in India.[20] The Government of India readily agreed to the suggestion and appointed Colonel Carson as Director of Transportation, Iraq.[21] Thus an important step was taken in the diversification of the functions of Movements and Transportation. Later in September 1941 Sir Godfrey Rhodes was appointed Director of Transportation, Iran.[22] Thus the chief features of the organisation of transportation were that the main executive responsibility for the work in Iraq and Iran fell on the General Officer Commanding Iraq Force, who had a Chief Administrative Staff Officer to assist him, and he in turn had two Directors of Transportation under him—one in Iraq and one in Iran. These had to deal with the following transportation agencies amongst others—Director General Iraq Railways, Director General Iranian Railway, River Navigation Companies, Port Director Basra, the United Kingdom Commercial Corporation and the Ministry of War Transport Committee at Basra. In addition many questions had to be settled through the medium of the Ministers in Teheran and Baghdad, and, where Russia was concerned, through the Foreign Office. Further the Wheeler Mission had to be consulted on certain matters when it began to function in November 1941. There were also two main supplying agencies for personnel and material required for transportation developments—India and the United Kingdom. In India both the Government of India and the Eastern Group Supply Council were concerned and in the United Kingdom the War Office and the Allied Supplies Executive.[23]

The reorganisation of the Movement Control was brought into force from 1 November 1941. The main features of this reorganisation were that the Assistant Quartermaster General (M), controlled four main sections—Movement Control Force H.Q.; No. 1 Movement Control Area Basra; No. 2 Movement Control Area Baghdad; No. 3 Movement Control Area Iran.[24]

With the formation of the Tenth Army in February 1942 a new

---

[19] W/D A.Q.M.G. (Movement) Force H.Q.
[20] Tel. dated 19.6.41 from Troopers to Armindia, File 40W—Sabine Transportation.
[21] Tel. dated 1.7.41 from Armindia to Troopers, File 40W.
[22] Tel. dated 20.9.41 from Troopers to Armindia, File 40W.
[23] Tel. dated 26.11.41 from Armindia to Troopers F. 730.
[24] Appendix 'G' W/D November 1941, W/D A.Q.M.G. (Movement Control) Force H.Q. For details see Appendices 21 and 22.

organisation of Movements and Transportation came into existence. Movements in both Iraq and Iran were under the control of the Deputy Director of Movements, Tenth Army. The Transportation Service in Iraq and Iran was controlled by the Director of Transportation, Iraq and Iran respectively. Director Transportation Iraq, Director Transportation Iran, and Deputy Director Movements Iraq and Iran were under the operational control of the Deputy Quartermaster General, Tenth Army. They came under the general supervision of the Deputy Quartermaster General, Movements and Transportation, G.H.Q., Middle East, who controlled the allocation of personnel, rolling stock, track and stores, as between the Tenth Army and the remainder of the Middle East Command and issued directives regarding major planning. The Major-General, Royal Engineers, Tenth Army, co-ordinated the development of Transportation with the other engineering projects, so as to ensure the best use of the available plant and material.

Deputy Director Movements was responsible for the through movement of stores, personnel and vehicles by land, sea, Inland Water Transport or air from the arrival within the area of the Tenth Army for delivery to the formations. He co-ordinated all demands for transportation and was the sole link for placing them on the various transportation agencies concerned. The Deputy Quartermaster General, Tenth Army, kept informed the Deputy Director Movements and Directors Transportation, Iraq and Iran, concerning the future requirements of the Commander so that facilities might be developed accordingly.[25] Directors Transportation, Iraq and Iran, were responsible for the collection of transportation information, the efficient working of the service, the execution of transportation projects, the command of transportation troops, the formulation of transportation plans in accordance with the directives from the General Headquarters and the control of transportation finance in consultation with the Financial Adviser.

In order that the Deputy Director Movements might exercise control at the ports over the through movement of stores the Docks Operating Companies came under the control of the Senior Movement Control Officer in the port areas. He was thus responsible for the efficient handling, stacking and loading of stores, for their safe custody and for the efficient working of the port labour. He exercised this control through the Senior Docks Officer on the port establishment, who was attached as a member of his staff. Directors Transportation, Iraq and Iran, however, remained responsible for the technical efficiency of docks troops, for the maintenance and provision of plant and gear, and for the planned lay-out of dock

[25] Appendix E, W/D March 1942 of A.Q.M.G. (Movement Control) Force H.Q.

development. The type and execution of construction were decided by the Major-General, Royal Engineers.[26]

War Transport Executive Committee

A very important part in the development of transportation was played by the War Transport Executive Committee. In October 1941 this Committee was formed for Iraq, Iran and all the territories bordering the Persian Gulf. The Chairman and Secretary of the Committee were the representatives of the Ministry of War Transport. The Senior Naval Officer, Persian Gulf, was represented on the Committee by the Naval Officer in charge Basra. The military side was represented by two officers representing Movements and Transportation. It was however intended to replace them by one officer who would devote his whole time to committee work and would represent all military interests in Iraq and Iran. Sir John Ward served in his private capacity and not as Port Director—his local knowledge and influence were invaluable, but obviously he could not be a member of the Committee in his capacity as an Iraq Government official. The United Kingdom Commercial Corporation had separate organisations in Iraq and Iran with headquarters at Baghdad and Teheran respectively. Their representative in Basra represented both the countries. Other members of the Committee were the Sea Transport Officer at Basra and a representative of the Royal Air Force. A representative of the Anglo-Iranian Oil Company served occasionally on the Committee whenever it was found necessary to do so.

The Committee was the central authority for receiving information regarding programmes of proposed civil imports, both for local consumption and in transit ; and projected movements of service cargoes and other cargo moving on Government account ; and, subject to operational secrecy in general, all transport requirements on the rail and river systems. The Commitee received information regarding movements and cargoes of any ships other than operational vessels. In the light of this information the Committee decided at what ports and berths and in what priority cargoes should be discharged and loaded with a view to the most efficient use being made of port and inland transport facilities. The Committee co-ordinated the operation of discharge and loading of ships and port clearance with a view to the most rapid turn-round of ships and distribution of cargo. The Committee also advised about the measures for the development of the port and inland transport facilities.[27]

---

[26] G.H.Q., M.E.F., Mov. & Tn. A/135/68 dated 10 Feb. 1942—Instruction concerning Movements and Transportation, F. 730.
[27] Report by Mr. Mactier, op. cit. ; also Tel. of 9 Sept. 1941 from S.S. to Basra, F. 730.

CHAPTER XLVI

Development of Roads and Railways

Management of Railways

The organisation of Transportation and Movement Control and the formation of the War Transport Executive Committee were important steps towards the development of the roads and railways. Another matter of vital importance was the management of the railways. The management of the Iraq railways remained in the hands of the Iraq Government, and Movements Control indented on the Traffic Manager for all military requirements. All the additional rolling stock and military railway personnel were placed under the general control of the railway executive. The Director General, Iraq Railways, and several of the senior staff, were British and were thoroughly co-operative, but the system of dual control of military personnel had its inherent difficulties. However, short of the army taking over the railways, which was politically not possible at that time, no better arrangement seemed feasible.[1]

The management of the Iranian railways remained nominally in Iranian hands, but British advisers, under the Director of Transportation, Teheran, supervised both the traffic management and maintenance. British control was therefore very much more direct in Iran than in Iraq, but the successful operation of the line depended very largely on the good-will of the Iranian railway employees, who proved very co-operative.[2]

In the beginning the Russians took no interest whatever in the Iranian railway and were content to let the British exercise a general supervision over the line north of Teheran.[3] This state of affairs however did not last long. On 24 October 1941, the British Military Attache, Teheran, informed General Wavell that the Russian authorities were pressing for the division of the railway into zones of influence—the Russians to control the northern lines as far south as Qum. He was of the view that this demand should be strenuously opposed as only by undivided operational control could maximum efficiency of the railway be assured.[4] General Wavell agreed with this view and represented to the War Office the desirability of retaining undivided operational control over the Iranian railways.[5]

[1] Report by Mr. Mactier, op. cit.
[2] Ibid.
[3] Ibid.
[4] Tel. dated 24-10-41 from Brit. Mil. Attache Teheran to Armindia, F. 730.
[5] Tel. dated 10.11.41 from Armindia to Troopers, F. 730.

On 15 December 1941, Lt.-General Quinan informed General Wavell that the Soviet Technical Commission had again pressed for the direct operational control of the entire northern section, including Qum, leaving the British in control of the line to the south. They were prepared to leave British workshop personnel in Teheran and perhaps elsewhere in the northern section but wished to appoint a Soviet Deputy and Iranian Director General. Further, they suggested the setting up of an International Control Commission consisting of Sir Godfrey Rhodes (Director Transportation Iran) Kraeivos (head of the Soviet Technical Commission) and the Iranian Minister of Communications. The Commission would deal with matters of policy and principle. Lt.- General Quinan concurred in the opinion of Sir Godfrey Rhodes that divided control would seriously affect the efficiency of the railway.[6] Thereupon the Governor-General of India informed the Secretary of State for India, on 19 December 1941, of his reactions to the Russian proposal. He concurred with Sir G. Rhodes that divided control would result in confusion and inefficiency. It was necessary to make urgent representations in Moscow to stop this demand in Russia's own interest, for the proposal, if accepted, would result in the serious slowing up of the supplies to Russia.[7]

A new turn to the discussion of this thorny question was given by the British Minister at Teheran, when, on 3 January 1942, he suggested to the Foreign Office, London, that one solution would be for the whole line to be controlled by the Americans. But as it would take many months for the American technical personnel to come to Iran the proposal would be viewed with considerable mistrust by the Russians. He therefore suggested that he should be permitted to take up the matter with the Soviet Ambassador. He frankly confessed that it would be fortunate if they could secure the line from Teheran inclusive to the Persian Gulf as the British section.[8]

General Wheeler's reactions to this proposal were rather guarded. He agreed that divided control would result in inefficiency, but added that American control would depend on the extent of the American interest in the use of the railway. General Wheeler had been, however, informed by the Russian Ambassador in Teheran, that Russia would not accept more than 2,000 lorries and 100 aircraft a month from U.S.A. by the Persian Gulf route. Consequently the American interests in the use of the Iranian railway were negligible. General Wheeler further maintained that if the Iranian railway was used for American supplies to Russia or for the maintenance

[6] Tel. dated 15.12.41 from Armindia to Troopers, F. 730.
[7] Tel. dated 19.12.41 from G.G. to S.S. F. 730.
[8] Tel. dated 3 January 1942 from Minister Teheran to Foreign Office London, F. 730.

IRAQ AND IRAN
TRANSPORT IN AID TO RUSSIA
DIAGRAMMATIC

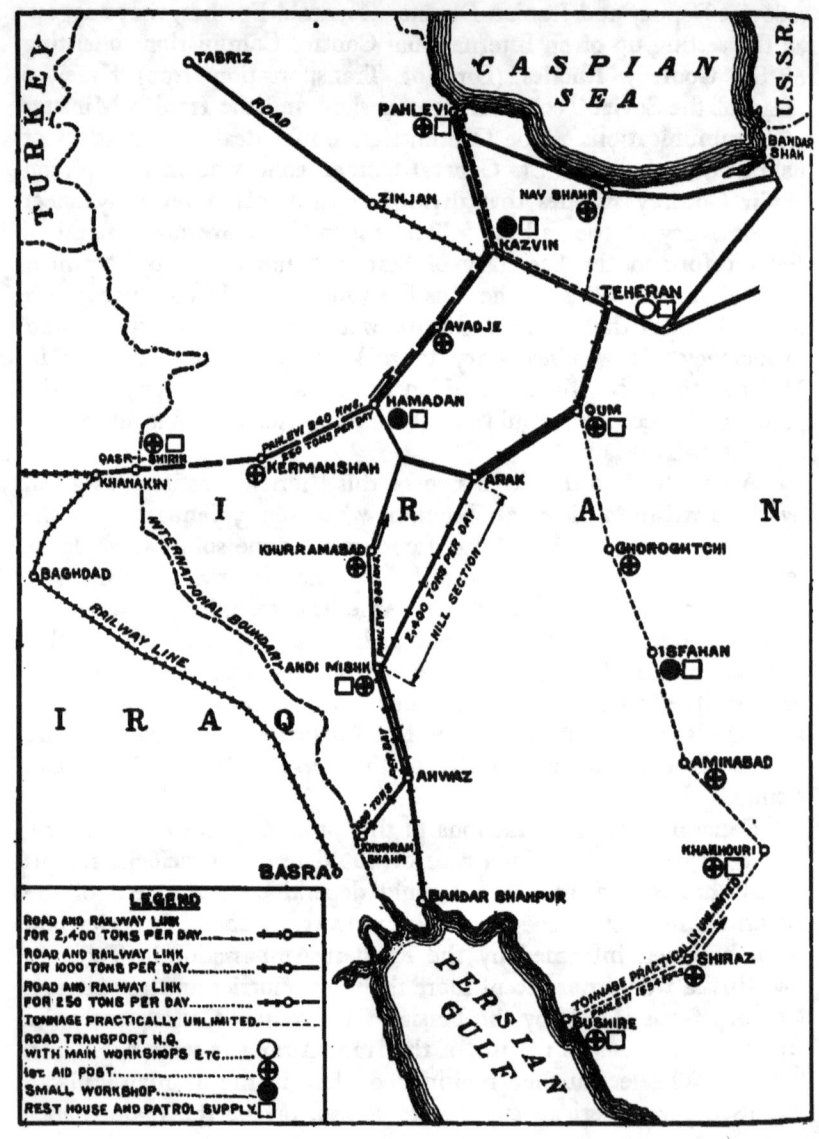

of British or American troops in north Iran, the Americans would have to take over full control. But that contingency was remote. So, after reviewing all these factors, General Wavell made the following recommendaions to the War Office on 13 January 1942:—

(i) Unified control was essential for the efficient operation of the railway.
(ii) As the Russians were unlikely to accept complete control over the railway it would be preferable to have full American control.
(iii) If divided control could not be avoided every effort should be made to prevent the Russian control from extending south of Teheran.[9]

But before any decision was arrived at on these proposals certain developments had taken place. On the same day that General Wavell informed the War Office of the above mentioned proposals he received information from Lt.-General Quinan that owing to continuous interference by Soviet troops he had ordered the withdrawal of British transport personnel from the Bandar Shah line, handing it over to the Soviet technical staff. He further reported that similar difficulties encountered in the operation of the Kazvin line would shortly result in the withdrawal of the British staff from that section also. It was imperative that an operating company and a workshop company should be despatched without delay to Iran to safeguard the position at Teheran.[10] Therefore, General Wavell requested the War Office to despatch additional British operating units from the Middle East to Iran to replace the 153rd Operating Company diverted to Malaya.[11]

General Auchinleck offered strong opposition to this proposal. The minimum requirements for Egypt-Palestine were six railway operating companies of which only two were available. One had been promised by the War Office. Still there was a deficiency of three operating companies. In view of these circumstances it was not possible to despatch any operating units to Iran. In fact it seemed doubtful if the British could displace the Russians on Bandar Shah (Caspian Sea) line or prevent them from taking over the Kazvin line. To engage in argument for operation rights, which the British were unable to carry out, would only lead to ill will. Accordingly, General Auchinleck recommended that they should accept the fact that the Russians would operate both the lines north of Teheran and the British would operate the railway south of it. He further recommended that the Railway Commission at Teheran (composed of the representatives of Iran, Russia and

[9] Tel. dated 13-1-42 from Armindia to Troopers, F. 730.
[10] Tel. dated 12.1.42 from General Iraq to Armindia, F. 730.
[11] Tel. dated 15.1.42 from Armindia to Troopers, F. 730.

Britain,) which was already controlling policy satisfactorily, should be made into a permanent commission of control, to which an American member might be added, if possible.[12]

General Auchinleck's straightforward views carried weight and the War Office seems to have veered round to them. A major hurdle however still remained, for the Russians were not prepared to agree to the proposal to make Teheran the dividing point between the British controlled and the Soviet controlled portions of the line. To resolve the differences the Soviet Ambassador in the United Kingdom held discussions with the Secretary of State for Foreign Affairs. The former explained the objections to the proposal, for this arrangement would leave the Soviet authorities in control of a comparatively short section between Teheran and the Caspian Sea. The Soviet Government maintained their view that Qum would be the best point of division but they would be prepared to allow the British authorities full use of the railway workshops at Teheran to which they attached special importance. The British Secretary of State for Foreign Affairs presented his case with skill. He had prepared a memorandum which set out in detail the overwhelming practical objections to dividing the southern line at Qum. The memorandum stated that while His Majesty's Government were convinced that the most efficient arrangement would be to maintain united operational control of the whole standard gauge of the Iranian railway system, it seemed to them clear that if there must be a division, it should correspond to the existing civil divisions of the railway and that Teheran should continue to be point of exchange between the southern and northern sections, as it was designed to be under peace-time conditions. The Soviet Government could not expect the British Government to agree that they should be cut off from Iran's capital. Moreover it might be necessary for the Allies to send troops back to Teheran in face of the Axis threat and it would then obviously be essential that the British should control the whole line from the south, since the British forces would be based upon it. Finally a division at Teheran would give the Soviet authorities not only the line to the Caspian but also the lines towards Tabriz and Meshed. The completed sections of these three lines were substantially longer than the line to the south.[13]

In reply to this memorandum the Soviet Ambassador communicated on 2 February 1942, to the Foreign Office, London, a memorandum giving the Soviet Government's observations. The memorandum asserted that although the length of the northern

---

[12] Tel. dated 17.1.42 from Mideast to Troopers, F. 730.
[13] Tel. from S.S. for Foreign Affairs to Ambassador Kuibyshev, dated 1.3.42, F. 730.

sector already completed was 1,090 kilometres, the Teheran—Shahrud line was only used for local traffic, and the main transit lines having a really great importance for the Allies had a length of about 770 kilometres. The Russian Ambassador in fact maintained that the division of the railway at Qum was technically possible and would have no practical disadvantages since the management was under the Anglo-Russian Board in Teheran. His Majesty's Government might fear that the division at Qum would be the first step towards extending the Soviet sphere of influence in Iran but he could give a most categorical assurance that his government had nothing of the kind in mind. He earnestly hoped that the British Government would meet his government's wish. It might be a small matter but it was 'symbolic' of the bonds ot friendship between the Allies.[14]

The Foreign Office, London, invited the opinion of the British Minister at Teheran, on this memorandum. The latter replied on 15 February 1942. He reiterated his views previously expressed. If the Russians controlled the railway as far as Qum the British would be squeezed out and the Russians would soon control the whole railway. The Soviet Government, however, wanted the lines up to Qum as a gesture of good-will.

The Secretary of State for Foreign Affairs, London sent a letter to the Russian Ambassador on 27 February in reply to the Soviet memorandum in which he mentioned that His Majesty's Government remained strongly of the opinion that the only acceptable criterion was as to what would give the best results in practice. There were overwhelming arguments, from the point of view of efficiency, in favour of retaining Teheran as the dividing point between the northern and southern sections. Teheran was not only the capital of the country but also the centre of the railway system, as well as the point of division in peace time. There seemed no advantage or indeed justification for dividing the southern section. The Soviet Ambassador was asked to inform his Government that the matter had been considered again most carefully but that His Majesty's Government regretted that they could not see their way to meeting the wishes of the Soviet Government on this point.[15]

No final agreement was arrived at but in actual practice the Russians continued to operate the line, north of Teheran and the British to the south, inclusive of Teheran. Then, as a result of the midsummer crisis of 1942, the British agreed to hand over the control of their sector to the Americans. The take-over commenced in January and continued for three months. From 1 April 1943, the Americans assumed the responsibility for the control of operations

[14] Tel. Foreign Office to Minister Teheran dated 10.2.42, F. 730.
[15] Tel. from S.S. to Russian Ambassador dated 1 March 1942, F. 730.

and maintenance of the Iranian State Railway between Teheran and the Persian Gulf ports.

Development of Railways

While discussion continued between the British and the Russians over the management of the Iranian railways, steps were being taken for the development of the railways, both in Iraq and Iran. Colonel Carson, the Director of Transportation, Iraq, took energetic measures to improve the capacity of the Iraq railway. Noticeable progress was made by the end of April 1942. Basra and Shuaiba bases were provided better railway facilities. The number of metre gauge and standard gauge locomotives put into service increased from 27 and 8 to 154 and 20, respectively, during the period December 1941-April 1942. The number of metre gauge wagons increased from 775 to 5,382 and the standard gauge wagons from nil to 378. The number of passing stations open to traffic on the metre gauge from Basra to Baghdad increased from 9 to 30. Forty miles of line was doubled between Basra and Baghdad. The military tonnage carried on the line Basra—Baghdad rose from 9032 to 27279 and the civil tonnage from 5067 to 12544.[16]

At the same time Brigadier Sir Godfrey Rhodes, Director of Transportation, Iran, took measures to improve the capacity of the Iranian railway. The Trans-Iranian Railway could carry only 200 tons a day; its capacity was to be raised to 2,400 tons daily for supplies to Russia alone by the spring of 1942. It was estimated that to develop it to carry from 600 to 750 tons a day, 168 locomotives and 3,800 (10-ton unit) wagons were required to run 12 trains daily.[17] All stations had to be greatly enlarged so that the heavy traffic might be efficiently handled. It was a single track and could take only a very limited number of trains. The doubling of the track was out of the question owing to lack of time and money. The deficiency to a certain exent was made up by adding new crossing and marshalling stations and sorting yards and by providing fuel and water facilities and signal equipment in large quantities.

The number of British locomotives put into service increased from 37 in January 1942 to 167 in April 1942. The number of British wagons increased from 317 to 1,561. The tonnage carried on the various sections of the railway line for the period February to April 1942 was as follows:—

	Feb.	April
Ahwaz—Andimishk	40,132	48,875
Andimishk—Teheran	27,658	38,183
Teheran—Zinjan	4,576	5,435.

[16] Development Reports, F. 730.
[17] Tel. dated 6.9.41 from Troopers to Armindia, F. 730.

Men of the Kashmir Rifles in Iran on the 'Aid to Russia' route

The Bandar Shahpuur—Teheran Express carrying war materials to Russia

Indian Troops in Iranian mountain passes

Further, 264 miles of the Zinjan-Mianeh railway line were completed and 73 miles of the Ahwaz-Khurramshahr railway line. Extension of twenty crossing stations and yards was also undertaken.[18]

It will be appropriate to mention here that although the railway line from Teheran to Mianeh was nearing completion the chances of completing the railway line to Tabriz became remote. It was estimated that the project would take almost two years to complete and would cost about forty million *tomans*. Over 30,000 tons of rail would be needed to complete the project. The Russians, therefore, favoured the improvement of the Pahlevi-Astara road; they erected about eighty wooden bridges—capable of carrying 20-ton loads—to help the connection of the road with their railway at Astara. Thus the improvement of Pahlevi-Astara road commended itself much more to the Russians than the completion of the Mianeh-Tabriz section of the railway, particularity as they could not have a wide gauge track.[19]

The midsummer crisis of 1942 brought home the realisation that the British alone would not be able to shoulder the heavy responsibility of developing the railway capacity in Iraq as well as Iran. Hence an agreement was arrived at by which the British concentrated their attention on the development of the Iraq railway and the Americans took over the operational control of the Iranian State Railway. By the end of December 1942, when the process of handing over the control of the Iranian railway to the Americans began, the British had succeeded in raising the capacity of the railway from the level of 200 tons daily to 1,500 tons. This progress had been achieved by doubling the number of roads in the yards at Andimishk, Ahwaz and Teheran, re-constructing crossovers and shunting necks, lengthening a large number of the existing loops, sound maintenance of the permanent way and constructing a large number of crossing stations.[20]

A railway line was laid out from Ahwaz to Khurramshahr with an extension to Cheybassi. Later, Cheybassi was connected with Maqil by a metre gauge railway line which crossed the Shatt al Arab by a bridge having a central span, which sank into the river to make way for the ships. Satisfactory though the progress was it fell far short of the 6,000-ton target now set by the Combined Chiefs of Staff. The Americans with their superior resources were soon able to accelerate the progress and attained the target of 6,000 tons in 1944 when the daily average of all freight hauled was 6,489 tons.[21]

---

[18] Development Reports, F. 730.
[19] The railway line to Mianeh was completed towards the end of 1942. There was a fair road (112 miles) leading from Mianeh to Tabriz, (Weekly Intelligence Summary No. 57 dated 4 December 1942).
[20] *Paiforce*, p. 99.
[21] *U.S. Army in World War II—The Persian Corridor and Aid to Russia*, p. 372.

In Iraq the British constructed early in 1943 a new railway line connecting Kut with Baquba, thus augmenting considerably the tonnage carried over the Khanakin route to Russia. The relaying of the railway line (in Baluchistan) increased the tonnage carried over the Nokundi-Meshed route to Russia.

Development of Roads in Iraq and Iran

Besides improving the capacity for discharge of the Persian Gulf ports and the development of railways, the improvement of roads was also taken in hand. At the end of December 1941, Lt.-General Quinan sketched a plan for the construction and maintenance of roads in Iraq for operational purposes.[22] Later, in June 1942 a new comprehensive programme was drawn up covering both Iraq and Iran. Fifty-one roads were selected for improvement. The following roads received top priority:—

		Specification
(i)	Mosul-Erbil	All weather
(ii)	Kirkuk-Tuzkarmatli-Diltawa-Baquba	All weather
(iii)	Baghdad-Falluja-Ramadi	All weather
(iv)	Baghdad-Mussaiyib	All weather
(v)	Khanakin-Kermanshah-Hamadan-Kazvin	All weather
(vi)	Mussaiyib-Hindiya junction	All weather
(vii)	Basra—Shuaiba	All weather
(viii)	Malayar-Sultanabad-Qum-Teheran	Gravel
(ix)	Nokundi-Zahidan-Kerman-Yezd-Nain-Isfahan	Track improvement
(x)	Isfahan-Dilijan-Qum	Gravel
(xi)	Zahidan-Birjand-Meshed	Gravel
(xii)	Dizful-Khurramabad-Malayar-Hamadan	All weather
(xiii)	Tanuma-Khurramshahr-Ahwaz-Andimishk	All weather
(xiv)	Jokar-Tuisarkan-Kangavar or Malayar-Nehavand-Kangavar	All weather
(xv)	Teheran-Kazvin	All weather
(xvi)	Kermanshah-Senneh	All weather
(xvii)	Senneh-Saqqiz	Single Track surface
(xviii)	Razan-Durud or Chalanchulan-Durud	All weather

[22] G/117/93 H.Q. B.T.I. Baghdad dated 27 December 41—Communications Iraq. F. 730.

(xix)	Kermanshah-Harsin-Khurramabad	All weather
(xx)	Baghdad-Baquba-Khanakin	All weather
(xxi)	Deir ez Zor-Chaddadi-Tell Afar-Mosul[23]	Improvement of track
(xxii)	Falluja-Saqlawiya	Gravel
(xxiii)	Tenth Army boundary-Ramadi	All weather
(xxiv)	Erbil-Rowanduz-Tabriz	Gravel
(xxv)	Senneh-Hamadan	Gravel
(xxvi)	Hamadan-Bijar	Gravel

In addition to the development of the road system in Iraq and Iran,[24] Lt.-General Quinan also made arrangements for the maintenance of the principal road routes in Iran for carrying supplies to Russia:—

(i) The Iranian Government (Ministry of Communications) would appoint approved contractors as their agents to maintain certain roads by which supplies would be sent to U.S.S.R.

(ii) A survey of these roads would be made to enable an estimate to be made of the cost of essential improvements and maintenance.

(iii) The Iranian Government would allot towards the cost of improvement and maintenance the amount previously spent on such work, based on the average expenditure for the last three years, and in addition such revenue as would be obtained from the additional motor transport to be operated over them.

(iv) The British Government would make up the difference between the estimated cost of maintenance of the roads and the sum to be spent by the Iranian Government. The total sum would be placed in the form of a special credit, which might be drawn on by the approved contractor or engineer in charge of the roads concerned.

(v) The Transportation Directorate would attach road engineers and accountants to the approved contractor to safeguard the interests of the British Government.

(vi) The United Kingdom Commercial Corporation would pay normal taxes for their lorries in the same manner as any other road transport operator.

(vii) A similar agreement would be made for the portion of Nokundi-Meshed route between the frontier and Meshed.[25]

[23] In July 1942 the amendment was made that the portion of this road Chaddadi-Balad Sinjar-Tell Afar-Mosul should be made into a gravel road.
[24] No. 258/F 15/56/Q1 H.Q. Tenth Army dated 6 June 1942, Road Development Programme, Appendix 'R' W/D Q. Branch, Tenth Army 1942.
[25] Tel. dated 4-10-41 from Armindia to Troopers F. 730.

Accordingly a tripartite agreement was arrived at between the British and the Iranian Governments and the Danish firm of Kampasax. The last were the consulting engineers acting in administrative and consultative capacity. They agreed to maintain and develop roads in Iran, excluding the route Nokundi-Meshed.[26]

Contracts valued at a little over £2,000,000 were given to about thirty different contractors for the development of roads. Later some more contractors were engaged. Reconnaissance of the roads had already been carried out by Lt.-Colonel A.J.R. Hill, R.E., who had arrived in Iran in September 1941.[27] A large number of coolies, with their shovels and wheel barrows, were employed for the improvement of the roads. The maximum number of coolies and donkeys employed was 67,000 and 14,000 respectively.[28]

Later, by an Anglo-American agreement made in August 1943, the construction and maintenance of the road Andimishk-Hamadan—Teheran became the joint responsibility of the British and the Americans. The United States played a very important part in the development of this road.[29] The road Malayar—Qum—Teheran was also improved; the sector Malayar—Qum upto the gravel standard, and the sector Hamadan-Malayar with a bitumen surface.[30] The Khanakin-Hamadan road was improved to the gravel standard.[31] The Bushire-Qum route was also improved but in course of time it ceased to be used for convoys. The construction of the Ahwaz-Andimishk road was taken in hand by the Americans as part of their project for improving the road Khurramshahr-Andimishk. They constructed before the end of 1942 a temporary road between Khurramshahr and Andimishk. And in 1943 they completed a permanent two-way highway between Khurramshahr and Andimishk with a branch road from Khurramshahr to Tanuma, which was further extended to Coal Island by British contractors with the help of the United States engineers.[32]

Development of the Nokundi—Meshed road

While the British and the Americans were busy developing the roads in the rest of Iran, the Government of India too played an important part in developing the roads in the eastern part of that country. In September 1941 the War Office had laid down the policy that the Baluchistan—Meshed route should be developed by

---

[26] Tel. dated 2.11.41 from Armindia to General Iraq, F. 730.
[27] M.G.R.E. Branch, H.Q. Tenth Army, dated 22 March 1942, to D.A. & Q.M.G.; File 8104.
[28] *Paiforce*, p. 108.
[29] *U.S. Army in World War II*—op. cit. p. 251.
[30] Letter dated 24 June 1942 from C.E. 202 Works Teheran to M.G.R.E. Tenth Army, F. 903.
[31] Ibid.
[32] *U.S. Army in World War II*, op. cit. pp. 250-51.

India up to 2,000 tons per month. The management of the route and the delivery of supplies to Russia by this route was to be the responsibility of the Government of India.[33] Fairly good progress was made so that by the end of February 1942 it was reported that about half the work of widening and metalling the road had been completed.[34] Further improvements were made so that by the end of 1942 the construction of the road was completed.[35] The maintenance of the road was the responsibility of the Danish firm Kampsax who kept it in very good condition.[36]

Development of the Zahidan—Qum road

Besides developing the above mentioned route the Government of India also tried to develop the route Zahidan-Kerman-Yezd-Isfahan—Qum. Early in October 1941, the Government of India explored the possibilities of opening an overland Line of Communication from India to Iran, on the general line Quetta-Zahidan-Kerman-Yezd-Isfahan-Qum. It was felt that the opening of this route would be of great importance as it would take the load off the ports and shipping in the despatch of supplies to Russia and movement of troops, military equipment and supplies to Iran and Iraq.[37] Accordingly, on 8 October 1941, the General Headquarters, India, ordered Western (Independent) District to make arrangements for a reconnaissance of the road.[38] The reconnaissance party was led by Lt.-Colonel K. Plomer, R.I.A.S.C., and its report was submitted in November 1941. It contained the following observations on the three sections of the route:—

(i) *Zahidan to Bam*

The only serious obstacle to the movement of troops on this route were two patches of soft, deep sand between miles 134-136½ and 152-156 from Zahidan. These stretches might be crossed only with considerable difficulty by a small number of vehicles at a time. Therefore, if only a temporary route was required, a suitable crossing would be made using army track netting fixed over planking. If, however, a permanent or semi-permanent route was required a pukka road would have to be constructed over these stretches, either of soling and metalling or of sleepers. In addition to these two patches of soft sand there was another factor which limited traffic on this route. At mile 78 from Zahidan the road crossed a pass and was narrow and winding for about 2½ miles. Over this stretch only

[33] Tel. 13074/G dated 13-9-41 from Armindia to West District, F. 698.
[34] Weekly Intelligence Summary No. 19 dated 13 March, 1942.
[35] Tel. dated 5/11/42 from S.E. 17 Works to Armindia, F. 567.
[36] Letter No. U.K.C.C./TPT/13 dated 30 March 1943 to Q.M.G. India, F. 567.
[37] Minutes of a meeting held at G.H.Q., New Delhi on 17-11-41, F. 742.
[38] No. 514/1/GS/M.O.4, G.H.Q. India dated 8 October 1941 to H.Q. Western District, F. 698.

single-line traffic was possible. A disabled vehicle would block the route until removed.

There was also a possible alternative route from Mirjawa to Bam via Kwash. This route was even more difficult but it was easier to improve.

(ii) Bam to Nain

There were no obstacles on this route.

(iii) Nain to Qum

There were two routes from Nain to Qum, via Isfahan or via Ardistan. The route via Isfahan (277 miles) had no obstacles. The route via Ardistan was shorter, being only 220 miles, but it included seven or eight nulla crossings, where spates were liable to occur and which in wet weather appeared likely to hold up traffic for a day or two. The route via Ardistan was in much worse condition than via Isfahan, which was the normal main road. The route via Isfahan was therefore recommended in wet weather.[39]

In February 1942, the War Office realised the urgency of developing this route. They informed General Auchinleck that increased enemy threat made the rapid movement of formations between the Middle East and India an urgent necessity. In view of the shipping shortage the early development of all possible overland routes was desirable. Therefore they suggested that General Auchinleck might examine, in conjunction with the Commander-in-Chief, India, the possibilities of using the over-land route from Baluchistan to Iraq via Nokundi—Yezd and Khanakin for the movement of troops.[40] On instructions from the General Headquarters India, Baluchistan (Independent) District made arrangements for a tactical reconnaissance of the route Quetta-Kerman. The report of this reconnaissance was submitted in June 1942, and stressed the fact that the country from Quetta to Kerman, a distance of 800 miles, was an area most suitable for mechanised movement, and could well be compared with the country between Alexandria and Benghazi.[41] Meanwhile another reconnaissance party from the headquarters of the Tenth Army had examined the road from Khusrovi to Kerman.[42] On the basis of these reports, early in July, Lt.-General Quinan decided to make the road fit to carry a division, but not for continuous heavy traffic.[43] By that time, however, enough progress had been made for the improvement of this route.

[39] Report on the route Zahidan-Qum by Plumrec, November 1941, F. 734.
[40] Tel. dated 27.2.1942 from Troopers to Mideast, F. 903.
[41] Report by Hurst on the tactical reconnaissance of the route Quetta-Kerman, F. 903.
[42] Letter dated 24 June 1942 from C.E. 202 Works Teheran to M.G.R.E. Tenth Army, F. 903.
[43] Minutes of a meeting held in Baghdad on 8 July 1942, F. 903.

The road Khusrovi-Kermanshah-Hamadan-Malayar-Qum-Isfahan-Aghda was brought up to the gravel standard, though progress on the section Aghda-Anar-Kerman was not satisfactory. The road Kerman-Bam-Zahidan was also improved with the exception of the desert section.[44] Not only had the road been improved considerably but the Anglo-Iranian Oil Company had also carried out the difficult task of establishing petrol dumps along the entire route.[45] The administrative and operational boundary between the North-Western Army (India) and the Tenth Army (Iran) ran from Meshed-Kerman-Bam to the coast.[46] The division of responsibility between the North-Western Army and the Tenth Army for troop movements was as follows: —

(i) Roadwork: Tenth Army for the whole route from Zahidan to Kerman.
(ii) Move of reinforcements Zahidan-Kerman: North-Western Army, India.

An outline plan for the movement of formations by this route was prepared early in 1942, and an agreement was arrived at between the Tenth Army and General Headquarters, India, for proper organisation on the route, and stages were fixed.[47]

On this road complete arrangements were to be made for replenishment of supplies, water, maintenance and medical aid, etc. The estimated time for the move of each formation (brigade group) from Zahidan to Baghdad was twenty days. India was reponsible for stocking the route from Zahidan to Kerman, while the Tenth Army was to manage the stock on the remaining portion of the route.[48]

---

[44] Letter dated 24 June 1942 from C.E. 202 Works Teheran to M.G.R.E., Tenth Army, F. 903.
[45] *Paiforce*, p. 110.
[46] 44729/G.S. (M.O.1) H.Q.N.W. Army to C.G.S., dated 27 June 1942, F. 903.
[47]

Zahidan		0 miles
Nasratabad Sipi		65 miles
Fehruj		103 miles
Tehrud		85 miles
Kerman		85 miles
Rafsinjan		87 miles
Anar		68 miles
Yezd		99 miles
Nain		98 miles
Isfahan		117 miles
Dilijan		115 miles
Sultanabad		85 miles
Tuisarkan		95 miles
Kermanshah		83 miles
Sar-i-Pul-Zuhab		87 miles
Baquba	...	99 miles
Habbaniya	... ...	87 miles

[48] Use of the route Zahidan—Iraq for troop movements, Appendix 'A', p. 29, F. 903.

CHAPTER XLVII

Inland Water Transport

Management

One other channel of transport besides the roads and railways was the system of inland waterways in Iraq and Iran, which it was essential to develop for organising transport on it. Such an organisation was intended to provide transport on the rivers:[1]

(i) between Basra and Baghdad (or Kut when the Kut—Baquba railway line was built),

(ii) between Khosroabad—Abadan and Khurramshahr—Ahwaz, and

(iii) harbour lighterage at Basra, Bandar Shahpur and Khurramshahr.

It was decided that the army should take over the direct management and operation of all craft on the Tigris and Karun rivers, and in the Shatt al Arab, with the exception of some indigenous sailing craft, and Anglo-Iranian Oil Company's bulk craft. This involved the setting up of a military organisation to handle the movement of practically all civil and military cargo by water in Iraq and Iran. The army had run such an organisation for the Tigris and Euphrates efficiently, if extravagantly, in World War I. Before deciding on setting up the military organisation, the alternative arrangement was considered of employing the existing firms who might operate river craft by expanding their organisation and running the river services under contract with the army. The only first class firm carrying general cargo on the rivers Euphrates and Tigris was the British Euphrates and Tigris Steam Navigation Co., but it had neither the personnel nor the technical organisation to expand upto the necessary scale. In addition, existing crews of river craft had proved unreliable under fire. It was, therefore, considered essential to have all inland water transport crew under military discipline,[2] and consequently an Inland Water Transport organisation was set up under Lieut.-Colonel Sudbury, who had extensive experience of commercial lighterage management.

Under the new arrangement the main port of discharge into craft for the Tigris and Karun rivers was Khosroabad, 15 miles below Abadan, which was an oil port, connected by pipeline with

---

[1] Report on Persian Gulf Ports and Inland Transport facilities and Organisation by Mactier, dated 1 Nov 1941, F. 730.
[2] Ibid.

Abadan, but was not in use. Three vessels could lie at the oil jetties (for easy access) and discharge both sides into craft. Khosroabad was 25 miles below Khurramshahr and 46 miles from Basra (Maqil). The extra tow was, however, compensated for by the fact that the port was below the Karun Bar and ships could therefore be accepted drawing 28' (neaps) as against 24' (neaps) at Khurramshahr or Basra. The area behind the wharves was also partly developed and was well suited for a camp for the necessary labour and for open storage of cargo.[3]

Increasing the capacity of the Persian Gulf ports and the development of inland water transport on the Tigris and Karun to the maximum extent as quickly as possible were of immense importance to Allied war strategy, both in respect of aid to Russia and maintenance of British forces. With it was vitally connected the development of the Khanakin—Teheran route which would carry the supplies to Russia. Heretofore the goods were carried from Basra in railway wagons to Baghdad, where these were ferried across the Tigris and hauled thence to Khanakin, the starting point of the highway to Tabriz. The ferry at Baghdad was a virtual bottleneck and limited the haul to 900 tons a day. To tide over this difficulty, it was considered desirable to carry the cargo in barges from Basra up the Tigris and to improve the facilities at Baghdad by constructing a barge wharf on the east bank of the river and provide a railway link to the Khanakin line. But, due to the scarcity of barges, the better alternative was to construct a new railway line connecting Kut with Baquba. The construction of this railway line helped in saving more than 200 miles of barge-haul. Goods could now be carried in barges from Basra to Kut, thence by rail to Khanakin. From Khanakin the goods were carried by lorries to Tabriz. This route played a very important part in the 'Aid to Russia' schemes.

The problem of the development of the inland water transport on the Karun river was vitally connected with the development of the Trans-Iranian railway. The port of Bandar Shahpur alone was not adequate to feed this railway. It was therefore necessary to construct a railway line to connect Khurramshahr with Ahwaz and another line to connect Ahwaz with Tanuma (close to Maqil on the left bank) where there were a number of barge wharves. In addition to these development schemes it was also necessary to develop the inland water transport on the Karun so that goods might be carried in barges from the port of Khurramshahr to the wharves at Ahwaz. This route however presented many difficulties for the barges plying on the river Karun found the channel very capricious and tortuous.

Besides the development of the inland water transport on the Tigris and the Karun, it was necessary to tackle the problem of

[3] Ibid.

harbour lighterage, viz., to unload and load the ships in the harbour so that they might not be detained in the Persian Gulf ports for an unnecessarily long period. As the Axis were taking a heavy toll of the Allied shipping there was an acute shortage; hence it was of vital importance not to detain the ships in the Persian Gulf ports for a long time.

Estimated Tonnage and Capacity

On 20 August 1941, General Wavell informed the War Office that in view of the commitments involved in the defence of Iraq, viz. maintenance of ten divisions and thirty squadrons R.A.F., it would be necessary not only to develop the ports of Basra and Umm Qasr but also to improve the railway line Basra—Baghdad and to develop the inland water transport on the Tigris. The maximum lift by the through service (Basra-Baghdad) during World War I was about 1,000 tons a day. It was unlikely that they would reach this figure owing to the difficulties of the supply of river craft. They were requisitioning all available craft in India and Burma but they could not reckon on a greater lift than about 500 tons a day into Baghdad for a long time to come.[4] After consultation with Lieut-General Quinan, General Wavell however revised his estimate, and on 2 September 1941 recommended to the War Office that inland water transport on the Tigris should be developed to carry 2500 tons a day.[5] On 5 September, Lieut-General Quinan recommended that the river facilities should be developed to carry 2500 tons daily through traffic to Kut and that a railway line should connect Kut with Baghdad.[6] On 17 September, General Wavell informed Lieut-General Quinan that His Majesty's Government had sanctioned the project for the development of the Tigris river to carry 2500 tons daily to Kut or 1500 tons through to Baghdad. The project of the railway Kut-Baquba was also sanctioned but was given low priority.[7]

On 26 September 1941, General Wavell communicated to the War Office his revised estimate that the maximum daily tonnage would be 3950 tons: 2500 tons from Basra to Kut up the Tigris and 1450 tons from Khurramshahr to Ahwaz up the Karun. 142 tugs and 400 barges would be needed to lift this tonnage. The available craft in Iraq and chartered from the Anglo-Iranian Oil Company and the Euphrates and Tigris Steam Navigation Company, were only 47 tugs and 161 barges. 35 tugs and 70 barges would be supplied from India and Burma before the weather deteriorated in March and prevented further despatch of the craft. The balance

[4] Tel dated 20.8.41 from Armindia to Troopers, F. 730.
[5] Tel dated 2.9.41 from General Iraq to Troopers, F. 730.
[6] Tel dated 5.9.41 from General Iraq to War Office, F. 730.
[7] Tel dated 17.9.41 from Armindia to General Iraq, F. 730.

of 60 tugs and 169 barges would have to be provided by the War Office. The prime movers should be twin screw tunnel type motor tugs, capable of towing the loaded barges, each carrying 300 tons dead weight.[8] The War Office appreciated General Wavell's efforts to develop the inland water transport but also urged him to move to Iraq by April 1942 (before the monsoon set in) the maximum number of craft available from India and Burma. He was further informed that orders were being placed in America for a large number of small shallow draught tow boats and barges for the Tigris.[9]

Development of Inland Water Transport (October 1941—April 1942)

We may now trace the organisation and development of inland water transport from October 1941 to April 1942. Prior to October 1941, work in this connection formed part of the duties of the Transportation Directorate. On that date a separate I.W.T. Directorate was created under Col. Subbury. There were only three officers available for the work, one was on a tour of inspection of the Tigris, the second was posted at Baghdad (as Staff Captain) and the third was at Basra (as Inland Water Transport Officer). Two other officers arrived in October and were made responsible for the engineering and administration departments, respectively. Another officer became available in November to organise and take charge of the Traffic Department. About that time ten subalterns without technical qualifications were provided and utilised on various jobs. In early January 1942 the officer strength was 38, and, though not quite adequate for all the work handled by it, this Directorate took over the Gray Mackenzie fleet and such portion of the Anglo-Iranian Oil Company's fleet as had been transferred to the I.W.T. Directorate. In mid-January No. 2 I.W.T. Group arrived from the United Kingdom and it was then possible to place British other ranks on all the large vessels for supervisory work. By the end of February the Traffic Control Establishment had secured a very great improvement in loading ships and barges. At the same time detachments of Marine, Engineering and Administration troops were sent forward as advance party to start work at the various stations which were to be developed (such as Kut) and a large party was sent to Qala Salih to open up the Narrows Control. Simultaneously the purchase of the fleet of the Karun Navigation Company was completed and its operation was taken over. Despite a grave shortage of supervisory staff, the control of Gray Mackenzie's workshop and slipway was also taken over. Thus the Engineering Department, which had hitherto been operating purely in a marine engineering capacity,

---
[8] Tel dated 26.9.41 from Armindia to Troopers, F. 730.
[9] Tel of 16.12.41 from S.S. to Defence Department India, F. 730.

assumed in addition the dockyard responsibilities.[10] By the end of April 1942, the Directorate was fairly well organised. There were 91 officers consisting of 1 Director (Colonel), 4 Assistant Directors (Lieut.-Colonels), 7 Deputy Assistant Directors (Majors), 36 Captains and 43 Lieutenants. There were 639 British other ranks, employed mostly as barge engineers, blacksmiths, boiler makers, carpenters and joiners, electricians, fitters, foremen, lightermen, millwrights, moulders, pioneers, plumbers, riggers, riveters, stevedores, stokers, turners etc. There were 1640 Indian other ranks also posted along with 2,857 local labour.[11]

The strength of the fleet of the inland water transport increased steadily. In October 1941 there were 125 craft available; of these 19 were towing units, 12 launches, 73 up-river barges, 6 harbour barges and pontoons, 14 service barges and 1 miscellaneous vessel. India supplied tugs and barges to augment the fleet. On 28 February, the first four paddle steamers from Calcutta arrived in the port of Basra. In March more craft arrived from India, including 9 paddle steamers, 2 tugs and 6 barges. Some more craft arrived from India in April; these included 3 paddle steamers, 2 tugs and 7 barges. At the end of April 1942 the fleet strength had risen to 546; of these 87 were towing units, 74 launches, 212 up-river barges, 59 harbour barges and pontoons, 33 service barges, 61 country craft and 20 miscellaneous vessels.[12]

There was also a noticeable improvement in the tonnage lift. In October 1941, the harbour lighterage disloaded was 4,000 tons and the total tonnage despatched was 7,072 tons.[13] By 1 April 1942, the position had improved considerably. The statement below shows the tonnage moved on the whole system[14]:—

Section	January 1942	February 1942	March 1942
1. Up Tigris	11,039	12,734	14,027
2. Up Karun	8,357	9,907	11,480
3. Down Tigris	1,634	2,467	4,149
4. Down Karun	2,787	7,040	5,515
5. Shatt-al-Hai	—	200	375
6. Harbour lighterage	11,088	24,318	27,884
Total tons handled	34,905	56,666	63,430

[10] Report of I.W.T. Committee of Review, April 1942, W/D I.W.T. Part I; and Monthly Summary of Progress from October 1941 to August 1942, W/D I.W.T. Part II.
[11] I.W.T. Organisation Strength Return dated 9.5.42, W/D I.W.T. Part I; and Monthly Summary of Progress October 1941 to August 1942, W/D I.W.T. Part II.
[12] Monthly Summary of Progress Oct 41 to August 42, W/D I.W.T. Part II.
[13] Ibid.
[14] Ibid, part 1.

I.W.T. Committee of Review

Lieut.-General Quinan, the Tenth Army Commander was not satisfied with the progress and ordered a review of the work on 21 April 1942. The Committee was to report on the following points:—

    (*i*) Whether the technical experience of officers and men was being properly utilised and what steps, if any, were necessary to improve these.

    (*ii*) Whether the available craft was being used to the best advantage.

    (*iii*) Whether any economy in staff and personnel was desirable.

The Committee was to consist of the Commander Line of Communication Area and Deputy Director of Movements, and was to be presided over by the Financial Adviser. Mr. Berry, the Inland Water Transport Adviser to the Government of India, was subsequently appointed to the Committee, which submitted its report on 24 May 1942. It drew attention to the slowness of improvement in the organisation of transport, which was ascribed to two main causes: (*i*) shortage of officers and men, (*ii*) shortage of tugs and barges. There was a deficiency of seven officers for workshops and slipway—two engineers (senior electrical engineer and engineer with Fitting Shop training) and five officers with the experience of motor launch shipwright, machine shop and repair work on vessels. On the traffic side there was a deficiency of 29 officers. There was also a deficiency of 20 British other ranks in connection with the night work supervision at Maqil. The small number of Indian other ranks was hardly adequate to meet even a fraction of the immediate needs. Of workshop operatives only 29 had been supplied by India against a sanctioned establishment of over 2500 for Basra and Kut. Of clerical staff, only a small proportion of total requirement had been provided. This shortage involved burdening some officers and others with clerical routine at the expense of their proper duties.

There was also deficiency of tugs and barges. For example, at the end of March 1942, out of 71 tugs requisitioned only 30 tugs were available for up-river cargo carriage. 25 tugs were out of commission. The Iraq tugs, which constituted more than 50% of the total, were generally in very poor condition. Though the condition of the tugs procured from the Anglo-Iranian Oil Company and India was very good, those from India arrived without their full complement of fuel tanks (some had none and most had only 25%); their running stores were inadequate, and they brought no spares, not even such vital items as paddle bolts and nuts.

There were no facilities for heavy repairs and overhauls. The Inland Water Transport Directorate took over the slipway and the small workshop (situated about half a mile from the slipway) of

Messers Gray Mackenzie on 1 March 1942. This was, however, not sufficient to cope with the demand for heavy repairs and overhauls. For this purpose, in August 1941, a well equipped workshop was to be provided on the Dockyard Island. But the plant, equipment and shedding material for this had not arrived, and work was not taken up. There was of course the A.I.O.C. workshop at Abadan, but it also suffered from certain limitations, the chief being the non-availability of layout. In September 1941, a proposal was made that the Quartermaster General in India would arrange for some 290 Indian workshop operatives to provide one full shift in the Abadan workshop but this scheme did not materialise. Similarly owing to the shortage of skilled labour, the Port Marine Dockyard was of no greater assistance than to maintain the Port Directorate's fleet.

Besides these maintenance shortcomings, an important factor which limited the tonnage lift from Basra to Baghdad was the imposition of additional tasks on the inland water transport. As for example, in order to obtain the greatest flexibility in the use of the craft, the Directorate was made responsible for the provision of craft for lighterage—not only at Basra but at all the Persian Gulf ports. Consequently its ST-5 was stationed at Bushire, MT-20 at Umm Qasr, MT-10 was lent to the Royal Navy; and flood conditions had necessitated retaining a tug for safety at Abadan, Khurramshahr and Baghdad. These, with MT-26 locked up in the Shatt-al-Hai, represented a loss in tonnage capacity of approximately 100 tons a day in March 1942. The towing of Mahaillas to Al Fatha represented a further loss in March of 70 tons a day. Water traffic was also restricted by the fact that through the Kut Lock no Indian paddlers could pass, and there was shoal water between Ba Ghilha and Baghdad, where Indian screw tugs could not ply owing to their deep draught.

The Committee recommended that the deficiency of officers and men should be made good by providing:—

(i) Deputy to Director at headquarters
(ii) Deputy to Assistant Director (Traffic)
(iii) Additional qualified officers for workshops and slipways
(iv) Additional Traffic officers
(v) Additional British other ranks for checking duties
(vi) Viceroy's Commissioned Officers, Indian Warrant Officers and Non-Commissioned Officers in camps and vessels for essential disciplinary and administrative purposes.

The Committee also recommended the publication of an order clearly defining the duties and responsibilities of Inland Water Transport, Movement Control, and other transport services. The Committee further recommended that representation should be made regarding:—

(i) urgent provision of shedding and plant for workshops on order from India,
(ii) stores and spares for vessels,
(iii) provision of Indian workshop operatives for Abadan workshops,
(iv) assistance by Port Marine Dockyard,
(v) urgent supplies for improvement of repair facilities.

Reorganisation of the I.W.T. Directorate

As a result of the report of the Committee of Review, steps were taken for the reorganisation of the Directorate. Even before the Committee had submitted its report the Director in consultation with the Committee and Brigadier Carson, the Director General of Transport, had outlined a scheme for the reorganisation of the Directorate. This was based on the view that the existing departmental organisation was too rigid to secure the best results, particularly during a period of shortage of staff. He felt that it would be possible to obtain better co-ordination and to utilise to better advantage the qualifications of individuals, if an area or regional administration were substituted for the system of administration by departments at the headquarters. The necessity for this was felt particularly as the introduction of sectional towage called for much greater supervision up-river. Hence a reorganisation was effected on 11 May 1942, which in outline was as follows:—

(i) The administrative department became the Directorate proper. In other words the Assistant Director Administration was responsible for all contacts with the other military formations and for the maintenance and continuity of all filing system and records. This involved attaching certain technical officers to the headquarters staff to deal with the departmental correspondence and the technicalities involved therein. By virtue of his office at the headquarters, the Assistant Director Administration deputised for the Director in his absence and operational officers were free from all staff responsibilities. The headquarters staff consisted of, among others, the Director, the Assistant Director Administration, Deputy Assistant Director Construction, the Camp Commandant Base (Ashar, Tanuma, Seraji and Khosroabad), and officers dealing with finance and accounts.

(ii) The rest of the staff was divided into three sections—Base, Forward Area and Engineering. The Assistant Director Base was responsible to the Headquarters for co-ordinating all demands for lighterage and transportation on the Shatt al Arab, the Karun river and in the Persian Gulf. He was also responsible for the allocation and movements of all vessels and barges within these limits. He was assisted by two Deputy Assistant Directors, one for the Base and the other for Karun. Other officers were posted at Ahwaz, Abadan and Bandar Gulf Port.

(iii) The Assistant Director Forward Area was responsible to the headquarters for co-ordinating the movements of craft and the disposition of the towing units on the Tigris, the Euphrates and the Shatt-al-Hai. In addition to his traffic responsibilities he was also accountable to the headquarters for the general development of Kut, Suwaira and Baghdad river heads. Three Deputy Assistant Directors were stationed at Kut, Baghdad and Amara, respectively.

(iv) The Assistant Director Engineering was responsible for the operation and maintenance of all repair facilities and for the disposition of the engineering personnel.[15] There was a Deputy Assistant Director in charge of stores. Many officers were assigned to the workshops.

The effect of this reorganisation was to throw on the various Detachment Commanders the complete responsibility for all operations within their areas. Headquarters Forward Area was established with a view to co-ordinating the administration of the various river detachments. The staff of the Forward Area consisted of one Assistant Director, covering the waterways, Al Qurna to Baghdad and above, a Deputy Assistant Director acting as an administrative officer, a finance and accounts officer, a quartermaster and a security officer. The Headquarters Forward Area controlled three Sub Areas, Amara, Kut and Baghdad. At Amara there were four officers. The Deputy Assistant Director, Sub Area Amara, covering waterways Al Qurna to Sheikh Saad inclusive, supervised the safe and expeditious movement of all craft in his area. The District Officer, covering the inland waterways, exclusive Kassarah to Al Qurna, was responsible for the safe movement of all craft within this area. The officer in charge, Narrows Control, covering the district Kassarah to Majar inclusive, was responsible for the safe movement of all craft within his area. Another officer was responsible for all traffic movements through Amara. At Kut were stationed three officers. The Deputy Assistant Director was responsible for the safe movement of all craft in this area. Another officer was responsible for all marine matters in the sub Area of Kut, inclusive of crewing of vessels and the proper operation of the Kut Lock. Another officer was responsible for all traffic movement through Kut. Three officers were to be stationed at Baghdad. The Deputy Assistant Director

---

[15] Appendix I.W.T. Committee of Review Report, dated 24 May 1942, W/D I.W.T. Part I.

commanded the Sub Area, two other officers were responsible for all traffic movements in Baghdad.[16]

The strength of the establishment continued to increase until in March 1943, the total number of officers was 145, including the Director, 2 Deputy Directors (one in charge of operations and the other in charge of engineering), 4 Assistant Directors and 14 Deputy Assistant Directors.[17]

Further reorganisation was commenced in December 1943 and was completed in March 1944. According to this new scheme the establishment consisted of 104 officers though the actual strength was 105 officers. The chief features of the new organisation were that the Director (Colonel) was assisted by three Deputy Directors (Lieut-Colonels), each respectively in charge of operations, administration and engineering. There were 3 Assistant Directors (Operations) in charge of conservancy, traffic and marine; 4 Assistant Directors (Administration) in charge of stores, accounts, administration and troops; 2 Assistant Directors (Engineering) in charge of dockyards and fleet maintenance and production. A large number of officers were stationed at the outstations—Kut, Maqil, Ashar, Khurramshahr, Abadan, Bandar Gulf and Amara.[18]

In December 1944 came another reorganisation. At that time the total number of officers was 77.[19] According to the new scheme headquarters consisted of six sections as follows:—

(i) *Commander*

This section was the Administrative Headquarters for the entire unit, and as such was the only proper channel of communication with outside authority, viz, Area Headquarters, General Headquarters, etc. For reasons of expediency certain outstations were permitted to communicate directly with the headquarters of the area in which they were situated, on matters affecting local discipline and administration; but it was an exception rather than the rule.

(ii) *Chief Engineer*

There were many engineering sub-sections, launch repairers, joiners and carpenters (shop), workshops, foundry and blacksmiths (shop), electrical, welding, planting, slipway, boiler making and marine engineering. The Chief Engineer was in over-all control over them.

(iii) *Senior Officer, Marine*

He was responsible for all Marine matters; for liaison with the

[16] From HQ I.W.T. Forward Area to Director I.W.T. dated 4 June 42; W/D May 42, Appx. I, W/D I.W.T. Part I.
[17] Bi-monthly Strength Return as at 1.3.43, W/D I.W.T. Part III.
[18] GHQ Paiforce order dated 18 March 1944, W/D I.W.T. Part V.
[19] Bi-monthly Strength Return dated 16 December 1944, W/D I.W.T. Part VI.

senior officer, labour ; for provision of marine (Dock) personnel ; and for contact with the senior traffic officer in respect of placing in commission of craft.

(iv) Senior Officer, Traffic

He was responsible for the efficient operation, either directly or through Gray Mackenzie & Co. Ltd. or the A.I.O.C. of that part of the fleet which was allocated to it and was in commission for traffic duties (excluding the vehicle ferries at Tanuma and Khurramshahr).

(v) Senior Officer, Stores

This section was unaffected by the reorganisation and continued to function as in the past.

(vi) Senior Officer, Labour

This was a new section of the headquarters combining the former Labour Control Officer's responsibilities and those of the Marine Personnel Officer (Camp Commandant, Marine) under one head.[20]

American Barges and Motor Launches

While the reorganisation of the Directorate was being carried out steps were also taken to increase the number of barges and motor launches. The problem of the shortage of barges and tugs was solved with the help of the United States. Already in November 1941, General Wheeler and General Wavell had come to an agreement that the United States would supply barges and motor launches. It was subsequently decided that knocked down prefabricated barges would be shipped from the United States to Kuwait (which boasted of a thriving native boat building industry) where a plant would be constructed to commence assembly operations. On 7 July 1942, the assembly of the first barge began. Henceforth the assembly operations continued with unabated vigour. The finished barges were towed by tugs or sailing ships for delivery at Basra or Khurramshahr. Satisfactory progress was made ; by the end of 1942, 213 barges were received from the United States at Kuwait, of which 186 were assembled.[21] By June 1943 when the Kuwait project terminated, 368 barges had been assembled. This was a substantial contribution indeed. In addition to supplying barges the United States also furnished initially 28 Eureka motor launches for towing the barges.[22] Thus American aid played an important part in the development of the water transport.

In addition to the American aid the United Kingdom and India

---

[20] Tel HQ I.W.T., dated 4.12.44, W/D I.W.T. Part VI.
[21] *U.S. Army in World War II*—op. cit., p. 112.
[22] Ibid, p. 111.

contributed their share to the development of such transport, and consequently the fleet was strengthened considerably so that at the end of December 1944 it had increased to 1102 craft of which 297 were towing units, 707 barges and 98 country craft.[23]

Total Lift

If we review the progress of the traffic operations for three years (from October 1941 to September 1944), we find that in the first year the total tonnage achieved was 680,869 of which 258,604 was harbour loaded and 422,265 despatched up the Tigris and the Karun. Lighterage discharged for the period was 262,076 and only 2,929 as 'Aid to Russia'. In the second year we find a marked improvement, the total tonnage being 1,469,801, out of which 761,534 was harbour loaded and 708,267 despatched. Lighterage discharged was 758,633 and 'Aid to Russia' 404,300. In the third year the total tonnage was 1,578,325 out of which 1,075,055 was harbour loaded and 503,270 despatched. Lighterage discharged was 1,076,004 and 'Aid to Russia' 822,364. Thus the grand total tonnage for the three years was 3,728,995 out of which 2,095,193 was harbour loaded, and 1,633,802 despatched up the rivers; lighterage discharged was 2,096,713 and 'Aid to Russia' 1,229,593. The following statement shows the record monthly effort[24]:—

Lighterage

Basra	59,277	March 1943
Khurramshahr	61,279	July 1944
Bandar Gulf	27,405	July 1944
Gross Lighterage	141,362	July 1944

Despatches

Up Tigris	23,339	July 1943
Down Tigris	17,923	March 1944
Inter Port	31,155	August 1944
Gross despatches	69,166	January 1944
Record gross tonnage	173,266	July 1944

Reviewing the period from January 1943 to March 1944, we get interesting information about the total contribution towards 'Aid to Russia'. The tonnage achieved at Basra was 232,931 out of which 107,311 was lighterage and 125,620 despatches. At Abadan the total tonnage was 74,658 out of which 4,680 was lighterage and 69,978 despatches. At Khurramshahr the total tonnage was 340,996

---

[23] I.W.T. Fleet List 1945 corrected to 31.12.44, I.W.T., W/D Part VI, December, 1944.
[24] Monthly Progress Report September 1944, W/D I.W.T. Part VI.

out of which 326,220 was lighterage and 14,776 despatches. At Bandar Gulf the total tonnage was 125,300 (i.e. lighterage). At Bushire the total tonnage was 40,025 (lighterage). Thus the total tonnage for the entire period was 813,910 out of which 603,536 was lighterage and 210,374 despatches.[25]

River Conservancy Operations

This marked improvement in the lift of the tonnage would not have been possible without river conservancy operations, by which shoals were dredged and 'bandals' (or barriers) of bamboos and reed matting planted in order to guide the stream into a narrow and deep channel in seasons of low water (from August to December). The report on the river conservancy operations during 1943,[26] throws interesting light on the working of the conservancy department. Reconnaissance of the river Tigris and Karun carried out during 1941-42 and training works and channel marking in 1942, enabled the department to appreciate the problems with which it was confronted in 1943. The report may be analysed under the following headings:—

Personnel

316 Bandallers (men who work in open boats or up to their waists in the water itself in order to plant 'bandals') and 29 Boat Pilots enrolled in India had arrived in Iraq. Unfortunately hardly 5% of the bandallers had any previous experience of work on the Indian rivers. The boat pilots had also not had much experience and therefore were employed as bandallers and on general camp duties. With inexperienced bandallers and with a greatly reduced staff, consisting of 1 major, 2 captains, 1 lieutenant, 1 sergeant, 1 corporal and three officers for dredging, the department had to tackle the problems of river surveying, dredging, training and marking.

Surveying

Surveys were undertaken to ascertain dredging and bandalling requirements and for the safety of the navigation on the Tigris and Karun rivers. In addition to this, surveys were carried out of Bushire harbour and anchorage, and of Masirah Island anchorage.

River marking

During the preceding years local firms operating on the rivers appear to have placed their faith in tug masters, who gained a knowledge of the vagaries of the channels by being constantly on

---

[25] 'Aid to Russia' Cargo, W/D I.W.T. Part V. See Appendix 22.
[26] Submitted by Major G. F. Willcox I.E.

the run. No effort was made to define or mark the deep-water channel with the result that during the 'dry' or low-river season drafts of towing units and barges had to be considerably curtailed. Military necessity, however, indicated a speedier turn-round of towing units with barges loaded to capacity, throughout the year. To achieve this, river training operations were carried out over shoal areas, and the channels were marked continuously. But progress was slowed down considerably due to the paucity of marking launches. The successful conveyance of river cargo depended largely on the marking and maintenance of channel marks in the 'dry' season and this work could not be accomplished with less than one reliable marking launch for every fifty miles of river. But the launches available for the work proved inadequate to cope with the demand and only the key shoals were attended to with any degree of efficiency.

Bamboo marking posts were used and, although they were frequently knocked down or washed away, were, with constant supervision, more economical and practical than moored floats which, when tried out, were more often than not stolen for the value of the mooring rope or wire. Shore transits, constructed from the two old oil drums, one superimposed upon the other, were in general use. These were easily carried and showed up well against a desert background.

'Bandalling' (Tigris)

In March, camp sites were selected at Abu Dood, Mandaliyah and Saiyid Abbas (in the worst section between Amara and Kut), the three key positions as indicated by the dry season of 1942, and parties consisting of 40 bandallers each were stationed there. Prior to their arrival in Iraq, the majority of the bandallers had had no experience in watermanship, but they soon acquired the art and showed remarkable improvement in handling the bellums. Sufficient quantities of bandalling material were received and, by the end of May, prism frames and the reed mats, framed with split bamboos, were ready for operations. The river reached its peak during the last few days in April and commenced falling in May, the average drop being about 2 inches per day. Current velocities were however too strong to enable a start to be made until the middle of June when the first bandal prism frames were placed across, the head of the sand now showing off the right bank in Saiyid Abbas reach. A Ganges type bandal was placed half a mile upstream of the Lower Camp. The accumulated sand deposits caused by the works were successful in narrowing the sectional area in the reach, thereby confining the channel to the path required. In June it was found necessary to extend the operations and additional camps were established at Sheikh Saad and Omaiyah. Personnel were increased to 180 between all the five camps.

Henceforth work proceeded apace in Abu Dood, Mandaliyah, Saiyid Abbas and Omaiyah. The officer in charge of the long Abu Dood reach had the personnel from both Sheikh Saad camp and Upper Camp to work with. Very extensive bandalling was carried out in this section and depths of at least five feet were maintained throughout a tortuous narrow channel.

Another officer, with headquarters at Mandaliyah camp, bandalled, marked and sounded the Mandaliyah, Saiyid Abbas and Omaiyah reaches. One great obstruction to bandalling in the broad reaches between Sheikh Saad and Omaiyah was the strong north-westerly wind, which prevailed throughout the months of August and September. On occasions the work was held up for as many as three consecutive days. The bamboos, of which the bandals were constructed, were not large or strong enough to withstand the pressure of wind and current against the reed matting skirting, and the collapse of these during the high wind ruined the efforts of weeks in a few hours. Narrow cross channels, running through the gaps in the damaged bandals, carried large quantities of sand into the main stream, thereby causing shoals, where there had been ample water. Maintenance of the bandals was extremely difficult under these conditions and entailed working long hours waist deep in the water.

Conservancy arrangements were also taken in hand on the river Karun. Bandalling personnel numbering nearly 90 Indian other ranks with accommodation craft, were despatched early in June for bandalling the Karun. Training commenced with the erection of bandals in Kut Abdullah reach with the intention of directing and deflecting the current into Kut Abdullah Bight to prevent the channel from running midstream through the sand, as it had done in 1942. This was successfully accomplished. The bandal parties were then moved to Ismailia crossing and to Ahwaz, where extensive operations were carried out. The bandals at Ismailia particularly required a great deal of attention as they were frequently collapsing due to high winds in the open stretch of water. Full use of road and rail facilities at Khurramshahr and Ahwaz did away with the necessity for a long river haul, and from 1 November 1943 traffic on the river Karun was abandoned. The bandalling personnel and materials were therefore collected and despatched to Kut.

The season's efforts proved conclusively that river training by bandalling was very effective over the localities worked, and good results could be obtained provided that bandalling was treated as an exact science so that the barriers were erected in conformity with the set of the current to assist the natural trend and not thrown across in a haphazard manner. Surface, sub-surface and under current floats, set-adrift in the reach upstream of the shoal, followed and plotted accurately on the field sheets, give reliable data from which to commence operations. Bandals then erected, to hold and protect the sands from scour set up by adverse current and wind effects, are quite successful provided they are carefully maintained and constructed progressively down the reach.

Dredging

Dredging formed an important part of the work performed by the Conservancy Department. Training works on the Tigris started early on the falling levels and the use of the suction cutter dredgers, S.D.1, S.D.2, S.D.3 and S.D.4 was confined mainly to harbour works and reclamation. The majority of these were in the Basra area, but activities extended to Kut, Khurramshahr and Bandar Shahpur also. The following is a list of the works undertaken:—

Basra area
1. Kibasi Basin entrance
2. Kibasi Basin reclamation
3. Tanuma P.O.L. Jetty site
4. R.E. House Creek
5. R.A.F. Slipway
6. Lighterage Wharf, Maqil
7. Ashar Dockyard reclamation
8. China Camp, reclamation
9. 'U' Craft Basin, Ashar
10. Hills Bros. reclamation
11. Ashar Dockyard creek
12. Basra Municipality reclamation
13. Ashar Slipway
14. Muftiyah reclamation
15. Robots Creek entrance

Khurramshahr area
1. Failiyah Creek entrance
2. Royal Naval jetties

Kut area
1. Kut Dockyard foreshore and slipway
2. D/S approach to Kut Lock

Bandar Shahpur area
1. New jetties
2. New lighterage wharf.

Dockyard Island at Ashar

While the Conservancy Department was concerned with maintaining a reliable channel in the Tigris and the Karun during the 'dry' season, the Engineering Department was busy with the task of the maintenance of the craft.[27] It was a very important job which the latter performed, for without maintenance and repair facilities the craft could not have been kept moving up the Tigris and the Karun. The Department set up a number of workshops on Dockyard Island, at Ashar.[28]

Achievements of the Directorate

Thus did the Inland Water Transport Directorate work and keep the Allied forces in Iraq and Iran well supplied with war material and essential stores as well as maintain the flow of British and American aid to Russia. The activities of the Directorate were mainfold and often entailed tremendous difficulties. But these were tided over and a steady traffic in goods was kept up the rivers of Iraq and Iran. The Government of India had supplied personnel, and barges and other craft, all that could be spared and drawn away from the Indian rivers, making the task of defending India difficult when in 1942 and 1943 river craft was required for use in the rivers of Bengal.

---

[27] I.W.T. Report on River Conservancy during 1943 by Major G. F. Willcox dated 25 March 1944, W/D I.W.T. Part V.
[28] For a summary of engineering activities at Ashar, May 1944, see Appendix 26.

CHAPTER XLVIII

Bases and Lines of Communication

Organisation of Headquarters Line of Communication Area

An account has been given of the development of the Persian Gulf ports, the roads and railways and the inland water transport. We may now turn to the development of the bases, the lines of communication and advanced depots. There were separate lines of communication in Iraq and Iran. In the former, Shuaiba was the base and Mussaiyib the advanced base; in Iran first Ahwaz and finally Khurramshahr was the base and Teheran the advanced base.[1]

The organisation of the line of communication of the Paiforce is of considerable interest. Headquarters Line of Communication Area (which initially formed part of the Headquarters Iraq Force) opened in Basra on 1 July 1941. Major-General G. de la P. Beresford C.B., M.C. was made the Commander. Meanwhile Headquarters Base Area was already functioning at Basra, with Brigadier C. Southgate, M.C. as the Base Sub Area Commander. Before the end of July, H.Q. No. 1 L of C Sub Area opened at Baghdad. Further development took place early in August when H.Q. No. 2 L of C Sub Area opened in Basra; in September it began functioning in Tanuma with an Advanced H.Q. at Ahwaz.

In October the organisation was improved considerably. H.Q. L of C Area and H.Q. Base Area continued to function as before in Basra/Shuaiba area. H.Q. No. 1 L of C Sub Area was at Baghdad; No. 2 at Ahwaz; No. 4 at Khanakin; No. 5 at Mosul and No. 6 at Kirkuk. In May 1942 further changes took place. H.Q. No. 1 L of C Sub Area was at Mosul; No. 2 at Kirkuk; No. 3 at Khanakin; No. 4 at Baghdad; No. 5 at Teheran and No. 7 in Basra—Shuaiba area. In July 1942, No. 5 moved from Teheran to Ahwaz and No. 6 opened at Abadan.

The organisation of the lines of communication underwent fundamental changes with the administrative reorganisation of the Tenth Army which came into effect on 15 August 1942. In order to free the Commander of the Tenth Army from the burden of the administration of the bases and lines of communication in Iraq and Iran, the control of the general administration of the ports, depots and communications behind the Tenth Army was vested in a senior Staff Officer of G.H.Q. Middle East, designated the Inspector General of Communications. At the same time there was created an Area

[1] Colonel W. H. Adcock: *Sappers in the Persian Gulf*, p. 56.

Command, known as Pibase (Persia and Iraq Base), to deal with the internal security and local administration of the Base Lines of Communication Area. But when the General Headquarters Paiforce opened in Baghdad on 15 September 1942, more changes occurred in the organisation of the lines of communication. The Inspector General of Communications and his staff were merged into G.H.Q. Paiforce while a Deputy Quartermaster General, Base and Lines of Communication, with a small staff was located at Basra. Major-General C. R. C. Lane, C.B., M.C., I.A., held this post. Further, Pibase area was divided into two area commands, covering respectively the Base and Lines of Communication Areas of Iraq and Iran.

Basra Base Reconnaissance Report

The development of the Base in the Basra—Shuaiba area was of great importance. The name Basra was generally taken to include a considerable area stretching from Maqil (which included the dock area) through Makina and Ashar to the old Basra city. Maqil and Ashar occupied about four miles of the river front on the right bank and this whole comprised the port area. The dock area was confined to Maqil, whilst on the river opposite Ashar were a number of mooring buoys, where ocean-going steamers unloaded into river craft. The Royal Air Force station was in Maqil adjoining and downstream the docks. Makina lay to the south of Maqil, about 1½ miles from the river. It contained the Royal Air Force hospital and the Levy Lines.

The area occupied by the Base of the Expeditionary Force of 1914-18 comprised generally the river front on the right bank from Maqil to Ashar and extended for some two to three miles inland. Some installations were on the left bank of the river. But in 1941 it was not possible to locate the permanent Base installations in the area occupied during 1914-18. Maqil and Ashar had become big business centres and therefore there were no suitable areas there to permit of considerable dispersion between the depots. Moreover, the intervening country was under intense date cultivation, and as a result the ground was water logged.

In order to select a suitable site for the permanent Base installations a reconnaissance party consisting of the representatives of India and the Middle East Command and led by Major-General Beresford assembled in Basra on 5 April 1941, and made a thorough examination of the various problems connected with the development of the Base. Their report is invaluable for its comprehensive analysis of the problems connected with the installation of a permanent Base which was now preferred at Shuaiba, instead of Basra, owing primarily to medical considerations. The Basra area was malarial and dysentery was endemic there, but the higher ground round the

Royal Air Force camp at Shuaiba (12-15 miles from the Basra port area) was free from either of these. Moreover, the location of the Base, well away from the heavily populated area of Basra and with its wide dispersion, would considerably reduce the risk of epidemic.

The limitations of the Base at Shuaiba were mainly three—lack of adequate water and electric power and inadequate communications. The R.A.F. Camp at Shuaiba was provided with electric power but no reserve from this supply was available for Base installations. Another difficulty was the provision of adequate water supply. Filtered water was carried from the R.A.F. station at Basra to the R.A.F. Camp at Shuaiba by a 6-inch pipe. As only 50,000 to 60,000 gallons per day were available from this supply for army purposes it was necessary to augment it. Communications between Basra and Shuaiba also required to be improved. One more or less all-weather road from Basra to Shuaiba existed. It followed the old railway formation through Zubair. It was necessary to construct a new all-weather road. The main Basra-Baghdad railway passed through the northern corner of the Base area, with a branch from Shuaiba junction into the R.A.F. Camp. A considerable number of old railway formations traversed the area Basra-Shuaiba. These would facilitate the establishment of the additional railways which might be required for the working of the Base area. The report, therefore, recommended that the permanent Base as well as the temporary Base should be located at Shuaiba. There was ample space in the Shuaiba area to locate the temporary Base without interfering in any way with the preparation of the permanent Base.[2]

The Plan of the Base

Having decided on a suitable site for the Base, the reconnaissance party next drew up a plan for its lay-out. The Base was to be of a size to maintain a force of three divisions (75,000 troops), but each depot would have sufficient area alloted to it to allow its expansion to maintain a force double this size (six divisions). Areas were allotted for Base units (Supply), such as Base Supply Depot, Petrol Sub-depot, Field Bakery, Field Butchery and Cattle Supply Sections. Areas were also allotted for transport units at Base, namely Mechanised Transport Units and Draught Bullock Companies. The Base Ordnance Depot was divided into three sub-depots, a Returned Stores Depot and Transit Depot. The lay-out of the Base Ordnance Depot permitted of expansion to the requirements for six divisions with dispersion of stores and workshops with intervals of 100 yards between buildings or dumps.

The reserves in Iraq were inadequate to meet the requirements

[2] Basra Recce Report, F. 519.

of the Base Ordnance Depot. The small quantities of stores that were procurable in the markets were required by the Iraqi army. The stockists carried on a hand-to-mouth trade. The leather produced was very inferior and boots and all leather stores were imported. Textiles, cordage and all requirements for an army had to be imported. As regards the lay-out of the Base Ammunition Depot the reserve of ammunition fixed for storage was approximately 35,000 tons, necessitating two ammunition depots, consisting of three and two sub-depots respectively. The five sub-depots did not admit of expansion; this would necessitate additional ammunition depots. In the plan the ammunition sub-depots were sited on the outskirts of the main Base area. It would have been advisable to locate these some miles away from other installations. However, in view of the initial difficulties of supply of water and electricity and good rail communications it was considered preferable to accept a less ideal solution and to locate ammunition sub-depots as close to the other installations as safety permitted.

As regards the medical facilities, the R.A.F. hospital at Makina was initially capable of accommodating 600 cases without additional building. It might later be developed to accommodate a Combined Indian General Hospital of 1,000 or more beds. The Base Depot Medical Stores might also be established in this area. Pending the establishment of the permanent Base all the sick were dealt with at this hospital. With the exception of the Post Quarantine Station, which was suitable and available for the treatment of infectious diseases in the vicinity of the docks, the remaining hospitals were to be established in the Base area at Shuaiba.[3]

Development of the Shuaiba Base

Headquarters (Works) Base Sub Area played an important part in the development of the Base. The first task was to augment the water and electric supply, and towards this end an eight-inch pipeline was laid from Maqil to Shuaiba and water started running through the pipeline for the first time on 1 July 1941.[4] Then attention was turned towards augmenting the water supply at Makina to feed the hospital and the adjacent tented camp area. The project was completed on 17 July 1941, an eight-inch pipeline connected the Maqil filtration plant to the Maqil Cistern and the latter to the Makina Cistern, thus ensuring an adequate water supply to Makina. Next, on 24 July, work commenced on an eight-inch pipeline (5½ miles long), which tapped the Maqil-to-Shuaiba eight-inch line near Shuaiba Fort Station and crossed northwards to the Base Ordnance

---

[3] For sketch map of the plan of the permanent Base at Shuaiba see Appx. O in Basra Recce Report, F. 519.
[4] War Diary, No. 1, E & M Company, I.E.

Depot and the Shuaiba marshalling yard.[5] In August 1941 another project was completed. The existing 6-inch pipeline carried filtered water from the port plant to Zubair; an 8-inch pipeline was also laid to carry it to Shuaiba. Additional projects were concerned with the laying of eight-inch pipelines to carry raw water from Maqil to the filtration plants at Shuaiba. The first filtration plant was completed in February 1942; eventually there were three filtration plants, each having a capacity of 600,000 gallons per day.[6] Thus adequate water supply was made available for the Basra-Shuaiba Base.

The problem of electric supply was also tackled with energy. The R.A.F. Camp at Shuaiba was provided with electric power but no reserve from this supply was available for Base installations. To meet these requirements small sets were installed in fourteen small power houses. Later a Central Power Station was set up to meet the growing needs of the Base.

With the availability of adequate supplies of water and electricity, the expansion of the Base took place rapidly. Of the Base installations the Base Ordnanace Depot and the Base Ammunition Depot were perhaps the most important. Due to the congestion at Maqil, all ammunition (with the exception of very small quantities) from the very beginning (May 1941) had been sent to Shuaiba for storage. Ammunition was stored in pits, which gave a certain amount of protection, but the ammunition was stored much closer than was desired or was required by Magazine Regulations. As the quantities increased, small packets or dumps were put in pits dotted about in that part of the perimeter which was allotted for ammunition. In course of time, however, the area allotted for the storage of ammunition was increased, thus providing greater dispersion for ammunition.[7] As regards the Base Ordnance Depot, the ordnance stores were initially divided between Maqil and Shuaiba. The more attractive items, including armament and scientific stores, were stored in buildings in the R.A.F. area at Maqil but non-attractive stores (about 60% of the total) were spread in the open at Shuaiba. Paradoxical as it might sound, the latter method of storage proved to be the better of the two. Iraq experienced late rains and in consequence all the low lying ground in the Maqil area was practically under water. The water level, which in that area was never many inches below the surface, seeped to the surface in many places, thus rendering a large area unfit for the storage of stores. The R.A.F. buildings at Maqil also were very damp and unsatisfactory. These were the initial difficulties which had to be faced

[5] Ibid; and Adcock: *Sappers in the Persian Gulf*, p. 23.
[6] Adcock: *Sappers in the Persian Gulf*, p. 29.
[7] War Diary D.D.O.S., Force H.Q., 1.5.41.

until more permanent storage was built at Shuaiba.⁸ Considerable improvement was made so that in September 1941 when the Deputy Director of Ordnance Services, Force Headquarters, made a report on the progress of the Base, he expressed his satisfaction at the noticeable improvement in the Base Ammunition Depot and the Base Ordnance Depot. About the former he remarked that the ammunition was well dispersed, some in pits and the remainder in irregular pyramids above the ground. As regards the latter, noticeably good were the mechanical transport stores in No. 1 Sub-depot, and Web Equipment Section in No. 2 Sub-depot. In No. 3 Sub-depot there was considerable congestion, and therefore it was proposed to move it to B.O.D. area.⁹

The Basra-Shuaiba Base was indeed humming with activity, as the Base Ordnance Workshop, the Engineers Base Workshop, the Engineers Store Base Depot, the Base Supply Depot, and the General Hospitals (Combined Indian or British) were all located there.

Advanced Base at Mussaiyib

While Shuaiba was being developed into a Base for six divisions, steps were also taken to develop an Advanced Base. In June 1941, an Advanced Base was visualised north of Baghdad in the Taji area. Taji was believed to be the only place in the Baghdad area which did not become flooded in wet weather. The project however never materialised, for planning began soon afterwards for meeting a possible Axis threat through Anatolia. The chief feature of the plan was to hold successive positions for a short period in the Mosul area, and then for a longer period immediately north of Baghdad. Therefore, it was not considered desirable to have an Advanced Base practically within a possible 'firing line'. Accordingly the area south of Baghdad was reconnoitred and eventually it was decided to have an Advanced Base at Mussaiyib. The plan was based on a system of a self-contained fortress area in north Iraq, and a southern fortress area in the Mussaiyib—Latifiya area, stretching north to within fifteen miles of Baghdad. Eventually two divisions were to be accommodated in the southern fortress area; they were to occupy certain defence works and were to be protected by large scale flooding. It was visualised that the Mussaiyib fortress area would be fully stocked for approximately 90 days. Administrative planning was based on a ten division target. If ten divisions were to operate in Iraq, Advanced bases would be required for four divisions above the Base at Shuaiba.¹⁰

⁸ Ibid.
⁹ D.D.O.S. Force H.Q., Tour Basra-Shuaiba dated 12-14 September 1941.
¹⁰ Minutes of a meeting held in 'Q' House on 13 March 1942 to discuss scheme 'Wolf', File 8056.

Administrative Planning for Bases

Early in May 1942, when the Axis launched the spring offensive and there was danger of the collapse of the Russian resistance and the consequent Axis threat to Iraq-Iran, the target for administrative planning for base developments in Iraq and Iran was reviewed by the War Office. Their decision was communicated to General Auchinleck who issued a directive laying down the final target for Iraq and Iran: 11 divisions (9 infantry divisions and 2 armoured divisions) and 30 squadrons R.A.F. for Iraq; and 7 divisions (6 infantry divisions and 1 armoured division) and 10 squadrons R.A.F. for Iran. The programme for base developments in Iraq and Iran was to be phased so as to complete, as soon as possible, the installations required for 9 divisions on the Iraq line of communication and 5 divisions on the Iran line of communication. The planned lay-out was, however, such that expansion was possible so as to cater for the final target of 11 divisions on the Iraq line of communication and 7 divisions on the Iran line of communication. Shuaiba and Andimishk—Ahwaz were to constitute the main base areas for the Iraq and Iran lines of communication respectively. Under certain conditions facilities at Ahwaz might be utilised to ease pressure on Shuaiba, and vice versa. On the Iraq line of communication requirements were to be divided between Shuaiba and the Advanced Base at Mussaiyib in the proportion of 2 to 1. In the event of operations ever taking place in north-west Iran, it might probably be necessary to establish an Advanced Base on the Iran line of communication in the Teheran—Sultanabad area. On the Iran line of communication, requirements up to 31 December 1942 (except in a certain contingency) would be wholly allotted to Ahwaz. The target for the construction of installations was laid down.

During the first phase (up to 1 June 1942) the target was for 4 infantry divisions, 2 armoured divisions and 30 squadrons R.A.F. in Iraq; and 2 infantry divisions, 1 armoured division, and 10 squadrons R.A.F. in Iran. During the second phase (by 31 December 1942) the target was for 7 infantry divisions, 2 armoured divisions and 30 squadrons R.A.F. in Iraq; and 4 infantry divisions, 1 armoured division and 10 squadrons R.A.F. in Iran. The final target, as already mentioned, was for 9 infantry divisions, two armoured divisions, and 30 squadrons R.A.F. in Iraq; and 6 infantry divisions, 1 armoured division and 10 squadrons R.A.F. in Iran.

In Iraq construction of the base installations was to be planned to cater for 30 days reserves at Mussaiyib for the divisions in Iraq, and the balance at Shuaiba. In Iran the construction of all reserves for the first four infantry divisions was to be at Ahwaz—Andimishk. This area was also to be planned to hold reserves for the possible armoured division, less 30 days which would be held at the Advanced

Base in Teheran—Sultanabad area. Construction to cater for the final target figure was to be at the Advanced Base.[11]

Development of the Bases

As a result of this administrative planning, the development of the bases—Shuaiba and Mussaiyib in Iraq, and Ahwaz/Andimishk and Teheran in Iran—was taken in hand. Shuaiba had already been considerably developed as a base; the Advanced Base at Mussaiyib required to be developed. Already some steps had been taken; in February 1942 a key plan for Mussaiyib had been prepared and in April 1942 orders were issued for the construction of the installations. The task of implementing the policy laid down for the development of the Base was delegated to Headquarters No. 1 L of C Sub Area.[12] The construction of the installations—Advanced Base Workshops, an Ordnance Depot, P.O.L., a reinforcement camp etc. was taken in hand. Considerable progress was made but eventually Mussaiyib was abandoned after the Axis had retreated from the Caucasus. Shuaiba in Iraq, and Ahwaz/Andimishk and Teheran in Iran, however, retained their importance for some time due to the 'Aid to Russia' schemes.

---

[11] Planning—Iraq and Persia; No. 258/1/99/Q.1 H.Q. Tenth Army dated 7 May 1942; File 8087; also Middle East Target for transformation and base developments, G.H.Q. MEF, dated 2 May 1942, File 8087.
[12] Scheme 'Wolf' dated 8 April 1942, File 8056.

CHAPTER XLIX

Supply

Organisation of Supply

The administrative problems of the Paiforce were many and varied. One of these was the maintenance of troops and the organisation of supply. This duty was entrusted to Colonel G. W. C. Hickie, O.B.E., Deputy Director, Supply and Transport.[1] He was initially assisted by two deputies (one for local purchase) and a small staff. They disembarked at Basra on 30 April 1941, and soon showed considerable energy in organising the Base Supply Depot and the Field Supply Depots. By 1 February 1942, when the Iraq Force came to be designated the Tenth Army, considerable progress had been made. The Base Supply Depot at Basra was organised with Sub Depots at Shuaiba and Maqil respectively and a Detail Issue Section at Maqil. There was an Advanced Base Supply Depot at Baghdad. There were Field Supply Depots at Mosul, Khanakin, Habbaniya, Kirkuk, Qaiyara, Ahwaz and Teheran.[2] The Distribution of the supply units was however defective. Thus the 14th Supply Personnel Company was distributed at Basra/Shuaiba, Teheran and Ahwaz; the 22nd Supply Personnel Company at Baghdad, Habbaniya and Ahwaz; the 23rd Supply Personnel Company at Kirkuk and Khanakin; and the 21st Supply Personnel Company at Mosul and Qaiyara.[3] It may be observed that with the exception of the two last named companies (which occupied a contiguous area) the others were very widely dispersed. To remove this defect a redistribution of the supply units throughout Iraq and Iran was carried out in March 1942. To simplify the supervision of supplies and P.O.L. installations, the whole country was sub-divided into areas, each of which was the charge of the Officer Commanding Supply Personnel Company in that area. According to the redistribution of units, No. 14 Supply Personnel Company with headquarters at Basra was responsible for the depots in area Basra, Shuaiba, Ahwaz, Abadan; No. 18 Supply Personnel Company with headquarters at Mussaiyib was responsible for the depots in area Mussaiyib, Latifiya; No. 22 Supply Personnel Company with headquarters at Baghdad was responsible for the area Baghdad, Habbaniya, L.G.5, Haffa; No. 21 Supply Personnel Company with

[1] War Diary D.D. S & T Force H.Q., April 1941.
[2] No. ST/1156/49 dated 15 Feb. 1942, Appx. 'F', W/D D.D. S & T.
[3] No. ST/1244/69 dated 4 March 1942, Liaison Letter No. 3, Appx. 'E' W/D D.D. S & T Force H.Q.

headquarters at Mosul was responsible for area Mosul, Qaiyara, Fatha; No. 23, Supply Personnel Company with headquarters at Kirkuk was responsible for area Kirkuk, Altun Kopru, Khanakin, Kermanshah; and No. 17 Supply Personnel Company with headquarters at Sultanabad was responsible for area Sultanabad, Teheran, Andimishk.[4] As a result of the reorganisation of the Supply Personnel Companies economical and efficient handling of Supplies and P.O.L. was ensured.[5]

Lay-out of Field Supply Depots

As a result of observations made during his visits to Supply Depots in Iraq and Iran, Brigadier Hickie, Deputy Director Supply and Transport, issued detailed instructions for the lay out of the Field Supply Depots. He directed that the practice of dotting the whole Supply Depot area with a series of small stacks at close intervals should be discontinued; and desired that a depot holding 20 days' reserves and 10 days' working stocks for a brigade group should be laid out according to the following principles:—

   (i) The depot should be divided into two sub-depots.

   (ii) Each sub-depot should be further sub-divided into two 'dumplets'.

   (iii) A dumplet should consist of a number of stacks contained in the minimum area possible consistent with ease of handling and checking up, and contain all commodities; but this disposal was conditioned by security consideration and availability of covered accommodation.

   (iv) Each dumplet should contain the minimum of covered accommodation necessary to safeguard against the sun those articles liable to perish in the hot weather, for example tinned goods (other than biscuits) and fruits, etc. During the winter months, such accommodation should become available for protecting articles liable to damage by rain, such as bagged supplies.

   (v) Dumplets should be not less than 100 yards apart, irregular in shape and staggered. Every advantage should be taken of ground conformation in siting them.

   (vi) Wherever possible, each dumplet should be wired in and some supply personnel should live within the enclosure as a safeguard against losses through theft or pilfering.

   (vii) The lay-out of large Field Supply Depots should follow the above principles except that such depots might be divided into three or more sub-depots, according to size,

---

[4] No. ST/1240/2C dated March 1942—Reorganisation of Supply Personnel, Appendix O, W/D D.D. Supply and Transport Force H.Q.

[5] For details of personnel etc. see Appendix 23.

with a number of dumplets to each sub-depot. Fewer dumplets, large in size, were preferable to a large number of small dumplets, provided that no dumplet contained more than 1,500 tons of supplies with a minimum distance of 150-200 yards between each dumplet.[6]

Director Supply & Transport, Paiforce

When General Headquarters Paiforce opened in Baghdad on 15 September 1942, Brigadier W. d'A. Collings, D.B.E., R.A.S.C. late Deputy Director Supply and Transport, Ninth Army, was appointed Director Supply and Transport, Paiforce.[7] Brigadier Hickie continued to serve as Deputy Director Supply and Transport, Tenth Army, until 26 January 1943, when he was succeeded by Brigadier P.A. Arden, C.B.E. As the operational importance of Iran increased, greater attention was paid to the organisation of supply depots. At Ahwaz was No. 13 Base Supply Depot, and there were Field Supply Depots at Kermanshah, Hamadan, Sultanabad, Darud, Khurramabad and Teheran.[8]

Types of Rations

The issue of rations to the troops formed a very important part of the duty of the supply personnel. The following were the five main types of rations:—

(i) 'Emergency ration' was a condensed form of food similar to a slate of chocolate in appearance, designed to keep a man alive in emergency and when no other form of rations was procurable. It was made up into a small compact pack which could be easily carried on the man. This ration was not intended for issue for day to day consumption, even for a limited period.

(ii) 'Battle ration' was a ration often wrongly referred to as 'hard rations' and was designed for use for a maximum period of seven days on active service conditions where there were little or no facilities for cooking. This ration was composed principally of preserved meat and biscuit and was therefore compact and easily transportable, in any form of vehicles. Since the gross weight of a day's ration for one man was only about 3 lbs the ration could be carried on the man in emergency.

(iii) 'Vehicle ration' was very similar to the 'battle ration' but

---

[6] ST/1129/92 dated 17.7.42 ; Notes by Brigadier Hickie ; Appx. L to W/D D.D. S & T Force H.Q.
[7] D.D. S & T Tour 24 Sept. to 5 Oct. 1942, Appx. A, W/D D.D. S. & T. Force H.Q.
[8] ST/205/55 dated 4 October 1942—Stocking of FSDs Tenth Army area, Appx. C, W/D DD S & T Force H.Q.

the commodities making this ration were slightly different. Its purpose was evident from its name and it was also a compact ration suitable for use on active operational conditions for a maximum of three days.

(iv) 'MEFS ration—hard scale' was the normal scale of rations but with tinned or 'hard' items substituted for fresh equivalents, e.g. tinned vegetables in lieu of fresh vegetables, biscuits in lieu of flour etc. Rations were issued on this scale to troops in operational areas, who could not be issued with the normal F.S. ration. Such troops were usually too far away from railhead and had insufficient cooking facilities to make it possible to issue to them or for them to be able to cook fresh vegetables, fresh meat or fresh fruit. Rations issued on this scale required little more than a fire and facilities for boiling water for the preparation of meals.

(v) 'MEFS ration—normal or fresh scale' was the ration normally issued to troops who had the ordinary Unit's cooking facilities and was the ration consumed by the great majority of the troops whatever their location. The ration scale included all the 'fresh' items, most of which required cooking before consumption.[*]

Local Provision

Local provision constituted another important duty of the Supply personnel. The local resources were successfully tapped by Paiforce to meet its requirements. Local provision was divided into two categories—(i) purchases made direct by the General Headquarters (Local Resources) to meet the general army requirements and for the purpose of building up reserves, as opposed to those of a purely local nature, (ii) those made locally for current consumption. As regards items in the first category, arrangements for their provision were made by the respective Assistant Directors (Local Resources) of Iraq and Iran, the latter being assisted in his task by the Deputy Assistant Director (Local Resources) at Teheran. It was proposed in October 1942 to have a Deputy Assistant Director (Local Resources) for Iraq also. It was also proposed, in due course, to have one Local Resources Officer for Iraq and one for Iran, each under the control of the Deputy Assistant Director (Local Resources) with a number of area representatives. Thus, initially, the establishment of the Assistant Director (Local Resources) provided for a central controlling body at the General Headquarters, without any representatives in areas, who might make local purchases or develop

[*] Extract from a note on a number of rations per ton, Appx. A to W/D September 1942 DD Supply and Transport.

the local resources. These proposals were intended to remove this defect and to enable the Paiforce to exploit fully the economic resources of Iraq and Iran.

The provision of items in the second category was the responsibility of the Assistant Directors, Supply and Transport of Areas, or the Assistant Director, Supply and Transport Tenth Army, where the area occupied was outside the Base and Line of Communication Areas. The Assistant Directors, Supply and Transport of Areas or the Deputy Director, Supply and Transport Tenth Army authorised officers of R.A.S.C. and R.I.A.S.C. to negotiate and conclude contracts and agreements for items in this category, subject to certain restrictions. The items in this category were fresh vegetables, fish (fresh for hospitals only), fuelwood (local), charcoal (local), onions, milk, butter, eggs, cream, ice, fruit (fresh—local), green fodder, hospital supplies, aerated water, bhoosa (Iran only), potatoes (Iran only), meat on hoof (Iran only), dressed meat (Iran only), and sale of hides and skins. Two methods only of purchase of items in this category were used: (i) purchase by formal contract (ii) purchase by local purchase agreement (previously known as informal agreement). Formal contracts were entered into wherever possible and purchase by local purchase agreement was reduced to an absolute minimum.[10]

P.O.L. Supply

P.O.L. supply presented no problem as the existence of the Anglo-Iranian Oil Company's depots and installations throughout the country ensured ample stocks of petrol and kerosene oil. No. 2 Petrol Depot and a P.O.L. section were in area Basra—Shuaiba, while P.O.L. sections were at Baghdad, Mosul (with a detachment at Kirkuk) and Sultanabad.[11] This was the position in November 1941. Later more petrol sections and Detail Issue Sections were set up. Also sites for reserves were selected at strategic places, such as Mosul West, Ninevah, Qaiyara etc. P.O.L. was stored in area Basra—Shuaiba in stacks, pits and tanks.[12]

The P.O.L. Section came under the administrative control of the Field Supply Depot Headquarters. Its main functions were[13]:—

(i) To receive all consignments of bulk and packed oils and lubricants despatched from base or other source of supply.

(ii) To arrange for their disposal, storage and camouflage.

---

[10] PI/383/ST/4 dated 18 October 1942—Local Provision, Appx. J, W/D D.D. S & T Force H.Q.
[11] Location of R.I.A.S.C. units on 13 Nov. 41, Appx. VIII, W/D D.D. S & T Force H.Q. Part III.
[12] Tour Notes of ADT (Pet) on visit to Basra/Shuaiba area, Appx. II, W/D October 1941.
[13] Notes on visit to F.S.D. Baghdad July 1942; Appx. T, W/D D.D. S & T Force H.Q.

(iii) To arrange for reconditioning or decanting of leaking containers.
(iv) To make issues to local units and convoys of all packed product ex Detail Issue Section.
(v) To issue supplies of packed products for forwarding to outstations.
(vi) To administer and control bulk Petrol Parks.
(vii) To check and receive, at R.O.C. Depots, oils filled in second-hand tins.
(viii) To operate the bulk kerosene and fuel oil installation at the Field Supply Depot when this was required.

The Detail Issue Section was responsible for the issue of all packed oils to local units and convoys against indents signed by a King's Commissioned Officer.[14]

Withdrawal of the Troops

While the Paiforce was engaged in its multifarious activities, such as organising and transporting aid to Russia and receiving and sending away to their destinations thousands of Polish refugees from Russia, besides maintaining occupational control over Iran, steps were taken to settle the main political issue, the status of Iran. It was settled at the Teheran Conference in November 1943, which was attended by President Roosevelt, Premier Stalin and Prime Minister Churchill. On 1 December 1943, the three great leaders issued a declaration confirming Iran's independence and territorial integrity. The declaration however could not be immediately implemented. Article 5 of the Treaty of Alliance with Iran (1942) laid down that "the forces of the Allied Powers shall be withdrawn from Iranian Territory not later than six months after all hostilities between the Allied Powers and Germany and her associates have been suspended by the conclusion of an armistice or armistices, or, the conclusion of peace between them, whichever date is the earlier. The expression 'associates of Germany' means all other Powers which have engaged or may in the future engage in hostilities against either of the Allied Powers". Thus, Allied troops were not withdrawn from Iran even when the war against the Axis Powers ended in May 1945, for the war against Japan and her allies (associates of Germany) continued till September 1945. After the cessation of hostilities with Japan there was no further justification for retaining Allied troops in Iran. Steps were therefore taken to withdraw them. The American troops were withdrawn from Iran by 1 January 1946, and the British and Indian troops by 1 March 1946. In Iraq 6,000 troops were left at Shuaiba (with the concurrence of the

[14] Tenth Army Consumption of important P.O.L. products for June 1942, Appx. C, W/D D.D. S & T Force H.Q.

Iraq Government) to guard stores and property, while other troops were withdrawn from that country also.

Shortly after the withdrawal of the British and Indian troops from Iran a serious situation developed. The employees of the A.I.O.C. had some grievances against the company. Their cause was taken up by a strong and aggressive local Tudeh organisation, which was supported by the Communists. Strikes and riots followed. To give protection to about 2,000 Indian employees of the Company and to protect the Abadan refinery against sabotage, British Government requested the Government of India to despatch a small force immediately. Consequently, Force 401, numbering 8,000 troops, was sent to Basra and was employed at Abadan and the oilfields. The situation was then brought under control.

When the National Government was installed at the centre in India, the Defence Minister put up a proposal on 6 February 1947, for the recall of all Indian troops from abroad. In that connection he wrote: "The question of the withdrawal of Indian troops at present serving overseas has been raised several times in the Legislature, and public opinion has persistently demanded that Indian troops should not be stationed in foreign countries. The reason for this feeling is that India wants to be on the friendliest terms with other nations and the presence of Indian troops in their territories impairs good neighbourliness and friendly relationship. It is necessary to take immediate steps to eliminate all causes which stand in the way of India maintaining friendly relations with other countries". This view was supported by the Prime Minister, who wrote on 8 February 1947: "There is now no particular danger of any disturbance near the oilfields. A possibility of a new situation arising is of course always there, but we can hardly keep troops abroad to gurad against future possibilities. That would mean an indefinite detention. I think we should suggest the retention of an adequate force to guard stores etc. only."

The British Government referred the matter to their Minister at Teheran who suggested that in view of the improved internal situation in Iran "it will shortly be possible and desirable to withdraw Force 401". He however added that as regards the troops in the Shuaiba Base the Government of Iraq had "no objection to these forces remaining in their territory". The British Government therefore decided that Force 401 should be withdrawn from Iran. They further decided that "as soon as Force 401 has been withdrawn the withdrawal of remaining land forces in Iraq should be resumed. The circumstances do not justify further retention of these troops in southern Iraq".[15] Thereafter the Indian troops returned to India.

[15] F. 110/47/DL

APPENDICES

APPENDIX 1

PROPOSED COMPOSITION OF SABINE FORCE

(EXCLUSIVE OF SYBIL FORCE)

January 1941

GENERAL ORGANISATION

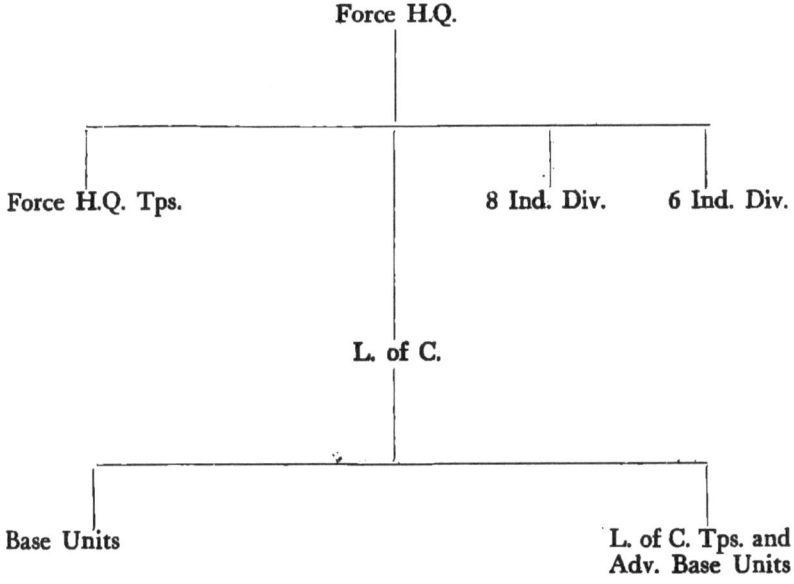

ORDER OF BATTLE

Force H.Q.
Force H.Q. Arty.
Force H.Q. Engrs.
Force H.Q. R.I.A.S.C.
Force H.Q. Employment Pln.
†8 Ind. Div.
†6 Ind. Div.
*Two Mob. Bath Units
*Two Mob. Laundry and forward decontamination Units

† Composition is given at the end of this Order of Battle.
* Not provided by India.

Force Troops

*One Mob. A.A. Bty.
*One Lt. A.A. Bty.
*Det. A.A. Bde. Sig. Sec.
*Det. A.A. Bde. Coy., R.A.S.C.
*One A/Tk. Regt., R.A. ⎫
*One A/Tk. Regt., L.A.D. ⎬ For 8 Ind. Div.
*One A/Tk. Regt., Sig. Sec. ⎭
*One A/Tk. Regt., R.A. ⎫
*One A/Tk. Regt., L.A.D. ⎬ For 6 Ind. Div.
*One A/Tk. Regt., Sig. Sec. ⎭
*One Med. Regt., R.A. 8 gun 8 How.
*One Med. Regt., L.A.D.
*One Med. Regt., Sig. Sec.
*One Svy. Bty., R.A. less one tp.
 H.Q. Engrs. Corps Tps.
 1 Fd. Coy., S & M
 5 Fd. Coy., S & M
 67 Fd. Coy., S & M
 141 Fd. Park Coy., S & M
*One Boring Sec. R.E.
*One Mach. Gun. Bn.
*One Mach. Gun Bn. L.A.D.
 One I.S.F. Bn. Basra Area
 Two I.S.F. Bns. Baghdad Area
*Force H.Q. Sigs.
 One Int. Corps H.Q.
 One Corps Sec. Int. Corps
*A.I.L. Secs.
 Liaison Officers Pool
 Two Div. Secs., Int. Corps
 Svy. H.Q. with an Army second Echelon
 One Ind. Fd. Svy. Coy. less reproduction sec.
 One Movement Control Group
 H.Q. Shipping Group
 One Shipping Sec.
 36 G.P. Tpt. Coy.
 37 G.P. Tpt. Coy.
*One R.A.S.C. Sec. Med. Regt., R.A.
*One R.A.S.C. Sec. A/Tk. Regt. R.A. } For 8 Ind. Div.
*One R.A.S.C. Sec. A/Tk. Regt. R.A. } For 6 Ind. Div.
 One Corps Fd. Amb.
*One M.A. Convoy
 One Fd. Hygiene Sec.
*Corps Postal Unit
*Field Cash Office
 Provost Coy.
*One Ord. Fd. Park
 Two Corps Secs.
 Two Div. Secs.
*One Army Fd. Wkshop. R.A.O.C.
 Two I.A.O.C. Mob. Wkshop. Coys.

*Not provided by India.

Base—Basra

One Army Tps. Coy.
One Artisan Works Coy.
*One Excavator Coy. R.E.
One Engr. Base Wkshop.
One Engr. Store (Base) Depot
*One E. & M. Coy. (L. of C.) less one sec.
One Printing Sec. S & M
One Rlwy. Construc. & Maint. Group
One Rlwy. Construc. Coy.
One Rlwy. Svy. Coy. less one sec.
One Tn. Stores Coy. less one sec.
One L. of C. Telegraph Coy.
*One W/T Det. G.H.Q. Sigs.
One M.A. Sec.
One Base Depot Med. Stores
One Fd. Laboratory
One Br. Conval. Depot
Two Ind. Conval. Depots
*One Br. Gen. Hosp. (600 beds)
Two Ind. Gen. Hosps. (1000 beds each)
One Ind. Gen. Hosp. (500 beds)
Five Comb. Gen. Hosps. (each 100 Br. & 500 Ind. beds)
Five X-Ray Units
Two Br. Staging Secs.
Six Ind. Staging Secs.
I.W.T. Barges
Three Hosp. Ships
*One Base Canteen
*One Fd. Canteen
*One Br. Wing H.Q. 2nd Echelon
One Mixed Reinforcements Camp
One Ind. Reinforcement Camp
Forty-one Mess Units (Officers)
One Rest Camp (Mixed)
Four Mess Units (Officers)
*One Mob. Bath Unit
*One Mob. Laundry and forward decontamination unit
One Provost Unit
One Prisoners of War Camp
*One Fd. Cash Office
*Br. Stationery Depot
Eight Labour Coys.
Base Military Dairy Farm
One Base Cinema
Four Mob. Cinemas
One Military Prison
Graves Registration and Enquiry Unit, L. of C.
*Base Ord. Wkshops.
One L. of C. Sec. for one port including Censor Sec. for two ports
Two Sup. Per. Secs.

* Not provided by India.

Advanced Base—Baghdad

H.Q. L. of C. Sub Area (with attached Censor Sec.)
One Sec. F.S. Police
H.Q. Sup. Per. Coy.
Six Sup. Per. Secs.
One Fd. Bakery
One Fd. Butchery
One Cattle Stock Sec.
One Cattle Cond. Sec.
One M.A. Sec.
One Reserve M.T. Coy.
One Sec. Petrol Depot
Two Comb. Gen. Hosps. (100 Br. and 500 Ind. beds each)
One Comb. Gen. Hosp. (200 Br. and 600 Ind. beds each)
Three X-Ray Units
One Fd. Hygiene Sec., L. of C.
Adv. Depot Med. Stores
One Br. Conval. Depot
Two Ind. Conval. Depots
One Fd. Post Office
Adv. Canteen Depot
Br. Rest Camp (for 500 other ranks)
Rest Camp
Two Mess Units
*One Mob. Bath Unit
*One Mob. Laundry and forward decontamination unit
One Provost Sec.
Vety. Det.
Adv. Base Ord. Depot
Adv. Base Ord. Wkshops
Adv. Base Ammunition Depot
*Two L. of C. Recovery Secs.
H.Q. Adv. Base Engrs.
Two Army Tps. Coys.
Two Artizan Works Coys.
*One Sec. E. & M. Coy.
One Wkshop. Sec. and two Adv. Park Secs.

Northern Railhead

Adv. Canteen Depot
L. of C. Pro. Unit
Four Sup. Per. Secs.
One Fd. Post Office
Railhead Det. (Corps Railhead)
Two Comb. Casualty Clearing Stations
Two Mob. X-Ray Units
Depot Med. Stores (Ind.)
Sigs. Det.
One Sec. Reserve M.T. Coy.
One Cattle Stock Sec.
One Cattle Cond. Sec.

* Not provided by India.

Basra to North by Rail

Two Amb. Trains (Metre Gauge) } Required for 200 miles journey
One Amb. Train (Standard Gauge) } above Baghdad and for 340 miles below Baghdad

Two Fd. Hygiene Secs.
*Two Mob. Bath Units
*Two Mob. Laundry and forward decontamination units
L. of C. Pro. Unit

Staging Post Samawa

Comb. Rest Camp (for 250 Br. and 250 Ind.)
Mess Unit
One Br. Staging Sec.
One Ind. Staging Sec.
Sigs. Det.

Basra to North by Inland Water Transport

Staging Post Amara

Rest Camp
Mess Unit
*One Sup. Issue Sec.
Br. Staging Sec.
Ind. Staging Sec.
Sigs. Det.

Staging Post Kut

Rest Camp
Mess Unit
Br. Staging Sec.
Ind. Staging Sec.
Sigs. Det.

Base Units for L. of C. Depots

Army Tps. Coy.
Artizan Wks. Coy.
Road Construc. Bn.
Wkshop. & Park Coy. (Less one Wkshop. Sec. and two Adv. Park Secs.)
Det. Engr. Base (Store) Depot
One Sec. Petrol Depot
H.Q. Sup. Per. Coy. and four Secs.
*Park of M.T., V.R.D.
Base Ammunition Depot
Base Ord. Depot

Additional Artillery

Arrangements were also under consideration for the despatch of artillery personnel to India, with a view to each division being provided

* Not provided by India.

with two field regiments and one anti-tank regiment. The third field regiment for each division would be provided from elsewhere than India. (All A/Tk. and A.A. artillery had to come from the United Kingdom; there were none as yet in India).

The two anti-tank regiments for 6th and 8th Indian Divisions are already shown under Force Troops in the Order of Battle.

On the assumption that each division could be provided with two field regiments and one anti-tank regiment, the additional artillery considered desirable was as follows:—

One more Med. Regt. for Force Tps.
One A/Tk. Regt. for Force Tps.
Two Army Fd. Regts. for Force Tps.
One Svy. Regt. for Force Tps.
Two Fd. Regts., to complete div. arty. in 6 and 8 Divs. (giving them a total of three each)
One A.A. Bde. H.Q. and Sig. Sec.

Two Mob. H. A.A. Regts.; each to comprise:—
   Two 3″ Batteries
   One 3.7″ Battery
   Regtl. Sigs.
One Light A.A. Regt. H.Q.
Three Light A.A. Batteries
One A.A. S.L. Regt.
} For Adv. Base (Force H.Q. and L. of C.)

One A.A. Bde. H.Q. and Sig. Sec.
One Mob. H. A.A. Regt.; to comprise
   Two 3″ Batteries
   One 3.7″ Battery
   Regtl. Sigs.
Three Light A.A. Regtl. H.Q.
Eight Light A.A. Batteries
} For Forward Areas

Composition of 8th and 6th Indian Divisions

8th Indian Division

H.Q. 8 Ind. Div.
H.Q. 8 Ind. Div. Arty.
H.Q. 8 Ind. Div. Engrs.
H.Q. 8 Ind. Div. R.I.A.S.C.
8 Ind. Div. Empl. Pln.

Cavalry
3 Cav.

Artillery
11 Fd. Regt. R.A.

Engineers
7 Fd. Coy. S & M
66 Fd. Coy. S & M
47 Fd. Coy. S & M

SIGNALS

8 Ind. Div. Sigs.

INFANTRY

17 Ind. Inf. Bde. H.Q. and Empl.. Pln.
1/12 F.F. Regt.
5/13 F.F. Rif.
1/5 R.G.R.
18 Ind. Inf. Bde. H.Q. and Empl. pln.
3/10 Baluch Regt.
1/2 G.R.
2/3 G.R.
19 Ind. Inf. Bde. H.Q. and Empl. pln.
1/1 Punjab Regt.
3/8 Punjab Regt.
2/6 G.R.

R.I.A.S.C.

8 Ind. Div. H.Q. Tpt. Sec.
8 Ind. Div. Tps. Tpt. Sec.
17 Ind. Inf. Bde. Tpt. Coy.
18 Ind. Inf. Bde. Tpt. Coy.
19 Ind. Inf. Bde. Tpt. Coy.

MEDICAL

Three Fd. Ambs.
Fd. Hyg. Sec.

I.A.O.C.

11 I.A.O.C. Mob. Wkshop. Coy.
15 I.A.O.C. Mob. Wkshop. Coy.
Two I.A.O.C. Mob. Wkshop. Coys.

POSTAL

41 Fd. Post Office
42 Fd. Post Office
43 Fd. Post Office
44 Fd. Post Office

PROVOST

8 Ind. Div. Pro. Unit

6TH INDIAN DIVISION

H.Q. 6 Ind. Div.
H.Q. 6 Ind. Div. Arty.
H.Q. 6 Ind. Div. Engrs.
H.Q. 6 Ind. Div. R.I.A.S.C.
6 Ind. Div. Empl. Pln.

CAVALRY

Poona Horse

ARTILLERY

'B' Fd. Regt. I.A.

ENGINEERS

57 Fd. Coy. S & M
58 Fd. Coy. S & M
48 Fd.. Pk. Coy. S & M

SIGNALS

6 Ind. Div. Sigs.

INFANTRY

26 Ind. Inf. Bde. H.Q. and Empl. Pln.
1/1 G.R.
1/19 Hybad. Regt.
1/9 G.R.
27 Ind. Inf. Bde. H.Q. and Empl. Pln.
4/8 Punjab Regt.
1/10 Baluch Regt.
5/12 F.F. Regt.
28 Ind. Inf. Bde. H.Q. and Empl. Pln.
2/1 G.R.
2/2 G.R.
2/9 G.R.

R.I.A.S.C.

6 Ind. Div. H.Q. Tpt. Sec.
6 Ind. Div. Tps. Tpt. Coy.
26 Ind. Inf. Bde. Tpt. Coy.
27 Ind. Inf. Bde. Tpt. Coy.
28 Ind. Inf. Bde. Tpt. Coy.

MEDICAL

Three Fd. Ambs.
Fd. Hyg. Sec.

I.A.O.C.

12 I.A.O.C. Mob. Wkshop. Coy.
   I.A.O.C. Mob. Wkshop. Coy.
36 I.A.O.C. Mob. Wkshop. Coy.
41 I.A.O.C. Mob. Wkshop. Coy.

POSTAL

35 Fd. Post Office
56 Fd. Post Office
59 Fd. Post Office
60 Fd. Post Office

PROVOST

6 Ind. Div. Pro. Unit

APPENDIX 2

PROPOSED COMPOSITION OF SYBIL FORCE

January 1941

GENERAL ORGANISATION

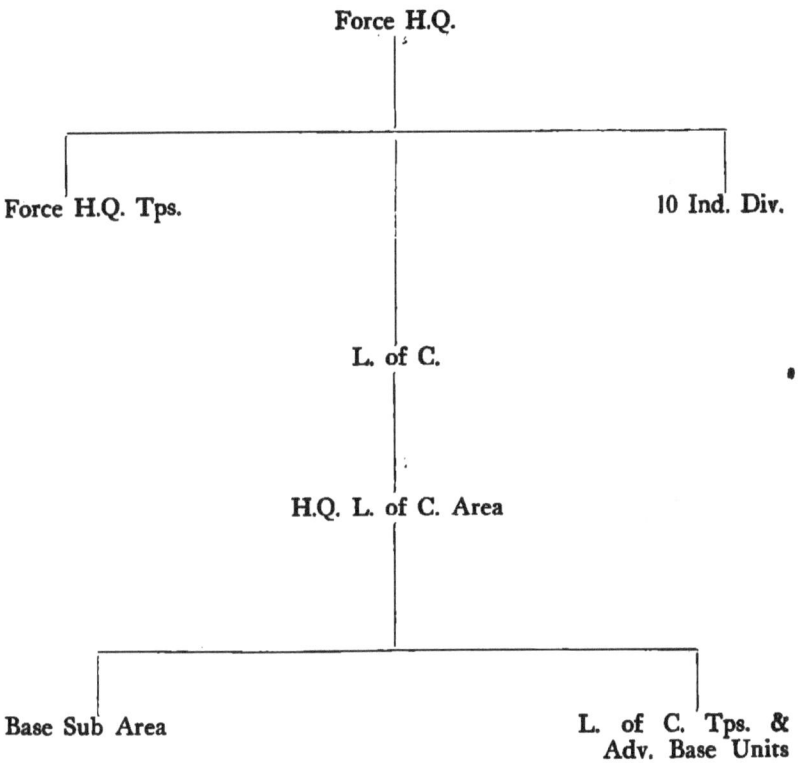

ORDER OF BATTLE

FORCE H.Q. AND FORCE H.Q. TROOPS

Force H.Q. including H.Q. L. of C. Area
One Int. Sec.
*260, 216 Secs. F.S.P.
A Echelon Movement Control Group and two Secs.
One Dock Sec.
*One A.I.L. Sec.

* Not provided by India.

ARTILLERY
*One A/Tk. Regt.
*H.Q. A.A. Bde.
*Two A.A. Regts.
*H.Q. Lt. A.A. Regt.
*Three Lt. A.A. Btys.
*Two Tps. S.L. Regt. (Searchlight).
*One Tp. 6 Svy. Regt.

ENGINEERS
One Bridging Sec. S & M

SURVEY
Svy. H.Q. with an Army 1st Echelon
One Ind. Fd. Svy. Coy.

SIGNALS
*One A/Tk. Regt. Sig. Sec.
*H.Q. A.A. Bde. Sigs.
*Two A.A. Regt. Sig. Sec.
*One Lt. A.A. Regt. Sig. Sec.
*One Det. S.L. Regt. Sig. Sec.

SUPPLY & TRANSPORT
*A.A. Bde. Coy. R.A.S.C. (less Det. for SABINE)
*One Sec. Bridging Coy. R.A.S.C.
*A/Tk. Regt. Sec. R.A.S.C.
Three Animal Tpt. Coys.

ORDNANCE
*H.Q. A.A. Bde. Wkshop.
*A.A. Regt. Wkshop. Secs. Base Defence
*Lt. A.A. Regt. Wkshop. Secs.
*A/Tk. Regt. L.A.D.
*H.Q. 1 Ord. Fd. Pk.
*Reserve Sec.
*Corps Sec.
*Div. Sec.

MISCELLANEOUS
*22 Mob. Bath Unit
*One Mob. Laundry Unit

10TH INDIAN DIVISION

H.Q. 10 Ind. Div.
H.Q. 10 Ind. Div. Arty.
H.Q. 10 Ind. Div. Engrs.
H.Q. 10 Ind. Div. R.I.A.S.C.
10 Ind. Div. Employment Pln.

CAVALRY
6th Lancers

ARTILLERY
157 Fd. Regt. R.A.
155 Fd. Regt. R.A.
"K" Ind. A.Tk. (2 plns.)

* Not provided by India.

ENGINEERS
9 Fd. Coy. S & M
10 Fd. Coy. S & M
41 Fd. Park Coy. S & M

SIGNALS
10 Ind. Div. Sigs. (less Inf. Bde. and Fd. Regt. Sig. Sec.)
15 Inf. Bde. Sig. Sec.
24 Inf. Bde. Sig. Sec.
25 Inf. Bde. Sig. Sec.
157 Fd. Regt. Sig. Sec.

INFANTRY
H.Q. 15 Ind. Inf. Bde. and Empl. Pln.
2/9 Jat Regt.
1/14 Punjab Regt.
3/16 Punjab Regt.

H.Q. 24 Ind. Inf. Bde. and Empl. Pln.
5/1 Punjab Regt.
2/6 Raj. Rifs.
5/5 Mahratta L.I.

H.Q. 25 Ind. Inf. Bde. and Empl. Pln.
1/5 Mahratta L.I.
2/11 Sikh Regt.
3/9 Jat Regt.

R.I.A.S.C.
10 Ind. Div. H.Q.. Tpt. Sec.
10 Ind. Div. Tps. Tpt. Coy.
15 Ind. Inf. Bde. Tpt. Coy.
24 Ind. Inf. Bde. Tpt. Coy.
25 Ind. Inf. Bde. Tpt. Coy.

MEDICAL
25 Fd. Amb.
29 Fd. Amb.
30 Fd. Amb.
10 Fd. Hygiene Sec.

I.A.O.C.
9 I.A.O.C. Mob. Wkshop Coy.
29 I.A.O.C. Mob. Wkshop Coy.
43 I.A.O.C. Mob. Wkshop Coy.
45 I.A.O.C. Mob. Wkshop Coy.

POSTAL
53 Fd. Post Office
54 Fd. Post Office
55 Fld Post Office
36 Fd. Post Office

PROVOST
10 Ind. Div. Pro. Unit.

BASE UNITS

H.Q. Base Sub Area
L. of C. Sec. Int. Corps for one port (incl. Censor Section)

ENGINEERS
Two Army Tps. Coys. S & M
One Wkshop and Park Coy. S & M
Two Artizan Works Coys.
Two Road Construc. Bns.
One Rly Construc. Coy.
One Rly Operating Coy.
One Rly. Svy. Sec.
One Sec. Tn. Stores Coy.

SIGNALS
One L. of C. Telegraph Coy.
*H.Q. 3 Coy. 4 L. of C. Sigs.
*1 Construc. Sec.
*32 D.R. Sec.
*26 Line Maint. Sec.
*30 Tech. Maint. Sec.
*85 Tel. Op. Sec.
*38 Hy. W/T Sec. (G.H.Q.)
*3 Lt. W/T Sec. (Corps)

INFANTRY
Jaipur 1st Inf. I.S.F.
Alwar Jey. Paltan, I.S.F.

SUPPLY AND TRANSPORT
One Cattle Sup. Sec. Cl. II
One Cattle Sup. Sec. Cl. IV
*One Bridge Coy. R.A.S.C. less one Sec.
Two Motor Amb. Secs.
*2 Heavy Repair Shop
*3 M.T. Stores Depot
H.Q. & two Secs. Petrol Depot
One Base Sup. Depot (A)
One H.Q. Sup. Per. Coy.
Eight Secs. Sup. Per. Coys.
One Fd. Bakery
Fd. Butcheries

MEDICAL
One Fd. Hygiene Sec.
One Depot Med. Stores
One X-Ray Unit
One Fd. Laboratory
One Br. Conval. Depot
Two Ind. Conval. Depots
One Combined Gen. Hosp.
*One Br. Hosp. (600 Beds)
One Anti-malaria Unit
Two Hosp. Ships
One Mob. X-Ray Unit

VETERINARY
One Vet. Hosp.

REMOUNTS
One A.R. Depot

* Not provided by India.

POSTAL
One Ind. Sec. Base Post Office

CANTEEN
One Base Canteen

PROVOST
One Pro. Unit

REST CAMP
One Rest Camp

LABOUR
Thirty-five plns.

MISCELLANEOUS
H.Q. 2nd Echelon
Field Accounts Office
Stationery Depot
Prisoners of War Cage
*One Mob. Bath Unit
*One Mob. Laundry Unit
*One Graves Registration and Enquiry Unit

REINFORCEMENT CAMP
One Mixed Reinforcement Camp

ORDNANCE
Base Ord. Depot
Base Ammunition Depot
One Base Cinema
Two Mob. Cinemas

L. OF C. AND ADVANCED BASE UNITS

WORKING ON L. OF C.
*One L. of C. Recovery Sec.
For M.T. see end of Order of Battle

No. 1 ADVANCED BASE

H.Q. L. of C. Sub Area
L. of C. Sec. Int. Corps for one port, less Censor Sec.

SUPPLY AND TRANSPORT
Cattle Sup. Sec. Cl. II
Cattle Sup. Sec. Cl. IV
Two Motor Amb. Secs.

MEDICAL
One Casualty Clearing Station
One Anti-malaria Unit
*Hospital Barges
Two Brit. Staging Secs.
Four Ind. Staging Secs.
One Fd. Hygiene Sec.
*One Mob. Bath Unit
*One Mob. Laundry Unit

* Not provided by India.

Postal
One Fd. Post Office

Provost
One Unit (two Ind. Secs.)

Rest Camp
One Rest Camp (Mixed)

Ordnance
Railhead Dets.

No. 2 Advanced Base

Supply and Transport
One Cattle Sup. Sec. Cl. II

Postal
One Fd. Post Office

Rest Camp
One Rest Camp

Ordnance
Railhead Dets.

Allotment of Mess Units

Allotted to serve

Force H.Q. (Indian Serial 71)
10 Officers' Mess Units
6 Warrant Officers' & Sergeants' Mess Units

H.Q. No. 1 L. of C. Sub Area (Indian Serial 72)
3 Officers' Mess Units
2 Warrant Officers' & Sergeants' Mess Units

H.Q. Base Sub Area (Indian Serial 74)
4 Officers' Mess Units
3 Warrant Officers' & Sergeants' Mess Units
3 Officers' Mess Units for three Rest Camps
1 Officers' Mess Unit for H.K. 2nd Echelon
17 Officers' Mess Units for one Mixed Reinforcements Camp

Allotment of Non-Divisional M.T.

Two G.P. Tpt. Coys. were allotted for the purpose shown below:
　Force H.Q. Tpt. Sec. and 3rd Line for 10 Div.
　Two Secs. for 2nd and 3rd Line for Force Tps. and two secs. for Base.

APPENDIX 3

LETTER FROM THE GRAND MUFTI OF PALESTINE TO HERR HITLER*

Baghdad
the 20th January 1941

To
    His Excellency
    The Fuhrer of Great Germany

Your Excellency,

England, that relentless and subtle enemy of the true liberty of peoples, has never ceased from forging for the Arab people, chains to enslave and to subjugate them, sometimes in the name of a perfidious League of Nations, and sometimes by the placarding of false and hypocritical sentiments of humanity for others, but always in truth for the most imperialistic designs, camouflaged behind the principles of a mendacious democracy and internationalism.

The Arab people have found themselves, by a geographical coincidence, in the centre of land and sea cross-roads, which form, according to the English, the principal knot of British imperial communications. For this, nothing was spared in creating perpetual obstacles to fetter the liberty and development of the Arab people. It may even be said, that the relative peace that has lasted for more than a century between France and England, is due to a great extent to the implied understanding between these two Powers to hold under their yoke the Arab populations, thus observing the law of an ignoble partition, which created in any case a balance of ambitions, without touching the sensitive artery of the 'sacred' British communications. Moreover, this partition of influence between France and England, helped to break the resistance and the reactions of the Arabs, by leaving them at grips with different and strong Powers. But the English policy was not able in the long run to defy the awakening of Arab nationalism from the incessant activity of England in creating for the Arab people new obstacles against the acquisition of their independence and liberty. Then came that lugubrious history of the last decades, which offer to the eyes of the world the spectacle of a continuous and desperate struggle.

In Iraq, England in her traditional policy of dividing to rule, conceived the project of installing a few million Hindus brought from British India,† side by side with the auchtochtonal Arab population. The project was foiled by a bloody revolution and England had had then to bow before a reality and devote her attentions to the immediate exploitation of Iraqi petrol. In a word, King Feisal I accepted a modus vivendi and signed, despite the opposition of the majority of the people, a treaty with England, thus buying the relative independence of the country, at the cost of petrol concessions. The attitude of Turkey,

---

* Translated for the CIS Historical Section from a photostat copy of the original letter in French by Lt.-Col. Mould.

† Note by the translater: Chevalley's Dictionary gives the translation of 'hindou' as Hindu, but it may mean inhabitant of Hindustan i.e. Indian.

towards annexing Mosul to her territory, dictated the necessity of this policy to the late King.

With regard to Syria, she was handed over to France to break her national unity and to impoverish her economically, in order to subdue, more effectively, her national spirit. After eighteen years of struggle, she was able to extract from France the lame treaty of 1936, recognising her independence but at the cost of unilateral concessions and reservations. Then, England rose to bar the path of liberty of Syria, and joined with Turkey to neutralise the effect of the Franco-Syrian Treaty; this was effected in agreement with the Jews, who feared an independent Syria side by side with her sister, Palestine, in revolt. The Anglo-French-Turco agreement was produced, from that time, against the Axis Powers. Thus, in 1936, there came the prelude to the question of Alexandretta and Antioch, which was destined to end by the cession on the part of France, to Turkey of the above-named region, and by the abolition of the *sine qua non* of the treaty of 1936 between France and Syria. Thus there arose, once more, a 'very democratic' game on the part of England, at the expense of Syria, despite the commissions and enquiry reports of the League of Nations, which were all favourable to the Syrian thesis.

In turn I pass to Egypt. England had already installed herself there from 1882, 'provisionally', because the people in revolt were demanding from the Khedive a national constitution, which would put restraint on the prodigality of the prince, and organise the budget according to the interests and needs of the country. But the so called democratic England occupied the country, to save the throne of the Khedive, under the pretext of assuring order at Alexandria, while perfidious Albion was spinning intrigues, with her own fingers, and fomenting trouble and disorders by means of her own 'agents provocateurs'. The truth is that it was a question of the Suez Canal and of the .... imperial communications. Egypt waited till 1936 to obtain also her lame treaty with the reservations which are known. This fact was not due to British generosity, but, far from it, simply to a rupture in the equilibrium of the forces in the Mediterranean, by Italy raising herself more strongly, and with greater menace to the British 'interests'.

Then comes Palestine, now after so many other countries of the Arab peninsula. You know her cause, Your Excellency, for she too has had to suffer from the perfidy of the English. It is a question of creating an obstacle to the unity and independence of the Arab countries, by putting them at direct grips with the Jews of the whole world; dangerous enemies, whose secret weapons are finance, corruption and the intrigues, which are, elsewhere, added to the British bayonets. For twenty years, we have found ourselves face to face with these different forces. Armed with an invincible faith in their cause, the Arabs of Palestine have fought with the most rudimentary means. Moreover, the Palestinian question has reunited all the Arab countries in a common hatred of the English and the Jews. If the common enemy is the prelude to the formation of national unity, one may say that the Palestinian problem has hastened that unity. From the international point of view, the Jews of the whole world have attached themselves to England, in the hope, that after her victory, she may be able to materialise their dreams in Palestine, and even in the adjoining Arab countries. By (your) aiding the Arabs to crush the Zionist aims, the Jews, and above all those of the United States, would be so demoralised, by seeing the object of their dream falling into annihilation, that they would lose their enthusiasm to help Great Britain, and would retract in face of the Catastrophe.

I beg Your Excellency to bear no grudge against me for my having related above, in a summary manner, the history of the Arab antagonism to England; for it appears to me necessary, to bring into relief the essential causes, which are agitating the Arab world against the English. I have, above all, been anxious to specify that these causes have their deep roots in primordial interests, and in vital problems, and not in futile questions with superficial and passing effects. The very warm sympathy of the Arab peoples, for Germany and the Axis, is henceforth a matter which is unquestionable. No propaganda can change this truth. Once liberated from certain material hindrances, the Arab peoples are everywhere ready to react, as is just, against the common enemy, and to rise with enthusiasm with the Axis, for the accomplishment on their part of the deserved defeat of the Anglo-Jewish Coalition.

Arab nationalism owes Your Excellency a debt of gratitude for having raised on several occasions in resounding discourses the Palestinian question. I am anxious in this letter to repeat my thanks to Your Excellency, and to assure you of the sentiments of friendship, sympathy and admiration, which the Arab people dedicate to you, Great Führer, and to the courageous German people.

I take this opportunity to delegate to the German Government my private secretaire, to open, in the name of the very strong and vast Arab organisation, and in my own name, the necessary negotiations for a sincere and loyal co-operation in all domains.

I may resolutely add, that the Arabs are disposed to throw themselves into the balance, and to offer their blood in the sacred struggle for their rights and their national aspirations, provided that certain preoccupations of a normal and material order are assured. It is a question of necessary precautions to be taken against a perfidious and powerful enemy and it is necessary to calculate means and strength in order to enter the struggle with the greatest chance of success. This foresight is indispensable, especially as England feels called upon to act and react with all her strength, in view of the strategical character of the Arab countries, which might otherwise endanger the imperial communications, and weaken all contact between India and the Mediterranean and Turkey by the Persian Gulf, while bringing about the exploitation, and flow of petrol to the profit of England.

I conclude by wishing Your Excellency a long and happy life and the brilliant victory and prosperity for the Great German People and for the Axis in the very near future.

I beg Your Excellency to believe in my sentiments of great friendship, gratitude and admiration.

Signed: Grand Moufti of Palestine
Mohammed Amin El Husseini.

APPENDIX 4

SUMMARY OF ORDER OF BATTLE OF IRAQ ARMY

15 April 1941

1st DIVISION—H.Q. at Baghdad
  Composition:
    Two Inf. Bdes.
    One Fd. Arty. Bde.
    One Mtn. Arty. Bde.
    One Divl. Cav. Sqdn.

  This Division was concentrated at Baghdad with the exception of the Divisional Cavalry Squadron at Jaloula, one Infantry Brigade at Mussaiyib and one Mountain Artillery Brigade at Diwaniya.

2nd DIVISION—H.Q. at Kirkuk
  Composition:
    One Div. Cav. Sqdn.
    Three Inf. Bdes.
    Two Fd. Arty. Bdes.
    One Mtn. Arty. Bde.

  All at Kirkuk except one Infantry Brigade and one Mountain Artillery Brigade at Mosul and one Infantry Battalion at Erbil.

3rd DIVISION—H.Q. at Baghdad
  Composition:
    One Div. Cav. Sqdn.
    Three Inf. Bdes.
    Two Fd. Arty. Bdes.
    One Mtn. Arty. Bde.

  Divided between Baghdad, Jaloula, Mansourat al Jebel (One Infantry Brigade at each). One Div. Cav. Sqdn. at Jaloula.

4th DIVISION—H.Q. at Diwaniya
  Composition:
    One (1st line) Inf. Bde.
    Two (2nd line) Inf. Bdes.
    One Mtn. Arty. Bty. (plus one Mtn. Arty. Bde. from 1st Division)

  Apart from a Mountain Arty Bde. at Diwaniya attached from 1st Division, the 4th Division had 1st line troops, one Inf. Bde. (less one Bn.) in or near Basra and one Inf. Bn. and one Mtn. Arty. Bty. at Amara.

  One complete 2nd line Inf. Bde. was at Diwaniya and a second with one battalion at Samawa was stationed at Nasiriya.

MECHANISED FORCE—H.Q. and all units belonging to the Force were normally stationed at Baghdad.

  Composition:
    Two Mech. Inf. Bns.
    One Mech. M.G. Coy.
    Lt. Tk. Coy.

Armd. Car Coy.
One Mech. Arty. Bde.

RIVER FLOTILLA OF IRAQI NAVY

Four Thornycroft gun-boats, each 100 tons displacement, each armed with:
One 3.7" How.
One 3" Mortars
Four M.Gs.

ARTILLERY BASRA AREA

One Mtn. Bty. 3.7" Hows. in Zubeila Barrack
One Mtn. Bty. (2.75") at Amara
One Mtn. Bde. (Two Btys. of 3.7" Hows.) attached to 4th Division and stationed at Diwaniya
One Fd. Bty. 18 pdr. at Zubair
One Mtn. Bty. 3.7" Hows. at Zubair.

(a) An Iraqi Inf. Bde. was composed of three Inf. Bns.

A Bde. H.Q. included one section of two A.A. Lewis Guns, and its War Establishment was:

5 Officers
15 Other Ranks
10 Animals.

(b) A 1st line Inf. Bn. consisted of:

H.Q.
H.Q. Wing
3 Rifle Coys. and
1 Support Coy.

Each Rifle Coy. had four pls., each of three rifle sections and one L.M.G. section. The scale of Brens in L.M.G. sections was in course of being raised from 2 to 3 *i.e.* from 24 Brens to 46 Brens per Bn. The Support Coy. had two M.G. platoons of 4 Vickers M.Gs. H.Q. Wing included one section of two A.A. Lewis Guns.

The War Establishment for a 1st line Inf. Bn. was:

26 Officers
820 Other Ranks
154 Animals.

(c) 2nd line Inf. Bns.

These units were intended for Base and L. of C. defence and Internal Security duties. They were composed of 3 Rifle Coys., each of 3 pls. consisting of 3 Rifle sections and 1 L.M.G. sec. (armed with Lewis Guns).

In place of a Support Coy. they had one M.G. pl. of 4 Vickers M.Gs. and also one A.A./L.M.G. section (total of 4 Vickers M.Gs. and 11 Lewis Guns).

APPENDIX 5

ROYAL IRAQI AIR FORCE AS ON 15 NOVEMBER 1940

Serial No.	Unit	Function	Location	Type	Serviceable	Reserve	U/S	Total
1	No. 1 Squadron	Army Co-operation	Mosul	Pegasus	9	—	—	9
2	No. 2 Squadron	General Purpose	Rashid	Vincent, Rapide Dragon, Dragonfly	7	—	2	9
3	No. 3 Squadron	General Purpose	Rashid	-do-	Reduced to Cadre			7
4	No. 4 Squadron	Fighter	Kirkuk	Gladiator	7	4	—	14
5	No. 5 Squadron	Fighter Bomber	Rashid	Breda 65	4	4	6	5
6	No. 6 Squadron	Medium Bomber	Rashid	Savoia 79	4	—	1	15
7	No. 7 Squadron	Fighter Bomber	Rashid	Northrop 8A	5	5	5	31
8	Flying Training School	Flying Training	Rashid	D. H. Moth	12	6 built 4 storage	9	
				Pegasus, Audax & Others	9	—	—	9
					—	—	17	17
		TOTALS:			57	19	40	116
		Percentages:			49.14%	16.38%	34.48%	100%

APPENDIX 6

FORCES IN AND AROUND BASRA

Place	Detail	
Fao	Two gun-boats Two pls. 1/7 Inf. Bn. (Subsequently reported to be 300 strong) One Sec. 2.75″ guns (reported to be two guns)	From 4 Div.
Zubair	Det. 1/7 Inf. Bn. (15 miles from Basra)	
Basra	H.Q. Shatt al Arab Comd. H.Q. River Flotilla Two Gun-boats H.Q. 7 Inf. Bde. 1/7 Inf. Bn. (less dets.)	
Tanuma (near Basra)	2/7 Inf. Bn. (Subsequently forces collectively at Zubair, Basra and Tanuma reported to be 5 Inf. Bns. and eight 3.7″ Hows.)	
Amara (110 miles from Basra)	3/7 Inf. Bn. 18 Mtn. Bty.	
Nasiriya (100 miles from Basra)	H.Q. 14 Inf. Bde. 2/14 Inf. Bn. 3/14 Inf. Bn. One Sec. 2.75″ guns	
Samawa (160 miles from Basra)	1/14 Inf. Bn.	
Diwaniya (just over 200 miles from Basra)	H.Q. 4 Mtn. Bde. 2/4 Mtn. Bty. 3/4 Mtn. Bty.	1 Div. attached to 4 Div.
	H.Q. 4 Div. H.Q. 15 Inf. Bde. 1/15 Inf. Bn. 2/15 Inf. Bn. 3/15 Inf. Bn.	4 Div.
Mussaiyib (230 miles from Basra)	H.Q. 2 Inf. Bde. 2/2 Inf. Bn. 3/2 Inf. Bn.	1 Div.
Baghdad (330 miles from Basra)	1 Div. 3 Div. Mech. Force Army Tps.	

Time and Space Table

1. **Troops within immediate striking distance of Basra**

FAO	Two Gun-boats
	Two pls. 1/7 Inf. Bn. (Subsequently reported to be 300 strong)
	One Sec. 2.75" guns (reported to be two guns)
Zubair	Det 1/7 Inf. Bn.
Basra	1/7 Inf. Bn. (less dets.)
	Two Gun-boats
	Three Port boats (one with 4" and two with one 12 pdr. each)
Tanuma	2/7 Inf. Bn. (Subsequently forces collectively at Zubair, Basra and Tanuma reported to be five Inf. Bns. and eight 3.7" Hows.)

    Note: The two bns. at Basra and Tanuma were separated by an unbridged river.

2. **Troops at Amara, Nasiriya, Samawa,** (*i.e.* those within a 160 mile radius of Basra)

Place	Troops	Distance	Time
Amara	3/7 Inf. Bn. 18 Mtn. Bty.	110 miles	48 hours, depending on availability of local motor transport
Nasiriya	2/14 Inf. Bn. 3/14 Inf. Bn. One Sec. 2.75" guns	100 miles	12 hours Railway
Samawa	1/14 Inf. Bn.	160 miles	16 hours

3. **Forces over 200 Miles Distant from Basra**

Place	Troops	Distance	Time
Diwaniya	2/4 Mtn. Bty. 3/4 Mtn. Bty. 15 Inf. Bde.	200 miles	20-24 hours By rail or Road
Baghdad	1 and 3 Divs.	330 miles	2-3 days; by Rail via Diwaniya or by road via Diwaniya or Amara.
Kirkuk	2 Div.	450 miles	4-5 days

    Note: (*i*) The Baghdad-Basra road via Amara was a 1st class road capable of taking M.T.
    (*ii*) The Baghdad-Basra road via Diwaniya and Nasiriya was a 1st class road capable of taking M.T. except for the stretch, Tal al Lehm-Nasiriya, which was uncertain.
    (*iii*) The Baghdad-Basra railway was a single line (metre gauge).

APPENDIX 7

MAIN DISPOSITIONS OF THE IRAQ FORCE
As on 20 June 1941

(A) MOSUL AREA

Mosul	H.Q. 20 Ind. Inf. Bde. 1 Bn. King's Own Royal Regt. 2/4 G.R. One Bty. less one troop, 3 Fd. Regt. R.A. 10 Fd. Coy. less one Sec. Ancillary units.
Kirkuk	2/7 G.R. One Sec. S & M
Haditha	One Coy. 3/11 Sikh Regiment One troop 3 Fd. Regt. R.A. One troop 13 Lancers.

(B) BAGHDAD AREA

Baghdad	H.Q. 10 Ind. Div. H.Q. 21 Ind. Inf. Bde. 4/13 F.F. Rif. 2/8 G.R. less one Coy. 3/11 Sikh less two Coys. 3 Fd. Regt. R.A. less one Bty. 157 Fd. Regt. R.A. One A/Tk. Bty. One Sqn. 13 L less one troop One Fd. Pk. Coy. 9 Fd. Coy. less one Sec. Ancillary units
Falluja	One company 2/8 G.R.

(C) LOWER IRAQ

Basra area ...	17 Ind. Inf. Bde.
Ur, Samawa and Diwaniya ...	24 Ind. Inf. Bde. less one Bn. 13 L less one Sqn. 32 Fd. Regt. R.A. 19 Med. Bty.
En route to Baghdad by rail	2/10 G.R. 25 Ind. Inf. Bde.

APPENDIX 8

TENTH ARMY ORDER OF BATTLE
1 February 1942

Under Command Tenth Army

Formations
Adv. H.Q. IV Ind. Corps
    6 Ind. Div.
        151 Inf. Bde. Gp. of 50 Div. (for Mideast)
H.Q. Tenth Army   Baghdad

Army Units

Artillery

Unit	Location
H.Q. 8 A.A. Bde. 8 A.A. Bde. Sigs. 8 A.A. Bde. R.A.S.C. Sec. 8 A.A. Bde. Wkshop. Sec.	Baghdad
H.Q. 17 AA. Bde. 17 A.A. Bde. Sigs. 17 A.A. Bde. R.A.S.C. Sec. 17 A.A. Bde. Wkshop. Sec.	Basra
61 Hy. A.A. Regt. (less one Bty.) 61 Hy. A.A. Regt. Sig. Sec. 61 Hy. A.A. R.A.S.C. Sec. 61 Hy. A.A. Wkshop. Sec.	Basra
83 Hy. A.A. Regt. 83 Hy. A.A. Regt. Sig. Sec. 83 Hy. A.A. Regt. R.A.S.C. Sec. 83 Hy. A.A. Regt. Wkshop. Sec.	Habbaniya (259 Hy. A.A. Bty. Baghdad)
87 Hy. A.A. Regt. 87 Hy. A.A. Regt. Sig. Sec. 87 Hy. A.A. Regt. R.A.S.C. Sec. 87 Hy. A.A. Regt. Wkshop. Sec.	Qaiyara (278 Hy. A.A. Bty. Kirkuk) (279 Hy. A.A. Bty. Mosul)
12 Lt. A.A. Regt. 12 Lt. A.A. Regt. Sig. Sec. 12 Lt. A.A. Regt. R.A.S.C. Sec. 12 Lt. A.A. Regt. Wkshop. Sec.	Mosul (34 Lt. A.A. Bty. Kirkuk) (36 Lt. A.A. Bty. Qaiyara)
16 Lt. A.A. Regt. 16 Lt. A.A. Regt. Sig. Sec. 16 Lt. A.A. Regt. R.A.S.C. Sec. 16 Lt. A.A. Regt. Wkshop. Sec.	Basra for Kirkuk (with one Bty. for Khanakin)
37 Lt. A.A. Regt. 37 Lt. A.A. Regt. Sig. Sec. 37 Lt. A.A. Regt. R.A.S.C. Sec. 37 Lt. A.A. Regt. Wkshop. Sec.	Baghdad (127 & 222 Lt. A.A. Btys. Habbaniya)
97 Army Fd. Regt. & Sig. Sec.	Habbaniya (under Comd. 10 Ind. Div.)

APPENDICES

121 Army Fd. Regt. & Sig. Sec.	Mosul (Under Comd. 8 Ind. Div.)
"A" Tp. 1 Svy. Regt.	Mosul
19 Med. Bty.	Habbaniya (Under Comd. 10 Ind. Div.)

ENGINEERS

H.Q. Corps Tps. Engrs.	Mosul
1 Fd. Coy. S & M	Qaiyara
5 Fd. Coy. S & M	Mosul
14 Fd. Coy. S & M	Mosul
103 Fd. Pk. Coy. S & M	Qaiyara
6 Army Tps. Coy. S & M	Basra—Shuaiba
49 Army Tps. Coy. S & M	Baghdad
52 Army Tps. Coy. S & M	Mosul
56 Fd. Coy. R.E.	Kirkuk (Det. Khanakin)
1 Pnr. Bn. I.E.	Pai Tak
3 Pnr. Bn. I.E.	Basra for Baghdad
4 Pnr. Bn. I.E.	Mosul (Det. Jebel Sanam)
7 Pnr. Bn. I.E. ...	Mosul
1 Bridging Sec. S & M	Habbaniya
3 Bridging Sec. S & M	Basra
5 Bridging Sec. S & M	Basra

SIGNALS

26 Corps Sigs.	Baghdad (Dets. Khanakin, H3, Erbil, Kirkuk, Kermanshah, Mosul, Qaiyara, Dashir)

INFANTRY

2/8 G.R.	Qaiyara for Basra (to come under Comd. L. of C. area)
2/10 G.R.	Due Latifiya 4 Feb. (to come under Comd. 1 L. of C. Sub Area)
3/9 Jat Regt.	Mosul for Baghdad (to come under Comd. 1 L. of C. Sub Area)
1 Indore Inf. (I.S.F.)	K.3 (Dets. Rutba & Pipeline) (under Comd. 1 L. of C. Sub Area)
2 Hybad. Inf. (I.S.F.)	Basra (under Comd. L. of C. Area)
Bikaner Sadul (I.S.F.)	Basra—Shuaiba (under Comd. L. of C. Area)

INTELLIGENCE

Force H.Q. G.S. Int. Sec.	Baghdad
5 A.I.L. Sec.	Habbaniya
7 A.I.L. Sec.	Mosul
266 F.S. Sec.	Baghdad

6 INDIAN DIVISION

H.Q. 6 Ind. Div.	Sar-i-Pul Zuhab
H.Q. 6 Ind. Div. Arty.	Pai Tak
H.Q. 6 Ind. Div. Engrs.	

H.Q. 6 Ind. Div. R.I.A.S.C.
H.Q. Div. I.A.O.C. Wkshops. 6 Div.
6 Ind. Div. Sigs.
6 Ind. Div. Sigs. Empl. Pl.
6 Ind. Div. Sigs. H.Q. Tpt. Sec. } Sar-i-Pul Zuhab
6 Ind. Div. Sigs. Tps. Tpt. Coy.
6 Ind. Div. Sigs. Pro. Unit
6 Ind. Div. Sigs. F.S. Sec.

Div. Recce. Regt.

Poona Horse   Basra—Shuaiba

Artillery

159 Fd. Regt. & Sig. Sec.
2 Ind. Fd. Regt. & Sig. Sec. (less } Sar-i-Pul Zuhab
   two Btys.)

Engineers

27 Fd. Coy. S & M	Pai Tak
57 Fd. Coy. S & M	Pul-I-Tang
58 Fd. Coy. S & M ...	Pai Tak
302 Fd. Pk. Coy. S & M	Pai Tak

Infantry

H.Q. 24 Ind. Inf. Bde.
24 Ind. Inf. Bde. Sig. Sec.
24 Ind. Inf. Bde. Empl. Pl. } Pul-I-Tang. (About 45 miles N.W.
24 Ind. Inf. Bde. Tpt. Coy.   of Dizful)
24 Ind. Inf. Bde. Wkshop. Sec.
1 Kumaon Rif.   (Dets. Haft Khel, Ahwaz, Bandar Gulf)
2/6 Raj. Rif.   (Det. Andimishk)
5/5 R. Mahratta   Hamadan. (Two Coys. Sultanabad)

H.Q. 26 Ind. Inf. Bde.
26 Ind. Inf. Bde. Sig. Sec.
26 Ind. Inf. Bde. Empl. Pl. } Baghdad for Kermanshah
26 Ind. Inf. Bde. Tpt. Coy.
26 Ind. Inf. Bde. Wkshop. Sec.

1/1 G.R.   Basra for Kermanshah Area
1/9 G.R.   Baghdad (Dets. Ur, Diwaniya, Samawa & Hashimiya)
1/19 Hybad. Inf.   Baghdad

H.Q. 27 Ind. Inf. Bde.
27 Ind. Inf. Bde. Sig. Sec.
27 Ind. Inf. Bde. Empl. Pl. } Pai Tak
27 Ind. Inf. Bde. Tpt. Coy.
27 Ind. Inf. Bde. Wkshop. Sec.

1/10 Baluch Regt.   Pai Tak (Det. Khanakin)
4/8 Punjab Regt.   Kermanshah (Two Coys. Pai Tak)
5/12 F.F. Regt.   Senneh (Two Coys. Pai Tak)

MEDICAL
25 Fd. Amb.   Andimishk (24 Bde.)
34 Fd. Amb.   Khanakin (26 Bde.)
35 Fd. Amb.   Pai Tak (27 Bde.)
6 Fd. Hyg. Sec.   Pai Tak

ORDNANCE
12 Mob. Wkshop. Coy. I.A.O.C. ...   Sar-i-Pul Zuhab
45 Mob. Wkshop. Coy. I.A.O.C. ...   Andimishk
51 Mob. Wkshop. Coy. I.A.O.C. ...   Baghdad

POSTAL
35 Fd. P.O.   Sari-Pul Zuhab (Div. Tps.)
54 Fd. P.O.   Ahwaz (24 Bde.)
56 Fd. P.O.   Baghdad (26 Bde.)
59 Fd. P.O.   Pai Tak (27 Bde.)

151 INF. BDE. GP.

H.Q. 151 Inf. Bde.   ⎫
151 Inf. Bde. Defence Pl.   ⎬ Kirkuk
151 Inf. Bde. Sig. Sec.   ⎪
151 Inf. Bde. L.A.D.   ⎭

ARTILLERY
74 Fd. Regt. R.A. Incl. Sig. Sec. & L.A.D.   Kirkuk

ENGINEERS
505 Fd. Coy. R.E.   ⎫ Kirkuk
235 Fd. Pk. Coy. (less Dets.)   ⎭

M.Gs.
C Coy. 2 Cheshire   Kirkuk

INFANTRY
6 D.L.I.   ⎫
8 D.L.I.   ⎬ Kirkuk
9 D.L.I.   ⎭

MEDICAL
149 Fd. Amb.   Kirkuk

R.A.S.C.
C Comp. Coy.   ⎫ Kirkuk
Sec. 11 Fd. Bakery   ⎭

POSTAL
Det. 50 Div. Postal Unit   Kirkuk

BASE AND L. OF C. UNITS
H.Q. L. of C. Area ...   Basra
H.Q. No. 1 L. of C. Sub Area   Baghdad
H.Q. No. 2 L. of C. Sub Area   Ahwaz
H.Q. No. 4 L. of C. Sub Area   Khanakin
H.Q. No. 5 L. of C. Sub Area   Mosul

H.Q. No. 6 L. of C. Sub Area	Kirkuk
H.Q. Base Sub Area	Shuaiba
H.Q. 2nd Echelon	Basra

ENGINEERS

H.Q. (Works) L. of C. Area	Basra
H.Q. (Works) A	Shuaiba
H.Q. (Works) B	Baghdad
H.Q. (Works) C	Mosul (Det. Baghdad)
H.Q. (Works) D	Kirkuk
H.Q. (Works) E	Basra
H.Q. (Works) F	Ahwaz
H.Q. (Roads) H ...	Teheran
51 Printing Sec. S & M	Baghdad
55 Printing Sec. S & M	Baghdad
2 Artizan Works Coy. I.E.	Basra—Shuaiba
3 Artizan Works Coy. I.E.	Shuaiba
6 Artizan Works Coy. I.E.	Shuaiba
9 Artizan Works Coy. I.E.	Shuaiba
10 Artizan Works Coy. I.E.	Baghdad
11 Artizan Works Coy. I.E.	Shuaiba
12 Artizan Works Coy. I.E.	Ahwaz
13 Artizan Works Coy. I.E.	Baghdad
14 Artizan Works Coy. I.E.	Mosul
16 Artizan Works Coy. I.E.	Tanuma
1 E. & M. Coy. I.E.	Shuaiba
2 E. & M. Coy. I.E.	Mosul
861 M.E. Coy. R.E. ...	Basra
207 Oxy. & Acet. Gen. Coy. I.E. ...	Basra—Shuaiba
1 Engrs. Base Wkshop. I.E.	Shuaiba
1 Engrs. Base Store Depot I.E. ...	Shuaiba
313 Steel Work Erection Sec. I.E.	Basra—Shuaiba (Det. Kirkuk)
304 Wkshop. & Pk. Coy. I.E.	Shuaiba for Baghdad (Dets. Baghdad, Mosul)
3 Army Excavating Coy. I.E.	Mosul (Dets. Samawa, Tell Kotchek, Qaiyara)
2 R.A.F. Excavating Coy. I.E.	Faidah (Dets. Shuaiba & Taza Khurmatli)
312 Well Boring Sec. I.E.	Jebel Sanam
316 Quarrying Coy. I.E.	Basra

SIGNALS

"B" L. of C. Sigs.	Basra (Dets. Baghdad, LG5, H3, Rutba, Teheran, Ahwaz, Habbaniya, Mosul & K3)
1 L. of C. Telegraphs	Basra—Shuaiba
Det. 2 L. of C. Telegraphs	Ahwaz
5 L. of C. Telegraphs	Baghdad (Dets. Kut al Amara, Latifiya, Ur, Khan Jadwal, Mosul. K3, Habbaniya, Kermanshah)
2 Ind. Const. Sec.	Mosul
1 Ry. Sig. Coy.	Ur (Det. Khan Jadwal)

Movements

1 Movement Control Area	Basra
2 Movement Control Area	Baghdad
3 Movement Control Area	Ahwaz

Transportation

H.Q. 1 Ry. C. & M. Gp. I.E.	Shuaiba
H.Q. 2 Ry. C. & M. Gp. I.E.	Baghdad
H.Q. 1 Ry. Op. Gp. I.E.	Basra
H.Q. 2. Ry. Op. Gp. R.E.	Ahwaz
H.Q. 1 Ry. Wkshop. Gp. I.E.	Baghdad
H.Q. 1 Docks Op. Gp. I.E.	Basra
H.Q. 2 I.W.T. Gp. R.E.	Khosroabad
973 I.W.T. Wkshop. Coy. R.E.	Khosroabad
940 I.W.T. Op. Coy. R.E.	Khosroabad
944 I.W.T. Op. Coy. R.E.	Khosroabad
103 Ry. Svy. Coy. I.E.	Baghdad
101 Ry. Constr. Coy. I.E.	Basra
105 Ry. Constr. Coy. I.E.	Baghdad
106 Ry. Constr. Coy. I.E.	Jaliba
120 Ry. Constr. Coy. I.E.	Baghdad
102 Ry. Op. Coy. I.E.	Baghdad
108 Ry. Op. Coy. I.E.	Basra
109 Ry. Op. Coy. I.E.	Basra
115 Ry. Op. Coy. I.E.	Basra
190 Ry. Op. Coy. R.E.	Ahwaz
114 Ry. Maint. Coy. I.E.	Shuaiba
121 Ry. Maint. Coy. I.E.	Al Khidhr
107 Ry. Wkshop. Coy. I.E.	Shuaiba
119 Ry. Wkshop. Coy. I.E.	Shuaiba
125 Ry. Wkshop. Coy. I.E.	Shuaiba
1 Ry. Mob. Wkshop. Coy. R.E.	Ahwaz
104 Tn. Stores Coy. I.E.	Basra
211 Docks Op. Coy. I.E.	Basra
212 Docks Op. Coy. I.E.	Basra
1 Docks Sec. I.E.	Basra
2 Docks Sec. I.E.	Basra

R.I.A.S.C.

500 Force H.Q. Tpt. Sec.	Basra
505 Force H.Q. Tpt. Sec.	Baghdad
35 G.P. Tpt. Coy.	Baghdad
36 G.P. Tpt. Coy.	Baghdad
49 G.P. Tpt. Coy.	Khanakin
50 G.P. Tpt. Coy.	Basra
51 G.P. Tpt. Coy.	Mosul
52 G.P. Tpt. Coy.	Qaiyara
53 G.P. Tpt. Coy.	Basra
54 G.P. Tpt. Coy.	Basra
57 G.P. Tpt. Coy.	Basra
58 G.P. Tpt. Coy.	Basra
62 G.P. Tpt. Coy.	Mosul
203 G.P. Tpt. Coy.	Khanakin (One Sec. Ahwaz)
204 G.P. Tpt. Coy.	Khanakin

501 G.P. Tpt. Sec.	Kirkuk
502 G.P. Tpt. Sec. ...	Kirkuk
15 M.A. Convoy (R.A.S.C.)	Basra
7 M.A. Sec.	Baghdad
8 M.A. Sec.	Basra
10 M.A. Sec.	Baghdad
11 M.A. Sec.	Mosul
12 M.A. Sec.	Khanakin
14 M.A. Sec.	Kirkuk
15 M.A. Sec.	Baghdad
16 M.A. Sec.	Baghdad
17 M.A. Sec.	Baghdad
53 Draught Camel Coy.	Basra
26 Mule Coy.	Basra
33 Mule Coy.	Basra
2 Base Supply Depot	Basra
H.Q. 14 Sup. Pers. Coy.	Basra
H.Q. 21 Sup. Pers. Coy.	Mosul
H.Q. 22 Sup. Pers. Coy.	Baghdad
H.Q. 23 Sup. Pers. Coy.	Kirkuk
3 Fd. Bakery	Basra-Shuaiba
4 Fd. Bakery	Baghdad
5 Fd. Bakery	Mosul
14 Fd. Bakery Sec.	Teheran
15 Fd. Bakery Sec.	Teheran
16 Fd. Bakery Sec.	Ahwaz
113 Sub Sec. Fd. Bakery	Basra
1 Fd. Butchery (Det.) ...	Basra
3 Fd. Butchery	Basra-Shuaiba
4 Fd. Butchery	Baghdad
5 Fd. Butchery	Mosul
1 Fd. Butchery IT ...	Basra-Shuaiba
113 Sub Sec. Fd. Butchery	Basra
Det. 8 Fd. Butchery	Kirkuk for Mideast
2 Petrol Depot	Basra
19 Railhead Sup. Det. ...	Baghdad
21 Railhead Sup. Det.	Basra
22 Railhead Sup. Det.	Ahwaz
4 Cattle Stock Sec.	Basra
22 Cattle Stock Sec.	Basra
23 Cattle Stock Sec.	Baghdad
25 Cattle Stock Sec.	Mosul
31 Cattle Stock Sec.	Qaiyara
32 Cattle Stock Sec.	Ahwaz
33 Cattle Stock Sec.	Basra
34 Cattle Stock Sec. ...	Kirkuk
20 Cattle Conducting Sec.	Ahwaz
21 Cattle Conducting Sec.	Kirkuk
22 Cattle Conducting Sec.	Baghdad
23 Cattle Conducting Sec.	Basra
24 Cattle Conducting Sec.	Ahwaz
25 Cattle Conducting Sec.	Mosul
26 Cattle Conducting Sec.	Basra
11 D.I.D. R.A.S.C.	Kirkuk for Mideast

MEDICAL

28 B.G.H.	Basra
35 B.G.H.	Baghdad
61 B.G.H.	Shuaiba
21 C.G.H.	Ahwaz
23 C.G.H.	Shuaiba
24 C.G.H.	Baghdad
25 C.G.H.	Baghdad
28 C.G.H.	Mosul
29 C.G.H.	Basra
31 C.G.H.	Ahwaz
32 C.G.H.	Shuaiba
33 C.G.H.	Kirkuk
34 C.G.H.	Ahwaz
35 C.G.H.	Baghdad for Mosul
36 C.G.H.	Ahwaz
37 C.G.H.	Shuaiba
64 C.G.H.	Baghdad
18 I.G.H.	Basra for Kirkuk
26 I.G.H.	Shuaiba
"Y" Hosp. Det.	Basra
7 C.C.S.	Khanakin
9 C.C.S.	Qaiyara
10 C.C.S.	Kirkuk
17 C.C.S.	Kirkuk for Mideast
22 Fd. Amb.	Baghdad
4 Br. Staging Sec.	LG5
8 Br. Staging Sec.	Basra
12 Br. Staging Sec.	Pai Tak
13 Br. Staging Sec.	Ahwaz
16 Br. Staging Sec.	Teheran
17 Br. Staging Sec.	Khosroabad
19 Br. Staging Sec.	Ahwaz
20 Br. Staging Sec.	Teheran
1 Ind. Staging Sec.	Ur for Khan Jadwal
5 Ind. Staging Sec.	Latifiya
6 Ind. Staging Sec.	Baghdad
7 Ind. Staging Sec.	Tanuma
8 Ind. Staging Sec.	Basra
15 Ind. Staging Sec.	Kirkuk
20 Ind. Staging Sec.	Bandar Gulf
21 Ind. Staging Sec.	Khosroabad
22 Ind. Staging Sec.	Khosroabad
23 Ind. Staging Sec.	Basra
24 Ind. Staging Sec.	Sultanabad
25 Ind. Staging Sec.	Habbaniya
26 Ind. Staging Sec.	Kermanshah
27 Ind. Staging Sec.	Baghdad
38 Ind. Staging Sec.	K.3
39 Ind. Staging Sec.	Umm Qasr
3 Br. Conval. Depot	Basra
4 Br. Conval. Depot	Ahwaz
6 Br. Conval. Depot	Latifiya
3 Ind. Conval. Depot ...	Shuaiba

4 Ind. Conval. Depot ...	Ahwaz
6 Ind. Conval. Depot	Latifiya
7 Ind. Conval. Depot ...	Basra
22 Ind. Conval. Depot	Shuaiba
23 Ind. Conval. Depot	Shuaiba
11 Fd. Hyg. Sec.	Basra
16 Fd. Hyg. Sec.	Ahwaz for Kirkuk
17 Fd. Hyg. Sec.	Kirkuk
21 Fd. Hyg. Sec.	Shuaiba
25 Fd. Hyg. Sec.	Ahwaz
34 Fd. Hyg. Sec.	Baghdad
4 Mob. X-Ray Unit	Khanakin
6 Mob. X-Ray Unit	Kirkuk
9 Mob. X Ray Unit	Qaiyara
5 X-Ray Unit	Basra
9 X-Ray Unit	Basra
10 X-Ray Unit	Shuaiba
20 X-Ray Unit	Baghdad
21 X-Ray Unit	Shuaiba
23 X-Ray Unit	Baghdad
24 X-Ray Unit	Mosul
25 X-Ray Unit	Kirkuk
26 X-Ray Unit	Ahwaz
4 Fd. Lab.	Baghdad
5 Fd. Lab.	Basra
8 Fd. Lab.	Shuaiba
10 Fd. Lab.	Baghdad
13 Fd. Lab.	Ahwaz
14 Fd. Lab.	Mosul
15 Fd. Lab.	Kirkuk
16 Fd. Lab.	Shuaiba
17 Fd. Lab.	Ahwaz
18 Fd. Lab.	Shuaiba
19 Fd. Lab.	Basra for Khanakin
3 Anti Malaria Unit	Basra
4 Anti Malaria Unit ...	Baghdad
1 Surgical Unit (E.N.T.)	Basra
1 Ophthalmological Unit	Mosul
1 Dental Surgical & Mech. Unit ...	Basra
2 Dental Surgical & Mech. Unit ...	Baghdad
3 Dental Surgical & Mech. Unit ...	Basra
7 Ind. Dental Surgery Unit	Basra for Mosul
8 Ind. Dental Surgery Unit	Basra for Baghdad
9 Ind. Dental Surgery Unit	Shuaiba
1 Depot Medical Stores	Kirkuk
7 Depot Medical Stores	Basra for Ahwaz
10 Depot Medical Stores	Baghdad
1 Base Depot Medical Store	Shuaiba
9 Amb. Train (M.G.)	Baghdad
10 Amb. Train (M.G.)	Baghdad
11 Amb. Train (M.G.)	Baghdad

ORDNANCE

31 Mob. Wkshop. Coy. I.A.O.C. ...	Baghdad (Army Tps. & 3rd Line)

APPENDICES

37 Mob. Wkshop. Coy. I.A.O.C.	Basra (Base Tps. & 3rd Line)
41 Mob. Wkshop. Coy. I.A.O.C.	Baghdad (Army & L. of C. Tps.)
52 Mob. Wkshop. Coy. I.A.O.C.	Shuaiba (Base Tps. & 3rd Line
2 Base Ord. Depot I.A.O.C.	Shuaiba
2 Base Amn. Depot I.A.O.C.	Shuaiba
11 A.O.D. I.A.O.C.	Baghdad
12 A.O.D. I.A.O.C.	Mosul
13 A.O.D. I.A.O.C.	Kirkuk
"Z" A.O.D. I.A.O.C.	Ahwaz
11 A.A.D. I.A.O.C.	Baghdad
12 A.A.D. I.A.O.C.	Mosul
13 A.A.D. I.A.O.C.	Kirkuk
"Z" A.A.D. I.A.O.C. ...	Ahwaz
Ry. Head Ord. Det. I.A.O.C.	Khanakin
Ry. Head Ord. Det. I.A.O.C.	Qaiyara
Ry. Head Ord. Det. I.A.O.C.	Teheran
Ord. Sub Depot I.A.O.C.	Khurram Shahr
7 H.R.S. R.A.O.C. ...	Shuaiba
1 Base Ord. Wkshop. R.A.O.C.	Kirkuk
1 Army Ord. Wkshop. R.A.O.C. ...	Shuaiba
5 Adv. Base Ord. Wkshop. R.A.O.C. ...	Baghdad
9 Port Wkshop. Det. R.A.O.C.	Basra
4 Ord. Fd. Pk. R.A.O.C.	Shuaiba
12 M.T. V.R.D. R.A.S.C. ...	Shuaiba
Det. 9 M.T. Stores Depot R.A.S.C.	Shuaiba
21 L. of C. Recovery Coy. I.A.O.C.	Baghdad
1 Salvage Pl. I.A.O.C.	Basra
2 Salvage Pl. I.A.O.C.	Shuaiba
3 Salvage Pl. I.A.O.C.	Baghdad
4 Salvage Pl. I.A.O.C.	Mosul
1 Base Laundry I.A.O.C.	Shuaiba
1 Mob. Laundry I.A.O.C.	Basra
8 Mob. Laundry I.A.O.C. ...	Basra
2 (Port Trust Laundry I.A.O.C.)	Basra
1 Mob. Cinema I.A.O.C.	Basra (For 6 Div.)
2 Mob. Cinema I.A.O.C.	Basra (For 8 Div.)
5 Mob. Cinema I.A.O.C.	Basra (For 10 Div.)
6 Mob. Cinema I.A.O.C.	Basra
9 Mob. Cinema I.A.O.C.	Basra (For Qaiyara)
11 Mob. Cinema I.A.O.C.	Basra (For Kirkuk)

Postal

"C" Base P.O.	Basra
7 Ind. Sec. Base P.O.	Baghdad
8 Ind. Sec. Base P.O.	Ahwaz
14 Fd. P.O.	Kirkuk
18 Fd. P.O.	Basra
21 Fd. P.O.	Shuaiba
22 Fd. P.O.	Habbaniya
57 Fd. P.O.	Khanakin
101 Fd. P.O.	Khosroabad
102 Fd. P.O.	Mosul
103 Fd. P.O.	Teheran

104 Fd. P.O.	Zubair
105 Fd. P.O.	Qaiyara

SURVEY

1 Ind. Fd. Svy. H.Q.	Baghdad
2 Ind. Fd. Svy. H.Q.	Mosul (Det. Baghdad)
4 Ind. Fd. Svy. H.Q.	Kirkuk (Det. Halabja)
1 Ind. Fd. Svy. Coy.	Baghdad
2 Ind. Fd. Svy. Coy.	Mosul (Det. Baghdad & Habbaniya)
4 Ind. Fd. Svy. Coy.	Kirkuk (Dets. Baghdad, Hindiya, Pai Tak, Ahwaz, Khanakin)
Base Map Depot	Basra
Central Map Depot	Baghdad

INTELLIGENCE

1 L. of C. Sec. Ind. Int. Corps	Basra
2 L. of C. Sec. Ind. Int. Corps	Baghdad
3 L. of C. Sec. Ind. Int. Corps	Baghdad
1 Iraq Composite F.S. Sec.	Basra
2 Iraq Composite F.S. Sec.	Baghdad
3 Iraq Composite F.S. Sec.	Baghdad
4 Iraq Composite F.S. Sec.	Shuaiba

PROVOST

2 Base Pro. Unit	Basra (One Sec. Ahwaz)
1 L. of C. Pro. Sec.	Baghdad for Kirkuk
2 L. of C. Pro. Sec. ...	Baghdad for Kirkuk
51 L. of C. Pro. Sub. Sec.	Ahwaz
52 L. of C. Pro. Sub. Sec.	Basra
53 Pro. Coy.	Baghdad
3 Base Pro. Unit	Basra
50 Pro. Sec.	Mosul

AUXILIARY PIONEER BATTALIONS

1 Aux. Pnr. Bn.	Basra
2 Aux. Pnr. Bn.	Mosul
3 Aux. Pnr. Bn.	Basra (Det. Ahwaz)
5 Aux. Pnr. Bn.	Baghdad (Det. Khanakin)
6 Aux. Pnr. Bn.	Mosul
11 Aux. Pnr. Bn.	Kirkuk
12 Aux. Pnr. Bn.	Mosul
14 Aux. Pnr. Bn.	Mosul

FARMS

Det. No. 1 Base Mily. Dairy Farm	Basra

MISCELLANEOUS

39 Br. Rest Camp	Basra
35 Rest Camp	Baghdad
36 Rest Camp	Khanakin
37 Rest Camp	Baghdad
38 Rest Camp	Basra

40 Rest Camp	Mosul
41 Rest Camp	Ahwaz
42 Rest Camp	Kirkuk
43 Rest Camp	Kermanshah
44 Rest Camp	Teheran
15 Rest Camp (Ind. Sec.)	Basra
"L" Ind. Transit Camp	Habbaniya
15 Reinforcement Camp	Shuaiba
16 Reinforcement Camp	Latifiya
17 Reinforcement Camp	Latifiya
2 Prisoners of War Cage	Basra
6 Prisoners of War Cage	Mosul
7 Prisoners of War Cage	Kirkuk
"A" Prisoners of War Camp	Basra
"M" Military Prison	Basra
1 Ind. Graves Registration & Enquiry Unit	Baghdad (Det. Mosul)
33 Mob. Bath Unit	Basra for Sar-i-Pul Zuhab
37 Mob. Bath Unit	Mosul
6 Fd. Accts. Office	Basra
5 Stationery Depot	Basra
3 Mob. Vet. Sec.	Basra

UNDER COMD. ADV. H.Q. IV IND. CORPS (For Operations only pending arrival of Corps H.Q.)

Formations:— 8 Ind. Div.
10 Ind. Div.
252 Ind. Armd. Gp.

Adv. H.Q. IV Ind. Corps ... Baghdad

8 INDIAN DIVISION

H.Q. 8 Ind. Div.
H.Q. 8 Ind. Div. Arty.
H.Q. 8 Ind. Div. Engrs.
H.Q. 8 Ind. Div. R.I.A.S.C.
H.Q. Div. I.A.O.C. Wkshop. 8 Div. ⎬ Mosul
8 Ind. Div. Sigs.
8 Ind. Div. Empl. Pl.
8 Ind. Div. H.Q. Tpt. Sec.
8 Ind. Div. Tps. Tpt. Coy.
8 Ind. Div. Pro. Unit

Div. Recce. Regt.

6 Lancers   Mosul

ARTILLERY

11 Fd. Regt. R.A. & Sig. Sec.   Buqaq
32 Fd. Regt. R.A. & Sig. Sec.   Mosul

ENGINEERS

7 Fd. Coy. S & M
66 Fd. Coy. S & M ⎬ Mosul
69 Fd. Coy. S & M.
47 Fd. Pk. Coy. S & M

INFANTRY

H.Q. 17 Ind. Inf. Bde. ...
17 Ind. Div. Bde. Sig. Sec. ...
17 Ind. Div. Bde. Empl. Pl. ...
17 Ind. Div. Bde. Tpt. Coy. ...
17 Ind. Div. Bde. Wkshop. Sec. ...
1 R.F. ...
1/12 F.F. Regt. ...
1/5 R.G.R. ... } Mosul
H.Q. 18 Ind. Inf. Bde. ...
18 Ind. Inf. Bde. Sig. Sec. ...
18 Ind. Inf. Bde. Empl. Pl. ...
18 Ind. Inf. Bde. Tpt. Coy. ...
18 Ind. Inf. Bde. Wkshop. Sec. ...
2/5 Essex ...
1/2 G.R. ...
2/3 G.R. ...

H.Q. 19 Ind. Inf. Bde. ...
19 Inf. Bde. Sig. Sec. ...
19 Inf. Bde. Sig. Empl. Pl. ...
19 Inf. Bde. Sig. Tpt. Coy. ... } Buqaq
19 Inf. Bde. Sig. Wkshop. Sec. ...
1/5 Essex ...
3/8 Punjab Regt. ...
2/6 G.R. ...

MEDICAL

31 Fd. Amb.   Mosul (17 Bde.)
32 Fd. Amb.   Mosul (18 Bde.)
33 Fd. Amb.   Buqaq (19 Bde.)
20 Fd. Hyg. Sec.   Mosul

ORDNANCE

15 Mob. Wkshop. Coy. I.A.O.C.   Mosul
34 Mob. Wkshop. Coy. I.A.O.C. ... Mosul
49 Mob. Wkshop. Coy. I.A.O.C. ... Buqaq

POSTAL

41 Fd. P.O. ... ⎫   (Div. Tps.)
42 Fd. P.O. ... ⎬ Mosul   (17 Bde.)
43 Fd. P.O. ... ⎭   (18 Bde.)
44 Fd. P.O.   Buqaq   (19 Bde.)

10 INDIAN DIVISION

H.Q. 10 Ind. Div.   ...   Erbil
H.Q. 10 Ind. Div. Arty   Habbaniya
H.Q. 10 Ind. Div. Engineers   Habbaniya
H.Q. 10 Ind. Div. R.I.A.S.C. Erbil
H.Q. Div. I.A.O.C. Wkshops.
  10 Div.   Erbil

APPENDICES 501

10 Ind. Div. Sigs. ...
10 Ind. Div. Empl. Pl. ...
10 Ind. Div. H.Q. Tpt. Sec. ... } Erbil
10 Ind. Div. Tps. Tpt. Coy. ...
10 Ind. Div. Pro. Unit ...

Div. Recce. Regt.
Guides Cav.   Erbil

ARTILLERY

3 Fd. Regt. R.A. & Sig. Sec. ...
157 Fd. Regt. R.A. & Sig. Sec. ... } Habbaniya
1st Ind. A/Tk. Regt. ...

ENGINEERS

9 Fd. Coy. S & M   Hindiya Barrage
10 Fd. Coy. S & M   Mosul (Under Comd. 8 Ind. Div.)
61 Fd. Coy. S & M ...   Mujara
41 Fd. Pk. Coy. S & M   Habbaniya

INFANTRY

H.Q. 20th Ind. Inf. Bde. ...
20 Ind. Inf. Bde. Sig. Sec. ...
20 Ind. Inf. Bde. Empl. Pl. ...
20 Ind. Inf. Bde. Tpt. Coy. ... } Qaiyara
20 Ind. Inf. Bde. Wkshop. Sec. ...
1 S.W.B. ...
3/11 Sikh Regt. ...
2/7 G.R. ...

H.Q. 21st Ind. Inf. Bde. ...
21 Ind. Inf. Bde. Sig. Sec. ...
21 Ind. Inf. Bde. Empl. Pl. ...
21 Ind. Inf. Bde. Tpt. Coy. ... } Hindiya Barrage
21 Ind. Inf. Bde. Wkshop. Sec. ...
1 D.C.L.I. ...
4/13 F.F. Regt. ...
2/4 G.R. ...

H.Q. 25th Ind. Inf. Bde.
25 Ind. Inf. Bde. Sig. Sec. ...
25 Ind. Inf. Bde. Empl. Pl. ... } Mujara
25 Ind. Inf. Bde. Tpt. Coy. ...
25 Ind. Inf. Bde. Wkshop. Sec. ...

1 Kings Own   Kirkuk (Det. K2)
1/5 Mahratta Lt. Inf.   Mujara (One Coy. Erbil)
2/11 Sikh Regt.   Mujara (One Coy. Falluja)

MEDICAL

26 Fd. Amb.   Qaiyara (20 Bde.)
29 Fd. Amb.   Hindiya Barrage (21 Bde.)
30 Fd. Amb.   Habbaniya (25 Bde.)
1 Fd. Hyg. Sec.   Erbil

ORDNANCE

11 Mob. Wkshop. Coy. I.A.O.C. ...	Qaiyara
28 Mob. Wkshop. Coy. I.A.O.C. ...	Erbil
29 Mob. Wkshop. Coy. I.A.O.C. ...	Habbaniya

POSTAL

48 Fd. P.O.	Qaiyara (20 Bde.)
49 Fd. P.O.	Hindiya Barrage (21 Bde.)
53 Fd. P.O.	Erbil (Div. Tps.)
55 Fd. P.O.	Mujara (25 Bde.)

252 IND. ARMD. GP.

H.Q. 252 Ind. Armd. Gp.	
252 Ind. Armd. Gp. Sig. Sqn.	
252 Ind. Armd. Tpt. Coy.	
15 Fd. Regt. R.A. & Sig. Tp.	
32 Fd. Sqn. S & M	
14/20 King's Hussars	
13 Lancers	
Hodson's Horse	
1/4 Bombay Grenadiers	
2 Lt. Fd. Amb.	Qaiyara
1 Wkshop. Sqn. I.A.O.C.	
14 Mob. Wkshop. Coy. I.A.O.C.	
35 Mob. Wkshop. Coy. I.A.O.C.	
"A" Sec. 31 Ind. Armd. Div. Rec. Coy.	
"B" Sec. 31 Ind. Armd. Div. Rec. Coy.	
103 Br. Pro. Sub. Sec.	
104 Ind. Pro. Sub. Sec.	
25 Fd. P.O.	

APPENDIX 9

TENTH ARMY OPERATION INSTRUCTION NO. 21
25 May 1942

(Supersedes Tenth Army Operation Instruction No. 19)

1. SCOPE OF INSTRUCTION

This instruction deals with the action to be taken by Tenth Army in the event of an enemy attack through ANATOLIA only. Although an attack through PERSIA from the CAUCASUS is equally possible, such an attack could not be delivered against Tenth Army as early as one through ANATOLIA. The steps to be taken to meet an attack through PERSIA are to be outlined in a subsequent instruction.

2 OBJECT

The object is to ensure the security of our bases and ports in IRAQ and PERSIA and of our oil supplies in south-west PERSIA and the PERSIAN GULF.

3. FORCES AVAILABLE

Tenth Army
  (a) 21 Ind. Corps. consisting of:—
      31 Ind. Armd. Div.
      CHINKARA (composed of H.Q. and two Armd. C Regts., dets. of inf. and arty. as decided upon by 21 Ind. Corps).
      8 Ind. Armd. Div.
      10 Ind. Div.
      One regt. med. arty.
  (b) 6 Ind. Div. (less one bde. gp.)
  (c) Three unbrigaded Inf. bns ; three I.S.F. bns.
  (d) Iraqi Army *(see Appendix 'A')*.

G.H.Q. Reserves
  One Armd. Div.
  One Armd. Bde. Gp.
  One Army Tank Bde.
  One Ind. Div.

4. ENEMY

(a) It is estimated that against IRAQ the enemy may employ up to 7-8 divisions of all natures supported by strong air forces and that he will advance from southern ANATOLIA in several columns on a wide front with the design of outflanking our mobile forces and defenced areas. His primary initial objectives will be ZAKHO, MOSUL, KIRKUK and BAGHDAD.

(b) It is expected that the enemy will attempt to secure intact the MOSUL bridge and railway tunnel as a preliminary to a rapid advance

Note: Ref. Map 1/1,000,000 sheets I-37, J-37, I-38, J-38.

on the one hand to KIRKUK and on the other to BAGHDAD, using armd., and motorised forces for the latter objective West of river Tigris.

(c) The enemy approach down the river EUPHRATES from ALEPPO and by the river KHABUR must not be overlooked and may even prove to be his main axis of thrust.

5. Conclusion

The forces available to Tenth Army are not of a strength to make it probable that they will be able to prevent an attack from ANATOLIA, on a maximum scale from penetrating into northern IRAQ.

6. Boundaries

With Ninth Army

TENTH ARMY excl. MALATYA—incl. KARACLI DAGH (KARADJA DAGH)—excl. HASSETCHE (ELHASEKE)—GAARET MOTTEB—thence IRAQ/TRANSJORDAN frontier.

7. Intention

(a) By resolute action on ground favourable to our troops, Tenth Army will impose on the enemy from the very first and as far forward as conditions will allow, the greatest possible delay and will inflict on him the heaviest possible casualties.

(b) Tenth Army will NOT allow the enemy in any event to establish himself south of the general line LESSER ZAB—FATHA—ANA.

8. Method

Delay

Essential delay will be imposed by:

(a) Covering and protecting as long as is practicable the northern aerodromes in IRAQ from which the R.A.F. are to attack heavily the enemy's most vulnerable communications in ANATOLIA.

(b) Thorough demolition of all types of communication and of all oil stocks and installations in S.E. ANATOLIA, N.E. SYRIA and NORTHERN IRAQ—as well as by early removal to the south of BAGHDAD of such war and other material as would be of operational value to the enemy.

(c) Holding positions, often in conjunction with demolitions in country unsuitable to enemy A.F.Vs., astride the enemy's main lines of advance.

(d) Seizing opportunities to counter-attack with armour or mobile columns whenever the enemy is at fault or a suitable situation is created by the action of our troops.

(e) Forcing the enemy columns into areas in which he will find it difficult to maintain them.

While imposing the maximum losses and delay on the enemy it is imperative that our own troops in the field should not be depleted to such an extent that on reaching the general line mentioned in para 7(b) above they will be too weak to hold it.

9. Initial dispositions

The process of delaying the enemy will start as far forward as possible, depending on the land and air forces available and on the attitude of the Turks.

The Plans of Tenth Army for its initial dispositions will provide for any of the following cases:—

CASE "A"

TURKEY resists German aggression and adequate army and R.A.F. resources exist for operations in Northern ANATOLIA in co-operation with the TURKS.

Opening move
(a) Air Striking Force, with an army component from Ninth Army is to move into TURKEY.
(b) When maintenance facilities permit, most forward tps. 21 Ind. Corps will occupy the general line ELAZIG (KHARPUT)—excl. MALATYA with a view to:—
   (i) Improving communications.
   (ii) Preparing demolitions on the main Turkish communications.
   (iii) Destroying oil stocks if this becomes necessary.

CASE "B"

TURKEY acquiesces in German aggression or collapses quickly— Attitude of the Turks if we enter from the South unknown.

Opening move
Most fwd. tps., 21 Ind. Corps seize and hold the general line DIYARBEKIR—excl. SIVEREK with the object of:—
   (a) Immediately destroying communications.
   (b) Delaying the enemy as far forward as practicable.

CASE "C"

The TURKS come in openly on the side of the Germans or the TURKS have strengthened their forces on the SYRIAN frontier with evident intent to come in on the GERMAN side and the entry of our forces into TURKEY will obviously be opposed.

Opening move
Foremost tps. 21 Ind. Corps will penetrate S.E. ANATOLIA as far as practicable with the object of:—
   (a) Carrying out demolitions.
   (b) Imposing the maximum delay on the enemy's advance.

10. GENERAL POLICY FOR THE CONDUCT OF THE BATTLE

CHINKARA will be the foremost body of 21 Ind. Corps in Cases A, B or C supported as necessary by troops specially detailed to deal with communications, demolitions and protection of the most forward landing grounds and R.A.F. installations.

CHINKARA being a particularly mobile force will not closely engage the enemy except on very favourable ground.

When CHINKARA has fought back to the general line MOSUL— TELL AFAR, Comd. 21 Ind. Corps has discretion to dissolve it as a force or retain it for further action. It is vital, however, to have a fresh mobile force to control the blowing of demolitions on rd MOSUL—FATHA and to fight successive delaying actions on those demolitions.

11. 31 Ind. Armd. Div., within its administrative circuit of action and the capacity of its recovery facilities, will initially oppose the enemy armoured and motorised formations in suitable areas West of river TIGRIS and later, based on the railway, North and N.W. of the general line FATHA—ANA.

It is NOT the intention that 31 Ind. Armd. Div. should incur heavy casualties early in the battle in the open country adjacent to the TURKISH frontier.

In the probable area of its operations this formation will forthwith make exhaustive recce. of ground and make such preparations as may enable it to cross natural obstacles and so gain added freedom of movement in contrast to the enemy who will not know of such crossing places.

12. 8 Ind. Div. will secure MOSUL bridge and with its own light columns and at least two bde. gps. Iraqi Army will operate South from ZAKHO in an offensive/defensive role, basing itself on prepared positions at FAIDA, NINEVEH and TWO RIVERS.

These positions should be completed forthwith to suit the above circumstances.

13. 10 Ind. Div. (less two bde. gps.) with two bde. gps. IRAQI Army will secure initially the MOSUL West defended area in order to support 31 Ind. Armd. Div. and CHINKARA.

Comd. 21 Ind. Corps has discretion to prepare a position at KISICK KEUPRI for this bde. gp. of 10 Ind. Div. to act in certain circumstances as an immediate pivot for the operations of 31 Ind. Armd. Div. from TEL AFAR area.

After withdrawal from the MOSUL area, the bde. group, 10 Ind. Div., is destined to garrison the defended position at TAJI. Comd. 21 Ind. Armd. Div. between MOSUL and FATHA.

14. FINAL STAND FOR BATTLE

To prevent the enemy establishing himself South of the line mentioned in 7(b), formations, when forced to do so, will withdraw fighting into prepared and stocked positions as under:—

8 Ind. Div.	ALTUN KOPRU	} One Bde. Gp.
(With three Iraqi bde. gps. under comd.)	DIBIS	
	TELL ALI	One Bde. Gp.
	FATHA	One Bde. Gp.
10 Ind. Div.	RAMADI—HABBANIYA	One Bde. Gp.
(With two Iraqi bde. gps. under comd.)	MUJARA CUT	One Bde. Gp.
	SAFRA	One Bde. Gp.
	TAJI	One Bde. Gp.
	FALLUJA Bridgehead	

The bridge site at SAFRA will probably be secured later by part of the G.H.Q. Reserve. One Iraqi bde. will operate under 10 Ind. Div. on L. of C. RAMADI—HADITHA excl. ABU KEMAL.

15. L. OF C. PROTECTION

(a) 6 Ind. Div. (less one bde. gp. in area KHUZISTAN—BASRA), with one Iraqi Bde. under Comd. will be responsible for L. of C. KIRKUK—BAGHDAD, both incl.

6 Ind. Div. will recce. and be ready to occupy in certain circumstances prepared bde. gp. positions at BAQUBA and HINDIYA.

The BAQUBA position will be completed by 8 Ind. Div.

The HINDIYA position will be completed by 10 Ind. Div.

(b) The defence of the adv. base at MUSSAIYIB and of combined Army/R.A.F. H.Q. at LATIFIYA will be the responsibility of two bns. Tenth Army Reserve with four Armd. Cars under a selected commander.

(c) Two Independent Bdes. IRAQI Army will operate under Comd. L. of C. Area protecting the EUPHRATES L. of C. with two bns. at DIWANIYA and one each at SAMAWA and NASIRIYA.

One Iraqi Bn., under Comd. L. of C. Area, based on AMARA, will protect I.W.T. on river TIGRIS. Four Iraqi gunboats will also operate under comd. L. of C. Area to protect I.W.T. on the rivers TIGRIS and SHATT AL ARAB.

One Iraqi Bn. will be employed on minewatching on the SHATT AL ARAB, in conjunction with Ind. Coast Defence Bn., under Comd. L. of C. Area.

(d) A defended staging post in the RUTBA area is being prepared by Tenth Army and will be held by an I.S.F. Bn.

Stocking of the post is the responsibility of G.H.Q.

16. IRAQI ARMY

Initial dispositions of IRAQI army formations and their roles are shown in Appendix "A".

17. WORKS POLICY

The present policy is:—

(a) To continue slowly with construction which has begun on roads North of MOSUL.

(b) To complete works on defences in the MOSUL West area to fit them for hasty occupation of the Inner Line.

In the Mosul perimeter new works of any kind will NOT be started.

Essential work in the hospital area will be finished off, now; the rest will be deferred.

It is imperative that the maximum amount of material and skilled labour be released from the MOSUL area for important work elsewhere.

(c) In general it is the policy that civil labour shall be used to the utmost for all works that remain to be carried out in order to release tps. for training.

18. AIR ACTION BY R.A.F.

(a) *Object*
  (i) Attack enemy communications and strategic objects to impose maximum delay on the enemy's advance.
  (ii) Give support to the operations of Tenth Army and G.H.Q. Reserve.
  (iii) Protect our L. of C., ports and oil installations from air attack.
  (iv) Protect shipping in PERSIAN GULF.

(b) *Intention*

Case "A"—In order to give air support to Tenth Army on the KHARPUT—MALATYA line our air forces must have use of aerodromes and L. Gs at DIARBEKIR. The forces so employed would be working on an O.L.G. basis.

(c) Case "B"—In the event of the DIARBEKIR—SIVEREK line being the furthest forward point reached by Tenth Army, the aerodrome at MARDIN and any L. Gs. in the neighbourhood must be obtained and made available for our forces which will operate on an O.L.G. basis.

(d) Case "C"—Air support can be given from aerodromes in the DUCKSBILL.

(e) In all cases, the maximum delay will be caused to the enemy by the bombing of his Ls. of C. and other important targets which from time to time appear.

(f) *Forces available.*

	Max.	Min.
S.E.F.	12 sqns.	4 sqns.
T.E.F.	1 ,,	—
L.B.	9 ,,	1 ,,
A.C.	3 ,,	2 ,,
M.B.	4 ,,	1 ,,
H.B.	1 ,,	—
B.T.	4 ,,	1 ,,
G.R.	1 ,,	1 ,,
N.F.	2 ,,	½ ,,

These figures include squadrons for PERSIA and the Persian Gulf.

The minimum figure is arbitrary.

19. DEMOLITIONS

These will be treated under three main heads:—
   (a) Tactical demolitions affecting the conduct of the battle.
   (b) Demolitions to implement a "Scorched Earth" policy.
   (c) Demolitions to deny to the enemy the oil facilities.

Responsibility for preparing, ordering and controlling demolitions will be organised on a basis of Zones and Areas. Formations will be allotted certain Zones and Areas according to their general tasks outlined in this instruction. The boundaries of these Zones and Areas have been drawn so as to fit in with existing demolition schemes. 21 Ind. Corps will be responsible for sub-allotting the responsibility for execution of these prepared demolitions North of the line incl. LITTLE ZAB—incl. FATHA—excl. SAFRA. South of that line execution will be controlled by Tenth Army.

Detailed instructions concerning the preparation of schemes in addition to existing ones are being issued separately.

20. SECURITY

It is of paramount military and political importance that the strength and initial battle dispositions of our forces and our intentions should not be disclosed to anyone below First Grade Staff Officer or equivalent.

It is essential that the above mentioned information should not be known to the enemy, TURKEY, or to the local inhabitants (incl. British) because the enemy may be induced to attack now, thus driving TURKEY into submission and bringing about a serious internal security situation in IRAQ and possibly in PERSIA as well.

As an additional and especially necessary measure of SECURITY all letters on policy arising out of the operation instruction will be dealt with and signed only by the heads of services and branches. Subordinates will be given orders and not full and lengthy reasons for them.

21. ADM.

An adm. instruction will be issued shortly.

22. ACK.

Brigadier
General Staff.

APPENDIX 10

REORGANISATION OF COMMANDS IN IRAQ AND PERSIA

H.Q. Tenth Army
23 July 42.

1. The organisation of command in IRAQ and PERSIA is being adjusted so as to reduce the present wide commitments of TENTH ARMY. To this end:—

(a) Tenth Army is to assume responsibility for PERSIA as far SOUTH and EAST as the boundary given in para 5 below.

(b) Ninth Army is to take over responsibility for IRAQ NORTH of and excl. the general line KHANAKIN—RAMADI and a new command to be known as PERSIA, IRAQ Base and L. of C. Area (PIBAS) is being created.

(c) PIBAS is to assume responsibility for IRAQ SOUTH of and incl. general line KHANAKIN—RAMADI and for the base areas in SOUTH PERSIA. Detailed boundaries are given in para 5 below.

(d) An echelon of G.H.Q. M.E.F. is to be established at BASRA under an I.G.C. who will be known as I.G.C. PERSIA and IRAQ.

2. Comd. PIBAS will be responsible for the local administration, defence and internal security of the area allotted to his Comd. He will also be responsible for the maintenance of Political relations with H.M. Embassy, BAGHDAD.

3. The functions of the I.G.C. (subject to general supervision by G.H.Q. and their direction as to policy) are as follows:—

(a) Control of all ports, rail, and I.W.T. movement in IRAQ and PERSIA.

(b) Control of all general administrative agencies, depots, etc., in IRAQ and PERSIA.

(c) Control of the working of the administrative services and provision for the troops in IRAQ and PERSIA.

(d) The maintenance to rail and I.W.T. head or to Army Depots of all troops in IRAQ and PERSIA in accordance with the requirements of the Commanders.

(e) All administrative arrangements and negotiations with U.S., N.A.M. and Civil Corporations, e.g. U.K.C.C., A.I.O.C. and M.W.T.

    The I.G.C. may conduct such political discussion as may be necessary on administrative matters with H.M. Embassies to the PERSIAN and IRAQ Govts. direct with approval of Comd. TENTH ARMY and Comd. PIBAS, or through their Headquarters according to the subject.

4. Orders regarding date of transfer of responsibility and war establishments required are being issued by G.H.Q. It is anticipated that the reorganisation will be completed by mid-August.

Note: Ref. Map 1/M Sheets J 37, 38; I 38, 39, 40, 41; H 38, 39, 40, 41; G 39, 40, 41 and F 40.

5. BOUNDARIES

(a) These are shown in the attached tracing Appx. 'A' and include the revised Sub-area boundaries.

(b) Between TENTH ARMY and INDIA incl. INDIA general line 60° EAST, NORTHWARDS from PERSIAN Coast HAMUN I JAZ MURIAN—BAM—Rd. BAM KERMAN—(excl. INDIA) KERMAN—KHOI I MURGHAB—JUIMAN—MESHED.

(c) Between TENTH ARMY and NINTH ARMY all incl. TENTH ARMY. The frontier between PERSIA/IRAQ to the point when it meets the boundary of PERSIA/IRAQ Base and L. of C. Area.

(d) Between PIBAS and NINTH ARMY and TENTH ARMY. All incl. to PIBAS. BANDAR ABBAS—BUSHIRE—ANDIMESHK—KHANAKIN—RAMADI—WADI MAHOMEDI—thence due SOUTH to SAUDI ARABIAN frontier—SAUDI ARABIAN frontier to PERSIAN GULF, BAHREIN, MASIRA and RASS-EL-HADD will be included in PIBAS.

6. RE-ORGANISATION OF SUB-AREAS

The revised location of sub-areas as shown below will be completed in all cases by 15 Aug.

Present Sub Area and H.Q.	New area of responsibility & nomenclature	New location of H.Q.	Under Comd.
No. 1 Sub Area MOSUL	TEHERAN Sub Area	TEHERAN	TENTH ARMY
No. 2 Sub Area KIRKUK	KIRKUK Sub Area	KIRKUK	NINTH ARMY
No. 3 Sub Area KHANAKIN	KERMANSHAH Sub Area	KERMANSHAH	TENTH ARMY
No. 4 Sub Area BAGHDAD	BAGHDAD Sub Area	BAGHDAD	PIBAS
No. 5 Sub Area AHWAZ	AHWAZ Sub Area	AHWAZ	PIBAS
No. 6 Sub Area ABADAN	PERSIAN GULF Sub Area	ABADIN	PIBAS
No. 7 Sub Area SHUAIBA	SHUAIBA Sub Area	SHUAIBA	PIBAS

General boundaries are as shown in Appx. A. Details will be adjusted mutually.

(b) On completion of this re-organisation H.Q. L. of C. Area will cease to exist as such, and will form the basis from which H.Q. PIBAS will be formed.

7. R.A.F.

(a) A.O.C. IRAQ remains responsible for the operation and administration of the R.A.F. in the whole of IRAQ, PERSIA, PERSIAN GULF and the DUCKS BILL area to SYRIA.

(b) The responsibilities of A.O.C. LEVANT are confined to the LEVANT and SYRIA less the DUCKS BILL area.

(c) The operational boundary is:—

A.O.C. LEVANT incl. MALATYA excl. KARACLI DAGH (KARADJA DAGH) incl. HASSECHE (EL HASSEKE)—GARRET MOTTEB—thence SYRIAN—IRAQ frontier to ABU KEMAL—QASR MUHAIWIR—thence a line due SOUTH to frontier of SAUDI ARABIA.

8. RE-ALLOTMENT OF TROOPS

(a) The detailed order of battle of—
   (i) Tps. remaining under Comd. Tenth Army
   (ii) Tps. passing to Comd. Ninth Army
   (iii) Tps. passing to Comd. PIBAS
   is given in Appendix 'B'.

(b) TENTH Army retains the right to call on formations of 6 and 8 IND. DIVS. located in IRAQ, under NINTH Army and PIBAS, for planning and recce in PERSIA.

9. MOVES

The detail of moves required to implement this re-allotment will be carried out in accordance with movement orders issued separately.

10. ADMINISTRATION

Administrative instructions will be issued separately.

11. INTER COMMUNICATION

Location of H.Q.

When the re-organisation has been completed H.Qs will be located as below:—

H.Q. TENTH ARMY	KHURRUMABAD
H.Q. PERSIA IRAQ BASE ...	BAGHDAD
H.Q. I.G.C. ...	BASRA
H.Q. NINTH ARMY	MAIN H.Q. as detailed by Comd. NINTH ARMY Sub H.Q. to be established at KIRKUK.

Sd/
Brigadier
General Staff.

APPENDIX 11

5 IND. INF. BDE. OP. ORDER No. 1
5 June, 1941

1. INFORMATION
   Enemy. For order of Battle and dispositions see Appx. A.

2. OWN TPS.
   (a) 28 Bde. A.I.F. and 21 Bde. A.I.F. are crossing the frontier at 0200 hrs. D 1 at METULLA and RAS NAQURA respectively.
   (b) Objectives Aust. Corps
      (i) to secure rd. ACRE—SIDON.
      (ii) to secure Rds. EAST to WEST in the LEBANON.
      (iii) to exploit towards ISKANDARUN.
   (c) One S.S. Bn. will effect a landing to secure Br. over R. LITANI.

   3. (a) A mob. Free French Force, Comd. Gen. Le Gentilhomme, is arriving IRBID 0800 hrs. D 1.
   (b) On capture of Line EZRAA—SHEIKH MESKINE by 5 Ind. Inf. Bde. Gen. Le Gentilhomme's force is advancing on DAMASCUS.
   (c) Col. Collet's Cav. Regt. crossing the Frontier at KAFR HARIB at first light on D 1 day and is operating in area between SHEIKH MESKINE and KUNEITRA.

4. TPS. UNDER COMD.
   (a) T.J.F.F. are under comd. 5 Ind. Inf. Bde.
   (b) Two Tps. Lt. A.A. Bty. are under comd. 5 Ind. Inf. Bde. from D-1 day.

5. INTENTION
   5 Ind. Inf. Bde., assisted by T.J.F.F., will:—
   (a) Secure the line of the Ry. from incl. NASIB—EL HAMME.
   (b) Open the way for the movement of Free French Forces northwards towards DAMASCUS by capturing EZRAA, SHEIKH MESKINE and KUNEITRA.

6. METHOD
   Operations will be carried out in three phases:—
   Phase A. The securing of the line of the Ry. and the advance to DERAA, FIQ and KUNEITRA.
   Phase B. The capture of DERAA.
   Phase C. The capture of EZRAA and SHEIKH MESKINE.

PHASE A

7. THE BDE., LESS T.J.F.F., WILL ADVANCE IN FOUR COLNS.

8. COLN. A.
   (a) Comd. Lt.-Col. L. B. JONES, D.S.O., 4 Raj. Rif. Tps. 4 Raj. Rif. in attached M.T.
   One Pl. Bde. A.Tk. Coy.
   One Sec. 18 Fd. Coy.

   Note: Ref. Map LEVANT SERIES 1/200,000.

(b) Task to secure a line about 800 yards from the outskirts of DERAA covering the line incl. track and Ry. DERAA—GHAZALE to track and Ry. DERAA—MUZEIRIB.

This line will be secured by 0500 hrs. D.1. day, and its occupation reported by code word TRICYCLE.

(c) Route MAFRAQ—EL BOWEIDA—ER RUMTHA—TURRA—cross tracks S.W. MZERIB STA—YADOUDE—DERAA.

(d) 4 Raj. Rif. will time their advance so that their tail clears ER RUMTHA by 0100 hrs.

(e) 4 Raj. Rif. will also be responsible for the capture of the Ry. Stn. at MZERIB and the Ry. Bridge at TELL CHEHAB until relieved by T.J.F.F. (see para 12 (a)). Two offrs of the Free French Forces will be attached to 4 Raj. Rif. to assist in this operation.

9. COLN. B.

(a) Will consist of all Tps. less those in colns A, C and D. For composition, Comd. and order to march see appx. B.

(b) Task 3/1 Punjab—To secure a line about 800 yards from the outskirts of DERAA covering the line incl. road DERAA-BASRA to track ER RUMTHA—DERAA.

This line will be secured by 0500 hrs, and its occupation reported by code word TANDEM.

(c) Route IRBID—ER RUMTHA—DERAA.

(d) All Tps. will be in M.T.

10. COLN. C.

(a) Comd. O.C., Coy. 1 R.F.
Tps. One Coy. 1 R.F. by march route.
Det. 18 Fd. Coy.

(b) Task—To secure the high ground in area EL'AL—FIQ, in order to deny to the enemy access to the Western portion of the Ry.

(c) Route—SAMAKH—KAFR HARIB—FIQ.

(d) FIQ will be occupied by 0530 hrs. and its occupation reported by code word BIKE.

11. COLN. D.

(a) Comd.—Lt.-Col. A.D.G. ORR, 1 R.F.
Tps.—1 R.F. (less one coy.)
One Pl. (British) Bde. A Tk. Coy.
11 Fd. Bty. (less one tp.)
One sec. 18 Fd. Coy. (less det with Coln. C)
Det 14 Fd. Amb.
9 Fd. Bty., A.I.F. (see sub-para f)

(b) Task—To capture and hold KUNEITRA.

(c) Route—SAMAKH—TIBERIAS—ROSH PINNA—JISR BENETT YACOUB—KUNEITRA.

(d) KUNEITRA will be reached by 0500 hrs. and its occupation reported by code word SCOOTER.

(e) All Tps. will be in MT.

(f) 9 Fd. Bty. will join coln. D at TIBERIAS *en route*, and will revert to and rejoin its own formation on capture of KUNEITRA.

12. T.J.F.F.

   (a) Will
      (i) secure all Ry. bridges and stations on the Ry. (excl. DERAA) from incl. frontier at JABIR—incl. EL HAMME.
      (ii) watch and patrol the line of the Ry. within these boundaries to prevent damage and sabotage by hostile elements.

   (b) For this purpose the Ry. will be divided into two main Sectors:—
      Sector 1. incl. JABIR—incl. WADI SHALLALA (but excl. DERAA itself) will be responsibility of mechanized Cav. Regt. with H.Q. at RUMTHA.
      Sector 2. Excl. WADI SHALLALA—incl. EL HAMME will be responsibility of Horsed Cav. Regt. with H.Q. at SAMAR.

   (c) The occupation of the line of the Ry. at NASIB and from excl. TELL CHEHAB—incl. EL HAMME will be effective as soon as possible after 0200 hrs. and its completion reported by code word PRAM.

The occupation of DERAA Station and the remainder of the Ry. line will not be undertaken until after the capture of DERAA, except that MZERIB STA and the bridge at TELL CHEHAB will be taken over from the 4 Raj. Rifs. at 0500 hrs. D 1 day.

13. ARTY.

   (a) 1 Fd. Regt. (less one tp.) will come into action in support of attack on DERAA astride track RUMTHA—DERAA immediately S.W. of frontier ready to engage enemy at 0530 hrs. Fire will NOT be opened without orders from Bde. H.Q.

   (b) An F.O.O. with each of 4 Raj. Rif. and 3/1 Punjab.

   (c) The two tps. Lt. A.A. Bty. will protect the area of Bde. H.Q. and 1 Fd. Regt. from 0530 hrs. D 1 day until capture of DERAA. For subsequent roles see under Phase C.

14. R.E.

18 Fd. Coy. less dets with colns A, C and D will remain in reserve at Bde. H.Q. until after capture of DERAA when it will move into the town and restore communications, repair demolitions and take over the water supply under orders of O.C., 3/1 Punjab.

15. R.A.F.

No direct or immediate support is available. A limited number of fighters and bombers will be available at call through Bde. H.Q. if urgently required. An A.I.L.O. will be attached to Bde. H.Q. upto end of Phase C, when he will be transferred to Free French Forces.

16. DESTRUCTION OF COMNS WITH DERAA

   (a) Two parties each consisting of the following in civilian lorries:—
      One officer T.J.F.F.
      One English speaking Sig. from Bde. H.Q.
      One English speaking Indian Sapper from 18 Fd. Coy. four men T.J.F.F.
will cut all Tele. comns leading out of DERAA by 0100 hrs. on D 1 day, under instructions to be issued separately to comds. personally.

   (b) The exchange at RUMTHA will be taken over by personnel Bde. Sig. Sec. at 0100 hrs. D 1 day.

17. CROSSING OF THE FRONTIER

(a) The Civil authorities are arranging to close the Frontier.

(b) Leading elements of Colns. A, B and C and dets of T.J.F.F. will all cross the frontier simultaneously at 0200 hrs. D 1 day, and will proceed to objectives at best possible speed compatible with secrecy and surprise.

(c) Fire will NOT be opened before 0500 hrs. D 1 day. All opposition which cannot be overcome by persuasion will be dealt with by the bayonet.

18. GUIDES

T.J.F.F. will provide one offr. to each of colns A, C and D as guides and liaison officers. They will join units on D 1 day and remain with them throughout operations.

PHASE B

19. CAPTURE OF DERAA

(a) At 0515 hrs. D 1 day a flag of Truce under Major H. S. J. BOURKE, 1 Fd. Regt. accompanied by an offr. of the Free French Forces and Mr. FOOT, will proceed from Bde. H.Q. to DERAA by car to demand the surrender of the town within a specified period of time.

(b) If this is successful tps. will act as in Phase C.

(c) If not successful, an intense bombardment (after registration) of the town and defences will be carried out by 1 Fd. Regt. and unit mortars as under:—
    Z to Z+10. H.E. Rapid.
    Z+10 to Z+15 Smoke
During this period the Inf. will advance to assaulting distance.

(d) On the conclusion of the arty. programme the Inf. will assault the town and occupy all Key points using the minimum force possible.

PHASE C

20. SUBSEQUENT OPERATIONS

(a) After the capture of the town the following Tps. will assemble about ATAMAN in M.T. under the Comd. of Lt.-Col. L. B. JONES, D.S.O., 4 Raj. Rif. and proceed forthwith to SHEIKH MESKINE.
    4 Raj. Rif. and attached Tps. (Coln. A)
    52 Bty. 1 Fd. Regt.
    One Tp. Lt. A.A. Bty.
    Det. 14 Fd. Amb.

(b) After capture of SHEIKH MESKINE a small garrison will be left there, the remainder of the Force proceeding to capture and hold EZRAA.

(c) It is expected that the Free French Forces will pass through SHEIKH MESKINE towards DAMASCUS about 1000 hrs. D 1 day.

52 Bty. and one Tp. A.A. Bty. will come under comd. Free French Forces as they pass through SHEIKH MESKINE.

21. 3/1 Punjab with following Tps. under comd. will hold DERAA with particular reference to air borne attack, and ground attack from the direction of BASRA:
>3/1 Punjab
>Bde. A/Tk. Coy. (less two Pls.)
>One Tp. 1 Fd. Regt.
>One Tp. Lt. A.A. Bty.
>18 Fd. Coy. (less two Secs.)
>One Coy. 14 Fd. Amb. (less dets.).

Administrative

22. LOCATIONS; ADM. UNITS AND L.O.B. PERSONNEL

Following units less specified dets. move to previously recced. areas near IRBID water point by 0800 hrs. D 1:—
>Rear Bde. H.Q.
>All 'B' Echs. (except 1 R.F.)
>5 Ind. Inf. Bde. Gp. M.T. Coy.
>14 Fd. Amb.
>17 Mob. Wkshop. Coy.
>Ord. Fd. Pk. Sec.

Routes to unit areas from main rd. and RUMTHA TRACK will be clearly sign posted.

L.O.B. personnel of all units except 1 R.F. will also concentrate in this area, concentration to be completed by march route by 0800 hrs. D 1 except in the case of 4 Raj. Rif. Major D. I. MORRISON, 3/1 Punjab will comd. L.O.B. personnel concentrated at IRBID, and will arrange to collect L.O.B. personnel of 4 Raj. Rif. from MAFRAQ in returned Tp. Carrying Tpt. as soon as available on D 1.

L.O.B. personnel 1 R.F. will move under senior L.O.B. offr. to JISR EL MAJAMIE by march route by 1000 hrs. D 1, where they will be att. to D.I.D. for sups.

23. TENTS, ACC., STORES AND BAGGAGES

L.O.B. parties will be responsible for closing tents, acc. stores and baggage left by units in present areas into L.O.B. concentration areas, where unit dumps will be established and guarded by 1800 hrs. D 1.

24. ATT. TPT.

2nd line M.T. of 5 Ind. Inf. Bde. Gp. M.T. Coy. will report to units as shown in Appx. C and D 1. Of the above, six 3-tonners may be retained with each unit until further orders: all other att. tpt. except coln. D must be released immediately on completion of task, to return to M.T. Coy.

25. AMN.

Amn. vehicles earmarked for Bde. Reserve will report to B.O.W.O. at Rear Bde. H.Q. from units except 1 R.F. by 0700 hrs. D 1.

A.P. for Colns. A, B and C is located immediately NORTH of T.J.F.F. barracks IRBID. A.P. for Coln. D is at A.R.H. JISR EL MAJAMIE.

1,200 Anti Tank mines are available at IRBID A.P. on demand.

26. SUPS.

Units at present hold 3 days H.S. (reserve) supplies. 2 days supplies will be returned to Sup. Pt. for surrender by 1200 hrs. D 1.

7 days H.S. (battle) supplies for this Bde. Gp. are dumped at IRBID.
Fresh rations will be drawn by units in the normal way from Sup. Pt. upto and including rations for consumption D 1 (*i.e.* drawn on D 1). In addition 1 days H.S. (battle) ration will be drawn on D 1.

Rations as follows will accompany units:—

On the man	cooked rations for consumption D 1
In unit A Ech.	remaining 1 day's H.S. (reserve) rations, as unit reserve.
In unit B Ech. (cook trucks)	1 day's H.S. (battle) ration, for consumption D 2.

Remaining dump of 6 days' H.S. (battle) and 2 days surrendered H.S. (reserve) rations will be drawn on by Sup. Sec. as S.R.P. for subsequent daily maintenance.

M.Ps. for Colns. A and B for drawing supplies for consumption subsequent to D 2 will be notified by signal.

Colns. C and D will be based direct on D.I.D. JISR EL MAJAMIE and F.S.D. at ROSH PINNA respectively.

27. P.O.L.

Units will proceed with full tanks and maximum vehicle reserve P.O.L. loads. P.O.L. vehicles will accompany A Echs.

P.Ps. are located immediately EAST of T.J.F.F. barracks IRBID, and at ROSH PINNA (for Colns. C and D).

Location of subsequent P.Ps. will be notified by signal.

28. WATER

Unit water vehicles will accompany A Echs.

Water Pt. for Colns. A and B is located 1 mile NORTH of T.J.F.F. barracks IRBID. Subsequent changes of location will be signalled.

Water Pt. for Colns. C and D are at SAMAKH and ROSH PINNA respectively.

18 Fd. Coy. S & M will be prepared to exploit suitable water sources.

29. R.E.

R.E. R.H. will be at KHIRYAT MOTZKIN. (HAIFA). Brigade repair materials will be obtainable there from 2/5 Fd. Pk. Coy. R.A.E.

Limited quantities of Dannert and Barbed wire are available at R.E. Stores IRBID on demand.

30. MEDICAL

Medical formations as under will form chain of evacuation. (See Appx. D).

With or At	Formation	Found by
Coln. A	R.A.P.	R.A.P. 4 Raj. Rif. with det. 14 Fd. Amb. (2 cars)
Coln. B	A.D.S.	A. Coy. 14 Fd. Amb.
Coln. C	R.A.P.	Det. 14 Fd. Amb. (A/S, nursing orderly)
Coln. D	R.A.P.	R.A.F. 1 R.F. with det 14 Fd. Amb. (2 cars)
IRBID	M.D.S.	14 Fd. Amb. (less A. Coy. and 4 cars) with det. Aust. M.A.C. (10 cars)
KINNERET	S.S.	12 I.S.S.
NAZARETH	C.C.S.	2/1 Aust. C.C.S.

31. VEHICLE RECOVERY

Unit L.A.Ds. will accompany A Echs.

L.R.S. will open 1st Line Recovery Post 2 miles WEST of ER RUMTHA, on rd. ER RUMTHA—IRBID, by 0600 hrs. D 1.

3rd Line Recovery will be by 1 Cav. Div. Ord. Wkshop. MAFRAQ.

32. PRISONERS OF WAR

P.W. taken during Phases A and B will be evacuated in returning-empty tp. carrying tpt. or other M.T. to P.W. Cage at T.J.F.F. barracks IRBID, whence they will be collected by Corps. Guard for this cage will be found under orders O.C., L.O.B. personnel from 0700 hrs. D 1. Separate cages will be constructed for senior officers, junior officers, French O.Rs., native O.Rs. and Germans.

P.W. taken by Colns. C and D will be evacuated to P.W. Collecting Park, YORK DRAGOONS lines, ROSH PINNA.

Location of P.W. Collecting Parks for subsequent phases will be notified by signal.

Notes for guidance on contact with French troops are attached (Appx. E).

33. REQUISITIONING

No requisitioning of supplies will take place without direct authority of Force H.Q., obtained through this H.Q.

Accommodation and other services will only be requisitioned in exceptional circumstances, through the local Civil Authority, by one officer specially detailed by name as Coln. Requisitioning Officer by Coln. Comds.

34. INTERCOMN.

(a) Adv. Bde. H.Q. will open near ARAB LEGION FORT NORTH of RUMTHA at 0330 hrs.

(b) On capture of DERAA will move to DERAA.

(c) Rear Bde. H.Q. will move to water point in IRBID defences by 0700 hrs.

(d) T.J.F.F. H.Q. opens IRBID D 1.

35. W/T.

(a) One W/T. set allotted to each 1 R.F., 3/1 Punjab and 4 Raj. Rif. and Coln. C.

(b) One W/T. set attached Bde. H.Q. for comn. to Force H.Q.

(c) One W/T. set T.J.F.F. attached Bde. H.Q. for Comn. to T.J.F.F.

(d) W/T. sets mentioned in (b) and (c) will report Bde. H.Q. by 1700 hrs D 1.

(e) *Frequencies.* Will be allotted later.

(f) Wireless silence will be observed till 0500 hrs. D 1 except in great emergency.

(f) *R.A.F. tender.*

36. L.Os.

(a) Unit L.Os. will report Bde. H.Q. at 1700 hrs. D 1.

(b) One Free French Officer will be attached to each coln. as a L.O. on D 1 day.

Sd/-
Maj.
B.M.

Time of signature 0200

APPENDIX A TO 5 IND. INF. BDE. OPERATION ORDER NO. 1
5 June 41

ORDER OF BATTLE OF FRENCH TROOPS IN SYRIA
(as known on 3 June 1941)

(A) FRONTIER AREA

 (i) BASRA   one coy. Senegalese Troops

 (ii) DERAA   one coy. LEVANT Troops
      two sqns. Moroccan Sepahis
      two 75 mm. and one 47 mm. guns.
      (A/Tk. role)

 (iii) EZRAA   one coy. Levant Troops
      one coy. Sappers

 (iv) SHEIKH MESKINE   one Bn. Senegalese
      one sec. 75 mm. guns (two)

 (v) KUNEITRA   one Bn. Senegalese
      one coy. Foreign Legion
       (a) one sec. M.Gs.
       (b) one sec. riflemen
       (c) one gp. 25 mm. A/Tk. guns
        (rifles ?)
      one sqn. Lt. Tanks (21)
      one sqn. Armd. Cs.
      (approx. 15 6-8 tonners)
      one Bty. Colonial Arty.
       two 65 mm. guns
       two 105 mm. guns

 (vi) Detachments and posts are believed to exist at the following places:—

   (a) NASSIB   25 morrocans from DERAA.
   (b) YADOUDE   34 —do—
   (c) MZERIB   20 —do—
   (d) TELL CHEHAB   30 —do—
   (e) MAKARENE   strength unknown.
   (f) FIQ   one coy. Senegalese from KUNEITRA.
   (g) JISR BENETT YACOUB   one sec. of SENEGALESE from KUNEITRA.
   (h) NERANE   one coy. Senegalese from KUNEITRA.
   (i) EL ALLEGA ...   one sec. —do—
   (j) TELL ABOU NIDA   Arty. in posn. —do—
   (k) AIN ZIOUANE   probably two coys. Senegalese from KUNEITRA.
   (l) DJOU KHADAC   half coy. Senegalese one 37 mm. gun. from KUNEITRA.
   (m) JAZSSAA   two coys. Senegalese from A.F.Vs.

(B) JEBEL DRUZE

Two Bns. Infantry
Four sqns. Cavalry } at the following places:—
Some Armd. Cs.

    (a) SOUEIDA   one sqn. Cavalry.
                                 two tps. armd. Cs. (8).
                                 possibly one bn. Infantry.

    (b) SALKHAD   one coy. Infantry.

    (c) GHAHBA   one sqn. Cavalry.
                                 one coy. Infantry.

    (d) RHARIYE   one sqn. Cavalry.

(C) DAMASCUS

Five Bns. Infantry.
One Gp. Cavalry.
Three Btys. 105 mm. guns.
One A.A. Bty.

(D) BEYROUTH

Four Bns. Infantry.
Three sqns. Cavalry.
One Gp. A.F.Vs.
Two Btys. Arty.
Four A.A. Btys.

(E) N. PALESTINE FRONTIER AREA

Five Bns. Infantry.
Four Sqns. Cavalry.

APPENDIX 12

IRAQ FORCE OPERATION INSTRUCTION NO. 6
21 June 1941

To
Major General Slim,
   Comd. 10 Ind. Div.

1. You will concentrate a force at HADITHA as soon as possible with a view to moving up R. EUPHRATES to ALEPPO, taking part in the operations now being carried out in SYRIA.

2. Secrecy is of great importance. The code name for the operation is DEFICIENT.

3. You will command the operation and will establish your adv. H.Q. in the first place at HADITHA. You will come under the orders of MILPAL from the time of your arrival at HADITHA, which you will notify to all concerned. Your force will continue to be maintained by BRITMIL IRAQ. 20 Inf. Bde. at MOSUL will remain under your comd.

4. Your force will be composed and initially disposed, as shown in att. Appx. A.

5. The force will be entirely carried in M.T. There will be no marching tps. All M.T. resources available at BASRA and BAGHDAD will be placed at your disposal at once and you will ensure that the most economical use is made of them. Adequate W/S facilities will be provided by Force H.Q. A high standard of driving and maintenance must be ensured.

Appx. B att. shows an M.T. allotment for tp. carrying which has been shown by experience to be more than adequate.

6. A.O.C. IRAQ is providing one Fighter Sqn. under your comd. from the time of your arrival at HADITHA. This Sqn. will operate initially from HADITHA and later from DEIR EZ ZOR.

7. Particular attention will be paid to A.A. defence. All available tracer ammunition is being sent to you at once. As no A.A. guns are available, the possibility of engaging aircraft with 18 pr. shrapnel will be considered.

8. You will send 15 days sup. and pet. and as much amn. as possible to HADITHA forthwith. A.Q.M.G. Force H.Q. will visit your H.Q. today to coordinate all administrative arrangements.

9. Force Sigs. are providing you with one long range W/T set and det., and are arranging for two 101 sets to be loaned to you by H.Q. 17 Inf. Bde.

H.Q. MILPAL is at JERUSALEM.

As far as possible wireless silence will be maintained until contact.

10. Maps are expected to be issued shortly.

Ack.

                                        Sd/- C. H. Boucher.
                                                Brig:
                                                G.S.

Note: Ref: Maps, 1/1,000,000 NORTH I-37—I-38
                                NORTH J-37—J-38

APPENDIX 'A' TO IRAQ FORCE OPERATION INSTRUCTION NO. 6

COMPOSITION OF COLUMNS, FORCE DEFICIENT

Adv. Div. H.Q.

Striking Force.
H.Q. one Inf. Bde. with Sigs., Empl. Pl., Bde. Tpt. Coy.
Three Inf. Bns.
13 L., with sec. Wkshop. Coy.
One Fd. Regt. R.A.
One Fd. coy. S & M.
One G.P. Tpt. Coy.
One mob. Wkshop. Coy.
One Fd. Amb.
Fd. P.O.

L. of C. HADITHA to DEIR EZ ZOR.
H.Q. one Inf. Bde., with Sigs., Empl. Pl. and Bde. Tpt. Coy.
Three Inf. Bns.
One A/Tk. Regt.
One sec. Fd. coy S & M and det. Fd. Park Coy.
One G.P. Tpt. Coy.
One mob. Wkshop. Coy.
One Fd. Amb.
Fd. P.O.

APPENDIX 'B' TO IRAQ FORCE OPERATION INSTRUCTION NO. 6

1. *To lift one complete Inf. Bn.*
    Unit tpt. plus 30 3-ton lorries
    H.Q. coy. 6
    4 rifle coys. at 6 = $\frac{24}{30}$

2. *To lift Fd. amb.*
    UNIT tpt. plus four 3-ton lorries.

3. To motorise one bn. in each bde. in order to make it more mobile *i.e.* no 3-ton lorries, see notes just issued by G.H.Q. India issued under 131/2/G of 20/6/41.

APPENDIX 13

21st INDIAN INFANTRY BRIGADE OPERATION ORDER No. 9

29 June 1941

INFORMATION

1. Intelligence Summary Appx. "A" Att.

2. No enemy ground tps. have been located in or South of DEIR EZ ZOR by air recce. A few trenches appear to exist South of DEIR EZ ZOR but no signs of life.

3. Enemy aircraft have bombed ABU KEMAL 28 and 29 June. It is to be anticipated enemy aircraft will be active and make frequent attacks to delay adv.

4. Under Comd:—
   127 Fighter Sqn. R.A.F.
   Det. 10 Div. Sigs.
   13 L.
   157 Fd. Regt.
   9 Fd. Coy.
   29 Fd. Amb.
   Det. 7 M.S.
   16 Mob. W/S. Coy.
   21 Ind. Inf. Bde. Tpt. Coy.
   35 G.P.T. Coy.
   17 Ind. Inf. Bde. Tpt. Coy.
   25 Ind. Inf. Bde. Tpt. Coy.

INTENTION

5. 21 Ind. Inf. Bde. Gp. will:—
   (a) Capture and occupy DEIR EZ ZOR.
   (b) Deal with any French Forces encountered.
   (c) Defeat and drive off any irregular forces such as those under FAWZI QAWUKJI which may appear.

METHOD

Phase 1

6. On the afternoon of 30 Jun. 2/4 G.R. less two Coys. with under Comd. a Sqn. 13 L will move out from ABU KEMAL to line of WADI ES SAWAB astride of rd. ABU KEMAL—DEIR EZ ZOR.

7. They will hold this posn. till 21 Ind. Inf. Bde. Gp. less dets. have passed through on 1 Jul.

Phase 2

8. Colns as under will move fwd. on 30 Jun. at 10 v.t.m. and 15 m.i.h.

Note: Ref. Maps 1/1,000,000 I 37 & 38
1" to 4 miles I 38 J, L & K
1/200,000 NI 37-XVII & XXIII

Nibe Coln

9. Comd. Lt. Col. H St. J Carruthers.
10. Tps.   One Tp. 4. 5 Hows. 157 Fd. Regt.
                   9 Fd. Coy. less two secs.
                   2/10 G.R.
                   One Coy. 29 Fd. Amb.
11. Will move from K 3 to ABU KEMAL.
12. Route   K 3—TRIPOLI PIPELINE to T.I.—AL QAIN—ABU KEMAL.
   S.P.   Junc. of Pipe Lines 5 miles S.W. of K 3
   S.T. ...   0430 hrs. To be clear of S.P. by 0600 hrs.
13. They will halt dispersed North of ABU KEMAL and clear of WADI RALQA (South of ABU KEMAL) night 30 Jun/1 Jul.

Puna Coln

14. Comd. Lt. Col. S.K. Furney M.C.
15. Tps.   13 L less one Sqn.
                   One Tp. 18 Pdr. 157 Fd. Regt.
                   Sec. 9 Fd. Coy.
                   4 F.F. Rif.
                   Coy. 29 Fd. Amb.
                   Det. M.A.S. (two Ambs.).
                   Det. 21 Ind. Inf. Bde. Tpt. Coy. (Amn., Pet. and Supplies).
                   R.A.F. Ground Party (as far as T 1 only).
16. Approx. number of vehicles 200.
17. Will move from K 3 to T 2 on 30 Jun.
18. Route   K-3—Track running South of HAIFA Pipeline to mile post 168 (about 19 miles from K 3) T 1—TRIPOLI Pipeline—T-2.
   S.P.   Rd. leading off S.W. from West gate.
   S.T. ...   0600 hrs. To be clear by 0730 hrs.
19. Halt for refill of water at T 1 before moving on to halt vicinity T 2 night 30 Jun/1 Jul. Halt will be South of Pipeline to keep clear of colns. moving along Pipeline.

Bde H.Q. Gp

20. Bde. H.Q.
C.R.A. will move from K 3 to ABU KEMAL behind NIBE Coln.
21. Approx. number of vehicles 50.
22. S.P.   West gate.
    S.T.   0730 hrs. to be clear by 0800 hrs.

Fund Coln

23. Comd. Major RODWELL R.A.
24. Tps.   157 Fd. Regt. less one bty.
                   Two Coys. 2/4 G.R.
                   29 Fd. Amb. less two Coys.
                   7 M.A.S.
                   Sec. 9 Fd. Coy.
25. Approx. number of vehicles 225.

26. Will move to vicinity of ABU KEMAL same route as for NIBE Coln.

27. S.P.   as for NIBE Coln.
    S.T.   ...   0815 hrs. to be clear of S.P. by 1000 hrs.

28. Halt dispersed behind NIBE Coln. on night 30 Jun/1 Jul.

TPT COLN "A"

29. 21 Bde. Tpt. Coy. less det. with PUNA Coln. Approx. number of vehicles 80.

30. S.P.   as for NIBE Coln.
    S.T.   1015 hrs. to be clear by 1100 hrs.
    Route   as for NIBE Coln.

TPT. COLN. "B"

30A. Comd.   Senior Tpt. Coy. Comd. to Comd.
     Tps.   17 Bde. Tpt. Coy.
                  25 Bde. Tpt. Coy.
                  501 G.P.T. Coy.
                  16 Mob. W/S Coy. less dets.

Will move to T 1 route as for PUNA Coln. and halt there 30 Jun/1 Jul. Approx. number of vehicles 185.

30B. Tpt. Coys. on arrival will revert to Comd. 10 Div.
    S.P.   as for PUNA Coln.
    S.T.   1045 hrs. to be clear by 1230 hrs.

Phase 3

31. On 1 Jul. Colns. will move as follows:—
    NIBE Coln. ...   Will pass through 2/4 G.R. position on WADI ES SAWAB not later than 0530 hrs. A Sqn. 13 L will come under Comd. NIBE.

32. Tasks   (a) To seize MAYADINE as quickly as possible.
                      (b) Thereafter to seize DEIR EZ ZOR as quickly as possible.

33. FUND Coln.   Will join up with 2/4 G.R. (Less two Coys.) after NIBE Coln. have passed through 2/4 G.R. posn.

34. Lt.-Col. Weallens will then assume Comd. FUND Coln.

35. Task   Will follow one hour behind NIBE Coln. as reserve.

36. PUNA Coln.   Will move from T 2 directed on DEIR EZ ZOR but will be prepared on orders of Bde. Comd. to move towards river EUPHRATES should NIBE or FUND meet opposition.

37. Comd. PUNA Coln. will issue orders for move of 13 L on wide front and be prepared for them to revert to Comd. H.Q. 21 Ind. Inf. Bde. at short notice.

R.A.F.

38. On 30 Jun Approximately one hour after head of coln. passes T 1 which time will be signalled by R.A.F. at T 1 to K 3 standing patrol of one Hurricane followed by two GLADIATORS will be found for a period of four hours.

39. A second standing patrol of two aircraft will be found from 1630 hrs. until dusk.

ADM—MED.
 40. 30 Jun.
  (a) PUNA Coln.
   All sick and wounded will be evacuated to T 1 by det. 7 M.A.S.
  (b) NUFA less PUNA Coln.
   All sick and wounded will be evacuated to 29 Fd. Amb. from where they will be evacuated to T 1 by det. 7 M.A.S.

41. 7 M.A.S. will concentrate at T 1 by 1900 hrs. 30 Jun at which time they will revert to 10 Div. Coln. Coms. will ensure that these dets. are despatched in time to arrive T 1 by 1900 hrs.

1 JUL.

42. All sick and wounded will be evacuated to 29 Fd. Amb. Div. is arranging normal rearward evacuation.

RECOVERY

43. All vehicle casualties will be evacuated to 16 Mob. W/S Coy. at T 1.

44. 16 Mob. W/S Coy. will detail one recovery sec. to each PUNA, NIBE and FUND.

TPT.

45. On 30 Jun. "B" Ech. will move grouped with their respective Colns. under orders of Coln. Comd.

46. On 1 Jul. "B" Ech. of NUFA less PUNA will be Brigaded and will move in rear of FUND Coln.

47. "B" Ech. of PUNA Coln. will move under orders of Coln. Comd.

SUPPLIES

48. Cooked midday meal plus at least one days uncooked ration will be carried by all units.

49. 21 Bde. Tpt. Coy. will carry three days rations. One fourth of his total stock of rations, pet and amn. will accompany PUNA Coln.

50. One days ration for 1/2 Jul. will be issued on arrival at tomorrows camps.

INTERCOMN.

 51. One 101 set to NIBE
  One 101 set to PUNA
  One 101 set to FUND
  One No. 9 set from Div. Sigs. accompanies Bde. H.Q. for Comn. to 13 L and landing ground.
  One F.S. 6 set accompanies Bde. H.Q. for Comn. to Adv. Div. H.Q.
  One R.T. tender accompanies Bde. H.Q. for Comn. with Aircraft in the air.

A/Maj.
B.M.

APPENDIX 14

LESSONS FROM THE OPERATIONS OF 10 IND. DIV. IN SYRIA[1]

TACTICAL

Mobility

The chief lesson from these operations was the tactical advantage that can be gained from the full and bold use of a completely motorised force. To gain this advantage movement must be bold and risks must be accepted. Thus, had the turning movement at Deir ez Zor been directed merely against a flank down the Palmyra road, it would have met with stubborn resistance; sent wide to the west and coming in from the north on the French rear, it achieved complete surprise and led to the capture of almost the whole of the enemy's guns, ammunition and transport.

Initiative

Mobility is of little use unless commanders, even junior commanders, are prepared to show initiative and act without waiting for orders from above. All commanders must be taught to react quickly to changes in the tactical situation. There is sometimes a tendency to inertness when action is needed. The pursuit on the left bank after the capture of the town was slow in starting and a chance of overtaking the only two enemy guns that escaped was lost. There was also the case of an Indian Officer who, meeting a superior number of French Armoured Cars, wirelessed to his commander to ask what he should do, thereby allowing the enemy cars to escape. On the other hand there were instances of drive and initiative, notably that of the column sent to intercept the French retreating from the north-east of Syria, which boldly and at great speed covered 200 miles from Deir ez Zor and drove the enemy across the Euphrates at Djerablous.

Air Attack

Even a small mobile force such as a brigade group has anything up to 800 vehicles, which in desert country however scattered, whether on the move or at the halt, offer a tremendous target to the air.

The force advancing on Deir ez Zor was opposed by a greatly superior air force. After the capture of the town our own small fighter contingent was either shot down or unable to operate in face of overwhelming numbers and more modern aircraft. The French, as the threat to Aleppo developed, concentrated their air heavy bombing and machine-gun attacks. It was evident that, even if resort were made to moving only at night, which saves casualties to men but not to vehicles, this scale of unanswered air attack would soon threaten to bring the advance to a stand still, if for no other reason, owing to the actual casualties to vehicles. Luckily the French confined their attack to the forward troops in an attempt to hold up the advance, and neglected the even more vulnerable administrative organization in rear.

[1] Summary of the operations for the capture of Deir ez Zor and the Euphrates Province between 30 June and 12 June 1941 by Major-General W. J. Slim, Commander 10th Indian Division.

The actual number of casulties was not high but the effect of constant air attack on morale, especially in certain administrative units whose personnel were untrained and largely unarmed, was serious and might, if combined with a vigorous ground attack, have been disastrous.

The lessons which stand out from this are two:—
  (i) It is unfair and unwise to push forward mechanised columns without adequate air support.
  (ii) Troops must in peace training be accustomed to low flying attacks by real aircraft.

Dispersion

Extreme dispersion (200 yards between vehicles) was forced on units by the scale of air attack. This rendered protection against ground attack, as was shown in the night affair at Raqqa, most difficult. Dispersion was in fact overdone. Dispersion in a unit area need not be more than 100 yards between vehicles but it is advisable, when tactically possible, to have considerable distances (500 to 1000 yards) between unit areas. If closer, an attack on one unit has an adverse moral effect on its neighbours who see the damage and casualties, and feel they are being attacked themselves. The lesson is that over dispersion in a unit can be as dangerous as under dispersion.

ARMAMENT

A.F.Vs.

The armoured cars of 13 Lancers were always singled out for low flying attack, whereas, it has been reported, the Marmon Harrington cars of the Royals were rather avoided by the French fighters. The reason for this was that each Marmon Harrington carries a vickers gun on an A.A. mounting while the Chevrolets have only a poorly mounted V.B. gun in an occasional car. Every A.F.V. should have an A.A. machine-gun.

In addition, every A.F.V., if it is going to meet other A.F.Vs. even of the lightest kind, must have some form of A/Tk weapon. It is not enough to have one A/Tk rifle per section. The .303 ammunition should be all either A.P. or tracer.

Transport Drivers

Most of the R.I.A.S.C. and I.A.O.C. drivers in the division and attached to it were unarmed. These men had to drive their vehicles for hundreds of miles through desert infested with Arabs on the lookout for loot. Many instances occurred of hold-ups and sniping. These men should be armed and trained to use their arms. The difficulty was met, with considerable success, by arming them with captured French rifles.

ADMINISTRATIVE

Amount of transport

The outstanding lesson on the administrative side was the necessity for keeping the number of vehicles with brigade groups down to a minimum. Actual fighting formations must be freed from the embarrassment of an unwieldy administrative tail. Administrative units should be kept well back, suitable arrangements being made to call them forward as may be required.

Traffic Control

If moves of 100 miles per day are undertaken, the standard organization for supply and for traffic control of a fully mobile force becomes impracticable. At few places is it possible to mark the route, instal communications or to provide traffic-control personnel. Units have got to find their own way. Several moves had to be carried out in thick dust storms with a visibility of not more than ten yards; such conditions mean that junior N.C.Os. must be able to find their own way. During the period of operations not a single vehicle failed to reach its destination through losing its way.

Recovery

Recovery over these big distances becomes a very difficult problem. The recovery vehicles available were quite insufficient to deal with the number of broken down vehicles. The problem was increased by many of the break down lorries themselves breaking down and by enemy action. More recovery vehicles are required and R.I.A.S.C. companies should have workshops, including recovery vehicles, of their own.

Petrol Consumption

In the initial advance on Deir ez Zor petrol consumption was far higher than was anticipated. This increase was due to a heavy duststorm which forced vehicles to travel slowly and to follow clearly defined but less good tracks in which there was much soft sand. A heavy wastage in petrol carried in 4-gallon tins must also be anticipated. Consumption worked out at 7 miles per gallon per vehicle.

Establishment of Vehicles

The transport for a division allows no margin for additional personnel and stores which are always likely to have to be carried. In practically the whole of the Mideast theatres of war it is essential to carry reserves of petrol and water. Interpreters, Political Officers, Publicity Officers and Tribal Officers are nearly always necessary; these all have to be transported with their servants and baggage, and messing arrangements made. The establishment of a division should take these factors into account and allow a more ample scale of transport equipment. In eastern theatres also tentage is nearly always necessary and transport must be provided for it.

Spare Parts

A very large number of vehicles were kept off the road for days and weeks simply for lack of spares. In many cases the repair would have been a matter of a few hours had the spares been available. "Cannibalisation" was carried out as far as practicable, but when mechanical transport is subjected to air attack, it is nearly always the same parts that get damaged, particularly tyres and radiators. Attempts had been made before operations began to get extra spares of both, but they were not available in the country. The situation regarding armoured cars would have been very serious had not a number of tyres, luckily of the unusual size required, been captured in Deir ez Zor. All armoured cars should be provided with 'run flat tyres'.

Communications

Operating over distances measured in hundreds rather than tens of miles, line communications become impossible. Moreover, the more mobile the force, the greater will be the number of detachments. The divisional wireless resources were unable to compete with the demand, the most serious occasion being the lack of touch between the two advancing columns on 1 July. If a set broke down mechanically or by enemy action, no spare set was available. For such operations more sets, more powerful sets and more wireless operators are essential.

During the operations the Divisional Commander had to control detachments at distances of over 100 miles from his headquarters, even when located most centrally. The provision of aircraft for communication is considered to be essential in operations of this nature.

Captured Material

There will always be a natural tendency for units and individuals, who have helped to capture enemy material, to seize what they can for their own use or as mementos. This at Deir ez Zor led to a good deal of avoidable destruction of valuable equipment, *e.g.*, wireless sets were wrenched from their stands, spare parts of lorries torn out, tools from workshops removed. Strict orders to prevent this must be issued beforehand.

APPENDIX 15

AGREEMENT FOR THE CESSATION OF HOSTILITIES IN SYRIA AND THE LEBANON

General Sir Henry Maitland Wilson, G.B.E., K.C.B., D.S.O., General Officer Commanding in Chief of the Allied Forces in Palestine and Syria (acting in the name of the Commanders-in-Chief, Middle East)—on the one hand, and

General de Verdilhac, Commander of the Legion of Honour, Deputy Commander-in-Chief of the French Troops in Syria, (acting in the name of the French High Command)—on the other hand

Have agreed to a convention which ends hostilities in Syria and the Lebanon, on which the following are the terms:—

1. Hostilities ceased on 11th July, 1941, at 2101 hours Greenwich Mean Time.

2. The Allied Forces will occupy SYRO-LEBANESE territory, the French Force will be concentrated in certain areas selected by a committee formed of representatives of both parties. This concentration will be completed by Tuesday 15th July, 1941, at 1200 hrs, at which hour Allied Forces will move to occupy certain strategic points. Up to the time of their repatriation the French troops will remain under French Command with a restricted establishment, which will provide for their maintenance from existing stocks. Special measures are foreseen for the JEBEL DRUSE, where, for security reasons, the French Troops will remain in garrison until relieved by British Troops.

3. In order to ensure public security, the occupation of the principal localities in SYRIA and LEBANON will be undertaken in accordance with a programme which will allow immediate replacement of French by the occupying forces.

4. Minefields, whether on sea or on land, will be disclosed to the occupying authority.

5. Full honours of war will be granted to the French Forces. The latter will retire to the selected areas with all arms, including guns, machine-guns, tanks and armoured cars, and their ammunition. All measures will be taken by the French command to prevent arms and ammunition being left unguarded on the battlefield or elsewhere. The French military authorities will give every assistance in recovering arms which may be in the hands of the population.

6. In consideration of the honours of war, French officers and non-commissioned officers, and soldiers, are permitted to retain their individual arms (rifles or carbines; revolvers; bayonets; swords or sabres). However the soldiers will not be allowed to carry ammunition. In each unit, for security reasons, a small quantity of ammunition will be retained. The gendarmerie will retain its arms and a limited amount of ammunition. All other war material including guns, coastal batteries, anti-aircraft guns and military transport will be stocked under British control. The latter will inspect this material and will have the rights to take over the material that may be required by them; the remainder will be destroyed by the French authorities under British control.

7. Prisoners of the Allied Forces will be forthwith set free, including those who have been transferred to France. As regards the latter, the British authorities reserve the right to hold as prisoners of war, an equal number of French officers, as far as possible of similar ranks, until those prisoners transferred to FRANCE have been released. The French prisoners will be released when the whole of the SYRO-LEBANESE territory has been occupied and the clauses of this convention fulfilled. They will then be enabled to join their units for repatriation.

8. The alternatives of rallying to the Allied cause or of being repatriated will be left to the free choice of the individual whether military or civil. In the case of the civilians who do not rally to the Allied cause, individual applications to remain in SYRIA or LEBANON will be considered by the British Authorities.

9. Executive officials, officials of the technical services and special service officers will remain at their posts so long as is necessary to ensure the continuance of the administration of the country and until such time as they can be relieved. They can then be repatriated if they so wish. Their services may be dispensed with if their work or attitude is not satisfactory.

10. The British Authorities agree to the repatriation by French ships of French troops and of French subjects, with the reservation that this repatriation will be limited to those who have opted therefor. The British Authorities reserve the right to control all matters relative to the repatriation of these people.

11. Holdings of French subjects to be repatriated will be transferred in accordance with terms to be arranged. These people will receive treatment not less favourable than that accorded to British subjects who have lately left for SYRIA.

12. French cultural institutions, including hospitals, schools, missions, etc., are assured that their rights will be respected. The rights of these institutions must not be allowed to conflict with Allied military interests.

13. All public services, including railways, tramways, public transport, electricity and water, will be maintained in operation and handed over intact.

14. All means of communication, including telephones, telegraphs, wireless and the submarine cable, will be handed over intact to the occupying authorities. The French command will have the use of telegraph facilities with FRANCE on the same conditions as the general public.

15. Port installations, naval establishments and all ships—including British—in SYRIAN and LEBANESE territorial waters, will be handed over intact to the occupying authorities.

16. All aircraft and air installations and equipment, in SYRIA or the LEBANON will be handed over intact. On the signature of the present agreement British aircraft are empowered to use any air base and alighting area in the LEBANON and SYRIA.

17. Fuel stocks shall be handed over intact. The quantity necessary for military transport will be placed at the disposal of the French Command.

18. Currency and other means of payment in circulation or in reserve, in possession of banks or other public authorities will be safeguarded.

19. The British Military Authorities reserve the right to take into their service the "Troupes Speciales du Levant" progressively as they are discharged by the French Authorities. The arms of these troops will be handed over to the British Authorities.

20. The British Authorities will not prosecute in any way native SYRIANS and LEBANESE who have been involved in the recent hostilities in a military or official capacity.

21. The carrying into effect of the terms of this Convention will be controlled and regulated by a "Commission of Control" which will sit at BEIRUT and will be composed of five members. Three of the members, including the President will be nominated by the British Authorities, the remaining two by the French Authorities.

This "Commission of Control" is empowered to appoint sub-commissions and to co-opt the services of such experts as may be necessary.

22. This Convention is drawn up in English and in French. In case of dispute the English text will be authoritative.

(SIGNED) H. M. WILSON.
General Officer Commanding-in-Chief,
Allied Forces in Palestine and Syria,
(Acting in the name of the Commanders-in-Chief, Middle East).

(SIGNED) DE VERDILHAC.
Deputy Commander-in-Chief,
The French Troops in Syria, (Acting in the name of the French High Command).

14th July, 1941.

APPENDIX 16

ORDER OF BATTLE, 8TH INDIAN DIVISION

25 August 1941

HEADQUARTERS

H.Q. 8 Ind. Div.
H.Q. 8 Ind. Div. Emp. Pl.
H.Q. R.A.
H.Q. R.E.
H.Q. R.I.A.S.C.

ARMD. TPS.

13 L.
One Sqn. 10 Cav.

SIGS.

8 Ind. Div. Sigs.

ROYAL ARTILLERY

3 Fd. Regt.
11 Fd. Regt.

R.E.

7 Fd. Coy S.M.
9 Fd. Coy.
47 Fd. Pk. Coy.

INF.

18 Ind. Bde.	*24 Inf. Bde.*	*25 Inf. Bde.*
H.Q. & Sig. Sec.	H.Q. & Sig. Sec.	H.Q. & Sig. Sec.
Emp. Pl.	Emp. Pl.	Emp. Pl.
3 Baluch	2 Raj. Rif.	1 Mahratta
1/2 G.R.	5 Mahratta	2 Sikh
2/3 G.R.	1 Kumaon Rif.	3 Jat

R.I.A.S.C.

H.Q.

8 Ind. Div. Tpt. Sec.
8 Ind. Div. Tps. Tpt. Coy.
18 Ind. Bde. Tpt. Coy.
24 Inf. Bde. Tpt. Coy.
25 Ind. Bde. Tpt. Coy.
51 G.P. Tpt. Coy. (Four secs.)
203 G.P. Tpt. Coy. (Three secs.)

MEDICAL

32 Fd. Amb. (with 18 Ind. Bde.)
25 Fd. Amb. (with 24 Ind. Bde.)
30 Fd. Amb. (with 25 Inf. Bde.)
20 Fd. Hyg. Sec.

ORDNANCE
15 Ord. Workshop Coy. (with Div. H.Q.)
50 Ord. Workshop Coy. (with 18 Inf. Bde.)
11 Ord. Workshop Coy. (with 25 Inf. Bde.)

POSTAL
41 Fd. P.O. (with Div. H.Q.)
43 Fd. P.O. (with 18 Ind. Bde.)
   Fd. P.O. (with 24 Inf. Bde.)
   Fd. P.O. (with 25 Inf. Bde.)

R.A.F. COMPONENT
164 (F) Sqn.
84 (B) Sqn.
244 (A/C) Sqn.
Det. 31 (BT) Sqn.

PROVOST
8 Ind. Div. Pro. Unit

L. OF C. TPS.
H.Q. 2 L. of C. Sub Area

APPENDIX 17

8TH INDIAN DIVISION ADMINISTRATION INSTRUCTIONS FOR THE ADVANCE ON 25 AUGUST, 1941

1. ORGANISATION

   (*a*) Line of Communication Area are responsible for concentration moves up to excluding D 1 Day.

   (*b*) 2 Line of Communication Sub Area are responsible for local administration of TANUMA, and will take over Line of Communication up to and including AHWAZ once Division Headquarters have moved forward.

   (*c*) 8 Division will be responsible for maintenance beyond AHWAZ.

2. MOVEMENTS

   From including D1 day Movement Control Staff of detached Echelon Force Headquarters will co-ordinate all movements ex B.S./S.B. to IRAN Area. Demands for despatch of personnel, supplies, stores, ammunition, mails will be submitted to Division Headquarters who will arrange despatch with Force Headquarters B.S.

3. SUPPLIES AND TRANSPORT

   (*a*) Ration issues will be from midnight to midnight.

   (*b*) 24 Infantry Brigade Group:—Cooked rations for D 1 and emergency rations for one day will be carried on the man.

   At least 7 days F.S. scale rations are being delivered at ABADAN on D 1 under orders of Force H.Q. All demands for replenishment ammunition will be placed on B.A.D. S.B. through Division Headquarters.

   2 × 3 ton lorries of 8 Division Troops Transport Company will be attached to 24 Infantry Bde. Transport Company with effect from 11 August 41, these lorries will be loaded by Division Troops Transport Company with 2nd Line ammunition load required by 4.5. troop of 3 Field Regiment. Ammunition sec. 24 Infantry Brigade Transport Company will proceed with full loads.

   Force Headquarters is putting in 7 days P.O.L. to ABADAN. In order to make full use of local resources 24 Brigade will report as soon as possible to Division Headquarter the amount of petrol available in ABADAN. Oils and lubricants are not likely to be available.

   (*c*) RAPIER:—One day cooked F.S. rations and one day emergency ration will be carried on the man.

   18 Brigade Transport Company will attach to RAPIER 4 × 3 ton lorries normally allotted for the carriage of 3 Baluch supplies. These lorries supplemented by lorries of 8 Division Troops Transport Company to be located on the East bank, will be able to carry two days F.S. scale plus two days hard scale for the whole Force less Squadron Guides and Sec. 203 G.P. Transport Company for which units similar rations will be on vehicles of 18 Brigade Transport Company ready to go forward.

   Comd. RAPIER will report when 2nd Line ammunition is required and whether it is to be delivered at TANUMA or ABADAN.

   2nd Line transport for carriage of supplies for RAPIER will report to Q.M. 5 Mahratta under arrangements to be made by C.R.I.A.S.C. 8 Division.

(d) *25 Infantry Brigade Group*:—Cooked rations for D1 and one days emergency ration will be carried on the man.

25 Infantry Brigade Transport Company and Detachment D.T.T. Company for 13 L and 3 Field Regiment will carry one days F.S. ration and one days H.S. ration in each echelon of Supply Section.

No. 2 Sub Area is providing one complete refill for ammunition for 8 Division at TANUMA. This ammunition will not be on wheels.

All available lorries (including blanket etc. lorries) of Pet. Sec. of 25 Infantry Brigade Transport Company will carry full loads of P.O.L.

(e) One Company Battalion 25 Infantry Brigade allotted for special task will take the unexpended portion and one days emergency ration on the man and three days H.S. in the planes.

(f) *BALUCOL*:—Unexpended portion and one days emergency ration will be carried on the man. At least three days H.S. will be carried in the planes and the balance in F.S. scale rations to complete 7 days will be delivered by plane in subsequent trip.

(g) *Res.*:—18 Brigade Transport Company will carry one days F.S. and one days H.S. rations in each echelon of Supply Section for all units of 18 Infantry Brigade Group.

Ammunition and Pet. Secs. will carry full 2nd Line loads.

(h) *SIBA guns*:—Transport for escort to these guns will be provided by 24 Infantry Brigade Transport Company who will also draw and hold the necessary 2nd Line ammunition for these guns.

(i) *General*:—All formation transport companies will ensure that their ammunition sections hold full authorised loads at all times. Division Troops Transport Company will carry ammunition in transport provided for the 11 Field Regiment on the basis of 16×25 pr. guns.

(k) *Adm.*:—Operations except in case of 24 Brigade Group will take place on bivouac scale. Tentage will be sent up as soon as possible. Brigade Groups (except 24 Brigade Group) and Division units not in Brigade Groups will report forthwith the weight of tentage at F.S. scale to be lifted.

4. ORDNANCE

(a) *Stores*:—A small first aid dump of ordnance stores is being created at TANUMA and is later being moved to AHWAZ.

All demands for stores will be submitted to Division Headquarters through O.W.Os. Dispatches will be made as in para 2. Forces in ABADAN and BANDAR SHAHPUR will indent direct of B.O.D. S.B. through Force Headquarters.

(b) *Salvage*:—Every effort will be made to return salvage, particularly tin plate, bottles and such captured warlike stores as are not required. Care must be taken to ensure that dangerous stores are so marked and packed separately from all other stores.

B.O.W.Os. will be responsible for the collection and return of salvage in accordance with detailed instructions issued by D.A.D.O.S. direct.

(c) *Maintenance of Vehicles*:—Ord. Mob. W/S. Companies will maintain units as under:—

11 Ord. W/S. Company	25 Brigade Group.
,, ,, ,, ,,	Division Troops not allotted to Brigades.
50	18 Brigade Group.

(d) All Ord Mob. W/S. Companies remain under Division Command. One section 11 Mob. W/S. Company will be held ready to move forward with B Echelon Transport 25 Brigade.

Light repairs forward of TANUMA will be carried out by L.A.Ds.

(e) *Recovery of Vehicles*:—25 Brigade Group and RAPIER. Vehicles beyond repair by L.A.D. will be towed if operations will not be delayed thereby, otherwise they will be abandoned. Loads will be transhipped into spare lorries of G.P. Transport Company. Locations of abandoned vehicles will be reported as early as possible to Division Headquarters who will arrange for recovery.

5. R.E.

(a) 6 lorries (4 from Division Troops Transport Company, 2 from 24 I.B.T. Company) will be loaded with R.E. stores as arranged by C.R.E. and will accompany Force RAPIER under Command.

(b) *25 Brigade Group*:—2 × 3 ton lorries in 25 I.B.T. Company for Engineer stores will be loaded under orders of C.R.E.

6. MEDICAL

(a) 25 Fd. Amb. (less one company) under command 24 Brigade. One company 25 Fd. Amb. under command Force RAPIER.

(b) 30 Fd. Amb. will remain under command 25 Brigade.

(c) 32 Fd. Amb. (less Det.) under command 18 Brigade till operations commence and then Division Reserve.

(d) Detachment 32 Fd. Amb. allotted to Major W. E. MAXWELL 3 Baluch as already ordered.

(e) The following detachment to be detailed from 30 Fd. Amb. will accompany airborne company of 25 Brigade Group (vide 8 Division O.O. No. 1 para 9(c)):
One S.A.S.
One nursing orderly.
One improvised Medical box to be drawn from 6 M.S.D. 20 Fd. Hyg. Sec. (less one sub sec.) will remain in TANUMA until further orders.
One Sub sec. 20 Fd. Hyg. Sec. under comd. 25 Fd. Amb. forthwith.

(f) *BALUCOL*:—M.O. 3 Baluch, one nursing orderly from 32 Fd. Amb. and improvised medical box to be drawn from 6 M.S.D. will accompany BALUCOL.

(g) *Evacuation of casualties*:—Fd. ambs. will evacuate to M.D.S. Comds. Fd. Ambs. will ensure that Division Headquarter is kept constantly informed of locations of A.D.S. and M.D.Ss.

(h) Two staging sections are being sent to B.S. and are allotted to 8 Division on arrival for formation if necessary, if improvised C.G.S. at AHWAZ by linking to M.D.S. of Fd. Amb.

Evacuation in rear of M.D.S. or improvised C.C.S. is being arranged by Force Headquarter.

(i) 11 M.A. Sec. (Force Troops) is being based on TANUMA for evacuation from AHWAZ area.

(j) Serious cases will be evacuated by air if possible. Demands for air transport will be submitted to Division Headquarter.

(k) Casualties in ABADAN will be held and reported to Force Headquarter to arrange evacuation.

7. Labour

Two labour companies are being held in readiness for despatch (one company to ABADAN and one company to AHWAZ) on demand from Division Headquarter.

24 and 25 Brigades will report if and when labour is required to be despatched.

8. Postal

Complete lists of officers of Headquarter Staffs and services and designation of all units are being handed to C Base P.O. by Area as soon as possible after D 1 day.

Reports will be submitted as soon as possible to area as follows:—

(*a*) By Division Headquarter: List of officers of Division Headquarter & Services.
List of units not under comd. Brigades.

(*b*) By Brigade Headquarter: List of officers of Brigade Headquarter including services.
List of units in Brigade Groups.

9. Surplus Baggage

Any surplus baggage will be collected at B.S. and stored under arrangements to be made by area. Applications for storage room will be made direct to area by Bdes. and Div. Tps.

10. Prisoners of War

P. of W. will be evacuated to B.S. where an improvised camp is being provided by area.

D.A.P.M. will arrange with 2 L. of C. Sub Area to establish P.W.C.P. at TANUMA west of the moat and inform all concerned of its location. A P.W.C.P. is being established on the right side of the main road approx. 300 yds. outside TANUMA. All concerned will arrange to send back P. of W. to this C.P. under escort, where they will be taken over.

Pro. unit only:—O.C. Pro. unit will keep in reserve one Indian Section to form the above P.W.C.P. when required.

11. Graves

Formations/units will be responsible for maintaining details of locations etc. of all graves. Firewood for cremation is being sent up with supplies and will not be used for any other purposes.

Locations of graves will be reported to 2nd Ech. periodically by unit/formations concerned.

12. Traffic Control

Area is providing from incl. D 1 day T.C.P. at TANUMA to work under orders of 2 L. of C. Sub Area. Ind. Sec. 8 Div. Pro. unit revert Div. control on D 1 day after handing over.

13. One Indian Sec. 8 Div. Pro. unit will be held ready on D 1 day to move forward with B. Ech. Tpt. 25 Bde. if ordered.

14. Canteen Stores

AHWAZ, ABADAN, and BANDAR SHAHPUR formations will send reps. to draw canteen stores ex BASRA. Cash will be paid and

10% discount allowed on the spot. In view of the above, units and formations are advised to open accounts with the bank in B.S., otherwise they may not have the necessary cash to draw the stores they require.

Det. NAFFI is being sent to AHWAZ as soon as possible to open bulk issue store. This is unlikely to be possible for some time.

15. FEEDING LOCAL POPULATION

Atta and other foodstuffs will not be sold or given to the local population under any circumstances.

16. LOCAL PURCHASE

Comds. 24 and 25 Inf. Bdes. and BALUCOL are authorised to make such local purchases as may be required. Details will be reported to Div. H.Q. Requisitioning may be resorted to if essential. Receipts for supplies so obtained will be signed by an officer not below the rank of captain and stamped with Bde. H.Q. office stamp or BALUCOL stamp.

Details will be forwarded to Div. H.Q.

17. MARTIAL LAW

G.S. Instruction regarding Martial Law refers only to the proclamation of martial law in the country. Local Comds. may apply local and temporary martial law in restricted area to control looting and incendiarism when the application is in effect part of a military operation. Attention is drawn to M.M.L. p. 444 Appx. 22 to the Law and Usages of War on Land.

APPENDIX 18

ORDER OF BATTLE, 10TH INDIAN DIVISION
25 August, 1941

HEADQUARTERS

10 Ind. Div.
10 Ind. Div. R.A.
10 Ind. Div. R.E.
10 Ind. Div. R.I.A.S.C.
9 Armd. Bde.
2 Ind. Armd. Bde.
21 Ind. Inf. Bde.
Hazelforce

CAVALRY

Household Cav. Regt. (9 Armd. Bde.)
14/20 H. (2 Ind. Armd. Bde.)
R. Wilts Yeo (9 Armd. Bde.)
Warwicks Yeo (9 Armd. Bde.)

ARTILLERY

15 Fd. Regt. (2 Ind. Armd. Bde)
157 Fd. Regt. (10 Ind. Div.) ⎫
19 Med. Bty. (10 Ind. Div.) ⎬ under comd. 21 Ind. Inf. Bde.

ENGINEERS

2 Cheshire Fd. Sqn. R.E. (9 Armd. Bde.)
32 Fd. Sqn. S & M (2 Ind. Armd. Bde.)
61 Fd. Coy. (10 Ind. Div.)
41 Fd. Park Coy. S & M (10 Ind. Div.)

SIGNALS

Det. Force H.Q. Sigs.
10 Ind. Div. Sigs.
9 Armd. Bde. Sig. Sec.
2 Ind. Armd. Bde. Sig. Sqn.
15 Fd. Regt. Sig. Sec.
157 Fd. Regt. Sig. Sec.
21 Ind. Inf. Bde. Sig. Sec.

INFANTRY

2/4 G.R. (21 Ind. Inf. Bde.)
1/5 R.G.R. (17 Ind. Inf. Bde.—2 Ind. Armd. Bde.)
2/7 G.R. (20 Ind. Inf. Bde.—2 Ind. Armd. Bde.)
2/10 G.R. (21 Ind. Inf. Bde.)

R.I.A.S.C.

2 Ind. Armd. Bde. Tpt. Coy.
20 Ind. Inf. Bde. Tpt. Coy.
21 Ind. Inf. Bde. Tpt. Coy.

H.Q. 10 ind. Div. Tpt. Sec.
10 Ind. Div. Tps. Tpt. Coy.
35 G.P. Tpt. Coy.
49 G.P.Tpt. Coy.
52 G.P. Tpt. Coy.
7 M.A.S.
10 M.A.S.
H.Q. 23 Sup. Pers. Coy.
205 Sub Sec. Fd. Butchery
Field Supply Depot

MEDICAL

166 Lt. Fd. Amb. (9 Armd. Bde.)
2 Lt. Fd. Amb. (2 Ind. Armd. Bde.)
29 Fd. Amb. (10 Ind. Div.)
Det. 8 Lt. Fd. Hyg. Sec. (9 Armd. Bde.)
1 Fd. Hyg. Sec. (10 Ind. Div.)
C.C.S.

ORDNANCE

Div. Sec. 10 Armd. Div. Ord. Fd. Park R.A.O.C. (9 Armd. Bde.)
2 Bde. Gp. Wkshop. 10 Armd. Div. Ord. Wkshop. R.A.O.C. (9 Armd. Bde.)
1 Wkshop. Sqn., I.A.O.C. (2 Ind. Armd. Bde.)
A Sec. 1 Armd. Div. Rec. Coy., I.A.O.C. (2 Ind. Armd. Bde.)
B Sec. 1 Armd. Div. Rec. Coy., I.A.O.C. (2 Ind. Armd. Bde.)
14 Wkshop. Coy., I.A.O.C. (less one Sec.) (2 Ind. Armd. Bde.)
16 Mob. Wkshop. Coy., I.A.O.C. (21 Ind. Inf. Bde.)
29 Mob. Wkshop. Coy., I.A.O.C. (10 Ind. Div.)
Adv. Ord. Depot
Adv. Amn. Depot

PROVOST

Sec. Cav. Pro. Unit (9 Armd. Bde.)
103 Pro. Sec. (Brit.) (2 Ind. Armd. Bde.)
104 Pro. Sec. (Ind.) (2 Ind. Armd. Bde.)
10 Ind. Div. Pro. Unit

POSTAL

Det. Cav. Div. Postal Unit (9 Armd. Bde.)
26 Fd. P.O. (2 Ind. Armd. Bde.)
49 Fd. P.O. (21 Ind. Inf. Bde.)
53 Fd. P.O. (10 Ind. Div.)

APPENDIX 19

PAMPHLET DROPPING OPERATIONS FROM 25 TO 28 AUGUST 1941

The work of the bomber squadrons, operating from Habbaniya, during the period under review consisted chiefly of pamphlet dropping on the cities and chief towns in the North, North-West and Central Iran, as follows:—

(i) On 25 August, Nos. 14 and 45 squadrons dropped pamphlets on Teheran and Kashan.
(ii) On 26 August, Nos. 11 and 14 Squadrons dropped pamphlets on Kazvin, Isfahan and Shiraz.
(iii) On 27 August, Nos. 11 and 14 Squadrons dropped pamphlets on Kermanshah, Malayar, Sultanabad, Khurramabad, Dizful, Hamadan, Qum and suitable smaller towns en route.
(iv) On 28 August, all three squadrons dropped pamphlets on Zinjan, Senneh, Takistan, Gulpaigan and Burujird.

PAMPHLETS DROPPED

August 25. 12 Blenheims of 45 and 14 Squadrons dropped propaganda leaflets on Kashan and Teheran explaining how the Iranian Government had failed to expel Germans from Iran.

12 Blenheims of 45 Squadron dropped 25,000 No. 1 pamphlets in Persian on Kashan. No anti-aircraft or air opposition. One aircraft returned owing to engine trouble. All aircraft returned safely.

Unfavourable weather prevented pamphlet operations by Blenheims of 11 Squadron from Shuaiba.

12 Blenheims of 14 Squadron, of which 4 returned prior to reaching objective owing to engine trouble, dropped 60,000 No. 1 pamphlets on Teheran. One aircraft force-landed in Iraq near frontier owing to engine trouble.

August 26. Bombers dropped pamphlets. Blenheims of 11 and 14 Squadrons dropped 105,000 propaganda leaflets on Isfahan, Shiraz and Kazvin.

6 Blenheims of 14 Squadron dropped 40,000 leaflets (pamphlet No. 1) on Kazvin. 10 Blenheims of 11 Squadron dropped 40,000 pamphlets No. 1 on Isfahan and 25,000 No. 1 on Shiraz.

August 27. 9 Blenheims, 11 and 14 Squadrons, dropped 170,000 No. 1 pamphlets on Kermanshah, Malayar, Sultanabad, Khurramabad and Dizful. Weather bad, visibility poor. 5 Blenheims of 14 Squadron dropped 50,000 No. 1 pamphlets each on Hamadan and Qum.

ENGLISH TRANSLATION OF LEAFLETS DROPPED IN IRAN

"Iranians. Thousands of Germans are living in your country. By a calculated plan they are holding important positions in industry. When Hitler gives the word they can sabotage the main sources of your revenues. They are organised by the German Legation and every man has special orders. You know they stirred up trouble in Iraq. They will not hesitate to do the same in Iran. This is exactly what happened in many European countries before they were invaded by Germany. Those in authority in Iran have ignored our repeated warnings of the danger of allowing those Germans to stay in your country, a danger not only to you but to Britain and Russia too. We are determined that the Germans must go and if the Iranians do not throw them out both Britain and Russia will. Our forces are irresistible. Iranians, we have no quarrel with you nor have we any designs on your country or your goods. We only wish to drive out those accursed Germans whose aim is to make your country a seat of war and misery. If you help us now we will help you both now and in the future.[1]"

SUPPLEMENTARY LEAFLETS

The following supplementary leaflets were suggested if situation demanded.

First for general use

"Iranians. British and Russia have demanded expulsion of German agents in your midst because they are precursors of war. Like you we wish to see peace preserved in Iran. We wish peace for our own sake. You must desire peace for yourselves. What does war mean? German agents prepared way for German armies in Norway, Holland, Belgium, Poland, Rumania and Greece. Then war came and Germans occupied those countries. They had been rich and prosperous. Now they are starving. When German conquest is easy Germans prey upon conquered lands like locusts. Fruits of the soil are reserved for victors, and vanquished go hungry. Where there is resistance, land is laid waste. Had Germans had time to secure hold upon Iran before arrival of British troops they would have hindered our advance, have destroyed not only railways and roads built at cost of taxes you have paid, but towns and villages of Iran in which you live. They would have slaughtered your cattle, burnt your crops and turned Iran into a desert. From such a fate we will save you as we have saved Iraq and Syria. We do not want your food. We will bring food for those who need it as we are doing in Syria. We do not want your goods but will open your ports to trade as we are doing in Iraq. We come as friends armed only against the common enemy".

Second for Iranian Troop Centres

"Soldiers of Iran. We are marching into Iran as your friends. We are doing nothing against your Country's freedom and well-being. All we want is to drive out and keep out the accursed Germans. You have no reason to fight against us and you cannot fight against our tanks, guns, airplanes. So do not be killed without reason. Many of you have been forced to leave your homes and join the army against your will. Now since there is no need for war, recruits and reservists can go home again. Those who stop with the colours will have regular pay assured them, officers will retain their rank. When Germans promised Rashid Ali in Iraq help they never gave it. One of their conditions was that Iraqi Army should pass under German control. We make no such demands. Army of Iran remains Iranian Army subject to its own national government. Soldiers of Iran, we come and our greeting to

---

[1] "As the Persian people were told by thousands of leaflets, it was no part of the allied purpose to take Persian lives, to interfere with Persian property or liberties; neither were there Indian or British lives to spare for such an adventure. Diplomatic relations with Persia were, in fact, never broken. The sole object of the Allies was to defeat the German intention; their weapons were not vast armies but resolution and speed".—*Paiforce*, p. 66.

you is 'Peace be with you'. Let your reply be 'And upon you be peace'. Then all will be well, but if any is so made as to oppose us, if any helps the accursed Germans, then our aeroplanes, tanks and guns will answer him and he shall be utterly destroyed."

During the four days of the campaign, nearly six lakh pamphlets were dropped. The number of leaflets dropped each day on the various Iranian cities and towns is given below:—

Date	Name of Town	No. of pamphlets dropped
25-8-1941	Kashan	25,000
	Teheran	40,000
26-8-1941	Isfahan	40,000
	Shiraz	25,000
	Kazvin	32,500
27-8-1941	Malayar	34,000
	Qum	41,000
	Sultanabad	34,000
	Hamadan	41,000
	Kermanshah	34,000
	Khurramabad	34,000
	Dizful	34,000
28-8-1941	Zinjan	40,000
	Senneh	40,000
	Takistan	40,000
	Gulpaigan	20,000
	Burujird	20,000

APPENDIX 20

TENTH ARMY ORDER OF BATTLE AND LOCATION STATEMENT AS ON 15 SEPTEMBER 1942

FORMATIONS

    3 Corps.
    21 Ind. Corps.
    6 Ind. Div.
    8 Ind. Div.
    31 Ind. Armd. Div.

H.Q. Tenth Army.		Khurramabad.
H.Q. Tenth Army Empl. Pl.		,,
505 Army H.Q. Tpt. Sec	R.I.A.S.C.	,,
508 Army H.Q. Tpt. Sec.	,,	,,

ARTILLERY

H.Q. 8 A.A. Bde.	⎫	
8 A.A. Bde. Sigs.	⎬	Kermanshah.
8 A.A. Bde. R.A.S.C. Sec.		
8 A.A. Bde. Wkshop. Sec. R.A.O.C.	⎭	
12 Lt. A.A. Regt.	⎫	
12 Lt. A.A. Regt. Sig. Sec.	⎬	Kermanshah.
12 Lt. A.A. Regt. R.A.S.C. Sec.		
12 Lt. A.A. Regt. Wkshop. Sec. R.A.O.C.	⎭	
34 Lt. A.A. Bty.		Husainabad.
35 Lt. A.A. Bty.		Kermanshah.
36 Lt. A.A. Bty.		Bisitun.
139 Lt. A.A. Bty.		Mosul.
19 Medium Bty.		Tuleh. (Under 21 Ind. Corps.).
1 Ind. A/Tk. Regt.		Kirkuk. (Under 8 Ind. Div.).
5 Mahratta A/Tk. Regt.		Sultanabad. (Under 21 Ind. Corps.).
No. 1 Tp. 6 Svy. Regt.		Kangavar.

ENGINEERS

Det 49 Army Tps. Coy.		Khurramabad.
56 Fd. Coy.	R.E.	Kirkuk.
3 Bridging Sec.	S & M	Kangavar. (Under 21 Ind. Corps.).
5 Bridging Sec.		Askaran. (Under 21 Ind. Corps.).
1 Pioneer Bn.	I.E.	Chariveh. (Dets. Pul-i-Tang, Pai Tak, Khanakin, Kermanshah).

SURVEY
2 Ind. Fd. Svy. Coy. — Zagheh. (Det. Mussayib).
4 Ind. Fd. Svy. Coy. — Hamadan.
Mob. Ech. 512 Army Fd. Svy. Coy. — Teheran.

SIGNALS
Tenth Army Sigs. — Khurramabad. (Dets. Teheran, Pahlevi Kermanshah).

201 Ind. Constr. Sec. — "
21 Ind. A.A.S.C. — Kermanshah.
G.H.Q. Liaison Sqn. — Khurramabad.
8 G.S.S. Sec. — "
9 G.S.S. Sec. — Tureh.

3 CORPS.
H.Q. 3 Corps.
3 Corps. Defence Coy.
3 Corps. Intall. Sec.
3 Corps. H.Q. Sigs.
3 Corps. H.Q. Sigs. L.A.D.
H.Q. 3 Corps. Arty.
H.Q. 3 Corps. Arty. Sigs. Sec. — Kermanshah.

ARTILLERY
156 Fd. Regt.

INTELLIGENCE
24 F.S. Sec.

POSTAL
3 Corps. Postal Unit — Kermanshah.

21 IND. CORPS.
H.Q. 21 Ind. Corps. — Hamadan.
21 Ind. Corps. Empl. Pl. — "
21 Ind. Corps. Tpt. Sec. ... R.I.A.S.C. — "

INFANTRY
17 Dogra M.G. Bn. — Hamadan. (Det. Kermanshah, Senna).
1 Afridi Bn. — Pai Tak.

ENGINEERS
H.Q. 21 Ind. Corps. Tps. Engs. — Askaran.
1 Fd. Coy. ... S. & M. — Kangavar.
5 Fd. Coy. " — Sarwandar.
14 Fd. Coy. " — Askaran.
30 Fd. Pk. Coy. ... I.E. — Askaran. (Det. Hamadan).

AUX. PNR. BNS.
2 Ind. Aux. Pnr. Bn. — Chariveh. (Det. Sarwandar).
14 Ind. Aux. Pnr. Bn. — Kangavar. (Det. Bisitun).

S. & T.
26 Mule Coy.   R.I.A.S.C.   Senneh.
33 Mule Coy.   ,,   Chariveh.
                                                        (Det. Kangavar).

POSTAL
R-17 Ind. Fd. P.O.   Hamadan.

6 IND. DIV.
H.Q. 6 Ind. Div.   } Sultanabad.
H.Q. 6 Ind. Div. Arty.
H.Q. 6 Ind. Div. Eng.   Kangavar.
H.Q. 6 Ind. Div. Regt. R.I.A.S.C.
H.Q. Div. I.A.O.C. Wkshops. 6 Div.
6 Ind. Div. Sigs.   Sultanabad.
6 Ind. Div. Empl. Pl.
6 Ind. Div. H.Q. Tpt. Sec.
6 Ind. Div. Tps. Tpt. Pl.   Hamadan.
6 Ind. Div. Rec. Coy.
6 Ind. Div. Pro. Unit
405 F.S. Sec.   Sultanabad.
DIV. RECCE. REGT.
6 Lancers

ENGINEERS
302 Fd. Pk. Coy.   S. & M.   Kangavar.

MEDICAL
6 Ind. Fd. Hyg. Sec.
POSTAL   Sultanabad.
35 Ind. Fd. P.O.

27 IND. INF. BDE. GP.
H.Q. 27 Ind. Inf. Bde. Gp.
27 Ind. Inf. Bde. Sig. Sec.
27 Ind. Inf. Bde. Empl. Pl.   Tureh.
27 Ind. Inf. Bde. Tpt. Coy.
27 Ind. Inf. Bde. Gp. Ord. Coy.   Sultanabad.
159 Fd. Regt.   Tureh.
27 Fd. Coy.   Pul-i-Tang for Tureh.
4/8 Punjab   (One P. Sultanabad).
1 Baluch   (One Coy. Andi-
3/15 Punjab   mishk).
35 Ind. Fd. Amb.   Tureh.
59 Ind. Fd. P.O.

8 IND. DIV.
H.Q. 8 Ind. Div.
H.Q. 8 Ind. Div. Arty.   Kirkuk.
H.Q. 8 Ind. Div. Eng.   Chariveh.
H.Q. 8 Ind. Div. Regt. R.I.A.S.C.
8 Ind. Div. Sigs.
8 Ind. Div. Empl. Pl.
8 Ind. Div. H.Q. Tpt. Sec.
8 Ind. Div. Tps. Tpt. Pl.   Kirkuk.
8 Ind. Div. Rec. Coy.
8 Ind. Div. Pro. Unit
406 F.S. Sec.

ENGINEERS
69 Fd. Coy.   S. & M.   Chariveh.
47 Fd. Pk. Coy.   Dibis.

MEDICAL
20 Ind. Fd. Hyg. Sec. ...   Kirkuk.

POSTAL
41 Ind. Fd. P.O.   Kirkuk.

19 IND. INF. BDE. GP.
H.Q. 19 Ind. Inf. Bde. Gp. ...
19 Ind. Inf. Bde. Sig. Sec. ...
19 Ind. Inf. Bde. Empl. Pl. ...   Mosul.
19 Ind. Inf. Bde. Tpt. Coy. ...
19 Ind. Inf. Bde. Gp. Ord. Coy. ...
346 Bty. 87 Fd. Regt. ...
1/5 Essex ...
6 F.F. Rif. ...   Kirkuk.
3/8 Punjab ...
33 Ind. Fd. Amb. ...   Mosul.
44 Ind. Fd. P.O. ...

31 IND. ARMD. DIV.
H.Q. 31 Ind. Armd. Div. ...
H.Q. 31 Ind. Armd. Div. Engs. ...
H.Q. 31 Ind. Armd. Div. Sig. Sqn.
H.Q. 31 Ind. Armd. Div. Regt. R.I.A.S.C. ...   Mosul.
H.Q. 31 Ind. Armd. Div. Tps. Tpt. Pl. ... ...
H.Q. 31 Ind. Armd. Div. I.A.O.C. Wkshops. ...

DIV. A.C. REGT.
13 Lancers   Bisitun.

ENGINEERS
39 Fd. Pk. Sqn.   ... S. & M.   Bisitun.

ARTILLERY
79 A/Tk. Regt.   ...   Bisitun.

S. & T.
36 G.P. Transporter Coy.   R.I.A.S.C.   Bisitun.

MEDICAL
1 Ind. Lt. Fd. Hyg. Sec.   Bisitun.

ORDNANCE
31 Ind. Armd. Div. Ord. Fd. Pk.   Bisitun.
31 Ind. Armd. Div. Sec. Armd. Corps. Wkshops.

POSTAL
45 Ind. Fd. P.O.   Bisitun.

3 IND. MOTOR BDE. GP.

H.Q. 3 Ind. Motor Bde. Gp. .... ⎫
3 Ind. Motor Bde. Gp. Sig. Sqn. ⎬ Bisitun.
3 Ind. Motor Bde. Gp. Tpt. Coy. ⎪
3 Ind. Motor Bde. Gp. Ord. Coy. ⎭

MOTOR REGTS.
2 L.   Bisitun.
11 Cav.   ,,
18 Cav.   ,,

ARTILLERY
144 Fd. Regt.   Bisitun.

ENGINEERS
31 Fd. Sqn.   ... S. & M.   Bisitun.

MEDICAL
3 Ind. Lt. Fd. Amb.   Bisitun.

POSTAL
3 Ind. Motor Bde. Fd. P.O.   Bisitun.

S. & T.
3 Ind. Motor Bde. Sup. Issue Sec.   Bisitun.

252 IND. ARMD. BDE. GP.

H.Q. 252 Ind. Armd. Bde. Gp. ... ⎫
252 Ind. Armd. Bde. Gp. Sig. Sqn. ⎬ Bisitun.
252 Ind. Armd. Bde. Tpt. Coy. ... ⎪
252 Ind. Armd. Bde. Ord. Coy. ... ⎭

ARMD. CORPS.
14/20 Hussars   Bisitun.
4 Horse   ,,
14 Horse

ARTILLERY
15 Fd. Regt.   Bisitun.

ENGINEERS
32 Fd. Sqn. S. & M.   Bisitun.

INFANTRY
1 Bombay Grs.   Bisitun.

MEDICAL
2 Ind. Lt. Fd. Amb.   Bisitun.

PROVOST
103 Br. Pro. Sub Sec. ...   Bisitun.
104 Br. Pro. Sub Sec. ...   ,,

POSTAL
26 Ind. Fd. P.O.   Bisitun.

MOSUL SUB AREA

H.Q. Mosul Sub Area ...   Mosul.

ENGINEERS
103 C.R.E. Works (Indian)		Mosul.
109 C.R.E. Works (Indian)		Kirkuk.
3 Army Excavating Coy.	I.E.	Mosul.
312 Well Boring Sec.	I.E.	Kirkuk.

S. & T.
H.Q. 21 Sup. Pers. Coy.	R.I.A.S.C.	Mosul for Khanakin.
112 Sup. Pers. Sec.	,,	,,
119 Sup. Pers. Sec.	,,	,,
139 Sup. Pers. Sec.	,,	,,
140 Sup. Pers. Sec.	,,	,,
141 Sup. Pers. Sec.	,,	,,
H.Q. 23 Sup. Pers. Coy.	,,	Mosul.
108 Sup. Pers. Sec.	,,	,,
130 Sup. Pers. Sec.	,,	,,
161 Sup. Pers. Sec.	,,	,,
25 Cattle Stock Sec.	,,	Mosul.
34 Cattle Stock Sec.	,,	Kirkuk for Sultanabad.
25 Cattle Conducting Sec.	,,	Mosul for Khanakin.
14 M.A. Sec.		,,
7 Mineral Water Sec.		Kirkuk.

MEDICAL
28 C.G.H.	Mosul.
33 C.G.H.	Kirkuk.
20 Br. Convalescent Depot	Penjwin.
24 Ind. X Ray Unit	Mosul.
25 Ind. X Ray Unit	Kirkuk.
14 Ind. Fd. Lab.	Mosul.
15 Ind. Fd. Lab.	Kirkuk.
4 Ind. Surgical Unit (E.N.T.)	Mosul.
1 Ind. Ophthalmological Unit	,,
3 Ind. Dental Mechanic Unit	,,
7 Ind. Dental Unit	,,
10 Ind. Dental Unit	Kirkuk for Khuramabad.
1 Ind. Depot Medical Stores	
2 Ind. Mobile Surgical Unit	
20 Ind. Fd. Hyg. Sec.	

ORDNANCE
516 Ind. Ord. Depot	I.A.O.C.	Kirkuk.
517 Ind. Amn. Depot	,,	,,
518 Ind. Ord. Depot	,,	Mosul.
519 Ind. Amn. Depot	,,	
4 Salvage Unit	,,	
2 Mob. Cinema	,,	
11 Mob. Cinema	,,	

POSTAL
14 Ind. Fd. P.O.	Kirkuk.
102 Ind. Fd. P.O.	Mosul.

MISCELLANEOUS
21 Ind. Aux. Pnr. Bn. ...	Kirkuk (Det. Kermanshah).
1 L of C Ind. Pro. Sub Sec.	Mosul.
2 L of C Ind. Pro. Sub Sec.	,,
1 Ind. Graves R & E Unit	,,
40 Mixed Rest Camp ...	,,
42 Mixed Rest Camp ...	Kirkuk.
50 Mixed Rest Camp ...	Mosul.
6 Ind. Prisoners of War Cage	,,
'A' Ind. Prisoners of War Camp ...	Kirkuk.
Town Major	,,

KERMANSHAH SUB AREA

H.Q. Kermanshah Sub Area		Kermanshah.

ENGINEERS
104 C.R.E. Works (Indian)		Kermanshah.
115 C.R.E. Roads (Indian)		Hamadan.
C.R.E. No. 2 Aerodrome		,,
801 Road Constr. Coy ...	R.E.	Khurramabad.
53 Printing Sec.		,,

S & T.
35 G.P. Tpt. Coy.	R.I.A.S.C.	Kermanshah (one pl. Durud).
51 G.P. Tpt. Coy.	,,	,,
62 G.P. Tpt. Coy.	,,	Vaisiyan.
375 G.T. Coy.	R.A.S.C.	Kermanshah.
442 G.T. Coy. ...	,,	,,
H.Q. 25 Sup. Pers. Sec.	R.I.A.S.C.	,,
118 Sup. Pers. Sec.	,,	Hamadan.
128 Sup. Pers. Sec.	,,	Vaisiyan.
211 Sup. Pers. Sec.	,,	Kermanshah.
212 Sup. Pers. Sec.	,,	,,
12 M.A. Sec.	,,	,,
16 M.A. Sec.	,,	Khurramabad.
6 Fd. Bakery	,,	Kermanshah.
Det. 5 Fd. Bakery	,,	,,
Det. 5 Fd. Butchery	,,	,,
23 Cattle Stock Sec.	,,	,,
32 Cattle Stock Sec.	,,	,,
70 P.O.L. Sec.	,,	Vaisiyan.

MEDICAL
12 Br. Staging Sec.	Kangavar.
16 Br. Staging Sec.	Kermanshah.
19 Br. Staging Sec.	,,
20 Br. Staging Sec.	Hamadan.

6 Ind. Staging Sec.		Khurramabad.
21 Ind. Staging Sec.		"
24 Ind. Staging Sec.		Hamadan.
25 Ind. Staging Sec.		Kermanshah.
26 Ind. Staging Sec.		"
21 Ind. Fd. Hyg. Sec.		Khurramabad.
13 Ind. Anti Malaria Unit		Kermanshah.
14 Ind. Anti Malaria Unit		"
1 Dental Surgical Unit (Br.)		"
1 Ind. Dental Mechanic Unit		"
3 Ind. Mob. Surgical Unit		"
11 Ind. Dental Unit		Hamadan.
12 Ind. Dental Unit ...		Teheran.
Det. 10 C.C.S. (Lt. Sec.)		Khurramabad.
36 Ind. Fd. Hyg. Sec. ...		Kermanshah.
170 Lt. Fd. Amb.		"
1 Mob. Cinema	I.A.O.C.	Kangavar.
9 Mob. Cinema	"	Kermanshah.

POSTAL

105 Ind. Fd. P.O.   Khurramabad.

CAMPAIGN

26 C.T.U.	Chariveh Pass (Under 21 Ind. Corps.)
27 C.T.U.	Kangavar (Under 21 Ind. Corps.)
32 C.T.U.	Kermanshah (Under 21 Ind. Corps.)
33 C.T.U.	Askaran (Under 21 Ind. Corps.)

MISCELLANEOUS

61 Ind. Garrison Coy.	Khurramabad.
43 Mixed Rest Camp	Kermanshah.
7 Mob. Bath Unit	Kermanshah (for 5 Br. Div.)
72 F.S. Sec. ...	Khurramabad.
Tenth Army Pro. Coy.	"
50 Br. Pro. Sec.	Kermanshah.
12 Ind. Aux. Pnr. Bn. ...	Khurramabad (Det. Askaran).
3 Ind. Mob. Vet. Sec.	Kermanshah.
Det. 42 Geological Sec. S.A.E. Corps.	Hamadan.

TEHERAN SUB AREA

H.Q. Teheran Sub Area   Teheran.

SIGNALS

Teheran Sigs. ...	Teheran.
2 Ind. L of C Telegraphs	Sultanabad.

ENGINEERS

C.W. Works 202	Teheran.
26 C.R.E. Works	Isfahan.
29 C.R.E. Works	Kerman.

S. & T.

H.Q. 17 Sup. Pers. Coy.	R.I.A.S.C.	Teheran.
113 Sup. Pers. Sec.		Sultanabad.
145 Sup. Pers. Sec.		Teheran.
168 Sup. Pers. Sec.		
14 Fd. Bakery Sec.		
15 Fd. Bakery Sec.		Pahlevi.
15 M.A. Sec.		Sultanabad.
17 M.A. Sec.		Teheran.
72 P.O.L. Sec.		Sultanabad.

MEDICAL

34 C.G.H.	Teheran.
18 I.G.H.	"
13 Br. Staging Sec.	Durud.
5 Ind. Staging Sec.	Sultanabad for Kangavar.
22 Ind. Staging Sec.	Durud.
1 Ind. Mob. Surgical Unit	Teheran for Khurramabad.
17 Ind. Fd. Lab.	"
22 Ind. Fd. Amb.	"
16 Ind. Fd. Hyg. Sec.	Teheran.
23 Ind. Convalescent Depot.	Sultanabad.
10 C.C.S.	Sultanabad (Lt. Sec. Khurramabad).
6 Ind. Mob. X Ray Unit	"

ORDNANCE

R.O.D.	I.A.O.C.	Teheran.
52 Mob. Wkshop. Coy.	"	"
3 Mob. Laundry	"	Pahlevi.

POSTAL

103 Ind. Fd. P.O.	Teheran.

MISCELLANEOUS

Det. C.M.P.	Teheran.
44 Rest Camp	"
31 Mob. Bath Unit	"
5 Ind. Aux. Pnr. Bn.	Durud.
12 Prisoner of War Cage	Sultanabad.

Sd/- M. Hayand Din Major,
for Lt. Col. General Staff.

APPENDIX 21

MOVEMENTS TENTH ARMY WORKING INSTRUCTION NO. 6.

ORGANISATION OF MOVEMENTS TENTH ARMY

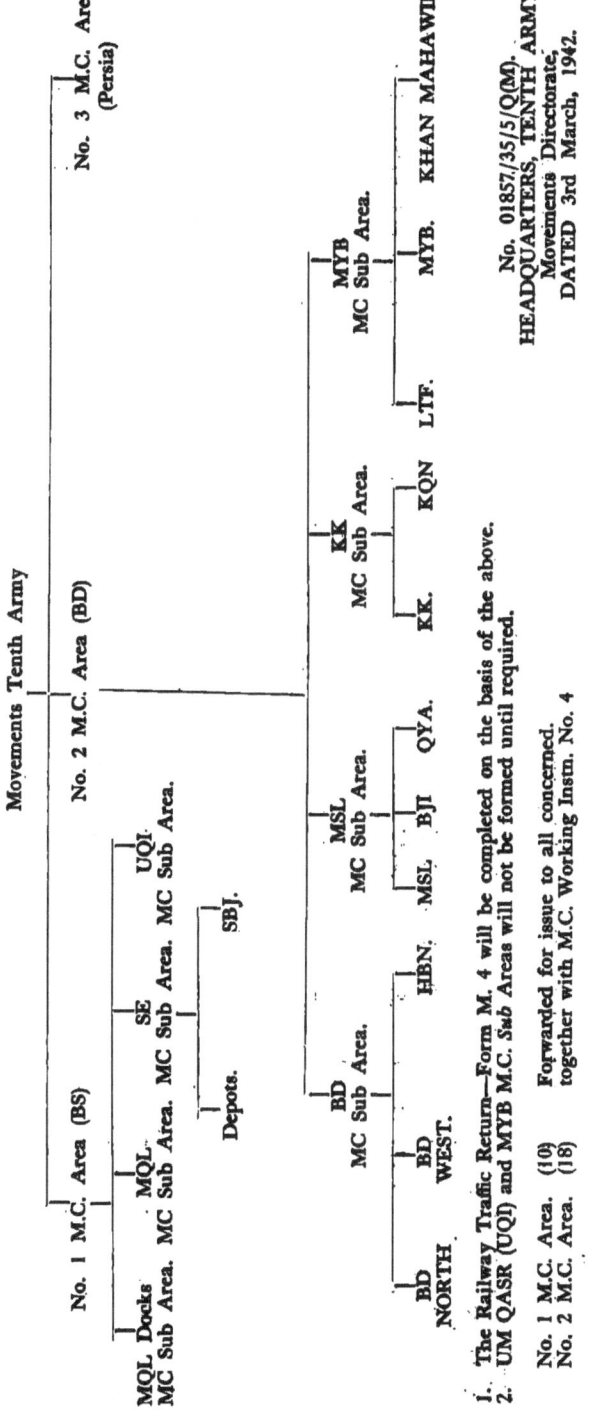

1. The Railway Traffic Return—Form M. 4 will be completed on the basis of the above.
2. UM QASR (UQI) and MYB M.C. Sub Areas will not be formed until required.

No. 1 M.C. Area. (10)   Forwarded for issue to all concerned.
No. 2 M.C. Area. (18)   together with M.C. Working Instn. No. 4

No. 01857/35/5/Q(M),
HEADQUARTERS, TENTH ARMY.
Movements Directorate,
DATED 3rd March, 1942.

Sd/-
Brigadier,
DIRECTOR MOVEMENTS.

556　CAMPAIGN IN WESTERN ASIA

APPENDIX 22
"AID TO RUSSIA" CARGO JAN. 43—MAR. 44.

LIGHTERAGE.

STATION	JAN. 43	FEB.	MAR.	APR.	MAY	JUNE	JULY	AUG.	SEP.	OCT.	NOV.	DEC.	JAN. 44	FEB.	MAR.	TOTAL
BASRA	—	2068	3943	3665	3309	4675	16143	11047	7995	3388	4807	10699	11376	9028	15128	107311
KHURRAMSHAHR	1907	8399	16222	14828	13908	12429	17877	17716	20995	31873	47160	29075	31836	27265	34530	326220
ABADAN	†3303	†431	86	—	153	27	34	94	310	112	—	—	130	—	—	4680
BANDAR GULF.	4414	2748	2934	2803	4832	3430	4015	4673	4070	7582	14677	14932	18556	12788	22846	125300
BUSHIRE	2609	5834	6980	7277	7892	6922	2511	—	—	—	—	—	—	—	—	40025
A. TOTAL	12273	19680	30165	28573	30094	27483	40580	33530	33370	42955	66644	54706	61898	49081	72504	603536
DESPATCHES																
BS - KUT	1895	7977	5959	7536	8816	7188	15970	15738	7679	1005	5304	9148	7177	5229	5597	112758
BS - AWZ	—	180	—	240	915	604	—	—	—	111	—	—	—	—	—	2050
BS - KRM	—	—	—	—	—	—	2347	1892	2843	280	340	668	653	783	1006	10812
B. TOTAL ex BASRA	1895	8157	5959	7776	9731	7792	18317	17630	10522	1396	5644	9816	8370	6012	6603	125620
ABN - AWZ	—	89	—	280	378	—	—	—	—	—	—	—	—	—	—	747
ABN - KRM	1657	2429	26	179	353	5367	55	—	90	627	28	303	853	4197	1919	18083
ABN - BS	—	—	—	—	—	—	8174	7303	5976	8960	8549	5996	5781	409	—	51148
C. TOTAL ex ABN	1657	2518	26	459	731	5367	8229	7303	6066	9587	8577	6299	6634	4606	1919	69978
KRM - AWZ	2543	3689	2032	456	2414	360	—	210	280	—	—	—	—	—	—	11984
KRM - ABN	—	—	—	—	10	30	30	—	100	2	12	—	—	362	482	1028
KRM - BS	—	—	—	—	—	—	—	—	—	—	—	—	370	1394	—	7764
D. TOTAL ex KRM	2543	3689	2032	456	2424	390	30	210	380	2	12	—	370	1756	482	14776
GRAND TOTAL	18368	34044	38182	37264	42980	41032	67156	58673	50338	53940	80877	70821	77272	61455	81508	813910
Percentage of TOTAL EFFORT	15.5	25.9	24.9	24.1	26.4	31.4	53.9	49.8	45.5	44.3	47.9	49.1	56.8	47.3	53.6	39.5

†Includes Khosroabad.

APPENDIX 23

REORGANISATION OF SUPPLY PERSONNEL

1. Attached, as Appendix 'A' to this letter, is the redistribution of Sup. Units throughout IRAQ and IRAN. The basis on which the allocation of Sup. Pers. Secs. has been made is roughly indicated; but Os.C. Sup. Pers. Coys. are at liberty to make such local adjustments as they see fit so as to ensure the most economical and efficient handling of supplies and P.O.L. Sub/Sections of the Field Butchery I.T. will remain in their present locations for the time being.

2. To simplify the supervision of Supplies and P.O.L. installations the whole country has been sub-divided into areas, each of which is the pre-occupation of O.C. Sup. Pers. Coy. in that area. This Officer therefore is in command of all Supply and P.O.L. personnel in the area other than those forming part of actual formations. The only exceptions to this are No. 2 B.S.D., SB and No. 2 Petrol Depot, MGL.

A sketch map of the areas is attached as Appendix 'B'.

3. It is emphasised that the O.C. of the Coy. is the Regimental Comdr. of all R.I.A.S.C. Supply Units inside his area and that therefore he will be represented at outstations by the Senior R.I.A.S.C. Officer of his command, whether that Officer be employed in the handling of Supplies, P.O.L. or Cattle. There is no question of one Sup. Sub. Unit working independently of another. It will be also noted that Cs.R.I.A.S.C. of mobile formations (i.e. divisions, Bde. Gps. etc.:) are in no way concerned with the working of base and L of C supply installations.

4. Although the H.Q. of No. 17 Supply Pers. Coy. is modified for particular use in connection with P.O.L. duties, the intention and policy is to utilize the H.Q. of each Supply Pers. Coy., as the controlling centre and authority in each area in connection with Supplies, P.O.L. (Except in the case of No. 2 B.S.D. and 2 Petrol Depot.).

5. The move of H.Q. No. 17 Supply Pers. Coy. to S.T.B. is dependent on developments in IRAN, and will not take place until specifically ordered. Until such a move is ordered H.Q. 17 Supply Pers. Coy. will be located at BD., and the control of Supply Units at AMK and TRN will be carried out by H.Q. 14 Supply Pers. Coy.

6. The final redistribution of units is shown in Appendix 'C', which constitute the orders to move sub units where necessary.

Sd/- ....
Lt. Col. Offg. D.D.S. & T.

Note: Appendix A to this letter referred to in para 1 above is given on the next page. Appendices B and C mentioned in paras 2 and 6 respectively are not reproduced here.—*Editor.*

APPENDIX 'A'

LAYOUT OF SUPPLY PERSONNEL

1. SB.   No. 2 Base Sup. Depot. (complete).

2. MQL.   No. 2 Petrol Depot. H.Q. and two Secs.

3. MQL.   H.Q. 14 Sup. Pers. Coy.
   MQL.   For F.S.D. and two D.I.Ss.   Three Sup. Pers. Secs.
   SB.   For F.S.D. and two D.I.Ss.   Three „   „   „
   AWZ.   For F.S.D. and D.I.S.   Two   „   „   „
   KRB.   All duties ...   One   „   „
   BS./SB.   One R.H. Det.
   AWZ.   ... One R.H. Det.
   In area.   Field Bakery   H.Q. and 5 Secs.
              Field Butchery (B.T.)   ... H.Q. and 4 Secs.
              Cattle Stock Secs.   Three.
              Cattle Conducting Secs.   Two.

4. MYB.   H.Q. No. 18 Sup. Pers. Coy. ... Three Sup. Pers. Secs.
              A.B.S.D.   ... Petrol Sec.
              A.B.Pet.D.   ... Sup. Pers. Sec.
   LTK.   D.I.S.   Two Sup. Pers. Secs.
              D.I.S.   ... One Sup. Pers. Sec.
                                          ... One R.H. Det.
   MYB.   Field Bakery   ... One Sec. & one
                                                           Sub-Sec.
              Field Butchery (B.T.)   ... One Sec. & two
                                                           Sub/Secs.
              Cattle Stock Secs.   ... One.
              Cattle Conducting Secs.   ... One.

5. BD.   H.Q. 22 Sup. Pers. Coy.
   BD.   F.S.D. & D.I.S.   Two Sup. Pers. Secs.
              P.O.L.   ... One Sup. Pers. Sec.
   HBN/LG5   F.S.D., D.I.S. & P.O.L.   Three Sup. Pers. Secs.
   K3/HFA.   F.S.D. & P.O.L.   Two Sup. Pers. Secs.
   BD.   One R.H. Det.
              Field Bakery   ... H.Q. and three Secs.
              Field Butchery (B.T.)   ... H.Q. and two Secs.
              Cattle Stock Secs.   One.
              Cattle Conducting Secs.   ... One.

6. MSL.   H.Q. No. 21 Sup. Pers. Coy.
   MSL.   F.S.D. and D.I.S.   Three Sup. Pers. Secs.
              P.O.L.   One Sup. Pers. Sec.
   FTA.   F.S.D. & P.O.L.   Two Sup. Pers. Secs.
   QYA.*   F.S.D.   ... One Sup. Pers. Sec.
              * for FTA as D.I.S. when QYA closes.
   MSL.   Field Bakery   ... H.Q. and three Secs.
              Field Butchery (B.T.)   ... H.Q. and two Secs.
                                              One Sub. Sec.
              Cattle Stock Secs.   One.
              Cattle Conducting Secs.   ... One.

APPENDICES

7. *KK.*   H.Q. No. 23 Sup. Pers. Coy.

KK.	F.S.D. & D.I.S.	Two Sup. Pers. Secs.
	P.O.L.	One Sup. Pers. Sec.
AKP.	All duties	One " " "
KQN.	F.S.D. & D.I.S.	One " " "
	P.O.L.	One " " "
KMS.	All duties	One " " "
KK.	Field Bakery	Two Secs.
	Field Butchery (B.T.)	Two Secs.
	Cattle Stock Secs.	One.
	Cattle Conducting Secs.	One.

8. *STB.*   H.Q. No. 17 Sup. Pers. Coy.

STB.	All duties	One Sup. Pers. Sec.
TRN.	F.S.D. & D.I.S.	Two Sup. Pers. Secs.
AMK.	F.S.D.	One Sup. Pers. Sec.
	P.O.L.	One P.O.L. Sec.
		One Sec.
STB.	Field Bakery	One Sec.
	Field Butchery (B.T.)	Two Sub Secs.
	Cattle Stock Secs.	One.
	Cattle Conducting Secs.	One.

APPENDIX 24

ENGINEERING ACTIVITIES AT ASHAR

May 1944

(i) SLIP-WAYS

All slipways were fully occupied during the month with the overhaul of the barges.

(ii) REFRIGERATION CRAFT

The construction of two Refrigeration craft was in hand.

(iii) STEAM SECTION

The reconditioning of some craft was completed.

(iv) DIESEL SECTION

Overhauling of ten craft was completed and work on five was proceeding.

(v) GRAY MACKENZIE'S WORKSHOPS

These workshops were kept busy mainly with the jobs for Diesel and Steam repairs.

(vi) MOTOR LAUNCH REPAIRS

Bi-monthly inspection of craft had beneficial results.

(vii) BARGE INSPECTION

A complete programme was made up, giving priorities for quick slipping and also for work requiring blocking up.

(viii) FLEET MAINTENANCE

Continuous inspection of all craft was being carried out.

(ix) WORKSHOPS (PRODUCTION DEPARTMENT)

Repairs and replacements for the Launch Repair Department were undertaken. Crankshafts and cylinder heads had the first priority. Seventeen shafts and thirty heads were completed. Bearings and clutch components were next on the priority list and received all possible attention.

(x) JOINERS AND CARPENTERS DEPARTMENT

The first of the new 'E' Pontoons constructed on Dockyard Island was completed. The second was also expected to be ready for service soon.

(xi) PLATING DEPARTMENT

Barge repairs continued to be the main occupation of this Department. Twelve were completed and repairs to six were in hand.

(*xii*) WELDING DEPARTMENT

'U' craft cylinder heads and shafts received priority. 39 heads and 4 shafts were completed.

(*xiii*) FOUNDRY

The first 'U' craft cylinder head was cast.

(*xiv*) BLACKSMITHS DEPARTMENT

Satisfactory progress was maintained.

(*xv*) ELECTRICAL DEPARTMENT

Maintenance and repair to workshop Motors mechanical transport and Launch Repair Department continued to be the main activity of this Department.

(*xvi*) M.T. REPAIRS

This Department gave good service to the mechanical transport and Plant.

(*xvii*) TINSMITH, COPPERSMITH AND PIPE FITTING SHOPS

The output and standard of work done continued to be very satisfactory

DOCKYARD

304 craft, including 21 towing units, 44 Eureka craft, 22 motor launches and barges received attention at the Dockyard.

Maintenance facilities were also available at the outstations—Amara, Kut, Baghdad, Khurramshahr and Bandar Gulf.

INDEX

Abadan, 315-26, 406; Iranian defences at, 315; invading force at, 315; attack on, 316, 327

Abdul Illa, Emir, becomes Regent of Iraq, 57; flies to Basra, 60; enters Baghdad, 112

Abdulla, Emir, 60

Agha Muhammad, 281

Ahwaz, reconnaissance of, 329; plan for the attack on, 331; 25th Indian Infantry Brigade's advance to, 332; air bombardment of, 332-3; fighter patrols at, 333; attack on, 334; Iranian surrender at, and armistice terms, 335; port of, 407

Aizlewood, Brigadier J. A., 305; plan of operations for the conquest of West Iran, 337-8

Alan Brooke, General Sir, Chief of the Imperial General Staff, discusses the Middle East situation with General Auchinleck in Cairo, 168

Aleppo, thrust by 10th Indian Division to, 227; Vichy troops at, 228

Alexander, General Sir Harold, becomes Commander-in-Chief, Middle East, 118

Allen, Major-General A. S., assumes Command of the 7th Australian Division, 210

America, see United States of America

American projects, 393-401

Amin Zaki, Major-General, Iraqi Chief of the General Staff, 70

Andimishk, 401

Anglo-Iraqi Treaty, 71

Anglo-Iranian Oil Company, 286, 299, 307, 310, 319; revision of concession to, 286

Anglo-Persian Agreement, 284

Anglo-Persian Oil Company, see Anglo-Iranian Oil Company.

Arden, Brigadier P. A., Deputy Director, Supply and Transport, Tenth Army, 457

Ashar, 82-3

Auchinleck, General Sir Claude, C-in-C, India, his proposals for expediting the planning of 'Sabine' and 'Sybil', 47; General Staff, India's view of his proposals, 47; on action to be taken in Iraq, 88-9; considers Iraq as a vital out-post for India's defence, 107; favours the occupation of Baghdad and control of North Iraq, 107; initial plan to meet Axis threat to Caucasia and War office appreciation, 125-6; assumes command of the Middle East, 131, 383; reviews the defence policy of Iraq—Iran theatres, 159-60; and reorganisation of the Commands in Iraq and Iran, 167, 360; discussion with Prime Minister Churchill and Chief of the Imperial General Staff, 168; declines to be commander of 'Paiforce', 168

Axis force, 364

Baghdad, advance of Habforce to, 109; armistice at, 112; anti-Jewish rioting at, 113; Indian troops move to, 114; 20th Indian Infantry Brigade advances to, 116; conference of 26 September 1941 at, 145; defence of, 154-5; General Corbett's plan for the defence of, 158; General Headquarters of Paiforce opened at, 168, 362; Advance Base Supply Depot at, 455

Bahmanshir ferry, 319

Balfour Declaration, 1917, 176

Bandar Shahpur, 327, 407

Bandra, H. M. S., 72

'Basloc', scheme prepared by G. H. Q., Middle East for the movement of Force Heron, 31

Basra, occupation of its port during first World War by the British, 15; difficulties in the occupation of, 48; 20th Indian Infantry Brigade plans for an opposed landing at, 66; Indian troops' landing at, 70; defence of by 21 Indian Infantry Brigade, 102; conference between General Wavell and General Auchinleck at, 106; development of the port assumes great importance, 383; reconnaissance report of by Major-General Beresford, 448

Bec du Canard, 256-7

Bedale (Force), organisation of, 338

Beirut, thrust by Free French force and 6th British Division to, 218-9

Beresford, de la P., Major-General G., Commanding 'Trout', 39

Berry, Mr., I. W. T. adviser to the Government of India, 435; becomes member of the I. W. T. Committee of Review, 435; and report of the Committee, 435

Blackburn, Colonel A. S., Commander 2/3 Machine-gun Battalion at Jisr Benett, 209; recapture of Kuneitra by, 209

Braim Creek, 316-17, 319

British Divisions:
    5th Infantry, 362, 373, 377-9
    50th Infantry, 360, 362
    56th (London), 362, 373, 377-9

British Brigades:
    151st Infantry, 360
    7th Armoured, 362, 377

British Projects, 380

Bullard, Sir Reader, British Minister at Teheran, 299-302; presses Iranian Government to take steps against Germans, 300; presents memorandum to the government of Iran, 305; Iranian Government's reply to, 306-7; submits note to Prime Minister of Iran regarding invasion, 307

Cangley, Colonel F. G., D.S.O., M.C., 412
Carson, Colonel Sir F., becomes Director of Transportation, Iraq, 413; improves the capacity of Iraq railways, 422; and reorganisation of I.W.T. Directorate, 437
Caucasia, Axis threat to, 125; Auchinleck's initial plan to meet the threat to, 125-6; appreciation by General Staff, India, concerning the threat to, 139; Russian forces in, 139; problems connected with the threat to, 130-40; possibilities of Axis attack on, 140; increased German threat to, 142, 363; Axis forces advancing to, 166; Axis victories in, 364
Chahar Zabar, preparation for the attack on, 347; Iranian surrender at and armistice terms, 347
Chatfield Committee, its report on India's defence policy, February 1939, 27
Cheybassi, 411; and its connection with Trans-Iranian Railway, 411; connection with Maqil, 423
Churchill, Sir Winston, discusses with General Auchinleck the situation in the Middle East, 168; tours Eighth Army front, and decides to introduce certain changes in the Middle East Command, 168
Clark, Major-General J. G. W; Commanding 'Habforce', 91; arrives at Habbaniya, 94; ordered by General Wilson to advance into Syria and occupy Palmyra, 220
Cockchafer, H. M. S., 72
Collings, Brigadier W. d'A., D.B.E., becomes Director, Supply and Transport of Paiforce, 457
Corbett, Lieut-General T. W., assumes command of 8th and 10th Indian Divisions, and 252nd Indian Armoured Group, 156; turns attention to defensive planning, 157; and construction of defences at Kirkuk, 158; decides to place his main reserves at Kirkuk and Fatha area, 158
Cornwallis, Sir Kinahan, British Ambassador in Iraq, 60; his advice to British Government on the course of action against Iraq, 61-2; advises against landing of troops at Basra, 64
Crimea, Nazis secure control over, 364
Cyrus the Great, 278

Damascus, Indian troops prepare for advance on, 209; instructions for the attack on, 212; capture of by the Allied forces, 217-18
D'Albiac, H., Air Vice-Marshal, 94
Darius the Great, 278
Defence of Indian Plan of 1927-28, 25
Deir ez Zor, plan for the attack on, 233-6; composition of 21st Indian Infantry Brigade Group for attack on, 233; three phases of attack on, 235-6; administrative arrangements for the attack, 236; Allied forces start operations against, 237; frontal attack on by 2/10 Gurkha Regiment, 241-2; Vichy bombers bomb the troops at, 242; Gurkha troops occupy Vichy positions south of, 242; 4/13 Frontier Force Rifles' attack from the rear, 242; capture of by British and Indian troops, 244-5; Vichy air attacks on, 245
Deraa, advance of Indian troops to, 191-2; capture of, 193
Donald H., Cannolly, Major-General, Persian Gulf Service Commander, 404
Dorquain, occupation of by 18th Indian Infantry Brigade, 326

Egypt, British Prime Minister's advice for the defence of, 166; Axis forces sweeping in, 364
El Alamein, battle of, 376; Allied victory at, 378
Endor Bay, Admiral, commander of Iranian naval force, 327
Esperance, H. M. S., 72
'Exporter', an operation in Syria by British Forces, 180
Ezraa, capture of by Indian troops, 196; capture by Vichy French, 208; attack on by Major Hackett, 209; Vichy garrison's surrender at, 209

Failiyah Creek, lighterage wharf at, 411
Feisal, Emir, proclaimed King of Iraq, 7; as administrator of Syria during 1918, 176; King Crane Commission recommends him to be king of Syria, 176; French compel him to leave Syria, 177, death of, 57
Feisal II, Succeeds King Ghazi of Iraq, 57
Falmouth, H. M. S., 72, 323, 325
Falluja, preparations for the capture of, 94; plan of operations, 95; attack on, 95; Iraqi troops, determination for the recovery of, 96; Iraqi troops withdrawal from, 96; occupation of by Habforce, 109
Fraser, Major-General W. A. K., Commands 10th Indian Division, 63; assumes command of forces in the Basra-Shuaiba area, 76; commands British troops in Iraq, 82; orders 20th Indian Infantry Brigade to secure Ashar, 82; gives ultimatum to Iraqi soldiers at Ashar to cease fire or face bombardment of the city, 84; hands over charge to Lieut.-Gen. Quinan and resumes command of the 10th Indian Infantry Division, 85
Fowle, Sir T., Political Resident of the Persian Gulf, on safeguarding places

of Imperial interest in the Persian Gulf, 28
Fawzi Qawukji, a reputed guerilla leader and an old opponent of the British, 92; fights against armoured cars of 'Kingcol', 92; fights with force 'Morocol' and retreats to Syrian border, 114; arrives at Abu Kemal, 231; his determined attack on Indian soldiers at Raqqa, 251

Galloway, Lieut-Colonel, 338
'Gentforce', 200; object of operation by, 200; advance towards Damascus, 210
Gilan, attack on, 347; Hazelforce commander at, 348; capture of, 348
Gillies, Colonel, U.S. Army railway expert in Wheeler Mission, 395
'Gocol', a mobile column of 'Habforce', 114;
'Golden Square', a team of four anti-British officers of Iraq Army, 59-60; its flight from the country, 111
Gracey, Brigadier D. D., Commanding 17th Indian Infantry Brigade at Mosul, 148; reconnaissance of Mosul area and proposals of, 148
Grozny, 369
Gurkha Rifles, 2nd, 3rd, 4th, 5th, 7th, 10th, 326, 328, 329, 335, 338, 340, 541 (See also under Indian Army)
Grobba, Herr, German Minister in Baghdad, 59
Glub, John Bagot (Glub Pasha), 92

Habbaniya, preparation for the battle of, 77; Iraqi forces in, 78; bombing of Iraqi forces at, 78; withdrawal of Iraqi forces from the airfield of, 80; end of fighting in, 80; defensive posts at, 159; Royal Air force at, 343
Habforce, a mobile force for operations in Iraq, 91; concentrates on the outskirts of Baghdad, 111; leaves Habbaniya for Syria, 116; crosses Syrian border to Palmyra, 118; capture of Palmyra by, 118-19, 220-5; Vichy planes attack on, 223; takes important part in the operation of Syria, 222-6; advances towards Homs, 226
Hackett, Major, 209
Haft Khel, occupation of by 18th Indian Infantry Brigade, 339
Harvey, Major-General C. O., 306, 313, 337-8; scheme 'Countenance' of, 313, 325; meets Iranian envoy and discusses cease-fire terms, 337; enters Ahwaz, 338; surrender of Iranians to, 338; message of congratulations at Ahwaz by, 339
Hassetche, 1/12 Frontier Force Regiment directed on, 263; French evacuation of, 264; occupation of by Indian troops, 264

Hazelforce, 342, 348
Heath, Major-General L. M., 'Rainbow' Commander, 39
'Heron', force, 30-1
'Herring', a force for operations in Iraq and Iran, 34; composition of, 34; administrative base for, 45; redesignated 'Sabine', 46; (see also Sabine)
Hickie, Colonel G. W. C., organisers supply to 'Paiforce' 455; issues instructions for the layout of the Field Supply Depot, 456; Deputy Director of Supply and Transport, Tenth Army, 457
Hill, Lt.-Col. A. J. R., Reconnaissance of the roads in Iran by, 426
Hughes, Brigadier F. E. C., Commander designate of the Persian Gulf, 122; reconnaissance of the Persian Gulf to study defence requirements and his recommendations, 122-3
Hutton, Major-General T. J., Chief of the General Staff, India, 51; represents C-in-C, India at the Middle East Conference, Cairo, 51

Ihsan (Ship), 319-20
India, external defence of, 25; concern in the defence of Iraq, 25; primary role of the army in, 26; plans and aims for the defence of Persian Gulf and Anglo-Iranian oilfields prior to September 1939, 27; Iraq and Iran as part of external defence of, 50; despatches troops to Iraq, 70-1
Indian Army:
  Divisions:
    5th Indian, 374, 376, 377, 379
    6th Indian, 360, 362, 373, 375, 376-8
    8th Indian, 305, 313, 334, 360, 263, 374, 377, 378
    10th Indian, 55, 360
    31st Indian Armoured, 362, 374-8
  Brigades:
    2nd Armoured, 306
    7th Armoured, 376
    9th Armoured, 305, 342, 353
    10th Indian Motor, 362, 376, 378
    18th Indian Infantry, 313-4, 320, 325-6, 330, 334-5, 337, 339
    19th Indian Infantry, 377
    20th Indian Infantry, 70
    24th Indian Infantry, 305, 314, 317, 323-5, 337
    25th Indian Infantry, 305, 314, 330, 333-5, 337
  Regiments:
    1/5 Gurkha Rifles, 340, 346
    1/2 Gurkha Rifles, 326, 328
    2/3 Gurkha Rifles, 326, 329, 335
    2/7 Gurkha Rifles, 340
    2/11 Sikh, 332
    3rd Field, 317, 326
    5/5 Maharatta, 326, 328

10th Baluch, 314, 317, 326
11th Field, 313
15th Field, 340

India—Middle East Conference, March 1940, reasons and aims of, 34; decision regarding force 'Herring', 34-5; Cairo Conference, March 1941, and its decision, 51-3; clash of views between India and Middle East Command, 53

Iran, geographical survey of, 271-7; climate, 272-3; communications, 275; population, 276-7; historical background, 278-88; under German influence, 121; aerodromes and emergency landing grounds in, 121; declares neutrality in the Great War (1914-18), 284; becomes battle-ground for Great Powers, 284; becomes member of the Council of League of Nations, 287; declares neutrality in the second World War, 287; military resources and organisation in, 289-98; efficiency and morale of the army of, 298; events leading to the action against, 123-4; 299-310; Soviet and British notes about invasion of, 308-9; Allied plans for the invasion of, 311-16; Iranian surrender at Ahwaz, 338; treaty, 353-5; American Technical Troops in, 354, administrative planning for the defence of, 382

Iran West, British plan of operations in, 340-44; operations, 343; Shah orders all resistance to cease, 351; Tripartite treaty with Russia and United Kingdom, 354; armistice accepted, 125; becomes occupied territory of the Allied forces, 125

Iranian Divisions:
    5th Kurdistan, 293, 344
    6th Khuzistan, 296
    12th Kermanshah, 293, 344
    13th, 344
    Regiments,
        1st Infantry, 291, 292
        2nd Infantry, 291, 292
        6th Infantry, 295, 345
        11th Infantry, 292
        13th Infantry, 292, 325
        19th Infantry, 292
        20th Infantry, 295, 345
        21st Infantry, 295, 345
        22nd Muzaffar Infantry, 293
        23rd Infantry, 293
        24th Infantry, 293
        30th Infantry, 292, 325
        37th Infantry, 295
        38th Infantry, 293
        39th Infantry, 293
        45th Infantry, 325
        9th Cavalry, 292
        23rd Cavalry, 293
        6th Artillery, 293
        14th Artillery, 293

Iraq, early history of, 3; early connection of British with, 4-5; during World War I, 6; British mandate over, 7; physical features, 9, 10, 17; population, 11; climate, 12; towns, 13; communications and economic resources, 15, 18, 21; local resources, 22; oil resources, 23; political development in 1941, 57; Axis infiltration in, 58; army and Air force of, 66-7; Indian troops in, 70-1; outbreak of hostilities in, 73, 78; operations, 79-106; collapse of Iraqi resistance, 111; Armistice, 112; becomes base of the British for invasion of Syria and Iran, 113, 220; military occupation of, 118; administrative problems for the defence of, 143-4; disposition and role of the force in, 152; effect of Japan's declaration of war, 156; Middle East Command, 156; IV Indian Corps in, 157, 159; role of Iraqi army in the defence of, 161-2; plan 'Wonderful', 162

Iraqi Ships, *Alarm*, a minesweeper vessel, 67; *Alert*, a control vessel, 67; *King Faisal I*, pilot vessel, 67

Italy, enters into Second World War, 359

Inland Water Transport—Iraq and Iran, management of, 430; development of, 433; review committee and its recommendations, 435-7; reorganisation of the Directorate of, 437-40; American barges and motor launches, 440; achievement of the Directorate, 446

Jamal Madfai, head of the new Iraqi administration, 112
Japan, outbreak of war with, 147, 156, 392, 406
Jebel Jebisa, 264-5
Jenin, Colonel, Commanding 1st Brigade of Free French, 209
Joint Planning Committee, 280
Jones, Lieut-Colonel L. B., Commander 4/6 Rajputana Rifles, assumes command of the 5th Indian Infantry Brigade, 200; message to Brigade Headquarters for help in the battle for Mezze, 216

Kala Dagh, 372
Kampasax, a Danish Firm, 426
Kanimbla, H. M. A. S., 306, 314
Karachi, C. K. D. plant at, 401
Karind, 21st Indian Infantry Brigade occupies, 349; Divisional Headquarters arrive at, 349
Karun, 444
Kerbela, 280-1
Kerch, capture by the Axis, 364
Kermanshah, geographical survey of, 352; Major-General Slim and Brigadier Aizlewood arrive at, 352; Gurkhas enter, 352
K-3, a force planned for the security of Anglo-Iranian oilfields in Iran, 32

Key, Lieut.-Colonel, plan for the movement of 'Heron', 31
Khalid, Arab leader, 279
Khanakin, preliminary reconnaissance at, 340; Armoured Brigade at, 344-2; Major-General, Slim at, 342
Khurramshahr, plan of operations in, 325; Iranian defences at, 325-6; forces and plan for the operations in, 326; Indian and British troops capture, 326, 327; port of, 407
Khusrovi, attacked and captured by 5th Royal Gurkha Rifles, 345
Khuzistan, British plan of operations in, 313; Iranians send reinforcements to, 313
Kingcol, 91; arrives at Mujara cut, 93; advances to Habbaniya, 93; attack on by German aircraft, 93; arrives at Kilo. 25, 93; moves out from Falluja and advances to Baghdad, 110
King Faisal I, a pilot vessel of the Iraqi Navy, 67
King-Crane Commission, 176
Kingstone, Brigadier J. J., Commander, Kingcol, 91; Commander, 4th Cavalry Brigade, and plan of operations against Palmyra, 222
Kirkuk, construction of defences at, 157-8
Kissoue, attack on by Free French force, 199; dispositions of Vichy troops in, 201; plan of operations at, 201-2; Free French and Indian troops attack on, 202; Punjabis attack on, 203; heavy counter-attacks by Vichy tanks, 203; Vichy troops push back 4/6 Rajputana Rifles to Tell Kissoue, 204-5
Krasnodar, 369
Kuneitra, captured by 5th Indian Infantry Brigade, 197; Vichy counter-attacks at, 205; strength of Vichy forces at, 207; Vichy tanks arrive at, 207; fierce attack by Vichy French forces, 208; Royal Fusiliers surrender to the Vichy French at, 208; situation retrieved at, 208-9; recaptured by Colonel A. S. Blackburn, V.C., 209
Kut Abdullah, 334, 337, 338;

Lane, Mr. H. W., reconnaissance at the oilfields area in the Persian Gulf, 43; his suggestions, 43-4; his recommended plan of operations, 45
Lane, Major-General C. R. C., becomes Deputy Quartermaster General, Bases and Lines of Communication, 361
Lavarack, Major-General Sir John, 210
le Gentilhomme, General, Commander, Free French Force, 198; wounded in the battle for Kissoue, 200; returns from hospital, and takes command of Gentforce, 217
Lilavati (Ship), 316, 318

Lloyd, Brigadier W. L. Commander, 5th Indian Infantry Brigade, 200
Macgregor, Lt. Col. L. E., as Commander, 1/2 Frontier Force Regiment, 260; orders three Rifle Companies to occupy Tell Aalo, 260
Manduwan, captured by Gurkhas, 325
Maikop Oilfields, 369
Makina, R.A.F. hospital at, 450
Maqil, plans for the defence of, 72; occupation of by Indian troops, 82
McMahon correspondence, 1915-16, 175
Mercol, a small detachment of 'Habforce', 115; engages Qawukji's force at Oseba and drives it across the Syrian frontier, 114
Messervey, Colonel F. W., General Staff Officer, 'Rainbow', 35; his reconnaissance of Basra-Abadan-Shat-al-Arab, and report, 35
Mezze, fighting between Indian and Vichy troops at, and the final capture of, 212-17
Middle East Command, 359, 361
Mohammad Riza Pahlevi, becomes King of Iran and co-operates with the Allies, 354
Montgomery, Field-Marshal Sir Bernard (Viscount); 168, 369
Mosul, arrival of German aircraft at, 97; plans for the defence of aerodrome at, 119; 8th Indian Division constructs defences at, 148; Brigadier Gracey proposes to fortify the approaches to, and his plans for the defence of, 148-51; General Wavell's visit to, 151; construction of defences at, 153
Mohammad Ali Mirza, 282-3
Mozdok, 369
Muqaddam, General, General Officer Commanding Iranian forces at Chahar Zabar, 351-2
Muhammad Hasan Khan, 281
Mussaiyib, advanced base at, 452; development of the bases at, 454
Muzaffar-ud-din, King of Iran, 282

Nadir Shah, 281
Naft-i-Shah, reconnaissance of, 345; attack on oilfields at, 345; captured by Gurkhas Rifles, 345
Najaf, 280-1
Nasir-ud-din Shah, King of Iran, 281-2
Noshirvan, King of Iran, 279
Nevasa, H. M. S., 72
Novikov, General, Russian Commander in Iran, 311
Novorossik, German occupation of, 369
Nuri-es-Said, General, 57; agrees to raise a force of ten Infantry Brigades for use in Iraq, 161
Nur-ud-din, Lt.-Col., Chief of Iraqi military operations, assumes command of the Iraqi Army, 111

Operation 'Deficient', task allotted to 10th Indian Division in, 227; commencement of, 228; and Air situation, 229; topography of the area of, 229-231
Operation 'Oakley', 107-8

Paic (Persia and Iraq Command), 168
Paiforce (Persia and Iraq Force), 360; General Headquarters open at Baghdad, 362, 448; Plan 'Wonderful' of, 363 (see also under plans); strength of, 376; arival of reinforcements for, 378; Aid to Russia scheme of, 379; organisation of supply for, 455-61
Pai Tak Pass, 340, 342-4, 346, 349; Iranian concentration at, and their determination to hold, 338; 'Bedale' force at and its organisation, 338; 21st Indian Infantry Brigade at, 345; bombing of Iranian positions at, 345; Iranian forces retreat from, 345; Major-General Slim arrives at, 345
Palang, Iranian Gunboat, 315-17, 319
Pibase (Persia and Iraq Base), 448
Palestine, plan for the defence of, 137-8
Palmyra, Allied garrison at, 222; Vichy French defensive positions at, 222; operations, 222-5; captured by Allied forces, 225-6
Persian Gulf, 291; principal ports of, 291; target import tonnage of, 390; developments of the ports of, 406
Plans:
    'Wonderful'; 162-4, 363; aim of the plan, 163; forces available for its implementation, 162; role of the air force in, 164; demolition schemes in, 164
    'Gherkin', 369, 373; aim of the plan, 369; forces available for, 373; plans A, B and C of, 375-6
    'Garment', 364, 369; basic dispositions of troops for, 365
    Plan 'A', reasons for the plan and its aims, 33
Plomer, Lt.-Col. K., 427
Polish Troops:
    Divisions:
        3rd Carpathian, 362, 373, 377
        5th Carpathian, 379
    Brigades:
        2nd Polish Army Tank Brigade, 379
        Polish Independent Infantry Brigade Group, 379
Powell, Brigadier D., Commander 20th Indian Brigade, 67; plans for oppposed landing of 20th Ind. Brigade at Basra, 67-9; decision to strengthen hold over Shuaiba and Maqil dock area, 81; orders 2/4 Gurkha Rifles to occupy Raqqa, 248; orders Lt.-Col. Clarke, to lead a column from Mosul to Jebel Jebissa, 264

Pownall, Lieut.-General Sir Henry, R., becomes Commander-in-Chief, Paiforce, 379
Pownall Committee, 26

Qamichliye, Vichy troops at, 256; 17th Indian Infantry Brigade's thrust to, 262; captured by 5/13 Frontier Force Rifles, 262-3
Qasr-i-Shirin, population of 343; geographical survey of, 343; attack on, 345; Gurkhas enter, 346
Qasr Shaikh, 330-4; attack on, 331-2; capture of the fort at, 331
Quinan, Lt.-General E. P., Commander designate of the force operating in Iraq, 75; duties and responsibilities of, 75; takes command of all the British Land forces in Iraq from Major-General Fraser, 85; orders Major-General Slim to capture Ur, 107; assumes command of all Land Forces in Iraq, 116; plans for holding Northern Iraq against Axis attack, 131-2; directive from General Wavell to, 142; issues revised directive to his troops, 152; and Plan 'Wonderful' for the defence of Iraq, 162; plan of operations against Iran, 305-6; arrives at Zibiri, 350; meets General Wheeler, 398; takes steps to implement Mr. Ward's recommendations for the development of ports, 409; plans for the development of roads in Iraq and Iran, 424

Radley, Lt.-Col. H. P., 30
'Rainbow', Infantry division forming part of 'Trout', 34
Rahmaniyeh, 333
Raqqa, captured by 2/4 Gurkha Rifles, 248; Vichy aircraft attacks on Indian troops at, 248; severe Vichy counter-attacks at, 249-51; determined attack by Fawzi Qawukji on Indian troops at, 251; Vichy French fighters machine-gun Indian troops at, 252; Casualties of Indian troops at, 252; R.A.F. co-operation in the battle at, 252-3
Rashid Ali el Gailani, becomes Prime Minister of Iraq, 57; virtual dictator of Iraq, 58; resigns the post, 57; *Coup d'etat* of, 59; becomes chief of the National Defence Government of Iraq, 60; executes secret treaty with the Axis, 72; objects to landing of Indian troops in Iraq, 72; flees from the country, 111
Rayak, 218-19
Rhodes, Sir Godfrey, becomes Director of Transportation, Iran, 413; improves the capacity of Iranian Railways, 422
Riza Khan (Riza Shah Pahlevi), 285, commanding Cossak Brigade, 285; overthrows old corrupt Government of Iran and becomes War Minister,

285; becomes Prime Minister, 285; National Assembly offers crown of Iran to, 286; assumes the title of Riza Shah Pahlevi, 286; improves administration and abolishes purdah system, 286-7; revives the claim to Bahrein islands, 299; and interview with representatives of Great Britain and Russia, 310; orders stoppage of all Iranian resistance, 351; abdicates, 354

Roberts, Colonel O. L., 78; assumes command of the Habbaniya garrison, 94; and plan for the capture of Falluja, 94

Rommel, General Erwin, 60, 166, 364, 369

Rostov, 364

Royal Air Force, 314, 335-6, 343

Russia, British Government's Aid to, 145; declines British offer of Staff conversations, 146; German attack on, 300, 359; Axis gains in, 369; supplies to, 390; aircraft assembly and delivery to, 398

Rutba, attack on and capture of, 92

Sabine Force, role of, 46, 48
Safaga, 385
Salmon, part of 'Trout' force, 34
Scheme Countenance, 313
Scheme Dover, 313
Seabelle, Ship, 316
Shahabad, 344; capture of by Hazelforce, 348
Shah Abbas the Great, 281
Shahpur the Great, 279
Shatliyat, 333
Shattforce, the riverborne troops, 104; returned to Maqil airport and Dock area, 105
Sebastopol, 364
Sheikh Meskine, advance of Indian troops to, 194; plan for the attack on, 194-5; attack on and capture of, 195-6
Sherif Sharaf, member of the royal family and regent of Iraq, 60
Shingler, Colonel, takes charge of U.S. Mission from General Wheeler, 403
Shirwan, 351
Shoreham, H. M. S., 319, 322
Shuaiba, 98
Slim, Major-General W. J., succeeds Major-General Fraser in command of 10th Indian Division, 102; orders Brigadier C. J. Weld to attack and disperse Iraqi police and troops at Habibshawi, 102; commands Northern Iraq, 116; arrives at Haditha, 233; takes command of West Iran operations, 342; discusses terms of truce with the Iranian envoy at Zibiri, 350; arrives at Kermanshah, 352; his note on lessons from the operations of 10th Indian Division in Syria, 527

Smart, Air Vice-Marshal H. G., Air Officer Commanding at Habbaniya, 74; and bombing of Iraqi force, 74, 78; wounded in car accident, 94

Smirnov, Mr., Soviet Ambassador in Iran, submits note to the Prime Minister of Iran regarding invasion, 308

Soden, Lt.-Col. J. N., 412
Southgate, Brigadier C., 447
Stalingrad, heroic defence of, 378
Sudbury, Lt.-Col., becomes Chief of Inland Water Transport organisation, 430; separate I.W.T. directorate under, 433
Sykes-Picot Agreement, 175
Syria, plans for the operations against, 118; invasion of by Allied forces, 118; fall of Damascus, 118; 21st Indian Infantry Brigade captures Deir ez Zor, 119; end of hostilities and Armistice, 119; General Headquarters, Middle East plan for the defence of, 137-8; physical features of, 171; topography of, 171; climate of, 172; communications in, 172; area and population of, 173; economic resources of, 173; early history of, 173; French rule in, 177; Damascus as capital of, 177; Franco-Lebanese and Franco-Syrian treaty, 177-8; admitted to League of Nations, 178; Axis influence in, 179-80; operations by British forces in, 180-1; Vichy forces in, 181-3; Allied forces in, 183-4; British plan of operations in, 184-90; role of R.A.F. in the operation, 190; commencement of the operation in, 191; 10th Indian Division faces administrative and communication problems during the operations in, 253-5; defeat of Vichy French and Armistice in, 267; terms of Armistice, 267; importance of the operations in, 268

Taha el Hashmi, succeeds Rashid Ali as Prime Minister of Iraq, 57
Teheran, military academy at, 289-90; arsenal at, 289; restrictions of bombing at, 315
Teheran Conference, declaration regarding Iran's Independence and territorial integrity, 460
Tell Aalo, reconnaissance of, 258; 1/12 Frontier Force Regiment's move to and capture of, 260-61
Tell Abiad, captured by 2/4 Gurkha and attached troops, 248-9; daylight air attacks by Vichy aircraft on, 249
Tell Chehab Viaduct, 191-2
Tell-i-Zibid, 337
Tell Kotcheck, Vichy troops at, 256; plan of operation at, 258; captured by Indian troops, 258
Tenth Army, 359, 362; administrative changes in the set up of, 360; Plan

'Garment' of, 364; Plan 'Gherkin' of, 370
Thomson, Group Captain D. L., 315
Tigris, bandalling of, 443
Trans-Iranian railway, development of, 385
Treaties:
Anglo-Russian, 284
Russo-Persian, 285, 309
Saadabad, 287, 304
Trout (or Sybil), a part of force 'Herring', 34; composition of the first Echelon of, 36; air and naval support to, 37; plans for movement and landing of, 38; plans for the operations of, 39; the role of, 49
Turkish Government, offers mediation in the Anglo-Iraqi dispute, 87; British Government's advice to, 87; Government of India opposed to mediation, 88

Umm-at-Tumair, 333, 337
Umm Qasr port, 383
Umm-ul-Ashiyeh, 334, 337
United Kingdom Commercial Corporation, carries supplies to Russia, 382; acts as agents for the Ministries of Supply and Food, 405
United States of America, 'Lend-Lease' aid to the United Kingdom, 393; Wheeler Mission of, 393; plans for the despatch of aircraft and related equipment to Russia, 398; takes direct responsibility for "Aid to Russia" through Persian Gulf, 404; development of the Persian Gulf ports by, 410
Ur, capture of, 109

Ward, Mr. A. M., becomes consulting engineer to the commander, Iraq force, 408; reports on the developments of ports, 408; inspects Anglo-Iranian Oil Company's site for a new port at Mashur, 409
War Transport Executive Committee, 415
Waterhouse, Major-General G. G., 70
Wavell, General Sir Archibald P., commends India's appreciation regarding occupation of Basra, 50; resumes temporarily the operational command of Iraq, 76; his views about policy to be followed in Iraq, 87; views about agreement with Rashid Ali, 90-91; criticises War Office appreciation about the Axis threat to Caucasia, 128; issues directive to Lt.-General Quinan to hold Northern Iraq against Axis attack, 129; becomes Commander-in-Chief, India, 131; opposes the idea of sending force to the Russian front, 146-7; visits Mosul, 151; his proposals to War Office regarding improvement of Railways in Iraq, 384-5; submits a detailed report to War Office regarding supply of mechanical transport to Russia, 396; discusses with General Wheeler about American projects, 396
Weld, Brigadier C. J., Commanding 21st Indian Infantry Brigade, 102; receives order from Major-General Slim to attack and disperse Iraqi police and troops at Habibshawi, 102; his plan of attack, 102; moves 21st Indian Infantry Brigade towards Baghdad, 116
Wilson, Captain A. B., 35
Wheeler, General, mission of, 393; discusses with General Wavell regarding American projects, 396; 400; visits Iraq, 398; discussion with Lt.-General Quinan and Air Officer Commanding at Iraq, 398; hands over charge of U.S. Mission to Colonel Shingler, 403
Wilson, General Sir Henry Maitland, assumes command in Palestine and Transjordan, 91; becomes Commander-in-Chief 'Paic', 168, 361; orders Habforce Commander to March into Syria and occupy Palmyra, 220; orders Habforce to advance towards Homs, 226; opens General Headquarters, 'Paic' at Baghdad, 361; tasks of, 362; prepares against the Axis offensive, 378; becomes Commander-in-Chief, Middle East and leaves for Cairo, 379

Yarra, H.M.S., 72, 326-7

Zibiri, fighting between Iranians and Habforce at, 350; request for truce by Iranians at, 350; Lieut.-General Quinan arrives at, 350
Zenobia, Ship, 319

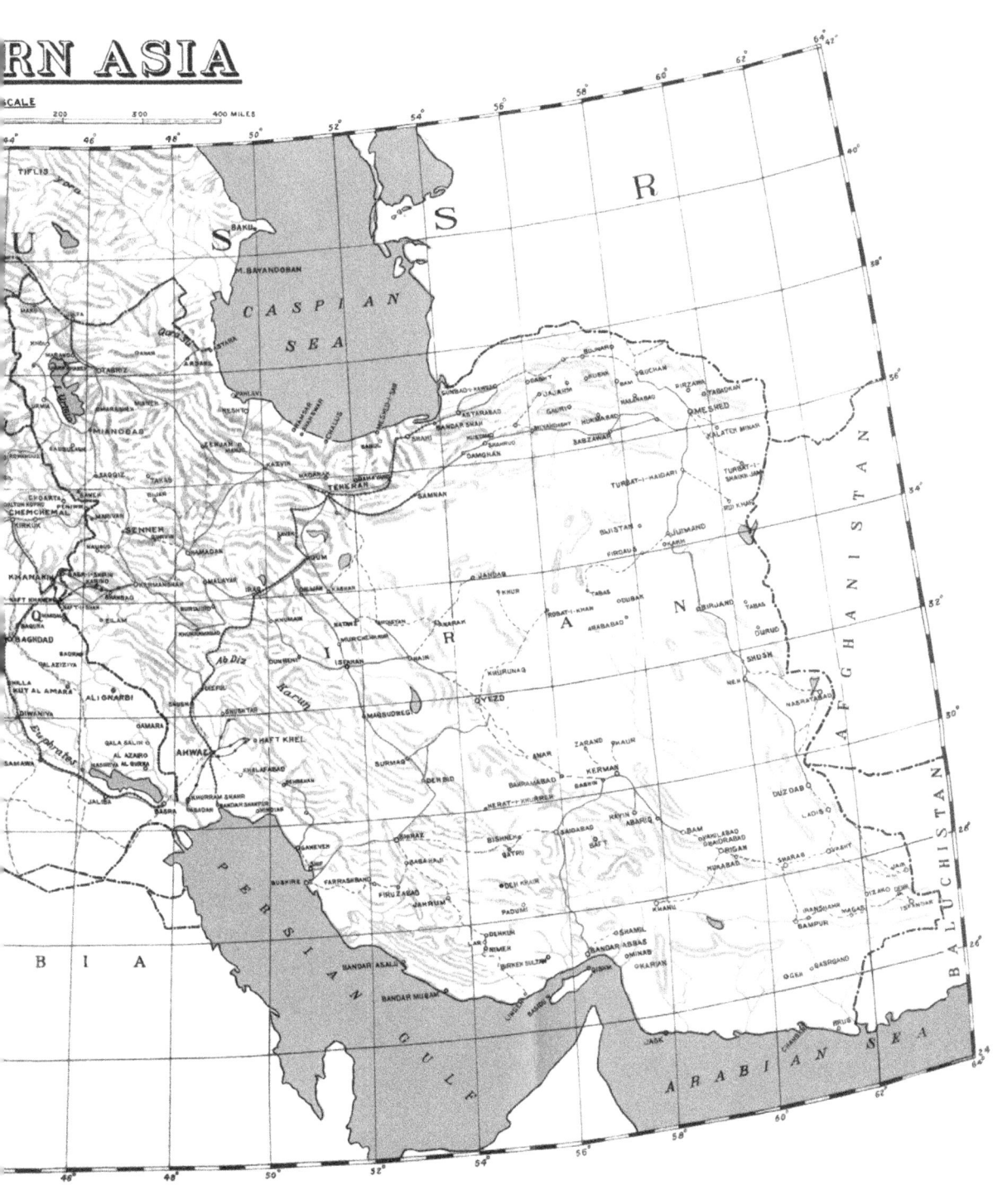

INDIAN DIVISIONS WON A FINE REPUTATION IN WORLD WAR TWO

Field Marshal Auchinleck, Commander-in-Chief of the British Indian Army from 1942, asserted that the British *"couldn't have come through both wars (World War I and II) if they hadn't had the British Indian Army"*.
British Prime Minister Winston Churchill also paid tribute to
"the unsurpassed bravery of Indian soldiers and officers".

Between 1945 and 1947, the Director of Public Relations, War Department, Government of India, published a series of short publications covering the individual histories of the WWII Indian Divisions. They followed a consistent format, having between 44 and 48 pages within illustrated soft card covers. They have an average of 50 monochrome photographic illustrations, and each has a full colour centrespread depicting a scene from the Division's wartime operations (drawn by official war artists). They were printed at various presses in Bombay and New Delhi, and each contains at least one map.

As condensed histories they are useful – particularly those which relate to Divisions for which no other record was ever produced.

The British Indian Army during World War II began the war, in 1939, numbering just under 200,000 men. By the end of the war, it had become the largest volunteer army in history, rising to over 2.5 million men in August 1945. Serving in divisions of infantry, armour and a fledgling airborne force, they fought on three continents: in Africa, Europe and Asia.

This Army fought in Ethiopia against the Italian Army, in Egypt, Libya, Tunisia and Algeria against both the Italian and German Army and, after the Italian surrender, against the German Army in Italy. However, the bulk of the British Indian Army was committed to fighting the Japanese Army, first during the British defeats in Malaya and the retreat from Burma to the Indian border; later, after resting and refitting for the victorious advance back into Burma, as part of the largest British Empire army ever formed. These campaigns cost the lives of over 87,000 Indian service-men, while another 34,354 were wounded, and 67,340 became prisoners of war. Their valour was recognised with the award of some 4,000 decorations, and 18 members of the British Indian Army were awarded the Victoria Cross or the George Cross.

RED EAGLES
The Story of the 4th Indian Division
9781474537520

During the Second World War, the 4th Indian Division was in the vanguard of nine campaigns in the Mediterranean theatre, Egypt, Eritrea, Syria, Tunisia, Italy and Greece. The 4th Division captured 150,000 prisoners and suffered 25,000 casualties, more than the strength of a whole division. It won over 1,000 honours and awards, which included four Victoria Crosses and three George Crosses. Field Marshal Lord Wavell wrote: "The fame of this Division will surely go down as one of the greatest fighting formations in military history."

THE FIGHTING FIFTH
History of the 5th Indian Division
9781474537513

As described in much greater detail in Anthony Brett James's book 'The Ball of Fire', the division saw active service in East Africa, North Africa and Burma.

GOLDEN ARROW
The Story of the 7th Indian Division
9781474537506

The role of this division is also duplicated by a much larger work: the book by Brig. M. R. Roberts. However, this booklet gives a good account of Kohima and Imphal and the crossing of the Irrawaddy. In 1945, the division was flown into Siam, so becoming the first Allied formation to re-enter South East Asia.

BLACK CAT DIVISION
17th Indian Division
9781474537483

This formation was committed to Burma from the early days when the British were in full flight from the invading Japanese. It remained in Burma right through to the end, when the starving remnants of the Japanese Army were making their own desperate retreat.

ONE MORE RIVER
The Story of the 8th Indian Division
Biferno, Trigno, Sangro, Moro, Rapido, Arno, Senio, Santerno, Po, Adige
9781474537490

The 8th Indian Division started its overseas service in the Middle East in the garrisoning of Iraq and then the invasion of Persia to secure the oil fields of the area for the Allies, before moving to Italy in 1943. Landing at Taranto, it pushed up the length of the peninsula in a series of major battles: breaking the Sangro Line, forcing the Rapido and turning the defences at Cassino, breaking the stubborn German resistance at Monte Grande and, finally, forcing the Po River. It won four VCs, 26 DSOs and 149 MCs along the way. During the war the 8th Indian Division sustained casualties totalling 2,012 dead, 8,189 wounded and 749 missing.

TIGER HEAD
The Story of the 26th Indian Division
Arakan, Ragoon
9781474537452

This is a history of the division said later by the Japanese to have been the opponent which they most feared. The 26th held the Allied monsoon line in the Arakan during two such seasons, repulsing every attack launched against it. Later it made a series of leap-frog landings down the coast to clinch the issue in the Arakan. It was the first division to enter Ragoon, invading the city from the sea.

THE TWENTY THIRD INDIAN DIVISION
"The Fighting Cock Division"
Burma, Malaya, Java
9781474537469

The Fighting Cock Division is well recorded in the book by Doulton. This book gives coverage of the heavy fighting at the Kohima Battle, the capture of Tamu, the reoccupation of Malaya in August 1945, and then its strange role on the island of Java – concurrently disarming the Japanese garrison, fighting the insurgent Indonesian nationalists, and caring for 65,000 former internees pending the arrival of a new Dutch administration.

A HAPPY FAMILY
The Story of the Twentieth Indian Division,
9781474537476

One of the few Indian divisions in the 14th Army trained specifically for the war in Burma. Raised in Bangalore in 1942, it commenced active operations in late 1943 and served from Imphal through to the end. It established the 14th Army's first brigade-head across the Chindwin and its second such brigade-head across the Irrawaddy. Its final task was to round up the Japanese in French Indochina.

TEHERAN TO TRIESTE
The Story of the Tenth Indian Division
9781783317028

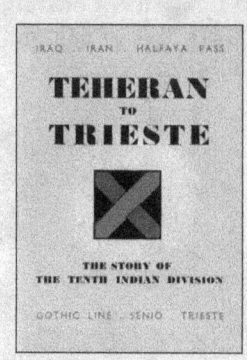

This History deals with the 10th Indian Div's exploits in Iraq (under Maj Gen "Bill" Slim) its role in the Libyan battles leading up to El Alamein, the following two years of garrison duties in Cyprus and Syria, and finally, its fighting services in the Italian campaign (from Ortona onwards).

THE STORY OF THE 25th INDIAN DIVSION
The Arakan Campaign
9781783317585

Formed in Southern India in August 1942 for defence of that area in case of Japanese invasion, the "Ace of Spades" Division had its baptism of fire in Arakan in February 1944. It served throughout the remainder of that campaign the climax being the battle of Tamandu. Its victorious fight for the Kangaw roadblock was considered by many to have been the fiercest battle of the entire Burma war, while its liberation of Akyab was the first convincing proof to the rest of the world that the tide had turned against the Japanese.

DAGGER DIVISION
The Story of the 19th Indian Division
9781783317035

Raised in the late 1941, the 19th was the first "standard" Indian Division. Its troops were the first to breach the Japanese defence line in Burma and to raise the flag at Fort Dufferin. It crossed the Chindwin in November 1944, driving on to Mandalay and Ragoon during seven months of continuous fighting. The 19th's exploits are graphically described also in John Masters' personal memoir, *The Road Past Mandalay*.